Double Feature Creature Attack

A Monster Merger of Two More Volumes of Classic Interviews

by Tom Weaver

McFarland
Classics

McFarland & Company, Inc., Publishers
Jefferson, North Carolina, and London

Front cover: Gary Clarke (werewolf), Robert H. Harris (victim) and Gary Conway (Frankenstein's monster) in a publicity shot for 1958's *How to Make a Monster*

Back cover: A giant spider menaces a moon maiden in the 1958 film *Missile to the Moon*

The present work is a reprint, under one cover, of the library bound editions of Attack of the Monster Movie Makers: Interviews with 20 Genre Giants, *and* They Fought in the Creature Features: Interviews with 23 Classic Horror, Science Fiction and Serial Stars, *first published in 1994 and 1995 respectively.* **McFarland Classics** *is an imprint of McFarland & Company, Inc., Publishers, Jefferson, North Carolina, who also published the original editions.*

Library of Congress Cataloguing-in-Publication Data

Weaver, Tom, 1958–
    [Attack of the monster movie makers]
    Double feature creature attack : a monster merger of two more
volumes of classic interviews / by Tom Weaver
        p.   cm.
    First work originally published: Attack of the monster movie makers.
Jefferson, N.C. : McFarland, c1994. 2nd work originally published: They
fought in the creature features. Jefferson, N.C. : McFarland, 1995.
    Includes filmographies and indexes.
    Contents: Bk. 1. Attack of the monster movie makers—bk. 2. They
fought in the creature features.

    [Both books] ISBN 0-7864-1366-2 (softcover : 50# alkaline paper)

    1. Science fiction films—History and criticism.   2. Horror films—
History and criticism.   3. Motion picture serials—History and criticism.
4. Motion picture producers and directors—Interviews.   5. Motion
picture actors and actresses—Interviews.   6. Screenwriters—Interviews.
I. Weaver, Tom, 1958– They fought in the creature features.   II. Title.
PN1995.9.S26W43   2003   791.43'615—dc21   2002043218

British Library cataloguing data are available

791.43
615
Weav

Manufactured in the United States of America

McFarland & Company, Inc., Publishers
    Box 611, Jefferson, North Carolina 28640
    www.mcfarlandpub.com

Double Feature Creature Attack

McFarland Classics

Adir. *The Great Clowns of American Television*
Anderson. *Science Fiction Films of the Seventies*
Archer. *Willis O'Brien*
Benson. *Vintage Science Fiction Films, 1896–1949*
Bernardoni. *The New Hollywood*
Broughton. *Producers on Producing*
Byrge & Miller. *The Screwball Comedy Films*
Chesher. *"The End": Closing Lines...*
Cline. *In the Nick of Time*
Cline. *Serials-ly Speaking*
Darby & Du Bois. *American Film Music*
Derry. *The Suspense Thriller*
Douglas. *The Early Days of Radio Broadcasting*
Drew. *D.W. Griffith's* Intolerance
Ellrod. *Hollywood Greats of the Golden Years*
Erickson. *Religious Radio and Television in the U.S., 1921–1991*
Erickson. *Syndicated Television*
Fernett. *American Film Studios*
Frasier. *Russ Meyer—The Life and Films*
Fury. *Kings of the Jungle*
Galbraith. *Motor City Marquees*
Harris. *Children's Live-Action Musical Films*
Harris. *Film and Television Composers*
Hayes. *The Republic Chapterplays*
Hayes. *3-D Movies*
Hayes. *Trick Cinematography*
Hill. *Raymond Burr*
Hogan. *Dark Romance*
Holland. *B Western Actors Encyclopedia*
Holston. *Starlett*
Horner. *Bad at the Bijou*
Jarlett. *Robert Ryan*
Kinnard. *Horror in Silent Films*
Langman & Gold. *Comedy Quotes from the Movies*

Levine. *The 247 Best Movie Scenes in Film History*
Mank. *Hollywood Cauldron: Thirteen Horror Films*
Martin. *The Allied Artists Checklist*
McGee. *Beyond Ballyhoo*
McGee. *The Rock & Roll Movie Encyclopedia of the 1950s*
McGee. *Roger Corman*
McGhee. *John Wayne*
Nollen. *The Boys: ...Laurel and Hardy*
Nowlan. *Cinema Sequels and Remakes, 1903–1987*
Okuda. *The Monogram Checklist*
Okuda & Watz. *The Columbia Comedy Shorts*
Parish. *Prison Pictures from Hollywood*
Pitts. *Western Movies*
Quarles. *Down and Dirty: Hollywood's Exploitation Filmmakers*
Selby. *Dark City: The Film Noir*
Sigoloff. *The Films of the Seventies*
Slide. *Nitrate Won't Wait*
Smith, L. *Famous Hollywood Locations*
Smith, R.D. *Ronald Colman, Gentleman of the Cinema*
Sturcken. *Live Television*
Tropp. *Images of Fear*
Tuska. *The Vanishing Legion: ...Mascot Pictures*
Von Gunden. *Alec Guinness*
Von Gunden. *Flights of Fancy*
Warren. *Keep Watching the Skies!*
Watson. *Television Horror Movie Hosts*
Watz. *Wheeler & Woolsey*
Weaver. *Poverty Row HORRORS!*
Weaver. *Double Feature Creature Attack*
Weaver. *Return of the B Science Fiction and Horror Heroes*
West. *Television Westerns*

Preface to the Combined Edition

It strikes me as funny that many of the movies discussed in these two books were made by people who expected that they would have a short theatrical run and then vanish more or less completely—perhaps even cease to exist. Well, their movies have not vanished—TV reruns, VHS, laser and now DVD have kept them alive and well, and a few of them popular beyond the wildest fever dreams of anyone involved. And now, wonder of wonders, even the interviews that these people have granted me refuse to quietly recede into the past; first published in magazines like *Fangoria* and *Starlog*, they were compiled and reprinted in my books *Attack of the Monster Movie Makers* (1994) and *They Fought in the Creature Features* (1995), and now re-reprinted in this mammoth McFarland special edition in its Classics series.

Each of these books has its own dedication, but this commingled collision of the two volumes is dedicated to the interviewees who, sad to say, have since dropped from the proverbial twig: John Archer, William Benedict, Charles Bennett, Lloyd Bridges, Richard Denning, Eugene Lourie, Jacques Marquette, Cameron Mitchell, Jeff Morrow, Vincent Price, Don Taylor, the irreplaceable John Agar, the irresistible Rose Hobart and the irrepressible Herman Cohen.

Tom Weaver
Sleepy Hollow, New York
January 2003

Attack of the Monster Movie Makers

Interviews with 20 Genre Giants

by Tom Weaver

RESEARCH ASSOCIATES:
MICHAEL AND JOHN BRUNAS

McFarland & Company, Inc., Publishers
Jefferson, North Carolina, and London

Original Library of Congress Cataloguing-in-Publication Data (Book 1)

Attack of the monster movie makers : interviews with 20 genre giants /
   by Tom Weaver
      p.   cm.
   Includes [filmographies] and index.

   [With Book 2:] ISBN 0-7864-1366-2 (softcover : 50# alkaline paper)

      1. Science fiction films—History and criticism.   2. Horror films—
   History and criticism.   3. Motion picture actors and actresses—
   Interviews.   4. Motion picture producers and directors—Interviews.
   5. Screenwriters—Interviews.   I. Weaver, Tom, 1958–
   PN1995.9.S26A94   1994   791.43'615—dc20   94-124

British Library cataloguing data are available

Manufactured in the United States of America

*McFarland & Company, Inc., Publishers
   Box 611, Jefferson, North Carolina 28640
      www.mcfarlandpub.com*

Dedicated to

EDWARD BERNDS

—the writer/director who gave me
my first-ever interview, and who made
it so much fun that I caught "the fever."

Preface

History is only a confused heap of facts.
—Earl of Chesterfield (1694–1773)

On that fairly accurate note, we're off together on another trip down Memory Lane—the memories of the stars, writers, producers and directors of the old horror and science fiction movies.

When I started on this kick several years ago, in some ways I had the field largely to myself; in fact, I wasn't at all sure I'd be able to find a magazine that would be interested in the sort of people I wanted to interview. Sure, from time to time there would be a chat with some well-known old-time movie maker or star in the occasional sci-fi or horror mag, but I wanted to be the *first* person to talk to the Richard E. Cunhas and the Susan Cabots and the Reginald LeBorgs—not the five-hundred-and-first guy to elicit the same old, dog-tired reminiscences out of, say, Roger Corman or Christopher Lee. It was *Fangoria* magazine, under the editorship of Dave Everitt, that took me aboard and enabled me to make a go of my newest hobby; and I'm still writing for that magazine (now in the capable hands of fearless leader Tony Timpone) a dozen years later. I've had a lot of great times interviewing some of my favorite stars and made a lot of new friends in those 12 years and I don't intend ever to forget that initially it was *Fango* which made it all possible. Nor do I intend to overlook the other magazines that have let me chat with filmmakers, air my opinions and spew my bile, most notably *Starlog* and its equally fearless commander-in-chief Dave McDonnell, whose affection for the old-time character players equals (surpasses?) my own.

Now *Scarlet Street, Cult Movies, Psychotronic* and several others have joined in the fray, sprinters in the race-against-time to put onto paper the memories of the old pros who might otherwise take their colorful tales to the next world (where, I'd like to think, interviewers like us have celestial counterparts scribbling away right now!). New to the next world since last we got together (in the pages of *Science Fiction Stars and Horror Heroes,* 1991) is that book's interviewee Robert Shayne, the no-nonsense Inspector Henderson of television's *Adventures of Superman,* who died December 2, 1992, at a reported age of 92. (Phyllis Coates tells me she's certain he was even older.)

Slowed down during the final years of his life by poor health and failing eyesight, Shayne still remained a popular convention regular, and even appeared as a blind newspaper vendor in episodes of the 1990-91 television series *The Flash*. During the half-century or so he spent in front of the cameras, Shayne worked in countless television episodes as well as approximately 100 movies — including four which are missing from his filmography in *Science Fiction Stars*: *See Uncle Sol* (Educational short, 1937), *The Meadville Patriot* (Associated Filmmakers/Astor, 1944), *Sea of Lost Ships* (Republic, 1953) and *Revolt in the Big House* (Allied Artists, 1958). Even toward the end, Shayne never let his health problems get in the way of communicating with fans; in fact, on *very* short acquaintance, he invited me to stay at his home whenever "work" (interviewing) brought me out to California. (I never stayed with him, but I was flattered by the offer.) Shayne was the kind of nice old guy the world is quickly running out of.

Writer Robb White *(House on Haunted Hill, The Tingler),* also featured in *Science Fiction Stars,* passed away while that book was in the final stages of production. This time around the same thing has happened to one of the all-time great actors (and, from every account, one of the all-time great people), Vincent Price. I never interviewed Price one-on-one; I knew I could hit him with a lot of questions that few if any interviewers had posed to him before, but he was so often interviewed by horror film fans that I could never bring myself to hound him. (Also, toward the end he gave every impression that he was finding his *too*-close identification with horror flicks demeaning — which it *was*.) Now that it's too late, that decision is shaping up to be one of my biggest regrets associated with this hobby.

Table of Contents

Preface vii
Acknowledgments xi

Merry Anders 1
Charles Bennett 17
Ben Chapman 31
Herman Cohen 45
Robert Day 85
Val Guest 99
Susan Hart 127
Candace Hilligoss 145
Rose Hobart 157
Betsy Jones-Moreland 175
Jacques Marquette 195
Cameron Mitchell 209
Ed Nelson 229
William Phipps 249
Vincent Price 267
Ann Robinson 289
Herbert Rudley 309
Harry Spalding 319
Kenneth Tobey 339
Lupita Tovar 357

Index 367

Acknowledgments

This companion volume to my earlier *Interviews with B Science Fiction and Horror Movie Makers* (1988) and *Science Fiction Stars and Horror Heroes* (1991) could not have been written without the generous assistance of many of the same people who have helped me in the past: Sincere thanks go to Mark Martucci, Paul and Donna Parla, Dennis Daniel, Mary Runser, Kevin Marrazzo, Glenn Damato, Don Leifert, Jon Weaver, Alex Lugones, Richard Valley, Joe and Jeff Indusi, Bandit, Carl and Debbie Del Vecchio, *Fangoria*'s Tony Timpone and *Starlog*'s David McDonnell (as well as all the other kind folks down at Starlog Publications; you know who you are), Tom Johnson, Greg Luce, Greg Mank, Gary Svehla and the whole FANEX crew, Ruth Brunas, Edward Bernds, Bernard Glasser, Rich Scrivani, John Antosiewicz, John Foster, Alex Gordon, Richard Gordon, Joe Dante and Joe Kane. Special thanks to my indefatigable filmography co-compilers John Cocchi and Jack Dukesbery, the best (and most detail-conscious) in the business.

Thanks also (as always) to all of my new interviewees; to the writers of the occasional angry letter (keep 'em coming!); to Research Associates John and Mike Brunas (the best in the world); and to the readership of loyal sci-fi/ horror fans which has helped me turn a parttime hobby (documenting schlock horror's history) into a fulltime racket.

Abridged versions of the interviews featured in *Attack of the Monster Movie Makers* originally appeared in the following magazines: *Merry Anders:* "Time Traveler," *Starlog Spectacular* #2, July, 1991; *Charles Bennett:* "The Oldest Working Screenwriter Explains It All," *Starlog* #193, August, 1993; *Ben Chapman:* "Creature King," *Starlog* #180, July, 1992; *Herman Cohen:* "How to Make a Teenage Monster Movie," *Fangoria* #109, January, 1992, "Field Trips to Terror," *Fangoria* #110, March, 1992, and "Crime & Crimson," *Fangoria* #111, April, 1992; *Robert Day:* "Director of Apemen," *Starlog* #164, March, 1991; *Susan Hart:* "The Bride of AIP," *Fangoria* #108, November, 1991; *Candace Hilligoss:* "Her Life Was a Carnival," *Fangoria* #118, November, 1992; *Rose Hobart:* "An Outspoken Interview with Rose Hobart," *Filmfax* #29, October/November, 1991; *Betsy Jones-Moreland:* "The Saga of the Corman Actress," *Fangoria* #126, September, 1993; *Jacques Marquette:* "Killer Brains & Giant Women," *Starlog* #187, February, 1993; *Cameron*

xi

Mitchell: "Cameron's Closet," *Fangoria* #103, June, 1991; *Ed Nelson:* "Full Nelson," *Fangoria* #104, July, 1991; *William Phipps:* "Tales from the Phipps Dimension," *Starlog* #172, November, 1991; *Vincent Price:* "Priceless," *Fangoria* #100, March, 1991; *Ann Robinson:* "In Martian Combat," *Starlog* #195, October, 1993; *Harry Spalding:* "Friend to the Fly," *Starlog Yearbook* #10, 1992; *Kenneth Tobey:* "His Favorite Things," *Fangoria* #124, July, 1993; *Lupita Tovar:* "Bitten in Spanish," *Fangoria* #119, December, 1992.

*I never did anything, in the twenty years I spent in the industry,
where I didn't have at least a bathing suit or covering of some sort.
Never did any semi-nudity or R-rated or X-rated or anything like that.
And maybe that's why I'm out of the industry!*

Merry Anders

ANOTHER IN THE LONG LINE of 1950s starlets who made their mark in SF and horror, green-eyed blond Merry Anders' genre career has truly run the gamut, from the medieval fantasy *Beauty and the Beast* to the futuristic *The Time Travelers* and the *Star Trek*-like *Women of the Prehistoric Planet;* from a frothy haunted house comedy like *Tickle Me* to the openly sadistic *Legacy of Blood* and *The Hypnotic Eye.* Long (and happily) retired from the industry, she treasures the memory of her 20 years in pictures and looks back (with the type of ency-clopedic film-buff's memory interviewers encounter too seldom!) at a unique career in *cinemacabre.*

Born in Chicago, Merry Anders (real name: Merry Helen Anderson) practically grew up in local bijous watching films and their accompanying stage shows with her movie-crazy mother and grandmother. The family relocated to Los Angeles in 1949 and, while attending John Burroughs Junior High School, Merry made the acquaintance of Rita LeRoy, an old-time film actress who convinced her to take a modeling course. Later, to help her with her modeling, she took dramatic lessons at the Ben Bard Playhouse and was "spotted" by a 20th Century–Fox talent scout in a Playhouse stage presentation. After several years at Fox, Anders turned freelancer, working in television as well as starring in a string of modestly budgeted Western, science fiction and horror films.

According to your publicity, you were "discovered" by a Fox talent scout while taking dramatics lessons at the Ben Bard Playhouse.

That's right. As luck would have it, there was a lady talent scout in the audience the night that we gave our presentation [*Little Women,* with Anders as Beth] for the parents and friends. Her name was Irma Bermudez and she was the secretary to Ivan Kahn, who was the head of talent scouts at Fox. I didn't know anything about it; I went back to school, and one day the follow-ing week, I got a phone call from Mrs. Ben Bard: "Did you contact Fox?" I said, "Did I contact *who?*" — I was that naive *[laughs]!* She said, "Darling, didn't you check the green room? There was a note in there for you to call Twentieth Century–Fox." So I called Fox, Ivan Kahn's office, and made an ap-pointment to see them. And everybody I knew tried to discourage me from going! The high school drama teacher said, "I'll give you the part of Emily in *Our Town* if you'll give up this phony movie business"; Rita LeRoy said, "Merry, they see three hundred fifty girls a week, all far more beautiful and slim and talented and decorative than you. Don't waste your time." But I didn't care. I went out there and they gave me six months of free drama lessons and made a screen test at the end of the six months. After I made the screen test, they said, "Call back in ten days."

So I waited the ten days, not even thinking of hassling these people. At the end of the ten days, Irma Bermudez called me and said *[in a cold tone of voice],* "They're running your screen test at four-thirty this afternoon, *if* you're

Previous page: **Merry Anders, during her early 1950s stint as a 20th Century–Fox starlet, strikes a pose at Santa Monica's Deauville Beach Club.**

interested. Would you like to see it?" Well, of *course* we wanted to see it—how exciting! My mother and I went over to Fox, and Irma was extremely cold. She had been such a wonderful friend that I couldn't quite understand it; Mother said to me, "You better find out why she's so upset." So I asked Irma, and she said, "Well, you didn't call back!" I said, "You told me to call back in ten days." Irma said, "Don't be silly! *Every*body calls, *every* day. To find out which producers and directors have seen the screen test, and how they voted." I said, "Do you mean to tell me that all the producers and directors at this studio have seen this test?"—I was flabbergasted, because I didn't know anything about the industry. Irma said, "By the way, the head of casting is going to see it with you, and then they want you to go and sign a seven-year contract immediately following."

What was your first film?

Wait Till the Sun Shines, Nellie [1952], which was produced by Georgie Jessel and directed by Henry King, who scared the living daylights out of all of us, he was so cross. I had a scene where I was to be married in the movie, and Henry King came up to me and said *[growling]*, "Why don't you smile?! You look like you're going to the gallows!" So I smiled, but the tears were welling up in my eyes, I was so scared.

One film at Fox that I was involved in—that never got made—was very interesting. They spent a lot of money and gathered together some very fine technicians for a movie that they were going to call *First of April*, with "talking" animals. We went in and prerecorded the lines and then they were going to go out and photograph animals moving their mouths so the lines could be dubbed in. I did the voice of a French poodle and spoke French—which was taught to me over a weekend by Natasha Lytess, who was Marilyn Monroe's drama coach. I also did the part of an old nag; I was supposed to be the mother of Kathleen Crowley, who played a filly. And Warren Stevens played First of April, who was a racehorse. But they never could get the animals to work out quite right and that was a shame, because we had all spent an awful lot of hours in that dubbing room.

You were at Fox for about three years.

Right. But everybody else at the studio either had more aggressive agents or were better prepared; they were all getting their nice raises. I was only up to one hundred twenty-five dollars a week, which meant a take-home paycheck of fifty-seven dollars and ten cents, and I was staying at that rate. So I went in to see Lou Schreiber, who was right under [production chief] Darryl Zanuck, and I said, "Mr. Schreiber, if I don't get my raise this time, I'd like my release." He said, "Do you think you're worth more money?" I don't know what made me say it, but I said, "If I am, I better get out and start making it; and if I'm not, I better get out of the industry." He said, "That's a very

Horror and science fiction films were a specialty for Merry Anders, who turned a love affair with motion pictures into a busy B-movie career.

good answer." Well, they let me know their decision two weeks later: They dropped my option. And I cried for three days and three nights, thinking I'd made the biggest mistake of my life *[laughs]*!

Then, after Fox, a lot of TV, including as a regular on a show called Trouble with Father.

It was very difficult working with [stars] Stu Erwin and June Collyer. They were married, and they had wanted their daughter Judy to play the part. So they were not too thrilled with *me [laughs]*! Incidentally, there was another beautiful young lady who was far more talented than I, that interviewed for the part of Joyce Erwin, and didn't get it. Possibly because she was much more assertive and would not have been as cooperative. Her name was Natalie Wood.

Your first horror film, The Hypnotic Eye, *was a bit ahead of its time in its gruesomeness.*

I enjoyed working on *The Hypnotic Eye*. That's when I worked with Jacques Bergerac for the first time, and through Jacques I was able to meet his brother Michel, who was later to become the head of the Revlon Company. Jacques thought it would be an ideal situation for me to meet Michel — Jacques was playing Cupid *[laughs]*. Jacques and his wife Dorothy Malone were going over to Michel's for dinner, and Jacques said that Michel would like very much to call me and have me over, too. I took a cab over to Michel's home, which was in the Hollywood Hills, and the four of us sat down to a very lovely dinner. That was the only time I ever saw Dorothy Malone — a charming woman and an incredible lady. I was in such awe of her I couldn't relax the whole evening long.

I think I was starstruck all my life. I was in the industry for twenty years and I don't think I ever stopped being starstruck.

Did you enjoy working with Bergerac and Allison Hayes in Hypnotic Eye?

Bergerac was adorable, he was a handsome and charming man, very agreeable and very helpful. I remember him asking for suggestions from people, he wanted everything to be right. And he was very personable and charismatic on the screen. I didn't work in that many scenes with Allison Hayes, but I felt she was a very fine performer and a very agreeable person. I worked more with Marcia Henderson and I liked Marcia very much.

How were you levitated in Hypnotic Eye?

A metal T square–type brace was fitted under the shoulder blades of my back and under my hips. I had a rod that hooked onto the heels of my shoes. Then it was all strung with wires. I wore a dress that was two sizes too large for me, to cover up the brace and everything. It was incredibly well-designed. But there was no head support, so of course I went out with a very stiff neck after about four hours of filming *[laughs]*! It was a very interesting experience!

Who did your acid-face makeup?

The sulfuric acid burns were done by a genius by the name of Emile LaVigne. He was just absolutely incredible, the way he had everything preplanned. What he used for the puffiness and the torn skin effect was cotton puffs. They were flattened out and applied to my skin with collodion. On top of that he put permanent papers [for hair setting] — he'd taken those and torn them, so there were rough edges, and placed them on top of the cotton pads with the collodion. Then he lifted the rough edges, so that it gave the effect of severe burns. It took three hours to do my face and my arms, up to my elbows, and I'm very grateful that we were able to do all of those scenes in one day, so that I didn't have to go around scaring everybody *[laughs]*. It was a lonely lunch hour!

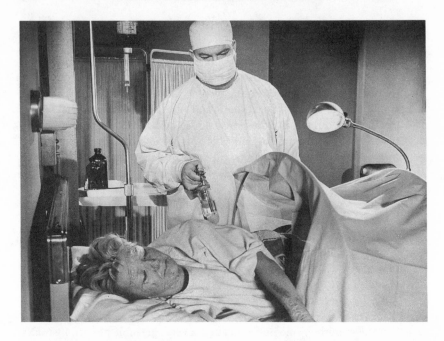

Talk about a run of bad luck: Not only is Anders' *Hypnotic Eye* character self-mutilated, her doctor turns out to be "The Great Impostor" Fred Demara!

You had another interesting co-star in Hypnotic Eye, *Fred Demara, "The Great Impostor."*

Fred Demara was a man who made a career out of assuming the identities of others—a schoolteacher, a prison warden, a surgeon, whatever—without any qualifications or formal education in any of those fields! He played my doctor in *The Hypnotic Eye,* and he was the kindest and gentlest man; I don't know how in the world he could have created so many different personalities and been that unnoticeable. He was just a phenomenal man, and a darling when they introduced me. He didn't seem terribly assertive, he was very shy and very quiet and soft-spoken. I just couldn't believe that he was "The Great Impostor," and that he had performed surgery and all these incredible things!

I count myself lucky to have been in *The Hypnotic Eye* because the producer was Ben Schwalb, and I worked with him in later movies; he called me in for the Elvis Presley movie *Tickle Me,* and if I hadn't worked with Ben Schwalb in *The Hypnotic Eye,* I don't think I would have ever had the opportunity to work with Elvis Presley. Ben was just a wonderful man to work for, he was very tasteful and a terrific gentleman—which you didn't run into too often in the industry *[laughs]*! He treated his people extremely well.

Why do you play such a minor role in Beauty and the Beast?

I interviewed for the part of Beauty, but [producer] Edward Small and [director] Edward Cahn didn't feel that I was particularly right for the part. They had selected Mark Damon for the male lead, and I don't think physically we worked well together as romantic leads. So Mr. Small made a very wise decision in selecting me for the aunt instead. It was a joy for me because I got the opportunity of working with Michael Pate, someone I had admired in films for such a long time. Michael was just delightful. He had so much Shakespearean background that he was giving me a lot of help; he suggested we do it with a very cultured accent, *à la* Shakespearean drama. The idea was just wonderful, and I enjoyed working on that very, very much.

Joyce Taylor ended up playing Beauty to Mark Damon's Beast.

Joyce Taylor I thought did a very fine job. She had just done *Atlantis, the Lost Continent* for George Pal, and I'm not sure that she was ready for smaller budgeted films *[laughs]*! I had worked on quite a few of them and had done some live TV, so I knew the importance of being cooperative; no temperament is allowed when you get on this type of picture. They don't have the money to put up with temper tantrums on the set!

Next was House of the Damned, *a good haunted house–type horror film with some of its "monsters" played by real-life sideshow performers.*

House of the Damned was for a director by the name of Maury Dexter; I did four films for him for [producer] Bob Lippert, and I liked working with Maury tremendously. He pretty much gave you your own way, he gave you a lot of leeway. And he had a wonderful sense of humor, and always had an excellent crew, fun people to work with, so that there wasn't much pressure on his sets. Maury went on later to work with Michael Landon on *Little House on the Prairie* and *Highway to Heaven.*

What can you remember about the circus performers [The Legless Man and The Legless Girl] that were in House of the Damned?

I enjoyed very much working with John Gilmore and Freda Pushnick. They mentioned having been with Barnum and Bailey — Freda and Johnny had toured with them and everything else. They had had quite interesting lives, I'm sure. Freda was just a torso — she had no legs or arms. She was so sweet, so dear. She had (I believe it was) her mom with her on the set of *House of the Damned,* and I got a chance to talk to them, just briefly, which I enjoyed. Johnny Gilmore's body was not formed beyond his chest, and he was able to "walk" around using his hands as feet. He was fully maneuverable; was capable of anything and everything; did not use a wheelchair; and he had the most incredibly beautiful hands, with long, tapered fingers. And a good sense of humor — an impish sense of humor, and the kind of beautiful, radiant smile that you see so rarely! He was a dickens, a delight to work with. I

Anders and Ronald Foster have understandable reservations about entering the *House of the Damned*.

corresponded with both of them after the picture was finished: Freda's mother had to write for her, but Johnny Gilmore had the most beautiful handwriting in the world. We corresponded for one or two years, and I was kind of sorry that I lost touch with them.

If you can stop and look beyond handicaps (or handi*capable,* if you will), you get to find out so often that there's a terrific personality with a lot of intelligence behind it.

You also had Ayllene Gibbons in House of the Damned, *as the Fat Woman.*

Ayllene was a wonderful woman to work with — she handled her lines extremely well and I thought she was quite good in the part. She gave the pathetic we're-so-lost-and-we-need-help effect. I've seen her in things since and thought she was fun. And then of course we also had a rather tall actor by the name of Richard Kiel, who went on to great fame as Jaws, the steel-toothed James Bond menace!

How did you become involved with The Time Travelers?

I had worked with [director] Ib Melchior before, when I did a picture called *The Case of Patty Smith* [1962] for Leo Handel. Ib was the associate producer on that one. That's where I first met Ib, so when *The Time Travelers* came up, he remembered me and decided that he wanted to use me. Ib was always very encouraging, very helpful. There were certain things that he wanted done a certain way, and he didn't say, "Damn it, do it *my* way," he said, "Let's try it *this* way," or "Let me give you some thoughts on this." He was a wonderful director.

So you enjoyed working on Time Travelers?

That was the movie that I probably enjoyed making the most. There were so many good people on that, such good performers; I just loved working with everybody. Preston Foster was a delight; he brought his guitar down on the set and he played all sorts of songs. Preston had written a song called *Two-Shillelagh O'Sullivan [laughs]* and he played it on the set. I told him I was crazy about it, and he gave me the sheet music and a record of it *[laughs]*! Dennis Patrick, who played the villain in *The Time Travelers*, had learned some Irish street dancing, and he was doing clog dancing on the set as Preston played the guitar and sang! And John Hoyt was fun to work with, too, because he had such a dry wit. It was a fun group to work with, which takes an awful lot of the pressure and the stress out of working on long, difficult scenes.

Was Philip Carey as "difficult" as some of his co-workers have indicated?

No, I liked Philip. He did have kind of a grand attitude and an aura about him, but I got a big kick out of working with him. He had an amazing amount of dignity in spite of the fact that he had a commercial for Granny Goose Potato Chips running at the time *[laughs]*. We did our best not to remind him or call him Granny Goose on the set.

Where were some of the places The Time Travelers *was shot?*

We worked at the Cathay Studio, a little soundstage down on Pico near Fairfax, and at a soundstage over in Glendale. Cathay was where we shot the scenes of the main auditorium in the "future" scenes, and also the scenes in the "present day" time travel laboratory; the cave sequences were done at

Preston Foster keeps co-stars Joan Woodbury and Merry Anders smiling between takes on *The Time Travelers*.

that little soundstage over in Glendale. We worked at the Pisgah Crater and Lava Flow, a lava field forty miles east of Barstow; we flew up there and did a day's location. There was a group of basketball players (they played the "mutants") chasing us across the field there, and we were told to wear shoes that we didn't care a great deal about because they would get cut up by the lava rock, which was razor-sharp. We had to run and run and of course I was huffing and puffing, but Philip Carey and Preston Foster were doing just fine. Of course *[laughs]*, their legs were longer than mine! And then some of the film was done on the U.S.C. campus. For a movie that was filmed in so many different locations, I think it came together amazingly well.

We were filming at the Cathay Studio the day that John F. Kennedy was assassinated. I had a little transistor radio and they announced over the air that he had been shot. We all gathered together for a moment of prayer, which I felt was unique because there isn't too much emotion or religion on a set. It was something that we were all quite devastated by. But work went on after that: We were behind schedule and we had certain schedules that had to be fulfilled on certain sets.

Part of the charm of Time Travelers *is knowing that many of the special effects were achieved on the soundstage, without optical work.*

David Hewitt was an unbelievable talent. He did the special effects, all of the miniatures, and all of the actual magician's illusions that are used as special effects throughout the picture. For instance, he devised the table that allowed them to remove the head of the android and replace it — that was quite a technique. Having been suspended by wires for *The Hypnotic Eye,* I know what's involved in lowering your head but keeping your body horizontal — you go home with a very stiff neck *[laughs]*! I think some of the things that he did were absolutely marvelous.

Any anecdotes about the film's android actors?

Their masks were very hot, because they were made out of a flexible rubber. And they were a little upset over the fact that some of them had to go home to their wives with shaven chests *[laughs]*! Some of 'em had to have their chests shaved almost every day, because their chest hair growth was very much like their beards. And then they also wore little pasties, so that they looked more like androids than humans. But they couldn't have anything except smooth skin on them if they were going to be playing androids.

How about the big battle scene at the end of the film?

It was amazing that it looked as active as it did, because there were not that many people on the set. It was a "cast of thousands" that was performed by probably a cast of *[laughs]* — dozens!

Any recollections about your semi-nude "ray bath" scene?

That was such a riot. I had the cutest little bikini bathing suit that I wore behind that screen and I was covered from head to toe, every inch of bare skin, with body makeup, but I felt like I looked nuder than anybody else in the scene *[laughs]*! And the other girls in the scene *were* topless — I began to wonder what kind of a movie I was doing! And I could never understand the significance of the scene, except that maybe it was necessary to make my character a little more human — a little less crisp and dried and dull. Uncanny as it sounds, we had one scene with Philip Carey saying the word *damn,* which was cut out of the movie the first times *The Time Travelers* was shown on TV, but the nude ray bath scene was left in, which made me very uncomfortable *[laughs]*!

I never did anything, in the twenty years I spent in the industry, where I didn't have at least a bathing suit or covering of some sort. Never did any semi-nudity or R-rated or X-rated or anything like that. And maybe that's why I'm *out* of the industry [laughs]!

What do you remember about Peter Strudwick, who played the malformed Deviant?

Oh, a delightful man, with a glib, cute sense of humor. He was a scientist in real life, and very gifted, and he had been born this way: He was born without his feet fully formed, and his hands had like talons for fingers. He was very agile, and handled it beautifully. He was just comfortable to work with and very professional for his first movie. He worked for the Rand Corporation, in their think tank in Santa Monica. At the cast party he told me that he was being teased unmercifully by his fellow workers at Rand, because he was a "big movie star" who had risen to fame from a laboratory.

You also got all your scientific equipment from Burroughs, right?

The scientific equipment we used in our "time travel" laboratory *was* provided by Burroughs. It was used for the first U.S. manned flight into space [Alan Shepard]—it helped plan that flight and also to track the John Glenn flight. It was apparently taken out of storage for *The Time Travelers,* and I don't know whether it was deep-sixed afterwards or what. We had a Burroughs representative on the set, so that they were able to make sure that we were using the vernacular correctly. At the time we did the movie, photon and ion drives were so new that the script had to be cleared before Ib Melchior could utilize some of these phrases. He had written about things that were so far into the future that they were just barely declassified. Ib was very exact in his research, and all this made it very interesting to work with. We were working with things that were actual, and gaining an education. I had no idea, with some of these things, what he was even talking about! I'm only now beginning to realize how new and how progressive Ib was in his research, and it just amazes me. He had a phenomenal background, but I didn't know any of this at the time I worked with him.

Have you been in touch with him in recent years?

Just recently, my husband and I were invited to his home for *koldt bord*—a "cold table," a Danish smorgasbord type of thing. Ib served herring which he'd prepared, salmon roe—Ib's a wonderful cook, and it was just incredible. Dennis Patrick was there with his lovely wife [actress Barbara Cason], Les Tremayne and his wife, Leo Handel and his lovely lady, Ib and his wife Cleo (a very elegant, wonderfully artistic, gifted woman). There were about ten people there, and they were the most interesting, well-educated, charming people I'd met in a long time.

What do you think of The Time Travelers *today?*

I probably see more substance in it today than I did back then. I felt very happy that the picture turned out as well as it did; I don't know whether it was accepted as much as I really expected it to be, because I thought it was really well thought out and well written, well photographed and well directed. A lot of people worked awfully hard to make it a good movie. They were agreeable and amiable, all professionals, and I think that's what made it turn out that well.

You also were in that haunted house comedy with Elvis Presley, Tickle Me.

To me, that young man was an absolute darling, down to earth and comfortable to be around. I brought my mother and my ten-year-old daughter down to the set, and Elvis Presley came down, pulled up a director's chair next to my mother and sat and talked to her for about forty-five minutes about how much he loved his mother and how great he thought it was that she came with me. And then he picked my daughter Tina up in his arms and took her around and showed her the set and talked with her for fifteen, twenty minutes. Tina was an absolute fan of the Beatles at the time *[laughs]*, but he broke through this because he was so kind and such a perfect gentleman.

Any memories of Women of the Prehistoric Planet?

Just that there were so many nice people to work with on that one; I wish I had been on the movie longer, because I really enjoyed the few days that I had on the set. I enjoyed working with Wendell Corey, because I'd been a fan of his for a long time. He had a very sarcastic wit and he'd say little things under his breath that would crack everybody up. He was concerned about the fact that his costume was so tight that if he bent over, he would rip his pants *[laughs]*! John Agar was so nice and Keith Larsen was just a darling to be around. But the thing that really impressed me about *Women of the Prehistoric Planet* was this one particular young man who was in it. I kept saying to myself, "God, that guy is so well-built and he has such a good presence on-screen!" Now, years later, I watch the film again on television and I darn near fell off the couch, because it was Robert Ito, who went on to star with Jack Klugman in the TV series *Quincy*—one of my all-time favorites! And all the years I'd been watching *Quincy*, I didn't realize he was the one I admired so much on *Women of the Prehistoric Planet*!

Your last feature was a "murder-in-the-mansion" horror film, Legacy of Blood.

That's one I hope will only run in the wee small hours of the morning *[laughs]*, although it was an exceptional experience because it had people in it like John Carradine, John Russell of *Lawman*, John Smith of *Laramie*, Faith Domergue, Jeff Morrow, Dick Davalos—some really capable people. The producer was a charming gentleman from Aruba named Ben Rombouts who had been in a very serious accident. Ben had been in the hospital, in a full body cast, for months, and he had some incredible doctors. And he wanted to make a movie so badly that he talked all of these doctors into backing this movie *[laughs]*! Ben and the director had us rehearse for six weeks before we ever put anything on film; we'd gather in a circle and do a read-around and talk about scenes and how important it was that they tied in logically. But when the film was edited together, it lost all the sense of what we had worked with on the rehearsing script; I almost felt like some of the scenes were out of sequence. I don't know whether it was the fault of the editor or if it was just running too long. I am so sorry that it never really made the money it was supposed to.

Where was Legacy of Blood *shot?*

We filmed that at the Van Valkenberg estate in Pasadena, which was the house that was used for the exterior of Wayne Manor on [TV's] *Batman*. We were one of the first filming companies to work inside there. We filmed on the grounds, too, and there was one scene that I had to do which involved wading into a fish pond with live goldfish that were six to eight inches long — very mucky, murky water — at twelve-thirty in the morning, which thrilled me. But it was a very dramatic scene and it was apparently very important to the plot. I knelt down into the water and skinned both knees, so we had to cover those with makeup because it was in the days of wearing short skirts. So for two or three days we covered my skinned knees with lots of makeup, and we kept filming *[laughs]*!

The day after the fish pond scene, Mrs. Van Valkenberg came up and she was watching one of the scenes that was being filmed. I was sitting in one of the bedrooms and she came in and sat down and she said, "I understand that one of the actresses on this film waded into the fish pond." I said, "Yes, that was me." She said, "Did they ask you if you could swim?" "No, they told me it was only hip-deep." And she said, "Oh, my dear, the thing is *bottomless!*" *[Laughs.]* She said, "If you'd moved over about two feet, you'd have gone down over your head!" Ah, the joys of being an actress *[laughs]*!

Did you get a chance to meet John Carradine on Legacy of Blood*?*

No, I didn't work the day that he did. But I have to tell you that, from what I heard from John Russell and Faith Domergue, who were on the set that day, the man came in letter-perfect with his dialogue. He did the scene two or three times, not because he wasn't right on target, but because of different mechanical difficulties. He knew every line in the script, never held up production and was just an absolutely consummate professional. I've only heard that about two or three people that I've worked with in the industry. Another great horror star that I worked with was Lon Chaney, Jr., who was in a Western

I did called *Young Fury* [1965]. A darling, kind, gentle man . . . who I think possibly wanted to seek the approval of his father, and who maybe never quite did receive the assurance from his dad that he was doing well. Maybe I understood him a little bit better than other people might because I never felt that I really had the approval of my father until I left the movie industry and got a regular job *[laughs]*! So I think I felt a kinship with Chaney.

Any regrets, looking back at a career that maybe wasn't all it should have been?

The only regret that I might have was that I wasn't able to climb out of my shell and trust my directors more, and allow myself to be more free in what I did. I held back because I was insecure most of my life. That probably sounds crazy coming from someone who spent so much of their life out on the screen portraying roles. But I was always hiding behind the characters. (I feel more secure about myself today.) But once I left the industry, I enjoyed having a steady job and that I didn't have to worry about someone saying, "You've got to lose ten pounds!" or "You've got to change your hair color!" or "I don't like the way you do your makeup!"

When people think of Merry Anders, they think of TV and what used to be called B movies. Is that okay?

I worked a great deal because I loved working with the people. I could spend seventeen hours a day on a set, stand until my feet hurt, and be so tired I'd think I was practically catatonic. Then I'd go home and climb into the tub and wash off the makeup, set my hair if it was one of those low-budget films where they didn't have a hair dresser—and go to sleep looking forward to going to work the next day. It was a wonderful experience, a wonderful twenty years. I loved the industry.

MERRY ANDERS FILMOGRAPHY

Wait Till the Sun Shines, Nellie (20th Century–Fox, 1952)
Les Miserables (20th Century–Fox, 1952)
Belles on Their Toes (20th Century–Fox, 1952)
The Farmer Takes a Wife (20th Century–Fox, 1953)
How to Marry a Millionaire (20th Century–Fox, 1953)
Titanic (20th Century–Fox, 1953)
Three Coins in the Fountain (20th Century–Fox, 1954)
Princess of the Nile (20th Century–Fox, 1954)
Phffft! (Columbia, 1954)
All That Heaven Allows (Universal, 1955)
Hear Me Good (Paramount, 1957)
No Time to Be Young (Columbia, 1957)
Calypso Heat Wave (Columbia, 1957)

Escape from San Quentin (Columbia, 1957)
Death in Small Doses (Allied Artists, 1957)
The Night Runner (Universal, 1957)
Desk Set (20th Century–Fox, 1957)
The Dalton Girls (United Artists, 1957)
Violent Road (Warners, 1958)
Spring Affair (George Bagnall Associates, 1960)
Five Bold Women (Citation Films, 1960)
The Hypnotic Eye (Allied Artists, 1960)
Walking Target (United Artists, 1960)
Young Jesse James (20th Century–Fox, 1960)
When the Clock Strikes (United Artists, 1961)
Secret of Deep Harbor (United Artists, 1961)
The Police Dog Story (United Artists, 1961)
20,000 Eyes (20th Century–Fox, 1961)
The Gambler Wore a Gun (United Artists, 1961)
The Case of Patty Smith (The Shame of Patty Smith) (Impact Films/Ellis Gordon/
    Topaz, 1962)
Air Patrol (20th Century–Fox, 1962)
Beauty and the Beast (United Artists, 1963)
Police Nurse (20th Century–Fox, 1963)
House of the Damned (20th Century–Fox, 1963)
The Quick Gun (Columbia, 1964)
A Tiger Walks (Buena Vista, 1964)
FBI Code 98 (Warners, 1964)
The Time Travelers (AIP, 1964)
Raiders from Beneath the Sea (20th Century–Fox, 1964)
Young Fury (Paramount, 1965)
Tickle Me (Allied Artists, 1965)
Women of the Prehistoric Planet (Realart, 1966)
Airport (Universal, 1970)
Legacy of Blood (Blood Legacy) (Universal Entertainment, 1973)

I've been a writer all my life, ever since I gave up acting in nineteen twenty-six. That's what I live for. If I couldn't write, I wouldn't want to live.

Charles Bennett

THE OLDEST EMPLOYED SCREENWRITER IN THE WORLD, Charles Bennett has had an amazingly wide-ranging writing career: It has reached from the mid–1920s (when he began to find success as a playwright in his native England) to the present day, and has included hall-of-fame titles like *The Man Who Knew Too Much* and *The 39 Steps* along with colorful exploitation items like *Voyage to the Bottom of the Sea* and *War-Gods of the Deep*.

Born just before the century turned (August 2, 1899), Bennett made his acting debut as a child in 1911, fought in France during World War I while still a teen and resumed his acting career after the war's end. In 1926 he dropped acting to concentrate on being a playwright, later turning one of his most famous plays, *Blackmail*, into a screenplay for production under the direction of Alfred Hitchcock. The affiliation with "Hitch" continued into the early 1940s, by which time both Bennett and the director were working in Hollywood. In the 1950s, Bennett began a long association with producer/director Irwin Allen, working on Allen's movies (*The Story of Mankind, The Lost World*, etc.) as well as on his TV series *Voyage to the Bottom of the Sea* and *Land of the Giants*; amidst these assignments he also penned the horror classic *Curse of the Demon,* based on Montague James' short story *Casting the Runes.* At 94, he's still writing, still razor-sharp, and always ready to share his candid memories of the highs—and occasional lows—of his remarkable life in the writing profession.

I know you must be regularly courted by interviewers who want to hear about your Hitchcock films and your other classics. How often do you hear from someone like me, who wants to know about The Secret of the Loch *and* War-Gods of the Deep?

[*Laughs.*] I never hear from anybody about those at all! As far as I'm concerned, they're forgotten. Certainly *The Secret of the Loch* is one that I thought no one could possibly remember—that was nineteen thirty-three, I think!

According to the credits, you co-wrote that with someone named Billy Bristow.

No, actually, she didn't do a damn thing, but she *was* around and I did do some pictures with her. So I think I gave her credit, yes. The picture was my idea. What had happened was, the Loch Ness Monster was just starting to hit the London newspapers and I decided that there might be a film in it. This was mid-winter, nineteen thirty-three. I got my car out and I drove to the Highlands of Scotland. I'll never forget passing over the pass of Glen Coe, a very wild pass in the Highlands, with this great drop on one side and the car skidding all over the place! Anyway, I got to Loch Ness, to Fort Augustus, where the monks were reporting that they had seen the monster. I got hold of the head of the monastery and I said to him, "I understand you saw the monster." He said, "Oh, yes, yes, yes, it was here this morning." "Oh, fine,"

Previous page: "[Writing is] what I live for," says still-active screenwriter Charles Bennett, now 94.

I said, "where is it *now?*" He said, "It's gone up the Loch. Go up there." So I drove up the Loch about fifteen miles to Urquart and I found the pier master of this broken-down pier; he was an old gentleman, I remember. I said to him, "Well, where's the monster? I understand it's around here." And the old gentleman said, "Oh, yes, yes, yes, it was here this morning. But it's gone back to see the monks down there!" *[Laughs.]* So I couldn't find the monster!

The other thing I remember is that by that time I'd been struck by the utter loneliness of the Loch—not a soul anywhere! I decided to go along the road on the south side of the Loch, a narrow road with weird little bridges. I followed it around looking for the monster, hoping to spot it. I didn't find the monster but I found a pub, and there inside were about ten newspapermen, some from Glasgow, some from Edinburgh and two or three from London. And I found the most beautiful Scotch whiskey in the world *[laughs]*! (*So* beautiful that when I came to California years later, I used to import this Scotch whiskey!) So at least *some*thing came of this trip!

After that, you wrote the film.

Yes, and it was terrible. I saw it again recently—I thought the picture needed cutting like hell and it was out-of-date. I was amateurish, I was a beginner then. But it's *amusing.* We used a lizard or something like that as the monster, and I suppose the picture made a certain amount of money—it was cheaply made. It was mainly shot at Twickenwood Studios and Loch Ness. A famous actor in those days, Seymour Hicks, played the lead and Milton Rosner directed it. This was at a time when the British government was saying that a certain amount of programs *had* to be made in Britain, so the American companies were financing cheap British pictures—we called them "pound-a-footers," meaning you made the pictures for one pound per foot of film. Then they were put in as second features to very important pictures. *Secret of the Loch* was made under those circumstances. It was a six-reel picture, I think, running about sixty-five or seventy-five minutes.

Do you believe in the Loch Ness Monster?

Oh, of course I do! I think too many people have seen it *not* to believe in it. It's been seen by thousands of people now. I wouldn't say that I necessarily believed in it at the time I wrote that crappy picture about it *[laughs]*, but I believe in it now!

What do you recall about writing The Clairvoyant?

Maurice Elvey directed it, and I think the producer must have been Michael Balcon of Gaumont-British. It was made as a Gainsborough Picture, but Gainsborough and Gaumont-British were the same company in those days. Whereas Gainsborough had its studios in Islington, the Gaumont-British studios were in Shepherd's Bush. I suppose I came up with the idea for

The Clairvoyant. I remember they said that they'd got Claude Rains coming over to do a picture for them, and they could also get the *King Kong* woman, what was her name?, Fay Wray. They had a lot of writers trying to come up with ideas, and I came up with the idea which they used: A "clairvoyant" who made predictions, but the events only happened *because* the guy had prophesied them. I was told to go ahead and write the story and screenplay, so I did.

According to the credits, it was based on a novel by Ernest Lothar.

I never read it. I never *heard* of it! But that sometimes happens: Often they would put the name of an author of a novel [on a picture] after the screenplay was finished, after the picture was finished. That happened with me with Cecil B. DeMille, on a picture called *Unconquered* [1947] with Paulette Goddard. When it was finished, it was "from a novel." And the novel was actually written from *my* screenplay! My screenplay wasn't written from the novel, the novel was written from my screenplay! But people thought it gave a picture more importance, to *say* that it was from a novel.

Your co-writer on Clairvoyant *was Bryan Edgar Wallace.*

Yeah, he was a . . . useless character. He was only there because he happened to be the son of Edgar Wallace. He couldn't write, he hadn't an idea in his head. I was happy with the picture when it came out; I haven't seen it for a long, long time now *[laughs]*!

One other thing I remember about *The Clairvoyant* is that I fell in love with the woman who was playing the second part, Jane Baxter. This is a funny story! I was doing what is sometimes called "writing just ahead of the cameras": I was in the studio, and the assistant director would come up and say, "Have you got any more pages?" He'd take them down to Maurice Elvey, the director, and they'd shoot them. One day, Claude Rains came up to my office and said, "By the way, Charles, have you noticed this girl who's playing the second part?" I said, "Yes, she's quite lovely." He said, "I only ask because she keeps on saying, 'That writer up there, he's so good-looking, I can't put him out of my mind.'" I thought, "*This* is very interesting!" So I went down to the set, met Jane Baxter, and we became very close friends. After the picture was over, one night we were having dinner on the lawn at the big hotel in Bray, and she said, "Do you know, Charles, how I met you?" I told her what had happened. She said, "No, it wasn't quite like that. Claude Rains used to come up to me every day and say, 'Have you noticed this writer? He can't put you out of his mind. . .!'" Rains was a practical joker *[laughs]*! He was on his way back to America on the *Normandie* and we sent a telegram to him that night, thanking him very much.

Who brought you to Hollywood? Some sources say it was Universal, others say David O. Selznick.

Universal brought me over in nineteen thirty-seven. I'd done, by that time, seven pictures for Hitchcock. Universal put me under contract for much more money than I was getting in England, so I couldn't turn it down. I came across, but it was about a year later that Universal was running low on funds and I dropped out of my contract and went to work for David Selznick, writing a picture for Janet Gaynor [*The Young in Heart,* 1938]. One night we were having an all-night conference on the thing, and Selznick said to me, "Charles, it's been suggested to me that I should bring over one of two English directors. One is named Alfred Hitchcock and the other is named Robert Stevenson. You've worked with both of them, who should I bring?" I said, "Bring them both!" *[Laughs.]* So, you see, it wasn't David Selznick who brought me over, but *I* brought *Hitchcock* over!

Another one of your early Hollywood films, They Dare Not Love *[1941], was directed by James Whale.*

James Whale didn't direct that film, strangely enough. He was thrown out after the first week, and Charles Vidor directed it — and *hated* it. (I didn't like it, either, quite frankly; I don't consider it one of my good pictures.) I had great respect for James Whale, I thought he was an extremely fine director, but he had [trouble from] Harry Cohn — the most revolting character in the world, with a foul tongue all the time. Cohn was head of the Columbia studios and he took a dislike to James Whale immediately, and threw him out after the first week.

How and when did you hook up with Irwin Allen?

I'd been directing a lot of television *for* Hollywood in England. When I came back, Irving Cummings was going to produce a picture called *Where Danger Lives* [1950] with Robert Mitchum and Claude Rains, and I was asked to write it. Irwin Allen knew somebody who worked for Howard Hughes, and Howard Hughes owned RKO, so somehow it was finagled into him being associate producer. Once the picture was made, after that, every picture he made (until *The Poseiden Adventure*) I wrote. I was his favorite writer. I couldn't stand him, he was a dreadful man, with the most horrible swollen head and everything. He always took other people's credits and things like that; he never wrote a damn thing himself, but he always put his name on pictures if he could.

Well, that takes care of my next question. I was going to ask if you two were friends!

Nobody could ever be a personal friend of his. But he had tremendous respect for me, and he never dared to cross me in any way. In fact, I remember a case at Twentieth Century–Fox when I actually threw him out of my office — and he was the producer, you know *[laughs]*! I said, "Get out of here. Get *out,* you're stopping me working." And he had to take it, because he knew that I could write and he couldn't. He was a horrible man. So there was no real personal relationship, no. He'd come to my house for drinks occasionally, yes, but then, so did many other people.

Whatever his failings, he was loyal to certain actors; the same ones turn up in a lot of his early movies.

Like Peter Lorre and people like that? Well, yes, when an actor was as good as Peter, naturally you'd employ him whenever you possibly could! It was as simple as that. But Irwin couldn't always get the actors he wanted. For example, I wrote the original screenplay of *Voyage to the Bottom of the Sea,* which later turned into a very successful television series. We had wonderful actors in it, but none of 'em ever played again for Irwin Allen except for Peter Lorre. Because they didn't like Irwin Allen. Joan Fontaine was one of the people that was in it, and she couldn't *stand* him *[laughs]*!

After writing these movies for Allen, did you visit the sets at all?

Oh, yes. I was usually in the studio [at 20th Century–Fox], because if he was shooting one picture that I had written, I'd be writing the next one at the same time. I had my own offices there.

Without wishing to dredge up too many painful memories, what can I ask you about Warners' The Story of Mankind?

That dreadful picture! I came back, again, from England and Irwin Allen implored me to work on that thing. I didn't realize quite how dreadful it was going to be, I didn't realize when I was starting off that it was really going to be just a collection of snippets from old pictures and things like that. It was dreadful, I hated the picture. But I'm a writer, I wrote it, I was being paid quite handsomely, so that was it.

Did it follow the book it was supposedly based on?

Certainly not! In fact, I never read the book—and I don't think Allen did, either *[laughs]*!

Vincent Price?

Oh, he was a very dear friend of mine, I was awfully fond of him. I had him in seven different movies and he's always been, to me, a fine, fine actor. But I don't know that he enjoyed playing the Devil in *The Story of Mankind*; I don't think *anybody* enjoyed any *part* of it. I know Ronald Colman hated it and I don't think Vincent Price liked it, either. No, nobody liked it, it was just a revolting picture and it should never have been made. And it was much too long. I remember the sneak preview at a theater in the Valley, and the wretched Jack Warner (who owned Warner Brothers) was there. At the end,

Montague James' *Casting the Runes* was the inspiration for Bennett, who had his own ideas about casting the movie.

we all went and talked about it around a table in a pub, and I said, "It's got to be cut. This is no good in its present form." Jack Warner said, "Oh, let's just put it out." And all his yes-men said, "Yes, Jack's right, let's put it out." So they did.

The worst scenes were the ones with the Marx Brothers.
    They were just given their heads. Nobody wrote the stuff, they were just told to do it themselves and that was it; the basic idea of Groucho Marx's segment was the sale of Manhattan by the Indians.

Were any of the historical vignettes to your liking? Do you have anything nice to say about The Story of Mankind?
    I have nothing to say in its favor at all *[laughs]*!

How did you become involved with Night of the Demon *[U.S. title:* Curse of the Demon*]?*
    I read the short story *Casting the Runes* by the late Montague James and I loved it, I thought to myself, "There's a movie in this." So I arranged with the James estate (with his wife, who lived in Africa) to buy the rights myself. I

bought the rights and then I wrote my own screenplay. My screenplay was ex-tremely good—my original title was *The Bewitched*. Actually, it turned into a very sad situation: I was in London directing the *Monte Cristo* TV series for Edward Small, and I was just about to leave to come back to Hollywood. I was leaving Thirty-nine Hill Street, which is just off Berkeley Square, and Hal Chester (who was a little producing man) was waiting in the foyer as I came by. He said, "Look, I can set this picture up with Columbia Pictures. Will you just give me your signature now?" I was on my way to catch a plane and like a fool, I signed it. When I got back to Hollywood, two days later I learned that RKO had given the okay for my screenplay to be shot, exactly as I wanted to make it, with *me* directing my own screenplay. But it was too late, I'd signed this paper on the way out to my plane, I'd signed it away.

Reportedly Robert Taylor and Dick Powell were both interested in starring at one point.
Robert Taylor certainly wanted to do it. In fact, it was his right hand man (whose name I now forget) who had set it up in my absence with RKO. Dick Powell also was very, very interested and talked to me about it a tremendous lot. But we never quite got down to a contract.

In the picture's main titles, you share the writing credit with Hal Chester.
Oh, no, I didn't *share* it at all, he just put his name on. He was in England, I was in America, there was nothing I could do about it. Hal Chester didn't do it any good, but I thought the James story and my screenplay were so good that he couldn't *entirely* ruin it! He did mess up the script, but never mind about that *[laughs]*!

Dana Andrews mentioned that Chester even tried to interfere in the directing.
[Laughs.] I'm sure he did!

In your original screenplay, were you faithful to the James story?
I tried to be, yes, but you *can't* be faithful entirely to a story like that. The fundamental idea was the guy being passed the runes, and then having to pass them *back* in order to avoid his coming death. That was the original story and from that I built my screenplay. [The movie makers] put in a mon-ster to look at, which made me very angry. I preferred that the audience should have to *imagine* the horror that was after this man, instead of *seeing* it. Hal Chester made quite a few *bad* changes, and they cut out some beautiful things, too.

What did you think of the special effects involving the demon?
They were not bad; considering how many years ago it was, they were pretty good.

The cast was also good.

Dana Andrews they had trouble with, but he was a good actor. For the Niall MacGinnis part, I wanted Francis L. Sullivan; he would have been better, *much* better. But MacGinnis gave a . . . *competent* performance, let me put it that way. The *idiot* thing that happened was that when it came to Columbia in Hollywood, they said, "Oh, we can't use [the title] *Night of the Demon* because it'll be mixed up with *Night of the Iguana.*" So they called it *Curse of the Demon.* I hated that title because it made it a B picture immediately, a title like that.

Did you ever meet director Jacques Tourneur?

I knew him very well and I was awfully fond of him. He was a very good director. But he got involved in some dreadful, *dreadful* picture which I should never have had anything to do with, *War-Gods of the Deep.* It was simply horrid, the worst thing I was ever involved in, I think. Jacques, the poor devil, got the blame for it, but actually he was not to blame at all. I had written a good script, and [while it was in production] I was asked to go to England to make alterations. The wretched American International Pictures came up with a lousy offer which my agent turned down, so they put on some other writer who *completely* annihilated the thing. It was dreadful, I should have taken my name off it. At any rate, poor, poor, *poor* Jacques got the blame—and he blamed *me* for not coming over *[laughs]*! But he was a great friend of mine.

But AIP did ask you to go to England and do some rewriting on War-Gods?

They wanted to send me to England, yes, but they wouldn't pay me any money. Their idea of money was absolutely so trivial that it would have *cost* me money to go *[laughs]*!

AIP credited War-Gods *to Edgar Allan Poe, but to me it was very Jules Verne.*

Oh, Christ, do we—*[laughs]*—do we *have* to talk about that film? Can't we forget it ever *existed*? It was supposed to be based on a tiny Poe poem; they said, "Can you take this and make it into a story?" Which I did—I did a pretty good story, as a matter of fact. And it was completely ruined when it came to a matter of my *not* going to England and protecting my own screenplay. Jacques Tourneur did a good job himself with an impossible script. The writer who did rework it put a chicken into the movie, as one of the main characters—oh, God, that was *awful*! That was stolen directly from *Journey to the Center of the Earth,* which was made by Twentieth Century–Fox. In *Journey,* it was a goose. But the chicken in *War-Gods,* that had nothing to do with me, thank you!

Who came up with the idea for the nineteen sixty The Lost World?

It was as simple as the fact that somebody suggested to Irwin that he should make *The Lost World*. He liked the idea of prehistoric monsters and things like that, so he asked me to write the script.

Did you reread the Arthur Conan Doyle novel?

Oh, I knew the novel by heart; I know *all* Conan Doyle's stuff by heart, I *loved* him. I knew him personally: I was playing Dr. Watson in *Sherlock Holmes in the Speckled Band* at a theater in Paris. I was only twenty-four at the time, and Conan Doyle was in front. He came 'round after the performance and said that I was the finest Watson he'd ever seen. So I must have been a pretty good actor at the age of twenty-four *[laughs]*! Of course, I never told that to Nigel Bruce, who played it so often with Basil Rathbone!

Allen hired one of the most famous stop-motion animators for The Lost World, *Willis O'Brien — and then Allen went ahead and used lizards in the film.*

I don't remember that. Quite frankly, I never went near that set, as far as I can remember. But there was no question of animation, no, the whole thing was special effects [with the lizards] — the Twentieth Century–Fox people were pretty good at that sort of thing.

These Irwin Allen pictures like The Lost World *got some bad reviews at the time, but audiences must have liked them.*

Oh, audiences *loved* them. And, to be frank, they *didn't* get bad reviews at all, ever — or, at least, I can't seem to remember bad reviews for them. (Not that I really bother much about reviews.)

What did you think of Claude Rains as Prof. Challenger?

He was wonderful — always. Claude Rains was always superb, whatever he did. I think Claude Rains was one of the best actors the world ever knew. I had him in seven different movies.

Some fans were disappointed that your Lost World *didn't end up with the dinosaur loose in London, the way the original silent* Lost World *did.*

Oh, God, we didn't do that, because the Conan Doyle *novel* doesn't end that way. The silent film ended with *that*? Then I guess I never saw it! *Our* ending was the escape of the people *from* the "lost world." I thought ours was a competent show; I didn't think it was very *good*, I didn't think it was very *bad*. It was *good enough*, let's put it that way.

Was Voyage to the Bottom of the Sea *your idea?*

Irwin's girlfriend had said, "Why not a movie about a big submarine?", and he told me that this was a good idea for a movie. So I wrote the story of it, and then I wrote the screenplay. It was as simple as that.

Inadvisably making its home in a pool of boiling lava, a fin-backed lizard rises to menace the stars of Bennett's *The Lost World.*

The Voyage *script involved a lot of scientific plot points. Is science a hobby of yours?*

I researched it a certain amount. It certainly wasn't a hobby, no; I'm not interested in science at all. I've spent my life writing all sorts of pictures, and many of them have entailed doing a lot of research.

In general, would you know as you were writing an Irwin Allen movie who would be playing the various roles?

I usually made suggestions myself; for instance, on *The Lost World,* it was I who suggested Claude Rains. And, yes, in all the films I used to suggest the cast, because I was working very closely with Irwin—my office was very close to his. Walter Pidgeon was excellent in *Voyage to the Bottom of the Sea;* he was my suggestion, too. Peter Lorre, and Joan Fontaine, also. And she *hated* it, and she blamed *me* for it! She was one of my closest friends, we used to ride horses together all the time, things like that. She was in my movie *Ivy* [1947] which Sam Wood directed at Universal, I adored her and she adored me, too. But she said she hated the part [in *Voyage*], and didn't like the picture.

Joan Fontaine (seen here with Walter Pidgeon) "hated *Voyage to the Bottom of the Sea,* and she blames me for it!" remembers Bennett.

Did you visit the sets of Voyage?

Oh, yes, I was in and out pretty frequently, particularly since Joan Fontaine was in it. And I also adored Peter Lorre. I had him in seven movies, and that's a lot of movies. The first time he was in a movie of mine was *The Man Who Knew Too Much* [1934]. He was an adorable, very kind, very gentle, very sweet man. Like Boris Karloff, another "very gentle monster." I was very fond of him.

Curt Siodmak told me Lorre was "a sadistic son of a bitch — liked to look at operations."

That's not true! Peter was a kind, very pleasant person with a big sense of humor, very delightful. I remember a funny thing about Peter, on *The Man Who Knew Too Much.* We had a secretary who was named Joan Harrison, and she had come down from Oxford. She was *supposed* to speak French very well, and Peter Lorre couldn't speak English but he *could* speak French and a smattering of English. So Hitch said to Joan, "Look, go and explain the scenes to Peter in French, so he'll understand them." So Joan did: She went to Peter, talked a lot of French to him, he listened very beautifully. And at the end of it he said, very kindly, "Please . . . I do not understand . . . speak English!" Her French was so bad, he had a better chance of understanding in English *[laughs]*!

You later worked on the Voyage to the Bottom of the Sea *TV show.*

I did a lot of them; I did about eight, when I had nothing better to do. I did 'em for the sake of the money *[laughs]*. I think I also did one or two of the series, oh, what was it called, *Giant Men?* What the hell was the name of that? Oh, yes, *Land of the Giants,* I did one or two of those. I also did one *Time Tunnel,* but I've forgotten what it was about.

How about Lost in Space?

That was my idea, but I never wrote anything for it. After we'd done *Voyage to the Bottom of the Sea,* I came up with the idea of a space picture—people were starting to go up into space then. I suggested to Irwin that *Lost in Space* would be a good idea for a movie. Well, I went off somewhere else, and Irwin stole the idea—instead of making it into a movie, he stole the idea and made a television series of it. It was as simple as that!

One TV show that you'd have been ideal for was Alfred Hitchcock Presents—*and you never wrote for them once.*

I never *wanted* to, quite frankly. I was a great, great friend of Hitch's and I preferred to remain a great friend, instead of getting mixed up with that particular show. Partly because the producer had been our secretary for so long, Joan Harrison. I couldn't *bear* the thought of working under my own secretary *[laughs]*!

In one of the Hitchcock biographies, it says that you called Psycho *"the work of a sadistic son of a bitch."*

I said that to Hitchcock's face. I was having drinks with him at his home in Bel-Air and I said that he was a sadistic son of a bitch. He said, "Charles, why do you say that?" I said, "Well, look at *Psycho,* look at that bathroom scene." He said, "Charles, you've lost your sense of humor." I said, "What are you talking about?" He said, "I didn't film that for drama, I filmed it for *comedy,* I wanted the audience to *laugh.*" What do you know about that?! Amazing! According to Hitch, he shot it for comedy!

Another actor who turned up in some of your Irwin Allen movies was Sir Cedric Hardwicke.

Oh, Cedric I adored, I was very fond of him. He played in a lot of my movies and he was a very, very close friend of mine always. And a very good actor indeed. I had him in the last picture I did for Irwin, which was *Five Weeks in a Balloon* [1962], and he was in half a dozen more of my pictures.

He starred in your King Solomon's Mines *in nineteen thirty-seven.*

I didn't really write that. My name was on it, but actually I took myself off it because I objected to having a woman going with the men. I was a fan of Rider Haggard and *King Solomon's Mines,* and in it the four main characters were men. I objected to having a woman coming along, looking as if she had just walked out of a beauty parlor. It was a damn silly idea. So I took myself off.

Anna Lee did a good job of playing the role.

Yes, she did, but, hell, it was wrong. The idea of dragging a woman across the desert...!

What's going on with the remake of Blackmail *that you recently wrote?*

The script is finished, and it's a very good script. It's now a question of finding the right cast. Making a picture in Hollywood now is a very difficult problem, because (no matter how much money you're putting into it) you've still got to get the right cast, and you sometimes find the actors you want aren't available for eighteen months or something like that. And then, if you get the actor you want, you find the *director* isn't available! It's a complicated business, not like it used to be fifty years ago when the actors and the directors were all under contract to the studios like MGM and Warner Brothers, and did what they were told.

And how is your autobiography coming along?

Fine, I'm about halfway finished, but this last week I've been in hospital over my damn injured leg. And that irritates me very much, because every day I feel I'm missing doing something. Either on the autobiography, or on a *new* screenplay which I am writing.

Are you going to keep on writing?

Yes, yes! As long as I possibly can, I will. I've been a writer all my life, ever since I gave up acting in nineteen twenty-six. That's what I live for. If I couldn't write, I wouldn't want to live.

*My conception, when I sat down and read the script
and discussed it with Jack Arnold, was, "Hey, this is
simply Beauty and the Beast." The Gill Man is really
a nice person, it's simply that he's in love with the
girl and just kills people that get in his way!*

Ben Chapman

MENTION THE *CREATURE FROM THE BLACK LAGOON* and deep-dyed science fiction buffs think of Ricou Browning, the amazing swimmer who played the modern merman in the underwater scenes, and who has frequently shared with fans his memories of working in this classic 1950s adventure. This, however, is only half the story. In the movie's on-land scenes, shot at Universal while Browning and the second unit were working in Florida's Wakulla Springs, the man in the foam rubber suit was Tahitian Ben Chapman, a low-profile Universal contractee who steps forward now for the first time to share *his* memories of playing the quintessential 1950s movie monster.

Chapman was born in Oakland, California, while his Tahitian parents were on a trip to the United States. He was raised in Tahiti, relocated to the United States in 1940 and went to school in the Bay Area of San Francisco. Working as a Tahitian dancer in nightclubs led to his first movie job, a bit in MGM's *Pagan Love Song* (1950); other small film roles followed before Korean War duty temporarily sidetracked his career. Talent scouts from Universal-International "discovered" Chapman upon his return, and for a year he became a U-I stock player — and, at 6'5", an ideal choice for *Creature*'s finny title role.

Was your dancing career your first brush with show business?

No, I've been around show business a long time. If you remember *Mutiny on the Bounty* [1935] with Clark Gable and Franchot Tone, the chief in there, Hitihiti, was played by my uncle William Bainbridge. He had appeared in a lot of other pictures: *Tabu* [1931], *White Shadows in the South Seas* [1928], quite a few more. I also had a cousin that I used to come down and visit, [actor] Jon Hall, who starred in a lot of pictures with Maria Montez, *The Hurricane* [1937] with Dorothy Lamour, on and on. His real name was Charles Locher, and he changed it to Jon Hall because we had an uncle named James Norman Hall, who was one-half of the [Charles] Nordhoff and Hall team that wrote [the novels] *Mutiny on the Bounty, The Hurricane* and a few others. In taking a stage name, he wanted to honor our mutual uncle. He couldn't take *that* name, because James Hall had that name, and he didn't want Jim or Jimmy Hall. So he took J-o-n, which is Scandinavian for James, and there was born Jon Hall. So I've been around show business, even in my youth.

Was English your first language?

I've always known four languages — fluent French, Tahitian, English and, in my youth, Chinese. In Tahiti, I spoke English at home, French at school, and Tahitian and Chinese in the streets. That was Tahiti in the thirties, when the South Pacific was really charming.

And your first movie role was in Pagan Love Song.

Previous page: Ben Chapman takes pride in "bringing life" to the greatest fifties movie monster, the *Creature from the Black Lagoon.*

That's right. I was hired on as a dancer; Robert Alton, who was a dance director, was also directing the movie. We got along famously, and he gave me an additional small part, as Rita Moreno's boyfriend. Then I went on to do a few other things at MGM. I was about to do *Bird of Paradise* [1951] at Twentieth Century–Fox when along came the Korean War and I was called up into the service. I went on to serve in the Marine Corps in Korea, going from the Inch'ŏn landing until I was sent home a year later. After I got back, I ended up a stock player at Universal-International.

How did you come to be under contract there?

I was appearing at a nightclub in Hollywood called the Islander Room, located at the Hollywood Roosevelt Hotel. My dancing partner was Tani Marsh; this was an all–Polynesian revue, by the way. A producer named Will Cowan came in one night, and asked us if we would appear in a Universal musical featurette which would be starring Pinky Lee, Mamie Van Doren, Lisa Gaye and the Miss Universe Girls. And I did do the short; it was called *Hawaiian Nights* [1954], and I played a young Polynesian chieftain in there. Later, I was asked to go under contract as a stock player.

How did you get the job as the Creature?

At Universal, there was a woman named Jonny Rennick who was head of casting, especially for wranglers and stunt men. We were talking one day and she said, "Benny, have you heard about this *Black Lagoon* picture they're going to make? Have they considered you at all?" I told her they hadn't approached me, and she said, "You're the only person who's right for it on this lot!" She knew I was a diver, a swimmer, etc., etc. — I had all the qualifications to portray the Gill Man. So eventually we went off and met with a group of people to talk about this; one of 'em, of course, was [director] Jack Arnold, another was [producer] William Alland, and then also a few other people. We sat down and talked, and they told me what would be involved; Jonny really went to bat for me, she told 'em, "This guy here *is* actually part fish!" *[Laughs.]*

How much were you paid to play the part?

I was making (I think) one hundred twenty-five dollars a week as a stock actor at Universal, but since *Creature* involved diving and swimming and a few stunts, I told 'em I was going to need a little bit more money. We settled on three hundred dollars a week.

The next stop, then, was the makeup department.

Right. I'd report in to makeup every day: plaster of Paris impressions of my body, testing various pieces and so on. It was tedious, but I enjoyed it. The suit was literally built right onto my body, to make sure that everything fit properly. This kind of caused me a problem, because I had to be careful not to gain or lose weight. If I lost weight, the suit would crinkle all over, and if I gained, or course, I'd have trouble getting into it.

Did you see any of the rejected Gill Man costume designs?

Yes, they did come up with different designs, different prototypes; the Creature went through all different "looks" before they settled on what is today the Gill Man. I was very fortunate to be there to watch the designs. A lot of days I didn't *have* to be at the studio, but I would come in just to hang around. Jack Kevan was most responsible for the costume, but Bud Westmore got most of the credit because he was the head of the makeup department.

Was the costume claustrophobic at all?

No—well, at least not for *me* it wasn't. It fit perfect, it was like part of my body, my skin. I *would* heat up, because I had a body stocking on and then the foam rubber outfit over it. In a situation like that, your pores cannot breathe, and when that starts to happen, boy, you're in trouble.

So how did you contend with the overheating?

On days when we worked on sound stages, what they would do was set up hoses, and there was someone there I could go to between takes and say, "Hey, do me a favor, hose me off." Because once you were into that suit, there was no taking it off! On the back lot, I would just stay in the lake to keep cool.

Ricou Browning's problem was trying to stay warm.

Oh, hey, I had *that* problem, too, during one scene that I did in the water at night. Let me tell you, it was freezing. And I do mean *freezing,* up in the hills, in the back lot there. I just had to get in the water and do it, but of course they had hot soup, they had heaters, hoses that would pump warm water. And I got off *easy* compared to Richard Carlson and Richard Denning—they were in the water just like I was, but they didn't have a foam rubber suit on, they were in their bathing suits! But we all survived; if you're a true actor, you're a trouper, and that's what you get paid for. I was getting three hundred dollars a week, which in nineteen fifty-three was a *lot* of money.

If you look at the film, you'll see that Ricou's stuff was kind of ... I'm not going to say *easy,* but it was a little bit more simple. Swim this way, swim that way; that great water ballet scene where he comes up underneath the girl; the scenes where the guys are shooting at him. There wasn't that much. Playing the Creature on land involved a lot more work.

Did you have any ideas of your own for the character?

My conception, when I sat down and read the script and discussed it with Jack Arnold, was, "Hey, this is simply Beauty and the Beast." The Gill Man

In his other vocation (Tahitian dancer), Chapman hulas with partner Lorraine Harris. Today he deals in Hawaiian real estate.

is really a nice person *[laughs]*, it's simply that he's in love with the girl and just kills people that get in his way! Jack and I worked together a bit to try to bring life to the Creature, rather than just make him a cardboard cartoon. We each had a few opinions, and we worked together on the character. This is what lent the picture some of its success, our taking this seriously and "breathing life" into the Gill Man and showing that he had feelings. For one thing, Jack wanted the Creature *not* to just stalk around, *clomp, clomp, clomp.*

He told me, "I want him to *glide*; he glides in the water, and also on *land*."
You can see it especially in one scene where there's a shot of the Gill Man's
feet walking across the deck of the *Rita*: The soles never come off of the deck,
or if they *do,* never more than a fraction of an inch. It kind of gives it that
"Moon-walk" look that Michael Jackson made famous *[laughs]*. We were doing the same thing, but walking *forward*. It was very hard to walk without
picking your feet up, so Jack Arnold thought up the idea of putting lead in
the bottom of the boots in certain walking scenes. That was a good reminder
for me not to lift my feet.

The toughest acting to do is when you cannot allow the people to see your
facial expressions, and there's no dialogue. So I had to do it all with body
language, and try to get this idea over to the audience—"Hey, I'm in love with
this girl and I simply want to take her away, down to my cavern, and live happily ever after." That was the whole idea of *Creature from the Black Lagoon*.

What was entailed in getting into the Creature outfit?

First of all, there was a one-piece body stocking that I would have to slip
into, like thermal underwear, or like the tutus ballet dancers wear. I'd stand
there, and my two or three attendants would put it on me. They'd slip the
legs on first, inch 'em up little by little so that every last bit of material fit into
each crevice of my legs. Then onto the torso, and the arms. The [Gill Man]
body and the [upper] arm and leg pieces were glued to this body stocking.

After that, the rest was pretty easy. I'd slip on the boots, which came up
to my calves. They zipped up from the bottom, then a fin would snap closed
over the zipper. The same thing for the hands; the zippers were on the sides
of the gloves, then fins would snap over *them*. These gloves then snapped onto
the body suit itself so that it would look like it was all one piece. The last thing
was the helmet, which had a zipper also through the back. A fin covered the
zipper there, too. Wherever you see fins, whether they're on the body suit,
the gloves, the boots or the back of the helmet, they're there to conceal zippers. It might take, on the average, two hours to get in and out of it.

Did you do all this in the makeup room or at the lake location?

Normally in the makeup room, in the main part of the studio. They
would get me into the complete costume—complete, that is, except for the
helmet. Then I would go down the stairs and onto one of those little trams
that they used to use to transport actors to and from the sets. I would have
to stand up on the tram—in fact, I could *never* sit down once I was in the suit.
They would put the helmet on me on the set itself. And once I was in that
outfit, I'd stand anywhere between twelve to fourteen hours a day. I'd come
in at seven o'clock in the morning and go home at ten o'clock at night, but
the total amount of time I'd spend in front of the camera on a given day might
be a matter of an hour, or it might be a matter of minutes.

Was vision a problem for you like it was for Ricou Browning?

There were different sets of eyes for different situations. The eyes of the Gill Man popped out, like contact lenses. For closeups, we had eyes that were "complete," that looked like regular eyes. These eyes I really could not see through, and they would have to direct me with lights. Somebody would stand off to a side or behind me with a flashlight; they'd ask me if I could see the light, and if I could, they told me, "Okay, just follow the light." For medium shots, I'd wear eyes that had pin holes in 'em; my visibility then was limited but quite clear. Then, of course, in the long shots, they would simply take out an eighth-of-an-inch hole, the size of the pupil itself, so I could see quite well. It all depended on how far away I was from the camera.

Do you remember any other costume-related problems?

Lunch time. I'd take the helmet, the boots and the gloves off, get onto a tram and go in for lunch. They had for me what they call a "stand-up" chair: It looks like a chaise lounge, except it stands straight up and has arm rests on it. I'd get into that, and there would be a very high table for me to eat off of.

Could you swim well with the suit on?

It was a *great* suit to swim in, because it had large fins for the feet and for the hands. By the way, if you look closely at some of the scenes, you'll notice that the "claws" on the webbed hands bend and flutter in the air; they're not real hard, like regular nails. It was very hard for me to grab something, and not spoil the illusion that they were real nails. For instance, in the scene where my arm comes up out of the water and I claw the bank, I had to be careful not to put too much pressure on them.

Do you remember stuntman Al Wyatt doubling for you in the fire scene?

Sure. I knew Al, he used to double for Rock Hudson. I came down to the set that day they were going to shoot it; Al had on the asbestos suit and they were getting ready to set him ablaze. But as they were setting up, I got called away. Actually, that's really *me* in that suit: Whit Bissell hit me with the lantern, and then it looks as though I'm on fire. But if you look very closely, you can see that that is a superimposed fire. It was Al Wyatt who was on fire, and somehow they were able to superimpose the flames over me.

Any mishaps or accidents while playing the Creature?

No, never. The only "stunt" that I had was when I grabbed Julie Adams and dove with her off the bow of the boat. Actually, that was Julie's stunt double [Polly Burson]. In falling off the boat with her, I rolled so that I broke her fall when we hit the water. I didn't want her to get hurt; I had this big padded suit on, so there was no way *I* could get hurt there.

The closest thing I came to having a mishap was during the fight scene on the beach with Bernie Gozier. He was supposed to swing at me with his

As Julie Adams watches, Chapman (unsuccessfully) tries to block Bernie Gozier's machete attack.

machete, and I was going to counter by grabbing his hand. We rehearsed it, and I told him he was going to have to help me; with the helmet on, I couldn't see that well. Well, he came down with the machete, I reached up and I missed his hand—and *bang,* right on top of my head. Of course, the blade was dull and the top of the helmet was quite thick, so there was no damage.

That was one of your best scenes on the beach there.

As I was walking out of the cave onto the beach, Jack Arnold told me to do no "acting" other than to just extend my arms forward; he wanted no animation on my part, he said it would be more eerie his way. After the Gill Man passes out on the beach, Richard Denning starts clubbing him with the rifle; actually he was hitting a gunny sack full of some kind of material.

Do you remember clunking Julie Adams' head against the cave wall in the grotto scene?

Yeah, I do. The cave set was very dimly lit, as you can see, and very narrow for two people to try to get through — especially with one carrying the other! The cave walls looked like rock, but they were made of plaster — but, still, it was very hard, like a wall. It was just one of those things: I was wearing the "medium" eyes, trying to carry her through there, when all of a sudden, *clunk*! And she let out a yelp, let me tell you — she saw stars!

How did the pulsating gills work?

Rubber tubes came into the back of the helmet, through the dorsal fin, and ran into the gills, where there were little "balloons" or air pockets. On the other end of the hose, there was somebody sitting off-camera with a little hand pump. We coordinated and worked together to create the effect. I would open my mouth and gasp at the same time that he would pump the gills; that way, it looked like the gasping was what made the gills flare out. It was just a matter of timing.

How did all the cast members get along?

Doing *Creature from the Black Lagoon,* we grew to be a family. Richard Carlson was a fine man, intelligent, a phi beta kappa man (I believe) from the University of Minnesota. Whit Bissell, nice man, also. Richard Denning — boy, talk about a handsome guy! He was married to Evelyn Ankers at the time. And Nestor Paiva was a great, gritty character actor; I mean, who could say anything bad about him? And Julie Adams was charming, too. All these people were just great, very professional.

And Jack Arnold?

Oh, Jack Arnold, too — he was a little tough at the beginning, but once we settled our differences about how to play the character, he turned out to be a sweetheart to work with. He made a lot of good movies, especially *It Came from Outer Space* — that's another classic right there. Directing-wise, he was *not* a tyrant, he would ask actors for input. Then he would give *his* input. Shake all the inputs together, and what came out was a successful movie called *Creature from the Black Lagoon.*

The Creature became quite a story on the lot; my God, did it! I was

Beauty (Julie Adams) looks none too happy about the romantic advances of her Beast (Chapman).

visited just about every day: Universal stars would bring guests onto the lot and say, "Let's drive out to the back lot and see the Creature." Someone would phone ahead and say that (for instance) Rock Hudson or Tony Curtis was bringing people back to see us. They'd have me swim out to the middle of the lake, and I would float there with just the top of the helmet and the eyes showing. I would look until I'd see them arrive, then I'd go underwater and come bursting up out of the water like a porpoise, then back under again. It would be tough for the people to get a good look at me. Then I would swim in towards them with just the eyes and the top of the head showing. I'd swim in this way, getting as close to shore as I could—of course it's becoming shallower and shallower. I'd swim in to where it was about a foot and a half deep and then all of a sudden I would stand right up and RRROOOAAARRR! Some of the guests would just about wet their pants *[laughs]*!

You also appeared as the Creature on TV's Colgate Comedy Hour *with Abbott and Costello and Glenn Strange, who played Frankenstein.*
    I remember standing around backstage with Glenn Strange and, being a buff of thriller movies, I knew that he had played Frankenstein. So I asked him

about that and we talked about it, and he asked me about the Creature. We talked about our careers in general and horror films particularly; he told me how he liked working with Boris Karloff. General chitchat about our careers— and hoping that we would go on to bigger and better things!

Why don't you get a screen credit on Creature?

The reason for this was a guy named Jack Smith. He was head of publicity at the time, and it was his idea not to credit either Ricou or myself. He wanted to give the illusion that Universal had actually gone to South America, to the Amazon, to the Black Lagoon, and captured a creature that they later named the Gill Man. He didn't want the audience to see in the credits that the Creature was a guy in a suit; he wanted 'em to *look* for that credit, *not* find it, and say to themselves, "They didn't say who played the Creature. They must've got a *real* one." That was [Universal's] thinking. I didn't go along with it; I mean, don't underestimate people, they're not so stupid that they'd believe this was a real monster *[laughs]*.

Was William Alland on the set much?

Yeah, Bill Alland used to come out. This was nineteen fifty-three, the time of the McCarthy hunt-for-the-Reds, looking for Communists. There were stories going around that Alland was a Communist, and everybody kind of poked fun. I don't know if he was ever officially accused or not; as far as I was concerned, he was a fine man. But evidently he didn't care for *me,* because I wasn't even considered when it came time to do the second Creature picture. I hope this doesn't sound like I'm letting my ego run away with me, but I thought I did a hell of a job on *Creature* and why *wouldn't* they have me on the second? But, hey, it was their movie.

Maybe it was because you weren't under contract to Universal anymore when the second one was made.

That's right, I was gone by then, but I did come back to talk to them about doing the second one and they said, "No, we're going to go with somebody else." That was the end of that—I've never been one to cry over spilled milk. Tom Hennesy played the Creature throughout *Revenge of the Creature* [the on-land scenes]. John Lamb was hired to play the Creature in some scenes, too; Johnny and I were very dear friends. If I remember correctly, John told me they still had my old Gill Man suits and they were trying to find guys that would fit into 'em. John and I were built exactly the same—same height, same weight, same measurements.

Why were you dropped by Universal?

There were one hundred twenty of us under contract to Universal, and a *lot* of us were let go; they came to us and said, "Hey, you have no talent."

Well, if that was the way they felt, that was okay with me. Our name for Universal in those days was "The Factory," because it actually *was* a factory for actors. One hundred twenty of us were under contract, and everybody was going to different classes, whether it be dancing or elocution or acting or fencing — God, they had classes for *every*thing! Of course, these were the great days of Hollywood.

What did you think of the Creature *sequels?*
They were so bad, Universal should have burned the film on 'em. Well, *Revenge of the Creature* was *f-a-i-r,* but the dumbest one was *The Creature Walks Among Us,* which was terrible. Burning his gills off, and putting him into a suit...!

Have you ever played any other monsters in movies?
Back in the seventies, when Lee Majors was doing his *Six Million Dollar Man* [TV] show, they did a segment here [in Hawaii], and I portrayed one of the men from outer space.

Do you take pride in having played one of the most popular movie monsters?
[Emphatically.] Yes — *very* much so. Even to this day, whenever I mention *Creature from the Black Lagoon,* there's always somebody who'll say, "God Almighty, what a great movie!" — which gives me pride. I enjoyed the experience very much, I had a lot of fun. Especially on the back lot, when we were out at the lake. Between shots, I was out there swimmin' around and having a great old time!

Did you realize at the time that these Creature films would become classics?
Well, I don't know about "these" films. Even if I had done [*Revenge* and *Creature Walks*], if they had been done as badly as they were — which I'm sure they would have been, because who am I? — I wouldn't have taken pride in 'em. (Don't get me wrong, I would *like* to have done the trilogy and be able to say I played all the Creatures.) But at the time, we just thought it was another movie, and it never entered my head that it would become a classic such as your *Frankenstein*s, your *Dracula*s, your *Wolf Man*s, your *Mummy*s.

Universal Studios was very famous for their thriller/chillers, and if you look at all of them closely, you can find their secret. Back in the twenties, Lon Chaney, Sr., made movies like *The Phantom of the Opera, The Hunchback of Notre Dame.* Then of course came the thirties, Boris Karloff doing *Franken-stein,* Bela Lugosi *Dracula.* We get now into the forties and there's Lon Chaney, Jr., doing the Wolf Man and the Mummy. Then, the fifties — science fiction. And in nineteen fifty-three, they decided they were going to do another thriller, and they were going to do this one in three-D. This was *Creature from the Black Lagoon.*

So if you look back at all of the thrillers that Universal Pictures made,

The Phantom, The Hunchback, Frankenstein, Dracula, The Mummy, and of course *Creature*: They were all very successful. And why? If you'll think about it, they're all Beauty and the Beast. The Phantom was in love with the girl; the Hunchback loved his Esmeralda; the Mummy had his Princess. They would never hurt the girl, only the people that got in their way. And the Gill Man was the same type of monster character. After that, of course, movies changed; Universal changed; stories changed; people's attitudes changed; and now the studios are not coming out with the quality thrillers they made before. Now it's all blood and gore. But in the old days, these Universal Pictures were all well done, and the best of 'em were all Beauty and the Beast. And *my* pride is that I was the original Creature from the Black Lagoon.

BEN CHAPMAN FILMOGRAPHY

Pagan Love Song (MGM, 1950)
Hawaiian Nights (Universal short, 1954)
Creature from the Black Lagoon (Universal, 1954)
Ma and Pa Kettle at Waikiki (Universal, 1955)

Chapman also appeared in a few of the Johnny Weissmuller *Jungle Jim* movies. On TV his credits include *Playhouse 90, Adventures in Paradise, Hawaiian Eye, Follow the Sun* and *Hawaii Five-O*. Clips of Chapman as the Gill Man are featured in *Fade to Black* (American Cinema, 1980) and *It Came from Hollywood* (Paramount, 1982).

*I've always believed that, in making a horror
picture, you gotta give the audience something
to laugh at before you hit 'em.*

Herman Cohen

I WAS A TEENAGE WEREWOLF. Or a Teenage Frankenstein. How to Make a Monster. Horrors of the Black Museum. There are very few 1950s horror films that are as well remembered as these near-legendary titles, and they represent only the proverbial tip of the iceberg in the amazing career of writer-producer Herman Cohen. The Detroit-born Cohen made his first films (including *Bride of the Gorilla*) during the early 1950s during his association with Realart Pictures honcho Jack Broder, and he continued to specialize in horror right on up through the 1970s; today he operates (with partner Didier Chatelain) Cobra Media, which also leans heavily toward the horrific in its roster of titles. In his first-ever truly comprehensive career interview, Cohen looks back over his years of filmmaking and divulges the deepest secrets behind some of exploitation's greatest horror hits.

What was your first job in the movie business?

My motion picture career began at our local cinema, the Dexter Theater in Detroit, as a gofer when I was about eleven, twelve years old. I started out by helping the janitor after school to get free passes for my family and me. Then the manager hired me to watch the exit doors on Saturday matinees, so nobody'd sneak in *[laughs]*! And when they were short an usher, and I was about thirteen years old, they put me in a uniform and tried to pin it down and what have you, because it was for somebody sixteen or seventeen. Then I went downtown to the big Fox Theater, which was *the* theater of Detroit, and I got a job as an usher there. Then I was made chief of service, then assistant manager.

Did your parents encourage your showbiz bug?

No, my parents really had nothing to do with it, and there was nobody in my family that was in showbiz, *per se*. While at school, I used to put on all the plays and I was in the glee club and choir, I acted (I played Tom Sawyer!), all kinds of things. I was captain of the monitors, captain of the safety patrol — anything in the way of extracurricular activities, I did. And once I was thirteen, I worked seven nights a week at the theater — after school I had to dash to Hebrew school for an hour, and then the theater was my life until late every night. I was picked up by the state labor board twice for working underage. One of my oldest sisters helped me write a letter to the State Labor Commissioner, John H. Thorpe, to ask for a special permit when I was fourteen. I wrote that this was going to be my career; I knew it even at that age. In fact, there was an interview with me in my high school paper when I was a junior, saying I was going to go to Hollywood and get into production.

Anyway, I wrote this John H. Thorpe for a special permit, saying in my

Previous page: As a producer for American International Pictures, Herman Cohen created a star (Michael Landon) — and a fear-film legacy not easily forgotten — starting with 1957's *I Was a Teenage Werewolf.*

letter, "Would you rather I be a member of a local drug store gang, or work in a theater where I am protected by the manager?", "This is going to be my career," all that jazz. I heard nothing. Then about three weeks later, the principal of our school said there was a car and a driver waiting to take me downtown to the Superintendent of the Board of Education in Detroit—he wanted to see me. They drove me downtown, and there was John H. Thorpe, the Secretary of Labor, who was down from Lansing—he wanted to meet the kid that wrote this letter! To make a long story short, he gave me a special permit to work to ten p.m. (Of course, once I got *that,* I worked till midnight!)

You could work in a factory or a sweatshop at fourteen, but you could not work in a theater, you had to be sixteen. Well, by the time I was sixteen, I was *managing* the place!

So you've been a movie fan all your life.

Oh, yes—I spent seven nights a week in a theater! And when I was a gofer for the operators in the projection booth, they taught me everything about the projection. In fact, one operator drank a lot, and I remember that many times I used to get up on a chair and make the changeovers for him on nights when he was drinking too much *[laughs].*

Were horror films your favorite type of film while growing up?

I had no favorite type of film; if the picture was good, I loved it. Including horror. As a kid, I always loved horror, and I used to scare my sister and kid brother going home from the theater!

How did you land your first job in Hollywood?

When I got out of the Marine Corps in nineteen forty-nine, I started working for Columbia Pictures, as sales manager in their Detroit branch. I didn't want to stay there in Detroit, but my mother wasn't too well at the time. When my mother passed away, then there was nothing holding me in Detroit, and that's when I came out to California. I got a job in the Columbia publicity department from Lou Smith, who I had been in touch with for years.

You produced your first films for Jack Broder's company.

Jack Broder owned theaters in Detroit, but I had never met him. But now that I was out in Hollywood, I was told by many people, "Gee, you ought to look Jack up," because he was an ex–Detroiter. He was the head of Realart Pictures, which was the company that had bought the Universal library. Then Jack Broder decided to go into production, and he was looking for an assistant, someone who would work very cheap. I went and had an interview with him, and he hired me. And that's how I got to work for him.

Anthony Eisley, who acted in one of Broder's pictures in the '60s, said that for a guy who made pictures, Broder knew amazingly little about them.

It's true. With all respect to Jack, Jack had money, and loved the business. When I was his assistant, it gave me an opportunity to learn all facets of the making of pictures. I got a lot of titles from Jack, instead of money *[laughs]* — I was vice-president of Jack Broder Productions, this, that and what have you, all at a very young age.

Do you remember what your duties entailed?
    Yes — *everything [laughs]*! Including, when Jack and his wife Bea would go out of town, moving into their house and taking care of their kids! Mind you, it didn't bother me, 'cause he lived at Eight Ten North Camden, which was a beautiful house in Beverly Hills with a swimming pool and a basketball court and everything. They had a black nanny and they had a black cook, but when he and Bea would go away, Jack wanted someone else to be there, too, to supervise the kids and just to be there in case of any problem. So he would ask me, and I didn't mind it because, when I did that, I would call up my friends and invite 'em to come over to go swimming. I played like it was my house! The cook would call to me, "Herman! What do yo' want me to make fo' yo' friends fo' lunch?" And she'd make whatever I asked for *[laughs]*! So I wasn't getting paid anything, but I was always hoping that Jack would go out of town!

You were "assistant to the producer" on Broder's Bride of the Gorilla.
    During the making of *Bride of the Gorilla* was the big *menage à trois* with Franchot Tone and Barbara Payton and Tom Neal. Barbara and I became good friends, and — well, what can I say? Even in those days, Barbara Payton, who was a gorgeous gal, was one step away from working Sunset Boulevard. And she was a bit strange — she thought she was a cat, and always wanted to play "cat" with me 'cause I was a young, handsome kid then. She would confide in me. At that time she had Franchot going (because of his money) and Tom Neal (because he was an animal!). We shot *Bride of the Gorilla* at the old Sam Goldwyn Studios, and I remember the gate calling one day to say that Tom Neal was there. And Franchot Tone was in Barbara's dressing room! So I had to keep the two of them from meeting!

This was before their big fight?
    Right, the fight took place after the picture was finished. But she was toying and playing with both of them during that time. Raymond Burr was also in the picture and he was a great guy, and Lon Chaney, too. I worked with Lon Chaney not only in *Bride of the Gorilla* but in *The Bushwhackers* [1952] and in *Battles of Chief Pontiac* [1952], which we shot in Rapid City, South Dakota. Lon Chaney was a wonderful man — he loved the business, he loved the outdoors. In fact, when we did *Battles of Chief Pontiac,* he refused to sleep in the hotel, he wanted to sleep with the Sioux Indians when we went on loca-

tion. We had to put up a tent for him and he slept in it, out on the location. In fact, right where Kevin Costner shot his film *Dances with Wolves* [1990]. I have fond recollections of Lon. He *was* Lennie in *Of Mice and Men,* just a big, overgrown puppy and a hell of a nice guy.

Was Curt Siodmak, the director of Bride of the Gorilla, *a good director?*
He was from Europe — a very serious man — and when he did *Bride of the Gorilla,* he thought he was doing *Gone with the Wind*! He was very serious about everything. He was the brother of Robert Siodmak, a big director, and I genuinely think he thought he was doing a big, *big* picture. He had a very thick accent, and, of course, to him I was "the kid" — "Hey, kid," "Listen, kid..." But he did do a good job on the picture, for what it was — we made it with spit. Of course, William Beaudine, who directed *Bela Lugosi Meets a Brooklyn Gorilla* for Broder, was one of the all-time terrific directors; he must have done one hundred pictures at Monogram and Allied Artists alone. He was such a pro, he was unbelievable; I learned a great deal from Bill Beaudine. A real no-nonsense guy from the old school.

You were associate producer of Brooklyn Gorilla.
"Associate producer" was just another title; actually, what I was doing was learning how to produce. On *Bela Lugosi Meets a Brooklyn Gorilla,* the guy that got producer credit, Maurice Duke, had two young guys that looked like Dean Martin and Jerry Lewis [Duke Mitchell and Sammy Petrillo] under contract, and that's why he got producer credit. I actually made the picture. And, oh, I hated it — I thought it was just a ridiculous idea. And Bill Beaudine hated the picture as much as I did; to him it was just a job. He said he did so much crap at Monogram and Allied Artists, that it didn't matter if he did another one! But Jack Broder, who knew Martin and Lewis, thought it was funny. We shot that at General Service Studios and our offices were right next door to Lucille Ball and Desi Arnaz, who were just starting *I Love Lucy.*

What do you remember about Lugosi?
He was very, very sick. He was an old man and not well, and his wife and son were on the set all the time, the wife giving him shots in the dressing room. I don't know what the hell she was giving him; at that time, I didn't know anything about drugs. But I *did* see syringes occasionally in the dressing room. Lugosi was a nice old guy, and he was happy just to be working. His wife and son would go over his lines with him, he was there when he was supposed to be — but it was sort of like he was "out of it." They brought him there, they told him what to do, he did it for the money — that's my recollection of Bela Lugosi. You couldn't have a personal relationship with him, or a personal conversation, because the minute he was through shooting anything on the sound stage, they would whisk him back to his dressing room.

Didn't Broder get in trouble, ripping off Martin and Lewis?

Oh, yes, we had trouble with Paramount and Hal Wallis. In fact, Jerry Lewis came over from Paramount to talk to Jack about it.

Did you think Mitchell and Petrillo were any good?

No, I thought they were a couple of rip-offs. And that's what the picture was, a cheap rip-off picture, and *[laughs]* I was embarrassed making it! However, in those days, I'd take credit on anything. With Jack Broder, I got credit on *Two Dollar Bettor* [1951], which was a good little picture with John Litel and Marie Windsor; *The Basketball Fix* [1951], another good picture, with Marshall Thompson, Vanessa Brown, John Ireland; *The Bushwhackers,* which was a hell of a good Western, with Ireland, Wayne Morris (remember *him?!*), Dorothy Malone, Lon Chaney; and *Battles of Chief Pontiac* with Lex Barker, Helen Westcott and Chaney, again. I think that was it, 'cause that was about the time I left Jack to form my own company.

What did James Nicholson do for Jack Broder?

That was when I first met James Nicholson. Jim owned the Academy Theater on Hollywood Boulevard, and at one point he became very ill. He had to go to the hospital for a long period of time, and when he came out of the hospital, he had lost his theater. Jim was a devastated man. At one time, Jim had been the manager in one of Jack Broder's L.A. theaters, and so Jack, who liked Jim, introduced us and said to me, "Herman, can't we use him in the company? He's terrific at advertising and publicity." I said sure. So Jim worked virtually as my assistant at that time—he worked in advertising in our offices during that period. And when I left Broder, Jim stayed and was promoted.

What did you have to do with the British film Ghost Ship?

That was one of the pictures I handled after I formed my first company. I met Nat Cohen, who was one of the heads of Anglo Amalgamated Films in England, and we formed a company to do some cheap pictures in London. (Nat was not a relative, by the way.) I would own 'em in certain territories [the Western Hemisphere] and they would own 'em in the rest [the Eastern Hemisphere]. The pictures involved were *Ghost Ship, Undercover Agent* [1953] and a couple more. I made a deal with Lippert Pictures, and they distributed these things for me here in the States. Then I told Nat, "Look, why don't I bring an American star over to London for the next picture? We'll get more money for it." Nat thought that was a good idea. He was hot, publicity-wise, for Phyllis Kirk, who was in *House of Wax* with Vincent Price—at that time, that was a big picture. So I signed Phyllis Kirk and I produced the picture, which was called *River Beat* [1954]. Bet you never heard of that one.

The first picture you produced stateside was Target Earth.

Target Earth started with me buying a short story called *Deadly City*—in fact, Jim Nicholson was with me when I found the magazine with the story in it at a newsstand on North Las Palmas. Jim took the story and started writing a treatment for it, and I bought the treatment from Jim, I think for two hundred fifty dollars. I changed the title to *Target Earth,* and then I developed the script with a writer named Bill Raynor.

Then I maneuvered to get a deal for financing, and two guys who were really nice to me were Harold Mirisch and Steve Broidy at Allied Artists. I was a young whippersnapper, in my early twenties, and I called up wanting to make an appointment with these guys—and they *saw* me! They read my first draft script, they liked it, I gave 'em the budget (which was under one hundred thousand dollars) and they said, "If you can get somebody to put up the balance of the financing, we'll put in X-amount of money." I flew to New York and got the head of DeLuxe Labs, Alan Friedman, to put up the money for the print order. And that's how I got the financing on my first independent picture. It really was something—everybody marveled that I put the damn thing together.

Then you got a film editor, Sherman Rose, to direct it for you.

Sherman Rose was "Pop" Sherman's nephew—Harry "Pop" Sherman, who produced all the *Hopalong Cassidy* Westerns. Sherman Rose practically grew up on a sound stage. He and his wife Kathleen worked a couple of the Jack Broder pictures, and I also met him at Columbia, socially. (And Kathleen Rose won an Academy Award for sound effects editor a few years ago, I want you to know. She's a great sound effects editor, one of the tops in the industry.) So I hired Sherman Rose to direct—that was his first directing job.

Where did you shoot Target Earth*?*

We shot at Kling Studios—Charlie Chaplin Studios—which is now A&M. And also we were on location all over the place. We shot on weekends without permits . . . my garage . . . you name it. We shot on the empty streets of L.A. early in the morning on four or five weekends, to get the scenes of the evacuated city. A friend of mine was a cop with the L.A.P.D., and he came with us one early Sunday morning in his uniform. (We didn't have any permits. We could've got in real trouble.) We cleared the streets in downtown L.A. The only problem we had was that there was a Catholic church right across from where we were shooting. There were no people on the street, we were shooting and then all of a sudden the church doors swung open and the people came piling out *[laughs]*! "Oh, God! Stop the cameras!" We forgot that they were all in there!

You had a good cast in Richard Denning, Kathleen Crowley and Virginia Grey.

It was a wonderful little family; they cooperated like crazy. They worked early Sunday mornings where we "stole" shots on the city streets, so on and so forth. Sherman Rose and I went out there, not with our crew, but with a hand camera, an Eymo, and shot it ourselves. Then we put in the sound afterwards.

How many robots did you have in that film?

We attacked L.A. with one robot *[laughs]*! David Koehler was a special effects guy that I've occasionally worked with, and he built the thing in my garage. (*Very* economically!) I also let Dave Koehler have several other jobs on the picture. The guy who wore the robot suit was my gorilla in *Bride of the Gorilla* and *Bela Lugosi Meets a Brooklyn Gorilla,* Steve Calvert; the first time I met him, he was a bartender at Ciro's on Sunset Strip. He just recently passed away.

Did the picture end up costing one hundred thousand dollars?

We did come in under budget; in fact, the Chemical Bank of New York gave money back to both Allied Artists and DeLuxe when we came in under budget. I think *Target Earth* cost about eighty-five thousand dollars. It took about a week as far as actual shooting, but then we did a lot of post-production. All the shots of Denning and Kathleen and Virginia and Richard Reeves on the streets and everything else, that was done in post-production.

Shortly after Target Earth, *you produced a number of pictures for United Artists.*

[Producer] Leonard Goldstein and his twin brother Bob had made a deal with United Artists to produce some pictures; Bob Jacks was also involved because at that time he was Darryl Zanuck's son-in-law. Anyway, Leonard died and Max Youngstein, who was head of production at the time, needed a producer very badly. He had seen *Target Earth* and another picture of mine, *Magnificent Roughnecks* [1956], and he'd seen the budgets. Robert Blumofe, who was an executive at UA, said, "Max, you ought to talk to this kid Herman Cohen." So Youngstein interviewed me, and to make a long story short, he signed a deal with me to produce four pictures for UA that Leonard Goldstein was supposed to produce. They were *The Brass Legend* [1956] with Hugh O'Brian, which was a Western; *Dance with Me, Henry* [1956], Abbott and Costello's last picture; *Fury at Showdown* [1957] with John Derek; and *Crime of Passion* [1957] with Barbara Stanwyck, Sterling Hayden, Raymond Burr and Virginia Grey. *Crime of Passion* got great reviews — some people said it was the best Stanwyck picture since *Double Indemnity* [1944] and all that. And it died — didn't do *any* business! I hadn't picked the stories, I was just under contract to produce 'em, but I felt terrible. So at the end of those four pictures, I wanted to go back to my own company.

It was during this time that Jim Nicholson left Jack Broder to form his own company. Roger Corman had produced a film called *The Fast and the*

Furious [1954] with Dorothy Malone and John Ireland, and gave it to Jim to release if he could get the franchise holders throughout the country. And Jim formed a company at that time called American Releasing Corporation.

Which later became AIP.

Right. Jim wanted me to be his partner—Sam Arkoff would have never been around if I had been Jim's partner! 'Cause Jim and I were close personal friends, even after I left Broder. Jim told me his ideas and this and that, and I said, "Jim, I can't come with you"—this was while I was in the midst of making those four pictures for UA. "But anything you need," I told him, "my secretary, my staff and I will help you." In fact, we did all his mimeographing and everything else at my offices!

Jim got an office at Six-two-two-three Selma in Hollywood, a one-room little office, and in another one-room little office was this attorney with a big fat cigar, Sam Arkoff. That's where Jim met Sam, in this building on Selma—Sam had a law office there. Jim told me that this attorney Arkoff said that if he got a piece of the company, he would do the contracts for 'em. That's how Jim and Sam got together.

And you were in a position to work with them once Crime of Passion *went bust.*

When *Crime of Passion* did not do business, I said, "Shit, I gotta do something quick to make some money." And Jim was asking me, "Herm, can you do a picture for us?" That's when I thought of doing a teenage werewolf picture; I felt that for a fledgling company which was trying to get the teenage market, it could be ideal. I came up with the title *Teenage Werewolf*, and Jim Nicholson added *I Was a*. And that's how I got involved with *I Was a Teenage Werewolf*.

Was Nicholson one to help creatively once a picture was underway?

The only thing Jim had anything to do with was the advertising campaign. He had nothing to do with the script whatsoever, or with the making of the picture—I wrote it with Aben Kandel. Aben was one of my dearest friends, and we worked very well together. To play the Teenage Werewolf, I signed Michael Landon to Herman Cohen Productions—and not just for one picture, I had him under personal contract for a multiple deal. But I released him to do *Bonanza*. I could have sold the contract, but I just ripped it up.

Two other actors who supposedly were up for the Werewolf role were Scott Marlowe and John Ashley.

Scott Marlowe was, but in the auditions and what have you, I felt that Michael Landon was the best. Landon was a hell of an actor, and he did a damn good audition. John Ashley was never up for *Teenage Werewolf.*

He *says he was, and that you gave him a part in* How to Make a Monster *as a sort of consolation prize.*

That's a lot of crap, I never even heard of him at that time. John was a kid who came out here from Oklahoma with a lot of money—his [foster] father was a very wealthy doctor. Jim Nicholson was going to use John in one of the AIP pictures, but it didn't work out. So when I was doing *How to Make a Monster* and it had a musical number scene, Jim said, "Herm, maybe you can use this John Ashley"—because AIP had committed themselves to use him in *some*thing. Jim sent John over to my office; I liked him and we rehearsed him, and that's how he was in *How to Make a Monster.* John was a nice guy, but he was never up for *Teenage Werewolf.*

Do you think Landon did a good job?

Oh, he was marvelous. At that time, he was living in one room with this gal Dodie, who he later married, and with her kid from a previous marriage. And they had about five or six cats in this one room! When I signed him, I took him to the Ranch Market, which was open twenty-four hours a day in those days, we went through there and I bought him whatever he thought he could use to eat. I got a big hug and a kiss in the parking lot when I drove him home, because he had no money at that time—he was broke, he was in tough shape.

And you got along with him well throughout the picture?

We got along great; long after the picture was finished, he used to come across to visit me at Raleigh Studios when they shot *Bonanza* at Paramount. We were very close friends until I went to London to do *Horrors of the Black Museum.* I was spending a great deal of time in London and he was busy at *Bonanza,* and we sort of drifted apart. These things happen.

Did he do all of his own stunts in the film?

He sure did. In fact, we thought he had almost killed himself in that gym scene, when he ran after Dawn Richards and jumped right into the bunch of iron chairs. That was Michael. It's funny, but when he had that makeup on, he said he felt like he *was* a werewolf. He was excellent. There was nothing he didn't do that we wanted him to do; in fact, he always wanted to do more.

Was he wearing a mask or makeup?

It was actually makeup, but there were a couple of appliances on the side. Philip Scheer was a makeup guy who used to work at Universal—that's why I hired him, because he knew about the old Wolf Man and Frankenstein makeups and what have you. He was like an assistant in those days there at Universal.

Gene Fowler, Jr., directed Teenage Werewolf.

When I was going to do *Teenage Werewolf,* I thought of Sherman Rose.

Michael Landon (notice the glove) takes on director Gene Fowler, Jr.'s, dog Anna in the exploitation classic *I Was a Teenage Werewolf.*

But throughout those years, he was going through a problem within himself, and he was having a problem with his marriage to Kate; I had to do a lot of directing on *Target Earth* myself. I gave him *Magnificent Roughnecks* reluctantly, and I did a lot of directing on *that,* too. He was a very shy guy, and his wife was pushing him, pushing him all the time to direct instead of cut. (He was a hell of a film editor.) Gene Fowler, Jr., and his wife Marge were very close friends of mine, and Gene Fowler wanted to direct—he hadn't directed any features before, he was a film editor. And I didn't know whether I should trust Sherman with *Teenage Werewolf* or not. So I looked at some of the stuff that Gene Fowler had cut, we sat and we talked, and to make a long story short, I hired him as the director.

Gene Fowler's wife Marge is an Academy Award film editor, by the way. I was the first producer in Hollywood to start hiring so many women for the cutting room. You've heard of Verna Fields? She was vice-president at Universal, in charge of post-production for years. I gave her her first jobs, as the assistant sound effects editor on my four pictures for UA. These people, Kate and Sherman Rose and Marge and Gene Fowler and Verna Fields and I — we were all close personal friends in those days.

Why did Aben Kandel use pseudonyms in writing these early pictures for you?

Aben and I wrote the scripts together and used a joint pseudonym. The reason for that is, Aben at that time was doing a couple of big things at MGM and Warners, so therefore he couldn't use his own name. But I didn't feel happy taking solo screenplay credit. So we decided not to use our real names. In fact, I almost did not use *my* real name as the producer of *I Was a Teenage Werewolf,* because after doing *Crime of Passion* and *Dance with Me, Henry* and the other pictures at UA, it seemed like a big step down. Friends of mine, like Harry Cohn's nephew Bobby Cohn, were saying, "Jesus, you're not gonna use your own name on *I Was a Teenage Werewolf,* are you? Herm, you'll be *ruined*!" So I started thinking, "Gee, maybe I better *not*!"; I was thinking of using [the pseudonym] "Ralph Thornton" as the writer *and* the producer. Then all of a sudden, Jack Benny, Bob Hope and various other comedians got ahold of the title and they started making fun of it. We started getting calls from *Time* magazine and *Look* magazine, and they wanted to talk to the producer of *I Was a Teenage Werewolf.* My secretary Donna Heydt (who was the wife of Louis Jean Heydt, the actor) said, "Herman, what do I tell 'em?" Well, when *Time* and *Look* and *Life* started calling for the producer, I decided that the producer was going to be Herman Cohen.

Did you get along well with Whit Bissell?

He was terrific in *Teenage Werewolf,* and *I Was a Teenage Frankenstein,* too. I just recently saw him at the Motion Picture Home; he and Aben Kandel are both out there and I had lunch with 'em a couple weeks ago. [Kandel died 1/28/93.] Whit Bissell is in great shape still. Whit was terrific to work with, a great gentleman. And even now, at the Motion Picture Home, *what* a nice guy! He's a class man: you ought to see how he is with the other older people at the Home. He even does their shopping across the street at the drug store for 'em.

Was I Was a Teenage Werewolf *called* Blood of the Werewolf *at any time?*

[Emphatically.] Never. In reference books, I've seen that and a couple other names for it, too. It was titled *Teenage Werewolf* from the beginning — I still have the original script. Jim Nicholson worked on the advertising campaign himself, came up and showed me a great ad on *I Was a Teenage Werewolf* and I said, "Jim, that's genius." We made the picture for under one hundred fifty thousand dollars and it grossed over two million dollars in the first two weeks.

Where was Teenage Werewolf *shot?*
We did a lot of it at Ziv in West Hollywood, where I had offices at the time. The high school was just a block away. The woods and all that were Bronson Canyon.

Were you on the set much?
All the time. I'm on the sets of *all* my pictures, *all* the time. If I'm not on the set, then my associate or my assistant or somebody is there, so if anything happens where they need me, they can call me and get me on there right away.

And that's why you're in a lot of these pictures, in bit parts?
[Laughs.] No, that was just for fun — a lot of the producers and directors do that. Sometimes I forget which pictures I'm in.

Teenage Werewolf *has an excellent music score by Paul Dunlap.*
Paul was a very underrated composer. I used Paul in a lot of pictures; in fact, prior to *Werewolf,* Paul did *Target Earth, Crime of Passion* and lots more for me. I got along with him very well because I'm very involved in music and with all my music composers. Paul would have been a hell of a top composer, but he was always involved with ex-wives and alimony, and he always had to work. So he would take anything that came his way. In my opinion, that really hurt him. He was also Sam Fuller's favorite composer.
Speaking of composers, I gave Elmer Bernstein one of his first pictures: He did *Battles of Chief Pontiac* when I was with Jack Broder. I met Elmer Bernstein at Schwab's Drug Store. I was having breakfast there and a friend came over and said, "Herm, I want you to meet this new young composer from New York," blah, blah, blah. We met, we talked and he wanted to know if I could someday come up to his place in Laurel Canyon and listen to some of his music. Which I did, and I was very impressed. So I introduced him to Jack Broder. Elmer's a very short guy — five feet five inches, five feet six inches or something. Jack was a very small man, too, but Elmer was even shorter than Jack! And I'll never forget Jack, with his hand in his pants (he always put his right hand in his pants as he was talking), saying to me with his little Yiddish accent, "Herman vhere did you find this *kid*? He's a *kid*!" I told him, "Jack, we

can get him very cheap," and he got all excited: "*Cheap*?! How much for the score?" Elmer did a hell of a score for us for *Battles of Chief Pontiac*.

Did you see the Highway to Heaven *TV episode where Michael Landon did his takeoff on* Teenage Werewolf?

Yes, I did, because we okayed it and sold them the piece of film that they used. I thought it was fun. I don't know what the ratings were like on that particular episode, but I think they were very high because I believe it was repeated several times.

Did you have a multiple picture deal with AIP?

No, it was just picture by picture, I never signed a multiple picture deal. Believe me, if one of my pictures had dropped dead, Jim and his people, which at that time was Sam Arkoff and Joe Moritz and so on, would have said, "Herm, we're not gonna do any more pictures with you!"

Sam Arkoff tells the story that a big Texas exhibitor asked for two new AIP horror pictures on Labor Day, and that I Was a Teenage Frankenstein *and* Blood of Dracula *were ready for him by Thanksgiving.*

That's true. *Werewolf* did terrific—in fact, the big Interstate circuit in Texas kicked it off and it just did great. I made personal appearances in Dallas and Houston and Austin. Bob O'Donnell [the head of Interstate] said to me, "If we can get another picture like this, I'll give you the Thanksgiving date." So in discussing this with Jim Nicholson, I said, "What if I did *I Was a Teenage Frankenstein*?" and Jim said, "Great!" I came up with the original story and got Aben in with me on the screenplay. And then Jim said, "Herm, if you've got a second feature to go back-to-back with *Frankenstein*, we'll have the whole program! We won't have to share it with one of the majors." So that's when I came up with *Blood of Dracula*, and we shot the two virtually back-to-back. O'Donnell gave us Thanksgiving in the entire circuit, with the kickoff at the Majestic in Dallas.

Herbert L. Strock directed the pair of 'em.

Herb was directing some Ziv TV shows at the time—*Highway Patrols* with Brod Crawford, a West Point show, so on and so forth. He was on the lot and I met him, and I felt that he was a director that I could get along with and work with. He was fast and quick, and that was what we needed—these were budget pictures.

Teenage Frankenstein *doesn't go over nearly as well as* Teenage Werewolf.

Both *Frankenstein* and *Blood of Dracula* were written and put in front of the camera in only four weeks, in order to make that Thanksgiving date. And there was a shortage of money at the time. So I had to really, really cut down.

So you made Teenage Frankenstein *very indoorsy to reduce costs.*

And *Blood of Dracula,* too. Well, we got out of the house a *little* on *Blood of Dracula*—although it was just outside on the lawn *[laughs]*!

On Teenage Frankenstein, *where did you shoot the scenes with the alligator?*

At Ziv, which is where we shot the whole thing. Actually, that's quite a story. We got the alligator from the Buena Park Alligator Farm, and it was an alligator that they had brought in from Texas. There it was owned by a guy that owned a roadside inn in a small town outside of Dallas. He would hire a waitress who had no family, he would swing with her and what have you, and then when he got tired of her, he would throw her in a pool in his basement where he had this alligator! That alligator had killed about *seven women*! This is a true story! And when I needed an alligator in *I Was a Teenage Frankenstein,* that's the one they sent me!

You shot that conclusion in color, which was very novel.

At that time, I thought that was quite inventive. We couldn't afford to make the picture in color, so I came up with that idea, and I talked Jim Nicholson into letting me spend a few extra bucks.

Did you think Gary Conway did a good job in Teenage Frankenstein*?*

He sure did—he did a *very* good job. In fact, *I* changed his name to Gary Conway. His name was Gareth Carmody, and I thought that was just too classy. I sat down with his mother and father, who were schoolteachers who came to meet the producer, and we changed his name to Gary Conway. Again, it was Philip Scheer doing the makeup; it was an appliance, in about four parts.

Do you stand by that Frankenstein makeup today, despite all the criticism it's gotten?

[Contemptuously.] Of course! Criticism never bothered me—I couldn't care less. Critics have to write something.

Didn't you ever run into problems with the censors on these older pictures?

Oh, sure we did! There were things that we had to cut out, but I can't recall what they were; it was a give-and-take situation. A wonderful guy named Geoffrey Shurlock used to be the head of the MPAA out here on the West Coast. He was head of it for twenty-five years, and of course everything had to be submitted to him—scripts in advance, and then the rough cuts when the pictures were done. Geoffrey and I became pretty good friends.

Take a look at my pictures. In my horror films, I never went for the *Texas Chainsaw Massacre* type of blood and guts and tearing stomachs out and what have you. Most of my horror I did with sound effects and music. You *thought* you were seeing what you were *not* seeing.

I thought I saw a smashed and bloody disembodied leg and hand in Teenage Frankenstein.

Oh, yes, but that wasn't really horror. I used to tell Geoffrey Shurlock, "Come on, Geoff, I'm doing this in good taste" *[laughs],* and I sold him on it. I had a lot of fights with his staff, so I always had to finish everything with him directly.

Why doesn't Whit Bissell try for a British accent when he's playing a British Dr. Frankenstein?

Actually, it depends upon the ear of the listener. Even today, when I talk to him at the Motion Picture Home, he sounds English to me. I spent the equivalent of fifteen years in England, and it depends what part of England you're from. He didn't have to talk like a Cockney or like the Royal Family to be "British." In the later pictures that I did with Michael Gough, I would try to have Michael talk "mid–Atlantic," so it wouldn't be too British—even though he *was* British!

At the end of Teenage Frankenstein, *there are crates in Whit Bissell's lab addressed to One-thirteen Wardour Street, London. Was that an in-joke reference to Hammer Films, which was headquartered there?*

No—that was the address of *my* office, which was in the same building! Nat Cohen and Stuart Levy, who were my partners in England, had the fourth floor at One-thirteen and Hammer had the sixth floor. Jimmy Carreras, the head of Hammer Films, was a wonderful friend of mine.

Six of your films had a teenager manipulated or transformed into a monster by an evil adult. What was it about that formula that you went back to it so often?

I have always felt that most teenagers think that adults—their parents, or their teachers, anyone that was older and that had authority—were the culprits in their lives. I know *I* felt that way when I was a teenager, and in talking to many teenagers, I found out that that was how *they* felt. (And even today—it hasn't changed, you know.) And so, in doing pictures primarily for the teenage audience, I thought that this theme would strike them just right.

And in some of your early pictures, you even had the songs and the comedy moments for the teenage audience.

I've always believed that, in making a horror picture, you gotta give the audience something to laugh at before you hit 'em.

Blood of Dracula *was also shot at Ziv.*

And also at a house I rented, someplace in Beverly Hills—that was the school in the picture. AIP didn't have its own studios or soundstages. When I

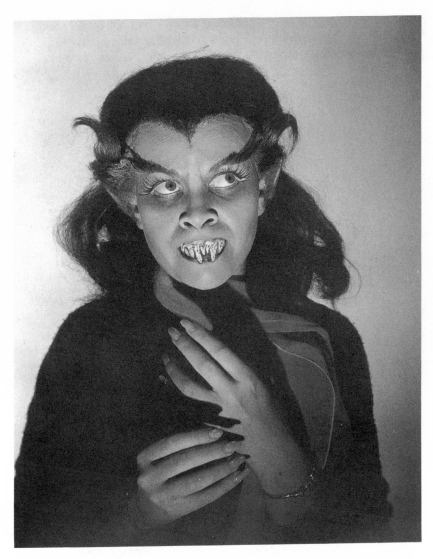

Vampiric girl student Sandra Harrison seemed more interested in Type A than straight A's in Cohen's *Blood of Dracula*.

did *How to Make a Monster,* I put up the sign that said AMERICAN INTERNA-
TIONAL STUDIOS over the gate, but that's actually Ziv. In fact *[laughs],* they
left the sign up long after the picture was over, so Jim and Sam would bring
people to Ziv all the time, as though it was *their* studio!

How did you go about rounding up the teenage casts of these movies?

We'd just put a call out to agents, and they submitted various young actors and actresses. I auditioned those that I thought I wanted to audition, and that's how I'd pick the casts. It's the way I pick any cast for any film.

Herbert Strock told me you had reservations about having Sandra Harrison play the lead in Blood of Dracula.

Well, I didn't have reservations about her originally, 'cause if I did, I wouldn't have signed her as the lead! But she was a pain in the ass once we got started.

When the Film Forum Theater in New York City recently scheduled Blood of Dracula, *she called the theater frantically begging them not to show it.*

Once I signed her, she suddenly thought she was Joan Crawford—which she *wasn't* [laughs]! As far as her acting went, though, she was fine. I wasn't that excited about the picture itself, personally, but it was going to be the second feature to *I Was a Teenage Frankenstein* and I had to get it done and get everything ready before Thanksgiving, for the opening in Texas. So I don't take pride in a lot of things that I did with *Blood of Dracula* because I had to slam-bang-rush it out.

Louise Lewis was good in Blood of Dracula, *as the evil teacher.*

Wasn't she? I had used her earlier as the principal in *I Was a Teenage Werewolf*; in fact, that's why I used her in *Blood of Dracula*, because she was so good in that first small part.

Why did you invoke the Dracula name in the title? Why not I Was a Teenage Vampire?

Because I thought *Blood of Dracula* was a damn good title. In fact, Jimmy Carreras tried to get me to change it [laughs]! He called me from London and he said [growling], "How dare you use *Dracula*! *Dracula*'s *my* title!" I said, "What do you mean, *your* title? Did you forget about Universal? How about *this* picture and *that* picture? What are you givin' me this shit for, Jim?" [Laughs.]

A two-in-one follow-up to Teenage Werewolf *and* Teenage Frankenstein *was a great idea. Who came up with* How to Make a Monster?

That was completely my idea. Many a night I would leave the studio late, and at that time you didn't have good security like we do now. Now we have so many guards they bump into each other [laughs]! But at that time, studios used to be very dark at night—a light here, a light there. And I thought to myself, "Gee, what a great spot to do a horror film." There were several studios at that time that were being taken over by conglomerates, so I thought that would be a good plot for it. I knocked out the original story and I hired Aben Kandel to do the screenplay with me.

Gary Conway (fifth from left), Robert H. Harris, Cohen and werewolf Gary Clarke join a colorful lineup of dress extras. Behind the scenes on *How to Make a Monster*.

Why Gary Clarke instead of Michael Landon as the Teenage Werewolf?

I was very pissed off at Landon, because I wanted him to do *How to Make a Monster* and he wouldn't. Michael got a lot of teasing for doing *Teenage Werewolf,* from all the young actors in that period. We had a whole group that used to meet at the Cock 'n' Bull for Sunday brunch: Natalie Wood and Robert Wagner, Jeffrey Hunter, Tab Hunter, Edd "Kookie" Byrnes and the gal that married him, Asa Maynor—it was a real fun crowd. Anyway, when *Teenage Werewolf* first came out, Michael was ribbed like crazy, because at that time they all wanted to be Serious Actors. When I approached Michael with *How to Make a Monster,* I certainly felt, for starting his career and getting him all this publicity, that he should have done it for me. And he didn't *want* to do it! So, like I said, I became pissed off at him at the time. But then, of course, everything got smoothed over; I was at his adopted son Mark's *bar mitzvah* a couple of years later and everything else.

So Gary Clarke took over as the Teenage Werewolf.

Gary Clarke had the same slight, thin build as Landon, and the same contour of the head. So Phil Scheer was able to do the same makeup that he did for *Teenage Werewolf* on Gary Clarke. Clarke did all right, he was very cooperative, and of course Gary Conway was, too. And Robert H. Harris, who played the crazy makeup artist, was a dream. A marvelous Broadway actor and a wonderful man personally; I wish I had had more things for him to do. I had seen him in a picture where he wore real thick glasses and he was playing a crazy guy who liked to start fires. I said to myself, "Who *is* that guy?" and I waited for the cast of characters at the end and got his name. And when I was about to do *How to Make a Monster,* I called him in.

Any anecdotes about the fire scene?
    It was tough to do, and we had to do it in one take. Going from black and white to color at the end of *Teenage Frankenstein* had worked so well that I decided to do it again: When Harris takes the two boys into his home in *How to Make a Monster,* I went to color again, from there to the end of the picture, about ten minutes. I thought the flames and the burning of the masks—all of Harris' "children" on the walls—would look better in color, which it did. That ending was talked about by a lot of critics.

Were the two studio executives in How to Make a Monster *meant to make Hollywood insiders think of Nicholson and Arkoff?*
    No. In fact, let me tell you something: I never thought of Sam Arkoff in any way, shape or form in those days. He had nothing to do with the making of the pictures. The fact that I went to AIP was because of my relationship with Jim Nicholson.

And now a big step up, with Horrors of the Black Museum.
    As I told you before, I had a very good contact with Nat Cohen and Stuart Levy of Anglo Amalgamated Films of England, where I did my first co-production, *River Beat.* Because of my contact with Cohen and Levy, I was virtually the agent that sold AIP pictures to Anglo Amalgamated, for release in the United Kingdom; and I was the first one to take Jim Nicholson and Sam Arkoff to London, to introduce 'em to Cohen and Levy.
    Anyway, I was reading a group of articles in the *Sunday Parade* about Scotland Yard's Black Museum. I went to London, and while I was there, a friend of mine that knew an inspector at Scotland Yard got me a special pass to go through the Black Museum. (They won't let the public go through it unless you're a V.I.P., a police officer or something like that.) From that, I wrote the original treatment of *Horrors of the Black Museum*; then Aben and I did the screenplay. I got Nat Cohen and Stuart Levy to agree to put up fifty percent of the financing of the picture, then I got Jim Nicholson and AIP to agree to put up fifty percent. That's how I got the financing to make the picture.

Black Museum *was the first color/CinemaScope picture for AIP.*
    I told Jim, "Hey, it's time for AIP to do a bigger picture. You can't keep doing these small pictures." In fact, it was right after *Black Museum* that they gave Roger Corman the okay to do his Edgar Allan Poes, because of the success

A highpoint of 1950s film horror: The shocking spiked-binoculars scene from *Horrors of the Black Museum*. (Pictured: Dorinda Stevens.)

of *Horrors of the Black Museum*. That's when AIP started going for bigger budgets.

Some sources list the producer of Black Museum *as Jack Greenwood.*

At that time, when an American did a film in England, we had to hire a British subject as a producer, plus other Brits, to qualify for a British subsidy. That's another reason why I was able to talk [AIP] into spending more money on the picture, because I was going to make it under British Eady. Therefore, Jack Greenwood was my "associate producer." Only in the United Kingdom prints did Jack Greenwood get producer credit, and I was the executive producer. Jack Greenwood was a hell of a nice guy, by the way, and I used him on a lot of pictures as my British counterpart.

How did you hook up with Michael Gough?

I saw him in a British film, in a small part; I think it was Hammer's *Horror of Dracula*. Now, initially, I wanted to hire Vincent Price to star in *Horrors of the Black Museum,* but we couldn't afford Price at that time. There were other people I was thinking about, too, like Orson Welles. Anyway, under British Eady, you're allowed to bring X-number of Americans in, but Nat

Cohen said, "Herm, why can't you use a British actor? If you bring an American over, we're gonna have to house him at the Dorchester, give him per diem, this and that. And there are so many British actors that can play this kind of role!" I remembered Michael Gough, I made a dinner date with him, we sat and we talked and I just flipped over him personally. He's a marvelous man, a wonderful person. That's how he ended up in *Black Museum*.

His bravura performances in your horror films won him lots of new fans.

I was so pleased when he won the Tony in New York [for *Bedroom Farce*] a few years ago. We're in touch all the time, although he hasn't worked for me since *Trog* with Joan Crawford.

The binoculars scene in Black Museum *still shocks today.*

You really don't see anything happen in that scene. After the girl screams, "My eyes! My eyes!" as the blood drips through her fingers, we then cut to a closeup of the binoculars on the carpet, with the needles extended. But you don't see it happen, you have to visualize it.

Whose idea was the binoculars scene?

Every instrument of murder in *Black Museum* was from an actual murder and is in Scotland Yard's Black Museum. The murder with the binoculars happened in the thirties, in Kent, which is outside of London. A young stable boy who was very much in love with his master's daughter was fired for having sex with her in the stables. And she would have nothing to do with him after that. When the Royal Ascot meet started the following year, she received through the mail a pair of binoculars, mailed from the Paddington Post Office. She took them to the window, she focused them, and the needles penetrated through her eyes and killed her. The stable boy was found, was tried and was hung. And those binoculars are in the Black Museum in Scotland Yard. The ice tongs, the portable guillotine [the other murder implements in *Black Museum*]—people don't realize it, but these were actual murders in England.

I thought America had the market cornered on outlandish murders.

Oh, no, no. The kinkiest murders are done in England [*laughs*]!

Ruth Pologe, who handled the publicity for *Black Museum* in New York, came up with the idea for me to bring the spiked binoculars over from England, and then at the airport in New York say that they were lost! She said, "That would hit the wire services and the front pages of all the papers!" So we did — of course, these weren't the *real* Black Museum binoculars, they were the binoculars that we had made for the film, but they were just as deadly. (In fact, I still have 'em today, under lock and key!) So that was the gimmick:

We suddenly "misplaced" them at the airport when I came from London, and we made the papers and everything. In fact, the assistant D.A. called me at the Hampshire House to talk to me about this, 'cause he had figured out that it was a stunt. (Of course, I never admitted it!)

You had a top-flight director of photography in Desmond Dickinson.
He was a real class cinematographer, and also a wonderful guy—we just got along terrific. That's why I used him so often.

And how about the director of Black Museum, *Arthur Crabtree?*
A nice Englishman. I needed a director who was English because we did the picture under the British Eady, but I wanted a director who was not going to be *too* British, who was not going to be in my way too much and who would do what I wanted done. Arthur Crabtree had just done *Fiend Without a Face* with Marshall Thompson, and on the basis of that, I interviewed him. The price was right and the old guy needed a job, and I hired him. And he was exactly what I wanted and needed as a good craftsman.

Why have you never tried directing?
Because I learned at a very early age that you can't do everything. I *have* directed, like on *A Study in Terror* when my director suddenly disappeared *[laughs]*—I've done it quite a few times during my career. However, I was head of my company and a real hands-on line producer, plus also head of the second largest theater in the world, the Fox Theater in Detroit, and other things that I was involved in. To be a director, you have to give one hundred percent of your attention, so I always just hired directors that I could work with.

How much did you have to do with the thirteen-minute prologue AIP tacked onto Black Museum*?*
That was Jim Nicholson's, not mine, and we did not use it anyplace but the U.S.A. Jim was looking for another gimmick, and he came up with HypnoVista. When Jim told me what he was writing and working on, I was reluctant to permit it to be tagged on, but I let Jim talk me into it; he said, "Herm, if it's really *that* bad, we'll take it off." We tested it in a few theaters and the audience went for it like crazy, hokey as it was. It helped make the picture a success, I guess, 'cause people were looking for gimmicks at that time. But when the picture was released on television in this country, we had to take it off because it *does* hypnotize some people. I saw it again recently and it *is* interesting, but my executive vice-president Didier Chatelain said, "Oh, God, is that corny!"

Right now, Martin Scorsese, Steven Spielberg and George Lucas are donating forty pictures to the Museum of Modern Art in New York, and Marty Scorsese has contacted me to tell me that he and the boys want *Horrors of the*

Black Museum as one of the pictures. They said they grew up on it and just loved it, and they thought there were a lot of inventive things done in the film. (Martin Scorsese said that, as far as he was concerned, that binoculars scene was one of the greatest scenes of any picture *[laughs]*!) In fact, Marty just talked to me the other day, because they're going over the negative in order to get a top print, and they've decided they're going to leave the Hypno-Vista business off, and go right into the picture after the main titles.

What was the rationale behind the horror-comedy The Headless Ghost? *It's not a funny picture.*

No, you're right, it isn't; I never liked that picture. While I was making *Black Museum* and we were near the end of shooting, Jim Nicholson called me from Hollywood and he was all excited about *Black Museum* even though he hadn't seen any of it—and *wouldn't* see it, until I brought it back from London. (In those days, he and Sam didn't spend the money to come across, and if they did, I wouldn't have shown 'em anything anyway!) Jim said, "Gee, if we only had a second feature..." I was awfully busy with *Black Museum* and with planning some other future projects, but he kept after me: "Herm, look, if you can knock out a second feature in black and white, just to go with *Black Museum,* we'll get the whole program from RKO, from Loew's, from Texas," blah, blah, blah. I told him I'd see what I could come up with.

I started thinking, "What the hell can I do?", and I thought maybe I should do a comedy. So Aben Kandel and I wrote this picture *The Headless Ghost* where these teenagers meet up with a ghost in a British castle. I got great publicity for using Richard Lyon in one of the leads—Louella Parsons gave us a headline story—because he was Bebe Daniels and Ben Lyon's son, who was acting in London. I met him and he needed a job badly, so we hired him. We knocked out that picture very, very fast; that's why the running time is so short, like sixty-five minutes. The director, Peter Graham Scott, was a film editor in London who always wanted to direct, and I needed somebody to do a fast job under my guidance. In fact, we started *Headless Ghost* as I was still finishing *Black Museum,* editing and cutting it. But I honestly don't recall too much else about this picture, it was so bad.

Was any of it shot on your Black Museum *sets?*

They were shot at the same studio, *Headless Ghost* in black and white and *Black Museum* in color, so we *did* reuse some of the sets after we redressed 'em. Then we also had to build some other sets, plus we went on location to an actual castle.

How often do you watch your old pictures?

I really don't, unless I happen to catch one at somebody's house. I haven't seen some of these pictures in twenty-five years. I don't have time to run yesteryear.

Around this same time, you announced you were going to produce Aladdin and the Giant *in London and in Europe, in Technicolor and CinemaScope.*

Originally, I was going to do that for AIP, but then it got put aside. I've brought it out many times since then—we almost made it for Warner Brothers, almost made it for E.M.I. in England. I've come so close on *Aladdin and the Giant* a half a dozen times, but I just never was able to put the picture together.

What did you have to do with Circus of Horrors?

I was involved in that through Nat Cohen. I had quite a bit to do with it—picking Anton Diffring and other things like that. I didn't get a credit—I didn't ask for one—but I was the executive in charge, representing the money, representing Nat Cohen and Stuart Levy, and I owned a piece of the picture. I was out on the set but it wasn't like it was one of my own personal pictures. I had a lot of respect for Julian Wintle, who got the screen credit as producer. Julian was a very classy producer for Rank who had his offices at Pinewood, he was quite a British gent but he did not know horror. So Nat Cohen asked me to be a part of the picture.

Next came Konga, *which you also made in England.*

Nat and Stuart Levy were so excited about the business that *Black Museum* did in England and in Europe (it was a very big hit there), they said, "Herm, can you do another exploitation type of picture?" Well, I had always flipped over *King Kong* and *Mighty Joe Young* and all that, so I came up with *Konga* and Aben and I started writing the script.

Konga *involved a lot more special effects than any of your other pictures.*

We did a tremendous amount of special effects with Rank Labs. I supervised them myself, all these special effects. For the scenes where Konga's a giant, the head of special effects at Rank Labs, a wonderfully clever guy named Victor Marguetti, developed a traveling matte technique that employed yellow sodium lights; *Konga* was the first picture that they used it on. Some of the special effects of Konga, when he's big, are really good, rock steady. *Konga* only cost about five hundred thousand dollars, in color, but the effects were so good that people thought the picture cost millions.

How long did it take to supervise the effects on Konga?

Eighteen months—over a year and a half to get those bloody special effects done perfect. It just went on and on and on, 'cause it was trial and error. AIP was after me constantly—"Where's the picture? When are we gonna get the picture?" They didn't realize how much fucking work was involved, 'cause they never used special effects at that time.

Herman Cohen—a giant of the horror/exploitation picture business, *and* on the miniature lab set for *Konga*.

The closest AIP came to special effects pictures prior to Konga *were the Bert I. Gordon jobs.*

Yes, but *Konga* was in color, and that's a whole different bag of beans. To have Konga hold Michael Gough, what I had to do there was matte five different scenes on one frame.

I assumed that you had built a giant ape arm.

Are you kidding? We didn't have money to build a giant *putz* at that time *[laughs]*!

You also had the actor in the ape suit on miniature sets, just as he was starting to grow.

For a cheap picture, those miniature sets that we built were pretty good. I worked my ass off; in fact, I don't think I ever worked harder on a picture than I did on *Konga*. And don't forget those giant plants that we had in the greenhouse scene. My art director Wilfred Arnold and I did a lot of research on all those plants—I had to go to all kinds of places with him, in the Kew Gardens, here and there. They were based on actual carnivorous plants. We had them made at Shepperton Studios. But it was exciting to do this on spit. We had to use a lot of ingenuity in place of money. Luckily, I had an enthusiastic crew with me.

I almost got thrown out of England 'cause of *Konga*. Once Konga grew into the giant ape, I needed to shoot the streets of London near the Embankment. Jack Greenwood and [production manager] Jim O'Connolly told me, "Herm, we can't get permission. The Metropolitan Police will shut us down." I was also told that you can't bribe an English bobby; unlike in New York, Chicago, Detroit or L.A., it won't work. So I had to take things in hand. I went to meet the inspector in charge of the precinct in Croyden, which is the jurisdiction of the Embankment area. I sat and visited with him for a long time, talked about all different subjects, on and on. Then we got to talking about television, and he said, "Oh, I wish I could afford a color television set." That was my opening—I went out and bought him a color television set, and I had it sent to his home. And suddenly I got permission to shoot on the streets in London! The thing that I *didn't* mention to him was that, at the finale, all hell was going to break loose—that we were going to shoot sub-machine guns, bazookas, etc., etc. I purposely didn't tell him this *[laughs]*!

It's always easier to get forgiveness than permission.

That's what I figured! We had permission to shoot from twelve midnight until five in the morning, each night for four or five nights. And on the last night, the night when we were going to shoot the finale, who should come out but the inspector, to have biscuits and a cup of tea with me and see how everything was going! I said, "Gee, it's awfully late for you to be up, it's like two o'clock in the morning." I wanted to get rid of him, I knew what was coming up! I did get rid of him, but there were also a couple of sergeants that were with me all the time—I didn't tell *them* what was going to happen, either!

Anyway, comes the final scene and we blaze away: I had told all my people, "Have the trucks ready, 'cause when we're done, we gotta split!" Which we did! Well, the nine-nine-nine [emergency number] got something like three hundred phone calls—people thought London was being invaded *[laughs]*! This was only fifteen years or so after World War II, and they were still worried. I had a lot of apologies to make—a *lot*. There were a few old women that claimed that the excitement affected their health, all kinds of shit. The Metropolitan Police gave me the addresses of the ones that were threatening to go to the Consul and what have you, and I had to go visit each of them in person and charm the bejesus out of them, which I did, fortunately. Jack Greenwood, Jim O'Connolly and I went and bought like twenty boxes of chocolates, which are terribly expensive in England, flowers, all sorts of crap for them. They took the candy and the flowers and kissed me goodbye *[laughs]*!

With a title like Konga, *people started making comparisons to* King Kong —
—which was *fine*, which was what I *wanted*! We paid RKO so that we could use in our ads the line, NOT SINCE KING KONG . . . HAS THE SCREEN THUNDERED TO SUCH MIGHTY EXCITEMENT! I paid RKO because I didn't want

them to think we were stealing it; we paid 'em twenty-five thousand dollars so there would not be any lawsuit.

After Konga, *you came back to Hollywood and made* Black Zoo.

That was an original idea of mine, and then I hired Aben Kandel to work with me and we did the script together. I built the zoo right here at Raleigh Studio [formerly Producers Studio] on North Bronson—the entire zoo that you saw in that picture was an interior set. (We have one of the largest sound-stages in town here on our lot.) We built the entire zoo exterior here on the soundstages so we could contain the animals. As a for-instance, when at the beginning you see the girl walking down the street, that actually was a public street. But when she gets attacked by the tiger, those were bushes we put up on the soundstage, because we had to control the tiger.

You must have an animal anecdote or two.

Well, one of our lions escaped during the shooting of the picture, and we had front page headlines in all the papers! Everybody said I must have done it as a publicity stunt, but it actually happened. A full-grown American mountain lion named Chico, three hundred pounds, broke loose and dashed out through a door. We immediately removed the cast and crew from the set, and someone was broadcasting warnings over loudspeakers for all the various studio personnel to take cover—this all happened just before lunch, and everybody was told to stay in their offices. The police were called and they surrounded the studio, and there was also a helicopter announcing over a speaker, telling the children at the nearby schools to get off the playgrounds and back inside the buildings! More than fifty police officers with their cars blocked off streets and were searching for him. And the lion's owner, Ralph Helfer, was asking 'em *not* to shoot the thing. This went on for an hour or two before they recaptured him—he had squeezed himself into a sub-basement under the soundstage, down through an electrician's crawl-hole in the stage floor. And he was scared stiff, the poor thing. Well *[laughs]*, at least we got a lot of free publicity out of it!

Did all these animals come from Ralph Helfer?

Yes. In searching for someone to provide the animals, I heard about him through other animal handlers. He was using a new technique for training wild cats for films, where they never used a whip, never did any beating. It was all through kindness and love and what have you. I went out to his animal training ranch, way out in the Valley in Saugus. I was there for hours with a couple of my staff, and I was so impressed with what he showed me that I signed him. We worked together on the script and we worked together with the animals. We had several African lions and lionesses, a tiger, a black panther, several cheetahs, a Himalayan black bear, oh, a whole menagerie.

How did your actors like working with the animals?

Some were afraid of them. But Michael Gough, who I brought here from London to do the film, loved animals, and the animals took to him beautifully. And I must say they took to me also. But we had to be very careful on *Black Zoo* (and on *Konga*, too, because that had chimps in it): When I interviewed any female in the picture, I had to ask when they had their periods. And right away, they shouted, "*What?!*" But if an animal smells blood, chimps especially, there can be trouble.

I've read that Michael Gough was bitten by the tiger.

No, I don't remember that; that sounds like a phony publicity release. However, a trainer *was* attacked by Zamba, one of our lions. One of the new young trainers was bringing Zamba from his cage to the soundstage to work in a scene, and when you bring an animal from place to place, you must have some meat in your hand. And you should walk *next* to him, never in *front* of him. This trainer was late in bringing Zamba out to the soundstage, and he was pissed off that Zamba didn't want to go. I was standing talking on the phone near the door, and I could see that Zamba did not want to go any further. That was when the trainer did a really stupid thing: He got in front of Zamba and said, "God damn it, *come here!*" and he started pulling on the rope. And Zamba *leaped*. Knocked him on his ass. The trainer put his arm up, and Zamba took a big bite. I was just a few feet away from Zamba, and I screamed for Ralph Helfer. Zamba stopped after he bit him—he realized what he'd done—and the trainer didn't move. Of course, Ralph and the other trainers came running like crazy and they lassoed Zamba. (Even Ralph didn't want to go near him, 'cause Zamba had blood dripping from his mouth.) The guy had to have seventy stitches. We calmed Zamba down, talked to him, brought him some food, and then he was fine. And I've got to hand it to Michael Gough: Two hours later, Michael was working with him in a scene.

You also did a lot of publicity with the cats.

First we were on the Johnny Carson show, when Carson was doing his show in New York. I brought Zamba and a tiger named Patrina to New York on American Airlines, and, of course, the animal trainers, four of them, two to an animal. I checked the animals into a suite at the Edison Hotel; I was staying at the Hampshire House myself, but for publicity purposes, we made like I was staying with the animals. (I have pictures of the lion standing at the registration desk, putting his paw print in the book like he was checking in.) This was all great publicity. Then I had two premieres, one in New York and another at my Fox Theater in Detroit. (In Detroit, they stayed at the Statler Hilton Hotel.) We built cages in the lobby of the Fox Theater and we had 'em there for three or four days.

Herman Cohen and one of the feline stars of *Black Zoo* amuse themselves between takes. (Notice that Cohen is *losing*.)

Did the cats enjoy all this?

Patrina the tiger was spooked coming on TV for interviews, spooked by the lights and the audience. We had to be very careful with Patrina. And Zamba—let's face it, if he turned his head the wrong way and you were there, he'd break your jaw. And they wanted *me* to pose for pictures with my head next to his and what have you! There was a big full-page ad we took in *Variety* that showed me with Zamba, and a caption, "Herman Cohen with Zamba. (Please note: Herman Cohen is on the right.)" *[Laughs.]*

Were you happy with the way Black Zoo *came out?*

Oh, very happy. It was a beautiful picture to make, because of the wild cats, and it was a very unusual film. I didn't like the title, but Allied Artists did. I didn't like it because I felt that people wouldn't know what *Black Zoo* was—the title doesn't really convey much. So because *Horrors of the Black Museum* had been so successful, in some territories I had Allied Artists put out some alternate ads in which *Black Zoo* was called *Horrors of the Black Zoo*. That's when our grosses jumped considerably. And it ended up being very successful.

Why did you stop making pictures for AIP after Konga?

Sam Arkoff told me, "We're not gonna make partnership deals anymore.

We'll give you a small piece of the profits, and a salary." That's when AIP was really in the black and doing great, because of the pictures that Roger Corman and I did for 'em. (And they told Roger the same thing at that time—"No more fifty-fifty!") And that's when I told Sam, "Goodbye!" *[Laughs.]*

What's the story on A Study in Terror?

I made a deal with two English distributors, Michael Klinger and Tony Tenser, who were talking about doing a Sherlock Holmes picture at the same time I wanted to do one. So we decided we'd do one together, and that I would make the film. Klinger and Tenser would have the United Kingdom and certain other territories to distribute it in, and I'd have the rest of the world. Then I in turn made a deal with Columbia Pictures, to be my partner in it. That's how *A Study in Terror* was put together.

Producer credit goes to someone named Henry Lester.

The Conan Doyle estate appointed Lester, who had to get a credit on the film. He was the representative to see that we didn't do anything in the script that would injure the Sir Arthur Conan Doyle name.

Study in Terror *did have an excellent script.*

Yes, it was very, very good. Donald and Derek Ford get screen credit for the writing but they *didn't* write it, although the idea of combining Holmes and Jack the Ripper was theirs. Michael Klinger and Tony Tenser had signed them for "their" Sherlock Holmes movie, but they didn't execute their script properly and I didn't like it. I hired Harry Craig, a writer that Adrian Conan Doyle [Arthur's son] and Henry Lester liked very much. He worked closely with me and James Hill, the director, on the final screenplay, which was based on the original story and screenplay by Donald and Derek Ford. Harry Craig didn't want a credit on *A Study in Terror* because he was doing a big picture for Columbia at that time.

Did Henry Lester or Adrian Conan Doyle pitch in creatively at all?

Not Adrian; Adrian just visited with his wife and friends for tea and lunch occasionally. But Henry Lester and I discussed many, many facets, and there were many things we wanted to do that he would say, "Oh, no, *no, Sherlock Holmes wouldn't *do* that!"

You mentioned before that you had to take over the direction one day.

Yes, I did, because Jim Hill had a habit of disappearing. He was a nice guy, but weird—strange. Nobody could get close to him. And he was always fidgety and very nervous. In fact, I talked to Carl Foreman about this and he said, "Yes, Hill disappeared on *Born Free* [1966], too!" And nobody knew where he went or what he did! So the assistant director had a tough time keeping tabs on him. Now, here we had this big fire scene upstairs in the pub, and we were all set for it. The special effects were ready, the fire department was standing by and everything else, and we had to be out of that stage that night—this was Shepperton Studios in London. That's when the a.d. came up to me and said, "Herm, I can't find Jim Hill!"

"Can't find the director?! Chrissakes, it's four-thirty in the afternoon!" And the a.d. said, "Well, he's disappeared!" I said, "Okay, *I'll* direct the scene." So we put the red light on, locked the doors, and I did the scene in one take—the whole bloody thing. As the firemen were putting out the fire, Jim Hill came back in and said, "I'm ready to—. Hey, what happened?!" I said, "We've already done the scene! Where in hell have *you* been? *Where* do you disappear, goddamn it?!" Well, believe me, he never left after that! He was so embarrassed, because the crew and everybody was laughing at him.

Did Study *have a bigger budget than some of your other British horror films?*

Oh, yes, it did, because of Columbia coming in with me. John Neville was marvelous as Sherlock Holmes, a fine actor; at that time he was running a theater in Nottingham. I had Donald Houston, Robert Morley, Anthony Quayle, Georgia Brown, Adrienne Corri—some top actors. I cast it myself, and I was very lucky to get the people that I did.

You sound pleased with A Study in Terror.

I was *very* pleased with the film. In fact, it turned out so well that Stanley Schneider, the president of Columbia Pictures, used *A Study in Terror* to show the studio what kind of a film could be made on a low budget. He ran it a half a dozen times for new young executives. (Which, by the way, Mike Frankovich was not too happy about. Mike was head of production in Hollywood, and he didn't like the fact that Schneider was showing *A Study in Terror,* which was not made in Frankovich's jurisdiction.) And I have a book on all the Sherlock Holmes movies that says *A Study in Terror* was the best Holmes movie which was ever made. But again, as with *Black Zoo,* I was not pleased with the title. Columbia insisted on *A Study in Terror;* I hated it. They wanted it because Sir Arthur Conan Doyle had written a book called *A Study in Scarlet,* but I didn't like the word "study" in there; I felt that the teenagers would think it would be like extra homework! Columbia fought me, and I had to go along with them in the end. My title was *Fog,* a nice, simple, one-word title.

Then Columbia went and . . . *[laughs]* fucked me up again! The big hit on TV at that time was *Batman,* so the head of advertising, Robert Ferguson, wanted to sell *A Study in Terror* almost like a comedy. On one of the one-sheets, he had POW, BIFF, CRUNCH, BANG, and HERE COMES THE ORIGINAL CAPED CRUSADER—which I didn't like at *all!* I wanted to sell it as horror, and so we had a big fight about the advertising. We did our own campaign for the

United Kingdom, France, Italy — Columbia had nothing to do with the picture there — and it was a much bigger hit over there than it was here.

I thought A Study in Terror *was crying out for a sequel. Were you ever tempted to do another Holmes picture?*

In those days, I never thought of doing sequels. I always wanted to do something different, something new. Several people did make Holmes pictures in the years following *A Study in Terror*; in fact, one which I have not seen called *Murder by Decree* [1979] prompted several people to call me or write me, telling me that the script was practically stolen from *Study in Terror*. And they even stole some of my cast — they had Anthony Quayle, and another actor, Frank Finlay, playing the same inspector he played in *my* picture!

How did you come to meet Joan Crawford, the star of Berserk *and* Trog?

I wanted to try to pitch the lead in *Berserk* to Joan Crawford, because I felt that Joan would be perfect for the picture. Joan was a very close friend of Leo Jaffe, the president of Columbia Pictures at that time, and I asked Leo if he would introduce me to her. He was the one who made the introduction, and that's when I became friends with Joan Crawford.

In writing Berserk, *were you thinking back to how well* Circus of Horrors *came out?*

No, that had no effect on it, I just felt that the circus would be a good backdrop for a horror story. I made a deal with the Billy Smart Circus in England, to use their circus in the film. We shot at Shepperton Studios, then we also shot at night at the circus, after the place was closed, for about two weeks.

Today Joan Crawford has the off-screen reputation that she does because of Mommie Dearest, *the book and the movie. What kind of lady did you find her to be?*

Fascinating. Exciting. In spite of her sipping hundred-proof vodka, she was very professional with me, and would never take a drink unless I okayed it. She always knew her lines and she was always on time. She would come in very early in the morning, like six-thirty, and she loved to cook: She made breakfast for her hairdresser, for her costumer, for "her team." She was strong-willed, she was tough — but, tough as she was, at the drop of a hat, she could be reduced to tears.

For her age, she looks great in Berserk.

Doesn't she? And doesn't she look great in the leotard? Edith Head designed that leotard for her as a favor.

Cohen and star Joan Crawford with the circus performers from *Berserk*. (Left to right, skeleton man Ted Lune, bearded lady Golda Casimir, Cohen, Crawford, strongman Milton Reid; front and center, vertically challenged George Claydon.)

Crawford's biographies say she was a lonely lady during this period.

Oh, yes, Joan was a very lonely lady, but we became very close friends, from the time of *Berserk* until she died. We went out a lot, in London and New York and here in L.A., in the years after I met her on *Berserk*.

She was taught everything at MGM, and one thing that she was taught there was that the producer is the boss. She always went to the producer if she had any problems, with the director or with any member of the cast or crew. As an example, one morning she called me, about two o'clock a.m. — woke me up out of a sound sleep — asking, "Herm, you have your script with you?" As if I go to bed with my script *[laughs]*! She said, "Go get your script! I'm working on tomorrow's scenes and you're sleeping!" I got the script, and she started in, "Now, on page blah, blah, blah," and she wanted to talk about it because, as I said, she was lonely. She would stay up late at night, sipping her vodka, going over her lines for the next day.

Then she said to me, "What time are you leaving for the studio tomorrow morning?" — we were shooting at Shepperton at the time. "Look, why don't you leave around five-thirty and pick me up?" I said, "Well, what's wrong with *your* car?" "Oh, there's something wrong with the car," she said. That was all b.s. It turned out that one of our prop men had to have all his teeth extracted, and she sent her Rolls-Royce over to pick him up — take him to the dentist —

wait for him — and take him home. Then she had it go to a Jewish restaurant in Soho called Isow's, where a lot of members of the industry would always go, and pick him up some chicken soup and bring it to his house! That's why she didn't have a car that day! So I had to call my driver, wake *him* up, and have him pick *her* up at five-thirty in the morning. She didn't tell me until after all this happened — in fact, it was the *prop man* who told me what Joan had done. But she was always doing this kind of stuff —

None of which you'll find in Mommie Dearest.

Right. Christina [Crawford] doesn't mention the nice things that Joan always did, especially for the crew. She was always very close to the crew, and knew all of them by their first names. When we were doing *Berserk,* Christina married Harvey Medlinsky, who was a director, and Joan gave Christina a check for five thousand dollars, told her to enjoy herself — I was right there at the time. And she gave her a big dinner party at Les Ambassadeurs, which was *the* restaurant club in London. *None* of this is covered in *Mommie Dearest.* (Harvey was married to Christina for about six years, and he said he never heard Christina tell *one* of these awful stories. It was her *second* husband who got her to write this book — they were broke and needed the money and what have you.) Joan ended up leaving Christina and [Joan's] son Chris out of her will, and that was a big mistake. Her attorneys should have advised her to leave them, say one thousand dollars, so they could not contest the will. (They *both* contested the will.) She was closer to her twins, the two girls, than she was to Christina or Chris. Joan had a lot of problems with Chris.

Did she seem to enjoy horror movies? She did What Ever Happened to Baby Jane?*, then two each for* William Castle *and for you.*

With Joan and with Bette Davis, they never looked at these pictures as horror films — not even *Berserk.* Joan just looked at it as a drama with some horrific moments. You had to be very careful — anyone who is a star never wants to feel they're going into a horror picture. You never use the word "horror" in front of them. In fact, the original title was *Circus of Blood,* and she hated that title. Fortunately, we came up with the title *Berserk,* which everybody loved.

Why *did* she do these pictures? Mainly she wanted to be Joan Crawford, mainly she just wanted to work. She was intrigued by the fact that *Berserk* was going to be shot in London, because she loved London and the Brits loved *her.* And in England, she was still the Joan Crawford of yesteryear, she wasn't "the old gal" there.

Were you pleased with the job she did in the picture?

Oh, yes. After she agreed to do the picture, of course we did a lot of changes on the script to make it fit her, and we had a lot of meetings prior to bringing her to London and shooting the picture. She was very much caught up in the idea of the story. Knowing what kind of a big star she was, I did not want to diminish her stature in any way. Joan always thought of yesteryear, so I assigned her a Rolls-Royce with a chauffeur. Even though it stretched the budget, I did whatever I could to make her realize that she was still Joan Crawford. She was revered in England, and we got great publicity there, not only from the tabloids but also *The London Times, The Sunday Times* and *The Observer.* Everybody did stories on her while we were shooting the picture.

Were you happy with the way Berserk *came out?*

[Laughs.] I've never been happy with the way *any* of my pictures have come out. I always want to do something over again. But *Berserk* was a huge hit — a very big success. In fact, we were one of the two top grossers for Columbia Pictures that year. But you keep asking me if I was "happy" with various pictures. We had pictures to make, we made the pictures, we did the best we could with the budgets we had, and there you are. That's the most you can do on a film.

Let me rephrase, then. Which of your horror movies were you least un*happy with? Is that a fair question?*

Well, it's a fair question, but there's no answer. Although, because it was period, and because I had a lot of fun with the research on Sherlock Holmes and Jack the Ripper, I enjoyed *A Study in Terror.* The most successful box office-wise was *Berserk* and then *Trog.*

So Trog *was also a nice experience, working with Crawford again?*

A great experience. *Trog* was based on an original story by Peter Bryan and John Gilling that I had bought, and then Aben and I wrote the screenplay. I changed the professor from a man to a woman; because we were so successful with *Berserk,* I wanted to do another picture with Joan. Fortunately, we got the same apartment for Joan that she had had during *Berserk* — Columbia Pictures owned this huge apartment at the Grosvenor House on Park Lane, and we rented it for Joan for *Trog.* Which was great, because she knew the whole staff — the maids, the waiters, everybody. It was like old home week. Joan also had a maid called "Mamacita," who went with her wherever she went.

Did Trog *cost as much as* Berserk *did?*

Trog cost *more* than *Berserk.* Between *Berserk* and *Trog,* I did *Crooks and Coronets* [1969] for Warner Brothers — Telly Savalas, Dame Edith Evans, Warren Oates, Cesar Romero, Harry H. Corbett — and that was a big picture. Then we did *Trog* for Warners. We shot at Bray, and also out on the English moors. The cave interiors were built at the studio.

Director Freddie Francis and producer Cohen flank the prehistoric star (Joe Cornelius) of 1970's *Trog*.

One Crawford bio says Trog's *budget was so low that portable dressing rooms were not sent on location, and that Crawford huddled in a car parked on the moors.*

Untrue. She had a huge caravan—and I have reason to remember that well! We were out on location and it was quite chilly out, and I was told by my assistant that Joan was deathly ill in her caravan. I had my car take me there immediately, I went in to see her and she was saying *[huffing and puffing]*, "Oh, Herm . . . oh! . . . get me a doctor . . . I can't work. . ." I told her I'd do it, and I turned to run out. On these caravans, the door is low, and I ran and smashed my head against the top of the door [frame]—knocked myself for a loop! Joan jumped up and yelled, "Oh, Herman, Herman, darling! Come here, lie down!" She got a cold compress for my head—"You rest! I'll work!"—and within an hour, she was on the set! She forgot that she was sick, now that she was taking care of *me*!

Did Freddie Francis do a good job for you as director?

Of course. Freddie had done some horror pictures for Hammer and for Max Rosenberg and Milton Subotsky, and he was a terrific director of photography—he just won an Academy Award for *Glory* [1989]. In asking him to do *Trog,* knowing what he had done, I felt that Freddie was right for it. Then when he read the script, and heard that we were going to have Joan, he wanted very much to do it.

During the making of *Trog,* I brought my three sisters over from the States, and Joan Crawford just took to them like they were *her* sisters. She gave a dinner party for 'em at Les Ambassadeurs, had a couple brunches, on and on. Joan was always "The Movie Star." There was many a Sunday when it was raining and cold in London, and a group of us from the film was going to go to a movie matinee. Joan said, "I'd love to see that picture," and I said, "Come on!" She said, "Oh, no, no, I'd have to get dressed." "No, you don't, just put a pair of slacks on." And she said, "I would *never* go out in a pair of slacks!" In other words, she *was* Joan Crawford. She just hated the young female stars that would go out on the street like they just got up. Whenever you saw Joan, *you saw* Joan Crawford. She wouldn't even dash to a movie with dark sunglasses on!

And her drinking was never a problem?

Well, on *Trog,* her drinking was worse than it was when we were doing *Berserk.* I had to reprimand her a few times for drinking without asking. (She had a huge frosted glass that said PEPSI-COLA — but inside was hundred-proof vodka!) In fact, when she arrived to do *Berserk* as well as *Trog,* she arrived with four cases of hundred-proof vodka, 'cause you can't get hundred-proof vodka in England. And when she arrived in both instances, she had something like forty pieces of luggage, and she had to arrange for Pepsi-Cola to send two trucks to meet the plane and pick it all up. These were *huge* cases, that she and "Mamacita" had packed themselves! And Joan knew where *every*thing was, she was *that* organized. Now, I guarantee you that she didn't open seventy-five percent of these cases while she was in England, but obviously felt that she had to have 'em all there.

She also had me come to New York and pick out from her own wardrobe what she should wear in these pictures — because she owned a big piece of both pictures, she didn't want us to spend any extra money on wardrobe. In her penthouse in New York, on East Seventy-ninth, she had a huge room, like a two-story room, with a ladder, and in it she kept all her clothes! And she knew where everything was, everything was catalogued! So we picked costumes out of there for both films.

And Trog *was a big hit again.*

It was *very* successful. Both *Berserk* and *Trog* came in under budget, on schedule, and again I say that Joan was very professional. When I hear stories today of Kim Basinger and some of the other young stars, I say, "Thank God for people like Joan Crawford and Bette Davis, all the old pros."

What can you tell me about Craze, *with Jack Palance?*

We had a very good cast in that: Palance, Trevor Howard, Diana Dors, Dame Edith Evans, Hugh Griffith. Jack Palance and I got along very well, but

Jack Palance and Cohen behind the scenes on the English-made *Craze* (a.k.a. *The Infernal Idol*).

everyone else was afraid of Jack — he has that aura about him. Freddie Francis was scared stiff of him, and any time a problem came up with Jack, Freddie called me immediately. The gals that were in the picture were scared, too, Suzy Kendall and Julie Ege. Jack had a sex scene with Julie Ege, and he got carried away and grabbed her so hard, one of her breasts started bleeding! I got him a flat right near my flat in London, and I remember that he loved Chinese food. I never ate so much Chinese food in my life, because virtually every night I had to find another Chinese restaurant for him! But as far as his work was concerned, he was very professional and he always knew what he was doing. And he's quite a thinker; you had to explain a lot of things to him, because he wanted to understand what the character was supposed to be doing, this and that. (By the way, he let me know from the beginning, when I first met him here in Hollywood before I signed him, that, "It's Jack *Pal*-ance like *balance,* and don't call me Pa-*lance!*" He let me know that very quick!)

Supposedly you, Francis, and Palance-like-in-balance were all going to do another film together, but it got called off when Craze *didn't do well.*
   No, not true at all. *Craze* did *very* well. But the thing with *Craze* was that I had a deal with National General for release in the U.S.A., and National General was sold to Warner Brothers. So the release was held up because Warner Brothers. had the pick of what films they wanted to release from what National General owned. They finally did pick *Craze,* but it took a long time.

Today you're busy with your new company, Cobra Media.
   The reason I formed Cobra Media was because the ancillary markets were becoming very big, and we were getting (to put it bluntly) *screwed* by various companies on the reports and moneys and what have you. We formed Cobra Media in eighty-two and we've had some very successful pictures, *Crocodile,* for instance. And we've also been very successful with a picture called *Watch Me When I Kill,* another horrific film, and a number of other biggies. We're putting together a package of films right now for the ancillary markets—for cable, for video, for pay-per-view.

Do you get much of a chance to be a hands-on producer these days?
   Not recently, except on pictures we've reedited, put music in, etc. I've paid my dues, and certainly I don't want to work for some company as a producer. However, we *are* working on two screenplays right now that I'm very excited about. One is really horror, and the other sort of leans toward horror. I will be producing these together with Didier Chatelain, my partner.

Are you going to be writing your autobiography soon?
   Not right away, because I might be doing those two horror films soon. But after that, what I've been thinking I might do is write a book like Roger Corman did, on all my horror films to date.

In making your AIP horror movies, did you suspect that in thirty or forty years they'd still have fans, and that some of them would be playing at the Museum of Modern Art?
   No, never. Never once. Never *thought* of it! But, let's face it, as long as there are new electronic devices being invented, who knows where our pictures are going to end up? I think it goes without saying that I'm very, very pleased.

If we'd have had more money, of course we would probably have been more elaborate with everything! That's the interesting thing that happens with these low-budget movies—that's why, so often, directors make their best movies when they don't have that much money. They have to use their imaginations instead.

Robert Day

THEY'RE SORELY MISSED IN THIS NEW ERA of film school hotshots, but years ago some of the best of what movies and TV had to offer was served up by journeymen directors. Their job wasn't to blow their own horns, to outshine their stars or to consciously work at building up an *auteur* reputation; they merely toiled at their chosen trade, bouncing from film to TV, from genre to genre and sometimes even from country to country.

Emblematic of this dying breed, globe-trotting Robert Day has directed numerous features and countless TV episodes since he broke into the business a half a century ago. Day worked his way up from clapper boy to camera operator to full-fledged lensman in his native England before giving directing a shot in the mid–1950s. His first film as director, the black-comic *The Green Man* (1957) for the writer-producer team of Launder and Gilliat, garnered fine reviews and a classic notoriety, and using this as a starting point Day went on to become one of the industry's busier directors. He relocated to Hollywood in the 1960s and now has moved again, from the smog of L.A. north to Washington, but Day still keeps his hand in, returning for the occasional directing assignment. Long-wed to actress Dorothy Provine, Day takes a self-effacing view of much of his work in films, but his output—which includes such well-crafted thrillers as *The Haunted Strangler, First Man into Space, Corridors of Blood* and the best-ever Tarzan film *Tarzan the Magnificent*—will continue to belie his modest appraisals.

How did you get hooked up with Amalgamated Pictures, producers of The Haunted Strangler?

That was through a guy named John Croydon. Amalgamated was run by three people: there was Croydon, there was an American involved, Chuck Vetter from New York—I don't know *what* happened to him!—and there was Richard Gordon, an English guy who lived in New York. We didn't see much of him, I think he was a sort of front man arranging the finance and the distribution more than anything else. John Croydon was the guy who asked me to make *The Haunted Strangler* with Boris Karloff. I guess they'd seen what I'd done already and liked it, and figured that I could probably bring it in on budget.

What kind of budget did you work with?

Oh, very little. Certainly not more than one hundred thousand pounds.

Where was Amalgamated headquartered?

We had an office at Walton Studios, which is where *The Haunted Strangler* was shot. We shot our interiors inside the studio and our exteriors on their back lot. *The Haunted Strangler* was my first film for them, then came *First Man into Space,* which we made not in a studio but in a house in Hampstead. And finally *Corridors of Blood,* with Boris Karloff again.

Previous page: **One of American television's busiest directors in the '70s, director Robert Day remembers well the early days of low-budget British sci-fi and horror films.**

Boris Karloff has had enough of asylum maid Jessica Cairns' off-key singing in a gripping scene from Day's *The Haunted Strangler.*

What can you remember about working with Karloff?

I met him for the first time on *The Haunted Strangler,* and he was a wonderful, wonderful man. We were very close friends, and we used to eat together almost every weekend—he would come to my house or I would go to his. He lived at that time in Cadogan Square in London, where he had an apartment. I just can't say enough good things about him—he was kind, gentle, not a bit like any of the characters he's played in movies. I directed the two films with Karloff, *The Haunted Strangler* and *Corridors of Blood,* we became friends and remained friendly thereafter.

Did he seem to appreciate his better-than-average role in The Haunted Strangler?

I think he treated every character, every script with respect; I know that he was very much involved in the portrayal of the character in *The Haunted Strangler.* He didn't treat it just as another role, he was very, very deeply interested in what he was doing. We discussed the characterization for hours and hours, the way he should look and everything.

If the budget had allowed for more elaborate special effects, would you have wanted a more monstrous-looking Karloff?

I thought he was just right. He had a little makeup on but mostly it was

Boris Karloff gave one of his (few) good 1950s film performances in director Day's *The Haunted Strangler* (British title: *Grip of the Strangler*).

just him, distorting his face. But if we'd have had more money, of course we would probably have been more elaborate with *everything [laughs]*! That's the interesting thing that happens with these low-budget movies—that's why, so often, directors make their best movies when they don't have that much money. They have to use their imaginations instead, and it works out very well so often.

The Haunted Strangler has scenes of strong violence. Did Karloff voice any objections?

I wouldn't say that he enjoyed it, but I had no complaints from him!

John Croydon has complained about Karloff's too-melodramatic style, but if Karloff was too melodramatic in Haunted Strangler, it was the fault of Croydon's script which called for it.

Right—exactly. Croydon was a little stuffy—in fact, he was a weird man, really strange. When I first met him, we had lunch at a restaurant in London, and I remember his dirty fingernails! And that's what always stuck in my mind—isn't that weird? He was just strange, and kind of sly.

I just enjoyed *The Haunted Strangler* very much. I was very cognizant of the fact that we didn't have much money to make the movie, so we were cutting corners all the time. So often, when I wanted to make a reverse shot, I thought, "Well, I *can't* do that because I don't have the time." And then also I had John Croydon up my ass all the time, talking about the budget and the schedule and so on. But I was pleased with the way the film came out—I mean, under the circumstances, and for the cost.

Are you a fan of horror films?

I'm not really a fan of horror now—I think I used to be. But to me it is so disgusting now, with contemporary horror movies, that I just cannot watch them. People getting cut up and all the graphic violence—I just can't stand it! But I liked them back in the old days.

How did you enjoy working on First Man into Space?

That was all right, but again we were so hamstrung with the budget. We had just no money at all. And the script wasn't very good—I didn't think it was, anyway. Actually, we had hardly any script when we started shooting! Chuck Vetter and I would meet after shooting, and prepare the next day's shooting—write the dialogue and everything!

How did the actors like this hectic pace?

Actors are usually used to that kind of thing anyway. I'm not saying by any means that they like it, but it does happen and professional actors can cope. Marshall Thompson was an okay guy; I don't know where they got Marla Landi. I never heard of her before *First Man into Space* and I never heard of her again *[laughs]*! What she did in the film was okay; it wasn't much of a part, anyway.

Did you have any say in casting?

Oh, yes. Again, it was always within the confines of the budget with those people. I didn't cast Marshall Thompson, I think he came with the package, but I helped to cast the remaining roles.

Were you pleased with the monster costume?

It was made of some plastic material, and then touched up with makeup afterwards. It was okay.

What fans don't like about First Man *is the way it shifts gears in mid-picture, from sober semi-documentary to lurid monster movie.*

Marshall Thompson (right) watches his mutated brother (Bill Edwards) take his last breath in *First Man into Space* (shooting title: *Satellite of Blood*).

I think that, to a degree, that was some of John Croydon's influence again. I hated the monster anyway, I thought it was dumb. My feeling at the time was, I thought that somebody could come back out of space with an aberrated mind, rather than the costume. I put that idea forward, but most of the people involved wanted the horror. Which I thought was almost a caricature. It's not one of my favorite movies.

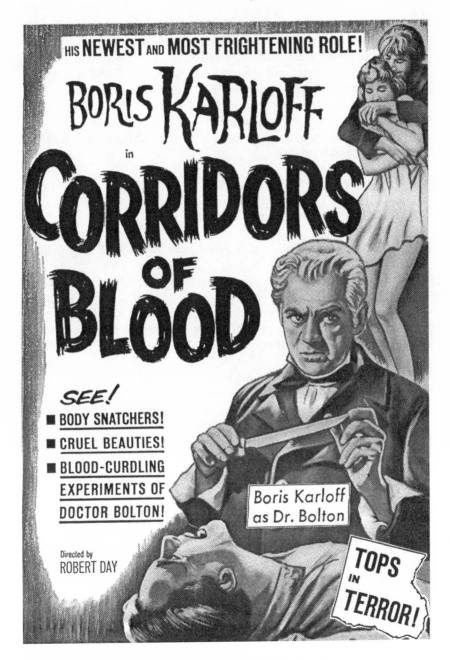

Day collaborated with Karloff a second time on *Corridors of Blood* (shooting title: *The Doctor from Seven Dials*), a historical drama with horrific flourishes.

Corridors of Blood *is another hybrid—a serious film about the discovery of anesthesia that suddenly detours into Grand Guignol.*

That's right, the same thing happened as in *First Man into Space,* where they wanted all this horror stuff again. By the time we got around to *Corridors of Blood,* we were shooting at the MGM British Studios in Boreham Wood, and we had a bit more money in the budget. How much more I have no idea, but I would think it was probably twice the budget of *The Haunted Strangler,* about two hunded thousand pounds. And the shooting schedule was a bit longer, about four weeks.

Any Karloff anecdotes on Corridors of Blood*?*

Well, he and I were deeply involved in characterization. I enjoyed it again, because of Karloff mainly.

Around this same time you also directed a fantasy/comedy called Bobbikins, *about a talking baby.*

That was a weird experience, from what I remember of it. The only thing I really remember about *Bobbikins* is that that baby drove me crazy all the time *[laughs]*! I would go home and think about what I could buy to attract his attention—I spent hours waving things and talking to him from behind the camera. It took all my energy!

How did you get interested in a career in the movies?

I've always been interested, ever since I saw my first movie. I just went from there! I remember that, even at just ten or eleven years old, I was determined that when the time came, I would get into the business. My father knew somebody at Warner Brothers in London and talked to them, and I got a job at Warner Brothers at Teddington, as a clapper boy. In the darkroom. Loading magazines and putting the numbers on scenes. That's how I started, and I went from there. That was nineteen-forty.

How did you climb the ladder to director of photography?

Just by hard work, I guess, and by having friends. Gradually I became an assistant cameraman, then a camera operator, and then on to photography. Then after being under contract to Warner Brothers for several years, I signed a contract with British Lion at Shepperton Studios, as a camera operator, and worked there for a long time. I worked with some good directors—I did a lot of work with Carol Reed, and Launder and Gilliat—I did *The Great Gilbert and Sullivan* [1953] and *The Constant Husband* [1955] with Rex Harrison for them. And then I didn't see them for a while and I went to Africa with Zoltan Korda to work on *Storm Over the Nile* [1956] and he kind of took a shine to me. I don't know if he was influential in talking to Launder and Gilliat subsequent to that, but when I went back to British Lion, Sidney Gilliat asked me if

I would like to direct a movie. I mean, it wasn't as sudden as *that,* but that was the bottom line. I said yeah, and then forgot all about it, really, because it was so outrageous. I went to the South Seas, to Western Samoa, working on a movie called *Pacific Destiny* [1956].

After I'd been there for two or three months, I got this cable from Sidney Gilliat saying they were about to make *The Green Man* and would I like to direct it? Of course I answered yes, but I was very sick. I had slipped on a reef and I cut my leg, got a tremendous cut which festered because of all the coral. Also, I was sharing a huge room with my assistant — they didn't have hotels there, it was like a huge government rest house that the whole crew was living in. My assistant and I had nothing to do in the evenings — there was just *nothing* in Apia — so we bought a couple of harmonicas and we used to play harmonicas in the evening. In bed, under the mosquito net! One night he was asleep and I was playing and I had a cigarette in my hand, too, and the next thing I knew I woke up and flames were all around me — I had set the whole thing alight! And I was covered in mosquito bites, I was awful. One became septic on my elbow and I had like a huge bag on my elbow with this damn infected mosquito bite! Anyway, to cut a long story short, that's how I arrived back in England — I'd lost many, many pounds and I was really in a bad state. But I guess the juices kept going, and the thought of directing *The Green Man* was a wonderful thought. Luckily, there was a long preparation time on the movie, so by the time we started I was in better shape *[laughs]*!

The Green Man *has a great reputation.*

It was tough, it was my first directing job. But it went well, and the reviews were excellent. Bosley Crowther in New York gave it a rave, and Pauline Kael loved it.

How did you get involved on Tarzan the Magnificent*?*

First Man into Space was running at a Leicester Square theater in Picadilly, [Tarzan producer] Sy Weintraub saw the movie and then contacted me to direct *Tarzan the Magnificent.* He came to my house in Roehampton, he and a second guy (I think he was an assistant director) and asked if I would be interested. I said, "Send me the script." So he did, and talked to my agent, and before I knew it I was in Africa!

They sent you the script? I thought *you* wrote it.

They sent me the original script, which I changed. I think that was my first time writing a screenplay.

Did you enjoy the opportunity of working on a Tarzan film?

It was okay. I was more interested in the action rather than Tarzan himself. Actually, this Tarzan phase is a period that I'm not that happy with in my career. I think it's just dumb, that's all. Especially what they did with him, making him talk—it's against the popular concept of Tarzan. But at that time, the business was really bad in England, and I guess those things came along when there was nothing else happening. It's not that I don't like them, I just wonder what the fuss is all about!

Maybe they were popular because Tarzan is such an immortal character.
    I don't know—it's like any legend, I guess. Maybe one reason that Tarzan has perpetuated is because people like to think of somebody going back to basics and living in the jungle. The fundamental aspect appeals to them. It's almost primeval, you know.

Did you enjoy the location trip to Africa on Tarzan the Magnificent?
    Yes, I enjoyed that. We shot *Tarzan the Magnificent* in Kenya. Part of the time we were based at Lake Nyvasha, which is a couple of hundred miles from Nairobi, and part of the time we were in Nairobi. Then we shot the waterfall scenes at a place called the Blue Posts, about two or three hours' drive from Nairobi.

Gordon Scott was your star in Tarzan the Magnificent.
    He was all right. I remember one funny incident—well, *I* thought it was funny!—on the first day of shooting. Gordon Scott got out of this limousine that drove him to the location, they made him up and he started flexing his muscles and all that stuff. Then they gave him the bow and the arrows that he had to use. And then when we were ready to shoot, he took his shoes off and all of a sudden he was hopping around because the ground was so hot *[laughs]*! I can't begin to tell you how funny it was, to see this guy jumping around—*ouch, oooch, ouch*—because he couldn't endure standing on the bare rock! I break up every time I think about it.

You also had John Carradine in Tarzan the Magnificent.
    Oh, he was wonderful, just great. But there was his drinking, you know. When we got back to England, there were some extra scenes to do, and at Shepperton Studios we shot a scene of Carradine and the actors who played his sons wandering through the swamp. And he was drunk as a lord in that scene, and he was reciting Shakespeare during the rehearsals! But he was a great guy.

Many fans consider Tarzan the Magnificent *the best-ever Tarzan film.*
    It makes me feel good that some people think that, yes. Naturally, I used to see the old Johnny Weissmuller Tarzan films when I was a kid; I thought they did a good job on those, and that Johnny Weissmuller was probably the

best Tarzan. That was a different era, of course; those early Weissmuller films were made at a time when we were just out of the silent period.

You shot Tarzan films all over the world. Did this create hardships, working in all these desolate locations?

Yeah, it did—it's not easy. You have to adapt to the surroundings and use the local talent—or what passes for it *[laughs]*! It was a lot cheaper, shooting in all these various places that we went to, especially at that time. And, of course, it was bringing new places to the screen, places that hadn't been seen in movies before. All the sound had to be added to these films after they were completed. We'd bring sound equipment along, because we had to get guide tracks, but we dubbed the whole movie, every time.

How about Jock Mahoney [Tarzan's Three Challenges] *as Tarzan?*

I thought Jock Mahoney did a good job but that he looked too old. He got pneumonia while on the picture. We carried on shooting, but, boy, was he sick! But Woody Strode did a good job playing the villain—he's great, isn't he? *Tarzan's Three Challenges* was shot in Thailand; we were in Bangkok, and in Chiang Mai, the northern province. We also shot in a sacred shrine, and that created all kinds of problems. Right at the last minute, they changed their minds and wouldn't let us photograph the monks, so we had to manufacture our *own* monks. We went into the town in Chiang Mai and got all the rickshaw drivers, we put bowls on their heads and cut their hair in a certain way, and used *them* as monks *[laughs]*!

Your next three Tarzan films featured Mike Henry.

We cast him in Los Angeles. We saw a lot of people looking for our new Tarzan, and I guess he came off best. The first film we did with Mike Henry was *Tarzan and the Valley of Gold,* which we shot in Mexico. The scenes in the ancient city were shot in Teotihuacán, which is a historic site, but we had problems. We got permission, but there again they reneged on the permission at the last minute and we had awful troubles day by day with the lawyers in shooting that. We went ahead somehow, I don't know how we did—I think Sy Weintraub was there in the background, talking to the lawyers all the time. They thought we were desecrating their holy ground by having Tarzan romping around there. It was hairy, but we got it done—although we did have to smuggle the film out! It was a great location.

The Mike Henry films are reviled by Tarzan purists—they say he isn't Tarzan, he's James Bond in a loincloth.

That was the trend at that time, the James Bond films and so on. And I must say I think I went along with it, too.

In these Tarzan films, much of your wild animal footage came from stock, right?

Yes, that's right. But when there was specific action with the animals, we'd have them on the sets. I remember that on one of the movies, *Tarzan and the Great River,* Mike Henry was bit by a monkey. We were in Brazil, we were working in a zoo in Rio and the scene called for Mike to be walking with a professor through the zoo and they come upon this chimp that Mike knew in Africa, that was now in captivity. The chimp came up to Mike, Mike embraced it, and as he embraced it, this chimp just bit his chin off! It was awful! We shot around Mike for a while, then I think the insurance took over.

Why are there no Janes in any of your Tarzan films?

I just don't know. I think it might have been because they wanted to keep him a free agent all the time, so he didn't have to return to that one nest.

Were you offered an opportunity to work on the Tarzan *TV series?*

I shot the pilot, with Ron Ely—that was shot in Rio as well. But I didn't work that show regularly. I'd had it up to my neck with Tarzan by then.

You also directed Hammer's remake of She *around this same time.*

That was my one and only time working with Hammer; they simply asked me to make the movie, although if you were to ask what made them think of me for it, I'd have to tell you that I just don't know. *She* was shot in London and Israel—all the desert scenes and the backgrounds for the special effects were all shot in Eilat, in Southern Israel, right on the ocean. The weather was right for it, anyway—it was hot, *boy,* was it hot! We were working in the Negev Desert.

Had you seen any of the earlier versions of She*? They date back to 1899!*

Yes, I did—I saw the one with Helen Gahagan [1935], and I saw one other one. I insisted on running them. I thought *I* did a better job *[laughs]*!

I'll tell you one interesting thing about *She*. While I was directing a movie called *Two Way Stretch* [1960] with Peter Sellers, Sellers was really involved with a guy called Morris Woodruff, who was a clairvoyant in London. And Sellers kept after me, saying, "You've got to go see Morris Woodruff." So eventually I did go to see him, and he told me some incredible things. He said that in a few years' time I would be making a movie written by a spiritualist; he said I would move to America; that I would be working for a producer with the initial W or M; and that I would marry a blonde and have a son in America. He told me all these things. Well, I made *She* in sixty-four which was written by Rider Haggard, who was a spiritualist; I'm living in America; I worked for both Sy Weintraub and for Quinn Martin, who brought me to America; I married Dorothy Provine in nineteen sixty-seven; and we have a son. Interesting, isn't it?

Day had to "watch the pennies again" while directing Hammer's remake of *She* (with Ursula Andress and Christopher Lee, pictured), but still feels that the film was superior to the more famous 1935 version.

Did that make you a believer?
   [*Laughs.*] No!

What can you tell us about the stars of She, *Peter Cushing and Christopher Lee?*
   Oh, I liked them very much, particularly Peter Cushing. He was a lovely man, just like Karloff. I also worked with him on *The Avengers*. Working with Ursula Andress was tough going at that time, because she hadn't had that much experience then. But it was okay.

She has a big-budget look —
   But did you know that that was made for two hundred forty thousand pounds? That was a fairly big budget film by Hammer standards, but we had to watch the pennies again.

Were you happy with the results on She?
   For what it was, yes. I understand it was a success at the box office.

You've also done plenty of "fantastic" television on both sides of the ocean, including The Avengers, The Invaders, Ghost Story *and* The Sixth Sense.

Oh, *The Avengers* was wonderful, I enjoyed it very much, enjoyed working with everybody there. *The Invaders* was fun, too; I felt the stories were quite good. That was a Quinn Martin show, and it was Quinn Martin who gave me my break in America. He'd seen my British movies and what I'd done on television, like *The Avengers,* and I signed a contract with him.

How does working in America differ from working in England, and around the world?

The industry is so cosmopolitan, wherever you go you meet the same kind of people. It's rather like the newspaper business—a reporter is a reporter is a reporter, anywhere. It's the same in the film industry.

Have you appeared in your own movies or TV shows?

Yeah, I was in *The Haunted Strangler*—I drove a horse-drawn cab. I was also in *Two Way Stretch,* and I played a scribe in a mini-series I did called *Peter and Paul* [1981]. There were more, but it's hard to remember.

Once in America, you immersed yourself in TV, and turned your back on features.

It's not that I turned my back on it, it's just that I was working so much in television I guess I got dubbed as a television director more than features. Right now we're living here in [the state of] Washington; Dorothy is from here, she was raised in Seattle. We used to come up here for vacations and I liked it so much I bought some property here, and when I couldn't stand Los Angeles anymore we moved up here, in nineteen eighty-one.

Are you happy with the work you've done in films and television?

Well, one is never really happy, one always wants to do better. I would like to do more good movies and good stories—I would like to read something that I want to do, a good story. Other than that I'm just at home enjoying myself, with my computer and my photographic darkroom. We just love it here.

When somebody asked me to make a horror film, my first reaction was, "Yes, but I want to do it differently." I tried to "think around it," "think sideways," tried to find a different approach to it. To make people who were the way I was want to see it.

Val Guest

ENGLAND'S HAMMER FILMS MAY BE MOST widely known today for their series of Dracula and Frankenstein snoozers, but in the days before Christopher Lee donned his vampire fangs and before Peter Cushing despoiled his first grave, the company leaned toward science fiction and produced its best three films: *The Quatermass Experiment* (U.S. title: *The Creeping Unknown*), *Quatermass II (Enemy from Space)* and *The Abominable Snowman (The Abominable Snowman of the Himalayas)*. All were based on television serials by writer Nigel Kneale and, just as importantly, all were adapted for the screen and directed by Val Guest, a reluctant dabbler in sci-fi whose remarkable aptitude made these films—and Guest himself—classic fan favorites. Returning to the genre in 1961, he added to his legendary canon what many consider his best-ever film, *The Day the Earth Caught Fire*.

Born in London in 1911, Guest began his career as an actor on the British stage and in early sound films. He ran the one-man London office of *The Hollywood Reporter* until an encounter with director Marcel Varnel led to a screenwriting job at Gainsborough Studios. Guest's directing career began in the early 1940s with a Ministry of Information short about the perils of sneezing(!), an inauspicious start to a lengthy roster of films which also includes (in the science fiction category) *Toomorrow*, *When Dinosaurs Ruled the Earth* and the wacky all-star spy spoof *Casino Royale*.

Your first entry into Hammer science fiction was The Quatermass Experiment *in 1954.*

And I very nearly didn't enter at all, because at first I wasn't going to make it. I wasn't interested. I think I was one of the very few people in the whole of England who hadn't seen the television series upon which it was based. [Hammer producer] Tony Hinds called me just as my wife Yolande [actress Yolande Donlan] and I were going on holiday to Tangier, and he said, "We want to do a film of *The Quatermass Experiment*. Would you like to make it?" I said, "Well, I don't know anything about it." He said, "Look, I'll let you have all the television scripts. I'll wrap them up for you, and you take 'em to Tangier with you and read 'em"—he wanted me to make *a* script out of it. So he met us at the airport and he gave us this great bundle of scripts, which I could well have done without on the plane *[laughs]*. In Tangier, I put it at the side of the bed, and it was there for a *week*. Yolande said to me one day, "What's this down here?" and I told her it was a science fiction thing Tony Hinds wanted me to do. She asked me, "Have you read it?" and I said, "No, no—that's not *me*, I'm no good for that sort of thing." And she said, "Well, *read* it. Since when have you been *ethereal*?" I couldn't answer that at all *[laughs]*, so I said, "All right, I'll read it."

Well, I read it—I *plowed* through it. I took it onto the beach with me, and I got absolutely hooked on it. I called Tony Hinds and I said that, yes, I'd do it. That's how I got onto *Quatermass*. Except for Yolande prodding me, I would never have done it.

Previous page: **Val Guest during his directing heyday.**

What made Hammer think of you for Quatermass?

I don't know. I'd done quite a lot of films for Hammer already and they kept coming to me now and then about all *sorts* of things.

Part of the money for the film came from an American producer named Robert Lippert.

[Laughs.] Robert Lippert was one of the — I don't want to say Poverty Row producers, but you know what I mean. He was one of the small independent producers working in Hollywood. Jimmy Carreras used to do quite a bit of work with Bob, and Bob used to give Jimmy [American] distribution of some kind in the early days of Hammer. Lippert was a nice enough guy and he had a girlfriend called Margia Dean who I was asked to put into the film. She was a sweet girl, but she couldn't act *[laughs]*. That's about all I know about Bob Lippert himself except that I think he made an *awful* lot of money one way or another, and if *he* did, I'm sure Jimmy Carreras did, too.

Are my ears playing tricks on me, or is Margia Dean over-dubbed throughout the whole film?

What probably happened was that she was not very understandable *and* the sound was bad, too. We did an awful lot of that film on location, and in those days Hammer didn't really have the power to stop Windsor Castle and everything, you know. We post-synched a lot of people, but the same voices.

What part of Quatermass Experiment *was shot in Windsor Castle?*

Not in the castle, in the city of Windsor. In the *shadow* of the castle, yes; in fact, we were about one hundred yards away when we shot the scene of Richard Wordsworth breaking into the pharmacy.

Was there American money in most of these early Hammer films?

Yes, there was. Jimmy Carreras was an incredible man. He would suddenly go to the art department and say, "Do me a picture with a dinosaur and a girl in its mouth," this, that and another. And the art department would come up with a great big, flamboyant poster. Then Jimmy would send it over to Lippert, or whoever he was working with at the time, and say, "How 'bout a picture about this?" And *that* was how he set up his pictures — he drew 'em out as posters. He did that for *One Million Years B.C.,* he did that for *When Dinosaurs Ruled the Earth — all* those things.

One of Lippert's associates, a writer named Richard Landau, gets screen credit for the Quatermass *script.*

Exactly what Dick Landau did was this: As we were working for the American market, when I had done my script, they would pass it to Dick and say, "If there's anything you want to Americanize, do it." So if I had put *got,* he would put *gotten*. It was things like that *[laughs]* — it was sheer nonsense! And *this* became a "co-script"! I can only tell you that on all the copies of the film that *I've* seen, my name is there [as screenwriter] and Landau's is not. But when we made it, I do remember either Mike Carreras or Tony Hinds saying, "Look, Dick Landau says that he ought to have his name on this. He's going to take it up with the Writers Guild." I said, "Oh, Christ, who cares? If it means that much to him, put his name on." I was told later that in America it only had Richard Landau's name on it.

Did you have any input on that first picture from Nigel Kneale?

Now, it's a strange thing about Nigel; I hear from all sorts of places that he's terribly unhappy about all his films. I don't know why that should be — maybe a hurt ego over the fact that some of his stuff had to be cut [to fit into a feature film running time]. For instance, when we did *The Abominable Snowman*, we let Nigel do the whole script. But, as I had to direct it, I had the final say on what happened. And I had to do all sorts of nips and tucks, because we could never have got away with it [the way Kneale wrote it] — people would have been up and out of the cinema. A brilliant writer, but one who writes stuff as though you were reading it in a book. An attention span, especially that of a science fiction audience, is *not* all that big *[laughs]*. So you have to make it a little bit more concise. And I don't think he was very happy with *that* film, either, even though he got sole credit on the screenplay.

But I really, honestly am sad about the situation with Nigel. He's a brilliant guy and he's had an enormous success with all these things — and he hates every minute of them. There's something rather twisted there, and it's sad that he doesn't enjoy the fruits of it all. I only met him a couple of times, that's all, and I can only vaguely remember what Nigel Kneale looked like.

If he disliked these films all that much, why did he keep going back to Hammer?

Money. *Money.*

Then he's got nobody to blame but himself if he doesn't like his subsequent Hammer films.

He seemed to have a chip on his shoulder, Nigel. See, at the beginning, he had a chip on his shoulder because he was not a screenplay writer and so they wouldn't let him write the screenplay. So therefore, automatically, everybody who was going to touch that piece of work was going to be a butcher.

In watching your Quatermass *films, we're struck by the overlapping dialogue, the realistic style — what directors and what films influenced you?*

I remember saying, when I told Tony Hinds I'd do *Quatermass Experiment*, "But only if I can do it *my way*." Tony said *[in a nervous voice]*, "W-well, w-what's your way?" I told him, "I would like to shoot it as though a television company had said, 'Go on out and cover this story.'" And I must say, to Tony's credit, that he said that would be all right. I wanted it to look as though it was [filmed by] handheld cameras; we didn't *have* to frame somebody absolutely in the middle—make it *real*. That is how that happened.

Now, the person who had influenced me there was Elia Kazan, who when he made *Panic in the Streets* [1950] did virtually the same thing. I was terribly impressed with that. And I think that's the thing that put the germ into my head. I've used that technique on an awful lot of movies, not just science fiction.

That rapid dialogue just pulls you through the film.

I'm glad you think so, because that's what I was hoping would happen on that. To me, there's nothing worse than hearing question-and-answer, question-and-answer. Also, it gives you *pace*. I think an awful lot of British films lacked pace in the old days—that was *one* of our faults. We all learned these techniques as we *[laughs]* got older and older and older in the business!

Did your actors have problems with it?

At the beginning, yes, there were a few heels dug in. Once they realized what we were doing, once they'd been to the dailies the following day and *seen* what we were trying to get at, there wasn't a problem, no. They were rather excited about it.

Howard Hawks was one of the first filmmakers who liked to have overlapping dialogue in his films. Were you inspired by those?

No. I mean, I admire Howard Hawks' work, but it doesn't ring a bell with me. Another person who did it, of course, was Orson Welles. Where that [overlapping dialogue] came from for me was *not* from any director or anything, but from the fact that that is a great way to get pace. And if you are doing "reality," in reality *none* of us wait for someone to finish the complete sentence. That is all part of the *cinema verite*, the *rapportage*, whatever you want to call it. Making you feel *you're there*.

Much as I admire Alfred Hitchcock's thrillers, they always seem very over-rehearsed, whereas in Welles' films everything seems spontaneous because of the overlapping, fluid dialogue.

[Laughs.] Well, Hitch was always over-rehearsed. I worked with Hitch on *The Lady Vanishes* [1938] and things like that, because his office was next door to mine in the old Gainsborough Studios. We *all* used to work on each other's

films there. Hitch used to say, "Give me five 'gizmicks,'" and we would think up five particularly startling moments—"gizmicks" was his word for that. Then he'd say, "Now find me five *unbelievable* locations." And that is how he would start his films, by finding an unusual location and just these "bumps," as we used to call them. Then the script was developed to bring in these "bumps," the locations and everything. He used to really work very hard at that, and then Hitch would draw every single shot at the side in his script. And when he had done *that,* he would say, "Oh, shit, now I gotta make it." He *hated* making films. He *loved* preparing them, he loved getting right up to the first day of shooting, and then he'd have been thrilled if someone else would then take over. He was an extraordinary, fantastic man.

What did you do on Lady Vanishes?

What happened at Gainsborough was, there were four of us under contract as writers: There was Frank Launder, Sidney Gilliat, myself and a fellow called Marriott Edgar, who was *my* writing partner. And every script that came up there would go around. Frank and Sidney wrote the *Lady Vanishes* screenplay, and that screenplay was pushed onto us; and the comedies that Marriott Edgar and I wrote were pushed onto Frank and Sidney. We read each other's scripts and added and suggested and things. Then, on *Lady Vanishes,* I also spent a lot of time down on the set and everything.

Did more money go into Quatermass *than into a run-of-the-mill Hammer?*

I don't really think so, no. On these Hammers, there were never any locations to speak of, most of it was done on the lot at Bray Studios. Or there was an old, empty hotel next door where they'd make all the "spooky" things—they used that in a million films. We were all very tight for money on *Quatermass,* and I think that we had probably gone a *little* over because of weather problems, shooting in Windsor and at Whipsnade Zoo. (That was about twenty-five miles away—that's a big location for Hammer *[laughs]*!)

I remember on the next-to-last day of the shooting on *Quatermass,* my assistant came to me and said, "You know, you haven't got [actor] Jack Warner tomorrow, guv." I said, "Why?" He said, "Tony Hinds won't pay for him." I said, "But he's a main character!" Jack played the cop who was in charge of the investigation throughout the whole film, and now he wasn't going to be around for the denouement! The assistant said, "Well, Tony won't pay for him, he hasn't got the money to pay his daily [rate]." I said, "You write your star out because you haven't got the money to pay for the *last day's* shooting?! That's absolute nonsense. Call Jack Warner, on *my* authority, and tell Tony Hinds that *I* will pay for his last day out of my salary." And that's what happened. I *didn't* end up paying out of my salary, no, Tony picked it up, but I really had to threaten that. Otherwise we wouldn't have had the end of that story. It would have been played with bit players.

Richard Wordsworth's striking performance as the mutating astronaut was one of the main assets of Guest's *The Quatermass Experiment* (American title: *The Creeping Unknown*).

Would you say that Hinds was more interested in the money than the product?

Strange thing about Tony. Tony used to write an awful lot of those thrillers and horrors and things, under an assumed name. And he *loved* the business. But when he was producing, he was much more [money-minded].

(Also, *Quatermass* was *not* one of his stories.) It was just one of those things. But I was great friends with Tony long after that—we got over that little squabble.

Did you have much say in casting?

Yes, I did. I had no say about the American stars who were given to us by the U.S. investors, but on the other people I did. In fact, I used to have a sort of a "rep" company that I used to use from one picture to another. I used to write little bits in for them in each film, and if they knew it was coming up, they'd try and keep themselves clear. We had some great people in those early days—people who became stars *over there.* Leo McKern and Sid James and people like that we'd keep busy.

Richard Wordsworth gives one of the best performances in Quatermass, *as the afflicted astronaut.*

He was *very* good, yes. He came from the Royal Shakespeare Company, and that was his very first film. I thought he had the right gaunt face. And he never stopped laughing throughout the years afterwards, saying that his very first appearance in a film was his hands coming out the door from inside a rocket ... pulling himself up ... and getting twenty-three hoses worth of water right in his face *[laughs]*! That scene with the rocket was shot on the lot at Bray. The gnarled old tree that we propped the rocket up against is still there. And the little girl in *Quatermass* turned into Jane Asher, who nearly married Paul McCartney.

Do you remember your budget or schedule?

Oh, nothing that Hammer ever did was much more than ninety thousand pounds. And the shooting was never more than about two, three weeks at the most.

What do you think of the special effects in Quatermass?

I thought dear old Les Bowie, who we used to employ from picture to picture, was brilliant. He would do "everything for nothing," because he was told he *had* nothing *[laughs]*, and he really worked like mad. He later did my special effects on *The Day the Earth Caught Fire.* Les was a wonderful craftsman—he did it all, practically in his own garage, and never failed to come up with something.

Quatermass's *claim to fame is that it scared a boy to death in Illinois.*

That was in the Guinness Book of World Records. I'd be interested to know what Nigel Kneale thinks of *that [laughs]*!

How big a hit was Quatermass?

Very big—one of their biggest. In fact, it started them off on that bent.

The Creeping Unknown was the American title. The most wonderful title was the one they used in Germany, and I wish to *God* we had used it; there it was called *Shock*. When I found that out, I thought, "What a hell of a title!"

In growing up and being a movie buff, were you a fan of horror and science fiction movies?

I'd love to say yes, but *no* — not till Tony Hinds said, "Read *Quatermass.*" I'm trying to think of all the things that I *had* seen and been taken by, but I can't honestly remember *any*. Maybe I'm missing one, but I can't remember any one that really stuck with me. I think that also is part of the reason why, when somebody asked me to make a horror film, my first reaction was, "Yes, but I want to do it *differently*." I tried to "think around it," "think sideways," tried to find a different approach to it. To make people who were the way *I* was want to see it.

You've made, what?, eighty-five films, and only a small handful are science fiction. And yet you may go down in the record books as "a sci-fi director." Is that all right with you?

[Emphatically.] Yes — sure! Why not? My God, just to "go down in the record books" is all right!

Next — obviously — came Quatermass II.

Everybody said to me — press, and people like yourselves — that *II* was far and away the best *Quatermass*. I didn't think so. I was very disappointed with *Quatermass II*. I didn't think it was a patch on the first one, because the first one had *freshness*. *Quatermass II*, I felt, was *reaching* somehow or other. But, it was very successful.

Did II *have a bigger budget?*

Yes, a little bigger budget. We were able to do more location work, and we had a *minutely* better schedule — I mean, probably another two days or something *[laughs]*! We drove down to the Shell Oil Refinery, where we shot a lot of that stuff. That was quite a long way away. That meant that the whole unit had to go down and be put up and paid location pay. The other locations were all based from Hammer, and you drove there in the morning and you drove back at night.

In nearly all the interviews we do, we hear how far imagination has to go to make up for the money that's not there.

Having no money means you have to use your head, that's all. The worst thing you can do, going into one of those, is think, "Well, this is a low-budget picture so they can't expect too much from us." That's *fatal*. You go into that picture saying *[through gritted teeth]*, "Nobody's going to say *this* was low-budget!", and you break your skull to try and overcome it. Everybody thinks up ideas that, if you had the lazy, easy advantage of just spending more dough, *no*body would have come up with.

Take [production designer] Bernie Robinson. I did a film with him called *Yesterday's Enemy* [1959], a war film set in the jungles of Burma, and we won an awful lot of awards with this. Our opening in London, at the Empire Cinema, was a big opening for the Burma Star Organization, Lord Louis Mountbatten was the guest of honor and everything. I sat next to Mountbatten during the showing, and he kept nudging me: "I know where you shot that and I *cannot* think where it was...!" Now, it was *all* shot at Shepperton or Bray, the whole thing! So this was that brilliant little man Bernie Robinson, who made a jungle on rolling trucks so that once the actors went through one part of the "jungle," we rolled our trucks and they were in an entirely *different* part! We built the swamp, the river, everything. And the Burma Star Organization and Lord Louis Mountbatten, who commanded over there, were absolutely convinced, not only that we were *there,* but that he knew exactly where we *were [laughs]*!

What arrangements did you have to make with Shell to shoot at their refinery? Did you shoot on days when they weren't working?

I honestly don't know, because that would have been the production department organizing that. I can't recall at any time having to hold up because of anything. It was a pretty empty place, as far as I can remember— there weren't an awful lot of people there. I think it ran itself, mostly.

One of the best scenes had that nosy investigator stumbling down from the top of the giant tank, covered with slime.

His name was Tom Chatto; he's become a well-known character actor in London, and his wife Ros is one of the top casting directors. I don't know what the hell kind of gunk they made up to smear all over Tom for that scene *[laughs]*—jelly, or something that looked like oil. He would come staggering down those steps, I'd say it was okay and my cameraman would say, "I'd like one more." And I'd say, "I'm sorry, Tom. One more." And *he'd* say, "Oh, shit...!" *[Laughs.]* He'd have to go all the way up the stairs again and be doused down again at the top while we cleaned the steps and the tank up!

Had you managed to catch the Quatermass II *serial on TV?*

No. It was far better that I didn't. Because then you're not bound by anything, you come in with a fresh eye. It's like an actor who's going to be in a new version of *A Streetcar Named Desire* going to see the Brando version. Absolutely fatal! Come in with a fresh approach. Or, again, if you're going to remake an old-time movie. I think it's quite fatal to go and see the original.

Tom Chatto, thoroughly "slimed" by the *Enemy from Space* (a.k.a. *Quatermass II*). According to Guest, the film "wasn't a patch on the first one."

How was Hammer thought of within the British film industry during that mid–1950s period?

Well, *my* feeling about Hammer was that it was one of the happiest "family" studios—I've never met anything like it ever again. You went into a family every morning. And that was a wonderful atmosphere. We *knew* that we had no money, we knew we had to make it look three times what it was costing, and we learned an awful lot of our trade through all that. We would be shooting in a small room and need to get a medium shot in there, and we'd have to get the cameraman to put his ass in the fireplace *[laughs]*! You learned what you could get away with and what you could make things look like. So it was fabulous. As far as the industry was concerned, I think that the industry looked down on Hammer a little. It was almost a laugh. They didn't do it with any derision, it was just like *[in a scoffing tone of voice]*, "Oh, well, it's a *Hammer*...!"

How did you like working with Brian Donlevy on these Quatermass *films?*

Oh, I got on with Brian fine. But so many stories have been concocted since, about how he was paralytic [drunk]. It's absolute *balls,* because he was *not* paralytic. He wasn't *stone cold sober,* either, but he was a pro and he knew his lines. There were times when he didn't know what the *story* was about, but he would say to me, "Give me a rundown up to here," I'd give it to him and he'd say, "Fine, fine." I never had any trouble with Brian, no.

Were you approached to do the third Quatermass film?

No.

What kind of a guy was James Carreras?

Jimmy was a fabulous character, no doubt about that—he had all the energy in the world. Enormous showman, terrific salesman. Didn't know anything about movies—didn't *profess* to know anything about movies. But he knew how to sell them and get 'em going. I was very fond of him. But he and his son Michael never got on—that was the sad thing about it. When Michael broke away [from Hammer], he swore that his father stopped him from getting jobs here and there. It was all very sad.

What do you recall about the proposed Hammer version of I Am Legend?

Mike Carreras was a buddy of mine then, and just becoming a producer around that time. Mike was one of the best producers I have ever worked for, because you knew that if you were out there on a lonely moor, that everything you needed was going to be there. You could rely on the guy completely and utterly. He did his homework.

Mike brought me the book *I Am Legend* one day and asked, "Do you think we'll ever get away with a film like this?" I said, "Let's try, let's see what we can do." The British censor *absolutely* said no, under no condition whatsoever would it be allowed. They then tried it on the American censor, and, of course, *no* again. It was completely blocked on both sides, unless great alterations were made. Now, I *think* Hammer had a script done, and that they tried the script out, and *again* they had terrible trouble. I don't know any more about *I Am Legend* than that, that we toyed with it at one time and that they were talking about having me direct it.

Hammer got into horror films much more than sci-fi. Were you ever asked to direct one of the Gothic thrillers?

No, not that I can recall. Somewhere along the line I might have been, because I was great chums with all of them and we used to spend weekends together *whatever* happened. I don't know if I'd have been very good at Gothic. I'd have started laughing, I think.

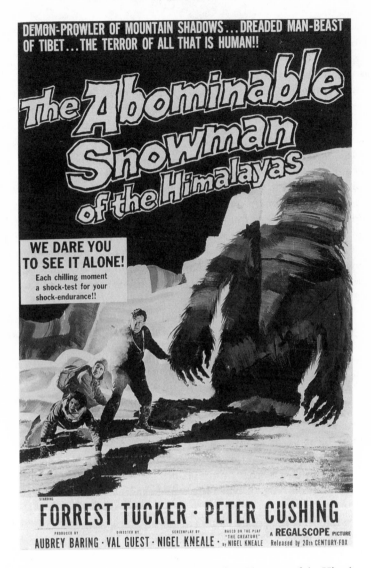

The best of the several 1950s films about the legendary Phantom of the Himalayas was Guest's suspenseful *The Abominable Snowman*.

Any memories of what led up to The Abominable Snowman*?*

No, just that it was something they sent to me; I think they sent me Nigel Kneale's script of it. I thought it was a very good idea, because there was so much going on [in the news] about the Abominable Snowman and there'd been so many people going up to the Himalayas: "Yes, we saw it," "No, we didn't." It was a topical thing, and I was very interested in doing that.

Were you under contract to Hammer?
No—*never.*

Where was Snowman *shot?*
    I went out with doubles and a full unit for a couple of weeks, up into the French Pyrenees, and we shot an awful lot of stuff up there. The rest was done at Pinewood Studios, on one of their vast stages in which Bernie Robinson had done a complete snowscape.

Your actors, Peter Cushing, Forrest Tucker and all—did any of them ever see the light of day, or were all their "outdoor" scenes shot on soundstages?
    I don't think they went out anywhere at all. The Tibetan village was shot out of doors—we built *that* for the film—but it was on the Bray lot. We had some bloody good lighting cameramen down at Bray. Arthur Grant did so many of my pictures—in fact, I took him *away* from Bray when I had my own company. A wonderful little cameraman, very quick . . . *cheap [laughs].* Now, when I say "cheap," what I mean is, he didn't demand five hundred arcs and all that sort of thing.

Did you have a lot of say in the photographing of your films, or did you leave it to the directors of photography?
    No, I would leave it to the director of photography. Once we had decided upon the mood we wanted to create on the thing, it was left entirely to him.

What can you tell us about Cushing and Tucker?
    Oh, Pete is an old chum. There's a man with the most incredible sense of humor. He'll be in the middle of a very dramatic scene—he's Shakespearean, he's everything—and at the end when you say *cut,* he'll suddenly go into a "Knees Up, Mother Brown" dance! And have everybody on the set in hysterics! He's nothing at all like you would expect. Wonderful, great, great character. And he was mad about props—we used to call him "Props" Cushing. He would work it all out and *not* tell you anything about it until the take, and then all these things would start happening. In that particular film, *Abominable Snowman,* when they show him the Yeti's tooth, none of us had any idea what was going to go on in that scene. But it sure went on! He took a tape measure out, he scraped the tooth with a nail file, he came up with a magnifying glass—all during the scene, talking the whole time. It was quite hysterical.

He and Tucker were sort of an "odd couple" in that film.
    They were complete, complete opposites. "Tuck" I made two pictures with, *Snowman* and *Break in the Circle* [1957], and he was a great big . . . *schoolboy.* In those days, he didn't have a drinking problem—or at least, if

he did, he didn't show it with us at all. He was a thorough pro, and I had no problems with him at all.

He really holds up his end in Snowman — *he's as good or better than Cushing.*
   He was very good. They used to kid each other a lot, Cushing and Tucker. Pete will kid anybody, and "Tuck" used to kid Peter Cushing. I remember we did a take and something went wrong, and I said we had to do it again. "Tuck" said, "Oh, Christ, that's the first time I've ever had to do a second take." And Cushing said, "Well, at least you're not a Method actor. They do it *seven* or *eight* times!" *[Laughs.]*

You went into the film intending not *to show the complete Snowman, correct?*
   Oh, absolutely. I refused positively to show the whole thing — I didn't want the audience to see the full figure, to see the full *any*thing. I thought that people were liable to laugh. Let *them* think they've seen the whole thing, and just let's show bits of it. Which is what we did.

Are any of these sci-fi films you made favorite films of yours?
   Yes, *Quatermass* and *The Day the Earth Caught Fire.* But not the other science fictions, I'm afraid.

Were you never tempted to "go Hollywood" while you were in your prime, à la, say, a Hitchcock?
   No, not really. I mean, I'd been over here and shot bits and pieces of films that I had to finish for various people — things like *Killer Force* [1975] that I made in Southwest Africa. But there was far too much to do over there in England. Also, I was in a very lucky position: To be able to write and direct your own movies, that's a pretty good position to be in. And then, every so often, to also *produce* and write and direct is *also* good. That makes it a situation where there's nobody else to *blame* but you. So, no, I never thought of leaving.

Where did the idea for The Day the Earth Caught Fire *come from?*
   It was something that had been going around in my head for a long time, that gradually we were fucking up the whole planet. I had always been very interested in what we are liable to do to ourselves without realizing it. We can be an awful bore about this, talking about Greenpeace and this and that. It was like the old Campaign for Nuclear Disarmament marches and all of that — it becomes a bore. And I thought, there must be a way of getting that same story over without being a bore.
   I wrote out the idea in a treatment form about *eight years* before I made the movie. And every time I made a movie and [the producers] said, "What

do you want to do next?", I'd tell them my idea and they'd say *[disdainfully]*, "Oh, Christ! No one wants to know about the Bomb!" No one would ever let me do it. For eight years I kept on with that thing, and eventually I talked somebody into it: I finally got Sir Michael Balcon and a couple of other people at British Lion Films to say yes, but what I had to do was put up as collateral a film of mine called *Expresso Bongo* [1960], which had made a *lot* of money and got us a lot of awards one way or another.

Did Day the Earth Caught Fire *have the biggest budget of all the science fiction films that you'd done?*

Do you know what that film cost to make? People just do not believe it. It cost us, in pounds sterling, just under two hundred thousand pounds, which at today's rate is four or five hundred thousand dollars. *Ludicrously* cheap.

This was made by your own company.

Oh, yes, it was a Val Guest Production. The first Val Guest Production was *Penny Princess* [1951], which I made for Rank, with Yolande and Dirk Bogarde. Our company was Yolande, myself and an actor who was in all our films, a very close friend of ours called Reginald Beckwith—a wonderful comedy character. As we formed that film company, Yolande was in a play in London called *To Dorothy, a Son*—she and Richard Attenborough, just the two of them on stage all night. It was a knockout success and it was running for about two years. We were getting this company together and Dickie Attenborough kept saying, *"Can't I come in this? Can't I come in with you?"* And we said, "No, Dickie, it's just the three of us. Sorry." "Oh, well . . . I suppose one day I'll have my own company. . . ." *[Laughs.]*

How did Wolf Mankowitz get involved on Day the Earth Caught Fire?

Wolf's been a chum of ours for a long, long time; a very brilliant guy. He's a writer with *bite*; he will churn you out twenty pages which you can whittle down to three *brilliant* pages. An undisciplined writer, but he has everything going for him. And there are certain subjects that you instinctively know he would be absolutely right to come in on. I brought him in on various pictures I've done. He's living now in Santa Fe—he moved there a long time ago and he's teaching as a professor there and writing books and things.

Did you have scientific advisers and people like that helping you on the picture?

Certain things that I wanted to know about, I asked certain people, yes, but I didn't have people working *with* me. What I did was, when I had the script, I would send it to (for instance) the weather people—I'd find somebody in a high weather office, and ask them to put me right if I'd used any wrong phrases. Or I would call somebody else and ask, "How long would it take an ice cap melting to get to the Atlantic?" Things like that I would ask, but, no, I didn't have a technical adviser.

Your SF films give the impression that, if these crazy things did *begin to happen in real life, what we're seeing is how they would be handled.*
I'm glad to hear that, because that's what we tried very hard to do.

Was there American money invested in Day the Earth Caught Fire*?*
Not a penny, no. It was all English money. And I was able to cast it exactly as I wanted to without having to take star names, which would have killed it.

Where were some of the places you shot?
All around London. One thing we did was recreate at Shepperton Studios the office of the *Daily Express* [newspaper]. We had *so* many stills taken of that office, and I said to my art department and my set designer, "Make [our set] look like *that*." We copied the *Daily Express* office absolutely, right down to the last piece of paper on the floor. I did three shots *only* of somebody walking down a passage in the real *Daily Express* building, and then we also shot in the entrance to the *Express* building.

We also shot in Fleet Street, and that was planned like a military operation. It *had* to be. To start with, we had to make it completely uninhabited. Fleet Street! We had to have boarded-up windows, dust, crap in the road, absolutely deserted, cars on the sidewalk left derelict—we had to do all that to make it look like the day before the end of the world. To do that in one of the busiest bloody streets in the world is not easy. So we planned it, and I must say the police were wonderful.

It was easy enough to get buildings to let us board 'em up (this was a Sunday), and to let us paste stuff on window panes to make 'em look cracked. What I told the police was, "I want no traffic; I want no cars parked on Fleet Street all the way from the *Express* office up to the law courts"—which has got to be a mile. They said, "We will have the street like that for you *for three minutes at a time*." They put NO PARKING signs all the way down, on both sides of the street; they were on stands which could be kicked over. So there was nobody parked at all, except our "dead" vehicles.

We rehearsed everything with all the traffic and the busses and everything going—we rehearsed it absolutely up to the time we had to shoot. Then we told the two cops that we were ready to go. They were both on motorcycles, one on each side of the street. They blew a whistle, which stopped everything [all traffic] at the top. Then they drove off up Fleet Street, hell-bent for leather, kicking these NO PARKING signs down so that you couldn't see them, they were all flat on the ground. Following them was our prop truck with the back down, and three prop men in the back with shovels shoveling all the crap into the road that they could get in. And the moment they disappeared 'round the corner at the top, I said, "Action!" (We had two-and-a-half minutes by then.) And we got our scenes that way. The instant that the time was up, the police let the traffic through again.

The big action scene in the film is the water riot.
    We staged the entire thing *again* in the studio. I remember that an agent (who was also a chum) called me one day and said, "Look, there's an awfully nice actor who needs a job and has got to pay his rent and he's a good actor and—can you give him a bit when you do your water riot?" I said okay. He arrived down there, we paid him something like twenty-five pounds—and it was Michael Caine. So Michael was in all those riot scenes, too, but he was only there for a day, day and a half, something like that.

Did you stage that big peace demonstration in the film, or just take advantage of a real one?
    We did take advantage of a real one, and then we went on another Sunday when there was nothing happening, with our own little bit of crowd, for closeups. We matched all the wardrobe off the people who had been there before. Very much the same way as I used newsreel shots of floods and riots and all that, and "rebuilt" tiny pieces of those scenes in a studio with people with the same umbrellas and the same whatevers. It sounds awful to say this, but I did what Oliver Stone has just done in *JFK* [1991] *[laughs]*!

Speaking of JFK, wasn't he quite taken with Day the Earth Caught Fire?
    John Kennedy asked for his own copy of it, and he screened it for two hundred foreign correspondents in Washington. And they asked if I could talk Arthur Christiansen, who was editor at *The Daily Express* and who played himself in the film, into going over and speaking to them. "Chris" went over, but *I* couldn't—I wish I could have gone, but I was busy on another film at the time. Christiansen was a legendary character in Fleet Street. Half the people who saw the film said, "Oh, he's awful in there!", and the other half said, "What an unusual performance!" *[Laughs.]* Poor "Chris," we had a terrible time with him, because he wasn't an actor and he couldn't remember his lines. I had to do some terrific cutting in that office, when he's talking to all the reporters. But a lot of people thought it came off as being an unusual character. Yolande always says, "Oh, you *ruined* it, putting him in!"

Did he get much help or advice from the "pros" there?
    I can only tell you that Edward Judd was a real horror with him. Judd didn't help at all; in fact, he kept saying, "Oh, shit," and walking out, and *that* doesn't help a guy when he's forgetting his lines. But that was Eddie Judd, I'm afraid. Eddie was very good and *Day the Earth Caught Fire* was his big break and it got him a contract with Columbia, but he was such a pain

Doomsday looms closer for Edward Judd (and the rest of the Earth's population) in Guest's environmentally aware *The Day the Earth Caught Fire*.

in the ass to everybody. He had an enormous opinion of himself, and he was his own worst enemy. Columbia just loaned him out here and there and then let him go.

Good actor, though.

Very good. Well, I put him in there because I'd seen him in a TV thing and I thought he had enormous talent. I thought, what an unusual type to use and launch off.

Any special memories of leading lady Janet Munro?

I always knew Janet as a very good little performer, and she had just finished her contract with Disney. She kept saying to me, "Oh, I want to grow up. I don't want to be Disney. I want to do a grown-up part." And I said, "Well, this'll do it for you." And she said, "You've got to tell me how to grow up, and put it on that screen." In the Disney movies, they used to make her tie her boobs down for all her parts, to make it look like she had none. (We got *those* out, to start with *[laughs]*!) She had a very tragic end. Very nice girl.

Stupid question of the day: What was the weather really like as you filmed scenes of all these actors broiling?

Pressbook ad for *The Day the Earth Caught Fire.*

I can tell you that on the day that we shot in Battersea Park, with everybody sun bathing, it was about fifty-eight, sixty degrees at most. And everybody was *freezing* — in *bikinis*! We told them to keep their coats on until we were ready to shoot. That whole scene of Janet and Eddie Judd on the grass — it was very cold weather. On the other stuff, Fleet Street and things like that, it wasn't all that cold, but in the scene where it was supposed to be the hottest day of the century, it was a very cold day!

Tell your story about shooting the fog effects.

The day that we did all that fog in Battersea Park, we had every fog machine we could get from every studio, all 'round this vast park on the Thames. We had all these machines going, hundreds of extras — the whole idea was that this strange mist was coming up the Thames and covering the whole of London. When we were very near the end of the shooting, we were suddenly invaded by about three or four police cars; the cops came up and said, "You must stop this *immediately!*" What was happening was, just on the other side of the Thames was the Chelsea Flower Show, which the Queen was opening. And they had all this fog, pouring all over Her Majesty *[laughs]*! The policemen said, "You have no right to do this! You didn't say anything about all this fog!" So I said to my assistants, "Go and argue with them. Keep 'em arguing as long as you can." They went and argued with the cops, and really had a high heated argument, while we got on with what we had left. And we shot it, *in* the fog, while my guys were arguing. Finally I came out and said, "Well, all right, okay, we're sorry. We'll stop." But, of course, we had finished by then!

Did you have anything to do with the yellow tinting on the opening and clos- ing scenes?

Yes, that was my idea, and it was written in the script. I *fought* against making the movie in color, I didn't want color, I thought color would kill it. But, I thought, what a difference it could make *if,* when the world is near its end, it is so hot that everything is this yellow shimmer. I thought that, if we could do the beginning and the end like that, it would make a difference. And they had terrible trouble doing it, because at that time, it was not all that easy to cut from color to black and white in a strip. They had to hand-tint the beginning and the end, and it became so expensive — we're talking about worldwide prints — that a lot of times they left it out.

The up-in-the-air ending was also terrific.

It was a terrible battle, getting them to agree to let me do that. I said, "You'll defeat the whole object of this film," and finally they let me do it, but then they said, "Well, can we have angels singing or something?" *[Laughs.]* I said I'd go that far, yes.

It was church bells, and that gave us the impression that the film seemed to be hinting —

— that maybe it was all right. But I refused to say *yes it was* or *no it wasn't.* I said, "All right, we'll give 'em a little feeling that *maybe...*"

Were you happy with all the special effects in the movie?

Yes. I mean, I can look at them and say, "Well, I'd have liked to have done this or that," but for what it was at that time, I thought Les Bowie did a very good job.

You wrote in films and filming *that you've never been happy with any picture once it was finished.*

Actually, that's not a complete quote. What I said was, I've never been completely happy with any film we ever made *because* you always sit and see so many other things you could have done. Which is quite normal, and doesn't mean that I'm *un*happy with a film. The day you sit at a film and think, "I could never have done anything better," I think you've had it.

Did all the positive reviews for Day the Earth Caught Fire *help your career?*

It would be nice to say yes, but I don't think so, no. I'll tell you what happened: Through my life, I have gone through a career where occasionally we've had, *oh,* a great big hit and wonderful press and everything, and you think, "Ah, now it's going to be easy." But it's not. All it does is that, for the *next* film, you can get in to see who you want to get in to see. Where, before you had done that, it's *tough* to get in to see who you want to see. It opens doors, but it doesn't make it any easier for you to make the pictures you want to make.

Was Day the Earth Caught Fire *profitable for you?*

Yes, it was, I'm glad to say. Universal released it in the U.S. and in England it was released by British Lion. Actually, Michael Balcon and Steven Pallos started their own distribution company, Pax Films, just for that picture, and then it went out through British Lion over there.

Do you have a favorite story about the making of Casino Royale?

[Laughs.] I could write a *book* on *Casino Royale!* It was an unbelievable experience in my life. I went on it under contract for eight weeks, and I was still under contract *nine months* later. [Producer] Charlie Feldman was a *madman.* There were days when you loved him and could hug him, and then other days you could *throttle* him! An extraordinary man, who would change his mind overnight—*during* the night, mostly—and call you at all hours.

They had bought a book called *Casino Royale,* which was a Bond book. *But,* when they went through it, they found that every single sequence in that book had been used in all the other Bond pictures. This was the only book that had "gotten away," the only one [Bond producers] "Cubby" Broccoli and Harry Saltzman didn't have. But they had used all the bits out of it, including the big card game!

You directed Woody Allen's segment.

Oh, yes—Woody and I sat down and wrote it all together. Then we took it all over to Charlie Feldman, who would go through it and send it back with all the gags cut out, having left all the buildups *[laughs]*! Woody would be in *tears*, Woody'd say, "How can a guy *do* this?", and I'd say, "Look, don't worry about it. Let him think he's cutting something. We can put 'em back when we shoot!" Which is exactly what we did. Woody has less confidence than anybody you would ever meet; you wouldn't think that, but it's so. You have to hold his hand and so on.

Did you work in collaboration with the other Casino Royale *directors?*

No, only to say, "Hey, don't use (such-and-such a star) Wednesday 'cause I need her!", that's all. It was a very strange set-up. At the beginning, it was just John Huston and me. One day, John said to me, "Is Feldman as mad as I think he is?" I said, "Oh, he's *madder*!" Huston said, "He's talking now about having a compendium of directors." I didn't know that *[laughs]*. "Oh, yes, it's not just us! There's a *compendium* coming along!" Then Charlie said to me he wanted a compendium of *stars* as well—a lot of stars, different segments and a compendium of directors. He gave me a script by Terry Sothern, a script by Ben Hecht, a script by Richard Maibaum—and he said, "Take all these away and see if you can get *one* out of 'em." It was an impossible job.

I ended up working on the film to the extent that Charlie said to me, "You've done so much on this, I'm going to give you a credit of your own: COORDINATING DIRECTOR: VAL GUEST." I said, "If you do that, I'll sue you." 'Cause people were going to say, "*This* is coordinated?!" *[Laughs.]*

Orson Welles was in the cast. What did he think of all this?

Orson Welles and Peter Sellers could not get on. And Orson Welles said one day, "Call me when that fucking amateur has finished." That gives you an idea of how they got on.

Was that your worst filmmaking experience in some ways?

Oh, no, not *worst*, I wouldn't say that. We had a lot of fun on it, and it taught you how to keep your head when all about you are losing theirs *[laughs]*. You have to be resilient.

Do you remember how you got involved on Hammer's When Dinosaurs Ruled the Earth?

It was a sorry day and I *do* remember it *[laughs]*. A lady called Aida Young was the producer of that; she used to be the production manager's assistant-cum-everything at Hammer. Aida called me at our little holiday pad in Malta and she asked, could she come over, would we be there? So she flew over and said, "Jimmy Carreras wants to do another dinosaur film." She brought over a few sheets of paper with ideas and things that matched up with the poster he'd sent to Hollywood. I thought it might be fun; I'd never done anything like that, so why not? I sat down and wrote a story. That's how I got involved, it was as easy as that. And I was *hoping* at that time that we could do it in Malta; then I could stay at my pad there and everything. But there were no mountains anywhere near there, and that didn't help! We shot it in the Canary Islands.

Maybe I'm not very good at working with a woman producer *[laughs]*. We didn't get on between us. After it was over, I was in on the editing, working with our editors as I always do, and then I went away onto another film and got on with my life. Then the editor called me up and said, "I don't like to tell you this, guv, *but...*" Aida Young had reedited the whole picture. But, what the hell, it's not as though we're talking about *Citizen Kane*! So I don't honestly know how it ended up, because I was too fed up with the whole thing to go and see it. I don't have much else to say about that, except I *loved* the animator, Jimmy Danforth — who I also believe was very unhappy with the film. But I thought we did rather well by him.

Was he unhappy as the picture was being made, or after it was all screwed up?
Well, I don't think it *did* get "screwed up" for *him*; he was nominated for an Oscar for that picture! Brilliant little man. Whether he wanted to have more to say in the film or *what* his complaint was, I don't know.

Did you at least enjoy the making *of the film in the Canary Islands?*
I enjoyed being in the Canary Islands because I love any location but, no, it wasn't a very scintillating company. As our star, we had a bimbo called Victoria Vetri, who was Miss Playboy or Miss Centerfold or something like that. She was a real nothing, and a very strange mixed-up lady, too. The rest of the cast were people I knew, like Pat Holt and Robin Hawdon — in fact, Robin Hawdon, who played the juvenile in it, played the office boy who died in *Day the Earth Caught Fire*. And he went on to become quite a good playwright.

Did Vetri give you a hard time?
She never gave me a hard time, the only tough time was *taking* her. It was tough to take her. She was a ... nitwit.

I don't like to say this to your face, but when I tried to watch the film, it was impossible. It's grueling, it's so bad.
It's awful, awful, awful. And they went and shot some more stuff, too.

Was that sort of prehistoric story even your "cup of tea"?

No, but like I said, I did it because I'd never done one and I wanted to try it. And, let me tell you, had I done that with Mike Carreras or even Tony Hinds, it would have been an entirely different picture. Absolutely. I would have gone in and said, "All right, let's try and get another angle on this— we've *seen* Raquel Welch. Now let's try and do something strange." But I couldn't, working under the auspices that I was. It was just sort of another *One Million Years B.C.*

Was creating a prehistoric lingo your idea?

Yes. I wish I hadn't thought of that. It was a sort of half-hearted attempt. It should have been followed by other things—which they didn't want to know about.

What can you tell us about your space musical Toomorrow?

That was a madhouse, with Harry Saltzman and Don Kirshner producing. They didn't talk to each other, they didn't like each other. It was an absolutely madhouse film, but it wasn't too bad a film—we launched Olivia Newton-John, who we found singing and playing a guitar in a nightclub. But there was so much going on behind-the-scenes during that film, with Kirshner wanting *this* and Harry saying, "Tell him you can't do it," all that sort of thing.

At the end of production, I was way over my contractual period— probably about six *months* over, and still working. Comes the time when the money's to be paid, Harry Saltzman says he doesn't have it. So *my* lawyer says, "Well, you better *find* it. Because the film is opening at the London Pavilion next week, and if you *don't* find it, we will enjoin the film so you can't open it." I allowed it to open, because I didn't want to stop it opening; it opened, and the following week I enjoined it; and it's been enjoined ever since *[laughs]*! The picture was not allowed to be shown until I was paid, and I was never paid.

My contract was with [a company] called Sweet Music, which was in Switzerland. And when we descended on Sweet Music, Sweet Music had nothing. What Harry had done was, he had put up his share of the Bond films to the Bank of Switzerland in exchange for money to back *Toomorrow*. But "Cubby" Broccoli, Harry's partner in the Bond films, and Harry had a contract which said that nobody else could be a partner in their Bond films. When "Cubby" found out that Harry had used them as collateral, they broke—that was the end of "Cubby" Broccoli and Harry Saltzman.

And now you're working on a remake of Day the Earth Caught Fire.

Winchester Films of England came to me about my proposed remake, and they had an idea of how to update it. I was very impressed, and I said I'd go along with them. At that time, I had Paramount, Warners and Twentieth

Currently living a chip shot away from a Palm Springs golf course, director Val Guest was England's most valuable contributor to the 1950s sci-fi/horror movie scene.

Century–Fox [vying for it]—*all* of them suddenly decided they wanted to remake the film. But it's much too nice down here in Palm Springs for me to be up there [in Los Angeles] arguing with all of them, so I leave this all to Winchester—they have done all the deals and things, and I just do the writing. We've done the first draft script, and brought it up to date. I don't want to say too much about what we've done on it, but it looks like we were slightly ahead of our time, because global warming is today a real concern.

You'll be directing?

Oh, no, no, I'm done with all that now. I've co-rewritten, and I'm co-producing.

Any closing comments? Proudest moments? Regrets?

Well, we've all got regrets about this, that and the other, but, yes, I'm happy, I think life has been very good to me. I think maybe I could have done more, and better, but I don't complain. I've had a very full life and a very interesting life. Somebody up there has been very good to me.

*It was at [our first] meeting that Jim Nicholson asked
me if I liked boats, and I said, "Well, yes, I love
boats." Had he asked me if I liked boa constrictors,
I would have said, "Oh, they're very nice!" He was
handsome, charming and the kindest man I'd ever met.*

Susan Hart

ACTRESS SUSAN HART STARRED (and showed off the type of figure that bikinis—even invisible ones—were invented for) in an assortment of horror and fantasy films in the 1960s. She debuted in the notorious *The Slime People* and later became a contract player at American International Pictures, where she was ideally (swim-)suited to her roles in way-out comedies like *Pajama Party, Dr. Goldfoot and the Bikini Machine* and the never-to-be-forgotten *The Ghost in the Invisible Bikini*. More importantly, she became the sweetHart—and later the wife—of the company's guiding light James H. Nicholson, and reigned as the First Lady of AIP during one of the more colorful eras in the history of horror, action and exploitation films.

Widowed but now happily remarried, her interests have shifted since the days when she was AIP's favorite Queen of Scream, first to country-western music (her 1981 "Is This a Disco or a Honky Tonk" made it to the Top 100) and now to ice skating, which she takes every bit as seriously as her earlier avocations. Taking a break from her daily ice routines, she gives us a rink-side seat as she reminisces about the films, the fun—and the intrigues—that were AIP.

How did you first become interested in pursuing an acting career?

I suppose my first step in that direction was going to the movies *[laughs]*! My mother gave me tap dancing lessons, ballet lessons, singing lessons, all the kinds of lessons that in those days mothers were prone to do to daughters that had naturally curly hair. I think I enjoyed all those things; I *asked* to do all those things. I wasn't enamored with school or schoolwork; these lessons seemed to put me in a happier mood. (I still do take lessons—right now, ice skating lessons.)

I had a relative by marriage who was in films in the late forties through the fifties. Her screen name was Noreen Nash. She was born and raised in Wenatchee and her brother was married to my sister. The first time I saw Noreen, I thought she was something from Heaven—she was probably the most beautiful girl that I had ever seen, and certainly that Wenatchee had ever produced. And I remember thinking, "Gee, does *every*body in the movies end up looking like that?" She was lovely—and she still is, by the way. So she was perhaps like an idol when I was a little girl. Of course, I didn't know that it took work and that one actually needed to *act* to be in the movies; as a seven- or eight-year-old, I just thought you had to be beautiful. So I remember meeting Noreen and thinking, "I would like to be in the movies like her."

We were spending the summers in Washington and winters in Southern California. I graduated high school—barely, as I recall *[laughs]*—and I worked at the telephone company in Palm Springs. One of my best girlfriends in those days worked at the *Desert Sun* newspaper. We saved up our money, working for maybe seven or eight months, and wound up with about nine hundred

Previous page: **She went from being Susan Neidhart of Wenatchee, Washington, to the First Lady of AIP: Lovely, leggy Susan Hart.**

dollars apiece to go to Hawaii—at that point, our dream was to go to Hawaii and learn to surf. (My big ambition was to be a great girl surfer.) We hung out with the beach boys and learned to surf—we spent about a month or so there. I came back to California, managed a dress shop for awhile, made enough money to go back to Hawaii and got a job in the International Marketplace, selling Hawaiian clothes. An agent named Morton Smith came into the shop one day and gave me his card, and told me that he was not only an agent but a photographer, too. He was doing a piece for *Playboy* on the Girls of Hawaii, and wanted to know if I would pose. I said, "Of course—as long as I don't have to take off my clothes." I told him that I loved to surf, so we went down to the beach at Waikiki the next day: I got on a surfboard and he took pictures from a catamaran. This was my first time in front of a professional camera-person, and the picture appeared in *Playboy*.

I stayed in Hawaii another month or so, and then came back to see my parents in California. I still had the agent's card, and decided at that point that, why not?, I'd give it a whirl. I had appeared in plays in Palm Springs, at the various playhouses and local community theaters and high school and so forth. I also sang on occasion, at weddings and, oh, various school things—I wasn't a very good singer, but maybe I was a little bit of a better actress because people thought I could sing. (I *was* a good actress—right?) I went in to see the agent and he was legitimate—he had an office on Sunset Boulevard and a small roster of clients. And that same day, I signed a year's contract with him representing me. I went out on an interview within about two weeks, and it was for a role on *The Joey Bishop Show*. It was about three lines, and I got it. That was my first job. Several others followed, always small roles for about a year—five lines here, three lines there. Then I worked myself up to maybe twelve lines *[laughs]*! *Laramie, 77 Sunset Strip, Cain's Hundred*—shows that were popular during those years.

This was all about the time of The Slime People.
  You had to remember *Slime People*, didn't you?

I'm afraid I have to rub your nose in that one for a little while—
  Oh, no, no, no—*The Slime People* was great fun! Bob Hutton had been a big star at Warner Brothers in the forties, he evidently wanted to direct a picture, and he had found a backer named Don Hansen who ran or owned a chain of dry cleaning establishments. (Don always wore a hat, a fedora-type hat—a real, *real* man's hat!) I remember meeting Bob Hutton at my agent's office, and I was scared to death! I knew, number one, that the picture was going to be non-union; number two, I had been told about all of these casting couches in Hollywood. (In television, it wasn't necessarily the truth, but I didn't know anything about movies.) I knew that Bob was handsome and experienced in the business, but I really didn't know what to expect. So that's

why I requested that he come down to *my* agent's office — and I suppose he was very pleased to do so, because who knows if he even *had* an office of his own to work out of? But Bob was super. I think I only had one meeting with him, and he made his decision fast — he wanted me for the role and I guess my price (which was very cheap in those days) was right. I believe I was supposed to be paid nine hundred dollars a week — or was it three hundred dollars a week for three weeks? It was a paltry sum, but it was more than I had seen for three or four weeks' work.

I went to the May Company with Robert Hutton, and we picked out an outfit for me to wear — I had to pay for it, thirty-four dollars, but I was reimbursed. I remember the outfit very well because I wore it for so many days. Bob Hutton was several years older than I was, so I tried to make myself look older. I wore my hair up and carried a huge black purse. Why on earth they had me carry that big purse through every single scene, including encounters with the Slime People, I have no idea! Where was I going — shopping *[laughs]*?? I also wore four-inch high heels while running over hill and dale to escape these weird creatures. Wearing those heels killed me — my feet were never the same again after the movie. (Looking back on this, I question if perhaps this very experience may have prepared me for the sure-footedness that ice skating presents me with today?) But, hey, it was great fun and the cast and crew were wonderful people.

Any memories of the Slime People themselves?

One monster was a charming young kid by the name of Jock Putnam. His stepfather was a very famous neurologist — in fact, in some circles, he's known as the father of neurology. His name was Dr. Tracy Putnam. He was instrumental in discovering a medication called Dilantin, which epileptics would be very familiar with. Jock was doing the sound on the picture and he was also playing a slime monster. And he talked his stepfather into playing the role of a famous scientist. I also remember Jock running around with a big tank full of dry ice or whatever, to create the fog that's everywhere in the picture. Everybody did that — well, not the girls, but anybody that was strong enough.

Where were some of these exteriors shot?

About forty miles outside of L.A., in a canyon around Agoura or Thousand Oaks. We would arrive at dawn. On two separate occasions, we couldn't shoot because someone forgot to bring the film. Organization was not a priority here.

What did you think of the Slime People costumes?

You know, even in person, the things weren't scary. Looking back on it, they were pathetic — well, at least *funny*! And I believe that they spent a great deal of money on those costumes — they were probably a big bite out of the

Hart shrieks at the clammy touch of one of *The Slime People* (Bob Herron).

budget. Jock used to get so hot in there, and when he'd take it off, he did not look well at all—ill, almost. Another fellow who also played one of the monsters smoked, and it was the wildest thing to see—he'd smoke through that costume! Long plumes of smoke would pour from the ears and "shoulders." Once they got him all locked in, he didn't want to take it off—it took maybe a half hour to get him into it. So he'd walk around the set, smoking through the nose hole *[laughs]*!

What about some of the other people in the picture?

Judee Morton, the girl who played my little sister, was my roommate in Hollywood for about two years; she was later nominated for an Emmy for a *Dr. Kildare* segment. We would go home after a day on *Slime People* and I would say, "Judee, gosh, do you think that they could give me some lines instead of just screaming?" And she would say, "What? *I'm* the one that's doing all the screaming." And we used to argue! I'd say, "No, no. *I'm* doing all the screaming. You have more lines than I do." But now looking back at it, she was absolutely right—Judee *did* do all the screaming in that film! We still talk from time to time. Bill Boyce, the marine in the film, was a good friend of Judee's from her home town, Shawnee, Oklahoma. I don't know what ever happened to him. And Les Tremayne also was a real gentleman.

Was Robert Hutton a good director?

To *me,* he was a good director; *any*body would have been a good director. I had never done a film before. He was not only directing, but he was also starring. So I suppose he was as good as anybody is able to be, who is doing both of those jobs. And he helped me as much as I, in those days, was capable of being helped. It was a very nice experience; I remember it being fun, I remember feeling like I didn't know what I was doing most of the time (or what I was *supposed* to do, or what it was all about). But the people that were there were all using it as a stepping stone. I didn't feel the way I might have if my career depended on this particular vehicle. I just knew that I was working and gaining experience, and, believe me, with the competition for any type of picture in those days, we all felt very fortunate to be working, Bob Hutton included.

Were you paid for The Slime People? *Hutton wasn't.*

I *did* get paid the first week, and we even had a makeup person the first week. All of a sudden, in the second week, we started doing our own makeup. And people started disappearing, like lighting men and carpenters. All of a sudden, the crew was down to maybe seven—not counting the monster! I don't know how much money they had for it, but I'll bet you that it wasn't more than about thirty thousand dollars. When it was all over, I believe I was owed fourteen hundred dollars.

In or around nineteen seventy, my husband Jim Nicholson and I were having some friends in for dinner. One of the couples happened to be Judee Morton and her husband Ian Fraser, who was and is a fine musical conductor/arranger. During the course of the conversation, Ian looked over at me and said *[in a thick British accent],* "Susan! I caught your film on the telly last night." I assumed he was referring to one of my AIP films. I said, "Oh, really? Gosh, I didn't know that they went to television that fast." I looked at Jim: "Am I in any pictures that you've already sold to television?" Ian said, "Oh, no, the one you did with Judee." I looked over at Judee and I kicked her a little bit under the table, signalling *her* to kick *Ian* under the table! *The Slime People* was something that I did not put on my resume, something that I didn't want Jim to know about. We'd been married for four or five years and I hadn't bothered to mention it. I didn't *lie*, but he didn't ask and I wasn't about to tell him *[laughs]*! But it was too late, Ian came out and said, "*The Slime People*! *The Slime People*!"—he repeated it three or four times! At first I feigned not knowing, but he kept at it: "Oh, God, it was *awful*, Susan! I just can't believe you *did* that, Susan!"

All the time this conversation is going on, Jim isn't missing a bite of his dinner. I turned to him and I said, "Well, gosh, Jim, I guess the cat's out of the bag now. I have to tell you." He said, "Tell me what?" I said, "Judee and I did a film a *l-o-n-g* time ago, and it wasn't exactly a great film..." He looked at me and he said, "I'm familiar with the film." Judee and I said in unison: "You *are*??" And Jim said, "Yes. We've been distributing it to television for the last five years."

What happens when you get your hand caught in the cookie jar? You either get mad or you go and sulk. I chose to get mad. I stood up from the table and I said, "Well, in that case, Jim Nicholson, you owe me fourteen hundred dollars!" *[Laughs.]*

The Slime People has a real Golden Turkey type of reputation today.

I don't want to say I was embarrassed over such a silly episode in my life, but I probably was. But time has a way of distorting any negative thoughts—at least, it does with me. Some people remember the negative, I try to remember the positive.

The Slime People was supposed to be opening in Los Angeles and I ran up to Seattle to get out of the city—as though anybody would even know or care who I was *[laughs]*! I went to Seattle to visit my brother, and my agent informed me that it was going to be sneak-previewing in Seattle! Of course my brother was all excited, and so we went to see it. There were maybe all of twenty-five people in the theater. And my brother reminds me—constantly— that he has never seen anybody sit so far down in their seat, for the full seventy-odd minutes or however long the thing was! But he got a big kick out of it, and so did the audience—it was kind of a hoot. But I remember seeing it that first time and badgering my brother, over and over: "Oh, please, Don, can we leave now?" I was embarrassed, not so much because of the film, but because I did a lot of things that were stupid.

Acting choices, you mean?

No, *lack* of acting choices *[laughs]*! Also, seeing yourself on the big screen can be a real shock—it magnifies everything that you see in the mirror that you wish was not there. In those days, so much emphasis was placed on the physical, and you had to be pretty vanilla-looking to be thought of as attractive. To me, I wasn't vanilla enough.

You took a year or so off from acting not long afterwards.

I was in the hospital for three months. I was very, very ill with pneumonia and I had streptococcus set in—I became poisoned. I lost about twenty pounds and they didn't know if I was going to live or not, and I lost all my hair. So for the next two years, I wore wigs, until finally my hair did come back. That's why I lost about a year in my career, mainly because I felt very self-conscious about my hair. It's different for men—people say, "Oh, he looks better." But a twenty-two-year-old girl bald is not exactly like a sixty-two-year-old guy with at least maybe some graying hair left over!

In nineteen sixty-three, I started getting back into it again—that's when I did *Dobie Gillis, The Beverly Hillbillies, Alfred Hitchcock.* I also had a small part in *For Those Who Think Young* and a small role in *A Global Affair* with Bob Hope. During those years, Paul Henning was producing *The Beverly Hillbillies,* and he was going to do a series on *Archie* and as I recall I was going to be Veronica. There was even some talk about perhaps marrying me off to Jethro in *The Beverly Hillbillies!* Mike Frankovich saw something that I was in, and that was how I got the role as a Hawaiian girl in *Ride the Wild Surf* [1964]. I went so far as to dye my hair black—blue-black—to get the role.

And not long after that, you met Jim Nicholson.

Jim Nicholson, who was then heading up American International Pictures, watched the rushes on *Ride the Wild Surf* because Columbia was perhaps going to be a competitor with the AIP *Beach* movies. Up until that time, I believe American International was the only company that was doing those types of films, and they did very well financially. Other studios were entertaining the thought of perhaps going them one better—spending more money, going three thousand miles further. Anyway, what Jim Nicholson happened to view were dailies of me. And—this is what I've heard from friends—he fell in love with me when he watched those dailies *[laughs]*! When I got back from Hawaii after making *Ride the Wild Surf,* I had an interview at American International; it was with [*Beach* series director] Bill Asher and Jim Nicholson. It was at that point that I was offered a very nice contract, and my agent Fred Briskin thought I should take it. So I signed with them.

Did you have your pick of roles at AIP?

Oh, gosh, no. *No,* no! You have to understand something: I was very torn about signing with AIP, because I had been under option for a time to Columbia, and I was told that they were going to be picking up my contract. When I went into my meeting with Jim Nicholson and Bill Asher, Jim offered me on the spot a very lucrative contract. Of course, I was feeling good because at that point I was technically with Columbia and I knew that I would probably be signing on Columbia's dotted line; plus, I had received quite good reviews from *Ride the Wild Surf.* Mike Frankovich, who had cast me in it, had at least *pretended* to have plans for me. So I was in a very good frame of mind at that particular time.

It was at this same meeting that Jim Nicholson asked me if I liked boats, and I said, "Well, yes, I *love* boats." Had he asked me if I liked boa constrictors, I would have said, "Oh, they're very nice!" He was handsome, charming and the kindest man I'd ever met. That was when he invited me onto his boat: Two or three weeks later, he had [director] Don Weis and his wife on his boat for brunch, and also myself and my agent, Fred Briskin. Our relationship started that soon, maybe a couple weeks after I met him.

Your first AIP film was Pajama Party.

There was something that left a very bad taste in my mouth about that picture. When they went back to do second unit stuff, nobody was around, so I think they shot somebody else's legs and inserted it in the final cut as though they were mine. That very well could have been something that happened as a result of the fact that I was Jim's girlfriend: Somebody working on the film might have been angry with me, and made that happen. It wasn't a very pleasant experience *[laughs]*!

People resented you for dating, and later marrying, Nicholson?

[Laughs.] Maybe. I was so naive in those days. I thought everybody loved me like I loved everybody, but it wasn't true at all, they *didn't*! I was greatly *feared—why* I don't know, but I *was*!

What was the atmosphere on the sets of these free-wheeling AIP Beach and Party movies?

That's exactly what it was, free-wheeling and fun. There was a great deal of camaraderie, and it was a wonderful feeling knowing that you were not saying goodbye at the end of a shoot, that you would be seeing these same people *[laughs]*—probably for the rest of your life! That's what you think when you're twenty; you think that the people you know, you will always know, and that the way life is, is the way that it will continue. It was a very closely knit group.

Did you enjoy going to England to make War-Gods of the Deep?

Of course. My mother went with me, and she stayed with me at the hotel there in England, the Carlton Tower. I had never been abroad before, so that was great fun for me and it was exciting for my mother. I was just happy that I was able to share those kinds of experiences with her. *War-Gods of the Deep* was wonderful; Tab Hunter and I had worked on *Ride the Wild Surf,* so it was fun working with him again, and David Tomlinson was just a kick.

What about Vincent Price?

You know, we didn't really have that many scenes in anything together, so the only occasion that I would have to know anything about him was just before we'd get ready to shoot, or perhaps on a social level with Jim. On a professional, working level, I think we had maybe two or three scenes at the most together, and not much dialogue. What I do know is that he was just a true professional through and through.

And socially?

Socially he was a lot of fun. I didn't go out with him as often as I would have preferred, but when I was married to Jim, we were in Europe half the time, because the company had many co-productions going in England, in Germany, in Spain. Most of our social life revolved around having people in for movies nearly every night of the week. And sometimes two movies a night. We'd see up to five hundred pictures a year! His life really centered around motion pictures—watching them, making them, talking about them and showing them. The times that we would go out to dinner with friends would be few and far between; most of our time was spent at our own house, having people in to share the films, dinner, coffee and conversation.

What kind of director was Jacques Tourneur on War-Gods?

I enjoyed working with him, he was absolutely lovely. We spent Thanksgiving [1964] together, as a matter of fact. The picture was shot in November-December, as I recall, because I remember having a Christmas tree in the hotel room. We'd shipped over everything; we even had Jim's cook accompany us on the trip so she could cook Thanksgiving dinner at the Carlton. We had an American Thanksgiving with all the trimmings. Anyway, Jacques was just lovely, and happy to be working.

AIP gave one-last-chance to direct to a number of older moviemakers.

Also to a lot of actors that weren't exactly being sought after, either. Jim always enjoyed doing that. Well, Vincent Price for instance. I don't suppose that Vincent mentions it, but AIP did pick up a lot of people, probably him included, whose popularity might have waned slightly had it not been for American International. Annette Funicello gained from it, Frankie Avalon— a lot of folks used AIP as a teething ring. Robert De Niro had a role in *Bloody Mama* [1970], Jack Nicholson wrote some scripts—he partially honed his craft there. And there's nothing wrong with that. But I think that sometimes people don't give as much credit to AIP as perhaps they should. Jim took chances on writers, actors, directors; brought people out of the woodwork; and I think he was responsible for a lot of actors' renewed popularity.

The producer on War-Gods *was Dan Haller—*

—who has also gone on to do really good things. He was an art director in the early days, and Jim thought Danny was very, very talented. Danny and George Willoughby co-produced *War-Gods of the Deep*.

Louis Heyward told me the two of them feuded.

Yes, but I don't know what the feud was about. I do remember George Willoughby being rather sour during the whole filming of that picture.

You had decorative, "fluffy" roles in a number of your pictures. Did you enjoy the change-of-pace straight role you had in War-Gods?

I enjoyed it, but somehow I always felt too young for that role and I don't know why. Like you say, it was a straight role and there wasn't a whole lot for me to sink my teeth into because she was just a simple girl. I did not really have a scene that was "mine" in that picture. I guess I *was* in there just for decoration, and I played nice, regular-type decoration. But not too much emoting was required.

What do you think of the film itself?

That it looks like a picture that was written as it went along. And I think that is the truth. Edgar Allan Poe was there, Vincent Price was there, the sets were there, the talent was there. The *story* wasn't *[laughs]*! Charles Bennett wrote the original script and it was good. But others added their two cents. It did receive very nice reviews.

War-Gods *may have been a bit muddled;* Dr. Goldfoot and the Bikini Machine *was just silly.*

Well, a lot of those pictures were rather silly. Silly albeit pure and entertaining. And they sure reeked of the vernacular of the day, the fashion of the day, and perhaps a lot of the attitudes in the early sixties.

Any special memories of Goldfoot *at all?*

Dr. Goldfoot was really a fun picture to make. I always felt as though I did a more-than-adequate job in that picture, and I think I have the reviews to back me up. I played a robot, a girl who was programmed to marry rich men and accumulate all the world's wealth. I was also programmed for different nationalities, and so consequently I took on the aura of whatever personality I was playing and I used a lot of different dialects in the picture. It was great fun and I felt very good about what I did in that picture. Now, I don't know about the picture *itself*; I think it made a little bit of money.

There was a sequel, so it must have made some *money.*

The sequel *[Dr. Goldfoot and the Girl Bombs]* was really rotten, as I understand it. The reviews were extremely negative and I doubt that it did well at the box office.

Did you enjoy working with the director, Norman Taurog?

He was probably one of the sweetest men I've ever met in my entire life.

Dull-witted spy Frankie Avalon begins to suspect that Susan Hart *might* be a robot in AIP's *Dr. Goldfoot and the Bikini Machine*.

He was so caring. I think of all the directors I've worked with, he was the most helpful; there was, again, a sweetness about him that I never really saw in any of my other directors. I didn't have very many of them, but none of them were as kind or as courteous as Norman Taurog. I think *Dr. Goldfoot* was an attempt by AIP to get out of the beach movie genre and into a new trend. One of the best scenes I've seen on film was with Vincent Price singing about the bikini machine — it was excellent. And I was told that it was taken out because Sam Arkoff thought that Vincent Price looked too fey. But his character *was* fey! By taking that particular scene out, I believe they took the explanation and the meat out of that picture. I would only love to see that footage again, but it probably disappeared long, long ago. It was a really unique explanatory scene and Vincent Price was beautiful in it, right on the money.

Wasn't someone killed during the making of Dr. Goldfoot?
    It was very, very hot up in the catwalks in the studio, and I guess one of the gaffers was overcome by the heat. He fell and landed about five or six feet from me — I remember hearing this *thud*. And I didn't know what happened until the next day, because they ushered me out very, very quickly and nobody told me until the next day. Maybe they thought I would be upset or

Doing Dr. Goldfoot's dirty work.

something. And I remember three or four people saying, under their breath, "Oh-oh. That's bad luck for the picture."

Bad luck for the gaffer, too.

[*Laughs.*] Oh, *extremely* bad luck for *that* poor chap! In those days, when someone died or was killed on a set, it was supposed to be very bad luck for the picture.

What can you remember about the Dr. Goldfoot *special that was made for ABC-TV?*

I believe that it was Ruth Pologe, who was head of AIP publicity in the New York office, who arranged for ABC to do a special relating to the picture. It was a half-hour show called *The Wild Weird World of Dr. Goldfoot,* and it had the highest ratings that night—everybody was thrilled about that. It was kind of a capsule presentation of the picture itself, with members of the cast doing maybe four or five songs. Tommy Kirk, who was *not* in the picture, *was* in this musical presentation of it, and I don't know why.

Where did you go on your world tour to promote Dr. Goldfoot?

Where *didn't* we go? London, Hong Kong, Italy, Spain—we went around the world! I remember landing in Frankfurt and running into Orson Welles. Both of our planes had been delayed about four hours, so we sat there and talked and had about six cups of coffee, and he was so nice! It was just the most delightful four hours, wonderful, wonderful fun.

What were your impressions of Sam Arkoff early on?

He had a good sense of humor and seemed to know enough about law to take advantage of people. He had no interest in making movies, only in making deals. Sam continues to take full credit for films he made with my late husband, which distorts true history. But he has to live with himself on that issue. Sam even tried recently to dismiss Jim's creativity by falsely claiming Jim was an alcoholic.

Only a few months ago, he was making derogatory remarks concerning Jim, like, "Jim would go home at night and sit there, and he'd have a drink or two, or maybe *more* than a drink or two, and he'd come in the next morning and say, 'What do you think of this title?'" And then Sam decided to twist the knife further and added, "Later Jim stopped drinking and after that, his titles weren't as good as they had been." I can't begin to tell you how many phone calls I received on those gems. I was shocked and hurt, and many of Jim's friends were simply appalled.

You were in London on your Goldfoot *tour when you announced you were marrying Jim Nicholson.*

Yes. Things were happening so fast in those days that I don't clearly remember it at all!

What became of two Susan Hart AIP films that were announced, Joan of Arkansas *and* Genghis Khan?

Joan of Arkansas I suggested to my husband, and he thought it was a fabulous title, a Jim Nicholson kind of title. We kidded around a lot about it, but it never got off the ground. *Genghis Khan* I wasn't aware of.

You were also going to co-star in Planet of the Vampires.

I was in Italy for two weeks the summer [1965] we were going to shoot that at Cinecitta Studios—I felt that it was going to be a very low budget, very yucky picture. And I remember Barry Sullivan got into a giant, violent argument with somebody, maybe Mario Bava. Why I didn't end up doing it, I can't remember, but I *do* remember being in Rome for a couple of weeks; meeting Mario Bava (a charming, colorful man); that the plot was explained to me in some fashion; and flying back to London *[laughs]*! That's all I recall and I'm shocked that it ever got made, because to the best of my recollection Barry Sullivan had some sort of a major problem either with the director or the producer.

What recollections of The Ghost in the Invisible Bikini?

The picture had been shot—without me—and it was such a mixed-up picture, it was not showable. You could make no sense of it! There was talk that one of the key production people was drunk through most of it; I don't know if that's true or not.

So after the picture was finished, they decided to put you in it?

After the picture was supposedly completed, it was unreleasable. I was not in the film at all initially; a month or a month and a half after they saw they couldn't do anything with it, the idea of shooting additional scenes with a ghost was thought up. I don't know who wrote my sequences; it was Ronnie Sinclair, the editor, who ultimately directed them. For my scenes as the ghost, they put a blond wig and a black velvet bathing suit on me and they shot me against a black velvet backdrop. I was told where the people were in the scene into which I would be superimposed, what kind of instruments people had in their hands, so on and so forth — this went on for about two weeks. And then they had Boris Karloff come in and we shot our scenes in maybe a week.

I don't think I'd have had the nerve to ask an eighty-ish actor like Karloff to climb into a coffin.

[*Aghast.*] You know, I wouldn't have *dared* ask! I saw *Ghost* again not long ago and I felt the same way, exactly — not when I was doing it, but now that I look back at it. *I* couldn't do it no matter *what* age I was!

Was Karloff fun to work with?

That was just a great experience. He was just so easy to work with! It was very natural working with him, and he was such a gentleman. Jim, too, liked Boris Karloff very much, got along well with him; in fact, I think Jim and he spent a great deal of time together, the same way Jim and Buster Keaton were good buddies.

Why did Jim Nicholson leave AIP?

He left AIP because his hands were tied in many respects. He had become an executive more than a filmmaker. He was very creative, he was always a hands-on type of guy as far as production was concerned. He knew what to make, how to make it, how to sell it, and had original ideas for what came next. He was wonderful with people; he liked the people that he had hired to work for him, and the people that he had hired liked Jim as much as he liked *them*. He was a very reciprocal type of person. He had loyalty like nobody I've ever met. People were extremely loyal to Jim Nicholson and he was extremely loyal to them. He required autonomy in his own specialized fields. He loved calling shots and he loved being responsible for his own bailiwick, which was all those things that I mentioned previously. What I think ultimately happened was that ... *other parties* got involved in his bailiwick. When that happened, I believe he lost his enthusiasm for working with those people who attempted to take away his expertise.

Scenes of Hart and Boris Karloff were added during post-production to help take the curse of incoherence off AIP's *The Ghost in the Invisible Bikini*.

Mr. Arkoff began hiring many people at American International at very large salaries, to do the very things that Jim Nicholson could do with his eyes closed. He was able to do this because, when Jim Nicholson got his divorce from [his first wife] Sylvia Nicholson to marry Susan Hart, he also gave up a lot of his stock, which put Sam Arkoff in the driver's seat in so far as the amount of stock held was concerned. So he allowed Sam Arkoff to do the driving, and I don't know how long AIP lasted after he left. I suspect that, after that point, producers simply came to AIP to make pictures; I would be surprised if American International itself made movies much after that. And the projects that *were* made after my husband left were many that he had chosen anyway. AIP was sold to Filmways in the seventies.

Jumping back a minute, why did you stop making movies for AIP after Ghost in the Invisible Bikini?

One of the reasons was because Mr. Arkoff informed me after I did four films that there was going to be no nepotism at AIP. And at that point, to go pound the pavement as Mrs. James H. Nicholson searching for roles at other studios probably wasn't worth it to me. I was at one time scheduled to do a picture for Jimmy Carreras, but that did fall through, and to this day I don't know what the film was. But that was the only thing that I rather pursued, a Hammer film [*The Lost Continent,* 1968] with Jimmy Carreras. (I personally found it difficult to be an actress, a mother *and* the wife of the president of AIP at the same time. Something was going to suffer.)

Also, I did not want to cause waves, and I think that may have caused waves. But I must say that I was in a state of shock when I was told that I was no longer going to be in pictures for that company because nepotism was not part of the bylaws of American International Pictures. I guess nepotism is in the eye of the beholder.

Everybody — including Arkoff — talks about the value of Nicholson's contributions to AIP. What would have been the point of subordinating him?
Ask Sam Arkoff.

Jim Nicholson later wound up with a deal at Twentieth Century–Fox.
He made a five-picture deal with Twentieth; I think he was one of the first producers that they allowed complete autonomy. He preferred never working on a studio lot; he preferred remaining his own person. Like using his own letterhead, his own stationery, and not the studio's. To hire his own publicity people. To make his own news releases. To totally produce. Well, they allowed him all of the things that he wanted, which included his own offices off the lot — he had beautiful offices at Nine-two-zero-zero Sunset Boulevard.

What were the five pictures?
The Legend of Hell House; Blackfather; Street People; The "B" People; and *Dirty Mary, Crazy Larry.* (The original title of that last one was *Pursuit* to begin with, and Jim changed the title. He thought *Dirty Mary, Crazy Larry* was kitschier, and he was right — as usual.) Anyway, they decided to go with *Legend of Hell House* first because that was the script that was ready, and that picture was shot in England. I made two or three trips to England with him.

And it was during Hell House *that he first became ill.*
Legend of Hell House was about three-quarters of the way through when Jim suffered his first seizure. It was later diagnosed that he had a malignant brain tumor. That would have been discovered in maybe October or November of nineteen seventy-two; *Hell House* was in its editing phase. And he died in December. *The Legend of Hell House* was put together ... released ... and did well. And then Fox decided to go with the next picture, which was *Dirty Mary, Crazy Larry* [1974]. Norman Herman and Mickey Zide were the two men left in charge of Jim's new company; they had been with Jim for about three months before his death.

I proceeded to get into quite a long lawsuit with them, which worked itself out after about three years. I think we all left the whole ordeal with bad tastes in our mouths. Since that time, I have spoken with Norman Herman and we are at the very least on speaking terms. He knows his craft very well and ultimately acted as producer on *Dirty Mary, Crazy Larry,* and I was always extremely upset because I was promised by Gordon Stulberg, the then-president of Twentieth Century–Fox, that Jim would without fail get screen credit since it was his original project. It was really his baby and everybody got credit except Jim Nicholson for it. I just about died when I saw the film and saw that Jim's name was left off of it.

And Dirty Mary, Crazy Larry *was a big moneymaker, wasn't it?*

It was Fox's biggest grosser in nineteen seventy-four and it helped finance *Star Wars. Dirty Mary* was the first picture, by the way, where they tested spending as much money on advertising as on the film itself. Which was the thing that AIP *always* used to do—spend a tremendous amount of money on their advertising and *[laughs]* not as much money on their picture as they should, really! But it was the first major motion picture ever done like that.

Would you have any interest at all in getting back into acting?

I would imagine that I'd be misleading you if I said I had no interest at all, because I will always have an interest in acting no matter who's doing it, somebody else or myself. Once you have experienced the fun of acting, it's something you never forget. In fact, I want to tell you something: Every actress that you will ever talk to in your lifetime that you ask that question, if they say *no,* they're probably fibbing!

SUSAN HART FILMOGRAPHY

The Slime People (Hansen Enterprises, 1963)
A Global Affair (MGM, 1964)
For Those Who Think Young (United Artists, 1964)
Ride the Wild Surf (Columbia, 1964)
Pajama Party (AIP, 1964)
War-Gods of the Deep (The City Under the Sea) (AIP, 1965)
Dr. Goldfoot and the Bikini Machine (AIP, 1965)
The Ghost in the Invisible Bikini (AIP, 1966)

Clips of Hart in *The Slime People* are seen in *It Came from Hollywood* (Paramount, 1982). Footage of Hart in *Dr. Goldfoot and the Bikini Machine* is seen in *Dr. Goldfoot and the Girl Bombs* (AIP, 1966).

*Your imagination is far more than what Hollywood special
effects people can do. Carnival of Souls played upon
fears that everyone can relate to.*

Candace Hilligoss

IF SOME ACTRESSES CAN WORK A LIFETIME and never achieve fame, does it seem possible that some can build a cult reputation on the basis of only a single film? It does when the film in question is *Carnival of Souls,* the micro-budgeted spookfest which has gone from lowly drive-in screenings in 1962 to playing at art houses and international film festivals in more recent years. Much imitated, never to be forgotten, the legendary Herk Harvey film continues to stand as a benchmark achievement in the annals of filmic horror, due in no small part to the haunting performance of its primary player, New York–based stage and TV actress Candace Hilligoss.

A product of Huron, South Dakota, Hilligoss was involved in acting from the early days of elementary school plays. After three years at the University of Iowa, she came to New York to study acting at the American Theatre Wing, and made her professional debut doing summer stock in Pennsylvania. She acted at the Cape Cod Playhouse, toured with Nina Foch in *Idiot's Delight,* turned up in New York TV shows and, as one of the world-famous Copa Girls, danced at the Copacabana night spot. In 1961 she was hired and spirited off to Lawrence, Kansas, to star in *Carnival of Souls,* and she later reinforced her horror rep playing the ingenue in Del Tenney's Connecticut-made shocker *The Curse of the Living Corpse.* Taking a break from her new avocation (novelist), she reminisces about her filmmaking experiences as well as her plans to reunite some of *Carnival's* principals in an all-new follow-up film.

How did you hook up with the people who made Carnival of Souls?

Sidney Berger was a graduate student at the University of Kansas at Lawrence who was helping Herk Harvey cast some of the smaller parts in *Carnival of Souls,* and Herk sent Sidney to New York to look for an actress to play the lead. Sidney called upon his friend Monty Silver, who was my agent, and said, "Would you have some actresses come in and read?" So I just auditioned in Monty's office, which was on the West Side in Manhattan. Sidney thought I was right for it. Now, *Herk* in his mind had originally envisioned a young Janice Rule; she was sort of the classic ingenue, with long dark hair. But when Sidney started casting, *he* saw *blond [laughs]*! I was not what Herk thought Sidney would be bringing back to Lawrence, and I think I was kind of a shock to him! Now, at the same time, I was being offered another picture, *Psychomania,* which originally was called *Black Autumn* (I think); Del Tenney was getting ready to shoot that in Connecticut. They were very interested in my doing a part in it, but I saw that the character had to be naked. *Carnival,* there was no nudity. So I chose *Carnival [laughs],* and an actress named Lorraine Rogers got the part in *Psychomania.*

If Carnival *hadn't come along, would you have done* Psychomania?

No, I probably wouldn't have. I would have found something else.

Previous page: **Actress/authoress Candace Hilligoss.**

Where did you stay while making Carnival of Souls?

In a hotel—the one hotel in Lawrence, which was on Main Street [*laughs*]!

Did you think Carnival *would be a good opportunity for you?*

[*Flatly.*] No. Because there were no known quantities attached to it. It was also very low-budget—under thirty thousand dollars—and movies of that sort usually don't take off, particularly if they don't have a major distributor. I felt it was going to be a take-the-money-and-run type of situation.

The people involved on Carnival of Souls—*did they seem to have confidence in themselves as feature filmmakers?*

Yes—why wouldn't they? They were very considerate, very sweet, like "innocents." There was a Mickey [Rooney] and Judy [Garland] attitude of "Let's put on a show!"

Did you *have confidence in* them?

I had no idea, because it all looked so strange on paper. I couldn't see what *they* were seeing in their minds, and I didn't know what they intended for it visually. And they wouldn't let me see the rushes, because they were afraid that somehow if I did see them, I'd become self-conscious. I had no idea what it looked like, because they wouldn't even let me *peek* at 'em!

How did you like working with Herk Harvey?

Herk was very together, very well-organized. Everything was on schedule, he got done what he wanted to do and so on. I'm sorry that he never went on to other movies, because he was very good with people. He did have some problems with me, I'm afraid: I was coming from a different training, which in those days was not familiar to people in universities. It was what he put down as "The Method." But I don't think he understood that the best acting comes from this way of working from the inside out. Many people in universities then were very used to a strong form of indication, which is working from the outside; more of what *I* felt was a superficial type of work. I think he didn't quite understand my terminology or my way of thinking. I had studied with Sanford Meisner and Lee Strasberg, and nowadays people are in tune with that style. But in the old days, to have someone come out and talk about "improvising" or "doing emotional memory" was so new, they didn't quite understand and it threw them a little bit. That made 'em very nervous.

And Harvey pushed you for a more conventional performance?

Yes, but I struggled hard to keep it very honest. He said, "I don't want people to really *care* too much about your character, because she's gonna come to a bad end." And I said, "But if they *don't* identify with her in some way, they won't sit with her for the whole movie. If they don't care, you'll lose your audience."

You shot mostly in Lawrence?

Lawrence, and Salt Lake City, Utah. I think we were in Salt Lake a week or ten days, and we stayed in motels there. It was very strange: There was a crew of five, and me, all traveling together, and when we signed registries, we all had different names and different addresses *[laughs]*! The whole picture took three or four weeks; we'd work seven days a week, sometimes around the clock. But they planned it that way. And because they were shooting in sequence, they said it would be all right if I looked more and more beat toward the end, because I would be dying anyway. And it would look good for me to be beat-up, and a little green around the gills. They thought that would add to the character *[laughs]*!

Besides Herk Harvey, who was the most creative person that worked on Carnival of Souls?

Herk credits Maurice Prather as the cameraman who set the tone and look of the film, but Reza Badiyi, who was the assistant director and the *other* cameraman, did a lot of the very complicated, tricky, almost "stunt" shooting: Hanging from rafters, dangling off the roofs of buildings upside down, lying on the ground and letting me almost drive over him. Really dangerous things. Herk had a good little crew overall. As he said, "Anyone can make a movie with two hundred people. Try making a movie with a crew of five!" *[Laughs.]*

What about the scene where you're almost run down by the van?

As a matter of fact, that van did come pretty close. That was in Salt Lake City: Herk stopped a man—a stranger—and asked him if, for twenty-five dollars, he would drive down the alley and almost hit me. The guy said sure. The first take we took, I was a little nervous; it's no fun to be hit by a moving car! And Herk said, "You know, Candace, you didn't let him get close enough. Do it again. And this time . . . kind of let him hit you." I said okay. So the second time, he *almost* clipped me. Herk said, "Oh, that was wonderful!" You know *[laughs]*, stunt people get *paid* to do this! And the stranger was thrilled; he got his twenty-five dollars and went on his way!

Real seat-of-the-pants filmmaking.

You bet. It was almost like the way Truffaut started making his movies. We'd be walking down the street, Herk and his crew of four or five, and he'd say, "We need a department store, and this looks like a very good one. Let's go in." *Today,* you would have to call the Chamber of Commerce, get a permit, this and that. *We* walked in, looked around, went upstairs on an escalator and found a saleswoman. Herk said, "Listen, for twenty-five dollars, would you keep people out of the dressing room area? We'd like to shoot some footage of this woman changing her clothes." The saleswoman said, "Of course! No problem!" Five men and myself crawled into a dressing room cubicle, and we shot the scene. Then we came out, and Herk went up to a woman customer and said, "Look, for ten dollars, would you look the other way when this girl tries to speak to you?" "Sure." No questions! We went up to a cab driver: "For ten dollars, drive away when this woman runs up to you."

The only place we had a problem was at the train station, where Herk said to a conductor, "This girl is going to run for the train. Would you slam the door in her face, like you don't see her?" For twenty-five dollars, the man said, "That sounds good!" But the word got up to someone in the office that people with a camera were down in the station. Some very official-looking man came down and said, "Wait a minute! *Waaaiiit* a minute!" — it was the first time we ran into anyone who questioned what we were doing. Herk, who has a very calm way about him, sat down with the man in the boarding area and talked to him awhile, the official got to feeling better and better, and by the time Herk was through, we had our permission again *[laughs]*!

This was all in Salt Lake City, right?

Yes. In Lawrence, everybody knew who we were and what was going on. The rooming house was a real house in Lawrence; it was empty at the time. A young couple now lives in it with a little boy. They said when they bought the house, the realtor pitched it to them by saying, "This is the famous house from *Carnival of Souls!*" It's become Lawrence's answer to the *Psycho* house *[laughs]*! When the couple moved in, it took the little boy a week to get up the courage to go upstairs. He probably never saw the movie, but he knew enough to be nervous!

The finale, at the big pavilion, was also shot in Salt Lake City.

That was the only time Herk had to call up the Chamber of Commerce and get permission. The Saltair pavilion was the largest open-air ballroom in the world, unused for years, and the Chamber of Commerce people said, "It's *so* ruined, so filled with torn decorations — would you like us to send a crew out to clean it up?" Herk said, "No, no, no — leave it! We love it just the way it is." They said *[hesitantly]*, "If we charge you fifty dollars ... would you be insulted?" An incredible bargain! Herk said, "*W-e-l-l,* if you have to, you have to." So we rented the entire amusement park, for a week, for fifty dollars!

Did you shoot both of your water scenes on the same day?

No. The first time was when I came stumbling out of the water, near the beginning of the picture. That was in warm weather, and I spent eight hours coming up onto that little beach there. First I'd go down, under the mud, and then I'd crawl up. That was still kind of Indian summer. When we came back to shoot the end of the picture, the scene where I'm shown dead in the car, it was cold weather and the men were in down jackets and ear muffs, and their breath was showing. I had on a cotton dress. I stepped into the water and it was like thirty-five degrees. I said, "I can't do it." Herk said, "You *got* to do it, or we've got no end for the movie." I said, "I just *can't* get in there!" So they *dragged* me into the water, and I was screaming all the way! A highway cop came along and he said, "What's going on? What's going on here?" They told him we were making a movie. The cop said, "You're going to put that woman out in that car, in the middle of the river?" Well, the cop got very nervous and upset, and decided that he'd better stick around! Anyway, they got me out into the car, and Reza was in a little rowboat with the camera, going around it. Reza said, "You know, she's supposed to be dead, but she's got goosebumps, and her bottom lip is trembling!" *[Laughs.]*

Did Herk Harvey and the others have future movie plans?

They hoped that *Carnival of Souls* would make money, and that they could start doing bigger and better-budgeted films. They were looking to launch a whole film complex there. But the film ended up with Herts-Lion, a crooked distributor, and unfortunately that took care of that.

Where did you see the picture for the first time?

In New York. Herk came to New York to find a distributor, and I came to one showing with my agent, Monty Silver. After the movie, Monty said, "You know, you're just too weird. You're *so* weird, I can't represent you anymore." I said, "Don't you understand, that's the character? I was *told* to act that way." But he was so upset—he said he had a reputation to protect. And he got up and walked out, and never spoke to me again *[laughs]*!

Eventually *Carnival of Souls* went to TV; in New York it became the *Million Dollar Movie* of the week, and it ran for a whole week, in prime time. Then, later, another local channel ran it, and someone from that channel told my new agent that *Carnival of Souls* and *Invasion of the Body Snatchers* with Kevin McCarthy were their two biggest moneymakers. They showed them every year, like clockwork, and they were always getting mail from people saying, "Please write and tell us when it's going to show again." People were crazy about it! From then on, wherever I went, people were staring at me and stopping me. One night I was on Broadway and Fiftieth Street at midnight, in the ninth month of my pregnancy, with my husband, and someone who looked like a Hell's Angel on a motorcycle hit his brakes and said, "Are you Candace Hilligoss??" I said, "No, no!" and my husband was saying, "Yes, yes!" He said, "I am so crazy about your movie! I am fighting with the Bleecker Street Cinema to get it in!" And then he took off *[laughs]*! All sorts of things like that happened!

Top: Hilligoss is about to be crowned by the mystery killer (director Del Tenney doubling for Roy Scheider). *Bottom:* As Dino Narizzano and Scheider battle it out, she ponders the problem of drowning with*out* getting her $50 wig wet. (Scenes from *The Curse of the Living Corpse.*)

Did the film's original release have a positive effect on your career?

[Shrugs.] It didn't have *any* effect. There was no publicity, no p.r., no agency pushing it; it was just out there on its own little legs. It should have done something for Herk Harvey, but it just went into this strange oblivion thanks to Herts-Lion, the distributor, who buried it, who played it at little drive-ins and so forth.

Were you paid for starring in it?

Yes, I was one of the few that was paid. I think I got two thousand dollars. Reza, for shooting it, got seventy-five dollars. Everyone else worked for a percentage. Next to the crooked distributor, I probably made more money than *any*body!

How did you get involved on The Curse of the Living Corpse?

I knew Del Tenney, who was a stage actor that had seen me work. He was already into making low-budget films; that was the era when they thought those kind of [horror] movies were easy to make. Del called up all his friends, "Let's get together and make a movie." He was going to be making it in Connecticut, so we didn't have to stay out of town, and so we said, "Well, okay, okay," and we did it. Like Herk Harvey, Del knew that those movies were easy sales, and could give you a good return on your investment. It was the end of an era.

What was Tenney like as a filmmaker, compared to Herk Harvey?

Del wasn't as experienced in the craft. He was okay, but he wasn't into it quite the way that Herk was; he wasn't looking for the values that Herk was looking for. He did *Psychomania* first, and he had wanted me for that; and then almost back-to-back he did *Curse of the Living Corpse* and *The Horror of Party Beach,* which had the sea monsters that looked like artichokes *[laughs].* We shot *Curse of the Living Corpse* in Stamford, Connecticut, at a home that was originally the home of Gutzon Borglum, the sculptor of Mount Rushmore. His studio was an annex of the home, with a big high ceiling. Del Tenney's wife was [actress] Margot Hartman, and her father had bought the estate. We used what had been the studio for Mount Rushmore to film the interiors; they had built all the sets in there. The outside — the yard and grounds — were the exteriors.

And you just commuted out there every day?

Right. We drove out from New York each day; Stamford is very close. I was pregnant at the time, and they were worried that my waist would be expanding. So they said, "What if we just keep building her chest out? Then her waist will look smaller." I said, "But then my head'll look small!" I was the ingenue, five and one-half months pregnant.

Did Del Tenney play the killer in all the early scenes? He told me that he did.

If he said he did, he did; he probably didn't want to bother Roy Scheider to put on all that gear. In my one scene with the killer, it was Roy. He had to throw me in the quicksand, and I was told to drown without getting my wig wet. They had no replacement for my fifty dollar wig, they said they'd need it again, and told me, "Whatever you do, don't get your wig wet." It is hard to drown without getting your hair wet.

Any memories of working with Scheider?

I got Roy his part in that. Roy and I had done a couple of shows together at Arena Stage, a national repertory theater in Washington, D.C. He was *so* broke—he and his wife had just had a baby. I remember him saying to me, "Oh, I don't know what to do. I've got seventy dollars to my name. What'll I do?" I said, "Well, a friend of mine is putting together a movie. You look evil enough. I'll suggest you for the villain." He thought that would be really great. I put him in touch with Del, and Del said, "Yeah, he looks like a young George C. Scott." So I got Roy in it. At the same time, I sublet my apartment in Hell's Kitchen to Roy and his wife, and I finally let them live there a month free. So I was very instrumental in getting Roy Scheider's career off the ground. And he *still* owes me seventy-five dollars *[laughs]*!

The whole cast of *Living Corpse* were at that time very well-working actors. Robert Milli was playing Horatio to Richard Burton's Hamlet; Hugh Franklin was in *Luther* with Albert Finney; Dino Narizzano was on a soap opera—*all* of us were involved in other projects. None of them ever thought that *Curse of the Living Corpse* would see the light of day. The Paramount Theater in midtown Manhattan had been showing *Love in the Afternoon* [1957] with Audrey Hepburn and Gary Cooper, and it was such a bomb that they pulled it. *Horror of Party Beach* and *Curse of the Living Corpse* had just opened in Texas and broke all box office records, and so this double-bill now moved into the Paramount. *Curse of the Living Corpse* was suddenly playing within just a few blocks of where all these actors were working! There was a life-sized poster of me, running in a negligee, with Roy Scheider in a black cape swinging a saber at me! Right out in front of the theater! And all these actors, on their way to do all their artistic *Hamlet*s and whatever, were so terrified that their fellow cast members would walk down and see them in *Living Corpse*! Richard Burton was so excited to learn that his Horatio, Robert Milli, was down the street in *Curse of the Living Corpse* that he and Elizabeth Taylor wanted to run down and see this movie! And Horatio, of course, pleaded with him not to go!

Also, we all felt that movies like this didn't get reviewed; then, of course, not only did *The New York Times* go to town on it, but also *Time* magazine felt it needed attention *[laughs]*! Even Les Crane, who had a midnight talk show, went on about it. The lesson was that you *cannot* do these movies and feel that they're not going to be seen, because someone somewhere — and not just kids — go to see these movies!

And what do you think of Living Corpse?
[Laughs.] No comment!

Why have you made only two movies?
Now, I didn't retire after *Curse of the Living Corpse*; I did go on to do some theater. Then later, it became too difficult. I was married at that time to an actor who was still struggling, and it became necessary for me to make a choice between a career and staying at home. I elected to try to hold the family together and to raise my daughters, Candace and Dinneen, so that *he* would be free to go on. I began to concentrate on my writing.

And what keeps you busy these days?
I've just finished seven years of working on a novel, *Dakota Ashes,* based upon a screenplay which I *also* did. (I was urged by producer Hal Wallis, before he died, to do the screenplay as a book, and become the next Edna Ferber!) It took me seven years of writing night and day, and I'm now trying to find some way, as an unknown, to get my novel published. It was based upon family stories and memories as told to me as a small child, about South Dakota when it was the Dust Bowl in the Great Depression. It's really *The Grapes of Wrath* in reverse: My story's about the people who stayed behind, and their fight to save the land, told through a love story.
Also, Reza Badiyi (the original cameraman and a.d. on *Carnival of Souls*) and I are now trying to find a way to raise the money to do the sequel to *Carnival,* based on a story which I wrote. It's a new story, but with some of the same characters in another wonderful ghost story. This would be the first time in cinema history that so many members of the original cast of a film came back to reunite this late in history, to do a sequel. We would also love, we would *adore* to be able to go back and use some of the original Lawrence, Kansas, locations. Herk would like to be involved, both on- and off-camera, but now he would like someone else to take over all the headaches that go with directing and raising the money. So Reza, who is a very prestigious Hollywood director of many television series and movies-of-the-week, would come on board as the director this time around. If you know anyone who has two-and-a-half million dollars burning a hole in their hip pocket, and who wants to make a very low-budget film with a built-in audience, tell 'em to call me as soon as possible *[laughs]*!

The recent reissue of Carnival *was a big hit, wasn't it?*
Not only was it a hit, it was reviewed by Siskel and Ebert on their TV show as though it were an establishment movie, and it was featured on *Entertainment*

A characteristic shot of Hilligoss as the aloof young beauty plagued by phantoms in the eerie cult favorite *Carnival of Souls*.

Tonight with Leonard Maltin. And became of the success of the reissue, it ended up at the Munich Film Festival. Herk Harvey flew over for it, and on a night when he didn't think anyone would show up (there was a European soccer match), *Carnival of Souls* was sold out and people were sitting in the aisles. They kept him on stage till about three in the morning, after the performance, asking him questions! It's now on British television; it's gone through Canada, Sweden, Australia, New Zealand, and it's on laser disc. It's also played on three of the major pay–TV stations.

What do you think of the picture today? Can you see the qualities which make it such a favorite?

Oddly enough, I almost see them more today than I did when we made it. In their wonderful "innocence," uncorrupted by the Steven Spielberg syndrome, they allowed the audience to ask the question, "Who am I and what would I be if I were dead? Would I have an identity?" That terror of being alone, the possibility that, when you're dead, you may go into a no-man's land — that fear is universal. Everyone's imagination goes to work. And their own personal terror comes through. Your imagination is far *more* than what Hollywood special effects can do. *Carnival of Souls* plays upon fears that everyone can relate to.

CANDACE HILLIGOSS FILMOGRAPHY

Carnival of Souls (Herts-Lion, 1962)
The Curse of the Living Corpse (20th Century–Fox, 1964)

I was a sort of Jane Fonda in my day, but without her dough or her clout. So, I got blacklisted.

Rose Hobart

BORN IN NEW YORK CITY IN 1906, Rose Hobart responded to the lure of the theater at a young age, went on stage at 15, then drifted to Hollywood to embark on a frequently less-than-satisfying movie career. Rebounding between the theater and films, she enjoyed critical acclaim while waiting for the star-making breakthrough which somehow managed to elude her.

Hobart film-debuted in the 1930 Fox version of *Liliom* and went on to appear in over 40 additional films, both in the A and B category. But by the late 1940s, her progressive social leanings (and participation in the Actors' Laboratory Theatre) had marked her for condemnation by the political witch-hunters of the day. After a period of being blacklisted, she returned to acting in the 1960s on TV's *Peyton Place,* and today she resides at the Motion Picture and Television Country House, not far from Hollywood. Not accustomed to pulling punches, the actress disarms interviewers with her candor, outspokenness and good humor.

How did you first become interested in acting?

I used to spend my summers in Woodstock, New York, where my father, a well-known musician, had a quartet. One year they decided to have a festival, and the guy who ran it invited Edna St. Vincent Millay. At that point in my life, I had never seen a play. I spent the entire two weeks they were rehearsing talking to her. After seeing the performance, I made up my mind in the middle of a daisy field that that's what I wanted to be — an actress. I think I was seven then.

The scene dissolves to when I'm opening in Atlantic City in *Liliom,* playing the child, with Eva Le Gallienne. There was a knock on the door and it was Edna St. Vincent Millay saying, "You made it!" She was absolutely wonderful. So that's how I got on.

Backtrack a bit to when you got your first job.

It was under peculiar circumstances. My mother was Swiss and had gone to England for a time to work as a governess as a way of earning a living. In those days, women didn't *do* that! One winter, we were having a terrible time financially. We spent a week on Long Island with some of her actor-friends whom she met in England — a man named Percival Vivian and his wife. They played colleges, universities, etc., as Shakespeare originally was done in England. That meant there was no stage, just everyone performing outdoors. They all had to be clowns and tumblers, too, because that's what they did in Elizabethan theater.

At the time, he was directing for chautauqua, which was in tents. They were set for a tour of one-night stands which was to start in Abbeville, Louisiana, and end in Billings, Montana, eighteen weeks after. Two days before they were to leave, his ingenue quit! He came home frantic. But his wife said,

Previous page: "My mother was Swiss and my father was Belgian, so I say I'm French by a geographical average!" — funny, feisty Rose Hobart.

"Do you want to listen to her [Hobart]?"—I had been busily learning the parts and rehearsing with her. So in sheer desperation, I got my first job.

I learned an awful lot and was very fortunate because one of the character players was a fine Shakespearean actor. He took me out to the Redwood Forest when we got to California and coached me on projection. By the time I got through with those eighteen weeks, I could be heard in a tent that seated a thousand people.

Where did you go from there?

When I got back, Mother said the only people she knew in show business were the Shuberts. She was a singer, and the Shuberts were putting out operettas and that kind of thing. So she took me to the office where I saw these beautiful women in black satin. A little man came out and said, "Can you act?" I told him about my eighteen weeks on the circuit. I went up to one girl and asked, "Who was that little man?" and, looking at me with utter contempt, she said, "J.J." It was Mr. Shubert himself!

I was sent with a note to the Shubert Theater across the street. I opened the door to it and there was a bare stage. And remember, I had never been in a theater because I had only played in tents! There was Eva Le Gallienne, to whom I handed the note. She yelled out into this totally black auditorium, "Hey, Pepe! The Shuberts are finally showing some sense!" Apparently, they had been sending over those beautiful girls in their black satin dresses— chorines looking for dance jobs—to play the child in the last act of *Liliom*. So I went on tour for that whole year with Eva Le Gallienne and Joe Schildkraut. Then I did a play called *Lullaby* [her New York stage debut, 1923], which was my first long run in New York.

Did you come to Hollywood after that?

No, I didn't come out here until 1929 when I was already an established actress in New York and was playing Grazia in *Death Takes a Holiday* with Philip Merivale [as Sirki]. (He was great, by the way; he really looked like a death's-head when they shifted the lights. It was incredible.) It was a metaphysical play; I was very moved by it. I wouldn't read my mail after each performance because almost every night I would get a letter from someone stating they had seen the play and had gone home to commit suicide!

Fox and Universal both wanted to test me. I signed with Universal because they offered to wait until I finished my run with *Death Takes a Holiday* that June. About a week later, Fox called to say that they had already assigned me to [the film version of] *Liliom* with Charles Farrell. I said to myself, "Oh, shit! How can I *not* do that?" That was *my play,* I knew every line in it. So I came out here ahead of my contract, did *Liliom,* and went back to my contract with Universal. Of course, they were furious at me for doing that. Unfortunately, the movie was not a success because Charles Farrell was just a boy with a ukulele who hadn't the foggiest notion what *Liliom* was all about. And his voice was about an octave higher than mine.

Any other memories of Liliom?

Yes, that I was photographed *appallingly*—I really looked quite awful through the whole picture. And I always wondered about it until I found out quite recently, by accident, that Janet Gaynor was supposed to do it, and had refused to play it. But the cameraman was her cameraman. And he was so upset at her not playing it—oh! What he did to me was really awful! I looked so terrible, that may be one of the reasons why it was a flop.

Did you enjoy your stay at Universal?

They put me in *East of Borneo* [1931], which really floored me. I thought I would never do pictures again! The shooting schedule for *Borneo* was just incredible. We did two solid weeks of shooting from six at night until six in the morning. I lost about fifteen pounds, so they had to put gauze in my evening dress so my bones wouldn't stick out! Everyone was fenced off, but I was with all of those wild animals. They all kidded me and said, "Don't be afraid!" They built a chute and shoved one of the big cats down it. But the cat got to the bottom, said to himself, "No way!" and backed right *up* the chute! You should have seen how fast those people came over to *my* side of the fence!

In one scene, there's a damn snake over my head. They had a boa constrictor there, and they wanted about ten feet of him hanging over my head. The snake man came up to me when they got it all set up, and said, "I wish you'd tell 'em not to take this. Boa constrictors only are awake when they're hungry; and if ten feet of him is loose, ten men on his tail aren't going to be enough." So I said to the director, "Have you talked to your snake man about this?" I had to convince him that I wasn't going to do it.

It really is a fun movie. Have you seen it recently?

I'm not sure I could stand it! The whole premise was idiotic, but I know it's *still* playing in Australia and Germany because I keep getting letters about it. Before we filmed, the studio sent a whole troupe over to Borneo to shoot the exteriors. But instead of jungle-looking, it was like the flats of New Jersey. There wasn't a tree in sight, not an animal, not anything. They filmed forty miles of absolutely nothing before they found any vegetation. The crew knew if they came home with that, they'd be fired. So they made up their own jungle with monkeys and things. There *are* no monkeys in Borneo! They brought back a wonderful scene with monkeys, and at the end of the scene, one of the monkeys took a cigarette out of his pocket and lit it *[laughs]*. They had hired some guys and put 'em in monkey suits! Everything in the picture was totally wrong.

I hated my stay at Universal. I fought with Junior [Carl Laemmle, Jr.] the whole time. The trouble with Junior was that he had no real talent and was a lousy administrator. His father was pretty good and had some idea what he wanted. But Junior didn't know his ass from a shotgun! After *East of Borneo,* they asked me if I wanted to leave. I said, "I sure as hell do! I want to get back to New York and the theater. This stuff with animals is ridiculous!" So I went to Junior's office to sign what I thought was a release. Fortunately, I had one of the top theatrical lawyers in New York, who was sharp as hell. He said, "Rose, read the small print, *please!*" And down at the bottom of this "release," in very small letters, it said that during the suspension of this contract, which could be continued by either party giving notice to the other in writing, I was not permitted to work for myself or in any other business whatsoever. So I said to Junior, "Screw you!" I stomped out of the office and slammed the door behind me. I found myself in another office, so I stomped through that and slammed *that* door. Then I found myself in a *third* office! It wasn't until I got home that I got the giggles.

Junior was really a good name for him. He was just a kid.

He was only around nineteen. I never saw him except for when he was bawling me out for not showing up or for losing weight and they had to spend so much money filling in the costumes. Junior really wasn't interested. He was a good Jewish boy, and when Father hands you the business, you run the business. He couldn't have cared less about it. Universal made a fortune off of me because they were always loaning me out to other studios. Finally, they let my contract lapse. The next day I was on a train heading back to New York.

How did you like working at Paramount when Universal loaned you out to do their Dr. Jekyll and Mr. Hyde?

I was just on the set and ready to work! That's what happened when you were loaned out. The whole business was very odd then, it was really paternalistic. If you were part of the family, all of the red carpets came out. If you weren't, you were damned lucky to get in the door!

How did you enjoy working with Rouben Mamoulian?

He really was a fine, fine director. There was only one thing that really bothered me about the way he directed. I figured he always must have dotted his *i*'s and crossed his *t*'s because when he finished a scene, he would always have to have something symbolic to finish it up with. That was really overdoing it! He died here at the Motion Picture Hospital a few years ago. I went to see him, but he didn't recognize me. I was warned by the nurse that he wouldn't, but it still broke my heart.

So what was he like personally?

He was very intense and had no sense of humor, unfortunately. That was true of many of the European directors. Otto Preminger was an absolute bastard because he had no sense of humor about anything, least of all about himself. The Europeans really think of filmmaking as an art, while most directors here think of it as just another job.

Miriam Hopkins was known for being difficult to work with. Did you get that impression of her?

Difficult is an understatement! I had no scenes with her, but I used to go on the set and hear about her endlessly from Freddie March. She was always upstaging everyone, all of the time. I don't even think she thought about it anymore because she was so used to doing it. She'd maneuver around until Freddie would have his back to the camera, practically. So in this one take in the music hall, Mamoulian set up a camera for a two-shot. But he also hid a camera behind her, behind a curtain. They took the whole scene, she upstaged him, and then she heard "Cut!", coming from behind *her.* She *wheeled,* and said, "Is *that* where the camera was?!" And Mamoulian said *[smugly]*, "Yes, *that's* where the camera was. *Print!*" *[Laughs.]* And she didn't do it quite as often after that! She was an excellent actress, though.

Have you ever worked with her?

No. You don't get to know the whole cast of a picture—but people think that you do, because you're all in the same picture. (I've been in movies with practically all the stars in the business—but I've never met half of 'em *[laughs]*—because I'd work with the "underlings"!) I only ran into Miriam Hopkins when I was handling the seating for an Equity ball, the fiftieth anniversary. I had a table for people who were working with me on the seating and the rest of it, and one of the people was a Negro, a friend of mine. Miriam Hopkins said, "I will *not* sit here," and I said, "Well, *don't,* then, girl. Go somewhere else." She *did* sit there, but when he asked her to dance, she *froze [laughs]*!

Fredric March had the reputation of being "all hands" where his female co-stars were concerned.

He had the worst reputation, but probably was the most faithful of all the husbands in Hollywood. He put on such an act! Oh, he'd kiss people behind the set, but that's as far as it went. Because he and Florence [March's actress-wife Florence Eldridge] had this incredible relationship. She knew what was happening, but her attitude was, "Oh, go ahead, have your fun."

Did you think the makeup on Mr. Hyde was effective?

We all saw the [1920] Barrymore version, which was the pinhead look. So they wanted to get away from that. I think it was the makeup man who suggested they go for the Cro-Magnon type regression rather than just inventing something.

Hobart is about to meet her fiancé's fearsome alter ego (Fredric March) for the first time, in the Rouben Mamoulian–directed *Dr. Jekyll and Mr. Hyde.*

Jekyll and Hyde *was a "lost" film for years, then only became available in a heavily edited version.*

The uncut version, which is now once again available, is great because the ending of the shorter version didn't make sense. What they cut out was what made the whole picture meaningful. The cut version isn't really good at all. You need those explanations.

Despite Fredric March's womanizing reputation, Hobart says he was "probably the most faithful of all the husbands in Hollywood." (A scene from *Dr. Jekyll and Mr. Hyde;* pictured: March, Hobart, Halliwell Hobbes.)

Your father in the film was played by veteran character actor Halliwell Hobbes.

He was just a charming English gentleman. I knew most of the English colony, including Ronnie Colman, Leslie Howard and Roland Young. They were incredibly beautiful actors. I loved all of them.

I was really fascinated with the guys who doubled for Freddie March and Halliwell Hobbes when they had the big fight in *Dr. Jekyll*. They were on the set for quite a long time and I got to know them. For instance, they got into a big argument one day over a hypothetical situation. Question: If you were doing fifty miles an hour on Mulholland Drive and you went off the bank, would you get hurt worse if you stayed in the car or if you jumped out? So one day, they did it! One of them stayed in the car and the other jumped out. The one who jumped ended up in the hospital for six months because the car landed on top of him and broke almost every bone in his body! But they really were great guys. I learned a lot from them. Stunt men are a breed apart.

Do you remember the cameraman, Karl Struss?

Again, he was a typical European. He concentrated only on what he was doing; he was always absolutely absorbed. Karl invented all kinds of things on that picture because the transformation of Dr. Jekyll into Mr. Hyde was really tough to do. Of course, the worst thing that happened to Freddie on that picture was when the makeup man (who should have known better) tried to make the masks. All of them were just *too* mask-like and Freddie couldn't move. So they just put liquid rubber on his face—*that* was the makeup. And when they took it off, his face came with it! He was in the hospital for two or three weeks, he was lucky he wasn't ruined for life. That's the kind of thing they used to do in those days, and that's why I hated pictures! They didn't give a shit about people.

Were you on the set when they shot the transformation scenes?

I was for some of them. I had gotten friendly with the crew, and when they did something special like that, I wanted to see what they were doing. Most of it was done with color slides over the camera lens which were gradually pulled out. Each layer of makeup was a different color, so you blocked out one layer by putting on another slide. They had to get Freddie exactly in the same spot every time. They finally drew the outline of his head on the wall.

Did you have any hint that he was giving an Oscar-worthy performance?

No, actually; nobody on the set anticipated that. First of all, he was very unhappy with it because that makeup was so rough for him to work in. He could only stay in that makeup about twenty minutes or so, and then he'd have to go relax—it *hurt*, finally. It was ruining his face, wearing that makeup.

Did you get to know Boris Karloff during those early years at Universal?

He was a lovely, true gentleman—the gentlest man I've ever known. Why he and Vinnie Price ended up as monsters, I'll never know. It's just incredible. Well, maybe that's why they're so good, because even when they played monsters, you *did* kind of like them, you felt sorry for them. I knew

Hobart acted opposite horror icons Boris Karloff and Basil Rathbone in Universal's lurid *Tower of London*.

Karloff when I was at Universal, and I used to watch some of the things he was shooting. I must have been on the set of *Frankenstein* because it feels familiar whenever I see it. I thought he was really a fine actor being wasted on all of that stuff.

A few years ago, they were selling the property of Elsa Lanchester out here. Of course, she played the Bride of Frankenstein. Well, she had this awful little replica of herself in that makeup [the Aurora model kit] which they were trying to sell. And I kept thinking, why would she want to be remembered as the Bride of Frankenstein with all of the other things she'd done in her life?

Were any of your scenes cut from Tower of London? *Your part somehow seems incomplete and your character simply drops out of sight.*

They must have been, because I worked on that for almost six weeks. When I see it now, I think, "They could have shot that in three days!" Universal was always a cheap studio and went on being that way even after the Laemmles left. They really didn't care about the pictures, they just cared about making the money. You can't do a decent picture like that.

Do you remember Basil Rathbone?

I worked with him even before *Tower of London*. We were both doing summer stock up in Newport, Rhode Island. I remember he and his wife Ouida used to give the goddamnedest parties out here when he was doing all of those Sherlock Holmes pictures. I think the thing that made his parties so special was that he was the first one (that I can remember) that used tents outside, so that you could go outside and do things out there — you weren't stuck in a room.

All of those English actors were terrible womanizers and they were always telling stories about their conquests. I remember Rathbone telling me one story about Marlene which really made me kind of sick — you don't do that, even if it's true. We always stopped for tea and I was the only one of the women invited to join the guys. And their conversation was getting dirtier every day. It was really getting *obscene*! One day when they had just finished one really bad one and they were laughing and having a ball, I decided that I couldn't put up with this. They were talking about gals that I knew, and *[laughs]* I also wasn't sure that they really did all the things that they said they were doing with 'em! I said, "How do I stop this?" to myself. Finally I asked, "What are the three most insulting two-letter words that a woman could say to a man?" And the answer was, "*Is it in?*" The reaction was fantastic because I knew exactly who had been asked this question and who had not. And they were so shocked that all conversation on the subject ceased for the rest of the time I was invited back. They were trying to outdo each other, of course. The boys were showing off. Actually, they were lying through their teeth!

Was Karloff one of the storytellers?

No, no, Karloff was never in that. He was a good family man and a British gentleman.

You played an emissary of the Devil in a very minor Columbia horror film, The Soul of a Monster *with George Macready.*

I remember spending all of one night shooting a scene on the back lot. I was walking down a street while black cats were supposed to hiss and all the street lights were supposed to buzz. We did that all night long—and it was colder than hell! They never warned me when all of this was going to happen, so I jumped each time. I wasn't meant to, as I was supposed to be *causing* it, so we had to do an awful lot of retakes. I enjoyed working with George Macready. We had previously done a play in South Carolina, an Elizabethan type of thing. Then, later on, I worked with him on *Peyton Place*. He was a great villain because he always underplayed. That makes the portrayal much more villainous, actually. Of course, he had that great scar which he won as a young man at the University of Heidelberg. They used to duel in those days, and that was his mark of distinction.

They shot three endings of that. I'm awfully sorry they didn't use the original one. In it, I fall out of a window, get run over, and the cat just gets up and walks away. That was the one I loved. They sent it out with three different endings to see which really appealed to an audience. But they ended up with a compromise.

Did you like playing a villainess?

I loved it. It was much more fun than playing those nice girls. I would have given anything to play the Miriam Hopkins part in *Dr. Jekyll and Mr. Hyde*. That's why Ingrid Bergman chose it in the MGM remake. Lana Turner loused up my part.

For that MGM version, Katharine Hepburn somehow wanted to play both parts.

I'm not very fond of Katie Hepburn. She was the original gal in the play *Death Takes a Holiday*. She was playing it in New Haven just before it came to New York, but they canned her and got me. I had two days to learn the part, and I had never even seen the play. No one had ever given me the script. I went out to New Haven, had a rehearsal one morning, saw Hepburn play it that night, and had to go on the Saturday matinee the next day. I was standing backstage waiting for my first entrance when I suddenly realized I couldn't hear what was going on on stage—next to where I was standing was a Victrola playing music. I ran up to the stage manager and said, "I can't hear my cue." And he said, "You're on!" I tore on stage and started talking all out of breath. I suddenly realized that that was the perfect voice for the part. And that's how I played it from then on.

Why was Hepburn fired from Death Takes a Holiday?

She was working with a very famous New York lady voice coach who told her that since she was playing this spiritual part, she must not let anyone touch her on the upper arm. Supposedly, the upper arm was the physical part, while the lower arm was the spiritual part. So that is what she was doing to the actors—while they were rehearsing, she wouldn't let anyone come near her. Needless to say, the producer was not happy! Then she wouldn't let me into the dressing room that Friday night to see if the costumes would fit me. I had to wait until she left the theater. I've never seen her since.

Did you ever see the movie version of Death Takes a Holiday, *with Fredric March?*

Not until many, many years after it was made, because I was so mad I wasn't playing my old part *[laughs]*.

Any recollection of The Brighton Strangler *with John Loder?*

Oh, sure—that was one of my favorites, actually, because it had an all–English cast. I loved that English group. I had a ball with 'em. Max Nosseck, who was the director, had a *thick* Austrian accent. For the very last scene, where I had to say, "Applaud, applaud!", he told me, "I want you to say, 'Applowed, applowed!'" I couldn't get that out of my head *[laughs]*, and I kept pronouncing it *applowed* when I tried it! They had to have about six takes because of me. And if he hadn't said anything, I'd have been all right!

John Loder was always a good actor, I thought.

He was excellent in that. It's interesting, the way certain people are very good actors but they never get to be really good stars. Because their personality isn't *alive* enough in some way. John Loder was very gentle and very sweet, but he never got to be the really important guy he should have been. He was just kind of dull, as a human being.

The bottom line, in a lot of cases, is sex appeal.

Well, look at Bogie, for God's sakes, who was the last person in the world who would have had sex appeal. And yet, *something* came across, and he was absolutely great. You just have it or you don't. And some gals, too. There are some girls that guys just slobber over, and women look at them and think, "She isn't that good...!"

I did a picture called *Conflict* [1945] with Bogie, and he was playing three games of chess, by *mail*, while that picture was being shot. He was a chess player, and apparently a very good one; the minute he wasn't acting in front of the camera, he was working out a chess play. Sydney Greenstreet was also in *Conflict,* and he had trouble remembering his lines in those days. And they kept changing the script, and that drove him crazy. So they never changed his stuff, they *couldn't,* because he just couldn't retain it. He had to learn his part before he ever came on the set, and that was *it,* kiddies—if you changed a *word,* he was dead!

He did a lot of his films with Peter Lorre, who ad-libbed all over the place, and that screwed him up like crazy!

Well, of course it did! I hate actors that ad lib, because it's really dirty pool. They always throw the other actors off.

You were originally cast as the entombed woman in Val Lewton's Isle *of the* Dead, *but had to be replaced by Katherine Emery after production shut down for a time. How much shooting did you actually do?*

We shot for about two weeks before Boris Karloff got sick and they had to stop shooting. And by the time they put it back into production again, I was on another picture, so I couldn't come back. They had shot all of my long shots first, and they used them at the end of the film, so I'm still in there. They were able to replace me without redoing everything they had done.

Did you have any acting scenes opposite Karloff in Isle *before it was closed down?*

Not that I remember, no.

Of all the directors you've worked with, do you have a favorite?

There were very few directors I worked for that I thought were really fine. Frank Borzage, who was the director of *Liliom,* was the one who taught me about working in pictures. He's the one who told me that the camera only picks up what you're thinking; emotion doesn't mean a goddamned thing. (*I* thought, "Oh, he's just used to picture actors who don't know how to act.") When we came to Liliom's [Charles Farrell] death scene, my big scene in the picture, Frank said, "Do you want to shoot or do you want to rehearse?" I said, "I think I know what I want to do with it. Can we just shoot it?" He said sure. So we shot it, and I gave a real theater performance—cried real tears and so on. And the crew was standing behind the lights with tears in *their* eyes— that's when I said to myself, "I did it!" But Frank said, "I'm sorry, we have to do it again"—there was some technical difficulty, he said. (I thought to myself, "Oh, shit!") We shot that closeup *thirty-six* times, one right after the other. Finally, Frank said to print takes eighteen and thirty-six. I said, "Frank, will you do me a favor? Will you print the first take?" He said he would.

We went into the projection room the next morning and saw the scene— it was an enormous head shot, a closeup of me. After about five seconds of watching the first take, I realized it was ludicrous. *Awful.* Absolutely nothing happened on my face—it was so frozen, it looked like a goddamned Benda mask. You could hardly hear what I was saying because I was really crying and the tears were muffling my voice. (Plus, sound wasn't very good in those days.) In the eighteenth take, when I was talking to myself with the camphor tears rolling neatly down my cheeks, it was perfect. I said to Frank, "Thank you so much for doing this. I never would have believed it if I hadn't seen it." And he said, "The one thing you've got to remember is that you must emote for that one first take before you can give the one that is great for the film." That's how I learned to be a movie actress.

Do you have a least *favorite director?*

Sylvan Simon. God, he was a bastard *[laughs]*! But I never worked with the *really* bad ones, like Otto Preminger and those guys. They were *real* stinkers.

How about a favorite actor to work opposite?

I guess Bogie, because I knew him best. I had played his wife twice in the theater, in New York. The interesting thing about him was that he was a *bastard* when he was a failure; before he became successful, he was an absolute stinker. That's why he had three wives before Bacall. But when he fell in love with Bacall, and was a successful guy, he turned out to be great. He's the only guy I know that improved with success *[laughs]*!

Do you have any recollections of the 1946 film The Cat Creeps?

I don't think it was very good. All I remember of that one was that my character couldn't stand cats. I love cats and even had a black one once.

How did you come to be blacklisted?

I was very political and was pretty horrified by the conditions out here. I belonged to Equity in New York before we had a Screen Actors Guild. At that time, actors were working twelve hours a day, and I thought, "We have to get a union. This is ridiculous!" I was a sort of Jane Fonda in my day, but without her dough or her clout. So, I got blacklisted.

Some kids from the high school around here came over to talk to the actors, and one or two of them knew about me being blacklisted. One of them said, "President Reagan said that there wasn't any blacklist." And I said, "Bullshit!" They were shocked, but I also think they were delighted. Reagan was president of the S.A.G. at the time of the blacklist. That's why I know everything that comes out of his face is bullshit! The man doesn't know anything!

At one point during the time I was blacklisted, I wanted to make sure that I would be able to get a passport if I wanted to go to Europe. So in order to get myself cleared, I privately went before the committee with my husband's Republican lawyer. They were bringing up such stuff that you wouldn't believe; papers that said things like, "Workers of the world revolt!" with my signature on the bottom. Of course, it wasn't my signature, it was printed. I thought, why don't they just *ask* me if that's my signature? My lawyer tried to get them to listen, but they threw him out of the room! He almost became a Democrat, he was so horrified.

They said I had been to a meeting of the Communist Party in Mexico City on such-and-such a date. And I said, "If you are interested, I was in a hospital in Culver City on that date, having my son!" When I finally got a transcript of my testimony, whatever I said to defend myself was cut out. It was just "...", and then it went on to something else.

How did you occupy yourself during the blacklist?

I'm just like a cat—I always land on my feet. I'd been told all my life that I couldn't have children because I had too much acidity in my system, etc. Then I suddenly found myself pregnant. I was forty-two, so I was really fascinated about being a mother. That was my next role for about six years until my son started going to school. Then I tried to get back into pictures, and that's when I *really* found out I was blacklisted.

Do you still feel repercussions from the blacklist years?

Sixty Minutes did a segment here about the Motion Picture Home, and the fact that I was blacklisted came up. Later, a guy came up to me here and he said, "I want you to know that I'm your friend." And I thought, *this* is a charming friend! There are people who were very happy to be warned about me because I'm a "subversive" character. I went around for days trying to figure out who was speaking to me and who wasn't. I finally said, "Come on, Hobart, you went through this before. Stop being silly and get back to normal!" So I went back to saying "Hi!" to everyone. Besides, half the people here can't see who you are anyway!

How many other actors are here at the Home?

Just me. Most of the other people here are [behind-the-scenes] people, or the wives or husbands of people that were in the business. That really startled me; I thought when I came here, "I'll be with my pals." No way.

Is this a nice place for you? Are you happy here?

Yes, actually. If you have to be somewhere like this, which I do, this is *it*, the *crème de la crème.* They really do everything they can to make us feel comfortable and they try to keep us happy. They have things every day that we can do, like painting; they take us out to concerts and certain other things. But the real problem is that there still isn't enough to do. All my life I wanted to be constructive, to help people, to do things for people. That's one of the reasons I wanted to be an actress. Most people sit here in their cottages, watch TV, go down to breakfast, come back, watch TV, go down to lunch, come back, watch TV, go down to dinner, come back, watch TV, go to bed. Well, that's not a life to me *[laughs]*. So it's very difficult.

How do you spend your time these days?

Rose Hobart at the Motion Picture Home in 1992.

I do a lot of writing. I wrote my autobiography, and a piece which I sent to *The New Yorker.* I have my first rejection slip, so I guess now you could say I'm an official writer!

ROSE HOBART FILMOGRAPHY

Liliom (Fox, 1930)
A Lady Surrenders (Universal, 1930)
Chances (Warners, 1931)
East of Borneo (Universal, 1931)
Compromised (Warners, 1931)
Dr. Jekyll and Mr. Hyde (Paramount, 1931)
Scandal for Sale (Universal, 1932)
The Shadow Laughs (Invincible, 1933)
Convention Girl (Falcon Pictures/First Division, 1934)
Tower of London (Universal, 1939)
Wolf of New York (Republic, 1940)
Susan and God (MGM, 1940)
A Night at Earl Carroll's (Paramount, 1940)
Ziegfeld Girl (MGM, 1941)
Singapore Woman (Warners, 1941)
Lady Be Good (MGM, 1941)
Nothing but the Truth (Paramount, 1941)
I'll Sell My Life (Select, 1941)
No Hands on the Clock (Paramount, 1941)
Mr. and Mrs. North (MGM, 1941)
A Gentleman at Heart (20th Century–Fox, 1942)
Who Is Hope Schuyler? (20th Century–Fox, 1942)
Gallant Lady (Prison Girl) (PRC, 1942)
Dr. Gillespie's New Assistant (MGM, 1942)
Salute to the Marines (MGM, 1943)
The Adventures of Smilin' Jack (Universal serial, 1943)
Swing Shift Maisie (MGM, 1943)
Air Raid Wardens (MGM, 1943)
The Mad Ghoul (Universal, 1943)
The Crime Doctor's Strangest Case (Columbia, 1943)
Song of the Open Road (United Artists, 1944)
The Soul of a Monster (Columbia, 1944)
Conflict (Warners, 1945)
The Brighton Strangler (RKO, 1945)
The Cat Creeps (Universal, 1946)
Canyon Passage (Universal, 1946)
Claudia and David (20th Century–Fox, 1946)
The Farmer's Daughter (RKO, 1947)
The Trouble with Women (Paramount, 1947)
Cass Timberlane (MGM, 1947)
Mickey (Eagle-Lion, 1948)
Bride of Vengeance (Paramount, 1949)

Rose Hobart (a.k.a. *Tristes Tropiques*) (Joseph Cornell short, 1939) is a cut-down version of *East of Borneo*. According to Hobart, she appears in long shots (as the mad Mrs. St. Aubyn) at the end of *Isle of the Dead* (RKO, 1945).

I liked Roger Corman. He's a monster, but he's a man with a great drive, a tremendous energy and tremendous charm. I wanted to kill him a lot of times, but I liked him.

Betsy Jones-Moreland

HOW OFTEN DOES IT HAPPEN THAT THE STAR of sci-fi and horror movies faces greater dangers when the cameras *aren't* running than they do in the pictures themselves? As part of Roger Corman's circle of actors in the late 1950s, Betsy Jones-Moreland coped with a sea serpent (in *The Saga of the Viking Women*), the Cookie Monster-ish *Creature from the Haunted Sea* and even with a disaster that brought about the end of the world (in *Last Woman on Earth*), but the cameras ought to have been facing the *other* way and recording her encounters with runaway horses and riptides, real-life mounted bandits, deadly manta rays (and good old Roger himself).

I was born in Brooklyn, New York—by accident. My mother's from the South, from Virginia, and I was supposed to be born in Virginia, but she got caught short in Brooklyn and that's where I got born. My real name is Mary Elizabeth Jones and I was born April 1, 1930. So I have been stuck all my life with being Mary Jones, born April Fool's Day, Brooklyn, New York. And if I didn't know how much my mother loved me, I would have thought that she had it in for me from the beginning *[laughs]*! I've never lived all that down! When I was in school—I lived in Madison, New Jersey—everybody had adenoid problems, and they would call me *[in a nasal voice]*, *"Mare-reee!"* And I hate the name *Mare-reee,* so in fifth grade I changed it to Betsy.

When did you decide that you were going to be an actress?
I never did, when you come right down to it. I weighed about one-sixty—which is not bad, because I'm five feet ten inches tall. I was zoftig, but I wasn't fat. But I also wasn't *thin*. I was working in New York, office work, public relations, publicity—I worked for *Howdy Doody* and *Gabby Hayes,* TV shows like that, for an organization called Martin Stone, which was the company that owned those shows. I wanted at that point to be in public relations and publicity for the rest of my life. Then I left there and went with Philip Morris, and I was distributing free cigarettes—they did that at all the fashion shows and all the shows of any magnitude in New York. You would put these little tiny packs of cigarettes around and you would talk to people and try to get everybody to change to Marlboro cigarettes.

Well, while that was going on, I was going to a beauty/exercise/"make-over" salon and losing twenty pounds, and that twenty pounds made all the difference in the world. A friend of mine, who was a costumer, made me an absolutely staggering costume and we went to a ball and won first prize for the most beautiful costume. That night, photographers and reporters came *pouring* out of the hotel where the ball was held—they kind of *trapped* me and pushed me up a flight of stairs, the flashbulbs popping and all that. They

Previous page: **Poor Betsy Jones-Moreland looks like she may be reacting to Roger Corman's newest directorial demand. (Photo from** *Creature from the Haunted Sea.*)

said, "Are you a showgirl or a model?" I said, "I'm not either, I'm a stenographer." And while *they* fainted, I thought, "They *really* think I could possibly *be* a showgirl or a model...?" Those words changed my life—that was the end of being a stenographer.

I was very, very shy. I was tall; I was awkward; in my teens, all my boyfriends came up to my boobs. It was *very* uncomfortable. I was so terribly shy, I couldn't talk to anybody. So I decided I'd better take an acting class—I'd better do *some*thing! I took an acting class at Carnegie Hall in New York. I had *no* intention of being an actress, I just wanted to be able to stand up in front of people and get over being tongue-tied and shy. One day I saw an ad for showgirls at what *had* been Billy Rose's Diamond Horseshoe (it was then called the French Casino). I thought, "Well, this ought to scare me to death!" So I went and auditioned for that, and I *got* the job, which I didn't *want*. I had no idea what being a showgirl involved or anything else, I was just trying to come out of my cocoon. Now here I was, *out* of it, and didn't exactly know how to handle that! I went home to Mother and said, "What'll I do?" and she said, "No *way* am I going to tell you what to do. You make up your own mind. We'll sit down and make a list, pros and cons. If you do it, most of the people that you now know will *never* speak to you again. On the other hand, if you *don't* do it, you will always say, 'What *if*...?' There is no way that I am going to make that choice *for* you." Which I think is one of the greatest things any mother ever did for any kid.

So I decided to become a showgirl and I did *that*; I was a showgirl at the Latin Quarter. One friend of mine had been in *The Solid Gold Cadillac* on Broadway, she got married and she was going to leave the show, and she called around to other showgirls and said, "Why don't you come on in and audition?" I went in and auditioned, and *again* I got the job; *again* I didn't want it, I still had it in my mind that I was going to do public relations and publicity, and that this showgirl bit was a passing thing. I took the job, I played on Broadway, I went on the road, and came to California. (By the way, Majel Barrett was my understudy in *Solid Gold Cadillac* on Broadway *and* on tour; we were roommates together all across the country.) Out here there was a lady agent who was a wonderful friend of my mother's, and she became my agent in California. And I became a movie actress! That's how that happened: I never decided to become an actress, it sort of happened to me, one step after another. And at each step, I was saying, "No, I don't want to do this." Each step was a *lark*, for the *moment*, for *today*, but I didn't want to act, I had this whole other life cut out for myself. But here I was, out in California, doing movies!

Where did -Moreland come in?

My mother's mother's name was Moreland, and my family in Virginia were all Moreland. When I went to join the [acting] unions, there *already* was a Betty Jones, and they won't let you have two names that similar to each other. So I put the -Moreland, which I've always loved, on the end of the Jones.

Most of your early movies were at Columbia. Were you under contract there?

I wished I had been, but I wasn't. They were putting me in front of the camera and grooming me — that is what I was *told.* They were trying to expose me without exposing me, and get me some experience. But then the whole business started to fall apart — that was nineteen fifty-five, when I first came out here. My first movie was *The Eddy Duchin Story* [1956], and I learned an awful lot in the few days I was on that picture. I always thought of Columbia as my home studio — that's where I started out, and I still feel very partial to Gower Gulch. None of it exists as I knew it anymore.

Roger Corman?

Roger Corman, as I have said many times — many, many, *many* times! — could charm snakes off bird eggs *[laughs]*! He could charm any*body* into doing any*thing* on the planet. I thought he had the most engaging smile of anyone I have ever known in my life, and he has a gift for making you feel like you're part of something important. Albeit it's *not* important and you're *not* part of it *[laughs]*, he makes you feel as though it *is* and you *are.* I think that's how he's gone as far as he has gone. He just has this incredible ability to charm people.

The first picture you did with him was Viking Women and the Sea Serpent.

At that point, Roger was going along making a movie every *month* — two weeks pre-production, two weeks shooting, two weeks pre-production, two weeks shooting. And, oh God, every picture that I did with Roger was *such* an adventure! When I would come home at night and try and tell people about it, I think they had a hard time believing me! Or when a picture was *over* and I had *survived* it — 'cause there was always a question of survival with Roger. You really had to check yourself every day to make sure you were still alive, because you're *always* in danger. There's always some goddamn thing about to kill you or eat you, or you were going to fall in a pit and never get up — there was always *some*thing.

There was a scene in *Creature from the Haunted Sea* with a manta ray. I had it put in my contract that I was *not* going to get into a tank, or any *other* place, with a manta ray, but there we were in the water together! Knowing Roger, he would have you *eaten* by the manta ray and still have the camera running, and say, "The bloody part, we'll fix it in the lab." That was his answer to everything, "We'll fix it in the lab." *Whatever* it was. If there were people running around in the background in a world that's supposed to be totally dead — "Don't worry about it, we'll fix it in the lab." If Roger exposed film —

it didn't matter what was on it, just so long as it was exposed—he was happy, he was just overjoyed. That was all he needed to do, expose the film. And anything that was *on* it, was a blessing. And I guess he always *did* "fix it in the lab"; somehow or other, it always got to the screen.

Anyway, on *Viking Women*, there was a girl who was supposed to star in it, Kipp Hamilton. The morning of the first day, we got into vehicles that were to take us out to the ocean—which at *that* point was somehow a lot farther away than it is now. There was nothing out there, no condos, no restaurants, no place to get coffee, no telephone, no *any*thing. It was a long time ago and nobody had really "discovered" the Pacific Ocean yet. We were at Cabrillo Beach, which is sort of "up" from Santa Monica, and at that point it was desolate—*nobody* went to Cabrillo Beach. There was a big undertow and it was very rocky and craggy, and quite *dangerous*, I guess.

Roger took us out into this wilderness—got us out of our vehicles—and Kipp Hamilton was not there. (By the way, neither was the key to the wardrobe truck!) So he waited, he stormed, he pounded. He had a baseball cap, and whenever things started to fly totally apart (which was at least once an hour), he would grab that cap and *slll-lam* it down on the ground! Well, no Kipp Hamilton. So finally he sent somebody to the phone, some phone a thousand miles away—it took a *l-o-n-g* time. And it turned out that Kipp Hamilton had had a call to do some other job, in New York, or *some*where. Anyway, not *there*, not on the coast with us. And she simply didn't come. Abby Dalton was supposed to play Kipp's sister, so when Kipp didn't show up, Abby got Kipp's part and Abby's [real-life] sister got Abby's old part. Abby and her sister were personal friends of Roger's and Abby's sister was home in bed asleep when Kipp did not show up and "the fit hit the shan." So Roger had her get out of bed and race to the location and become her sister's sister in the film. They also had to send back to Hollywood for the key to the wardrobe truck, which was like sending back to Mars, we were so far out. So Roger was in high dudgeon right off the bat.

Talk about the ship-launching scene.

The rudder on our Viking ship fell off; the girl who was supposed to be holding onto the rudder had long fingernails, and of course they all snapped when the rudder broke. Well, this ship wasn't seaworthy, and we floated out into the ocean in it. And *sat* there. No way to get back. *No way.* We thought we were going to end up in Hawaii! Roger was going crazy, up and down the beach, storming and screaming. We could see him waving his arms, we could see him ripping the cap off, throwing it into the sand. We knew that what was coming out of his mouth were things we were glad we weren't there to hear *[laughs]*. (And *we* were out there cussing in our own way!) I had gotten bloody beforehand running up and down the beach, over rocks and so on, and I was not *about* to put my feet in the water 'cause there were sharks out there.

Also, we had on leather costumes that were left over from some John Derek movie. They were *leather*. We are now in *salt water*, so the leather *shrank*. We were in the hot sun; we were in these already-abbreviated costumes; and they abbreviated even *more*. There *were* no doubles [duplicate costumes]; forget doubles! On a Roger Corman picture, you're lucky if you have anything *single*, let alone double. We didn't have anything else to put on, so for the rest of the picture we were sort of shrunk. We also lost our shoes so they *stayed* lost—that was the end of the shoes *[laughs]*!

Also, I should tell you that I am not very good in the sun, I never *have* been—I get sunstroke and heat prostration. When it got hot that day, I collapsed, I passed out. So they shot around me—it was one of those Roger Corman things! I started again, tried to launch the boat . . . and, again, the sun got me. Finally, [actor] Jay Sayer took a reflector that they had been using and he brought it over to me, and set it up so that it shaded me. If he *hadn't*, I don't know what would have happened to me. Nobody else was paying the slightest bit of attention to me. Not that I *need* attention on a movie set, but I didn't want to *die*!

You launched a second ship at the end of the movie, but that was shot the same day?

Right. The second ship was a longboat, a hollowed-out log—a *very* heavy thing. We were all supposed to push it out into the surf and then jump into it. It was the end of the day and the surf was coming in really big. The stuntmen had nothing but absolute contempt for actresses—they wouldn't save your life no matter what, they're not the least bit interested in being friendly or in being concerned about your well-being. But my agent also represented a man who *was* a stuntman on that show, and this stuntman came over to me and said, "No matter *what* happens, do not let go of that boat. Hold onto that boat no matter what it does, because if you let go of it and it hits you in the head, there is a riptide here. They'll never even find your body. *Do not let go*." That was the second launching we had to go through.

It was that way every day, every day was an adventure. Also, we were always running one step ahead of the unions. Roger would keep one long gallop ahead of the unions, they were always trying to come and shut him down because he was always working with not-enough-crew and the crew doing the wrong things and everybody was doubling and doing this, that and the other thing that they weren't supposed to be doing. The unions frowned upon that sort of thing. Of course, I didn't know diddly-squat, and I certainly didn't know anything about the crew and who's supposed to do what. Each day we were shooting at a totally different place, and I didn't realize until later that we were shooting at each location for only one day for a very good reason!

After the beach, you shot at Iverson's Ranch.

Between life-threatening experiences on *Viking Women,* Jones-Moreland giggles as she comes to Brad Jackson's rescue. Susan Cabot (right) is not amused.

Roger thinks horses have brakes. He does not understand that horses *don't* have brakes. We [the Viking women] had these eight-foot steel spears and Roger would gallop us into a pile of rocks—a *big,* dead-end pile of rocks—at Iverson's Ranch. And we were supposed to put on the brakes. Well, the horses don't know that! And we've got eight-foot steel spears comin' up our rear ends! There were a whole bunch of stuntmen on horses behind us, chasing us, and we would practically *splatter* ourselves all over these rock faces. We were all tired; we were riding bareback; our legs were *raw* from riding. (We'd already had riding scenes on the beach the day before.) We were not *any* of us used to that, and our legs were *way* beyond the point of shaking. It was very dangerous, because we were riding rough territory.

And at least one person did *get injured, right?*
    A *couple* of people got injured; Richard Devon shattered his knee, I think he still has problems with that. And Abby Dalton's sister fell off her horse. Now, this is a girl who was riding her own horse—she and Abby had sent home and got their own horses. Abby's sister pitched over the head of her horse during one of these "brake jobs" and plowed her head right into a

rock. The first-aid man came flying over—he really liked the Dalton girls very, very much and he was beside himself. He went *flying* down into the scene to try to shield her, because there were many more horses coming and he didn't want her to start to come to and put her head in the path of all these horses. Everybody went galloping on by and he had his body over the top of her, trying to keep her down. She was unconscious; she had to be taken away. And when Roger went to the hospital to see her—she was not even conscious yet— he tried to get her to sign a release, that he was not responsible or liable for any of this. (I was not there so I can't swear to this, but this is what I was told.) That was Roger to the core *[laughs]*! [June Kenney came in at this point and took over the part.]

Any memories of Susan Cabot?

I *loved* Susan Cabot, I got along with her just fine. We had lots of fun together. We were sitting on the beach that first day and we were having lunch under a tree after that boat adventure, and we were still in these damp costumes. Very short costumes, getting shorter by the second. And a lizard ran right up an embarrassing part of her anatomy. She didn't bat an eye, she sat there and toughed it out. The rest of us were screaming hysterically, having fits laughing, falling down—she just sat there, and waited for it to leave. I *loved* her for that, and I have never forgotten it.

Richard Devon was very outspoken when he talked to me, and he said that Corman was a monster on the set when things weren't going his way.

Roger was *real* put-out if things didn't go his way. But he was *never* abusive. I've worked with directors who *are* abusive, and he was never that. He would scream at everybody *equally [laughs]*, he didn't find *one* person to whip. I worked with another director later on that liked to find *a* woman, and then beat the crap out of her—humiliate her, and beat her down. The stronger the woman, the more they gotta do it.

Did you see Viking Women *when it came out?*

Yes, I did. What did I think of it? I thought I was wonderful; I thought I was terrible. I thought it was the most wonderful thing in the world; I thought it was a piece of trash. *All* those things go through your head. There's a scene where the girls are incarcerated, and somebody says to me, "We've got to get out of here." I was supposed to say, "But how?" But because I had come from New Jersey not too long before that, I said, "But *hhhooowww?*" All in the nose—nasal New *Joisey*. Everybody in the theater laughed, and I thought I was going to *die*! God Almighty, I thought I would never live it down!

You didn't work for Corman for several years after Viking Women.

When we were on *Viking Women,* I kept track of my hours. I had been

Jones-Moreland and Haze weather a rear-projected sea squall in the campy *Viking Women*.

a secretary and a stenographer and an office person, and I was accustomed to doing that. I kept track of my hours and I felt that I should be *paid* for those hours—we went way the hell beyond the hours we were supposed to work. Well, when I said I wanted to get paid for these hours, and I *didn't* get paid for 'em, I went to the Screen Actors Guild. Everybody said, "You'll *never* work for Roger again!" I said, "The man's a crazy man. Who the hell would *want* to work for him again!" Not working for him again wouldn't have bothered me at all. But I *did* like him, I liked Roger. He's a monster, but he's a man with a great drive, a tremendous energy and tremendous charm. I wanted to *kill* him a lot of times, but I *liked* him. I never felt hostile toward Roger, but I wasn't going to be "had" by him, either—I worked for that money, I earned it and I wanted to get it.

Did you get that extra money?
    Oh, absolutely. Then time passed, and I did *A Streetcar Named Desire* on stage in Hollywood—I played Stella and Virginia Arness [wife of James] played Blanche. We were extremely successful and I got some *staggeringly* good reviews, which just blew my mind. The day after some of the reviews came out, Roger called me and he said, "I have been testing a title for a movie for two years. People are ready to beat down the doors of the theaters to get to

see this movie. This is the most excitement there's ever been for any title that I've ever done." I said, "What's the title?" He said, "*Last Woman on Earth.* I want *you* to star in it." He told me that we were going to San Juan, Puerto Rico, we were going to stay at the Caribe Hilton, we were gonig to do *this* and we were going to do *that.* "It's going to be in CinemaScope and Technicolor; I have *never* had this much money to spend before; this is my first big picture and I want you to star in it." I said, "All right. Send me a script," so on and so forth. I read the part in the script about going in the water with manta rays and I said, "None of that for *me,* thank you!" Other than that, I signed and I went.

I got to Puerto Rico . . . I got off the plane . . . I was supposed to be met at the airport, and there was no one there to meet me. I had this enormous amount of wardrobe (I had seventeen wardrobe changes) and I literally dragged it through the airport, *crying,* I was so goddamn mad. It was hot . . . it was wet . . . it rained every twenty minutes (that is *not* an exaggeration) . . . and it was *humid.* I was furious. Anyway, they finally took me out of the airport and they took me to the location where they were shooting that day, out in the jungle. Here I see for the first time in my life real thatched roofs, houses up on stilts, chickens, three and four generations living in a one-room house— it looked like a movie set, except it wasn't a movie set, it was real. No fences; cows wandering from property to property, from house to house; they used palm fronds and coconut husks to cook outside. People had said to me, "Don't put your foot down on the ground in the jungle. There will be ten million bugs on you before you can get your foot back up off the ground." I said, "For God's sake, I've got to *shoot* in the jungle. How am I gonna *not* put my foot on the ground?!" You just cannot believe the bugs—I *lived* with a can of bug spray in one hand the whole time.

And, of course, you ended up not staying at the Hilton.

[Laughs.] No, we stayed in a house, all . . . of . . . us . . . in . . . a . . . *house, one* house, with *one* bathroom. The entire company had to come back from work and everybody had to go to the bathroom, 'cause there weren't any bathrooms in the jungle, believe me. And if there *had* been, you wouldn't have used 'em, because a barracuda would have gotten your parts *[laughs]*! So everybody would come back and use the bathroom and the toilet *immediately* plugged up—that would always happen. We were always out of hot water because there were twenty or twenty-five of us trying to take a shower! Well, [director of photography] Jack Marquette and two or three of the others *promptly* moved out. *I* didn't have the clout to move out; Roger said, "Stay in this house," I stayed in that house. *Finally* I got the hell out of there, but I stayed for as long as I could. I was doing my own makeup, my own hair, my own wardrobe, my own everything. Looking at the movie today, I can't believe how good my hair looks in that movie *[laughs]*, considering that I had

Not unexpectedly, Jones-Moreland's status as the *Last Woman on Earth* is the source of some discussion between Robert Towne (enjoying the upper hand) and Tony Carbone.

absolutely everything working against me. I had no mirror, no nothing. I had to dress and undress on the beach in the middle of everything and everybody — there was no trailer or anything like that.

The second day in Puerto Rico, my ankles swelled up to be the size of my thighs. I had a terrible reaction to the water. Well, I ran all over the place, running to doctors, trying to get pills, anything. And the *first shot of the movie* was between my ankles, with me putting sun tan oil on my legs! My ankles looked like elephant ankles, they were so swollen. Then there were those goddamn air tanks that we had to carry on our backs. Roger was too cheap to have 'em pumped out so that they would be light; he didn't want 'em pumped out 'cause then he would have had to pump 'em back *up* again! They were very heavy, sixty or seventy-five pounds, and at one point the three of us [Jones-Moreland, Tony Carbone and Robert Towne] had to jump in the water with these tanks on. Supposedly we were jumping off a boat, but actually we were jumping off a dock. The Puerto Rican crew was standing up on the dock. Well, I can't swim, not worth a nickel, and this thing started to pull me over backwards. I'm gulping water, gulping water. And we're practically in a sewer — we were in a place where people lived on their houseboats. This was *not* the best water to have going in your eyes and your mouth! I'm swallowing water and choking, and I cried out, "Throw me a rope! Throw me a rope!"

And they threw me a rope—both ends. *Both ends*! And I was so goddamned *mad*! Tony and Robert Towne finally helped me, they kept me up—they could swim and I couldn't. (Bob Towne could swim like a fish.) I finally got the damn tank off and got up there, and I stood toe-to-toe with Roger and I cussed a streak. A *streak*! 'Cause I damn near drowned in that sewer, and I was *not* happy about it! That was *one* of my days with Roger.

Did the fact that your leading man [Towne] was also the film's writer cause any problems?

No. It was 1959 and I guess the drug culture was starting, and he was kind of involved with a lot of people who were doing ... things like that. I don't mean that *he* was on drugs on the picture, I don't mean that at all, but he was sort of "spaced," I had the feeling that he was always off on a cloud somewhere. If anybody had said to me that this man was going to go on to win Academy Awards, I would have said they were stark raving mad *[laughs]*! However, he had things to say—you *had* to know that. There was something about Bob that you *knew* that he had things that had to be said. There are some lines from *Last Woman on Earth* that *to this day* I remember, and quote to myself. It was his first sale of a script, as far as I know, he was just beginning, and that sort of pleased me, the fact that we were all puppies in a basket together, all doing this "wonderful" movie. ('Cause Roger made us think it *was* a wonderful movie!)

And Tony Carbone?

He was a wonderful actor. I met him for the first time way before *Last Woman on Earth*: [Producers] Clarence Greene and Russell Rouse were going to do a TV series, Clarence asked me to come in and read with a bunch of actors, and Tony was one of 'em. I was very impressed with him and I liked him very much. I thought he was a very exciting, dynamic, *interesting* actor and that the others were sort of white bread—totally blah. I didn't know Tony at all but I thought he was a great choice for the series. Clarence Greene tried to explain to me that an actor coming into the home every week [on TV] needed to be a blah one—then you could bring in the more dynamic people to play *off* the blah one. That was the thinking at the time, you wanted white bread coming in every week, you didn't want anything that was going to rock the boat. Tony was much more a rocker-of-the-boat. I just thought that was awful, because he was such a good actor.

Was Corman less of a "traffic cop" and more of a director on Last Woman*?*

He made a couple of noises in that direction. I think that was around the time when he was going to [acting teacher] Sanford Meisner, and I thought, "Well, boy, now I'm gonna get directed, this is gonna be great, it's gonna be Elia Kazan time!" I thought we were going to get Direction with a capital D.

Well, *no*, that didn't happen. Roger does not direct—maybe he did later, but he didn't then. He moved the camera, he got it from Place One to Place Two, and if you happened to be in the shot, that was fine, but he didn't tell you what to *do* in that shot. On *Last Woman on Earth,* it was business as usual and "We'll fix it in the lab!"

Let me tell you about the bandits. We were shooting in the jungle, and all of a sudden, all the Puerto Rican guys started to disappear—they would just vanish into the weeds! We didn't know what the hell was going on. Then these small horses with people on them came *flying* by! And they were *bandidos*—they were *really* bandits! I thought it was a joke the first time, but it was no joke. The Puerto Rican guys took off and I stood there like an idiot— what did I know? They went by ten feet from me, fifteen feet max. Two or three days later, the same thing happened again; by that time, of course, I knew what was coming when I heard the horses' hooves, and I was fascinated. I didn't run and hide behind a tree, I was just fascinated! I couldn't believe my eyes—the romance of it all was more than I could stand *[laughs]!*

Any other near-fatal memories of Last Woman on Earth*?*

[Laughs.] There was a scene where Bob Towne comes up to my hotel room to give me legal briefs or something. I've been drinking, I'm loaded, and I'm walking on a bannister on the balcony. First of all, you have to remember that we're all sleeping in this house, we're all up half the night trying to get into the shower and go to the toilet, the toilet's not working. I then had to get up at the crack of dawn to get ready to go out and shoot—do my hair, do my makeup, do all this stuff. I was getting very little sleep. We get to this scene, which we shot at the Caribe Hilton as I recall, and we were on the top floor. And I was walking on the bannister, like an *idiot,* doing the tipsy, gonna-fall-off routine. Jack Marquette was shooting it from the floor *up,* not from the top *down* where you could see how high up I was. And I realized later that I could have been standing on a *chair*—or *any*thing! I didn't need to be walk-ing on a goddamn bannister, thirty floors above the ground or however the hell high that hotel is! This is why I say, you have to pinch yourself and be sure you're alive every day when you're working for Roger—this kind of thing goes on all the time! I don't know what in the world possessed me to do it!

The other thing I remember is Jack Marquette saying, "Betsy, you've got deep circles under your eyes. You're going to have to put on some Erase." Erase was a makeup that you'd use to hide the dark circles under your eyes—it goes on underneath other makeup. And I said, "Jack, I have got half a tube under each eye. There is no more that I can put on!" And he said, "Well, Betsy, there's nothing I can do for you." And this is one of my big scenes *[laughs]!* What a *hell* of a way to go into your big scene, thinking that you're supposed to be as beautiful as you can possibly be, and you're told by the cinematog-rapher, "There's nothing I can do for you." Lord Almighty!

Did you have any live sound in that film?

[Laughs.] Oh, God, you just had to ask that. A *year* or so after we made that picture, Roger calls—this is ten thousand miles and at *least* twelve months later. He says, "We have no sound. 'Beach' Dickerson didn't get any sound. You gotta come in and wild-track it." *Not* loop it—wild-track it. We didn't have [a guide track], we didn't have *anything* to go by. We just had to throw in some words and just *hope* that it matched the mouth somehow or other! I stood there with tears running down my cheeks and the microphone in front of my face, trying to figure out *some* way to put *some*thing to make *some* kind of sane marriage between my voice and what was on the film! And it broke my heart, because if I *had* done any good work [in *Last Woman on Earth*], that took care of it! If *any* of it had been any good, that blew it right out of the water.

Years passed. *Years!* Then all of a sudden Roger called again and he said we were going to do some added scenes—the film had to be longer for TV. By this time, I was heavier, and my hair was darker. (By the way, Roger had originally wanted me to go blonde for the movie, and I don't look good as a blonde. I wish that I did, but I don't. So I had my hair streaked and it looked great, *I* thought.) Anyway, when we shot these additional scenes on a beach in Malibu (or wherever), I was a totally different person. I *tried* to be the same person but I was much more mature—that girl [in the movie] was a dip, and I couldn't *be* a dip anymore somehow! This was the scene where I'm sitting on a rock and Tony Carbone finds the dead girl on the beach, and then comes back all a-twitter. That whole sequence was added on much, *much* later. Roger got all three of us back together, me and Tony and Bob. We just had to add minutes, so there's a lot of scenes of us just walking up the beach. We also shot another added scene in some little bar on Santa Monica Boulevard.

Also, all the stills that I've seen from *Last Woman on Earth* were taken while we were shooting the extra scenes, they were *not* taken in Puerto Rico. I'm heavier in those pictures, my hair was darker, and it was not nearly the way it was style-wise in the movie.

Was there ever a movie where you had a better role than the one in Last Woman on Earth*?*

No. Uhn-uh. My favorite scene in the movie is the scene where I run after the baby chicks. That, and where I'm cutting the fish. I think I looked best in those two scenes.

Were you enjoying the experience of working in Puerto Rico?

I fell in love with the Puerto Ricans. Because of the humidity and the climate, I can understand their totally different tempo. I adjusted to *theirs* better than Puerto Ricans adjust to New York. *Their* tempo is a hell of a lot *nicer* than ours in New York. I ended up having a lot of friends in Puerto Rico in a very short period of time. You *cannot* run around tap-dancing to New York tempo in Puerto Rico, 'cause you will simply drop dead. It is too damn wet, it's just *unspeakably* humid, and the bugs are everywhere. There are groups of dogs, fifteen or twenty of 'em, that lie in the middle of the roads when you get a little bit out into the country. They lie there and they don't move — you can be going any-number-of-miles per hour that you want and they don't move, you have to drive around them. It's unbelievable!

There was one young Puerto Rican boy who had a crush on me, and he would go down to the water — the beautiful Caribbean sea — and throw a line in the water and pull in fish. One day he said he wanted me to have one of the fish for lunch. He cooked it out of doors at his house and brought it to me on a beautiful leaf, and told me how good the fish would be and he wanted me to eat it. Well, I'm not a big fish eater, but I thought, "I'm *not* going to create an international incident, I am going to eat this fish, and if it's the last fish I eat, if I choke to death on the bones, that's just gonna have to be the way it is!" *[Laughs.]* I started to eat the fish, and all the Puerto Ricans were standing around saying, "The head is the best, and the eyes the sweetest." And I thought, "Oh, my God, what have I gotten myself into here?!" Well, of course, I ate the whole fish, I ate the head, I ate the eyes and they were absolutely fine — it was a *great* delicacy, *marvelous*. And they were just cheering me as I went on, and it made for very good feelings amongst us — because there was so much anti–American sentiment at that point. There were riots in 1959, there had been riots before that — we were not the most welcome people on the planet Earth. So any little thing I could do, like eat the eyes of the fish, was for the good *[laughs]*!

How did Creature from the Haunted Sea *come about?*

Creature from the Haunted Sea was shot because, after *Last Woman on Earth* was done, Roger had some film left over; that's all *that* was about. Roger called back to Hollywood and he told a writer [Charles Griffith] to rewrite a picture that Corman had already shot twice, once in Hawaii [*Naked Paradise,* 1957] and once in the snow somewhere [*Beast from Haunted Cave,* 1959]. He told the writer, "Rewrite it for Puerto Rico and we'll shoot this picture again." He told us he had the film left over and he said, "Let's spend five more days here and we'll shoot this other picture," which we did. Roger was supposed to be in it, he was going to play my brother and he was going to play it like an idiot. Then at the last minute, this kid named Robert Bean came down from Canada (as I recall) and he played the part. Robert Bean was fine, but I wish that Roger had done it — I think it would have been a lot of fun.

The only problem with that movie is that it started out to be a takeoff on everything Roger had ever done before. It was to be a comedy, a laugh a minute. Then all of a sudden, somewhere in the middle of it, that got lost and it got to be serious! You never knew whether it was a fish or a fowl, and it turned out to be — foul, I guess *[laughs]*!

Did your paycheck double when you agreed to do a second picture?

No, no. We did *Creature* in only five days. *Last Woman on Earth* took two weeks, I think.

So what about the experience with the manta ray?

I literally had to go into the ocean where we saw the sharks and the manta ray. We had been shooting in the jungle and Roger had some of the guys construct a platform out in the ocean; they wanted me to go out onto this platform (which was supposed to be part of the boat) and then fall off of it. All the Puerto Ricans came running out of the water screaming, "Manta! Manta! Manta!" We looked out and right under the surface of the water we could see this big black shadow. I said, "Oh, God, Roger, I can't go out there—" He said, "Just *do* it! Just get in the goddamn water! I don't want to hear any more about these fucking fish!" And I was so mad at him that I thought, "If a goddamn shark comes along and takes off my leg, I am going to beat Roger to death with the bloody stump!" I was just fit to be tied! And yet I have always *liked* Roger—you can't help but *like* Roger! He never did harm to me. He tried to *screw* me in that I wasn't going to get my money and that kind of thing, but who doesn't do that?

Most of the people I've interviewed have that sort of attitude toward him. The one who came away with a real healthy dislike was Richard Devon.

Well, Richard got really badly hurt on *Viking Women*; the last time I talked to him, he was still suffering from Roger making him do something that was not necessary to begin with, and not *sane* secondly. I've never disliked Roger at all. I remember I was utterly *stunned* when he started importing ["artsy"] pictures from Sweden. I said, "Roger *who* is distributing these pictures?!" I couldn't believe it!

Were you doing much improvising and ad-libbing in Creature?

Yes, I think we were. Every day was a new adventure, and we didn't quite know from minute to minute what we were doing.

Did you find playing comedy appealing?

Yes, I did. I'd like to know a lot more about it than I do, I've never felt secure. I also sang in that picture; that was my singing debut *and* my singing end.

The fact that the film was a spoof—did that make it more fun to work on?

Yes, it did—especially since it was a spoof of *Roger*.

What do you remember about the Creature itself?

Not very much. It was all made of chicken wire and Brillo pads; the footprints were made with a toilet plunger. I don't remember who played it.

According to Jones-Moreland (seen here with Tony Carbone), *Creature from the Haunted Sea* wasn't a fish, so it must have been "foul."

What does a picture like Creature from the Haunted Sea *do for—or to—an actor's career?*

Probably bottoms it out. I just assumed that nobody would ever see it. In the beginning, because it *was* going to be a "sophisticated" spoof and it *was* going to be an inside joke, I was not ashamed of it. Later, when it *didn't* turn out to be that way, when it got off the track and got dumb, then I wished that I'd never heard of it. You're there, the camera's running, you just do whatever you gotta do and you just go on.

Jacques Marquette told me that, once the pictures were done, getting out of Puerto Rico was the toughest part for you guys.

We finally got to the point where Jack, who was the cinematographer, hid the last reels of the films. He *hid* them, because we didn't have tickets to get home, we didn't have money to get home, the crew wasn't getting paid. We were truly stranded. Roger was going on to other things—and we *weren't*! Roger talked to his brother on the phone a lot, and the brother, I understand, is even tougher. Good cop, bad cop—*he's* the bad cop. Roger and his brother were going to go on and do something else, and his method of operation was to leave everybody [connected with the finished pictures] and go on. I don't think that was really Roger's m.o. Jack hid the film—he stashed it in a freezer or something—and he wouldn't let Roger have it until we not only got our checks, but we got our checks cashed and we had the money in our hot little hands, to do with as we pleased!

One other story: I found out that *Last Woman on Earth* was going to premiere in San Diego. I went camping with friends of mine, we went down and spent the night in the mountains, and came down to the theater in our fatigues and so on. I'm sure the poor manager of the theater could have killed me, could have shot me dead. He probably thought that this glamorous person was going to appear, and in I walk in army fatigues, wild hair, sunburned (and having a wonderful time). The double feature was *Last Woman on Earth* and *Little Shop of Horrors*. So I will always feel a close kinship to Jack Nicholson, because of that moment when our two pictures came out together!

Did Corman ever offer you a part that you turned down?

No, but a funny thing happened later. I had done a soap opera called *Morning Star* on NBC and I had money in the bank, and that's when Roger called my agent and wanted me to do a part in *The St. Valentine's Day Massacre* [1967]. Jason Robards was the star and he was very insecure as a *movie* actor, and Roger wanted to make him feel *very* secure. Roger wanted me to play one of the reporters in Robards' first scene—Robards' first scene was going to be shot at some big mansion that Roger rented. Roger offered me some amount of money, I forget how much, but I had money in the bank and I was being very snotty at the moment and I said to my agent, "There's not enough money!", meaning that there wasn't enough money in the *world* to tempt me to get onto another Roger Corman picture and get killed, which is what was in my head. (Also, it was a small part and I had starred in this soap opera for a year and I didn't want to bring myself down to a small part.) Well, *he* thought I said, "*It's* not enough money"—there is a world of difference. So Roger doubled the price and then I thought, "Well, *okay,* I can't turn *that* down!" So here I was, the very experienced "old hand," gonna help Jason Robards *[laughs]*!

By the way, I hope that nowhere along the line have I made it seem that I don't like Roger. You cannot help liking Roger, he has such great charm, and you can't beat the fact that he started out with a nickel and a half and built what he built. He discovered people, he employed people, he *used* people. Yeah, he *used* people—he found talented people that needed to work and were not working and he *used* them, but *he gave them work.* I want to make all that clear, because it'd be easy to mistake a lot of what I'm saying for Roger-bashing. By no means do I intend to do that. You can't *not* like Roger. You have to be *lured* by that wonderful, wonderful smile and that ability to make you feel important. *Anybody, anywhere* has got to respond to that—I don't care who you are, you have to respond to that feeling that he's taking you in and you're part of the family and your input is important. He just *generates* that, and I don't even think he *works* at it, I think it just *happens.*

What do you recollect about working on The Outer Limits ["The Mutant"]*?*
   That was shot about a block and a half away from my old house on Tuxedo Terrace in Hollywood, up in Bronson Canyon—the cave where we shot *Viking Women.* The first night that we were there, my voice went hoarse, I lost my voice from screaming in that cave. I had one hell of a time—it was very cold and very damp. It was very difficult from then on to sound like anything but a frog *[laughs]*!

You were also in the famous Route 66 *episode with Boris Karloff, Lon Chaney and Peter Lorre.*
   We went to Chicago to shoot that, just after Labor Day as I recall. Peter Lorre and other actors of that sort, Humphrey Bogart and so on, were always loved by "the darker side," if you know what I mean. The Mafia. The hoods of this country. Those actors were always treated with great respect and love and devotion. We went one night, Peter Lorre and I and I forget who else, a whole bunch of us—we were taken by "gentlemen" from that world to a nightclub, to dinner, and we were treated like royalty. Absolutely like royalty! Peter Lorre wasn't allowed to pay for anything, there was no way that anybody like Lorre could ever pay for anything when the *other* kind of people were around. And everything was done first class. It was very interesting. You sort of had a feeling there was an undercurrent *all-l-l-l* the time, that other things were going on that you didn't know about and didn't *want* to know about, but you'd read about them in the paper tomorrow. There'd be little exchanges at the other end of the table, somebody would step out from the shadows and whisper in somebody else's ear, and you thought, "Oh, God, somebody was just macheted somewhere!" *[Laughs.]*

Did you get the feeling that Lorre knew more than you did about what was going on?
   I don't think so, I don't think he was part of it. I think he was like a mascot. He was a pet, but *not* a pet who knew anything! Peter Lorre was wonderful fun. I have not too many other recollections about that *Route 66* except that George Maharis got *very* sick. Very, very, *very* sick—he had hepatitis. I *think* that in the episode before that, they had him in the water at night in the cold. He got real sick, and they would *not* take care of him. They would not double him or do any of the things they needed to do to protect their star. And so in the middle of our shooting, he took off! Nobody could find him. We were there, as I recall, an extra two weeks, on salary, *all* of us. Finally he was found, or allowed himself to be found, or came back; he had tried to recover. They were not good to him.

Talk about Betsy Jones-Moreland today.

I did seven *Perry Mason* [TV movies], which I was *very* grateful for. We shot them in Denver and I played the judge. And I have a kennel in El Monte and I do rescue work; I have dogs and cats and a few chickens and ducks, and I try to find homes for animals that people can't keep anymore. I've formed a not-for-profit organization — *believe* me, it's not for profit *[laughs]* — and everything I make goes into it and much more besides. I get food donated to my organization and I try to spread that out amongst other people who are doing rescue work. That's the biggest thing that I do: I can't personally rescue hundreds of animals, but I have been feeding hundreds of animals for a long time and I feel *real* good about that. It started out when I lost a cat in nineteen sixty-six, and in trying to find that cat, I went around to the pounds and saw what was happening to so many animals. You can either say, "I was never here . . . I will walk away . . . I will forget that this happened," and put it out of your head, or you can say, "I have to do something about this." I chose the latter and it changed my life, and of course it totally ate up my career. (Ate up everything *else,* too.) But it's very satisfying, makes me feel good. It's something that I'm very proud of and that I work very hard at.

BETSY JONES-MORELAND FILMOGRAPHY

The Eddy Duchin Story (Columbia, 1956)
The Best Things in Life Are Free (20th Century–Fox, 1956)
The Garment Jungle (Columbia, 1957)
Operation Mad Ball (Columbia, 1957)
The Saga of the Viking Women and Their Voyage to the Waters of the Great Sea Serpent (AIP, 1957)
Screaming Mimi (Columbia, 1958)
Thunder in the Sun (Paramount, 1959)
Day of the Outlaw (United Artists, 1959)
Strangers When We Meet (Columbia, 1960)
Last Woman on Earth (Filmgroup, 1960)
Creature from the Haunted Sea (Filmgroup, 1962)
The St. Valentine's Day Massacre (20th Century–Fox, 1967)
The Hindenburg (Universal, 1975)
Network (United Artists, 1976)
The Last Tycoon (Paramount, 1976)
Joni (World Wide Pictures, 1980)

I think from time to time that a sequel to
The Brain from Planet Arous *would be*
worth doing. Know any investors?

Jacques Marquette

IN A SHORT BUT ACTIVE PRODUCING CAREER, Jacques Marquette was responsible for three of the most conspicuous low-budget sci-fi/horror films of the frantic 1950s: *Teenage Monster*, a "werewolf" Western (also directed by Marquette); *The Brain from Planet Arous*, featuring John Agar and a giant floating brain; and the all-time cult classic *Attack of the 50 Foot Woman*.

Born in Brooklyn in 1915, Marquette moved to Hollywood in 1919 and attended Hollywood High School. Breaking into the business as a "gofer" for his older brother Joe, a newsreel cameraman, Marquette's first job was assisting his brother on coverage of the 1933 Long Beach earthquake. Later, after a World War II stint as a cameraman for the Air Force's Film Division, Marquette accepted a $69-a-week job at Technicolor Labs as a technician. By 1957 he had moved up to camera operator on various studio pictures and was still facing the difficulty of climbing to the next notch of director of photography. It was at this time, according to the filmmaker, that his "interest in sci-fi and producing all merged into a new project known as Marquette Productions."

What were your first jobs in Hollywood after the War?

First as a technician at Technicolor Labs. Soon I was in Technicolor's camera department, which in those days meant *on the set*—the old three-strip color required Technicolor people, not studio employees, on the camera. I was a camera assistant on many color films like *Anchors Aweigh* [1945], *Niagara* [1953], etc. Finally, film crews on color films went back to studio personnel and I went to work at Twentieth Century–Fox as an assistant cameraman. There I met actor Jeffrey Hunter, and he coaxed me into serving as camera operator, director of photography and co-producer on *Living Swamp* [1955], a Disney-style documentary film on Georgia's Okeefenokee Swamp. After that, I returned to Hollywood now advanced to camera operator, first on Warners' *The Helen Morgan Story* [1957]. I "operated" on many films thereafter but wanted to advance to director of photography—which was not easy to do at the time.

What made you decide to get into the business of making movies?

I'd been working in the business for quite a while, and I was seeing some of the ineffectual things they were doing with a pretty good amount of money. For instance, an actor's agent could talk a producer into almost any amount of money they wanted—particularly if the producer was "stuck" on that one actor. They would pay probably ten times the amount they would have to pay at *scale*—that's the minimum amount of money any actor gets if he belongs to the Screen Actors Guild. This went through the whole business. Cameramen, actors, producers—their agents would up 'em, up 'em, up 'em. I knew a hell of a lot of people in the business that were not working (and would

Previous page: Cinematographer Jacques (now Jack) Marquette, long active in movies and (especially) television, once combined his love of science fiction and a desire to make movies into a short-lived producing career.

like to keep working), that would be *more* than pleased to work for scale. Consequently, I got together with a writer-friend of mine, Ray Buffum, and we wrote *Teenage Thunder* [1957], a drag race movie. Sweet old guy, Ray; I paid him out of my pocket for it.

And you also raised the money to make the film.

I had been raising the money all along. I finally got it all together, hired a director named Paul Helmick and cast it. We shot about two days when all of a sudden I got a phone call from an outfit in New Orleans called Howco International. Somehow they'd gotten a copy of the script — I don't know how! — and they wanted to talk to me about getting together. They wanted to contribute to make it, and they would distribute it. I had a board of directors, about five guys, and we talked this over — it was like money from heaven, because we knew damn well that we were thin on what we were doing. And, naive as we were in business, we went for it. Howco made up the contract and it seemed okay. We made the picture, made the prints, Howco released it and it did pretty good.

"Did good" for them or for you?

[Laughs.] For *them*! Howco was a dishonest outfit, one of too many distributors who take your product and "creatively account" their costs, leaving you, the independent producer, without a dime. After *Teenage Thunder* — but *before* we knew what thieves they were — Howco wanted to make some more pictures with us. I told 'em, "Well, you'll have to put up *all* the money. We don't have the money to do it" — 'cause we hadn't received any money from Howco on *Teenage Thunder* yet. So I had Ray Buffum write another story, *The Brain from Planet Arous*. I wrote about twenty pages of a treatment, because I wanted to give Ray an idea of what I was trying to do. He got the idea, and he did real well. Eight days, we shot it in; we paid everybody scale.

Where did your idea for Brain *come from?*

It was a story which I had sort of halfway stolen from *Amazing Stories*. I used to read that, *Astounding Science Fiction*, all of those — I loved science fiction. One of them ran a story about a guy on the beach in the summer, and this thing came out of the ocean, went up into his foot and took him over. So I used that idea. John Agar and Robert Fuller are scientists working out of a house in the desert, and their equipment tells them that radiation is emanating from one of the mountains in the desert nearby. When they get there, they're attacked by the Brain from Planet Arous, which kills Fuller and takes over Agar's body. We shot those scenes in the cave at Bronson Canyon.

According to The Hollywood Reporter, *your shooting title was* Superbrain.

We never called it that. What *The Hollywood Reporter* and *Variety* would do is this: They'd call me up and ask, "What pictures have you got start-ing?" I'd say, "Well, we're about to do. . ."—whatever it was. They'd say, "What other ones are coming up?" "At the moment, we don't have any other ones." And then they'd say, "Well, just make up some titles and tell 'em to me!" *[Laughs.]* Honest to God!

What was your budget on Arous?

The budget, as I recall, was about fifty-eight thousand dollars. I did all the optical effects in the camera; otherwise, it would have cost probably five hundred dollars for *one* effect.

Where did you shoot your interiors?

My neighbor Walter Studt was an optometrist, and he had a much bigger house than we had. We used his house, and also part of the backyard, I think. We were there about three or four days. (Part of the film we shot in my house, too.) This neighbor also came up with the silver contact lenses for John Agar to wear when the alien brain was in control of his mind. John Agar didn't like 'em, but he wore 'em—he had no choice! It was very uncomfortable for Agar, the lenses could not be worn for more than fifteen minutes at a time.

What do you remember about your brain prop?

We told the people who were going to make it what we wanted, and that we wanted lights inside. It was made of plastic and held up with wires. Later on, after we finished the picture, my kids got a-hold of it and put on a show. They'd get other kids together, charge 'em five cents and put on a show with the brain in there *[laughs]*!

Where'd it eventually go? In the garbage?

That's right. That's where everything eventually goes *[laughs]*!

Dale Tate, the associate producer, was also the voice of the brains.

That's right. Dale Tate was a guy that worked for Consolidated Film Labs, which did all the processing of our films. He was dying to be an actor, but never quite made it. He did the voices for the brains and also played a scientist. Later on, he played the TV announcer in *Attack of the 50 Foot Woman.*

What made you think of Nathan Juran as director?

I think we had worked together on something in the past. We got together and talked a little bit, and I hired him. He worked for scale, too.

Next you did Teenage Monster, *a Western with a werewolf-ish monster.*

That one we originally called *Monster on the Hill.* We hired a director, looked at all the locations, did all the casting; I was going to photograph it,

According to Marquette (and everybody else!), the problem-plagued horror Western *Teenage Monster* was the least of his 1950s films.

and we were going to start on a Monday. The director came up to me on Sunday and he said, "Jack, I can't do the picture. I've got a fourteen-week deal at Universal, and I have to take it." Well, what could I do? I called another board of directors meeting, and they said, "It's too late to stop it, and we can't call in another director on one day's notice. *You* direct it, Jack." It was one of those things—when you've got the ball, you've got to run. So I became a member of the Screen Directors Guild, five thousand dollars worth, and I went ahead. It was my first and only directing job.

Who dreamed up the plot for Teenage Monster?
I think that just came from a talk I had with Ray Buffum. We talked a little about it, and he took it from there. To play the Teenage Monster, we hired Gil Perkins, with whom I'd worked in the past. He was basically a stuntman from Australia, a real nice guy. He was about six feet five inches tall and I knew I needed a tall guy for the monster. We had special boots on him that raised him up about four more inches, and so (in relation to other people) he was pretty tall. We couldn't give him any dialogue, other than the grunts and groans and stuff like that.

Watching the film, it looks as though Perkins is delivering dialogue, even though grunts and groans is all we hear.
No, the grunts and groans were intended from the beginning. There *was*

some dubbing. The women in the film [Anne Gwynne and Gloria Castillo] were supposed to intuitively understand — almost like a pet dog — what the creature meant and wanted. English was not spoken by the creature on the set, he grunted and emoted, but this is what was intended, poor dubbing and looping aside.

Where was Teenage Monster *shot?*
We were shooting out at a place called Melody Ranch, which was a big old Western street way out in the Valley. I'd hired another cameraman — I didn't want to have *that* chore, too! — and the first day of shooting was all what we call "day-for-night" scenes. The editor got the rushes the next morning, and he came driving out to where we were shooting and he said, "We can't print any of this stuff, we can't do *any*thing with it." Shooting day-for-night is an *art,* and this cameraman evidently didn't know how to do it. He had under-exposed the film so much it couldn't be printed, there was no image on it! Howco found out about it and they said, "Fire the cameraman." I said, "No, I'm not going to do that. He's just given me another job to do" — which was to watch *him*! Anyway, what had been an eight-day picture was now a seven-day picture, because a whole day had been lost. But I went ahead and completed it, and it was *bad,* naturally. For instance, when situations called for a closeup or a tight two-shot instead of a master shot, we couldn't do it, we had to stay with the master. We couldn't "punch up" situations that *should* have been "punched up" in a closer shot, I knew I had no time to do it. *Teenage Monster* was produced on a budget of fifty-seven thousand dollars with a full I.A. [the International Alliance of Theatrical State Employees] union crew.

How was the special effect of the falling meteor achieved?
With sparklers. Held by my hands with a black felt covering, then superimposed over the landscape shots.

After these three films, you figured out that the people at Howco were only looking out for themselves.
[Laughs.] It was the typical thing. The exhibitors cheat the distributors, and the distributors cheat the producers. For instance, just recently when Art Buchwald sued Paramount over *Coming to America* [1988]; even the *judge* said how ridiculous the accounting was. It's always been that way. For each picture, Howco would send me producer's reports which showed the amounts of money received in the different areas where the pictures had played. And it was almost impossible to figure out if the pictures were profitable or not. Maybe there'd be thirty or forty different areas where the pictures were released, and (for instance) some of the drive-ins reported rain, which means no income from there on those days. The majority of the problem, in *my* case,

was that I had no real business experience. We tried to force the issue in a suit against Howco, and one of their claims was that the pictures was "cross-collateralized." (There was never anything in the contract that said that, but that's what they claimed.) That means that if one picture makes a profit and the other makes a loss, Howco "evens it out." There are so many areas where they can cheat you; you can't tell how many theaters the thing played in, or how many nights or days it played, unless you had somebody there taggin' along. We just got our salaries, on all three pictures. On paper, *Teenage Thunder, The Brain from Planet Arous* and *Teenage Monster* all lost money and returned nothing to the thirty investors in Marquette Productions.

Why did you photograph these films, when you already had all the producing responsibilities?

The dual roles of director of photography and producer grew out of my previous role as a camera operator. My career in the film union hierarchy was stagnated. To jump the next step up to director of photography required (by union rules) that a producer hire me as d.p. and (by union contracts) producers can only do that when nearly all available d.p.'s are working. So, as producer, I hired *myself,* at an opportune time.

Did you derive more creative satisfaction directing, producing or photographing your pictures?

Photographing was always the most satisfactory task. Producing — secondarily. Directing was not my favorite job — dealing with agents, actors and egos was not enjoyable. In photographing, I feel more directly involved with the medium and process of filmmaking, rather than the personalities and bureaucracy that seem, so often, to get in the way.

Who came up with Attack of the 50 Foot Woman?

If I remember right, Bernie Woolner had the idea for that, and we had this friend of mine, Mark Hanna, write it. (Nice sweet guy. He still owes me two thousand dollars!) Bernie was one of the producers on *50 Foot Woman,* he was the one that actually put all the money situation together. He was a theater owner in New Orleans — I think he had two drive-in theaters, which then were very lucrative. (Drive-in owners could take a picture, play it, and then tell the distributor, "We got fogged in, we couldn't play it." Then they'd keep all the money! As I said before, that was typical of exhibitors.) Anyway, Bernie was a real sharp guy, and he'd made at least one or two pictures years before.

Talk about your special effects on 50 Foot Woman.

Making Allison Hayes fifty feet tall was another optical effect. We had to shoot the background that she was going to be walking in front of, then we had to shoot her separately, on a stage covered with black velvet. We had to light her so that she was totally lit all over, because anyplace where there was

A big hand for the little lady: Allison Hayes has a close encounter in Marquette's *Attack of the 50 Foot Woman*.

dark or shadow, the background image would bleed through. The lab would put the two together. We built a giant hand for her; the miniature electrical tower; and also a miniature house. We either built these things ourselves, or we paid to have 'em built. We also built the interiors of the outer space giant's spaceship; that was built out of pegboard. The giant was played by a guy named Mike Ross, who also had another part in the film, as the owner of the bar. The last time I heard of him, he was a used car salesman in the San Fernando Valley.

Where was the film shot?

Partly in an old house near Beverly Hills, a house that was sort of built like a castle. We did quite a bit of it in there. It was very expensive to rent the place, like five hundred dollars a day. The exteriors were mostly shot in a canyon near my residence in Tarzana.

Nathan Juran directed again.

"Jerry" Juran was another one of these directors (they're basically all the same) who don't give a goddamn about your budget. That's *your* problem. They want to shoot on and on and *on*. So he and I went through arguments like you can't believe. I said, "Keep it up and you're gone." And I meant it, too—I had no choice.

He must have been better on Brain from Planet Arous, *or you wouldn't have rehired him for* 50 Foot Woman.

There was a *beginning* of that argument with him on *Arous.* Juran was good in the respect that he knew what he was doing and he completed each day's work in the proper sequence and in the proper time — *until* he got to certain things, and then he'd get a little stiff about 'em. That's when I'd lower the boom.

He did both pictures under the name Nathan Hertz.

He's like so many people, they have a real ego. He felt that his name was well-known (or *some*thing!), and he would be put down if people saw that these were his pictures. He didn't want people to know that he would make that cheap a picture.

Any memories of star Allison Hayes?

She seemed like a very nice gal, very willing. Not like a lot of the actors and actresses today; today, they think they know more than the producers or the directors and they don't give a damn about the budget. After the picture was done, she became involved with this director, a guy I didn't think could even direct traffic. She got hooked on this guy, who was about five feet three inches tall; *he* never got a divorce from his previous wife and he was boozing pretty good. At the rate he boozed, he has to be dead by now.

The 50 Foot Woman *script ended with Hayes crushing William Hudson in her giant hand while Hudson shoots up her face with bullets.*

I chose, together with Juran, to omit this ending in favor of a slightly less violent one. It seemed at the time too violent, and not really necessary to serve the purposes of the plot.

Most of the humorous business in the film is not *in the script. What made you decide to "spoof it up"?*

No "spoofing" was ever intended. It was an exploitation film, simply that. Think of it as an honest period piece.

And the fact that people derive so much fun from it — does it hurt your feelings that people laugh at the film you made seriously?

No. I made it seriously, and I made it in the contingency of what I had to make it with. I know that *initially* people didn't laugh at it; *I* didn't laugh at it. But you have much more "intellectual" people that look at it and laugh. They have no idea of what it was like at that particular time. You can look at comedies from forty years ago today, and *some* of that comedy stands up. *Most* of it doesn't.

Allison Hayes' growing techniques are revealed in this behind-the-scenes glimpse at the special effects of Marquette's *Attack of the 50 Foot Woman*.

You released 50 Foot Woman *through Allied Artists.*

Right. We had a budget from Allied Artists of ninety-nine thousand five hundred dollars to complete it. When we completed it, it came in at eighty-nine thousand dollars. There *were* a few optical effects I would have liked to improve, but unless you do it right at the time that you're shooting it, you have to go *back* to do it over again and, my God, the expense is terrific. Allied

Artists told us we should go back and improve some of the effects. Well, it would have probably cost twenty thousand dollars. I said, "My friends, *that's* the picture. Period." So they had to buy it, what could they do?

Was Allied Artists a more honest place to work for than Howco?
Oh, yes, far more. Allied Artists reported over four hundred thousand dollars at the box office on *50 Foot Woman*. I think I owned twenty percent of that picture, and my share finally ended up about eighty thousand dollars net.

You photographed several films for Roger Corman. How did you hook up with him?
Roger Corman's "legend" is well-earned: He's too stingy to believe. I had worked on one of his pictures where what he had done was this: There was an independent picture [*Diary of a High School Bride,* 1959] that Roger either had something to do with, or maybe he just found out about, and Roger had his eye on the sets. He had one of his writers knock out a screenplay that would make use of *this* picture's sets! So as soon as the first picture quit, *he* went in there and used every set they had and he made his own picture, which was *A Bucket of Blood.* I think that was my first time working with him. Later on, he decided he was going to make two pictures in Puerto Rico [*Battle of Blood Island* and *Last Woman on Earth,* both 1960] and I was going to be the director of photography. He drew up all the contracts and I was to get two percent of each picture's gross; he didn't want to pay me, he wanted me to defer. You can't do that; [by union rules] I had to be paid at least scale. I got off the plane at Puerto Rico, and Roger was right there. Whenever you arrive in Puerto Rico by plane, Puerto Ricans give you a free drink at the airport—"Welcome to Puerto Rico!" Well, *Roger* was there for the free drinks *[laughs]*!

He said to me, "Do you realize that the cost in Puerto Rico is twenty-five percent *more* than it is in the United States?" I said, "What are you trying to tell me, Roger?" He said, "I've rented a house, a big mansion, and we're all going to stay in this mansion" [rather than at a hotel]. I said, "Oh? I don't think *I'll* stay there." We went to look at it: The place had about four or five bedrooms, and in each bedroom they had four or five army cots. It was like a dormitory. I also remember that there were two big deep-freezers in the "mansion," filled with all kinds of frozen food. I said, "Wait a minute. Where are we going to put all the film?"—we had to keep the film frozen as much as possible before the high humidity got to it. So we threw all the goddamn frozen stuff out of the freezers and put the film cans in there. Then they went and got some more freezers and put the meat back *in,* which means it's refrozen meat!

I told him, "Roger, I'm not staying here." This was still five days before we were supposed to start shooting, so he had plenty of time to get somebody else to come. So Roger and I got into his Volkswagen and he showed me another place I could stay if I wanted, a cabana on a major hotel. A cabana off the swimming pool. No bathroom, no place to eat, and there would have been drunks and people using the pool until two, three in the morning. No way! Finally, after all day looking at all these different horseshit places, he took me to the Caribe Hilton. I said okay, I'd stay there. *Now* what happened is that, all the people that were staying at the "mansion" came into town on the weekend. They'd come to my hotel and eat dinner with me, and I'd sign the check for all of 'em *[laughs]*!

Corman ended up making three *pictures there.*

It was so cheap to make pictures in Puerto Rico that Roger did decide to make a third picture *[Creature from the Haunted Sea]*. By this time, I was ready to go home; I told him, "If this third picture takes over eight days, I'm gone. I can't stay. I've got commitments and so forth." He said, "Okay, we'll do it in eight days." Meanwhile, his secretary never paid the bill at the Caribe, the bill for me and the other people I'd signed for. I told Roger, "Your girl hasn't paid the bill. They won't let me out until the bill's paid." He said he'd talk to her. *Another* couple of days go by, and still the bill is unpaid. I said, "Roger, if this bill isn't paid, you're not going to be able to release *any* of these three pictures you've made because part of 'em *is going to be missing.*" 'Cause I had the negatives *[laughs]*! *That's* when Roger finally paid the bill and I went home!

Did he at least give you creative freedom in how you shot these films?

Roger did give me complete photographic freedom—he was too busy with logistic problems to solve. As long as my suggestions did not cost any extra money, it was fine.

How did you get involved on Flight of the Lost Balloon?

Barney Woolner and I had done *Attack of the 50 Foot Woman* together and that was very successful, so when he got *Flight of the Lost Balloon* going and realized that he couldn't do it all by himself, I had to put in money. I put in (I forget how much) cash, and then also I put my house up as collateral with the film lab. Then we went ahead and started to make the picture in Puerto Rico. One incident that stands out in my mind about *Flight of the Lost Balloon* was the day we shot a scene where the two stars, Marshall Thompson and Mala Powers, were supposed to run over to the hot air balloon, climb in and take off. (Of course, we didn't *have* a hot air balloon, just the basket and some straps going up from it.) We rounded up all the blacks we could get and we had them playing cannibals, and they were supposed to be chasing Marshall and Mala and trying to catch the balloon. Instead, they're standing and just running in place *[laughs]*! Nathan Juran was directing, and I said to him, "We can't get by with this!" And he looked at me and said *[sneeringly]*, "Let 'em write letters." He had *that* kind of an attitude.

Marquette's main memory of *The Strangler* involves star Victor Buono's avoidance of the shower.

Just the opposite of the problem he gave you on Attack of the 50 Foot Woman.

Well, by that time he was probably getting very annoyed with me because we were running into problems in Puerto Rico; a lot of the people that we'd hired there were striking.

Any memories of photographing a thriller called The Strangler *[1964]?*

That was for a director named Burt Topper, with whom I've worked a few times. One thing I remember about *The Strangler* is that we were working on a stage at Paramount, and it was a scene where Victor Buono (who *was* the Strangler) was supposed to go into a shower that this woman [Diane Sayer] was in. The woman was supposed to be nude. And Buono said, "No way I'll go in there with her nude." He wouldn't go in there *[laughs]*! So that loused Burt up!

How about shooting Burnt Offerings *with Oliver Reed?*
    That was a thing we did in Oakland, in a big old house up there. The director was Dan Curtis, and this supposedly was his "biggie." He would have us set up in a corner for a shot of a whole room. We'd get the room lit properly, which might take a half hour or more. Then he'd come back and say, "No, now I want to do it from *that* corner over *this* way." *[Laughs.]* One day we were having lunch, and Curtis' assistant came over and said that Curtis' daughter had jumped off a building in Pasadena—committed suicide. Drugs. He said, "We're shutting down the production." So everybody went home. Some time later, they were ready to start back up, and my agent felt that I should be paid for all the time that production was shut down—which, by union rules, I *was* entitled to. I said, no, this shutdown was *not* the type that called for that, and they didn't have to pay me anything for the time we didn't work. The next thing I know, I find out that they don't want to use me for the balance of the picture. It wasn't until later that I found out that, sure enough, my agent had sent these earlier letters [demanding full payment]. So I got rid of *him*.

Of all your pictures, 50 Foot Woman *is the one with the big following. Is it your favorite of the bunch?*
    No, I liked *The Brain from Planet Arous* best, maybe because I wrote the initial treatment. I like science fiction so much, and I thought that was more "authentic" to science fiction than the others. It was exciting to see it realized. I think from time to time that a sequel would be worth doing. Know any investors?

I don't like gore pictures, I won't see them.
I make 'em, but I don't have to look at 'em!

Cameron Mitchell

NO ONE EVER SAID THAT LIFE WAS FAIR (especially not in the film business!), but it's still a cruel irony that Cameron Mitchell, the intense, dark-haired leading man of many a celebrated Broadway play and Hollywood hit, should wind up the human emblem for the low-rent horror and slasher flicks of the recent past. Over the past dozen years, he has appeared in such dross as *The Toolbox Murders, Frankenstein Island, Space Mutiny* and *Screamers,* a far cry from the caliber of films and the type of celebrities with whom he was associated during the 1940s and 1950s when he was a rising star at MGM and Fox. The only one who *isn't* complaining, it seems, is Mitchell himself: Now in his 70s, he's only too happy to still be working steadily, and in some ways, he says, he is pleased about having enjoyed some of the unique acting opportunities which an actor gets only by working the wrong side of the Hollywood tracks.

Scotch/German/Irish Cameron McDowell Mitzel was born in Dallastown, Pennsylvania, one of seven children of a country minister. At 18 he told his parents he wanted to become an actor, and was promptly disowned by his father who intended for Cam to become a minister like himself ("He forgave me when I did the voice of Jesus Christ in *The Robe*!"). Arriving in New York with a thick Pennsylvania Dutch accent (he had never used a telephone or an elevator, or been in a movie house or a restaurant), Mitzel held the usual variety of odd jobs (42nd Street movie house usher, mail clerk, dishwasher) while at the same time beginning a letter-writing campaign to all the big-name Broadway producers and actors. The legendary husband-and-wife acting team of Alfred Lunt and Lynn Fontanne took an interest in Mitzel (Fontanne got him to change his name), and he stage-debuted in the Lunt/Fontanne play *The Taming of the Shrew* in 1939. After doing his part in World War II (as an Air Force bombardier), Mitchell got an MGM screen test through the auspices of actor/director Richard Whorf, an old friend from his stage acting days, and was signed to a Metro contract the following day. Mitchell appeared in a number of MGM films and then reached what he considers the apex of his career when he appeared as Happy Loman in the Pulitzer Prize–winning stage production of *Death of a Salesman* (1949) under the direction of Elia Kazan.

After several more years in Hollywood, Mitchell broke into TV (he starred in NBC's long-running *The High Chaparral*) and began globetrotting, turning up in dozens of mini-budgeted horror and action items in every corner of the world (including 30 films made behind the Iron Curtain!). Now filling the void left by John Carradine as the patron saint of rock-bottom horror movies, Cameron Mitchell looks back over a long career in horror, sci-fi and exploitation.

Your first science fiction film was Flight to Mars, *made in 1951.*

Flight to Mars I made for Monogram, and they had high hopes for it. We had to shoot it in like five days, and I remember I said to them, "How the hell can you shoot this in five *days*?", but they did! The technical stuff—the miniatures and special effects—were done by another unit. It was fun to work at Monogram, and they knew it was gonna make a ton of money, which it did. And, by the way, it was that picture that put the Mirisch brothers on the map.

Previous page: **From Hollywood classics** *(Death of a Salesman, Les Miserables, Love Me or Leave Me)* **to rock-bottom exploitation fodder: The Cameron Mitchell story.**

Men meet Martians on the Red Planet in Monogram's Cinecolor *Flight to Mars*. Left to right, Morris Ankrum (in spacesuit), John Litel, Virginia Huston, Cameron Mitchell, Richard Gaines.

Flight to Mars opened the door for Walter Mirisch, who zoomed to the top as a producer not long after doing this one little film.

Did you enjoy working with costars Marguerite Chapman and Arthur Franz?
　　Marguerite Chapman was a doll, an absolute doll; Arthur Franz, I haven't seen or heard from him in years. I remember that I really enjoyed doing that film; I don't know why, but I did! It was interesting because it was primitive and it was second-class, but a lot of the things that they did in the real space program *we* did in that film *[laughs]*! I'm embarrassed to look at it today because my performance was awful.

How did working at Monogram compare to working at the larger studios?
　　They weren't calling it Monogram then, they had a fancy name for it, Allied Artists—years later, a picture I did with Mario Bava, *Blood and Black Lace,* was a big hit for them. Needless to say, the larger studios were better— Lesley Selander [director of *Flight to Mars*] was strictly a B picture director, of course, and you had to go very fast. I do remember that John Litel, who was a good actor, was in it, and he had a lot of scientific razzmatazz to say.

Well, he was having trouble, and starting to perspire *[laughs]* — it happens to an actor! Finally I went to Selander and I said, "For God's sake, write it on a board for him — put it on a card!" That's what they finally did, and he got it.

The producers promised a sequel, Voyage to Venus.

Voyage to Venus was never made. But I remember that they did talk to me about it.

Did you enjoy working in these older sci-fi and horror films?

Many years ago, I liked every picture — and today, I don't like *any* *[laughs]*! As a kid, to see a movie was a joy for me, and there *were* no bad films — to my mind, every film was great. I used to see triple features when I was in New York, going to drama school; you saw three pictures for a dime. I made six dollars and seventy cents a week, and had to live on that, but for a dime I could see three movies! So I used to sit through 'em twice, no matter what they were. Today I don't like any movies. I don't like Stallone, I don't like (what's his name?) Clyde Westwood, I don't like Bronson, none of 'em. They made 'em better in the old days. I watch American Movie Classics to see guys like Gary Cooper, who was a very underrated actor, Clark Gable (I did three films with Gable), Spencer Tracy, the true greats.

In general, do you enjoy science fiction in films or literature?

Some of it is very good, like Ray Bradbury's stuff; George Orwell's *1984* was good. Yeah, I do enjoy it. I saw a flying saucer years ago, and I do believe in those things.

Where did you see a flying saucer?

In the Saskatchewan, about forty years ago. I've also been operated on by a doctor, a very religious man, by the name of Alex Orbito in Manila. I had heard about him, and when I got a chance to do a film in Manila, I really went not to make the film as much as to see Orbito, because I knew I had to have a big operation. He performed it, and it worked. He operated on me with his hands — he did three big operations, cut me with his fingers. He's now a close friend of Shirley MacLaine — in fact, she wrote a whole chapter about him in her book.

At Twentieth Century-Fox you appeared in the classic musical fantasy Carousel.

That was from the play *Liliom* by Ferenc Molnár. Originally Frank Sinatra was supposed to play the lead part in that, and we were all on location in Boothbay Harbor, Maine — beautiful place. Frank and I had left California on a Thursday, and on Sunday Frank *quit*. But we had prerecorded all of his songs, including a duet with me! It was a comedy number and we had a long sustained note, and I was very nervous about it because I'm no singer, and I

Exhibitor Edwin Zabel and Mitchell, joined by actresses Barbara Ruick and Joanne Woodward, at a showing of Mitchell's musical/fantasy *Carousel.*

had heard that Frank only did things one time. But it came off. We had a one hundred fifty-piece symphony orchestra conducted by Alfred Newman and I was scared to death, but luckily we did it.

Why did Sinatra walk off the picture?

Several reasons. One, I think, was that he wanted Judy Garland to play the girl, but Shirley Jones got the part—she had done *Oklahoma!* [1955] and she was a very nice girl. The second thing was, we were going to do the picture in fifty-five mm, but the camera made so much noise that we had to do it twice, once in fifty-five and once in thirty-five. And Frank's basic reason for walking off the film was that he felt he should be paid twice if he had to do it twice. They sued him, and he settled the lawsuit by agreeing to do *Can-Can* [1960]. I heard his recordings, by the way, all of them, and when I saw him recently in Palm Springs I said, "Frank, I wish to God you had done *Carousel* because I never heard you in such great voice." And he said, "Cameron, that was the greatest my voice ever has been in my life." Gordon MacRae sang it on the nose, Gordon had a great set of pipes, but he didn't have what Frank had. I still think that Frank's sorry he didn't do it.

Well, when Frank walked off the picture we were stuck in Boothbay

Mitchell unveils James Whitmore's hideous *Face of Fire*.

Harbor without a leading man. And at one point the director and all the executives wanted *me* to play that part, and I thought I was gonna get it, but I was sold out by my agent at MCA and they finally gave it to Gordon MacRae. And that was the last film Gordon made.

Carousel *was a very expensive picture, wasn't it?*
    Carousel was the most expensive film made until *Cleopatra* [1963] — the film cost a fortune. Because they redid some of the musical numbers six times, and that's money! And when they ran it for the first time for Darryl Zanuck and Buddy Adler and all the other Fox executives, they all said, "Jesus, what a mistake we made. If we had put Mitchell in there, we'd have had a new star." That's true. I've missed out on a lot of things like that.

One of the better horror films you did was the Swedish-made Face of Fire.
    The original story was written by Stephen Crane, author of *The Red Badge of Courage,* and was called *The Monster.* In the story, "the monster" was a black man from the South, which gave it an added dimension, but for the film they made him white and James Whitmore played him. [Director] Albert Band, going over to Sweden on the plane, met Clare Boothe Luce, and she told him *The Monster* was one of the three best stories she had ever read.

How did you enjoy working in Sweden?

I loved working in Sweden because we worked at Svensk Filmindustri and I met Ingmar Bergman — they pronounced the *g* like a *y*, Ingmar *Ber-ry-mon*. He reminded me so much of Kazan. We had a deal, we were going to do *Siddhartha* by Hermann Hesse in India, and I was very excited about it. But at the last moment, he pulled out — Hesse was still alive, and Bergman said, "I'm so insecure. I can only do my own things." Finally somebody did a terrible, synthetic, sugary version of *Siddhartha,* but, boy, it could have been a great film.

Why was Face of Fire *done in Sweden?*

Because I think they had most of the money there. It was shot in a town outside of Stockholm, a little town that looked like early America, and we did the interiors at Svensk Filmindustri in Stockholm, where Bergman did all his films. It was tough shooting, because we had a lot of rain — I think we had three good days in four months, and they were Sundays so we weren't working *[laughs]*! But I enjoyed my trip to Sweden, I love Sweden and I love the people there. I went back there later, after *The High Chaparral*, and they treated me like a king. There's a certain crayfish there for three weeks of the year, which you eat with fresh dill, and I once made a trip from Rome to Stockholm just to eat three dishes of that!

Were you happy with your performance in Face of Fire?

Yes, I liked it, I like that kind of low-key stuff. I also liked James Whitmore; the girl who played my wife, Bettye Ackerman, was the wife of Sam Jaffe. Robert Simon, Royal Dano, Richard Erdman — it was a fairly good cast. I felt *Face of Fire* was a pretty good film, although it probably could have been better. I don't think that I've ever been happy with anything I've done, I always see things I could have done better. I can't recall ever seeing a film I've made that I felt was absolutely right from my point of view, and I've never been truly happy with a performance. The closest I think I came was when I played Barney Ross in *Monkey on My Back* [1957], which was one of the first films on drug addiction.

You made a number of films for Mario Bava in the nineteen sixties, most notably Blood and Black Lace.

I did about six films with Mario Bava, I loved him, I thought in many ways he might have been the best director — certainly the best one I've worked with in Europe, and maybe the best of them all.

Better than Kazan?

I thought Mario was one of the greatest directors in the world. I've worked with Kazan, Orson Welles (I did his last film, *The Other Side of the Wind*

[1976]), John Ford, I've worked with the best. Bava's right up there. And when I think of the limited money he had and the corners he had to cut, it's unbelievable! He never had a really good script, but he could make a film out of anything. I remember the vampire film with Barbara Steele, *Black Sunday*—Bava was the first to use slow motion with the black horses and the coach and all that, and in actuality that was shot on a soundstage and they had about twenty feet to run and that was all! Only Bava with his mastery, his know-how, could have done that—he was a miracle man in the film world. He would use a little boy's wagon as a dolly, he did incredible things with nothing. I did one picture for him called *Knives of the Avenger* [1967] which was really a hodgepodge, but he made it so good—even with the dubbing, it was good. He was so clever! He made the first face mask—he could make a mask of your face and put it on anybody else. I always felt we would get together to make one of the great pictures of all time, but unfortunately we never did and he passed away. His son is now directing.

Bava certainly was a good cameraman.
   He was a *very* good cameraman. In *Knives of the Avenger* I wear a mask, an armored mask, you can't see my face, and I rape a young girl; I later meet her, and she doesn't know that it's me. Anyway, on the day we shot the rape scene, she had a couple of pimples on her face and I said to Mario, "Maybe we oughta shoot this in a few days..." He said, "*Che? Che?* Son of a bitch!" That's all he knew in English, "son of a bitch!" I said, "Mario—her *face!*" He said, "*Va bene!*", he put two or three lights in, and, by God, she looked gorgeous. I felt that the way he shot *Blood and Black Lace* was unbelievable, and it came out so good.

How close were you two personally?
   We were very close personally, very friendly. I really think that I was his favorite actor, because he would always call me. He was really a wonderful man and I loved him personally. There's a Mario Bava cult all over the world.

Blood and Black Lace *was fairly successful at the time.*
   Blood and Black Lace was a big release, made a lot of money. Eva Bartok was the female star, and I liked her very much—there was a big scandal about her years before, when she had had a baby by a leading member of the British royalty. We shot *Blood and Black Lace* in Rome.

How does working in Europe compare to making films in Hollywood?
   I loved Italy; you make better films in Hollywood, but I loved the Italian people, they were wonderful and friendly. I did a lot of co-productions with them in the Iron Curtain countries.

Nutty nobleman Cameron Mitchell demonstrates his carnivorous plants to anxious onlookers in *Island of the Doomed* (a.k.a. *Maneater of Hydra*).

Many of the Italian horror films make up for what they lack script-wise and acting-wise with rich color, lighting effects and striking decor.

Then it all comes down to who directs it. I felt that Bava was always in good taste.

Any general comments about the amount of globetrotting you've done?

Well, it's one way to see the world! I feel like Willy Loman, because I'm always packing my suitcases *[laughs]* — I don't think anybody's traveled more than I have. And I don't think anybody's made as many films as I have; I must have made close to three hundred.

You're adding in TV.

I'm talking strictly about *features*. I've never counted them, but I think I've done a thousand TV shows! Maybe this is awful to say, because I should have been more selective.

In what countries have you had the best filmmaking experiences?

I would say Italy; parts of Africa; Mexico I enjoyed. I had some pretty bad experiences in Yugoslavia; some terrible ones in the Philippines, because it's so hot over there you almost can't work.

Do you speak the languages in all these countries?

Yes, I did—I *had* to, in some of these films. I didn't know the tenses or grammar, but I could make myself understood. Many directors I worked with, including Bava, didn't know English at all. And so for other American actors, I could translate for them, too. I speak pretty good Italian, German and Spanish. You pick up that stuff—you *have* to.

Horror-wise, you next turned up in Island of the Doomed.

Island of the Doomed has made a lot of money for that producer, Jorje Ferrer. We shot it in a big estate near Barcelona; it was a dreadful film, but it's made a lot of bucks. Every time the producer needs money, he leases it to a cable company, and it's kept him going! I enjoyed playing the villainous Baron, although I didn't think the dubbing was very good.

What else can you recall about where the film was shot?

It was a very expensive house; the producers paid the people who owned the place five thousand dollars, which then was a lot of pesetas—and, believe me, the owners were sorry, because the crew did a great deal of damage. The crew laid dolly tracks and stuff like that; they cleaned the house before they left, but they didn't fix what they broke.

Did you enjoy working on the film?

Yes and no. It was a German/Italian/Spanish coproduction, and I enjoyed being in Spain. I saw a bit of Ava Gardner while there.

Around that same time you made Autopsia de un Fantasma *in Mexico.*

Right, with Basil Rathbone and John Carradine. Basil Rathbone in his mind was Don Quixote, and if you think about it—he was about seventy then—he *was* a perfect Don Quixote. That face, that aquiline nose! It's a damn shame that nobody ever did the real *Don Quixote* with Basil Rathbone, he was a brilliant actor. He was very neat, very well educated, read many books—and he was a great fencer, really one of the world's best. In *The Mark of Zorro* [1940], they had one of the greatest fencers in the world doubling Tyrone Power, but Rathbone did his swordwork himself, he was that good. The fencing scenes in *The Mark of Zorro,* because of Basil, were the best I've ever seen. And he was really one of the nicest men I ever met.

Did Rathbone seem unhappy to be in Autopsia de un Fantasma?

Not at all. We enjoyed it, and we had a good time in Mexico City—this was before the smog came, when it was still lovely. I don't think either Rathbone or Carradine spoke Spanish, or, if they did, just *poco [laughs]*—a *little.* And the director was an interesting man, Ismael Rodriquez—a bit crazy, a real wacky sense of humor. *Autopsia de un Fantasma* was a comedy which really did not come off, but it had its moments.

Mitchell says that his suggested script changes helped to turn the trick in the shock schlocker *Nightmare in Wax.*

You've worked in a few films that featured John Carradine. What were your impressions of him?

I liked John, he was a good old ham. I like ham if it's good, like Charles Laughton, one of the finest, a marvelous actor. Carradine was a fun person to work with, but he had a terrible arthritic condition in his knuckles and his feet—his toes curled up under the soles of his feet! He was playing the Devil in *Autopsia de un Fantasma,* and he tried to be light and limber. And of course it came across very funny—he was a very old, limping Devil *[laughs]*! Which really added to the humor, which Carradine was not even aware of!

Do you recall how you got involved on Nightmare in Wax?

I'm sure somebody just called me and asked me. [Director] Bud Townsend and I had worked together on a TV series called *The Beachcomber*—he directed about twenty-eight of 'em. They were having trouble with the script on *Nightmare in Wax,* and I told Bud, "Don't worry, we can fix anything"— we had fixed many terrible scripts on *The Beachcomber*. So on the first day of shooting I went to the Movieland Wax Museum in Buena Park, which is where the film was going to be made, I read the script for the first time and Bud said, "Well, Cam, you missed this time. There's no way we can save this." In the original script, my character skins the people—but if you skin people, there's a lot of blood, right? Well, it was impossible — you wouldn't have seen anything but blood, and I don't think anybody would allow us to do a film where we skinned like twenty people! It was way overboard in bad taste.

Then I said, "Well, gimme a few minutes. Let me think about it." So it was my idea to make a dream sequence out of it: The film opens with a phone call and ends with a phone call, and it was all a dream. That saved the picture, because it could not have been made the way it was written. I also created the scenes with the red-headed girl [Victoria Carroll] in the wax museum, where we're talking; the scene in the car, after I've killed her and I'm talking to her corpse. Those scenes I thought were interesting. We had all these ideas and we could have done more with the picture, but we just didn't have time. When you consider that we did that from scratch, it was a hell of a film.

Any problems entailed in shooting at a real wax museum?

No, it was really quite a thrill, especially because they had the Rolls-Royce there from *Sunset Boulevard* [1950], a picture I love, one of the greatest films ever made. What I thought was clever in *Nightmare in Wax* was when I was putting the finishing touches on these wax dummies, we were actually using the real people — they had to stay perfectly still. And they came out beautiful, especially some of the girls — they looked like works of art. Berry Kroeger was in it, he was a good actor; Anne Helm was a good actress, and she was very big then; Scott Brady played a detective; we had a pretty good cast. And, as I said, I also liked working with Bud Townsend. That was the first film that he did, and he was a very intelligent and fast director and he should have been one of the great ones in the business. He was damn good, and I loved Bud.

In nineteen seventy-seven, you did a very muddled suspense film called Haunts, *with May Britt.*

That was a strange film — I didn't understand a lot of it, and I don't know what [director] Herb Freed was trying to do. But they cut the end of it. At the end of the film now, the uncle, the part that I play, goes to the sink and turns the faucet and blood comes out. Then he hears the shower running, he walks over to it and parts the curtains, and there May Britt is, nude, and they embrace. The embrace was cut — taken out of the film — and I don't know why. It should have been left in — that would have shown that he was as crazy as she was, that madness ran in the family. It was an interesting film.

What can you tell me about May Britt?

She was wonderful, and lovely to look at. For the nude scene she covered her nipples — she looked naked, but there was tape on the nipples. We shot *Haunts* in some very lovely country above San Francisco, where no one is allowed to make any improvements — you have cattle grazing on farms by the sea up there. It was a great location.

Do you remember appearing in The Swarm *for Irwin Allen?*

Irwin Allen you can have *[laughs]*! I did a lot of work for Irwin, but I thought *The Swarm* was dreadful. It cost a lot of money, but the bees—it looked like there were two hundred and that's all! They had this all-star cast and a geriatric love story between Olivia de Havilland and Fred MacMurray, which didn't make much sense. And I remember Irwin Allen wanted me to cut my hair, to get a military haircut, and I said, "Okay, Irwin, for sixty thousand dollars, I'll cut it." So naturally I didn't cut my hair *[laughs]*!

Many horror fans probably remember you best for The Toolbox Murders.

Boy, did *that* make money! The producer, Tony Didio, he's now a big Hollywood producer. I have been in so many horrible little films that have "made" people! He now smokes ten dollar Cuban cigars, he goes to the Cannes Festival every year, and he made his fortune off that picture!

Did you actually play the killer in the murder scenes?

Yes, I did. In the scene where I chase the nude girl, we used a gal who was a porno star [Kelly Nichols]. I shot her in the head with a nail gun.

Does the type of gore seen in pictures like this influence young viewers?

I'm sure it does. I don't like gore pictures, I won't see them. I *make* 'em, but I don't have to *look* at 'em!

Was it a challenge playing this type of murderer?

I think I did enjoy the challenge. The scene where I sing to the girl I'm holding prisoner was my idea; I thought that actress was quite good, Pamelyn Ferdin. The lollipop I carry around, anything weird like that was my idea! A lot of the odd touches that were any good were mine *[laughs]*! The human touches—'cause even a killer is human, you know.

What about the sequel that we've been threatened with for years?

It's supposed to be done—I read that in the papers all the time.

What do you think of horror film fans?

Horror fans are interesting people. They love these kinds of things! I don't know how I got hooked up with this horror thing, 'cause I never thought of myself as a horror actor, but I am. I mean, once Vincent Price is dead, nobody's done more than I have!

You played a comic book–style mad scientist in the campy Supersonic Man.

I liked the director and the producer of that film, and I had a wonderful time doing it in Madrid. The dubbing was dreadful, and it was badly sold—it was a takeoff on *Superman* [1978], and it didn't quite come off. But the people involved on that were nice people.

What about The Silent Scream*?*

The Silent Scream made a lot of money; they tell me it's done over sixty million dollars. It had to have something going for it to do that kind of business; I thought Denny Harris, the director, was a creative guy. I remember them shooting the opening scene in slow motion, and thinking it wasn't much of an idea until I saw it. They did a hell of a job there and really set a mood for the picture.

Without Warning*?*

I don't remember much about that, except that I did have to wear some gross makeup. One film that I did around that same time was *The Demon,* and that I thought was a pretty good film; we shot that in Africa. *The Demon* had a kind of an E.S.P. angle to it, and I played an army colonel who's called in on a case. It was an interesting film, not all bad.

Raw Force, *about kung fu zombies?*

We shot that in Manila. It's so humid there because you're almost on the equator. You can go out to some of the outer islands and get a breeze, but most of the things I did were in Manila, and you couldn't really act. The only place where you were *halfway* comfortable was in your air-conditioned hotel room, because even in cars, even though they had air conditioning, you just perspired. I don't want to have to go back *there* again!

Cataclysm*?*

I went up to Salt Lake City, Utah, to work in that; Phil Yordan wrote and directed. Many years earlier he wrote the screenplay for a picture I was in called *No Down Payment* [1957]; if *No Down Payment* had been sold properly, I might have been close to getting an Oscar nomination. *Cataclysm* had to be done and redone four or five times, I don't know why, and I haven't seen it. Marc Lawrence was in that, too, playing two parts—I have no idea why they did that, but I thought he was very good. I think *Cataclysm* might have had some interesting things in it.

Do you still try to pitch in creatively on any of these horror things?

Oh, always. Some of the scenes are terrible! Years ago I helped out on a very good film called *Ride in the Whirlwind* [1965] with Jack Nicholson and Millie Perkins; I got top billing in that, and some people said it was the best Western ever made. They made it for like seventy thousand dollars and they shot it in Utah, and they lived on nothing. I got quite a bit of money out of 'em for the money they had, 'cause I didn't know how much of a skin-and-bones operation it was. It was written and produced by Jack and he was very good as an actor, and he was getting ready to *quit*! I really saved his skin: I said, "Jack, you *can't* quit, you're too good." I told him, "Beg, borrow or steal the money, but take this to a festival in Europe." He did, and it ran for thirteen months in the Champs Elysées in Paris! That's how he wound up in *Easy Rider* [1969]; instead of getting out of the business, he became one of the biggest stars. He owes a lot of that to me, I really helped him.

Are directors open to suggestions on these newer, schlockier pictures?
Some of them are, some of them aren't. The intelligent ones are.

Screamers? Frankenstein Island?
Don't remember 'em.

Blood Link, *with Michael Moriarty?*
I remember doing that in Berlin, and I'd never been there; I'd been to Germany, but never Berlin. And I loved Berlin, it was wonderful. I enjoyed doing the picture but I don't know what happened to it and I never saw it. The director, Alberto De Martino, was pleasant and the producer, Italo Zingarelli, was the Commissioner of Wines and Spirits for Italy. And he is as big as Orson Welles *[laughs]*!

One of your best supporting parts in recent years was as the gang boss in My Favorite Year *[1982].*
I'll tell you how that happened: I was having lunch one day with an Egyptian director in the MGM commissary, and Mel Brooks came by. "My God!" he said. "The star of my favorite picture!" I asked, "Mel, what's your favorite picture?" and he said, "*Gorilla at Large!*" At first I laughed, and then I understood because Anne Bancroft [Mrs. Brooks] was in that, and she is very good and very sexy in the film. Then he said, "Listen, how would you like to play Jimmy Hoffa in a movie?" and I said, "I would love to." [Director] Richard Benjamin did a helluva job on *My Favorite Year,* and as I did my scene I was not aware of the grunts and animal noises I was making—it was just the way it happened. I thought it was a great picture and that Peter O'Toole deserved the Award that year.

You've worked with Fred Olen Ray a time or two, most prominently in The Tomb. *Is he a good director?*
Well, he's a nice guy *[laughs]*! And for the amount of money he puts into these pictures, I guess he does all right.

You had another sadistic role in an anthology horror film called The Offspring.
I enjoyed making that because the Civil War is one of my favorite topics. We couldn't do the story of Sherman's March but we did the next best thing, a sergeant as wicked as Sherman, and I played that part in the film. Do you

A carnival background and a rampaging ape (George Barrows) added to the flavor of Fox's 3-D *Gorilla at Large* (1954) with Mitchell and Anne Bancroft.

remember the house that the maimed children lived in? In actuality, Sherman spent several nights in that house. We shot it there in Georgia, and I thought my segment of the story was good. And the kids, I thought, were wonderful.

Is it fun to work with today's aggressive, hurry-up young directors, or just hard work?

   It depends. Sometimes it's fun and sometimes you die gettin' up at 4:30.

Deadly Prey? Teenage Exorcist?

[Laughs.] Don't remember either of 'em!

Have you ever turned down a role?

I turn down a lot of things. In the last week alone, I must have turned down six offers — not that any of them were great things *[laughs]*! But I've just signed with a new agency, Contemporary Artists, I have a good agent and I'm very happy with him.

Do you think you'll ever retire from the business?

I can't really answer that . . . I don't think I could ever retire. If the right vehicle came along, I think the vinegar would work and the fire would still burn. But it doesn't burn for mediocre films anymore — I would like to do something good. And I think I will always like to do something good. But it's very difficult today to find a good script, to find a good director, and to find the kind of production we had years ago.

One of your newest flicks is Space Mutiny *with John Phillip Law.*

I had to wear a beard longer than Moses and it was awful. I couldn't eat, I couldn't smoke, I couldn't do anything *[laughs]*! I haven't seen the film.

What hopes do you have for your acting future?

I did a play at the Burt Reynolds Theater in Florida several years ago, *Family Planning,* written by Bill C. Davis, who I think is the finest young playwright in America. The play was about an old caretaker in a very poor old folks' home — it's a great part for me — and the play is about the fact that we don't know what to do about senior citizens. But it isn't all sad, it also has a lot of laughs and it's just the way life is. It's the only play I've ever done where, every performance, we got a standing ovation. Because it is a terrible thing, the way we treat seniors, and I feel that this play that Bill wrote could make a statement about that. This could be Academy Award time for me if we were to do this as a feature, and that is what we are trying to do. It's really very touching and funny.

Even though you're now in this low-budget rut, you've got a lot to be proud of overall.

It was my honor to be the first actor to read aloud the words of supposedly the greatest play in the history of the American theater, *Death of a Salesman.* I read it for Elia Kazan and Arthur Miller at the Taft Hotel, which was next to the Shubert Theater, in nineteen forty-eight. Kazan was directing a Kurt Weill musical, and between the matinee and evening performance we met in his room, we ordered dinner, they threw the script in front of me and Kazan said, "Read." I said, "The whole script?" and he said, "Yep." So I read the whole play, beginning to end, including all the characters. And they sat there with smiles on their faces, and not one word was changed. It was my privilege and honor, and luck I guess, to have been the first actor to read those wonderful words aloud. And I'm unique in another way: I did *The Taming of the Shrew* with Alfred Lunt and Lynn Fontanne, and that's considered the greatest comedy ever made. Sydney Greenstreet was in it, Celeste Holm, Richard Whorf, Thomas Gomez — a bunch of good people. So it was unique that I did the best tragedy and the best comedy.

Do you feel you've lived up to your early promise as an actor?

Sometimes yes. I came to Hollywood when Brando came out, and Montgomery Clift, and I was considered the third good Broadway actor from *Death of a Salesman,* and I feel that if I had been more selective my career might have fared better. I had a great, low-key part in a Kazan picture called *Man on a Tightrope* [1953], and the picture he did after that was *On the Waterfront* [1954]. And I was supposedly the number one choice for the lead and Brando was number two. But Kazan had a fight with Darryl Zanuck — I was under contract to Zanuck — and they didn't talk for like five years, so I lost *On the Waterfront.* So I've come close to some big things. But on the other hand, the way things have turned out, I did get a chance to experiment, and as an actor, a pure actor, I could do and try many things which you couldn't do in a major film. I have been lucky in many ways.

CAMERON MITCHELL FILMOGRAPHY

The Last Installment (MGM short, 1945)
The Hidden Eye (MGM, 1945)
A Letter for Evie (MGM, 1945)
They Were Expendable (MGM, 1945)
What Next, Corporal Hargrove? (MGM, 1945)
The Mighty McGurk (MGM, 1946)
High Barbaree (MGM, 1947)
Cass Timberlane (MGM, 1947)
Tenth Avenue Angel (MGM, 1948)
Homecoming (MGM, 1948)
Command Decision (MGM, 1948)
Leather Gloves (Loser Takes All) (Columbia, 1948)
Adventures of Gallant Bess (Eagle-Lion, 1948)
The Sellout (MGM, 1951)
Smuggler's Gold (Columbia, 1951)
Death of a Salesman (Columbia, 1951)
Man in the Saddle (Columbia, 1951)
Flight to Mars (Monogram, 1951)
Japanese War Bride (20th Century–Fox, 1952)
The Outcasts of Poker Flat (20th Century–Fox, 1952)

Okinawa (Columbia, 1952)
Les Miserables (20th Century–Fox, 1952)
Pony Soldier (20th Century–Fox, 1952)
The Robe (voice only; 20th Century–Fox, 1953)
Powder River (20th Century–Fox, 1953)
Man on a Tightrope (20th Century–Fox, 1953)
How to Marry a Millionaire (20th Century–Fox, 1953)
Hell and High Water (20th Century–Fox, 1954)
Gorilla at Large (20th Century–Fox, 1954)
Garden of Evil (20th Century–Fox, 1954)
Desiree (20th Century–Fox, 1954)
Strange Lady in Town (Warners, 1955)
Love Me or Leave Me (MGM, 1955)
House of Bamboo (20th Century–Fox, 1955)
The Tall Men (20th Century–Fox, 1955)
The View from Pompey's Head (20th Century–Fox, 1955)
Carousel (20th Century–Fox, 1956)
Tension at Table Rock (RKO, 1956)
Monkey on My Back (United Artists, 1957)
All Mine to Give (RKO/Universal, 1957)
Escapade in Japan (Universal, 1957)
No Down Payment (20th Century–Fox, 1957)
Face of Fire (Allied Artists, 1959)
Inside the Mafia (United Artists, 1959)
Pier 5 — Havana (United Artists, 1959)
Three Came to Kill (United Artists, 1960)
As the Sea Rages (Raubfischer in Hellas) (Columbia, 1960)
The Unstoppable Man (Sutton Pictures, 1961)
Last of the Vikings (L'Ultimo dei Vichingi) (Medallion Pictures, 1961)
Dulcinea (Nivi Films, 1962)
The Black Duke (Il Duca Nero) (Production Releasing Corp./Eldorado Pictures, 1963)
Caesar the Conqueror (Giulio Cesare il Conquistatore delle Gallie) (Medallion Pictures, 1963)
Erik the Conqueror (Fury of the Vikings) (AIP, 1963)
Dog Eat Dog (Ajay Film Co., 1964)
The Last Gun (Jim Il Primo) (British Lion/Spanish, 1964)
Blood and Black Lace (Sei Donne per l'Assassino) (Allied Artists, 1965)
Ride in the Whirlwind (Favorite Films, 1965)
Minnesota Clay (Harlequin, 1966)
Hombre (20th Century–Fox, 1967)
The Treasure of Makuba (Producers Releasing Organization, 1967)
Autopsia de un Fantasma (Rodriquez/Peliculas Nacionales, 1967)
Knives of the Avenger (I Coltelli del Vendicatore) (World Entertainment Corp., 1967)
Island of the Doomed (Maneater of Hydra) (Allied Artists, 1967)
Nightmare in Wax (Crown International, 1969)
Rebel Rousers (Four Star Excelsior, 1970)
Buck and the Preacher (Columbia, 1972)
The Big Game (Comet, 1972)
Slaughter (AIP, 1972)
The Midnight Man (Universal, 1974)
The Klansman (Paramount, 1974)

Political Asylum (Panamericana Films/IF, 1975)
Haunts (The Veil) (Intercontinental, 1977)
Viva Knievel! (Seconds to Live) (Warners, 1977)
Slavers (Lord Films/ITM, 1977)
The Swarm (Warners, 1978)
The Toolbox Murders (Cal-Am, 1978)
Texas Detour (Cinema Shares International, 1978)
Supersonic Man (Topar, 1979)
The Silent Scream (American Cinema Releasing, 1980)
Without Warning (The Warning) (Filmways, 1980)
Cataclysm (1980)
Captive (1980)
The Demon (Gold Key–Holland, 1981)
Texas Lightning (Film Ventures International, 1981)
Screamers (New World, 1981)
Raw Force (Shogun Island) (American Panorama, 1982)
My Favorite Year (MGM/United Artists, 1982)
Frankenstein Island (Chriswar, 1982)
Kill Squad (Summa Vista, 1982)
Blood Link (Zadar Films, 1982)
The Guns and the Fury (A&Z/Bordeaux, 1983)
Killpoint (Crown International, 1984)
Prince Jack (LMF Productions, 1985)
The Tomb (Trans World Entertainment, 1985)
Low Blow (Crown International, 1986)
The Offspring (From a Whisper to a Scream) (Conquest Entertainment, 1987)
The Messenger (Snizzlefritz, 1987)
No Justice (Richfield's Releasing, 1989)

Night Train to Terror (Visto International, 1985), a horror anthology, features Mitchell in a much-abridged version of *Cataclysm*. Mitchell also appears frequently in made-for-home video movies like *Swift Justice, Ninja Nightmare, Memorial Valley Massacre* (1989) and *Easy Kill* (1990) as well as made-for-TV movies. This list represents only a starting point for future compilers of his extremely convoluted (and confusing) filmography.

*I was always looking to sustain myself [in the business]
for a long period of time rather than ever being
a "star," so to speak, or going for "The Big Time."
That was never very important to me ... I have six children
and eleven grandchildren, a very happy marriage — it's been
that way for forty years. And that kind of solidification
was more important to me than being an unhappy star.*

Ed Nelson

A REALISTIC ACTOR JOINING THE ROGER CORMAN stock company during the maverick director's 1950s heyday came on the scene knowing that short pay and long hours were two of the few certainties attached to the job. In store for Ed Nelson was one of the widest assortments of roles enjoyed by any of the Corman regulars, from scientist to caveman, from gang leader to attorney, and from cops and robbers (sometimes in the same picture) to the giant fiberglass crustacean in *Attack of the Crab Monsters*. Behind-the-scenes, too, Hollywood newcomer Nelson tried his hand at many trades, working without credit (and sometimes without pay!) as a screenwriter, stuntman, location manager, wardrobe and prop man, alligator wrestler, cameraman and even producer (on Corman's *The Brain Eaters*).

Happily, it all paid off for Nelson, who went on to become one of television's most recognizable faces (1500 + performances, including five years on TV's hottest nighttime soap opera, *Peyton Place*). Backstage at the Catskill Actors Theatre in Highland Lake, New York, where he's appearing with Beverly Garland in a stage production of *The Gin Game*, Nelson is more than happy to talk about the days before his TV successes, when he paid his dues in movies like *A Bucket of Blood*, *Devil's Partner* and *Night of the Blood Beast*.

When was your first encounter with Roger Corman?

I met him when he came to Louisiana to do *Swamp Women* [1956]. At that point, I didn't know he was just starting out in the business; all *I* knew was, when everybody wanted to go to town 'cause it was Saturday, I would volunteer to stay in the jungle and watch the equipment. Roger was very grateful, and he helped me out a great deal in those early days. He's every bit as cheap as everybody says he is—that's what he calls "frugal." They tell a story about Roger, who I love dearly, that he made two or three pictures before he found out you could go "Take Two" *[laughs]*! I did a lot of work for him, for free, so that I could get parts in his pictures. Just like Jack Haze and Dick Miller and all the rest of 'em. He used us and we used him. But it was no more than that—it hardly ever got personal.

A lot of people have that attitude about Corman; people like Richard Devon just couldn't stand him after a while.

Well, Richard was brighter than a lot of us *[laughs]*, and I could understand that from him—Richard is theater and he's a noble person. I don't have time, really, to dislike Roger, I have no reason to. He was very kind to me. Yeah, he used me, but so what? I mean, I used him, too, if you want to use the term *used*. But I didn't know of a single person that worked with Roger and really was personal with him. I didn't know who went home with him and sat up and played cards—you know what I'm saying? Nobody, as far as I knew.

Previous page: **Before his days of TV prime-time success on *Peyton Place*, actor Ed Nelson had a baptism of fire in Roger Corman's notorious exploitation movies.**

So what exactly did you do for Corman on Swamp Women?

I did everything on that picture: I was the location manager, I wrestled the alligator, I held it up in the water so that Touch Connors — Mike — could wrestle it. The guy that brought that alligator out ran an alligator farm / snake farm on Highway 90, outside of New Orleans; now he is one of the wealthiest men in America, and lives in a compound with high walls outside of Atlanta. Very paranoid — he has guards with guns and carries guns and knives on him. A very short guy with a lot of muscles — and he invented Nautilus.

Two of your first films — Swamp Women *and* New Orleans Uncensored — *starred Beverly Garland.*

Beverly Garland was one of the first "stars," so to speak, that I ever worked with, and she has been consistent from that day to this. An underrated actress; even though people know who she is, people don't really know the work she can do. We've been very good friends over a period of time and I think the world of her.

Your very first film was The Steel Trap *[1952], wasn't it?*

That's right, I was an extra in that. *The Steel Trap* had a great director-and-producer husband-and-wife team, Andrew and Virginia Stone, and that was the first picture I was ever in. They were shooting at the old New Orleans airport and were using extras like crazy. Joseph Cotten and Teresa Wright were going to run up to the ticket counter, past a line of people, because they had to get on that plane — he had robbed his own bank and now she has convinced him to return the money, and he has to get the money back in. And it's turning out to be harder to get the money back in than it was stealing it in the first place *[laughs]*! I was the last one in the ticket line, and just before the first rehearsal the director Andrew Stone looked down the line and said, "You!" Everybody turned their heads looking back, back, back — I didn't know I was last, *I* looked back, too! I pointed to myself and said, "Me??" He said, "Yeah, come up here." So I came up, in front of my fellow New Orleans actors. Stone said, "You get in the front here." And here I am at the front of the line, at the ticket counter, and Joseph Cotten is gonna come up and stand next to *me*! And Teresa Wright! My God!!

So they rehearsed once — "Cue Joe and Teresa. Come on!" They come running in and the camera pans with them up to the counter and Joe goes into his dialogue. "Okay, good rehearsal," Stone says. Then he looks at me and he says, "You. What are you doing?" I say, "I beg your pardon?" He says, "What are you doing?" I say, "Well, I'm doing the same thing I thought I was doing at the back of the line." He says, "You're in the front of the line now!" When you see that picture, you'll be amazed, because I do the biggest non-acting job — I close my eyes real slow and open 'em real slow, almost do a half-yawn and I don't pay any attention to these people who come runnin' up screaming! It's absolutely embarrassing. Stone said to me, "Listen, I'm gonna give you some advice. Don't act." That was my first picture.

After you did Swamp Women, *how did you hook up again with Corman in Hollywood?*

I went to see him right away, because he and the crew were very good to me. I mean, I did a lot of work for 'em down there in New Orleans for very little, and I guess they thought I could make it. So I came out and I knocked on his door. He knew I had had training in production, so I gathered his wardrobe, I got his props together, I'd help rewrite the scripts—

So you worked on a lot of Corman pictures that you didn't act in.

Well, sure!

Where did you learn production?

In nineteen fifty-two, I went to New York to study direction and production. There was a school there called S.R.T.—School of Radio Technique—and it was live medium. You worked camera, direction, you worked switching, you worked the boom, everything. And I learned all about the production side of television there. It was a very good school. At the end of the six months, they put on a one-hour program and they invited all the network people in to watch it.

In nineteen fifty-three you were back in New Orleans working as an assistant director at WDSU-TV.

WDSU was the only station in New Orleans at the time, it was the NBC flagship of the South and I was the floor manager there. One of the guys working out there, doing a fifteen-minute sustained show, was Dick Van Dyke.

Then between nineteen fifty-four and nineteen fifty-six you narrated a show called N.O.P.D.

N.O.P.D. was a series that a buddy of Jack Webb's, Stacy Harris, starred in. It was shot in New Orleans and it was shot with a group that used to do the trailers for motion pictures—Motion Picture Advertising was the name of the production company. I wrote some of those because the guy that wrote 'em was drunk half the time and he couldn't come up with 'em, so he hired me for one hundred dollars a script. Because I narrated that series, I knew I couldn't act in it also, so I wrote one where the heavy didn't have any lines— but you saw him throughout the episode. So I played in that one. (And I had acted in a couple of other ones before they decided I was going to narrate it.)

You arrived in Hollywood with one hundred five dollars in your pocket.

Well, it was in my *wife's* pocket *[laughs]*. We had three kids at the time,

Stardom at last: Somewhere underneath all that heavy fiberglass, Ed Nelson is playing the title role in *Attack of the Crab Monsters*.

and I got a job—I never felt that I couldn't get a job, earn enough to support my family.

What did playing the crab in Attack of the Crab Monsters *entail?*

Weight, mostly. The crab was made by Dice, Inc., and it was a heavy piece. What they did was, they had piano wires on the end of every elbow of the crab, and on a long stick way up in the air they had these wires connected. And people out of the frame would be holding these sticks. They would alternate picking them up and lowering them, so the legs would move. That worked fine. Inside the crab was a hole no bigger than maybe four feet, and I would get in there. They would put pads on my shoulders and I would bend over and pick up the body of the crab and walk along, in a squat. In my hands I held two wires which worked the eyelids, and I could pull on those and the eyes would open and close. So I had that double job. Roger would set the camera up so that there would be rocks in front of the lens, down low, so that you wouldn't see my feet. And it worked pretty good.

Most of the time.

Yeah, there *is* one place where you see my feet, and I'll tell you where it is. The girl scientist, Pamela Duncan (the first plastics I ever saw in my life, incidentally, Pamela Duncan wore)—she is in a scientific lab, and she shows one of the professors stills of the Crab Monster that she has taken and she notices that the crab is pregnant. You cut to one insert of the photographs of the crab, and in that insert you can see my feet hangin' out the bottom. I saw it on the big screen in downtown L.A., and I said *[loudly]*, "There're my feet!"—people were lookin' at me *[laughs]*—!

What was the crab made of?

It was fiberglass, and I would say it weighed like a hundred forty pounds, something like that.

You also played the ensign who brings the scientific team to the island.

And that's one example I always give of one of the most impossible lines I ever had to say in my life. We were shooting a scene on the beach at Malibu where one of my men was killed falling out of a motorboat. And Roger had me yell to the other guys in the boat, over the surf, with emotion (because the dead guy was supposedly a friend of mine), "Bury him!" I mean, the boat was sixty feet away and the surf was pounding, and Roger wanted me to holler, "Bury him!" with emotion! How the hell *[laughs]*...! Chuck Griffith played the guy who fell out of the boat; he also wrote the picture.

Another one where I played two parts was *She Gods of Shark Reef* [1958]. I swam across San Pedro Harbor and climbed up a dock or something, doubling for one of the stars. Then I played a guard and got into a fight with the guy I just doubled for!

Would you go out and see these movies after they were made?

I've seen some of them; I think I might have seen all of them. I wouldn't go see 'em today, I don't think *[laughs]*.

You had minor roles in several non–SF Corman pictures, like Rock All Night *[1957].*

Did you know that in that movie Russell Johnson really shot me with a wad—a blank? We'd already done it two or three takes, I ran by Russell and he turned, *pow,* and shot me, without aiming off to the side which is what you're supposed to do. The wadding went through my sports coat, through my shirt, and into my back. I may still have the scar, on the left side of my back. I went to the hospital and they took the wadding out. And, you know what?, they didn't use the take where I really got shot, they used the one where I pretended.

There's another scene in there where Roger had Mel Welles beating breadsticks on the counter to the music—which he didn't have. Later on, Roger put the music in and the breadsticks don't go to the music! Talk about lookin' like an ass *[laughs]*!

Teenage Doll *[1957]?*

I put rubber hoses up into my nostrils to play that blind man, so people wouldn't recognize me, 'cause I play a cop in that, too.

How about Carnival Rock *[1957]?*

They brought a New York actor in for that, an older man [David J. Stewart]. He looked at me on the set one day, on the side, sitting in his chair with his name on it, and he said, "My God, what I couldn't do with a face like that..." I had some plans for it myself! He thought I was gonna waste it, you know what I mean? — that was the connotation *I* got out of it! I felt like saying, "Well, what're you doin' with yours?"

Dick Miller hated him.

This guy was easy to dislike. Dick's still around and working — I like ol' Dick, he was very nice to me the last time we were together. He's married to a swell gal.

I, Mobster *[1958]?*

I, Mobster I remember because Stosh was in that from *Stalag 17* [1953] — Robert Strauss. I had done the play in earlier years, and so I was anxious to meet him and all. And in that picture I invented — or I thought I did — a bit where, in taking my hat off, I hold it for just a moment in front of his face and I sucker-punch him, *boom.* And it worked out really great. It's nice to invent little bits of business like that.

You were back to science fiction with Teenage Caveman.

We had a tough time in that. I was like Number Two Bad Caveman. The Number One Bad Caveman was a great heavy, had a pockmarked face — Frank deKova. When we were running, Roger had us bunched up so tight together that we had to carry our spears straight up and down. Well, Frank wouldn't do it. He kept carrying his spear [horizontally]. I was the second guy and, Jesus, he was almost gouging me with the thing *[laughs]!* So Roger says, "Frank, will you carry the spear straight up and down?" Frank grumbles and curses under his breath, we try it again and he carries it down again. Roger's yelling, "Nelson! Keep in close! Keep in close!" I holler back, "I can't keep in close, the guy's gonna *get* me!" All I had on was a sheepskin! So I go to Frank, "What the hell's the matter with you?" And Frank grumbled, "Well, no Number One Bad Caveman carries his spear up in the air like that..." I told him, "He'd carry it up in the air if the director *told* him to carry it up in the air!" Jesus!

Was that just the way deKova was?

No, it's just that he was upset, or because Roger had him runnin' through the bushes with Mexican sandals on, made out of rubber tires—he was just angry at that moment, that's all.

Did Robert Vaughn seem to be enjoying himself?

No, not really. He's not the type of actor that enjoys himself anyway. Bobby's not a happy person; he always plays the erudite, sophisticated prick, and he was a little bit like that in real life!

Later on in *Teenage Caveman,* there's the scene with the dogs—it was incredible. A guy comes out in a truck with a bunch of dogs in the back— Roger got this guy, who was a "dog wrangler" *of sorts.* I think the guy went down to the pound *[laughs],* 'cause he had mastiffs, he had Doberman pinschers, Russian wolf hounds—! So this guy is out there throwing meat to the dogs out of a leather bag, and he says, "Who's fightin' the dogs?" Somebody says, "The fellow over there, Nelson." The wrangler says *[growling],* "Tiger, get over here! Fang, come here! Killer, let's go!" I thought to myself, "Jesus Christ—Tiger, Fang and Killer!" Besides three other ones! So he says to me, "Look, watch out for Missy here, 'cause she's the one, she'll go right for the throat." I said, "Well, uh, hey, I don't have any padding on—"

He interrupts me, "You're not carrying that spear, are you? I wouldn't let 'em see ya with the spear. The dogs see ya with the spear, they're gonna become very aggressive." I said, "Well, it doesn't stand to reason, here come the dogs and I throw the spear away!" The wrangler goes, "Yeah, well, I'm just tellin' ya fer yer own protection, you figger out the rest." *[Laughs.]*

This is a true story, as God is my witness! I said, "Roger, look, before I hear the dogs I get tired or somethin' and I lay the spear down. Or something like that. I can't throw the spear away!" I mean, it's tough enough I had to fight these dogs! Roger said okay, okay. And, you know Roger, we gotta get it on the first take—we were losin' the light, or he only had the dogs for ten minutes, or some damn thing. So I put the spear down, I hear the dogs coming, I brace myself and I go, AAAARRRRGGGGHHHH!, like that. The dogs stop—stare at me—and they *take off*! They take off in the opposite direction, and they run away from the guy! He never caught all of 'em, he caught like four or five of 'em.

And then you had to do it over again.

Yeah! And the wrangler's complaining, "He scared my dogs!" I said, "Scare your *dogs*??" What the hell, *I* was scared, too! Roger called over Jonathan Haze and Dick Miller and all those guys, and he said, "Grab a dog! Everybody grab a dog!" They grabbed the dogs and Roger got a waist-shot of me and they threw the dogs into the frame, onto me. The dogs now are so frightened they're pushing against my body to get away from me, and I'm havin' to hold onto them and force one of 'em's mouth open and stick my arm in it! Now, if you watch that movie, you'll see that those dogs are afraid I'm gonna choke 'em to death with my arm. It's one of the funniest things that ever happened to me, and that was *Teenage Caveman.*

Susan Cabot's gripe with Corman was that he had no regard for actors' safety.
You had to watch out for yourself, but you generally have to do that anyway—not as much today as in those days. He didn't want to hurt anybody, but if anyone got hurt, they could recover—he wasn't gonna *kill* anybody. He didn't have a great deal of knowledge in those days about safety; I'm sure he's much more aware of it today than he was then. I mean, he didn't have much knowledge of *any*thing in those days—what he had was a great deal of courage [to become a moviemaker]. And he had connections who would release his stuff.

Did you have any contact during those years with Jim Nicholson and Sam Arkoff?
No, not much, other than I worked for them on several other pictures over the years. Nicholson was a very thin man, and Arkoff of course quite the opposite! Sam I saw quite often later on because he liked to go to Mardi Gras, and being from New Orleans I was there most of the time, too. We used to have some chats about the old days.

Any memories at all of Invasion of the Saucer Men?
[Laughs.] Just that Frank Gorshin and I got along great, and struck up a friendship that lasted many years.

Your acting career wasn't enough to support a family for a while.
Oh, no, I did the other things. But we lived way out of the city, and I think that was very smart, too—inadvertently! We lived out in Pomona because it really was less expensive, and that was a long way out in those days. Consequently, the kids weren't into the "Hollywood thing"—they just went off to school like everybody else, and it worked very good. And I could get jobs out there. I met a wonderful guy who had a cab company there, he knew I was an actor and I could take the cab whenever I wanted and if I had to take off to make a movie, fine. That worked out great. Then every year at the Fair Grounds we had the largest county fair in the world, and I'd sell beer and ice cream in the grandstands at the races. And jobs like that. But mostly drove the cab in Pomona, to make ends meet.

You also worked with Jack Nicholson during this early period, in a picture called The Cry Baby Killer *[1958].*
In it, Jack played a guy who held a pretty girl hostage in the back of a restaurant, in a storage room, and I was a TV news reporter who came on the scene, *[in an announcer's voice]* "live, to bring you the drama of this hostage

situation." But Jack was so strange, in those days even — the crew hated him. Poor Jack was defeated, I think, after that picture for two or three years — he went off to the Northwest or someplace to "find himself." About ten years ago, we were on a flight together coming back to Los Angeles from Vancouver and he was very nice to me. We recalled those old days and the rough stuff we had together. He was very good to me and he's always been one of my favorites, and certainly one of my favorite actors.

What was it about working with Roger Corman that made many of his co-workers feel that they should be out making movies on their own?

I don't know, I suppose they thought that if Roger could do it, *any*body could. Obviously, that's not true. I never felt that way; I never wanted to do it. I mean, I produced *The Brain Eaters* only because I needed the money. I knew I could do it — I could always produce a picture. But I just don't like it, it's not my bag.

So how exactly did The Brain Eaters *come about?*

Roger Corman called me into the office and he said to me that he and Bruno VeSota (who was going to direct this picture) needed a producer. But we had to do it non-union, we had to do it with N.A.B.E.T. crew rather than I.A. And since Roger knew that I had been in production for many years, he felt that I could produce the picture. I'm vague about the figures, but the budget was astronomically small — it was something like thirty thousand dollars to make the picture. And I would come up with all of the who's, where's and why's.

I was living in Pomona, and I knew a lot of the folks there — the mayor, chief of police, people like that. So I asked them to help us, and they did — they volunteered a lot of equipment that normally you'd pay for. Like the hospital facilities — we made a contribution to the nurses' fund, and shot some interiors at the hospital. All the policemen, all the guns, all of that stuff was donated because we contributed to whatever charity they had. I had a carpenter/neighbor/buddy of mine make the half-shell [the alien craft] — it was only half because we only photographed it from one side. When we went to the other side, we just turned it around! It was close to thirty feet tall, and he made it for like two hundred fifty dollars. We used sheet metal — aluminum sheets — around a wood structure, then we rented the scaffolding that we used alongside it.

You and VeSota cast the picture, right?

Yep. A lot of my friends, and friends of Bruno's, did the picture — played ghouls and things like that. And of course Leonard Nimoy, who was a buddy of mine, played the old man that protected the Brain Eaters. We shot all the interiors of the vehicle that came from "inner Earth" in my garage, with the

Nelson gave producing a shot in 1958, putting together—and starring in—the non-union *The Brain Eaters* with Joanna Lee.

lights off—just in darkness, with one light on Leonard. And, you know *[laughs]*, I never paid Leonard for that day. I owe him about forty-five dollars, or whatever it was I promised him.

The Brain Eaters was originally not called *The Brain Eaters*—Roger loved our original title so much he took our title off of it and Bruno and I had to make up *The Brain Eaters*. The original title of *The Brain Eaters* was *Attack of the Blood Leeches*—that was the title Roger loved! So he took the title to make another picture [*Attack of the Giant Leeches*]—he got somebody to hack out a script for him.

Tell us how you made the Brain Eaters themselves.

We made the creatures out of a little toy wind-up beetle that was around in toy stores at the time and quite plentiful. They had antennae and, if they bumped into a piece of furniture, they would turn and go the other way. We put crepe hair on 'em, and pipe cleaners for their antennae.

Were you happy with the way they looked on film?

No, not really. But we were not trying to make a flawless picture, we knew we had limitations and we just tried to make it the best we could with the money we had available. Most of the time you never saw the creature, it was always on the back of somebody's neck, under their clothes. Also, I knew what they really were, so it's hard to judge [laughs]!

So just about the whole thing was done in Pomona.
     Right. We shot in a very famous park in Pomona called Ganesha Park — we got permission from the local park people. Remember the scene where we finally get rid of the machine — "electrocute" it? We did that in my backyard, using telephone lines as the high tension wires. We lit 'em and threw a line over the telephone wires going to my little tract house.

How much did you get paid on Brain Eaters?
     I got (I think it was) one thousand dollars a week for the part, and to be the producer also. Because of the non-union crew and all, we could work long, long hours, so we did that, but I always made sure that we fed the crew well — having been on crews so much, I knew that was important. So we always went to a restaurant and let 'em order whatever they wanted. And we always had a lot of good food on the set, a lot of beer and stuff like that, so they wouldn't mind being there. And they did a good job, they worked very hard on it. One day the camera operator didn't show up, and we had to shoot. So *I* shot that day. I didn't have a light meter or anything, so I went down to the store and bought a thirty-five mm light meter that had settings for CLOUDY, HAZY, CLEAR, BRIGHT SUN [laughs]...! That's what I used, and it came out perfect!

Did you supervise the picture in post-production?
     No, Bruno did — I have very little knowledge of that. Bruno and Roger together, probably. I understood that Roger sold the film to AIP for something like two hundred thousand dollars — and then later on he got an offer of three hundred thousand dollars. He was quite upset that he didn't wait!

Do you have any inkling how well it did for AIP?
     No, but [laughs] I don't have any trouble believing that it made money!

An SF writer named Robert Heinlein claimed the film plagiarized a story of his.
     Never even knew about it.

So you enjoyed working with Bruno VeSota on Brain Eaters.
     Dear Bruno, he was a wonderful guy — had nine children. He was only married like three or four years but he had a set of twins, and triplets —! He had a great face, but [squeaking] had this terrible, terrible voice! A sweetheart of a guy — he died way ahead of his time, he was so overweight.
     I later did another picture with Bruno, a thing called *Valley of the Redwoods* [1960] that we shot in Eureka, California. We were staying at a hotel

way out in the middle of nowhere, and a bunch of gals that worked at a lumber mill, in the office, invited us to a cafe in Eureka—"on Saturday night it really moves." I wasn't interested, Bruno wasn't interested, but a couple of the younger guys were. And I had to get us the car. Gene Corman said, "No way"—he didn't have the insurance and all of that, and he was afraid that we'd all get drunk and wouldn't be at work the next day. Or that we'd get into trouble. I said, "Look, Bruno's gonna be with me. How much trouble could I get into with Bruno?" I mean, the guy weighed like four hundred pounds, he was like five feet tall—! Gene hemmed and hawed and I said *[calmly]*, "Gene, I'm takin' the car. I can hotwire it—steal the thing—or you can give me the key and nobody'll know the difference." "Okay, okay, it's over there on the dresser. . ." It was a little Studebaker wagon. The two young guys sat in the back, Bruno in the front and I was driving.

We got to this place, the Blue Moon Cafe, and it was a long shotgun bar—it just ran forever. From the bar to the wall was five feet—I mean, it was just the bar, the stools, and enough room to walk by and hang your coat up. We were there for quite a while, and a guy came over and was talking to Bruno. (Looked like he was gay.) The other two guys were talking to these gals, and I was in there telling "Hollywood stories." Now, Bruno and the guy took off, and I thought to myself, in my own sick mind, "Bruno, poor guy, what the hell can he do, he's four hundred pounds." I mean, he's not going to go with some secretary, eighteen years old, from the lumber yard *[laughs]*! Bruno said *[in a squeaky voice]*, "I'm gonna get some cigars, Eddie." "Right, Bruno, right!"

Half an hour goes by. There's a mirror that runs the whole length of the bar, I look up at it and in comes two cops. These two cops come in and they're talking to everybody (there's not that many people in the bar) as they're working their way down: "Is your name Wilson or Nilsson?" they're asking. "My name is Nelson," I tell 'em. "Are you from Hollywood?" "I'm with a film crew that's shooting outside of town." "You got a buddy, a big fat guy?" "Yeah—he's a sweetheart of a guy," I said. The cop said, "Well, we got him in a padded cell." Oh, my God, I said to myself, poor Bruno.

I told the two cops, "Okay, no problem, I'll come right down and we'll straighten this thing out," and I got my coat. We get out front—we could see the police station from where we were—but the street's one-way. So we gotta drive a-l-l the way around the park. I get in the police car and I hear over the radio, "This guy's giving us a lot of trouble down here." I told the cops, "I don't understand! Bruno's one of the sweetest pacifists—he's a non-violent person!" We get to the police station and we go in, and I can hear him screaming in the back of the place! I get in the back and he's got one cop on each arm and he's flailing 'em around the room! I grabbed him and I yelled, "Bruno! Bruno!"

And he busted out laughing. And the *cops* started laughing. These were

No girl was safe
as long as this
HEAD HUNTING THING
roamed the land!

NIGHT
OF THE
BLOOD
BEAST

Unforgettable poster art for a movie Nelson doesn't remember at all, AIP's *The Thing* **inspired *Night of the Blood Beast*.**

two cops that were buddies of Bruno's, that he'd met at a roadblock three days before when he went to get some cigars! He went into the police station and said, "Listen, why don't we rig this up for Nelson?" I'm telling you, I was out of it, it worked so well. I'd already started to sweat, I could already hear Gene Corman bawlin' me out —! Then on the way back to the location in the car, Bruno, big as he was, leaned back against the seat *[Nelson arches his back]* to straighten his pants — his crotch — and broke the back of the seat in this little Studebaker. Broke the seat! Oh, my God, Corman is gonna kill me, I told myself. We got back, claimed total innocence, finished the picture. But that was the joy of Bruno and that picture.

What do you remember about Night of the Blood Beast?
　　Not much *[laughs]*.

It was one of the first films of Bernard Kowalski, who was twenty-eight at the *time.*
　　I've worked with Bernie a lot — he's a wonderful guy. Even back then, so early on, he was a very confident young man, very knowledgeable.

Blood Beast *was for Gene Corman. How was he different from Roger?*
　　They were very similar, as far as I was concerned, and I think they had

Nelson is braced for action in AIP's *Night of the Blood Beast*.

just about the same amount of knowledge. They always treated the work "light-heartedly," as far as I was concerned—I never had any problems with Roger or Gene. And having just come out from Louisiana, I can remember some very kind things that Roger did for me. Gene was very much like that, too.

Beverly Garland resents the fact that, when Corman moved up to slightly better pictures, he left some of his old stock players behind. Was it that way with you?

I guess—I don't know. I know I never worked for him again *[laughs],* but who knows why? But also, money is a question—my money went up, and I'm sure Beverly's did, too.

So he was looking for more affordable people.

Oh, absolutely. He never took headliners, people who wanted big money. The ones that he did get, people like Vincent Price, he probably worked 'em for one week, and then the rest of the picture was with the other people.

What's the story on Devil's Partner?

Devil's Partner was made by a guy named Hooker—he made a famous little picture that made millions of dollars, *The Littlest Hobo* [1958]. *Devil's Partner* was his second picture, and it was directed by Charlie Rondeau—big guy, pretty much of a bullshitter *[laughs].* But we got along fine.

Richard Crane and Jean Allison are on hand as *Devil's Partner* Ed Nelson takes his last breath. The 1958 film, co-written by Bowery Boy Stanley Clements, collected dust for three years before its 1961 Filmgroup release.

You played a dual role in that, as an old man and a young man.

Yeah, it was a Faust story. And I lived with goats *[laughs]*! I remember them shooting the transformation effects [from old to young] — I had to hold my head still while they took some makeup off, shot a few frames, took some more makeup off. *À la* Dr. Jekyll and Mr. Hyde — lap dissolves. The makeup didn't take that long to put on — an hour, maybe two.

Do you remember where that was shot?

No, but it was out in the San Fernando Valley somewhere, out in the sticks. I don't think I ever saw the picture.

You had a good heavy role in Soldier in the Rain *[1963], one of your better pictures.*

There were some great things in *Soldier in the Rain* — I loved the fight scene that I did at the end, that was one of the great fight scenes of film, they say. They had me rigged up on a wire so Jackie Gleason could pick me up over his head. And then the fight scene between Steve McQueen and me, at the bar — a wonderful stunt coordinator figured that out for us. That's where I met my stuntman (he's dead now), Howard Curtis — he was killed in a parachute leap. He was my stuntman from then until the time he died.

Did you hurt your back in that fight scene? It looks as though you did.

I don't remember—I may have. Those were the days when you wore bruises and such like a medal; today, the guy takes off three weeks. But in those days you got a little extra joy out of doing those things. I came up through the Westerns, too, and in those days we fell off the horses—not at full gallops, but we reared and did things like that. We were physical people, and they cast us a lot of times because of that.

Do you remember working with Boris Karloff on Thriller?

[Emphatically.] Sure. I did a lot of those—I had been at Universal under contract for awhile, and the producer of that show, Bill Frye, used me quite a bit in other things later on. I was glad to get on *Thriller,* 'cause I wanted to work with Mr. Karloff so badly. He only came in and worked the show Tuesday, Wednesday, Thursday—Thursday night he would fly to London, stay in London two days, then fly back on Monday. He was very, very nice to the cast, but I just—*pestered* him, almost, sitting with him and talking about the old days and talking about his friend Bela. He would tell me how sad it was, that Bela had been almost the number one actor in Europe, and when he came to the United States, because of his language problem, he became this *creature* here! How sad that was, Mr. Karloff thought. So I just loved working with him—he was a very gentle man. He had window flowers in his flat in London, and he loved to talk about flowers!

How about Twilight Zone?

Twilight Zone I did only one, and it was a classic—they reran the hell out of it. It was called *Valley of the Shadow* and it was ninety percent "my" show, so to speak. A wonderful script. I was pleased to do that, because it was a hot show at the time.

You were also on The Outer Limits, *in an episode called* Nightmare.

Yeah, I remember that, too—that was one of Marty Sheen's first jobs. We shot it over on Melrose Avenue, at one of the independent studios, and one day when we went to lunch we talked John Anderson into going in his creature outfit *[laughs]*! And we almost caused a traffic accident on Santa Monica!

Going into Peyton Place—*would you call that your Big Break?*

No, I think my big break's in front of me. *Peyton Place* was the biggest break I had at the time, although we didn't know it at first—don't forget, the reviews on *Peyton Place* were hideous. *Terrible!* As a matter of fact, as a joke one time, after the show became number one, Ryan O'Neal and I cut one of the *TV Guide* reviews out and sent it back to the reviewer on bread, with mayonnaise *[laughs]*!

Once you started working real regular in TV, you hardly ever made movies again. Was that by choice?

That's just more or less the way things worked out. They say if you're in television, people are not going to use you in motion pictures. Generally that's true. And usually directors and producers who are in television, when they make the jump to motion pictures, they don't bring their people along — they have a whole new entourage. Like what Beverly [Garland] said about Corman. That's just the way it goes. And so there's no way to measure [your worth as an actor]: You can't measure it by the final result, you can't say, "Well, if I was any good, I'd be way up there." Because a lot of guys that are "up there" aren't any good at all!

And vice versa.

Yeah. Of course a guy can look good in a twenty-five million dollar picture — they shoot every scene about eight times, six different ways, and they take eight months to do it! Now, to find out if he's any good or not, I'd like to see him in a *Highway Patrol.* Done in two and a half days. With a bad script. And a new director.

I've done some films you don't know about because they've never been released — one with Brooke Shields called *Brenda Starr,* and then I just finished one in Asheville, North Carolina, *The Boneyard* with Phyllis Diller. That one, I think, is not going to be around in the United States *[laughs].* It was made, really, for Japan — that's where the money came from — and it was a monster picture. I'm sorry you won't see it, 'cause they had a wonderful ten-foot Phyllis Diller monster *[laughs]* — it looked just like her, only ten foot high! And a guy inside, up on stilts. Incredible! But who knows what it looks like on film. These were "monster people" — they make creatures in Asheville. They have their factory there, and they make some wonderful ghouls and creatures. [*Brenda Starr* was finally released in 1992. *The Boneyard* went directly to video.]

So what's ahead for you?

I don't know what's ahead; I put so many restrictions on my agent this last year that I hardly get called for *anything!* But I'm going to take 'em off, and see if I can work a little more. They're calling me always about soap operas, asking me if I'm interested in doing another one. I'm not. It isn't hard work, it's just the quality of 'em is so poor — five, six, eight people writing the same character, it doesn't make sense. I watch them, and they're terrible for the most part. I hate to do something I wouldn't watch.

No regrets, then, that you never fully made "The Big Time"?

I was always looking to sustain myself for a long period of time rather than ever being a "star," so to speak, or going for "The Big Time." That was never very important to me. Also, because I had a lot of children, I had to work a lot. I couldn't sit out and turn down a lot of things, and wait for the big plum. Which didn't bother me a great deal. Once in a while it bothers me, when I see other contemporaries that have gone on and done very well by doing that—by *not* taking everything. But, hell, I have a lot more to show for it, in the long run. I have my eleven grandchildren and my six children, a very happy marriage—it's been that way for forty years. And that kind of solidification was more important to me than being an unhappy star.

ED NELSON FILMOGRAPHY

The Steel Trap (20th Century–Fox, 1952)
New Orleans Uncensored (Columbia, 1955)
Swamp Women (Woolner Bros., 1956)
Bayou (Poor White Trash) (United Artists, 1957)
Hell on Devil's Island (20th Century–Fox, 1957)
Invasion of the Saucer Men (AIP, 1957)
Teenage Doll (Allied Artists, 1957)
Carnival Rock (Howco, 1957)
Attack of the Crab Monsters (Allied Artists, 1957)
Rock All Night (AIP, 1957)
She Gods of Shark Reef (AIP, 1958)
Night of the Blood Beast (AIP, 1958)
The Cry Baby Killer (Allied Artists, 1958)
The Brain Eaters (AIP, 1958) Also producer
Street of Darkness (Republic, 1958)
I, Mobster (20th Century–Fox, 1958)
Teenage Caveman (AIP, 1958)
T-Bird Gang (Filmgroup, 1959)
The Young Captives (Paramount, 1959)
A Bucket of Blood (AIP, 1959)
Valley of the Redwoods (20th Century–Fox, 1960)
Elmer Gantry (United Artists, 1960)
Judgment at Nuremberg (United Artists, 1961)
Devil's Partner (Filmgroup, 1961)
Killers' Cage (Code of Silence) (Sterling World Distributors, 1961)
Soldier in the Rain (Allied Artists, 1963)
The Man from Galveston (Warners, 1963)
Time to Run (World Wide, 1973)
Airport 1975 (Universal, 1974)
That's the Way of the World (Shining Star) (United Artists, 1975)
Midway (Universal, 1976)
For the Love of Benji (Mulberry Square, 1977)
Acapulco Gold (R. C. Riddell, 1978)
Brenda Starr (Triumph Releasing, 1992)

*People ask me how we were able to
keep a straight face making* Cat Women
of the Moon. *Well,* we didn't!

William Phipps

IN THE EARLY DAYS OF 1950S SCIENCE FICTION, before the floodgates opened wide, one of the first people to become identified with the genre was actor William Phipps. Aside from furnishing the voice of Prince Charming in Disney's cartoon classic *Cinderella* (1950), Phipps also hid his boyish face beneath a beard as the star of Arch Oboler's end-of-the-world melodrama *Five*; made a token appearance in Oboler's *The Twonky*; encountered Martians in both *Invaders from Mars* and *The War of the Worlds*; and took on the Abominable Snowman as one of the leads in *The Snow Creature*. Probably most notoriously, he even grappled with Moon maidens set on world conquest in the almost indescribable *Cat Women of the Moon*.

Hailing from St. Francisville, Illinois, Phipps knew from boyhood that he was destined to be an actor, and appeared in several plays in grade school and at Eastern Illinois University. Hitchhiking to Hollywood in 1941, he worked on the stage and later in films, beginning with RKO's *Crossfire* in 1947. In the nearly half-century since, he has amassed a list of credits that is nearly staggering, not only in films but also in television, commercials and in voiceover work (he provided the narration for the special 190-minute TV version of David Lynch's *Dune*). Aggressively feisty, William Phipps has some surprising things to say about some of the biggest names in science fiction.

How did you get interested in becoming an actor in the first place?

That's kind of the wrong question. People in my profession will understand this, but I don't know if you will or not: I never thought of *becoming* an actor, or of being interested in acting. I always *was* an actor. Either you are or you aren't. I always just felt, "I *am* an actor." The first thing I did was in the second grade, when I played Bluebeard—the man that killed all of his wives *[laughs]*! Then I did a couple of plays in high school; went on to college (Eastern Illinois University in Charleston, Illinois), and did some plays there. At college, I was president of the freshman class—every office that I ran for, I was elected. The one office that I was *not* elected to was the president of the drama society, because the advisor to that, Dr. Robert Shively, said, "Oh, we can't elect Bill. He's going to go to Hollywood this summer"—I had told everybody that I was going to Hollywood to become an actor, and everybody took me seriously *[laughs]*! And so I *had* to go, to save face!

Did you get work there right off the bat?

I did a play out here called *Families Are Like That*—that was in forty-one—so I've been in Hollywood fifty years. Right after that, World War II broke out, so I was interrupted by three years in the Navy. (Across the Pacific sixteen times, on six different ships.) Then I came back and I started in at the Actors' Lab, which was a very famous school. It was *the* school, the only one

Previous page: The boyish-faced William Phipps began his science fiction career as the star of *Five* (pictured), written, produced and directed by radio's Arch Oboler.

that was considered any good at that time. (And I don't think there's been a better place since.) They had body work, fencing, speech, pantomime, the whole bit. I went there on the G.I. Bill. I did a play there, and Charles Laughton and Mrs. Bertold Brecht came to see it 'cause they were getting ready to do the play *Galileo. Galileo* had over fifty speaking parts, and so it was hard to cast. So Charles Laughton saw me and came backstage and asked me to do the play with him because he thought I was a terrific actor. And Mrs. Brecht, too—"Ah, yah, so, you *vunderful!*" So I did the play—I played Andrea, who was Galileo's [Laughton] number one pupil. It premiered at John Houseman's Coronet Theater on La Cienega Boulevard in Hollywood.

Your first fantasy film work was as the voice of Prince Charming in Disney's Cinderella.

I auditioned for it. They recorded me at a sound studio at Disney, and Walt Disney heard the tapes before he met the people. I later met him, and I did the film.

After the picture was done, Disney had a nationwide contest where the winner would get to come to Hollywood for free and have a date with the man whose voice brought Prince Charming to life—in other words, me! I don't know how they selected the winner; I suppose the people that entered it competed in some way. (*How* I don't remember—didn't care then—don't care now *[laughs]*!) I met the winner for the first time on the stage at the Pantages Theater in front of a full house, thousands of people, on coast-to-coast radio—*Art Linkletter's House Party*. I was in white tie and tails, and top hat. While I was backstage in the wings, waiting to go on, I noticed that there were a lot of mannequins—for what reason they were there, I don't know, they were for some other production, I assumed. There were several of them, female mannequins, and they were naked. And I was pretending to make love to them while on my hands and knees, in white tie and tails and top hat! Art Linkletter's announcer Rod O'Connor was so broken up, laughing so hard, so distracted, that he had trouble announcing the show. Rod and I thought that was hysterical—but I don't know what the *other* people around us thought *[laughs]*!

Anyway, she and I went out on our date. They gave me (I think) one hundred dollars pocket money and gave me a limousine and a driver, so we could go anywhere we wanted. We went to Ciro's and the Mocambo, which were the two most famous places on the Sunset Strip at the time, and we went to the Trocadero, too. At the end of the night, around midnight, the limousine driver and I took her back to the Roosevelt Hotel, where she was staying. And then the chauffeur took *me* back home—a rooming house we called the House of the Seven Garbos, a home for fledgling *actresses,* where I lived in a room in the basement for seven dollars a week! The next day I went to the tuxedo rental place and turned in my stuff. I was a pauper again!

Several articles that came out about Five *called you a radio actor. Were you?*

You know, I'm so amazed that there are so many "authorities" in this business that seem to know every-fuckin'-thing about it. I was *never* a radio actor—I wasn't then, I never became one and I'm not one now. I hadn't done *any* radio at all at the time of *Five.* When Arch Oboler was casting *Five,* he had Leo Penn—Sean's father—signed to do the lead. Then Oboler went to Charles Laughton looking for advice on casting the mountain climber. Laughton had an acting group by this point, a group that I was very active in. Oboler asked him, "Who's your best person?" and Laughton said, "Bill Phipps." We were doing a play at that time, Chekhov's *Cherry Orchard,* and I was playing Petya, the perpetual student, so I had a scraggly beard. Oboler came to see the play, and then he had me come up to his place in the mountains above Malibu—a ranch, the buildings all designed and built by Frank Lloyd Wright. I was all prepared to test for the part of the mountain climber, and when I got there, Arch said, "I want you to test for the lead." I said, "You've already got somebody for that part, I thought." He said, "Well, nothing's set in *concrete.*" So I tested for the part of Michael. Arch Oboler liked my test and he paid off Leo Penn.

Oboler said he turned down name stars when he did Five. *He wanted unknowns.*

You'll have to make up your own mind about that. I would take it with a grain of salt. For one thing, he couldn't have *paid* a big name star *[laughs]*! He had a very limited budget, so he *had* to go with unknowns. He paid all of us S.A.G. minimum, and the only reason I did it was because I was getting top billing and a percentage. Then, too, *Five* was a non-union film, so I don't think that many big stars would go out on a limb with that. When we were making the picture up at Oboler's ranch, union people from all the different guilds came to see him, and there were big objections. What Oboler finally did was sell the picture to Columbia and pay off the unions.

Did that leave him any profits from Five?

Yeah, but I don't think very much. I had a percentage of the picture—a percentage of *his* profits—and I *did* get some money, I don't remember how much. But I think that he came close to breaking even, that he didn't make very much money.

Were all of your scenes shot on the ranch?

There, and also some down on the beach, which was just down the hill. The empty city that Susan Douglas and James Anderson go into was Glendale. My car was one of the abandoned cars sitting on the street. It was a real shoestring production.

How much of a shoestring? How hurried were you?

We weren't hurried, but he didn't have any expenses, though, because we were all staying there at the house. And he had five students from U.S.C., kids who had been students of the very famous montage director Vorkapich, for the crew. (I'm sure Oboler, in his cheap way, went to U.S.C. and said, "I'm making an experimental film, non-union," and he got the best students.) They all doubled in brass—in other words, they all did *everything*. They gripped and they lit and they assisted the cameraman, everything the crew normally does. And there was a very ugly incident on *Five*: College students will be college students, they're not people of long professional standing in the business. One of the crew, a very nice fellow name of Art [presumably assistant director Arthur L. Swerdloff], said something that Oboler didn't like and Oboler *hit* him. With his fist. Cut him real bad—nasty gash, blood, the whole bit. I wasn't there to see the blow struck, but I was there shortly afterwards and saw the guy—Oboler had broken his glasses and cut him all up. And there was a big lawsuit over it. That was a terrible thing; no matter *what* the guy said or did, there's no excuse for that. But that's Oboler for you.

You've *[laughs]*—you've got me started on Oboler now. I never thought much of the man. I thought he was silly, about as silly as *The Twonky* is.

But initially, going into Five, *were you looking forward to working with the Great Arch Oboler?*

I didn't know a thing about him. Never heard of him. Years after *Five*, I appeared on an album that he did called *Drop Dead*, and a lot of it was scripts from his old *Lights Out* radio show. I just didn't think they were any good! And I appear on *The Chicken Heart*, which is the *famous* one! I played this *Chicken Heart* segment for a writer-friend of mine, John Paxton, who wrote *Crossfire* [1947], *The Wild One* [1954], *On the Beach* [1959] and so on. I played it for him and he said, "It all sounds phony, it's terrible! And as much as I think of your acting, Bill, *you* even sound false on there. I don't believe you." I agreed with him, and if you play it, I think it'll bear me out.

When it comes to Oboler and this genius bit, I don't see it. Never did. I don't think he was a genius at all. Not by any stretch of the imagination *[laughs]*! When Oboler directed, he didn't so much watch as he *listened*—he was a radio man. He always had the earphones on. Sometimes a scene would end, you'd look over at him and see that he wasn't even watching.

Did you and he get along all right?

Oboler had a "hands-off" thing with me. He didn't want to clash with me; he had clashes and run-ins with everybody else. Why *not* me? I have my own theories about that, but I couldn't really tell you why. I was his leading man—

So it wouldn't pay to clash with you.

Well, but he *could*. He clashed with Susan Douglas—very, very badly. She was one of the biggest pain-in-the-asses I ever worked with!

With her, then, he might have been in the right?

Except I think he had the hots for her! The nearest thing I had to a run-in with Oboler was a very interesting one. We were shooting on the beach and I had a microphone under my shirt. I was doing my dialogue and Arch came up to me and said, "Bill, I want you to do that again, but use your lower register"—meaning, bring the voice down, and use my normal voice, the way I'm talking to you now. I said, "I am." He said, "No, you're not." This went on for a few hours, doing it over and over; he kept saying, "I want you to get it down." It got to be where I was saying, "But I am," and he was saying, "No, you're not." It was a standoff, an impasse. I never came unstuck, though, I kept very calmly saying, "I *am* speaking in my normal voice, Arch." Then, the next day, he played it all back and it was just perfect, natural and normal. He came up to me and apologized. But, coming from him, it wasn't really an apology. In fact, he *didn't* apologize, he admitted he was wrong. No— that's *still* not right, 'cause Oboler Could Do No Wrong. What happened was that he told me that what I did *was* the lower register. Boy, that was delicious to me *[laughs]*!

And, by the way, I never, ever, *ever* called him Mr. O. or Mr. Oboler. He was Arch. Most of the others called him Mr. O., because they were scared, I suppose. *I* wasn't scared of him.

In what way was Susan Douglas a pain in the ass?

Oh, she wanted this and she wanted that, she wanted her own way and nothing was right. She bellyached and bellyached. She was just a thoroughly unlikable person. Thoroughly!

James Anderson, who played the bad guy?

James Anderson was at the Actors' Lab when I was, and he was in Laughton's acting group. Jimmy Anderson was a very nice, very talented person, but a person out of control. He'd let his emotions carry him away, he would get almost irrational at times. He was a very heavy drinker and he died very early—it was brought on by dissipation.

And what's your opinion of the film?

Oh, I never did like it. I didn't like the script, didn't like the picture, still don't. I quarrel a lot with the writing. Oboler did a lot of sermonizing, and there's a lot of sermonizing in the picture. But it always rang shallow with me.

Did you feel it would be a successful picture?

No, no, I did not. I had no hopes for it at all.

In the late sixties, a theater in North Hollywood decided to run *Five* and *The Twonky* as a double-bill. They invited Oboler, and Oboler invited me. I didn't really want to go, but I did because he made a special thing of wanting me to be there. Hans Conried, who was the star of *The Twonky,* he was there, too. When something like that happens, people come from out of the woodwork, buffs of these things; there was a full house. During an intermission, Oboler spoke, and do you know what he did? After asking me to be there, he introduced Hans Conried to the audience but not me *[laughs]*! I suppose he thought that would hurt me, but, you know what? It didn't. I didn't care. Oboler was a ... he was... Oh, hell, he was a *creep [laughs]*!

Did appearing in Five *help you move up the Hollywood ladder?*

Who knows? You never know. But the premiere of *Five* was the first premiere that was ever televised—television was in its infancy then. I was still living at that same rooming house that I mentioned before, which was called the House of the Seven Garbos. I wore a tux and went to the premiere with the seven girls who lived there, all of them dressed in rented furs. The girls were Suzan Ball; Ann McCrea, who was a regular on *The Donna Reed Show* for years; Valerie Cote, who is now the wife of John Guedel (Guedel produced Groucho's *You Bet Your Life*); and four others. So I got fantastic publicity out of *Five*, all over the United States, probably the world. So that can't *hurt [laughs]*!

Speaking of the House of the Seven Garbos, I wasn't the only male there, there was also Hugh O'Brian and Leonard Nimoy. O'Brian was ostracized, because he was like an octopus, and because he was so *cheap*! Every girl that lived there, when nobody else was around he would paw them. So after a while he was just "frozen out"! And Leonard Nimoy used to drive me up the wall! I was already in movies, and he used to follow me around and pester me to death. I used to *hide* from him, honest to God *[laughs]*!

You have an unbilled bit part at the end of Oboler's The Twonky.

He called me one day and said he wanted me to appear in a scene, the last scene in the movie, where a bunch of guys barge in in their white coats and take Hans Conried away to the nuthouse. Oboler wanted to know if I would play one of the guys, as a "good luck" thing—we had done *Five* together, and I guess he was happy with *Five* and what I did in it. So, would I do it as a gesture? I figured, so what? Sure, I'd do it. And that's all I did in the picture.

And did you see the film?

I saw it when it came out, but I don't remember too much about it outside of the fact that I thought it was a silly film and I got very bored with that animated TV set running around the house. It just didn't make sense.

You had another small part, as one of the soldiers, in Invaders from Mars.
     That was produced by Eddie Alperson, one of several movies I did with him — he was a big fan of mine. I don't remember too much about *Invaders* except that on a soundstage at Republic they built a whole floor that was like the surface of the earth — they brought in dirt and everything. But it was done way up off the floor of the stage, so that underneath it there was a whole world of tunnels, like a rabbit's warren or a prairie dog town, and there were all kinds of entrances and exits. It was hard work: I wore a helmet and a uniform and I carried a lot of equipment, and it was hot and sweaty and miserable. And I was on that picture for quite a while.

Any memory of the director, William Cameron Menzies?
     I never got to know him, but my memory of him is that he was always lost in thought, like he was far away someplace.

How do you feel about science fiction in general?
     Just this morning I was talking at breakfast with a director friend of mine, Jack Hively; he was just the executive producer of a new film called *The Giant from Thunder Mountain* with Richard Kiel and Jack Elam. I was telling him, "Thinking back, I have been involved with a *lot* of science fiction. I didn't try it, I didn't plan it that way, and I remember that at the time it was happening, I would remark on it with wonder. How is it that I kept getting in?" — *Five, The Snow Creature, Invaders from Mars, The War of the Worlds,* etc. It just happened, and I *still* don't have an answer *[laughs]*! But I'm happy about it because I like doing science fiction, and I like watching it — I like the visual possibilities. It's exciting to do.

Was Cat Women of the Moon *exciting to do?*
     [Laughs.] People ask me how we were able to keep a straight face making that movie. Well, we *didn't*! Marie Windsor did, and so did Victor Jory, because they took themselves so seriously, but Sonny Tufts, Douglas Fowley and I had a ball. We were laughing and making fun of things all the time, trying to make the day as pleasant as possible. We shot it in five days, and I remember on the last day, we quit before the picture was really finished. That was it — they pulled the plug — because it was quittin' time and they didn't have any more money and couldn't go another day. Or another *hour* *[laughs]*!

The conclusion of the movie takes place off-camera. Victor Jory chases some Cat Women out of camera range, you hear gunshots, and then you hear him yell, "The Cat Women are dead."

Susan Morrow (left) and her fellow Moon maidens roll out the red carpet for Earthman Phipps in the 3-D camp classic *Cat Women of the Moon.*

Wasn't that wonderful? That's the thing that really stays with me about *Cat Women*, because I thought then, as I think now, "Boy, what a shitty way to end a movie!" *[Laughs.]* It just stopped! The director, Arthur Hilton, was a very, very nice man, though; he was a short man, and he walked with a pronounced limp. He was an editor before he became a director. And one of the producers was a fellow by the name of Jack Rabin, who had an optical special effects lab and he did work for lots of other studios. He had those facilities already, in his own business, so there was ninety-eight percent of the budget right there. That's how the picture came about.

Do you remember your first impressions of the spaceship set, and some of the props?

[Laughs.] When I saw that spaceship set, I thought I was workin' for Soupy Sales! And that giant spider! They held it up with big ropes above us on the cave set and dropped it down on our heads. At the time, we thought it was the most outrageous, absurd thing in the world—how did spiders get on the Moon?! It was all just incredible—I thought, "How can anybody put this in a movie? It's gonna ruin it!"

What can you recall about the attitudes of some of the other actors involved, like Marie Windsor and Victor Jory?

Well, Marie Windsor has never been one of my favorite people, I'll tell you that right now. A couple of years ago, I did a play called *Daddy's Dyin' ... Who's Got the Will?*, and I played the title role. *The L.A. Weekly* picked it as the outstanding drama of the year, and gave us its top award. There was a big dinner and presentation, and the mistress of ceremonies was Estelle Getty. Del Shores, the guy who wrote the play, and I sat together at a table; and before things got started, Marie came by and said hello to me. Estelle Getty was calling up the different presenters, and Marie was one of them. So when Estelle called her to present us with our award, Estelle mentioned *Cat Women of the Moon* and how it was a cult film nowadays, blah, blah, blah. And Marie even commented upon it. Now, she could so easily have said, "And one of my co-stars is sitting right over there, Bill Phipps." She did not—she did not say a word about it—and yet *I'm* getting one of the awards *[laughs]*! You know what that is? It's a person who relates everything to themselves.

It's surprising she acknowledged it at all. She can be a little touchy about Cat Women.

Well, that's Marie Windsor for you. If she had any class at all, she'd be tickled to death about *Cat Women of the Moon*. Look at Elsa Lanchester; what if she took that attitude about *Bride of Frankenstein,* where she walked around with her hair standing on end? She didn't; in fact, she had the [Aurora] model kit sitting on her mantelpiece! Me, I'm glad that *Cat Women* does have this kind of Worst Film reputation today, that it's funny and cultish and people can laugh at it. What do I care? Why should *any*body care? And if it embarrasses Marie Windsor, I feel sorry for her.

And Victor Jory?

Oh, what a pompous ass. Terrible! The day before we started shooting, he and I happened to walk into a little coffee shop which was on the Goldwyn lot. I was very young at the time, and Victor Jory said, "Sonny Tufts is gonna do this picture, eh? Well, he'd better not take a drink while he's working, 'cause I'll knock him on his fuckin' ass!" I remember thinking at the time, and I still do, what a thing to say! And what a thing to say about a fellow actor, before he's *done* anything! Sonny Tufts was a known carouser and heavy drinker, but so were a lot of other people. But they *worked*! In other words, Victor Jory was trying to establish himself as top dog, but that didn't mean shit to me.

Did you like Sonny Tufts?

He was a marvelous fellow, and he had the greatest sense of humor of anybody I've ever known. He should have been in vaudeville! They always made him like the amiable leading man or second leading man–type, but that wasn't really his nature at all. He was a funny, funny guy, and wonderful to be with. I loved him. Also in the cast was Susan Morrow, who played one of the Cat Women, the one I have a little romance with. Do you know who her sister is? Judith Exner, the lady that was having an affair with John F. Kennedy and the Chicago mob boss [Sam Giancana] at the same time, and wrote a book about it!

And, on the opposite end of the SF spectrum from Cat Women, *what can you tell me about* The War of the Worlds?

I have wonderful memories of that, because Byron Haskin and I became very good friends. Before I met Byron, I met his wife Terry at Preston Sturges' nightclub, a fabulous place called the Players. She had seen *Five* and was very impressed with me, and so she introduced me to her husband. I ended up doing a number of things with Haskin, like *The First Texan, The Boss* [1956], even some TV, but *The War of the Worlds* was the first one. Paul Birch, Jack Kruschen and I were three townspeople that were in a lot of the early scenes, and we're also the first three people killed by the Martians. Jack later got an Academy Award nomination for *The Apartment* [1960], and Paul Birch was a wonderful actor and a really nice man. One of my lines is the nearest thing to a laugh in the whole picture—"Welcome to California!"—and I immediately get zapped! We shot those scenes indoors, on a stage at Paramount.

Did you meet George Pal at all?

George Pal was very much the European, mannerly gentleman, very cordial, always smiling, very accommodating—"How good to see you," "How nice of you"—and you never knew who he was or what he was or what he was thinking *[laughs]*! *You* know the type! There was something very indeterminate about him. I remember that Byron Haskin used to give himself all the credit for making these pictures good or making them a success, always intimating that George Pal just got in the way. But Pal was a great promoter and he was the one that got them off the ground, got the backing and the financing and etc.

Haskin's notorious for taking the credit for other people's contributions to movies.

I'll tell you something about Haskin. You can always spot a liar when they say certain things. Haskin was always saying, "And I can show you proof," or, "You can ask so-and-so," things like that. You don't talk like that when you're telling the truth. He would lie about things for no reason. He was a cameraman and he was great in special effects; he was a good mechanic. But as a director I don't think he could handle anything poetic or sensitive or warm or touching. Things like that would have been completely out of his realm.

Did you have any inkling, as you were making War of the Worlds, *that it would be a classic?*

You never do. And a lot of times, when people *do* think they're making a classic, that's usually the kiss of death *[laughs]*!

Next you were one of the two leads in the first Abominable Snowman film, The Snow Creature.

The director on that was W. Lee Wilder; I first worked with Willie on a TV series called *Gangbusters,* and he said to me then, "I'm gonna do a movie"—meaning *The Snow Creature.* He told me a little about it and he said he wanted me to play the detective, and of course I thought to myself, "Oh, sure"—you hear this kind of stuff every day. But then he contacted me when he was about to do the movie, and we did it. I liked him, by the way, very much—he was very open and direct, very warm and friendly. (The opposite of Oboler.)

Do you recall the end of the movie, when I shoot the Abominable Snowman, down in the sewers? You don't actually see me shoot the gun, there's a big closeup of the gun going off. Well, the problem was that the gun wouldn't fire. Little things like that will make an impression on you, because *[laughs]* I remember thinking to myself, "How in the fuck can they get all the way down here, under the city, in these sewers, and not know that they have a gun that won't work and ammunition that won't fire??" It was idiotic, it *upset* me, because I've never had it happen before or since, and I've fired guns thousands of times. But I remember Willie saying to me, "Don't worry about it, I can fix it." And he did, he put in the closeup.

Were you still associated with Charles Laughton when he directed The Night of the Hunter?

Oh, yes. After Laughton and [producer] Paul Gregory bought the book *The Night of the Hunter* by Davis Grubb, Charles asked me to come over to the house, and he handed me the book. He shut me in the library and he said, "Don't come out 'til you've read it!" *[Laughs.]* So I read it, and I told him, "My God, this'll make a great movie...!" He was all hot to approach Gary Cooper to play the preacher; Laughton had done a movie with Cooper and Tallulah Bankhead called *Devil and the Deep* [1932] years before. He wanted Cooper, but I kept saying, "No, I think Robert Mitchum would be great." But he didn't know Mitchum.

So you kept after him?

I kept working on him and working on him, that Mitchum had to play this part. And he wouldn't hear of it. Finally he said, "Well, have you got his phone number?" I did. So I called Mitchum, and I put Mitchum and Charles on the phone together. Laughton told him, "This character's a shit—a real meanie. So, if you play it, you've got to play it in a way that you don't give the little kids nightmares!"

After they got off the phone, Laughton handed me the book and said, "Here, take this out to him." I said, "Nope. I won't take it to him." He said, "What do you mean?" and I told him, "I won't take this book to Mitchum unless you go with me." "No, no, no, no!" he cried out. This went on for an hour or two, but I was adamant: "I will not take the book to Mitchum unless you go with me."

So he drove out with me; I had a Mercedes roadster at the time. Laughton lived in Hollywood, up the hill from Hollywood Boulevard, and Mitchum lived way out west in Mandeville Canyon. We parked in the interior of the grounds where Mitchum lived, and I went up to the door with the book. Mitchum answered the door and I said, "Here's *The Night of the Hunter*." He said, "Come in. Say, who's that in your car?" "Oh, a friend of mine came along." Mitchum looked and looked and then he finally walked out to the car, and he of course saw who it was and invited Laughton in for a drink.

Mitchum had some relatives over at the time, and several days after that he said to me, "When those relatives told me they wanted to come over, I said, 'What do you want to come over for? It's dull here on Sunday, nothing ever happens.' Then all of a sudden Charles Laughton walked into the room!" It made a liar out of him, made him feel like a fool *[laughs]*! Because for Charles Laughton to walk into a room, believe me, it was like leading an elephant into a living room. Wherever he went, he would stop traffic — people would just stop and stare. He had that kind of presence, as you can very well imagine.

How come Laughton directed only one movie in his career?

About that time, he directed some big successes on the stage — *The Caine Mutiny Court-Martial*, Shaw's *Don Juan in Hell* — and I remember he was saying he didn't care about acting anymore, he wanted to spend the rest of his time directing. (He was not an old man when he died, you know — he died at the age of sixty-three.) So he was looking forward to directing a lot more movies — whatever came up, whatever he got hold of. Once I got him and Mitchum together, but before he started doing *Night of the Hunter*, at a projection room at Nosseck's Studio he ran every classic picture he could get his hands on, just to "bone up" on directors' techniques. All that stuff, I saw with him — silents and everything. I went with him every day.

Did he like the way The Night of the Hunter *came out?*

Oh, yeah. I was on the set several times, and here's another anecdote about the film that you may not know. He would never say *cut*, unless the camera ran out of film. "Everybody be quiet; get settled; if you're standing up and you're uncomfortable, sit down; if you're sitting down and you're uncomfortable, stand up *[laughs]*; if you've got a cough or a cold, leave; but I want it quiet until this camera runs out of film." Then he would start a scene. I remember being there one day for a scene with Mitchum and Shelley Winters.

They started it, but Charles interrupted, "No, no, that's not right. Do it again and *this* time..." blah, blah, blah. Most people would have said *cut*. But in order to start up again, they have to call "Quiet!" again, they have to slate it again, lots of things. That all takes up a lot of time, and it also breaks the mood, breaks the rhythm. Laughton did all that preparatory stuff *once,* and then never stopped until the camera was out of film. That way, he got a lot better work out of people. Still today, very few people do it that way.

In the late nineteen sixties, you dropped out of the business for several years.

My problem at that point was, I wasn't a juvenile anymore; I didn't look old enough to be a father; I was sort of in no-man's-land. I dropped out for five years and moved to Hawaii. I arrived in Maui in nineteen sixty-nine and came back here in March of seventy-five. While I was over there, at one point they were shooting *Hawaii Five-O* and they were trying to find me, and I got the message two weeks later. The people said, "Why don't you try to get work in this series?" and I said, "Either you're in this business or you're out of it. I am *out.*" I wanted to see if I could get out, cut the umbilical cord, forget about agents and managers and casting people and the Screen Actors Guild, etc., etc. —I wanted to get out of the *reel* world and into the *real* world and see what would happen! I had a couple of commercial fishing boats when I was over there; I also had a radio program, and a cable TV program for a while. I had a wonderful time.

You made your comeback as Teddy Roosevelt in TV's Eleanor and Franklin *[1976], and later appeared as a regular on the short-lived* Time Express *[1979].*

That was very exciting. It was created by Ben Roberts and Ivan Goff, who did *Mannix* and *Charlie's Angels,* and who wrote one of the best Cagney pictures of all time, *White Heat* [1949]. *Time Express* was a mini-series, we did four of them, and they had a lot of back-up scripts. It starred Vincent Price and his wife Coral Browne, and it had a great format: People would get lured to the train station downtown on some pretext, and they'd come up to the ticket office, where there'd be fog swirling around. The ticket master in each episode was Woodrow Parfrey, and he would greet them by name and have their tickets ready. Now they would get on the train and suddenly they'd be talking to Vincent Price, and he'd take 'em to his car. His car was the most elaborate, swankiest car that you ever saw—from the eighteen hundreds, with the bright red cushions and upholstery, beautiful woodwork and all that stuff. Price would get around to saying, "Remember when such-and-such a thing happened in your life..." Now, the format of it was that they could go back in time to any turning point in their lives in hopes of changing their futures.

And you ran the train.

Right, I was the engineer of this diesel streamliner. My name was

Phipps (center) co-starred with Vincent Price, Coral Browne (Mrs. Price) (seated), Woodrow Parfrey and James Reynolds in the short-lived teleseries *Time Express.*

Callahan and I did it with an Irish brogue, and I was dressed in the engineering uniform of the eighteen eighties—the striped cap, red bandana, the works. I had been on an old steam locomotive that went off of a trestle into a river 'way back in eighteen ninety, and I perished with it. But now here I was, back on the Time Express!

Well, I thought, "Vincent Price, Ben Roberts, Ivan Goff—it *can't* miss!" And we weren't doing a pilot, we did four! I remember saying to Vincent Price, "God, I'd like to be in a really big, hit TV series before I die," and he whispered, "So would *I!*" *[Laughs.]*

Phipps (now billing himself as William Edward Phipps) in a recent pose.

You were also in another SF pilot that didn't take off, Space Force *[1978].*

It was first called *Fort Leo,* then they changed it to *Space Force.* That was a good experience. The two leads were Fred Willard and I and we were on a space station; I was the commander and Fred was under me. It was written and produced by Norman Stiles and John Boni, two writers from *Sesame Street.* I would have been the star of the series, and we thought we were all in like Flynn. But unbeknownst to Norman and John, the same studio and the same network were also making another science fiction pilot with Richard Benjamin and Buzz Henry, called *Quark.* Norman and John were intimidated when they found out about that; they didn't know we had competition, they thought theirs was the only one being made. I imagine because of the Richard Benjamin name, and Buzz Henry's, that they got priority; *Quark* got picked up and several episodes were made, and *Space Force* wasn't. And I think we would have had some wonderful stuff happening on there.

Your overall career: If you had it to do all over again, what would you do differently?

You know *[laughs]*, I was asked that once before, and I answered by saying, "Well, you do what you have to do." Which, when you think about it, is *not* a flip answer; it really boils down to that. I always knew that I was an actor, and you have to have that inner knowledge to go ahead and "do what you have to do." I never did what a lot of actors have done (right or wrong, smart or dumb, I don't know): I just went with it. Whatever came along, whether it was *Cat Women of the Moon* or *War of the Worlds* or *Five,* I'd stick my toe in the water and if it felt okay, I'd do it. I never thought about what any of these would do for my career, never thought ahead to whether it would be a success or what it would do for me. I never had any kind of plan or blueprint, never tried to capitalize on anything. But I kept busy throughout a forty-year career, and I'm still busy today. I know that I've always been a good actor, I know that I am now, and I know I still get work. And I have the respect of my peers. Hey, what more could you ask for?

WILLIAM PHIPPS FILMOGRAPHY

Crossfire (RKO, 1947)
The Arizona Ranger (RKO, 1948)
Train to Alcatraz (Republic, 1948)
Desperadoes of Dodge City (Republic, 1948)
Belle Starr's Daughter (20th Century–Fox, 1948)
Station West (RKO, 1948)
They Live by Night (The Twisted Road) (RKO, 1948)
The Man on the Eiffel Tower (RKO, 1949)
Scene of the Crime (MGM, 1949)
Cinderella (voice only; RKO, 1950)
Key to the City (MGM, 1950)
The Outriders (MGM, 1950)
Rider from Tucson (RKO, 1950)
The Vanishing Westerner (Republic, 1950)
The Red Badge of Courage (MGM, 1951)
No Questions Asked (MGM, 1951)
Five (Columbia, 1951)
Fort Osage (Monogram, 1952)
Rose of Cimarron (20th Century–Fox, 1952)
Loan Shark (Lippert, 1952)
Flat Top (Monogram, 1952)
Invaders from Mars (20th Century–Fox, 1953)
Julius Caesar (MGM, 1953)
The Twonky (United Artists, 1953)
Fort Algiers (United Artists, 1953)
Northern Patrol (Allied Artists, 1953)
The War of the Worlds (Paramount, 1953)

Savage Frontier (Republic, 1953)
Cat Women of the Moon (Rocket to the Moon) (Astor, 1953)
The Blue Gardenia (voice only; Warners, 1953)
Red River Shore (Republic, 1953)
Francis Joins the Wacs (Universal, 1954)
Riot in Cell Block 11 (Allied Artists, 1954)
Executive Suite (MGM, 1954)
Jesse James vs. the Daltons (Columbia, 1954)
Two Guns and a Badge (Allied Artists, 1954)
The Snow Creature (United Artists, 1954)
The Indian Fighter (United Artists, 1955)
Rage at Dawn (RKO, 1955)
The Violent Men (Columbia, 1955)
Smoke Signal (Universal, 1955)
The Far Horizons (Paramount, 1955)
The Eternal Sea (Republic, 1955)
Lord of the Jungle (Allied Artists, 1955)
The Man in the Gray Flannel Suit (20th Century–Fox, 1956)
The First Texan (Allied Artists, 1956)
Great Day in the Morning (RKO, 1956)
Lust for Life (MGM, 1956)
The Wild Party (United Artists, 1956)
The Boss (United Artists, 1956)
Kiss Them for Me (20th Century–Fox, 1957)
Badlands of Montana (20th Century–Fox, 1957)
The Brothers Rico (Columbia, 1957)
Escape from Red Rock (20th Century–Fox, 1958)
The FBI Story (Warners, 1959)
Black Gold (Warners, 1963)
Showdown (Universal, 1963)
Cavalry Command (Parade, 1963)
The Kidnappers (Manson, 1964)
Harlow (Paramount, 1965)
Dead Heat on a Merry-Go-Round (Columbia, 1966)
Incident at Phantom Hill (Universal, 1966)
Gunfight in Abilene (Universal, 1967)
Valley of Mystery (Universal, 1967)
Homeward Bound: The Incredible Journey (Buena Vista, 1993)

Phipps also appeared in additional footage shot for the American television version of Hammer's *The Evil of Frankenstein* (Universal, 1964).

*I know of so many people who are miserable
in this business—really miserable—and I never could
understand it, because they're so bloody lucky to be
in and to stay in it. I really think it's a wonderful business.*

Vincent Price

HE REQUIRES NO INTRODUCTION IN A BOOK OF THIS SORT: Vincent Price was a living legend to fright film fans for most of the 50-plus years since he took the horror plunge with Universal's *Tower of London* in 1939. In the years since, he played a variety of roles in approximately 100 films, made all over the world, but it was as a screen villain—sometimes haunted, often heinous, occasionally humorous—that Price made his most popular and acclaimed pictures. And in recognition of his preeminence in the horror field, Vincent Price was the very special guest of honor at the May 1990 *Fangoria Weekend of Horrors* in Los Angeles where, following an introduction by the one and only Roger Corman, the screen's foremost aristocrat of evil received ovation after ovation during an on-stage interview with director Joe Dante.

Per Price's request for a "different" type of interview, the questions (devised by Dante and yours truly, and supplemented with questions from the audience) were an eclectic and wide-ranging bunch, touching on his horror movies, the 1982 Disney short *Vincent* (shown at the tribute), his dramatic and comedy roles, the work he'd done on stage and the music scene, and more. (Price died after a long illness in October 1993 "closing the book" on the screen's great horror stars.)

How did you come to be involved with the Disney short Vincent?

Somebody sent me from Disney a storyboard for *Vincent* and I thought it was such a wonderful idea—I loved the story. So I went over to meet [director] Tim Burton, and Tim is kind of a mad fellow, a wonderful, mad little fellow. He had this marvelous idea and he showed me a little mockup of Vincent, the character, and then read me the script. And I said, "I will do it." Because I think this is something that you must do when something like it comes along. So I went in and did the narration for him. It won a lot of prizes for Tim in little festivals, all over the world. One of the reasons he did *Vincent* was that he was fascinated with (as he called it) "the Vincent Price persona"—how I was able to hide behind the evil. I think it's a wonderful film.

I'm going to do another film for Tim very soon, called *Edward Scissorhands,* and I'm playing the professor who creates Edward Scissorhands. He's a marvelous fellow, really brilliant talent, this boy. Wonderful designer—he's sent me other things that he's designed, and we've sort of kept in touch. [*Edward Scissorhands* was released in 1990.]

You are also the voice of the haunted house in the new Euro Disneyland.

They asked me if I'd do it and I asked, "In what language?" and they said, "French." I said, "*Mais oui!*"—that's about as much French as I speak *[laughs]*! They sent the script to me and they spelled it all out phonetically, and I learned it—I got French friends to come in and help me, and I had a terrible time because it's all sort of in pseudo-verse. I really had a big three weeks of work

Previous page: Vincent Price reigned as King of Horror Films in the 1950s and 1960s, beginning with the starring role in Warners' 3-D blockbuster *House of Wax* (pictured).

Out of the musty mufti of AIP's creepy Poe series, Price played a fanatical peacemonger in the company's science-fictional *Master of the World*.

to get it right, I got over to the studio—and they had changed almost every word of it *[laughs]*! But I got through it and I think it's going to be very nice, and it's kind of fun to be part of Disneyland.

When you made the Three-D House of Wax, *was that the point at which you had to decide whether you wanted to be a stage star or a movie star?*
 Yes. I was offered a wonderful play in New York called *We're No Angels,* and it was a big, big hit, and every time I'd go by that theater in New York [after turning down the role], I'd say, "Did I do the right thing?" But it was playing and it was about to go off after a year, and *House of Wax* is *still* playing after forty years *[applause]*! I don't know, really; you always wonder whether you've done the right thing or not. But I think I did, because I loved

House of Wax, it was great fun to make. And it was fun to be part of the growing technology of the motion picture industry.

The famous story about House of Wax *is that the director, Andre de Toth, only had one eye —*

—and he couldn't see any of the Three-D effects! He'd go in and look at the film, and he'd ask, "What are all those people screaming about?" He never saw a thing!

One of your co-stars in that film was Charles Bronson.

Yes — Charles *Buchinski.* He was wonderful in it; he had no dialogue, but he was awfully good *[laughs]!*

Did you think he would go on to bigger things?

Yes, I did — he really has a wonderful face. We did another picture together, *Master of the World,* and I think Charlie was practically a deaf mute again *[laughs]!* And I saw one of his first pictures as a great star and he was almost a deaf mute in *that [laughs]!* He didn't talk very much, he talks more now.

In preparing to do House of Wax, *which was a remake of* Mystery of the Wax Museum, *did you look at Lionel Atwill's performance?*

No, I think that's a big, big mistake. No, I've never seen *Mystery of the Wax Museum* unless I saw it as a kid — it came out when I was a youngster. So [in preparing for *House of Wax*] I never did see it — on purpose — because I didn't want to copy Lionel Atwill. And *House of Wax* was a different story.

While *House of Wax* played for about thirty weeks at the Paramount Theater in New York, I was doing a play and I used to sneak into the back of the movie theater. And I'd have more fun watching the people with these silly Three-D glasses on *[laughs].* And they couldn't tell who I was, because *I* had glasses on, too! I'd always pick two teenage girls to sit behind, 'cause their reactions were marvelous. At the end of one of the showings, these two girls were riveted and they were moving forward in their seats. And when finally I'm thrown into the vat of wax and I'm burned up and the steam comes up and it says THE END, I leaned forward and I said, "Did you *like* it?" Right up into orbit, they went *[laughs and applause]!*

A lot of people might not remember that you were directed by Alfred Hitchcock in an episode of his television series.

I was really terribly excited about working with Hitchcock, he's one of the great movie makers of all time. There were only two of us in it [Price and James Gregory], just two characters, and I thought it was going to be wonderful. It was a very elaborate thing called *The Perfect Crime,* and I was really very thrilled to think of Hitchcock telling us what to do.

His entire direction was, he came on the set one day and he said, "Faster." *[Laughs.]* And so we did it a little faster and he said, "That's better. A little bit faster." Then he went over and slept *[laughs]*! I've read four books about Hitchcock recently and he slept all through everything—or gave the appearance of sleeping. He set things up so brilliantly that he didn't really have to watch very carefully.

Another director people might not remember your working with was Orson Welles, who directed you on stage when he was twenty-two.

Yes, after I had done *Victoria Regina* and a couple of other plays, I joined the Mercury Theater with Orson. And I did two plays which were really wonderful: *The Shoemaker's Holiday*, which is a very bawdy Shakespearean farce, and *Heartbreak House* by George Bernard Shaw. Wonderful cast, we had, and he was a brilliant director, Orson—mad as a hatter, but brilliant *[laughs]*!

Angel Street was one of your major successes on Broadway, and it was eventually made into the film Gaslight *[1944]. But you didn't end up playing the lead in the movie, Charles Boyer did.*

You never get a chance in the movies to play the same leading role that you've done on Broadway, or very seldom. But I did the play, and it ran for five years. It was an extraordinary story, a real theatrical story. The Shuberts [the theater owners] hated the play so much when they came to see a run-through that they refused to print the tickets for Monday. So the play opened on Friday, and Saturday the reviews were raves, one hundred percent. I've never read reviews like that in my life—"The best melodrama of all time" and so forth. And there were no tickets! The line outside the box office was there and the girls in the box office were writing the seat numbers down on slips of paper!

Finally Sunday came around. My wife was out on the West Coast and I called her from New York and I said, "Isn't it wonderful?" There was a dead silence and then she said, "What do you mean wonderful? It's the greatest tragedy of all time." I said, "The play is a *hit*! It's the biggest hit in town! What's this tragedy bit?" She said, "*Pearl Harbor.*" I had read the papers, but I'd only read my own notices, I hadn't read about Pearl Harbor *[laughs and applause]*. Isn't that a terrible story? Almost every show in New York closed sooner or later right after that, except *Angel Street,* which ran five years.

You also wrote a play yourself.

My God, how did you know that?

Poet's Corner. Were you happy with it?

I loved it, I had a wonderful time. I was up in a famous summer theater called Skowhegan in Maine and I showed it to the director at Skowhegan (I'd worked there before) and he said, "Well, it needs some work, but I like it and

I'll do it—if you'll play in it." I said, "My God, I can't play in it—I'd be so nervous and self-conscious." So he put me in a small part.

Well, I was a disaster, because every time somebody else would open their mouth and say one of my brilliant lines, I'd go [Price gasps with awe]. Or if it was a funny line [Price bellylaughs]—and I wasn't meant to laugh! But it was fun to do. I never tried another one, but it wasn't too bad.

When you did Victoria Regina *with Helen Hayes, there were two other great screen villains-to-be in the cast, George Zucco and George Macready. How did you enjoy working with them?*

Oh, they were wonderful. *Victoria Regina* I had done in London first, in a little theater, and then [American producer] Gilbert Miller came to see it and decided to buy it for Helen Hayes. And it was of course the peak of her career—this was fifty-five years ago. (I was only ten years old, playing Prince Albert [laughs]!) It was a wonderful play. George Macready played my brother, and became one of my best friends. He was a wonderful villain. I remember when he did *Gilda* [1946], a critic said he was "an icicle dressed by Wetzel." (Wetzel was a great men's tailor.) And George Zucco was also a really great villain.

When people see Invisible Man movies they often think, "How much work does this really involve?" Like, when you're not there, do you come in those days?

You come in. It's endless! *[Laughs.]* There's a scene in *The Invisible Man Returns* where I take the clothes off a scarecrow, because I'm only invisible if I'm naked. (It's very cold!) I have to undress this scarecrow and put the clothes on myself, and it took nine hours. Today they have blue screens and chroma-key, but the way they did it in those days, the set was built and the camera anchored and they draped the whole set in black velvet. And then I was draped with black velvet. And whatever I put on myself, I put around the black velvet. But it took forever, because anytime you'd make the smallest mistake, you could be seen. So it was very laborious, and rather boring!

Is it true that the director of The Invisible Man Returns *didn't speak English?*

Joe May spoke very, very little English. Thank God I spoke a little German—we could curse at each other. He was a great director in his day in Germany, but he really did have a bad time here because he didn't speak very much English at all. I saw *The Invisible Man Returns* in a theater and there were two fellows in front of me, and at the end, when I returned to visibility, one of 'em said, "That'll teach you not to drink ten-cent whiskey!" *[Laughs.]*

There was a wonderful triple bill that I went to see about ten times: the original *Invisible Man* with Claude Rains, myself in the second one, and a cartoon called *The Invisible Mouse* [1947]. Which was heaven, because they used all the tricks: The cat even put flour on the floor so that the feet of the mouse would leave tracks *[laughs]*!

You worked with another great director, James Whale, on what is generally regarded as not *his finest hour,* Green Hell *[1940].*

Probably one of the ten worst pictures ever made. If you ever get a chance to see it, you must, because it is hysterical. I had a line where I am going up the Amazon with Douglas Fairbanks, Jr., who was playing a character named Brandy. For some unknown reason, going up the Amazon, I say, "Brandy, do you think it is possible for a man to be in love with two women at the same time, and in his heart be faithful to each, and yet want to be free of both of them?" *[Laughs.]* Opening night, the audience fell on the floor—it was hysterical! It was the funniest picture in the whole world!

Another one of the funniest pictures in the world is Champagne for Caesar *[1950], in which you played a mad soap tycoon* [applause]. *And in* His Kind of Woman *[1951], you gave another wonderful comic performance.*

I loved playing comedy, but I looked like a villain. And they were all villains, really, those comedic parts. But I love comedy, and I think it's much more difficult to play comedy than the straight roles. *His Kind of Woman* is really a funny film; I play a movie star who believes in himself, believes that everything he does is true. Mr. [Howard] Hughes didn't direct the picture but he fell in love with the character that I was playing, and six months after we finished the whole film, he called me back and built a set which cost at that time two hundred fifty thousand for that scene where all the Mexican policemen and I go down in the sinking boat. The policemen all go underwater, I'm standing on the prow and I turn around and say, "Stop mumbling and abandon ship!" And their heads pop up out of the water *[laughs]*! It cost him two hundred fifty thousand to add that scene and he loved it—*loved* it!

You were hilarious in Tales of Terror, *in the wine-tasting contest.*

That's a funny scene, I must say. They hired a fellow to come on the set and show us about wine-tasting, because people don't really taste wine, they *drink* it. And so he was showing us all these fancy things. So all Peter Lorre and I did was just exaggerate them a tiny bit, and they were hysterical. I loved doing that.

George Sanders is a person about whom much has been written—some of it by himself—describing what "a dreadful man" he was.

He wasn't. He was a dear man, a wonderful man. One of the first pictures I ever did *[The House of the Seven Gables]* was with George, and I knew him really intimately and was very, very fond of him. He pretended to be a dreadful man, but he was a brilliant raconteur, spoke Russian superbly (he was born in Russia), he was a wonderful pianist, had a beautiful singing voice. But he really didn't care. I remember one day he said to me, "I'm going to Egypt to do a film," and I said, "Is it an ancient film or a modern film?" He said, "I

The cast of *Tales of Terror* discussing a scene (or maybe just posing for a publicity shot!) behind the scenes: Debra Paget, David Frankham, Price and production assistant Jonathan Haze.

really don't know yet, old boy." I said, "Well, aren't you going to find out before you go?" He said, "Really doesn't matter. You smoke cigarettes *this* way *[Price holds up a hand]* if it's an old film and *this* way if it's modern." *[Laughs.]* I loved it!

Who instilled in you your appreciation of the arts?

I went to college in the East, I went to Yale; it was during the Depression, and there really were no jobs. And I thought that being a teacher would be a wonderful job, and what I would love to teach is visual arts. So I majored in the arts, in the history of art, at Yale, and then when I got out I taught school for a couple of years—and found out how little I knew! So I went over to England, to the famous Courtauld Institute, which was just started at that time, and I stayed there for two years and started in the theater then, too. But it's really my hobby, I know a lot about art. I don't know much about anything else, but I know a lot about art!

Have you ever tried your hand at painting?

I took it up about six months ago and I quit about five and a half months ago *[laughs]*! I have no talent whatsoever!

Do you ever seek out and watch your old pictures?

Every once in a while, if it was one that I enjoyed making. The ones with Roger Corman I loved, because we had such a good time making 'em. We worked hard, really hard—oh, boy, he was a slavedriver! But it was wonderful fun, because he had it so carefully planned. He had Danny Haller doing the sets and Floyd Crosby on the camera, he got wonderful people around him and he just did a superb job. And, again, they were great fun.

When Ray Milland was asked how he liked working with Roger, he said, "I can't remember, because the pictures were made so quickly that I have hardly any memories of them."

Roger did make pictures very quickly, but they were made thoroughly. They were brilliantly designed and brilliantly thought out. He was one of the best directors I ever worked with in my life. [Mr. Corman was present at the tribute.]

Which of the pictures you made for Roger was the most satisfying to you?

Well, I kind of loved *The Masque of the Red Death*. We had one of the great cameramen in England [Nicolas Roeg] and we had a wonderful cast. And all the extras were from the Royal Ballet—but that you can do in London, you can't do it here. You'd have to bring 'em out from New York! But it was a very exciting film, and I found it fun to work on.

Another fan favorite is The Tomb of Ligeia, *which was written by Robert Towne.*

I think *The Tomb of Ligeia* was closest to Poe—it was *very* close to Poe, as a matter of fact. Roger and I had often talked about the idea of doing a film in an actual location. We had this wonderful twelfth century abbey and most of it was done right in there.

Pit and the Pendulum?

Pit and the Pendulum I think was one of Roger's triumphs, because that

Price, a script girl and Roger Corman on location in England for AIP's *The Tomb of Ligeia.*

is a really difficult thing to bring off. You know, one of the problems with doing Edgar Allan Poe is that those are short stories, and you've got to make them into long films! And Poe doesn't take the trouble to explain why people are where they are, so you have to explain that. It was a very difficult film to do, *Pit and the Pendulum,* but I enjoyed it.

Were there Poe stories that you would have liked to have done with Roger Corman, but didn't?

Yes, I would love to have done *The Gold-Bug* with Roger. *The Gold-Bug* was the first detective story—Poe was an extraordinary writer, and it would have been fun to do that "version" of him. Because a lot of people don't recognize that something like sixty-five percent of Poe's work is satirical—it isn't heavy, it isn't horror, it's satirical work. I did a television show one time called *An Evening with Edgar Allan Poe,* and in it I narrated a Poe story called *The Sphinx.* It's about a man who thinks that he sees a monster, and it turns out to be a little moth.

Tell us a little about Dragonwyck *[1946].*

If only one Vincent Price movie still exists a thousand years from now, *he* wants it to be *Dragonwyck* (1946).

Dragonwyck I think was one of the best pictures I ever made *[applause]*. It was Joe Mankiewicz's first picture [as director] and it was the fourth picture that I'd done with Gene Tierney; I also did *Laura* [1944] with her, and I think that's really one of the best pictures ever made *[applause]*. It's not a pretentious picture, but it was perfect — the best thing that Otto Preminger ever did.

Did you enjoy working with Gene Tierney?

Yes. I did four pictures with her *[Hudson's Bay* (1940), *Laura* (1944), *Leave Her to Heaven* (1945), *Dragonwyck].* She was divine. You know, when you see *Laura,* it isn't dated at all. Gene Tierney didn't date! Her hair was sort of contemporary, no matter what period...! It's almost fifty years ago that we did *Laura,* and *Laura* holds up—it's just as modern today as it was then, largely due to Gene Tierney. She was wonderful to work with but she had a rough time [in life].

Your "typing" in the late nineteen-fifties as a horror star began with your association with William Castle. He brought a sense of fun to going to the movies, a kind of showmanship that is sadly missing today.

He was a *great* showman. There was a wonderful article in one of the airplane magazines not too long ago about "What Happened to Show Biz?", and it brought up Bill Castle and the things that he did. The crazy things, like *The Tingler [applause].* But he was wonderful! I mean, who would ever do a black-and-white movie and have one scene in color, where the lady turns on the water in the bathtub and it's *bloo-oo-ood [laughs]*! Wonderful!

When Castle would come to you with a script, would he already have the Gimmick in mind?

Yes, I think so. Like *House on Haunted Hill,* with the emerging skeleton *[applause]!* When he was looking for a haunted house, he went out and found a great Frank Lloyd Wright house—one of the most modern pieces of architecture in the world—and he used this as the haunted house! And there's nothing like that first scene, where all the guests that I've invited arrive by hearse...! He was a nutty fellow, but great fun and very inventive.

The opening night of *House on Haunted Hill,* I was in a little theater in Baltimore. In the movie, I reeled this skeleton in using a winch, and then there'd be a real skeleton in the theater that would shoot over the audience. Well, I was in this theater with a great many young people in it—and they panicked! And they knocked all the seats out of the theater *[laughs]*! They just took down the first five rows. I loved it!

You were on The $64,000 Question *a number of times, on art. Was that before or after the quiz show scandals?*

It was before the quiz show scandals. *The $64,000 Question* had a very good premise: The contestant would be a person who was, say, an actor or a shoemaker or whatever, who knew about some other subject. *One* other subject. Then, because it was so popular, there came shows where a guy knew about *everything.* Well, I never could believe that, I couldn't go along with that for a minute. Ours was very honest—at least, it was with me. I studied—I never put down books on art. I studied the whole time I was on it!

Could you tell us a little about Peter Lorre?

[Holding his nose and imitating Lorre.] Peter? *[Laughs.]* The greatest imitation I ever heard of Peter Lorre in my life was by Peter Lorre. He held his nose and talked like that, and that sounded just *exactly* like Peter Lorre *[laughs]*! At his funeral, I read the obituary address for him, because all of his friends were dead — Humphrey Bogart and all of them were gone, and I guess I knew him as well as anyone at that time. He called himself a "face maker," and he always denigrated actors. He always played 'em down, said we're face makers, we're nothing else, we really don't have a brain in our heads. But he was a wonderful actor.

He also loved to rewrite the script. One time, in one of Roger's films, there was a scene where all Peter and I were doing was getting from one place to another, and there was some exposition there. I always know my lines and I was saying them, and Peter was sort of vaguely saying something else, I don't know what it was. And I said, "Oh, for Christ's sake, Peter, *say the lines!!*" He said, "You mean that, old boy? You don't like *my* lines better?" I said *[sharply]*, "No!" So he said all the lines — he knew every line in the script! But he didn't like to say them *[laughs]*!

Boris Karloff found Lorre a little off-putting, because he would not stick to the script.

Yes, it's very annoying, it really is. Because no actor is funnier than a good writer.

Basil Rathbone?

Basil — I sound like Pollyanna, don't I? — he was one of the nicest men that ever lived *[laughs]*! I did a picture with him called *Tower of London [applause]*, years ago, he was Richard III and he was absolutely marvelous in it. And he did a wonderful thing, sort of to keep everybody's spirits up (it was a rather heavy play and too many stars in it). He got us all together, all the cast — being the star, he could do this — and he said, "Let's make an agreement amongst ourselves. Let's never tell a dirty joke that we didn't hear after we were fourteen." Well, we'd all go home at night and think of all the dirty jokes that we'd heard before we were fourteen. And they're *very funny [laughs]*! They're not particularly dirty but they're very funny, and we'd come on the set the next day and tell these stories...! Basil was a sweet man — a great prankster and joker, but a wonderful actor.

What were some of your most difficult films to make?

I did a couple of pictures in Italy, which shall be nameless —

Queen of the Nile *[1964] with Jeanne Crain?*

God Almighty! And another one with Ricardo Montalban called *Gordon, il Pirata Nero* [1962] — "Gordon the Black Pirate." I said, "Why *Gordon?*"

[Laughs.] Gordon, what kind of terrible name is that? Well, Gordon, I finally found out, was because of Byron, who was Lord Gordon—he had lived in Italy. On *Gordon* they lost the soundtrack, so we dubbed it. But we had so many different nationalities in it that we had to hire lip-readers in everything but Watusi *[laughs]*—it was impossible! I don't think anybody ever saw it.

What was it like doing The Last Man on Earth *in Rome?*
    The problem doing *The Last Man on Earth* was that it was supposed to be set in Los Angeles, and if there's a city in the world that doesn't look like Los Angeles, it's Rome *[laughs]*. We would get up and drive out at five o'clock in the morning, to beat the police, and try to find something that didn't look like Rome. Rome has flat trees, ancient buildings—we had a terrible time! And I never was so cold in my life as I was in that picture. I had a driver and I used to tip him a big sum to keep the car running, so I could change my clothes in the back seat.

How about The Abominable Dr. Phibes?
    Dr. Phibes, and *Dr. Phibes Rises Again,* were really funny pictures, I think two of the funniest pictures ever made. Scary, but funny—each one of the murders had a little fillip to it that made it funny. But the guy who directed it [Robert Fuest] was a madman—and wonderful. He would say, "Do this" and you did it, because there was nothing else to do! It was so mad and so crazy but they were great fun to do. I loved doing those two *[applause]*.

How did you and Charlton Heston get along when you worked together?
    Charlton Heston? Who's he *[laughs]*? Oh', *that* one! Charlton and I got along all right. We did a couple of television shows—the first *Playhouse 90* and a few other ones—and I did *The Ten Commandments* [1956] with him. I always loved him because he was practically brand new to the screen and he was telling DeMille how to direct *[laughs]*!

How about Errol Flynn?
    I did two films with Errol, one with Bette Davis called *The Private Lives of Elizabeth and Essex* [1939], which was one of the biggest films made in its time. It was exciting because it was the very beginning of my movie career and I was thrilled to be working with Bette. And with Errol, who was a little difficult, but an extraordinary, charming man. Charmed the pants off every girl that he ever met *[laughs]*—and the dress, too!

How did you get involved with Alice Cooper and his Welcome to My Nightmare *album?*
    I did a show for a long time called *The Hollywood Squares,* and on

Price's horror bow, as the foppish Duke of Clarence in Universal's *Tower of London*.

Hollywood Squares you met *every*body *[laughs]* — everybody in the *world*! It was great fun because the comics were all on it, and I love comics. Alice and I became friends, and he asked me if I would do this thing. Just like Michael Jackson asked me to do *Thriller* — which is still the biggest-selling album in the history of the medium *[applause]*. I notice that I am now sort of the grandfather of the raps, or the *great*-grandfather *[laughs]*! *Thriller* was a wonderful rap, really marvelous.

Can you tell us about working with Diana Rigg in Theater of Blood?

Diana Rigg—she's a killer, that girl, one of the most sexy and attractive ladies I've ever met in my life. She took over my spot in *Mystery!* as the host; I'd done it for eight years and I thought that was enough of that, and so she's come in and is doing it now. She's awfully good, a wonderful actress.

You've worked a number of times with your fellow Geminis Peter Cushing and Christopher Lee, and you're very close to both of them.

Christopher, when you first meet him—if you don't get along right away, he's a rather pompous man *[laughs]*. He's very sort of British and terribly sort of proper. For some reason or other, we got along wonderfully, and we're like two girls—we get on the telephone together and we crack jokes. We save up jokes and gossip and all kinds of things! I don't think he does that with anybody else—we just have the best time together and I'm devoted to him. Peter Cushing is a very proper man, a very sad man—he lost his wife years ago and he's never gotten over it. But we're all born within a day of each other—not in the same year, as they hasten to point out *[laughs]*!

What was it like to work on the set of the old Batman *series?*

Egghead *[laughs and applause]*? I've run into a large amount of criticism over the years, people would say, "Why did you *do* such a crappy thing as *Batman?*" Well, *Batman* wasn't crappy, it was one of the funniest shows ever on the air, really hysterical *[applause]*. They were broad, they were farcical, but they were wonderful. I must get a hundred pictures of Egghead a week to sign—*Batman* is all over the world now, they replay it in England, in Germany, everywhere. I'm so sick of that picture of me holding the egg...! *[Laughs.]*

What did you think of the new version of The Fly?

When the new *Fly* opened, I thought they were going to call it *The Zipper [laughs]*. Anyway, when it came out, I got a lovely letter from Jeff Goldblum saying, "I loved your *Fly*, hope you like mine." *[Laughs.]* I thought that was very sweet, it was an adorable letter. And he loved the original *Fly*. So I went to see his, and I thought parts of it were marvelous, up until the end. Then he didn't turn into a fly, he turned into a glob. And there was nothing left of him. I really thought they went too far. And it lost credibility.

I have a feeling that horror films must be logical. You must be able to believe some part of them—not all of it, but you must be able to believe that this could happen. Otherwise, it's not frightening.

Being that you're the true master of classic horror, what is the attraction for you for horror and terror?

You. People who enjoy it. And when they're made with the imagination that Roger Corman put into 'em, and that the other people I've worked with put into 'em, people love 'em. They're like fairy tales—they have a quality of the unreal and yet they're real. They scare you and you scream and then you laugh at yourself. I think they're great fun.

There are no derogatory stories about you.

There are very few, because I like people. And I think that if *you* like people, you get along with people and they don't dislike *you*. I know of so many people who are miserable in this business—really miserable—and I never could understand it, because they're so bloody lucky to be in and to stay in it. I really think it's a wonderful business and people should be very grateful for being part of it.

A thousand years from now, there's only one Vincent Price picture surviving. Which one do you think it should be?

I think *Dragonwyck [applause]*. *Dragonwyck* was a very difficult part to play, because he's a crazy man, a monomaniac, and yet didn't know it. So it was a challenge to play it. I think *Dragonwyck*'s a very good film.

Conqueror Worm *reportedly was a very troubled film to make; your conflict with the director stemmed from the fact that he had originally wanted someone else for the part—*

—and *told* me so *[laughs]*! When I went on location to meet him [Michael Reeves] for the first time, he said, "I didn't want you and I *still* don't want you, but I'm stuck with you!" *That's* the way to gain confidence! He had no idea how to talk to actors. He came up to me one day after a take and he said, "Don't shake your head!" I said, "What do you mean? I'm not shaking my head." He said, "You're shaking your head!! Just don't shake your head." Well, that made me so self-conscious that I was poker-faced—and, as it turned out, he was right! He wanted it *that* concentrated, so it would be that much more menacing. He could have been a wonderful director . . . such a sad, sad death. . .

When I made that picture in England, it was called *Witchfinder General*, from the title of a novel. And when I came back here, I wanted very much to see it and I kept looking in the paper to see if it was going to be released. And when it was released here, they called it *Conqueror Worm*. So I started to look around, to see where the hell they got this title. And I found it. I read it one day in a book of poetry and I thought you might like to hear it because you're going to *[laughs]*!

> Lo! 'tis a gala night
>   Within the lonesome latter years!
> An angel throng, bewinged, bedight,
>   In veils, and drowned in tears,

Sit in a theatre, to see
A play of hopes and fears,
While the orchestra breathes fitfully
The music of the spheres.

Mimes, in the form of God on high,
Mutter and mumble low,
And hither and thither fly—
Mere puppets they, who come and go
At bidding of vast formless things
That shift the scenery to and fro,
Flapping from out their Condor wings
Invisible Woe!

That motley drama—oh, be sure
It shall not be forgot!
With its Phantom chased for evermore,
By a crowd that seize it not,
Through a circle that ever returneth in
To the self-same spot,
And much of Madness, and more of Sin,
And Horror the soul of the plot.

But see, amid the mimic rout
A crawling shape intrude!
A blood-red thing that writhes from out
The scenic solitude!
It writhes!—it writhes!—with mortal pangs
The mimes become its food,
And seraphs sob at vermin fangs
In human gore imbued.

Out—out are the lights—out all!
And, over each quivering form,
The curtain, a funeral pall,
Comes down with the rush of a storm,
While the angels, all pallid and wan,
Uprising, unveiling, affirm
That the play is the tragedy "Man,"
And its hero the Conqueror Worm.

—Edgar Allan Poe

[Applause and standing ovation.]

VINCENT PRICE FILMOGRAPHY

Service DeLuxe (Universal, 1938)
The Private Lives of Elizabeth and Essex (Elizabeth the Queen) (Warners, 1939)
Tower of London (Universal, 1939)

Continued clashes with the film's director may account for Price's dour demeanor in this shot from AIP's *Conqueror Worm*.

Green Hell (Universal, 1940)
The House of the Seven Gables (Universal, 1940)
The Invisible Man Returns (Universal, 1940)
Brigham Young—Frontiersman (20th Century–Fox, 1940)
Hudson's Bay (20th Century–Fox, 1940)
The Song of Bernadette (20th Century–Fox, 1943)
The Eve of St. Mark (20th Century–Fox, 1944)
Wilson (20th Century–Fox, 1944)
Laura (20th Century–Fox, 1944)
The Keys of the Kingdom (20th Century–Fox, 1944)
Leave Her to Heaven (20th Century–Fox, 1945)
A Royal Scandal (20th Century–Fox, 1945)
Dragonwyck (20th Century–Fox, 1946)
Shock (20th Century–Fox, 1946)
The Long Night (RKO, 1947)
Moss Rose (20th Century–Fox, 1947)
The Web (Universal, 1947)
Up in Central Park (Universal, 1948)
Abbott and Costello Meet Frankenstein (voice only; Universal, 1948)
The Three Musketeers (MGM, 1948)
Rogue's Regiment (Universal, 1948)
The Bribe (MGM, 1949)
Bagdad (Universal, 1949)
The Baron of Arizona (Lippert, 1950)
Champagne for Caesar (United Artists, 1950)
Curtain Call at Cactus Creek (Universal, 1950)
His Kind of Woman (RKO, 1951)
Adventures of Captain Fabian (Republic, 1951)
The Las Vegas Story (RKO, 1952)

House of Wax (Warners, 1953)
Casanova's Big Night (unbilled guest appearance; Paramount, 1954)
Dangerous Mission (RKO, 1954)
The Mad Magician (Columbia, 1954)
Son of Sinbad (RKO, 1955)
Serenade (Warners, 1956)
While the City Sleeps (RKO, 1956)
The Vagabond King (voice only; Paramount, 1956)
The Ten Commandments (Paramount, 1956)
The Story of Mankind (Warners, 1957)
The Fly (20th Century–Fox, 1958)
House on Haunted Hill (Allied Artists, 1958)
Return of the Fly (20th Century–Fox, 1959)
The Bat (Allied Artists, 1959)
The Big Circus (Allied Artists, 1959)
The Tingler (Columbia, 1959)
House of Usher (The Fall of the House of Usher) (AIP, 1960)
Master of the World (AIP, 1961)
Pit and the Pendulum (AIP, 1961)
Naked Terror (voice only; Joseph Brenner, 1961)
Tales of Terror (AIP, 1962)
Convicts 4 (Reprieve) (Allied Artists, 1962)
Confessions of an Opium Eater (Souls for Sale) (Allied Artists, 1962)
Tower of London (United Artists, 1962)
Rage of the Buccaneers (The Black Buccaneer; Gordon il Pirata Nero) (Colorama
    Features, 1963)
The Raven (AIP, 1963)
The Haunted Palace (AIP, 1963)
Twice-Told Tales (United Artists, 1963)
Diary of a Madman (United Artists, 1963)
Beach Party (unbilled guest appearance; AIP, 1963)
Queen of the Nile (Nefertite, Regina del Nilo) (Colorama Features, 1964)
The Comedy of Terrors (AIP, 1964)
The Masque of the Red Death (AIP, 1964)
The Last Man on Earth (AIP, 1964)
The Tomb of Ligeia (AIP, 1964)
War-Gods of the Deep (The City Under the Sea) (AIP, 1965)
Taboos of the World (voice only; AIP, 1965)
Dr. Goldfoot and the Bikini Machine (AIP, 1965)
Dr. Goldfoot and the Girl Bombs (AIP, 1966)
House of a Thousand Dolls (AIP, 1967)
The Jackals (20th Century–Fox, 1967)
Conqueror Worm (Witchfinder General) (AIP, 1968)
Spirits of the Dead (voice only; AIP, 1969)
The Oblong Box (AIP, 1969)
The Trouble with Girls (MGM, 1969)
More Dead Than Alive (United Artists, 1969)
Cry of the Banshee (AIP, 1970)
Scream and Scream Again (AIP, 1970)
The Abominable Dr. Phibes (AIP, 1971)
Dr. Phibes Rises Again (AIP, 1972)

Theater of Blood (United Artists, 1973)
Madhouse (AIP, 1974)
The Devil's Triangle (voice only; Maron, 1974)
Journey into Fear (Stirling Gold, 1976)
It's Not the Size That Counts (Percy's Progress) (Joseph Brenner, 1978)
Scavenger Hunt (20th Century–Fox, 1979)
Days of Fury (host and narrator; Picturemedia Ltd., 1980)
The Monster Club (ITC, 1981)
House of the Long Shadows (Cannon, 1983)
Bloodbath at the House of Death (Wildwood, 1984)
The Great Mouse Detective (The Adventures of the Great Mouse Detective) (voice
    only; Buena Vista, 1986)
The Offspring (From a Whisper to a Scream) (Conquest Entertainment, 1987)
The Whales of August (Alive Films, 1987)
Dead Heat (New World, 1988)
Edward Scissorhands (20th Century–Fox, 1990)

Clips with Price from *The Bribe* are used in *Dead Men Don't Wear Plaid* (Universal, 1982). *It Came from Hollywood* (Paramount, 1982) includes an abridged version of the Price-narrated *House on Haunted Hill* trailer. Price's scenes in *Forever Amber* (20th Century–Fox, 1947) were reshot with George Sanders. His cameo appearance was cut out of *Bustin' Loose* (Universal, 1981). His 1989 feature *Backtrack* was released theatrically in Europe (as *Catchfire*) but went directly to cable and video in the United States in 1991. He also narrated numerous shorts and documentaries, many on art.

[The War of the Worlds] *was a big responsibility and I
was very inexperienced, so they took a big chance on me.*

Ann Robinson

YOU DON'T HAVE TO STAR IN A *lot* of movies to become a famous actress, sometimes you just have to be in the right *one*. Ann Robinson's fling at film stardom in the mid–1950s put her at the head of the casts of such *un*remembered titles as *Gun Duel in Durango, The Glass Wall* and *Gun Brothers,* but her starring stint in George Pal's knockout science fiction adventure *The War of the Worlds* has, all by itself, made her one of the top female science fiction stars.

Growing up in the proverbial shadow of the studios, the California native acted in grade school plays and later fibbed her way into the movie business as a stunt woman. She was part of Paramount's "Golden Circle" of new stars in the early 1950s but had only one leading role at the studio, in Pal's *War of the Worlds.* In 1977, after falling away from acting to attend to marriage and motherhood, she masterminded the movie's 25th anniversary celebration at the Holly Theater in Hollywood, and in 1989 she took up arms again, backing up Richard Chaves and the rest of the cast in TV's *War of the Worlds* in *their* battle against the newest wave of Martian marauders.

Your publicity says you thought about a career in medicine while you were in school. True?

That's not true; you can't believe any of that publicity stuff. When I was a little girl, I think I wanted to be a policewoman *[laughs]*! I guess acting was always interesting to me, but I didn't realize that I would ever have a chance to *be* in a movie. I liked plays and at school I always entered into plays 'cause I liked the attention, I liked showing off. The first play that I can remember being in was *Snow White,* which we did in the eighth grade at Flintridge. I was one of the ladies-in-waiting who tells the story. But I don't really know if I had any particular ambition or not in *what* I would be when I grew older.

How did you break into show biz?

As a stunt girl and an extra. One of the first films I ever did was called *Black Midnight* [1949] with Roddy McDowall. I was on a horse, doing the stuntwork for some young actress. (That's what I did the best, horseback riding.) I also doubled for Shelley Winters, when a stagecoach or a buckboard turned over in a movie called *Frenchie* [1950] — little things like that. Another one was *The Story of Molly X* [1949] where I doubled for June Havoc — in fact, that might have been my very first job as a stunt girl. I had to escape from Tehachapi State Prison, over a fifteen-foot barbed wire fence. I didn't know *any*thing about stuntwork — I had lied like crazy to get the job, telling everybody how experienced I was! I looked and I thought to myself, "What have I got myself into?", but when you're that young and stupid, nothing fazes you *[laughs]*! I took a big brown wool army blanket and threw it over my shoulder, I climbed the fence and I threw the blanket over the barbed

Previous page: **Ann Robinson and Gene Barry in their signature screen roles — the leads in George Pal's *The War of the Worlds.***

wire. (I got "prickled" quite a bit, I got stuck here and there.) So now here I am up on top of the fence, and I'm saying, "Now how the hell do I get down?" I could hear the assistant director yelling, "Jump, damn it, the film is running!" And so this stupid girl jumped. Fortunately, all the sod was plowed very deeply so that, if anyone *did* escape, they could follow the footprints. So, when I jumped, I didn't hurt myself. By the way, before we did the scene, all the prisoners from that side of the compound were made to go someplace else, so they couldn't see me climb the fence. They didn't want 'em to see how easy it was for an inexperienced stunt girl to climb over *[laughs]*!

And how about your first movie acting job?

I did my first bit in *A Place in the Sun* [1951]: I was an extra and director George Stevens walked by and said, "Who has an S.A.G. card?" I said, "I do!" And he said, "Fine. Stand there, and when Elizabeth Taylor walks through the door, say, 'Hello, Angela.'" That was my first bit. After that, I don't know if I went back to being an extra or not; I probably did, but I don't recall. Then, down the line, I read in the newspaper or somewhere that they were casting at the Circle Theater. I went down and auditioned; I'd never been in a play like *that* before, this was semi-professional now. I got the part, and we were there about ten weeks. The play was called *The Wind Without Rain,* with Marty Milner, written by Ivan Tors.

All the talent scouts in those days went to plays (they still do, that's still the best place to get "discovered"). Milt Lewis from Paramount came, and he said, "When you're finished with the run of the play, come over and read for us." I *did* read, several times, but I didn't seem to be material for them at the time. But Milt liked me a lot, he thought I had potential—he was a sweetheart. One day Robert Walker was doing some retakes [for *My Son John,* 1952] at Paramount; director Leo McCarey was there and they had a complete crew. But Robert Walker became ill. Milt Lewis called me up and said, "How fast can you get down here? We've got a whole crew standing by, doing nothing, and we can make a screen test!" This was all Milt Lewis' plan. I hurried down, they ran me through wardrobe, I wore some beautiful gown that belonged to Joan Fontaine, they fixed my hair, ran me through makeup and sent me to the set. Milt said, "Do you have anything memorized?" I said, "Well, yeah, but it's got three parts in it." He said, "Make it a monologue." So, *on the spot,* I was able to incorporate all three parts—I was talking and saying all three characters' dialogue, just changing the tenses and all. We managed to get through it, and a few days or a week later, Paramount said they were interested in signing me.

You were part of a group of actors called the Golden Circle.

The Golden Circle started back in the twenties or thirties; it was Paramount's group of "stars of the future." Then in the forties and fifties they had new groups, with Susan Hayward and Robert Preston and William Holden—a whole lot of them. *Everyone* in the first and second group became a star; the only one who really became a star in the third group—*my* group—was Barbara Rush. By the way, Ann Robinson is my real name, but when I first went into the business, I found out that I couldn't use it—there was another Ann Robinson in the Screen Actors Guild, a stunt woman. I dropped the -son and went as Ann Robin for awhile. I went under contract to Paramount as Ann Robin. Then, when they did *War of the Worlds,* they said they didn't like that name and they were going to change it to Susan Roberts. I said, "Oh, my God, haven't you had enough Susans around here? Why can't I just use my own name?" They said, "What is it?" and I told them, "Ann Robinson." And they said, "Okay—works for us!" That's how *that* took place.

What did a Golden Circle player do when he—or she—was not in a movie?

They had a room called the Fishbowl—it's still there at Paramount, but now it's all filled with electrical equipment, they use it for a storage room. Back then, it had all props—pianos and couches and things that you might need to do scenes. We used to memorize scenes and do them every week, and the heads of the studio would come in and sit and look at us. They'd sit behind a glass wall, in this darkened theater, and watch us.

Did you have to test for your part in The War of the Worlds?

Yes. I don't think George Pal was particularly impressed with me at first—my hair was very, very short, bright red, and I just didn't look like what George had envisioned a library science teacher to look like. So I had to read for the part—here we are, back in the Fishbowl again! I did a radio play on tape called *Alter Ego*, where I had to do two voices. I played two girls; one was a sweet, innocent, adorable creature who had an inner self, an inner voice—she was possessed. And this awful, *horrible* creature came out of her and told her to murder her boyfriend [Vince Edwards]. So she stabbed him with scissors (and ended up being hanged!). I still have a copy of it and it isn't half-bad, considering the fact that I was inexperienced and just doing it from instinct. The drama coach, Charlotte Clary, told George Pal, "I want you to listen to this recording that Ann did." So he listened and he was *very* impressed. Gene Barry thought it was a trick, he said, "Oh, she's recorded it twice, it's a trick." And so Charlotte told me to go in the Fishbowl and do it again, for George Pal. I've never been really nervous, but twice in my career, my legs gave out from underneath me. Once was when Gene Kelly wanted me to walk down the stairs as a showgirl in *An American in Paris* [1951] and I couldn't walk down the stairs in a bathing suit and high heels because Gene Kelly was staring at me. The second time was when I had to go into the Fishbowl and read for George Pal. (Gene Barry and the director, Byron Haskin, were there, too.) I had to sit down, my knees gave way, I got so nervous.

But I repeated what I had done on the tape and he realized it wasn't a trick, I was able to do it all by myself. That impressed him, and he said, "Well, we'll *make* her look the way we want her to look." He was afraid my short, bright red hair — my "poodle cut" — would date the picture. So they put these ghastly hair pieces on me, these terrible bangs and this awful hair hanging down my back, and if *that* hasn't dated the picture, nothing will *[laughs]*!

Anyway, after they decided they liked me, *then* we did have to do a screen test, Gene Barry *and* I together, from the movie. We did the farmhouse scene — sitting down, having the eggs. That was our screen test, I guess to see how we looked together, or to see how we looked in Technicolor.

Do you happen to know what other actresses might have been up for the role?

Oh, everybody that was in the Golden Circle. They read a lot of people. But they wanted unknowns. George Pal didn't want a well-known person. I asked him once how I got the part and he said, "Because I wanted *you* . . . and because my *wife* approved!" By the way, I met his wife Zsoka, too, and she was a lovely, gracious woman.

Was it shot mostly on the lot?

Yes, everything was done on Stage eighteen except a couple of things on the back lot. Gene Barry went downtown, to Sixth and Hill or Eighth and Hill on a Sunday morning and did some shots down there, running through L.A. They did that around six o'clock on a Sunday morning when there was no traffic. Then we did some things in the Hollywood Hills, up on location. And we went to Arizona to use the Arizona National Guard, who were on maneuvers. All that stuff you see with us running around tanks and things was done in Arizona — that's what we did first. I always figured they had us do *that* first so that if we got flattened by one of those tanks, they could recast pretty easily *[laughs]*!

What about the "exteriors" at the crater at the beginning?

That was all Stage eighteen. Even the miniatures were done on eighteen — *and* the farmhouse. With the exceptions I mentioned, there wasn't anything that wasn't done on Stage eighteen. (Sounds like Hangar eighteen where the government supposedly has all the U.F.O.s hidden!)

What kind of guy was Pal?

The most wonderful man in the world. I'd never met such a kind, sweet gentleman. Brilliant, soft-spoken — he was *everything*, everything anybody could imagine, just the nicest person in the world. Not a mean bone in his body.

His "rep" these days is that, if he'd been a little less sweet and a little more tough, he could have gone a lot farther than he did.

I think everyone took advantage of him, no question about it. MGM took advantage of him, and so did Warner Brothers. And I'm not sure he was treated very well at *Paramount* at the beginning—he wanted to do *War of the Worlds* and Paramount threw it in the trash! Cecil B. DeMille pulled it out of the trash and said, "You're crazy if you don't do this," and I believe that DeMille was responsible for convincing them that George should do it.

Was he on the set much?

Every day, absolutely. And so was Byron Haskin. You never saw any discord or harsh words. And Byron was adorable, *so* nice. This picture was a big responsibility and I was *very* inexperienced, so they took a big chance on me. I've heard that an awful lot of people don't like [my performance]—fans and people like that—but then a lot of people think I was *great*!

So Haskin was a good director for you?

He was very, very nice and very helpful. And he taught me lots of little camera tricks, like how to use my eyes in a suspenseful manner, and *not* to over-mug. He taught me how to move my eyes first, and *then* my head—things that would add a little suspense to the scene, but things that an inexperienced young girl wouldn't think to do.

Was Pal giving Haskin directorial suggestions?

Oh, I would imagine so, they had *lots* of conferences. They worked extremely well together. The associate producer was Y. Frank Freeman, Jr., and he also was a very nice man—very quiet, but a good friend and a nice person. His father was one of the heads of the studio.

Are Pal and Freeman really in the movie, playing bums?

Yes, they are—they're listening to a radio out in front of some store. But I *think* that that was actually shot for *When Worlds Collide*.

Was War of the Worlds *perceived as a "big" picture for Paramount while it was in production?*

Oh, yes, because it was a George Pal picture. It was a big, *big* picture and everybody treated *us* very big—"star treatment." I was terribly excited, this was big stuff. Lots of publicity and attention—it was wonderful. They took great pains with this, every step of the way.

How long were you on the picture?

We started in pouring-down rain the first or second day of February nineteen fifty-two. They had to bring Gene Barry out of Laurel Canyon in a weapons carrier because everything was flooded—we were having torrential rains. It was quite an opening day! How long did we work on it? Two or three months maybe,

I *really* don't know—we didn't work on it physically as long as it took for the special effects. It came out on the twenty-fifth of November, nineteen fifty-three.

Have you ever read the H.G. Wells book?
No.

How was acting opposite Gene Barry?
Oh, he was great. I just felt so good with him—he was strong and protective and helpful. He'd come from Broadway and he was a song-and-dance man, and he was *awfully* kind and *awfully* nice to me, and helped me out a lot. My son and his daughter took ballet lessons together twenty years ago, and so one day he came to pick her up. I ran over to his little Mercedes and he couldn't believe who was running across the lawn—he was just *so* tickled to see me. Then, when he was doing *La Cage aux Folles* down at the Pantages in Los Angeles, I went to a matinee one day. I went to the stage door and wrote down my name, and in case he didn't remember my name, I put *War of the Worlds* underneath it! I wasn't taking any chances *[laughs]*! And he came *racing* to the door, grabbed me by my hand and dragged me through—he hugged me and kissed me and said, "Look at you! Look at you!" He was just so kind, so sweet! He dragged me around to meet all the cast members—he said, "Did you see *War of the Worlds*? This is my leading lady!" He's such a neat guy! He's in Palm Springs now and friends of mine see him quite often. I, being a mountain person, not a desert person, will *not* go to Palm Springs. It's ninety or one hundred degrees at twelve o'clock at night!

According to Byron Haskin, Barry was "terrible" in War of the Worlds.
I thought he was great. And he never looked more handsome. I don't think they could have cast anyone else who was as good as he was, or suited the part better.

Was Lee Marvin really considered for that part?
Yes. But he didn't know it! Years later, my son was working on *The Mike Douglas Show* and he told me Lee Marvin was going to be on. I said, "Ask him about being up for that part in *War of the Worlds*." And it was all news to Lee Marvin, he hadn't had the slightest idea.

What about Les Tremayne?
I "grew up" listening to Les Tremayne on radio, the same way I grew up with George Pal and his Puppetoons. And suddenly here I was with my "heroes" that I knew when I was a little girl! Les and I used to sit and he'd reminisce about *Orphan Annie* and *Jack Armstrong,* and he would tell me all the characters he played. And we would play games about who the sponsors were—Ovaltine for *Orphan Annie,* on and on. I loved him! And he and I still

do see each other off and on and he looks just the same, he looks *wonderful*— mustache, full head of hair, distinguished and, of course, that *voice.*

If you had been picking your own parts in those days, what kind of parts would they have been?

Gee, I don't know. I was so inexperienced, I don't know *who* I identified with — I was so swept up in the whole thing, things like that didn't occur to me. I couldn't sing and dance, as much as I would have loved to, and I never pictured myself as being a comedienne. (Everybody compared me to Ann Sheridan in looks; in fact, Warner Brothers wanted to hire me to do the Ann Sheridan part in the *Kings Row* TV show, but I had signed with Edward Small to do *Fury* with Peter Graves.) So I imagine that it would have been normal, regular dramatic parts.

Did you have an "approach" to your War of the Worlds *role?*

Oh, I just did what I was told to do. I never even heard of the expression "approach," it was really just flying by the seat of your pants. I was so young, what was there to call upon? I was really playing *myself* as if I were a young girl at that time, living in a small town. It was a nice, *quiet* era anyway, the fifties — everybody was just *nice!*

Were you still living at home at that point?

I was. My father didn't believe that unmarried women should live by themselves. I don't think he did me any favor, though, because I should have learned how to manage my affairs, my money and rent, that sort of thing. Things were too easy for me. The first time I moved away was when I married and went to Mexico. And *that* was quite a departure — living in a foreign country and *barely* speaking the language.

How much money were you making at Paramount?

Hah! One hundred twenty-five dollars a week, that was my contract. But I was making twenty-five dollars *more* than the other contract players, and I don't know why. And they didn't put me on hiatus, they paid me right straight through, fifty-two weeks, and again I have no idea why — maybe I just had a good agent! And when I was loaned out to do *The Glass Wall* [1953], Vittorio Gassman's first [American] movie, they charged the other studio one thousand dollars a week for my services. But *I* still got one hundred twenty-five dollars!

Apart from War of the Worlds, *did you make any other movies at Paramount?*

No. When I was loaned out to do *The Glass Wall*, I thought, "Gee, my career's on its way. Another studio, another group of people want me!" I got a little full of myself, I thought it was so great.

The Martian (Charles Gemora) in *The War of the Worlds* **indulges in an** *E.T.*-**ish impulse to reach out and touch someone — unsuspecting Ann Robinson.**

What was your best scene in War of the Worlds?

Everybody likes the sitting-at-the-breakfast-table, cooking-the-eggs scene. That's probably the *nicest,* the most *normal.* I wasn't over-acting, I was just being a normal girl, none of this screaming and running around. It was a nice, quiet scene and a *thoughtful* scene. It was such a departure from all the hysteria and noise and racket — finally you have these two people talking to each other. By the way, my character, Sylvia, and Gene's, Clayton Forrester, we were thrust together, we were *not* lovers. He was stuck with me through the whole movie! Everybody keeps saying there was a romantic interest. Sylvia might have had a crush on him when she was doing her thesis, and she was tickled to death to meet him in the opening scene, but they were never, *ever* sweethearts, or fell in love with one another. It was a nice scene when he held her in his arms and she was sleeping; I liked *those* types of scenes.

Your best-remembered scene is the one with the Martian.

Charles Gemora was the Filipino chap who played the monster. He must have made that costume to fit his own body, because he was a slight individual. He put that latex suit over his head and body — it came down to his hips. His fingers reached as far as the elbows, where there were three little rings attached to wires — that would make the suckered Martian fingers open and close. He knelt on a wooden dolly and very gently they rolled him into the scene. He couldn't see very well — in fact, maybe he couldn't see out of that tri-colored eye at *all*. Then that big arm of his was placed upon my shoulder — someone had to do it *for* him, place his arm on my shoulder, and then get out of the shot. I could hardly feel it, it was so gentle. We had to do that several times to get accustomed to it. Gene Barry pulled me away from him, Gemora got yanked out of the shot on the dolly and Gene threw a hatchet. Then in the next shot, you see the Martian's shadow run by and you see the hatchet sticking out of his chest. And I always thought, "This guy might have been nice!" Maybe we ruined a chance for peace because Gene Barry got overzealous and threw that hatchet! This Martian was just coming up behind me to tap me on the shoulder — he wasn't aggressive, he wasn't mean. Of course, the Martians *had* blown my uncle apart, along with a bunch of other people, but maybe *this* guy was the nice one who wanted to negotiate. And Gene "thanked" him with a hatchet in the chest *[laughs]*!

My biggest surprise was when I came on the set one day and they had the "cobra" there — the ray-zapper. That's the only prop that was life-sized. I walked up to look at it and somebody turned the damn thing on — and it scared me to *death [laughs]*! The light came on and noise came out of it and, Lord!, I jumped. They had great sport with me *that* day!

Do you remember where you saw the picture for the first time?

Yes, at the sneak preview at the Fairfax Theater on Fairfax and Third Street in Los Angeles. Everybody [involved in the making of the movie] was probably there. Those were the days when they passed out cards for you to write your opinion on, and leave in a little box when you walked out. I remember standing there in the lobby, and not a person recognized me. It was a riot!

Why did you leave Paramount?

[Laughs.] Because they *asked* me to! When my contract was to be renewed in September-October 1953, it was not renewed. George Pal, Frank Freeman, Jr.,

people like that begged [Paramount]—they said, "The movie hasn't even come out yet, what are you *doing?*" It did no good. I don't know what I did, I don't know what happened, I don't know if I stepped on someone's toes, if somebody was jealous, if somebody was angry with me. In those days, you didn't do *any*thing wrong—in the Golden Circle, you couldn't even smoke or drink, even if you were twenty-one. But somebody got a bee in their bonnet, somebody didn't like me, and they were *adamant* about not renewing my contract. So to this day it's a mystery. Then later, in November when the picture was out, Paramount wanted me to tour! It was so strange, they had to hire me back because they needed me to publicize the movie. So they paid me two hundred dollars a week to tour!

Who else toured with the movie?

Just me. I went to New York for the opening at the Mayfair Theater. I remember there was a Saturday or a Sunday when all the publicity people left me alone in New York City—they just headed for the hills on the weekend. I'd never been there before—I got lost on the subway, took a hansom cab ride, all that sort of stuff. I was walking in Times Square and saw myself two or three stories high on this big billboard for *War of the Worlds*—it was just incredible. I took pictures of it and there was a soldier there, and I asked him if he would be kind enough to take a picture of me with this theater in the background. Afterwards he said, "What did you do that for?" I said, "Well, you see that great big character over there? That's me." He said *[sarcastically]*, "Sure it is." I said, "Well, we'll go across the street to the theater, there are some pictures of me out in front."

After that, I said, "You want to see the picture?" and he said, "Sure." But the line to get in was around the block for two miles, three or four people deep! So I went up to the ticket-taker and I explained to him that I was Ann Robinson and I was in the movie and Paramount said I could come and see it if I wanted to. I'm sure he thought I was a dingdong. So he called the manager and I said the same thing to *him*. He said, "Who's the soldier?" and I blurted out, "Oh, he's my *cousin!*" Because all of a sudden I realized I had "picked up" a stranger—I was so embarrassed, so humiliated, that they might think I had picked up some soldier off the street! (He looked a lot like Jimmy Lydon, oddly enough—that's how I remember the kid.) The manager scratched his head and he said, "Do you have any i.d.?" So I showed him my California driver's license and he said, "Well, you don't *look* like her but I guess you can go in." *[Laughs.]*

What other cities did you visit?

The entire eastern seaboard, all the way down to Norfolk, Virginia. I remember arriving there late at night, and Paramount forgot to pick me up. I had spoken to a young man on the plane and he said, "You're going to Norfolk

When her interplanetary telecommunicator is on the fritz, Queen Juliandra makes do any way she can. Ann Robinson behind the scenes on *Rocky Jones, Space Ranger.*

and you've never been there before? Let me tell you something: This is a navy town, you've got to be careful." So now here I am waiting—Paramount forgot about me. About a half-hour, forty-five minutes later, back comes this young man with his wife—his wife had picked him up and they had left, but this guy somehow *knew* that something would go wrong. He and his wife took me to my hotel, and he said, "I'll tell you what to do. You move your bed in front of that door, and don't come out till morning." And all night long, my phone was ringing and notes were being slipped under my door! It was just a *sea* of sailors in white suits, and I was scared to death *[laughs]*!

On TV's Rocky Jones, Space Ranger, *you were a regular as Juliandra, an alien queen. How did you get that part?*
I probably went out on an interview; I don't exactly remember. Maybe they said to themselves, "Gee, she's been in a great big science fiction Paramount movie. We'd be dumb not to hire her for *our* show." And so I got the part. Richard Crane [Rocky Jones] was a very charming man — very personable, very likable, and very much to himself. He wasn't outgoing or gregarious and he wasn't a flirt. Just a nice person.

Where were these shot?
Out at the Hal Roach Studios in Culver City. And these were quick — you'd learn fifteen, twenty pages of dialogue for a half-hour show, and they shot one half-hour show every three days or so. It was almost like working on a soap, *very*, very fast. It was a case of memorizing your lines, hitting your mark and staying out of the other guy's key light — *that* is the secret to television!

Was it fun working that fast?
Yeah, I guess. See, we weren't doing Ibsen *[laughs]*, it was just fun. As long as you didn't hold up production by not knowing your lines, as long as you didn't stutter, everything was fine. [Producer] Roland Reed was a very nice man; he used to always tease me about going on his yacht, knowing perfectly well I wouldn't go. He was just a nice guy. I had a cat that scratched my face and gave me impetigo, which is terribly contagious. We had to shut down the whole production because I could have spread it through the cast. That sweet man paid for all my medical bills — he sent me to a doctor to have special X-ray treatments. (Later on in life they can possibly *kill* you, but who knew then *[laughs]*?) He didn't bat an eye — it had to cost him a lot of money to close down production and pay my bills and it wasn't even his fault, it was *my* cat. He was a lovely man.

Sounds like you've had a lot of luck meeting nice producers.
I really did. I think I had some sort of an attitude, or an upbringing, or an *aura* about me — people didn't bother me. Nobody molested me, nobody approached me. Either I was totally sexless *[laughs]*, or they thought to themselves, "No, she's not the type." No casting couches, nothing like that! I was either terribly innocent and people realized it, or I was totally unappealing.

What about the Rocky Jones *director, Hollingsworth Morse?*

He was really nice, too, a gentleman. I remember going to his house years ago with a boyfriend of mine, I had to pick up something, and he had a magnificent home in Beverly Hills with wonderful souvenirs of every place he'd ever been on locations. I was very impressed with the man.

You also played Juliandra's evil sister Noviandra. Did you enjoy that?

Oh, God, yes! I was Bette Davis, I was Agnes Moorehead, I was John Barrymore—I was all of them rolled up into one. I chewed up the *walls*, it was *wonderful*! I did everything but *snarl*! I was so awful, I was so corny! I *loved* doing something like that—but I didn't get paid any more for doing two parts *[laughs]*. To play opposite me when Juliandra and Noviandra were in the scene together, they got a girl about my height and build for over-the-shoulder shots. They didn't have that wonderful electronic stuff that they have now, where you can walk right in and put your arms around each other. But for the time, I thought it was done very well [with a split-screen]. Those episodes with the bad sister were, I guess, the ones that were the most fun.

Whose idea were your sexy costumes?

I got to tell 'em what I wanted. They said, "What kind of a skirt would you like to wear?" and I said, "I want something slit up the leg." I really had a neat figure and a nice, tiny waist—those were the years of the waist-cincher. And because I wore my hair parted in the middle, they fixed a skullcap for me.

Did anybody wonder if maybe you were too *sexy for a kids' show?*

Well, look at the comic books, look at how they draw those bosomy heroines. No one ever objected to *those* round hips and full bosoms. Look at the Phantom and his girlfriend, living in that cave with him—she was well put together! So they never objected to drawing women who looked like women. I didn't show any cleavage—it was just a nice, long leg and a narrow waist. I didn't have bosoms hanging out—I didn't *have* bosoms in those days *[laughs]*!

I had some great publicity pictures taken at Warner Brothers one time. I was trying to get out of the image of the straw hat and the cute little girl, I said, "Please put me in a black negligee." And so they had me in pillows, lying around with this laaaazy look on my face and my hand through my hair and my hand on my hip. And I was trying to pull the top down as low as I could, to get some cleavage. And when I saw the final pictures, they were all air-brushed out. I looked like a *boy*!

How busy were you acting-wise in the nineteen fifties?

I did a *lot* of work in the fifties, a lot of television shows—all of 'em. I can't think of any that I *didn't* do! But then I ran off to Mexico in nineteen fifty-seven and blew my career right out of the water—I married a very famous

Robinson in a sultry 1950s glamour pose.

Mexican matador, Jaime Bravo, and had two children. When I got back home, Hollywood had passed me by. I just ruined it, I blew it. I should have stayed around and paid more attention. Now I realize why they call it "the business" — because it *is* a business. I thought it was all fun and games and glamour, and I didn't take care of it *as a business*. We had two sons, Jaime, who is a director with ABC Sports, and Estefan, who's a back-up singer with a singing group called Human Drama. Both of them are doing what they like to do and they're very good at *what* they do; Jaime's won three Emmys! Their father and I were

The *War* 25th anniversary re-premiere, attended by Forry Ackerman, Zsoka and George Pal, Les Tremayne and Robinson, was such a success that the actress hopes to arrange a 50th celebration, too.

married until nineteen sixty-seven, and now I'm married since nineteen eighty-seven to Joseph Valdez, who's a real estate broker.

So you did very little acting in the nineteen sixties?

After my second son was born in nineteen sixty-three, I think I did a *Gilligan's Island* and that was about it. Motherhood suddenly took over. Then in the seventies, I found out that *War of the Worlds* was going to be reissued. I went to Paramount and I said, "Why don't you do a 'premiere' for the twenty-fifth anniversary?" The Paramount publicity people said, "Gee, that sounds like a good idea—but *you* do it." I said, "Yeah, but *you* pay for it!" And they said okay—they gave us a budget of two thousand dollars. So we did it—my husband-to-be and I put that twenty-fifth anniversary on. And there was a lot involved—you have to hire off-duty policemen, you have to rent klieg lights, rent barriers, get insurance, champagne, flowers, a cake . . . a *lot* of work! Well, the thing snowballed; it got so big, so huge, that a lot of people started *asking* to come. It was shown that night [September 7, 1977] at the Holly Theater on Hollywood Boulevard in tandem with *When Worlds*

Collide, so we had some stars from *that*; George Pal flew in from Europe, Les Tremayne, people came from all over the country, all over the *world*. It became so huge that Paramount was absolutely flabbergasted that we put this thing on. They'd never seen anything like it in their lives — people were lined up all over the street. And the Holly was only a seven hundred–seat theater!

Had all the years of being kicked around by Hollywood changed Pal at all?
   No, he was the same wonderful man. By that time, he'd decided to move his office to his home so he wouldn't get ripped off anymore. Everybody was coming in and stealing his storyboards. Like Forry Ackerman, he liked people and trusted everyone, and they walked off with everything! So in his later years he had his office in his home, so nobody could look over his shoulder and steal his ideas.

And that "re-premiere" also helped you to get back into "the business"?
   Yes, it did. I got a job on *Police Woman* and I did a running part on *Days of Our Lives,* a soap opera. Somewhere down the line I found out that Paramount had something up their sleeve about *War of the Worlds* — we contacted them and they said *[gruffly]*, "Send us a picture." They were so *cool*. So my husband took some great pictures of me, they were eight by tens the next day, and they were in Paramount's hands a day later! And the day after *that*, Paramount said, "Let's do lunch" — and they signed me on the spot. Working on the show was fun — it was *great*. Those people treated me like royalty — I can't imagine being treated any better, I got top-drawer star treatment. [Producer] Sam Strangis and his son [Greg] are just charming people, and Richard Chaves was so adorable. It was just a thrill. We shot up in Toronto.

You were also in a low-budget item called Midnight Movie Massacre.
   Here's what happened on that. Robert Clarke and I went to Kansas City, Missouri, to star in a movie version of the old television show *Space Patrol* for [producer] Wade Williams. The director who Wade had selected, thinking that the guy knew what he was doing, made a wonderful, beautiful bunch of scenes. But when they were edited together, there was no continuity. Meanwhile, Wade's backers were saying, "We'd like to get our investment back," so Wade had to capitulate and make it something kids would like. So Wade made *Midnight Movie Massacre,* about a monster that eats up everybody in a movie theater, and *Space Patrol* became the movie-*within*-a movie in that. I saw Robert Clarke just the other day, and as much as we both love Wade Williams, Bob said, "I have a mental block about that movie!"

On this, the fortieth anniversary of War of the Worlds, *tell me what your opinion of the movie is today.*
   I've gotten more mileage out of *War of the Worlds* than Vivien Leigh did with *Gone with the Wind*. And now — in a totally different genre, of course —

Ann Robinson (seen here in a current shot) still enjoys the occasional TV role, as well as looping dialogue into features (*The Dead Are Alive, To Begin Again,* many more).

here I am, up with the classics! So how can I *not* be proud of the movie? Even Gene Barry, as wonderful as he was in *La Cage,* is going to be remembered one hundred years from today for *War of the Worlds.* As long as there are still prints and laserdiscs and videocassettes, it'll still be playing. It was a wonderful movie and a wonderful experience. My husband and I had a great time doing that fortieth anniversary "premiere," and in ten more years, we're going to do the fiftieth!

ANN ROBINSON FILMOGRAPHY

As Ann Robin:

The Story of Molly X (Universal, 1949)
Black Midnight (Monogram, 1949)
Frenchie (Universal, 1950)
Peggy (Universal, 1950)
An American in Paris (MGM, 1951)
A Place in the Sun (Paramount, 1951)
Goodbye, My Fancy (Warners, 1951)
Callaway Went Thataway (MGM, 1951)
I Want You (RKO, 1951)
The Cimarron Kid (Universal, 1951)

As Ann Robinson:

The War of the Worlds (Paramount, 1953)
The Glass Wall (Columbia, 1953)
Bad for Each Other (Columbia, 1953)
Dragnet (Warners, 1954)
Gun Brothers (United Artists, 1956)
Julie (MGM, 1956)
Gun Duel in Durango (Duel in Durango) (United Artists, 1957)
Damn Citizen (Universal, 1958)
Imitation of Life (Universal, 1959)

Basil Rathbone had sunk low [by doing The Black Sleep*],
and I think he found it uncomfortable to accept the
lesser members of the hierarchy as being social equals.
Now, I'm accusing him of a kind of snobbery and I can't
be* sure *that that's an accurate evaluation ... but at
least that was my feeling at the time.*

Herbert Rudley

No OTHER HORROR MOVIE, not even Universal's campy "monster rallies" of the 1940s, had a cast to compare with the lineup of fright film luminaries that turned out for 1956's *The Black Sleep*. And consequently no leading man ever appeared with as many great ghouls in a single session than the hero of *Black Sleep*, stage and screen actor Herbert Rudley.

A former Philadelphian, Rudley left Temple University at the end of his second year, journeyed to New York and won a scholarship with Eva Le Gallienne's Civic Repertory Theatre. He made his first stage appearance in 1928 and went on to do many more, including the Judith Anderson/Maurice Evans *Macbeth* (with Rudley as Macduff). He repeated his stage role in *Abe Lincoln in Illinois* in the 1940 Hollywood version, appeared in over two dozen films since, and also worked regularly in TV (including a two-year stint as husband to Eve Arden on NBC's *The Mothers-in-Law*).

How did you get the leading man part in The Black Sleep?

The director, Reginald LeBorg, had apparently seen some of my other work, and when he was engaged by [producer] Howard Koch to do the film, he called me in for an interview and wanted to know if I'd be interested in working with him in that particular picture. I was a working actor at that time, and I said, "Certainly!" And it became a very happy association.

Wasn't that heroic role a change of pace for you, movie-wise?

That's kind of a hard question to answer. You see, I have never been a personality actor, I've always been basically a character actor. The range of my acting career has gone from A to Z rather than from A to B. From one point of view, that [being an "A to B" actor] was an asset; it can be helpful in some ways if you're known for playing a certain type of role, whether it's a heavy, a leading man, a comedian or whatever. When you're established along those lines, you're called for anything that might come up in those arenas. People didn't quite know who *I* was, because whatever role I was involved in was totally different from most of those other roles; it was not predicated upon a personality. Now, I'm not denigrating that approach; there've been some wonderful stars created out of that approach. But I was theater-trained, and as a person in the theater, each role was an adventure in itself. It was stepping out of your own personality into the character. I was basically a character actor, and therefore I never established a persona as an individual.

To answer your question — boy, did I take the long way around! — yes, it was different, but so was every *other* role that I played.

What did you enjoy about working on The Black Sleep?

Previous page: Stage and screen actor Herbert Rudley played an uncharacteristic "monster fighter" role in the all-star horror free-for-all *The Black Sleep,* with Patricia Blake.

Basil Rathbone, Patricia Blake and Herbert Rudley don't look like they wanted their picture taken. Publicity shot from *The Black Sleep*.

I think the interesting thing about *The Black Sleep,* as opposed to a great many of the other horror films, is that it was predicated upon a script which had an element of warped but actual reality. In other words, it was not so far beyond the ken of probability that you had to dismiss it, or accept it with a big jump of imaginative acceptance. It was based on a simple but basically realistic concept. Now, it *did* go far afield in the subsequent development of the story, but it was rooted in some sort of off-key reality as opposed to so many of the other horror films which were *per se* just horror films. So everything that was done in relation to the film had that basis in some sort of elemental truth — distorted though it might have become! I think that was true for Howard Koch, who was the functioning producer, and also for Reggie LeBorg. He strove to keep in touch with an essence of reality throughout that film. I think he was successful at that, and that that's one of the reasons why *The Black Sleep* has become kind of a celebrated film of its genre.

How quickly was the film shot?

Oh, very quickly. It was a low-budget film, and we had it done in ten or eleven days.

The big draw for fans, of course, is the all-star horror cast.

One of the interesting things about the all-star cast of horror people was in relation to Bela Lugosi. He played the mute butler in that, and, amusingly enough, he had numerous discussions with Reggie, pleading for a chance to "break his silence" and speak, even if it was only a couple of words. He did not want to feel that he was playing a voiceless character. Reggie was very touched by that, I remember, and he tried to explain to him that that was the character—Reggie couldn't suddenly switch and have him talk, because it would destroy the basic concept of the character. I think Bela knew that from the beginning, but it was just a case of actor's ego—everybody else was talking, why the hell couldn't he [laughs]?

Could he have handled a speaking role at that point?

I think he could have, within certain limitations. Now, Akim Tamiroff, of course, had a ball, and he was marvelous in it. He had no problem with silence—his problem was *verbosity [laughs]*! But he was not responsible for it, it was written that way.

Did you have any chance to socialize with Lugosi?

No, I did not. As a matter of fact, I had very little socialization with anybody outside of Reggie and Howard Koch. That included even Basil Rathbone, with whom so many of my scenes were played. But I have never been an actor who could not disassociate himself from the function in a particular project. I've always been married—many times! [laughs]—and my life was not devoted to the social life of mingling with actors *per se*. There have been a few exceptions, like Gregory Peck, whom I had a long-standing relationship with—we went all the way back to a play of Irwin Shaw's called *Sons and Soldiers* in which Greg played my fantasy son.

When I came out to Hollywood, I had no concept of "the Hollywood scene." I had been theater-trained and theater-bred. And in the theater, there is no caste system. I came out here in forty-two to make *Rhapsody in Blue* (and that was only because I thought I was going into the Army, and I wanted to make a few bucks to leave for my wife and child). I had known, from New York, a number of people who had subsequently become out in Hollywood big-name writers, producers, directors and so on. I used to invite them to evenings at my home, along with actors who were making maybe five hundred, seven hundred fifty dollars a week. I remember [Philip and Julius] Epstein being present at one of these evenings—I must have had maybe thirty or thirty-five people there, all of varying groups, representatives of different phases of the theater from an economic point of view. Phil came over to me and said, "Herb, what the hell are you trying to do? Revolutionize Hollywood?" I said, "I don't know what you're talking about." He said, "Well, look at the group of people you have here tonight. You've got the three or four thousand dollars a week writers, you've got a producer who's making five thousand dollars a week—and then you've also got people who are bit players!" I said, "But they're my *friends!*" And he said, *"You can't do that in Hollywood.* There's a caste system." I said, "Oh, fuck off—don't give me that shit!" I was really very put out by it.

It wasn't until many years later, in my relationship with Greg Peck, by the way, that this came home to me. He would on occasion be invited to my place and I would be invited to his, and one evening, he invited me to a big party at his place. I got there, and only the *crème de la crème* of the motion picture industry was present—*except for me.* And I suddenly realized how valid that comment about the caste system was. Because *I* suddenly became uncomfortable—this was the only time in my relationship with Greg that I did. *So* uncomfortable that, though Greg continued to attempt to maintain our relationship, I veered away from him. I just didn't feel that I could mix comfortably in that upper echelon. I was just a working actor. I was a *respected* actor, but I was not in the star category, I was not important in that sense. And we drifted apart as a result of that. Which was a lesson to me. I had been naive.

Basil Rathbone gave a lot of parties, too. Were you ever at any of those?

No, I was never invited to a party of Rathbone's. As a matter of fact, I don't think Basil socialized with *any*body in the cast of *The Black Sleep.* I have a sneaking suspicion that this was at the nadir of his career, and that he had sunk to a level which was uncomfortable for him. The reverse of what I was telling you about myself. Rathbone had sunk low, and I think he found it uncomfortable to accept the lesser members of the hierarchy as being social equals. Now, I'm accusing him of a kind of snobbery and I can't be *sure* that that's an accurate evaluation of his position, but at least that was my feeling at the time. He would leave the studio as quickly as possible. (But then *[laughs],* so did I!)

Did you enjoy your scenes with him?

Oh, yes, he was a professional and he was excellent. There was no friction, no attempt to take advantage of a fellow actor in a scene. He was a very generous and nice person to work with.

He may not have thought much of The Black Sleep, *but he gave a very good performance in it.*

He did—he gave an *excellent* performance in a role which could very easily have become a caricature. And that was a mark of his professionalism, his ability and natural talent. I thought he was marvelous in it. I never worked with him before or since.

You were both in The Court Jester *[1956].*

Well, yes, come to think of it, and there *were* a few scenes in which we were both involved. But we had no real contact.

Lon Chaney, Jr., can't be bothered to set aside his cigarette for this publicity photo with Rudley for *The Black Sleep*.

How about Lon Chaney?

Not much recollection. My whole approach as an actor was that I had a job to do, and I was concerned with doing it to the best of my then-ability. And that was the end of it. There were no lingering social aftermaths, at least on my part, in the main. John Carradine I admired; as a talent, I think he was quite extraordinary. And as an intellect, he was quite *brilliant*. His classical knowledge was outstanding. I think he deserved a much better fate than what he got.

Your leading lady, Patricia Blake, didn't seem to go too far in the business.
I was not impressed with Patricia. I don't know whatever happened to her. She was pretty, and she had a nice personality, but I didn't think she had any plusses from the point of view of abilities.

LeBorg told me his one problem on Black Sleep *was that the horror stars were trying to outdo one another.*
That's true. But I think, in the main, that he did an excellent job of keeping control. Reggie had a Prussian background, and *[laughs]* when his authority was challenged, he was quite capable of handling that. As a matter of fact, I think that that aspect of his personality may have had something to do with his lack of acknowledged success in the industry, as opposed to his ability. We talked so much, and he very often told me about his experiences, that I had the feeling that he got into a lot of trouble because of that. He was bucking the system. And he didn't have the acceptable requirements. For example, when Bette Davis bucked Warner Brothers, she was in a position to make her rebellion effective. Reggie, when he would rebel against the institution, was not in that position. And I think he suffered because of that. I think his ability was far above what his success was.

He left Universal because they kept giving him horror pictures to direct— then, right after he left, Universal dropped the horrors and started doing more prestigious films!
It was really kind of sad. He should have been more creatively productive in a higher level of film than he was relegated to. He was a very, very interesting man.

The Black Sleep *was a big moneymaker.*
Yes, it was, especially in relation to its investment — which was minuscule *[laughs]*! I saw it when it came out and I thought that overall, considering the minimum amount of time and the minimum amount of money that was expended *in* that time, it was a *very,* very good film. There were things about myself that, in retrospect, I was not too happy about, but *again,* it was a melodramatic situation (to say the least!). I think I may have gone overboard on a few occasions, although I attempted to stay within realistic bounds. And I don't think Reggie let me get *too* far out of hand! Reggie got as much out of that film as could have been expected, if not more.

Reggie LeBorg and I became very close friends. Out of that relationship, we developed a writing combination, and based on an idea that he had about Mary Magdalene and Matthew, we wrote a religious script. Initially, he had hired a writer who was very well-known in the industry to collaborate with him on it. Reggie knew that *I* wrote, and at the end of work one evening, he asked me to read it and tell him what I thought. I felt that the idea was fascinating, but that the development was very poor. I told him so, and he asked me, "What would *you* have done with it?" I began to improvise, and as a result of that, he said, "I think your ideas are marvelous. Would you like to collaborate with me?" I said, "You already *have* a collaborator." (Collaboration is a difficult thing, very close to marriage; if you have a third party in there, it's not a very advisable program!) "However," I said, "if you feel that strongly about it, and if you can relieve yourself of your other obligation, I'd be very interested in doing it with you." So he bought the other writer out and we collaborated on it. Reggie was a multi-talented man, and I was extremely fond of him and respectful of his ability.

What are you doing these days?

I retired in eighty-four or eighty-five. I was given a television script to read with a certain part in mind, I took the script home to read it, and it included a list of the characters with a minuscule description of each. One was described as "a middle-aged man of thirty-five." I thought to myself, "Something is very screwy here. When does a man of thirty-five become middle-aged?" I realized that the handwriting was on the wall, and that I would very soon be faced with a choice: Either to be retired, or to be unemployed. I chose retirement.

These days, I'm enjoying my release from having to prove myself. I play a good bit of golf, and I continue to do some writing. My wife and I have a very active social life. I am, for the first time, happily married—this is my fourth attempt, and the one that I think will last. (We've been married thirty-five years, and went together for four years prior to that.) And occasionally, when my wife gets a little out of hand, I tell her, "Look, honey, you're my next-to-last . . . !"

HERBERT RUDLEY FILMOGRAPHY

Abe Lincoln in Illinois (RKO, 1940)
Marriage Is a Private Affair (MGM, 1944)
The Seventh Cross (MGM, 1944)
The Master Race (RKO, 1944)
Rhapsody in Blue (Warners, 1945)
A Walk in the Sun (20th Century–Fox, 1945)
Brewster's Millions (United Artists, 1945)
Decoy (Monogram, 1946)
Hollow Triumph (The Scar) (Eagle-Lion, 1948)
Casbah (Universal, 1948)
Joan of Arc (RKO, 1948)
The Silver Chalice (Warners, 1954)
Artists and Models (Paramount, 1955)
The Black Sheep (United Artists, 1956)

The Court Jester (Paramount, 1956)
Raw Edge (Universal, 1956)
That Certain Feeling (Paramount, 1956)
Tonka (Buena Vista, 1958)
The Bravados (20th Century–Fox, 1958)
The Young Lions (20th Century–Fox, 1958)
The Big Fisherman (Buena Vista, 1959)
The Jayhawkers! (Paramount, 1959)
Beloved Infidel (20th Century–Fox, 1959)
The Great Impostor (Universal, 1960)
Hell Bent for Leather (Universal, 1960)
Follow That Dream (United Artists, 1962)
Falling in Love Again (International Picture Show, 1980)

The thing I remember most about writing [horror and science fiction] was how much fun it was. It's an interesting kind of writing because you don't use much of your own life and experience in it; it's out of your head, it's fantasy, it's imagining. I was very fortunate that so much of what I wrote got on the screen.

Harry Spalding

THE NAME MIGHT NOT BE INSTANTLY RECOGNIZABLE, even to diehard fans of science fiction films, but throughout the late 1950s and early 1960s, writer Harry Spalding was right-hand man to Robert Lippert, the exhibitor-cum-mini-movie mogul who (under his Regal Films and Associated Producers banners) was responsible not only for the swarm of *Fly* films but also a flock of other B titles in that same period. Spalding started out as story editor to Lippert, then built up to screenwriter of *Curse of the Fly*, *The Day Mars Invaded Earth*, *The Earth Dies Screaming* and many more.

Born in Victoria, British Columbia, and brought to the States when he was six, Spalding credits his interest in writing to his mother, who read the classics aloud to him when he was still a child. His affinity for fantasy and horror subjects also dates back to his youth, when he was enamored of then-new films such as *The Lost World* and the Lon Chaney classics; the first "grown-up" magazine to which he subscribed was *Amazing Stories*. Early on, Spalding did some short story and newspaper writing, then went into the theater business as a film booker/buyer in San Francisco. Working in this capacity brought him in contact with Lippert, who asked Spalding to read and critique scripts that his company was preparing to shoot in Hollywood. In 1956, when Lippert got the go-ahead to make a steady flow of low-budget features for bottom-of-the-bill 20th Century–Fox release, Hollywood's doors opened wide for Spalding, who moved down from San Francisco to become part of the Lippert unit.

Bob Lippert loved movies from the beginning, all his life long. He got started when he was a kid in high school: He had a sixteen mm projector, so he was in charge of running films at school assemblies. He'd acquire a film on, say, a Thursday and, being a natural-born dealmaker, he'd show it Thursday night at the Elks, Friday afternoon at the school, Friday night at the American Legion, Saturday at the Presbyterian Church...! As one of his suppliers said, "If we were lucky, we'd get it back by Wednesday!" He always loved theaters—which he pronounced "the-*a*-ters" to his dying day. I first got to know him in the late forties.

How did he get started as an exhibitor?

He got hold of a small theater but had trouble getting films, so he sued his opposition, Fox West Coast, which was run by the Skouras brothers. He won his suit, and got enough money to get himself going. He started acquiring theaters and then, after awhile, he fell in love with the idea of going down to Hollywood and making movies. I always felt that that was the connection between he and Spyros Skouras. The Skouras brothers had taken over a theater circuit in trouble and built it into a dominant corporation. With these similar backgrounds, Spyros and Bob got along. The whole deal with Fox was between Lippert and Skouras, it did not involve the other people over at Fox

Previous page: Screenwriter Harry Spalding (a.k.a. "Henry Cross"), the brains behind such horror and science fiction favorites as *Witchcraft, House of the Damned* and *Curse of the Fly.*

During his story-editing days, Spalding was involved on "Terror-Topping, Supershock Thrill Sensations" like this Lippert/20th Century–Fox twin bill.

at all. If Bob had a problem, he called Skouras, and if Skouras wanted something done, he called Bob. It was very much a personal deal. The initial Regal deal called for one hundred twenty-five thousand dollar budgets, more under different circumstances. That went on for quite a while. Then, when that expired, Associated Producers came about — and they made even cheaper pictures than *Regal [laughs]*! That's when I got involved as a writer. Then at the *very* end, he co-produced a few things in England, which he put into the Fox deal.

He always seemed to have good luck with science fiction.

Rocketship X-M was one of the best science fiction things that he did; then he had a dinosaur picture called *Lost Continent* which he also had good luck with. Then he did *The Creeping Unknown* with Hammer—that was "before Hammer was Hammer." Bob and James Carreras hit it off. Carreras had a property called *The Quatermass Experiment,* and so Bob and Carreras together made that. In England, it was released as *The Quatermass Experiment* and here it went out as *The Creeping Unknown.* Of course, Hammer went on to bigger and better things in a hurry, but that was really the beginning of it.

Richard Landau, an American who'd worked for Lippert before, gets a writing credit on Creeping Unknown.

Landau had to have come in through Bob; he had been friendly with Lippert for years, and had worked for him at different times. The film starred Brian Donlevy and Margia Dean, whom Bob furnished—that was *his* end of it. Under England's Eady Plan, an American partner could only provide a very limited amount. What the financial arrangement was, I don't know.

Can you say why Lippert's name isn't in the credits?

Curiously enough, he didn't really care too much about credits. Also, if you were going to get the Eady Plan money, they were very persnickety about the percentage of non–English contributions to the film. Lippert had a good, healthy ego, but he really wasn't all that concerned about getting screen credit and that sort of thing, as many people are. His attitude towards Hollywood was always "pretty boys" and "pretty girls" and "don't take it too seriously."

He went without screen credit on The Fly *as well.*

Essentially he *did* do that first one, but it was kind of a strange thing. [Director] Kurt Neumann was a very talented man and a very cultured one—he played the piano, knew a lot about music, understood art. But he had the German background and he was fiercely independent. He was one of those people that just did not feel like fitting into "the Fox arrangement" or "the Metro arrangement" or what have you. He just loved to be out there, picking something with possibilities, and putting a deal together. And he had a lineup of people who worked with him when he found something. He also had a friend (whose name I forget, I'm sorry to say) who liked spotting properties and telling Neumann about 'em. Neumann probably paid him finder's fees and things like that, but the main point was that this gentleman just enjoyed being "part of the action." Anyhow, I came to work one Monday morning, and Kurt Neumann was there already. He handed me a copy of the newest *Playboy,* which contained a short story called *The Fly,* and said, "I've got an appointment with Bob at ten. He'd like you to read this." I read it, and loved it.

The phone rang and it was Bob, and he asked me, "How'd you like it, kid?" I said, "It's great, Bob, but I imagine everybody in town is already dickering for it." But that did not turn out to be true — *nobody* was dickering for it. So Lippert went right to work on the thing, and got an option, and set up the deal. But he didn't *complete* the deal, because he had to talk to Fox first. We were the small tail on the big dog and the production people at Fox hated to have Lippert find something that they overlooked! Fox got hold of it and read it, and wanted it. They simply made a deal with Bob: "*We'd* like to make this, but *you* buy the property" — it would be cheaper if Lippert bought it than if Fox did, naturally. So Bob and Fox worked out some financial arrangement, Kurt Neumann was included as director and producer, and it was made as a Fox picture, in color.

Who brought in James Clavell as screenwriter?

Kurt had James Clavell — always *James*, never *Jim* — whom none of us had heard of. As I remember, prior to this, Clavell had written one script (*with* somebody else) which was never produced, for RKO. Clavell's first draft [of *The Fly*] was, I think, the best first draft I ever saw, it needed very little work. Kurt practically shot it "as is," it was a really great job. Kurt produced and directed, with no further involvement by Lippert. The picture did very well.

Any other recollections of Clavell?

I remember him talking about an idea he had for a novel. He had been in a Japanese prison camp during the war, and the thing that had interested him was that the people who got along best in the prison camp, the ones who *survived* the best, were the same people who would probably land in jail in *normal* life! The very things that made them undesirable citizens made them great survivors in prison camps — and that became *King Rat,* his first novel, and subsequently a picture. Clavell was also very anxious to direct, and Lippert had an idea that he wanted to do — a war story in Asia, more or less modern-day. So Clavell wrote the script, and again the first draft was practically perfect — he's one of the few writers I ever ran across that had that facility. Lippert was having trouble getting a director, and I said, "Why don't you use Clavell?" He thought about that for a while, and the next thing I knew, Clavell came in the office and said, "Thanks very much!" And he did direct the picture, which was called *Five Gates to Hell* [1959]. During the main titles, there's even some fine print saying, "With thanks to Harry Spalding," which he just sort of sneaked in *[laughs]*! Then, of course, he went on from there. I was up at his house one time, a lovely house up in the hills, with a great view — and he said, "I always get a kick out of looking at this. It represents a hundred typewritten pages!" *[Laughs.]*

Lippert had no misgivings about using a first-time director?

The great advantage for Clavell was, we were used to this sort of thing.

Being a small Fox unit, we used to have thrust upon us the relatives of the Fox brass, who wanted to be producers, directors or whatever. We used to call 'em the Sons of the Pioneers. We had quite a number of them over the years, so we knew how to do it. We used to put the film editor up there with a new director, and we'd get certain cameramen who were good at working with new directors. All the director really had to do was work with the actors, because he would turn around and the cameraman would say, quietly, "I think you should get a reverse on that." And of course the director would say, "What's a reverse?" *[Laughs.]* But Clavell was quick to learn.

Arch Oboler went after Fox, claiming that The Fly *was very much like some story he'd written way back when.*
  I didn't know that; never even heard of it.

Were you on the set of The Fly*?*
  I don't know whether I was ever on the set at all. I *was* involved on the script but not to my usual extent, because Clavell did such a great job. In fact, probably most of the few changes that *were* made to that first draft were changes to fit in with production problems of one kind or another. I remember they brought the Fly mask over to the office, and I did put it on *[laughs]*! It was just a plain head mask, the simplest kind of a prop.

What was Lippert like? Edward Bernds told me that, if there was such a thing as reincarnation, then Lippert used to be a pirate.
  I used to accuse *Clavell* of being that, a reborn pirate! Clavell was very ambitious, very talented—never forgot an enemy! He had a little plaque on his desk, TIME WOUNDS ALL HEELS. But, back to Lippert. He came from Alameda background, lived with his mother all his early life. He loved movies and theaters, and when he was nineteen he married his wife Ruth, who was an Irish girl, seventeen, if I remember correctly. Ruth's father protested vigorously, and it wound up in court when the father wanted the marriage annulled. The judge asked, "Why do you want the marriage annulled?" and the father said, "He's too young, he doesn't have a steady job. I want someone who can support my daughter." Lippert took two thousand dollars out of his pocket, held it up and said to the father, "Well, here's two thousand dollars. How much have *you* got?" And the judge was convinced! That's the kind of guy that Lippert was.
  He was the quintessential entrepreneur, really; even in school, turning the sixteen mm into a going thing. And then, following that, he got into the giveaway dish business, selling dishes to the theaters to give away on Dish Nights. All his life he spent buying and selling theaters, buying and selling film, opening exchanges. He was an easy man to get along with, but he was totally concentrated. He and I had a pretty good relationship, 'cause we were

Robert L. Lippert, production manager Harold Knox and Spalding during the threesome's filmmaking heyday.

both from San Francisco, we both knew the theater business, all that kind of thing. As a matter of fact, Lippert's employees were kind of his family a good deal of the time. He really took that attitude. But he had no interest in the world at large; what he was interested in was what he was going to do tomorrow. This is not to disparage him; it's just that he concentrated on the bottom line at all times. Like others of that kind, he was a little "innocent," in a way, because he was so concentrated in the one area he was successful in. As a result, some people didn't understand him. They'd come out of meetings with Lippert scratching their heads! He had certain people that he trusted, and *un*like a lot of people, he didn't like "yes men" around. Unfortunately, he was *too* fond of making deals. If he had made fewer deals and concentrated more on the ones that he did make — in other words, made bigger pictures — he would have probably been better off, and his reputation would have been better.

Did he seem to have a soft spot for science fiction?

Yeah, he liked that kind of picture — because he'd had some success with it, for one thing. There were other angles about it that he liked, too. For example, if you're doing a rocket-to-the-moon film, basically you only have one set. And that's very cheap, you see *[laughs]*!

Where were Lippert's headquarters?

Oh, we moved around—he also liked to buy real estate *[laughs]*! He didn't believe in ever having offices in a building he didn't own. We were in Culver City right across from MGM at one time, we had offices on Wilshire Boulevard, we had offices in Beverly Hills. Actually, it was a very small staff of half a dozen or so, including Jack Leewood, a producer and troubleshooter for Lippert. Bill Magginetti was production manager and Jodie Copeland film editor. And the story editor—me. (Also, I was running some theaters for Bob in my spare time *[laughs]*!) We brought everything else in from the outside, hiring as we needed.

Were you involved on Lippert's Kronos *and* She Devil?

Kronos, no. *She Devil* was going on while I was there, but I was really not much involved on that, either.

The Unknown Terror? Back from the Dead?

Unknown Terror, not that I recall. I worked with Charles Marquis Warren on *Back from the Dead;* Warren did the directing and Robert Stabler did the producing. It was based on a novel [*The Other One*] by Catherine Turney, who also wrote the script. The only thing I remember about that involves Warren and his sardonic sense of humor. He was not a man who loved everybody, and he particularly didn't like lady writers with convertibles and huge dogs in the back seat—which is the way Catherine Turney arrived at Lucey's, a restaurant across from Paramount, where we met to discuss the script. This lady loved her dog and worried about it and brought it over with her. Halfway through this meeting, there was a problem involving a dog in the script. I made some suggestions, Stabler made some suggestions—and Warren settled it: "Why don't we just *kill* the dog?" Catherine *blanched*—but killed the dog anyway!

Any recollections of Space Master X-7?

That was produced by Bernard Glasser and directed by Ed Bernds. I remember that we had to go over budget on the script, but actually the thing I remember more about the overall situation there was that they did a very good job. Ed Bernds was just great to get along with, a capable writer and director, and Bernie Glasser had lots of production experience. In an outfit like ours, where we were making a lot of pictures with a small staff, it was great to have units that you could turn the picture over to, and not worry about anything other than acts of God. When we decided to make *Return of the Fly,* I suggested them, and Lippert went along with that idea. He liked both of them, too. The big problem on *Return of the Fly* was figuring out where to start. *The Fly* was a one-shot deal, an accident. It's not like a Frankenstein Monster, someone you could revive.

Also, you killed the original Fly pretty thoroughly in the first movie.

Yeah, we crushed the hell out of him in a press! So we were really puzzled, how do we make a sequel to this thing?! We finally got (sort of) a reasonable answer, setting it years after the first *Fly* and having the son recreate his father's experiments. Ed Bernds wrote every word of the script, I'm not taking any credit along those lines, but we would kick things back and forth and bring back memories of other films that might have something that would possibly help us. And it worked out quite well. They shot it over at Fox and it had a higher budget than the usual one hundred twenty-five thousand dollars. It went smoothly, and the picture was very profitable.

Did you have a chance to meet Vincent Price while making Return of the Fly?

Yes, as a matter of fact, we had lunch with Price. It was strange to sit with this man who had a huge art collection, and the ability to discuss practically *any*thing that you could think of — and know that the public perception of him was as an evil monster *[laughs]*! They couldn't have been more dissimilar, the screen man and the real man, who was a pleasure to be with.

I had another experience like that on *Witchcraft*. I wasn't in England when *Witchcraft* was being made, but I went over subsequently on something else, and stayed for two or three days at the Thames Court, which was a big house that had been turned into a hotel. It was run by a man and wife, and when she found out I was connected with the movies, we started talking — "Bob Hope stayed here once," things like that. She said, "The one I remember the best was Lon Chaney, Jr. He was here making a picture *[Witchcraft]*, and you know the terrible people he plays in the movies" — she admitted that she was a little worried, having him going up and down the halls in her hotel! And, she said, the first time she met him, he *was* coming down the hall: "He spread his arms wide and said, 'Let's dance!'" She said he was the most lovely man *[laughs]*!

Once the Regal setup came to an end, Lippert called his company Associated Producers.

This was around nineteen fifty-nine, and television was a factor. As I understood it, Lippert and Skouras had the thought that they would make a bunch of pictures for one hundred thousand dollars or less apiece. At the time, film companies tended to sell features to TV in blocs of thirteen. A bloc from Fox would include a big picture, half a dozen medium-sized pictures — and then they wanted to sneak a few of these Lippert cheapies in at the bottom, and it would be profitable in the long run! The market soon changed and the TV people lost interest in the smaller pictures, but it worked for a while.

Anyhow, when that was decided, we knew that we couldn't continue to operate on the old basis, so it became a house operation. Maury Dexter was the production manager for the company; he'd been an actor, and was anxious to direct. I had been story editor, and I was anxious to write. So we were both there, and we became the nucleus of the thing, because the organization wasn't in a position to go out and bid in the open market for writers and so forth. We didn't have the money to pay 'em; then also, as in the case of (let's say) *The Day Mars Invaded Earth,* we used practical sets. In other words, we didn't go onto stages, and therefore we didn't have to pay any studio costs. When we had an idea for a picture, Maury and I would look over the situations, and see what could and couldn't be used. For *Day Mars Invaded Earth,* the script was written to the Doheny Mansion, to get the maximum out of the thing once we had rented it. Except for the opening office sequence—which was shot in one of our company offices—the entire film was shot at Greystone, built by the Doheny oil family in nineteen twenty-eight for what was then a staggering price for a residence, three million dollars. It had a pool, greenhouse, stables, movie theater and bowling alley. We rented it for around two thousand dollars a day and tried to use everything.

And we were doing six pictures a year, don't forget, so that meant a fresh, original script every two months. Now, that doesn't mean that you had two months *to write* the script: You had to come up with the idea, then you had to get it approved. Fortunately, Maury was a very talented guy and he knew production thoroughly. He was imaginative, he got along very well with crews, and he was unflappable. He'd run into things that would absolutely *destroy* the average director, and to him it was business as usual! He was, and is, a very, very capable guy. He later became a right-hand man to Michael Landon—directing for him, production-managing for him—and had a very successful career with him.

Was The Day Mars Invaded Earth *your first script?*
    It was the second script I ever wrote and the first in the sci-fi genre. There was quite a lot of talk about Mars at that time—little green men and that sort of thing! I thought to myself, "Well, nothing that *we* know could live on Mars, if what they say about it is correct. If there's any life on Mars, then it's an abstract kind of life." And from that, I developed the idea of the "abstract life" coming down the beam to Earth, creating duplicates of human beings and so on. Of course, it had all *kinds* of advantages: It could all be done at the one place, and all the main characters play two parts!

    Now, you have to understand that, for *me,* this was an absolutely fabulous opportunity. Not that the pictures were that great, but who ever gives you a chance to sit down and write scripts, and see every single one of them made, and find out where you went wrong and where things worked out? Of course, with pictures like these, you're very restricted: You can't shoot at night, you can't have snow, you can't have rain, you have to be able to "work" the location, and you have to be able to shoot the film in seven days. That's the most we'd have. The scripts would run around one hundred, one hundred five pages, and in seven days, that's a lot of pages a day to do. Also, one of Lippert's favorite sayings was, "Talk is cheap, action's expensive." So you'd get characters in a room and have 'em do twenty pages of dialogue; that's an awful lot easier than car-chasing and violence, which we couldn't really afford in those days.

The girl playing Kent Taylor's teenage daughter [Betty Beall] had a lookalike stand-in, didn't she?
We *did* use identical twins, which caused quite a stir on the set. They were a couple of nice youngsters with little or no experience. Mostly they worked in TV commercials. Casting them certainly made life a little easier for Maury Dexter.

The downbeat ending of Day Mars Invaded Earth *comes as a surprise.*
Everybody loved that. The picture still shows up on TV now and then, and gets mentioned in articles, which always pleases me. I always liked that one; I saw it again recently, and I was surprised how well it still plays. Kent Taylor loved it. He came up to me one day and said he'd given the script to his daughter the night before and asked her to read it, and she thought it was great. On the set, he would do *any*thing for us, in addition to acting, because he loved that particular story.

Part of Lippert's formula was using stars who were well past their prime.
Lippert — or Fox, as the case may be — would *always* say, "We have to have a recognizable 'name' in here, not just a bunch of guys named Joe." But the Recognizable Names didn't necessarily fit the script. That was the big problem with *Curse of the Fly*: Claude Rains was who I had in mind when I wrote it, not expecting to get him. It should have had a Claude Rains or a Herbert Marshall, and what we got was Brian Donlevy, who was a tough New York–type. He's the best Brian Donlevy–type around, but he's probably the poorest Claude Rains that ever walked *[laughs]*! That used to happen quite often. We had to use actors for their *one-time* name value, regardless of how badly they were miscast. At this stage of the game, many really didn't care, and a lot of 'em would just "phone it in." Kent Taylor was not that way, he liked to work, he enjoyed it. But a lot of those pictures could have been greatly helped with better casting, regardless of "name value."

How did House of the Damned *come about?*
Somebody quite high up in the business told me once that he would have given a lot for that script; not necessarily to shoot it exactly as written, but he loved the whole idea of the old circus owner taking in these sideshow freaks in their dying days. Here's how it came about: I was talking to somebody about Tod Browning's *Freaks,* and whoever I was talking to said, "You couldn't make that now because they don't have freak shows anymore." I took

that little thought home with me and I wondered, "Well, if they don't have freak shows anymore, where *are* all these people?" That thought turned into *House of the Damned.* We got hold of a house up in the Hollywood Hills, a place that once had a lurid reputation. You went down a two-lane little concrete road to a *cul de sac*—not very big. And there this building was, tall and narrow. With *a* door. You opened the door, and there you were in a little foyer with an elevator. That was it. In the Prohibition days, it was a speakeasy—with all the stuff that went with the speakeasy business. And the way it was set up, they had absolute control of everybody coming in *and* going out. The man who was renting it at the time was a great collector of antiques. He had this place full of things he'd bought from the William Randolph Hearst estate, stuff that Hearst had picked up all over the world. And he was quite pleased and fascinated: Not only did he have all this Hearst stuff in his very strange house, but now he had a whole houseful of freaks working in there!

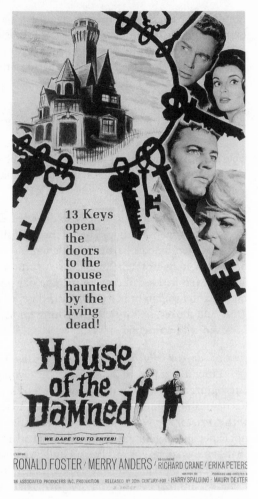

Tod Browning's old-time circus melodrama *Freaks* provided the inspiration for Spalding's creepy *House of the Damned.*

House, *I thought, was one of the better Lipperts.*

It's the one I would like to have done all over again. It had a nice ominous "feel," but it was a picture that you couldn't shoot properly in seven days, it was something you really had to work on. Especially *after* making a picture, you begin to see opportunities that you hadn't thought about before. The third act didn't look bad on paper but sorely lacked conflict and climactic action in actual fact. The freaks should have been used much more and been more integrated into the story. However, since they are basically handicapped people and not actors, this would have been almost impossible for Maury on a seven-day shooting schedule.

Did you know what kind of "freaks" you'd be using before you wrote the script?

No, no. In Hollywood, it doesn't matter *what* you want, there's an agent representing it. And there was a guy that represented freaks—I guess there *were* still some carnivals and freak shows around. I met them all at the time, of course, but the only one I remember is Richard Kiel, who later played Jaws in the James Bond films. He was a very soft-spoken, very mild sort of man.

Some of the later Lippert pictures were made in England.

In England, he could get Eady Plan money, and he could get *rid* of a good deal of the responsibilities, because the English producers were basically in charge of shooting. Lippert met a fellow named Jack Parsons, who was in the theater business over there; Jack was dying to get into pictures. So they got together. *Witchcraft* was the first one of those I was involved in.

Where did the idea for that come from?

When I was in San Francisco, there was a graveyard that dated back to before the Fire. It was full—no new bodies had been buried there for years. Somebody decided it would make a fantastic real estate development, so they offered to move all the bodies to another cemetery. Of course, great-grandchildren came out of the woodwork *[laughs]*, and it was a big news story in San Francisco. And it always stuck in my mind; thinking in terms of horror, I wondered, "If you ran a bulldozer through here, what might you run across?" I had that on the back burner for a long time—there was nothing I could do with the idea under the old Lippert program. But for an English horror film, it was perfect, because they did have that whole witch business back in Cromwell's time.

That's another one that came out particularly well.

I had more time, and they got a good director, Don Sharp. I met Don later, and he said he thoroughly enjoyed it. He realized the thing very well—they had about fifteen days to shoot in England, as compared to the seven here. And it got some very good reviews in England; *Sight and Sound* compared it to the Val Lewton pictures. So it helped Don quite a bit. The big ending was the scene of the house burning, which goes back to the burning of the witches in the first place. Instead of having "phony" flames coming out of a set, they found a suitable house that was going to be destroyed and made a

Yvette Rees as the witch in the Spalding-scripted *Witchcraft*.

deal. They burned the actual house to the ground! It made a very effective ending for a small picture.

Any memory of Spaceflight IC-1?
     That one was made in England, too. Like a lot of movies, that was based on ideas that came out of the newspapers. There was talk back then that if people were ever going to fly to Mars, they'd have to be frozen for the trip and revived once they got there.

Recollections of Lippert's Hand of Death?
     That script originated with an Eastern company which was a good customer of Fox. Wishing to accommodate him without involving the parent company, Fox passed the project on to us. They did this now and then with relatives or friends who wanted to get into the movie business. Gene Nelson had done some acting for us and very much wanted to direct. Bob decided to give him a chance with *Hand of Death*, which got Gene into the Directors Guild. It was his first directing assignment and led to many, many more. I had almost nothing to do with that one.

Were you involved at all on The Cabinet of Caligari?
     [*Laughs.*] Steven Scheuer in his movies-on-TV book gave *The Cabinet of*

Caligari one half a star and characterized it as an "aberration." The perfect word!

One of the major agencies in Hollywood represented the remake rights to the all-time internationally famous film masterpiece *The Cabinet of Dr. Caligari.* They shopped it all over town with no takers and finally brought it to Bob Lippert. Everyone in our organization hated the whole idea, but Bob decided to take a chance. The next thing we knew, he'd hired a European director no one had heard of and installed him at the Goldwyn Studios.

It certainly was an odd sort of film for Lippert to try to do.

Bob got out of his depth very quickly in this thing — all his friends said, "Bob, for Christ's sake, don't start remaking the classic motion pictures of all time!" But Bob got stubborn, as he sometimes did, and he decided he was going to go ahead and do it no matter what *any*body said. He then found out that they were probably right *[laughs]*! I inherited the job of sort of unofficial liaison. The director hired Robert Bloch, who had just written *Psycho,* but soon had a falling-out with him. He then wrote a script himself, interesting in a Freudian way, but completely uncommercial. The "aberration" continued, including a fistfight at a cast meeting, because by now Lippert was in too deep to drop it. I wrote a report which fortunately ended my usefulness as liaison and someone else got stuck with the job. When the picture was finished, the Fox sales and publicity staffs had no idea what to do with it. The reviews generally were scathing. It was as if Roger Corman had decided to remake *Citizen Kane.*

My pleasantest personal memory of a very *un*pleasant project was of opening a door to go onto a Goldwyn stage and running into a young man coming out. He stepped back and politely held the door for me. It was Elvis Presley, who was shooting *Kid Galahad* [1962] on an adjoining stage. My teenage daughters were delighted.

Wasn't Lippert involved with The Last Man on Earth?

I was involved on *several* last-man-on-Earth–*type* pictures. When I first came down here to Hollywood, Charles Marquis Warren and Robert Stabler had an option on a book by George Stewart called *Earth Abides,* which was a last-man-on-Earth story. It would have been a bit expensive to make at the time, but nevertheless it was a good story. Unfortunately, before much happened, Metro made another last-man story, *The World, the Flesh, and the Devil,* so that pretty much killed *Earth Abides.* Then later on, I went through the old cliché of finding a book in a second-hand bookstore, a paperback of *I Am Legend* by Richard Matheson — another last-man-on-Earth story, several years old. I talked to Bob Lippert about it, and he liked the idea. (Last-man-on-Earth stories have very small casts, which makes 'em quite reasonable *[laughs]*!) So I got in touch with Dick Matheson, who is a very nice man, very

Alien robots *and* the living dead walk our streets in *The Earth Dies Screaming*. Left-right: David Spenser, Virginia Field and (reacting to a gunshot) zombie Vanda God-sell.

talented. He had an idea which I love to this day: Make one of the major scenes the last man on Earth trying to make friends with the terrified last *dog* on Earth. It typified the whole story.

Meanwhile, a deal was made to shoot it in Italy, so it got out of our hands altogether. I had to go back to Matheson and tell him that, which didn't make him too happy. Didn't make *me* too happy, either. American International made it as *The Last Man on Earth,* with Vincent Price, and they had their own approach. Matheson was talking along the lines of *Cat People* — using the audience's imagination. American International had the attitude of putting as many vampires at the window as they could afford!

You later wrote an English picture for Lippert that was half-alike, The Earth Dies Screaming.

That, I thought, was the worst title in the world. Somebody said that as a joke, and somehow it just *stuck*! That's the way things sometimes worked in those days. It had a good director, Terence Fisher, but apparently they had a lot of trouble on the set. What the problem was, I really couldn't say, because I wasn't there. And I've always wished that picture would kind of go away, because I hate that title so much *[laughs]*!

A menagerie of mutants — but no Fly — furnished the horror in the English-made *Curse of the Fly*. (Pictured above: Mary Manson, Carole Gray.)

Lippert went to the well once too often with Curse of the Fly.

Lippert was co-producing these ninety thousand dollar wonders, and *he* came up with this one: He said, "Why don't we do another Fly? We have the rights." I said, "Bob, how can we do a third Fly? We were lucky to be able to do a *second* one!" He said, "Well, you can handle it, kid!" Actually, considering the basic problem, it wasn't all that bad a script. As a matter of fact, Don Sharp said that the opening ten pages, where the girl [Carole Gray] is coming out of the insane asylum, was the best opening he'd ever had on a film.

So what was "the basic problem"?

The problem was that you really needed a Claude Rains kind of guy to play that main part — remember I told you that I had Rains in mind when I wrote it. And from the word *go,* you didn't believe Brian Donlevy, who ended up in that role. This threw a pall over the whole thing. I gathered that Don Sharp felt it wasn't working, and that he had lost confidence, or felt depressed by what he was getting. And he had rather *liked* the script, originally.

Who put Donlevy in there? Lippert?

Right. Bob tended to do what had worked before; he was a very practical guy. Donlevy had worked fine for *Creeping Unknown;* Lippert was about to do this similar picture *[Curse of the Fly]* in England; and the two things went together in Bob's head. Donlevy was getting very little work at that time. I saw the picture, and I don't remember liking it very much; I might like it better now than I did then. But it was very difficult writing a script here in Los Angeles for a production in England. It goes out of your hands, and they go ahead and make it. It's supposed to be a collaborative medium, but there was no collaboration there. You didn't get a chance to sit down with the director — or with *any*body — to discuss things, to pick *their* brains. So I was kind of uncomfortable with those, except for *Witchcraft,* which came out better than I had expected.

Did you worry that the audience might feel gypped by a Fly movie with no Fly?

I don't remember whether I worried about that or not. I *do* remember Donlevy complaining bitterly that he'd spent his whole life in movies, and the only thing anybody ever remembered was *The Great McGinty* [1940]!

Did they do any rewriting on these English pictures?

Not much, no. But it would have been all right with me if somebody had wanted to, under those circumstances. (On one of 'em, I forget which one, they shot the first draft with no revisions, and I objected a bit on *that*!) *They* [the English filmmakers] felt uncomfortable with it, too, I think. They didn't know quite what my relationship with Lippert was, they didn't want to hurt my feelings, things like that.

Why did you use the "Henry Cross" pseudonym on some of these pictures?

That was very simple. I wrote eighteen original scripts in three years, and I didn't want people to start thinking that the only writer in Hollywood was Harry Spalding! So there were maybe nine Harry Spaldings and nine Henry Crosses. That was the primary reason.

Why did you leave Lippert?

He closed down his production company and moved back to the Bay Area. I sat down with Bob and talked with him about it, and said, "I think I'd like to stay here." He said, "Great, kid, fine." I used to see him after that, up in San Francisco, from time to time. Then I went to Europe for a couple of years, and eventually wound up at Disney.

While at Disney, you co-wrote The Watcher in the Woods.

My wife Jean is a great mystery story reader, and one day she said to me, "I think this novel *Watcher in the Woods* would be pretty good for Disney." So I read it, and she was right. I took it over to a producer at Disney, and *he* took it to Ron Miller, Disney's son-in-law, who was in charge of motion picture

Filmmakers line up a low-angle shot of Bette Davis in this glimpse behind the scenes from *The Watcher in the Woods*.

production. They bought it, and I did the first draft. Disney at that time had a policy of doing a certain number of pictures in England, for various reasons; and this, they figured, was ideal for England. They turned it over to an English director [John Hough] who had done several things for them; and English directors always use English writers, in my experience. So I was *out* and they were *in*.

Did they retain what you had written?

Basically, there wasn't that much changed. *My* feeling was that you couldn't show the audience the Watcher, you had to let them imagine it. They got caught in the trap of trying to show it. That was the major difference. After all, we were all working from the same novel, the same material. I wound up with a co-credit on it, which was fine. I also kidded them that the least they could do was give my wife a finder's fee—which they laughed heartily about, and changed the subject!

Given all the limitations you've had to work with, have you enjoyed writing science fiction and horror films?

The thing I remember most about writing them was how much fun it was. I've always felt that way. They're really fairy tales for adults, and in a sense they take me back to my childhood when I loved *The Phantom of the Opera* and those things. It's an interesting kind of writing because you don't use much of your own life and experience in it; it's out of your head, it's fantasy, it's imagining. I was very fortunate that so much of what I wrote got on the screen, and gave me a chance to (hopefully) improve as time went on. It was just a lot of fun all the way along the line, and I have no regrets.

I feel I've had a career. Maybe not a great career, but what the hell. I won't retire, I'll just be found one morning, dead, with one shoe on and one shoe off. And with a script clutched in my hand!

Kenneth Tobey

WHAT DO THE MONSTERS FROM 20,000 Fathoms, from Another World and from Beneath the Sea have in common? Apart from the fact that they were nameless horrors threatening mankind in the Fabulous Fifties, the one other thing they share is that all were vanquished by movie and TV veteran Kenneth Tobey.

Born in Oakland, California, Tobey was headed for a law career when he first dabbled in acting at the University of California Little Theatre. That experience led to a year and a half of study at New York's Neighborhood Playhouse, where his classmates included Gregory Peck, Eli Wallach and Tony Randall. Throughout the 1940s, Tobey acted on Broadway and in stock, and in the late 1940s he made his Hollywood film debut in a Hopalong Cassidy Western. Since then he has appeared in 75 (or more) features and on countless TV series (including one of his own, the high-flying adventure series *The Whirlybirds*), but the monster-busting days when he took on vampires, dinosaurs and Martians remain his most enduring on-screen accomplishments.

Let's start out with me telling you how glad your fans are that you're so busy again lately.

It seems to *you* like I'm busy, but it seems to *me* that I haven't worked this year *[laughs]*! But last year [1991] was the best year I ever had.

Financially?

Yes, financially, *and* as far as doing some pretty good work. The last one that came out is *Honey, I Blew Up the Kid* and I played a walk-on in it, practically — an extra — and I got one of the best notices of anybody in the picture! "They were lucky to get Ken Tobey, the old tried-and-true..." — you know, all that crap *[laughs]*. I was a security guard in that. Then, in *Single White Female,* I have even *less* to do: I played a night clerk in a hotel. I ad-libbed quite a few lines, but I had only one written line. Also I did a two-parter on *L.A. Law* and I did a picture called *Desire and Hell at Sunset Motel* — hell, I'm pickin' up the crumbs now! (Actually, I had a pretty big part in that.)

Would you say that some of these roles you're getting lately in movies by young directors are thanks to The Thing*?*

Most of 'em. It's a golden oldie now and it's still got a lot of fans, and I don't have to tell you that that's very gratifying.

Even though The Thing *was a popular movie, in general it didn't do too much for the careers of the people in the cast.*

No, it didn't shoot me to stardom, you're right about that!

Previous page: They axed for it — the Things, Beasts and Its that threatened mankind in the 1950s, only to be beaten back by Kenneth Tobey. (Photo from *The Thing from Another World*.)

Did you have to compete with other actors to get the role? Did you have to test for it?

No. I did do a lot of testing, but I did it with people that were cast *around* me, Dewey Martin and so forth. I'd done a picture for Howard Hawks called *I Was a Male War Bride* [1949] that was supposed to be a daily job, but Cary Grant and Ann Sheridan laughed so hard at what I did (I have no idea *what* I did!) that Hawks kept writing in new scenes for me. And at the end of the picture he said to me, "You know, I'm gonna star you in a picture someday." Nothing more was said. So I kept my eyes and ears open as far as his next picture, and when I read about *The Thing* in a paper, I called him and he said, "I was just gonna call you. Come on in and see me." So I don't know if there were any other people up for it. I know a lot of people *hated* me 'cause I got it.

Other actors who would have liked the role?

Scores. I'm not gonna name 'em because that wouldn't be nice. I think Margaret Sheridan and I were the only two that didn't have to test [for leading parts]. I'm sure that some of the old character actors that Hawks knew didn't have to test, either.

When I first talked to Hawks about *The Thing,* he said, "Why don't you come in today?" I came in and Hawks was talking to a little short guy. And I had my brains blown when the secretary or somebody called this guy "Mr. Faulkner." I realized right away that's who it was, William Faulkner, because he looked exactly like his picture on the cover of books. I'd been a student of Faulkner's, but I never got a chance to talk too much to him because he was hurrying off to his first drink of the day *[laughs].* He drank quite a bit, he was depressed out here. But Hawks loved great writers and did everything he could for them.

And Faulkner had a hand in The Thing, *you believe.*

Oh, yes. I know he was asked to write a treatment, but I'm not sure if he did, or if it just wasn't what they wanted. I realized then that even great writers are not always accepted on the first draft, either.

Margaret Sheridan had been under contract to Hawks since nineteen forty-five, and yet The Thing *was her first picture.*

And almost her *last,* as far as I remember. She wasn't aggressive about pursuing her [acting] career. She made quite a bit of money hair modeling and stuff like that. Margaret was a wonderful girl; she died a few years back. Robert Cornthwaite [who played Dr. Carrington] was a lovely man and a good actor, *still* working, still doing nice things. Douglas Spencer ["Scotty"] was Ray Milland's stand-in for years and years, and *The Thing* was his big chance. I know he did a Western after *The Thing*—I didn't see this, I only heard about it—and he had the reins tied around his fingers. And the goddamn horse lurched so quickly forward that it tore his finger out—literally tore his finger right out of his hand.

Was he good to work with on The Thing?

I had a little trouble with him, but otherwise he was fine. Somebody had taught him how to get upstage and all that crap. I don't do it and I don't want anybody else to do it to me.

Do you think The Thing *would have worked as well if Hawks had put established stars into it?*

No, I don't, I think he had the right idea. I mean *[laughs]*, Tyrone Power could have played my part pretty easily, but I don't think it would have had the same impact. It was more believable with*out* name actors. At least, that's the story I'm getting now when they won't cast me in some of these new pictures—"No, no, you're too well-known!"

Was James Arness really *as embarrassed about* The Thing *as people say?*

[Emphatically.] Yes, he *was*. He was so embarrassed about all the makeup, he never came and had lunch in the RKO commissary with us! (I have no idea where he did eat; maybe he brought his lunch.) But he was a *very,* very nice man. I was down on my uppers at one time and I got a small part on an episode of his TV show *Gunsmoke,* and he *knew* I was having trouble. And, doggone it, he called an end to shooting that day at six o'clock just so I'd have to come back the next day and do (maybe) one line or something. So I got two days' pay instead of one. That was wonderful of him, and I'll never forget him for that.

Whenever you worked with Arness subsequent to The Thing, *did you feel free to mention the film, or did you think it was a sore subject?*

It didn't come up. *I* would have mentioned it, but I just never thought of it. I had nothing to ask him or tell him.

What did you think of Arness' makeup?

I was a touch disappointed. I think they should never have shown a closeup of what it looked like. Showing that detracted from the mystery and the scariness. The makeup itself—well, to me it looked like a big guy with a green face! Look, both the Greenway boys [makeup men Lee and Dan] have passed on, and they did a lot of good work, so I don't have to worry about them.

Did you ever meet Howard Hughes?

Oh, yeah. This was quite a bit before making *The Thing.* I met him at about three-thirty in the morning! He had an aide call me at about two-thirty in the morning, and I'd come home a little . . . inebriated. I told the aide, "I

More-than-heroic he-man, less-than-helpless heroine: Tobey and Margaret Sheridan in a nostalgically sexist posed shot from *The Thing*.

can't meet a man like Hughes at *this* hour" — I told the guy I'd been out playing and so forth. He said, "He just wants to look at you." I told him, "Oh, I look *awful*!" — I'd just been awakened from sleep. The aide said, "He just wants to *meet* you." So I thought, well, I'd better go or he might say *no* [to casting Tobey in *The Thing*]. So I went over there and he took a look at me, and said, "Okay." That was *it* [laughs]! This was at Hughes' little office across the street from RKO, a terrible little office — he probably *owned* the whole block! I walked in and he stared at me, looked me up and down, and said, "Okay." That was my Howard Hughes experience.

All the time that you were up in Cut Bank, Montana, waiting for snow, how did you pass the time?

We played poker, and I went for long walks; we entertained each other. Sometimes we'd go through a scene, under Hawks' direction; we'd see how it started and see if it played. There were two guys up there, radio personalities who were pretty clever, George Fenneman and Paul Frees—they played two of the scientists. Paul Frees entertained us quite a bit, he was a very funny man.

You stayed at a hotel up there?

[Laughs.] Well, up *there* it was called a hotel; down here, it would be called a rooming house! You didn't have too many of the comforts of home, that's for sure. We flew up there on a chartered plane, one of Howard Hughes' own planes. He owned TWA then, and they had all Constellations. He took an old, tired Constellation and gave it to us to go up and back. And the Indians up there made me an honorary Blackfoot when I got off the plane! They gave me all sorts of stuff—Indian mementos which I later gave to some kids down here. Things like declarations written on leather. I forget what my Indian name was now, it was something like Running Star or some other ... idiot name [laughs]. We ended up shooting the snow scenes at the RKO Ranch down here, with phony snow, and we all got pretty overheated. It was a hundred degrees when we shot it and we had on all that crap—fur coats and hats and so on. What they used for ice was photographic solution; photographic solution, when it hits the air, freezes, almost like dry ice. It was a very, very tough few days. That was towards the end of the shooting.

You also blew up the "saucer" in that scene.

And when that blast went off, we were *really* ducking! When I yelled, "Hit the deck!", it wasn't a written line, I wanted everybody to get down!

In scenes where your breath is showing because of the "cold," Robert Cornthwaite says you were actually blowing out cigarette smoke.

No, that's not true; maybe he was thinking of someone else. We worked in the Ice House in downtown Los Angeles, which is where ice was made. It was very old then; it's forty years older *now*, if it's still standing. The only reason we worked there was because Hawks wanted to see our breath coming out of our mouths, but it was kind of tough to do that. The Ice House was about thirty degrees, so naturally our breath *was* showing, but all of our bodies warmed it up in there to like thirty-eight or forty degrees, so our breath *stopped* showing. So what we'd have to do was take a gulp of hot soup or hot coffee on "Action!", take a second to get ready, and *then* blow it out. That produced the foggy air.

Was the scene of the Thing on fire also shot there?

No, that was shot on a stage at RKO—on a stage that I just worked on when I recently did Bob Newhart's new show. That fire scene was kind of scary, really. I was trying to protect Margaret Sheridan—then that damn mattress caught on fire, and I disappeared in a hurry! And so did *she,* I guess *[laughs]*! That shows how brave us actors are! The stuntman that was put on fire had a little tank of oxygen under all that crap he had on, and he had a tube going into his mouth. But he only had one minute of oxygen in it, 'cause otherwise it would take too big a tank. So we shot the scene in about seven or eight takes, because he kept running out of oxygen. That stuntman's name was Tom Steele, he was a real good man.

Did you ever read the original short story?

Yeah—*Who Goes There?* by John Campbell. And I was very impressed by that story, although our show is nothing like it. It was a terrifying story.

How long were you on The Thing*?*

Nineteen weeks—that was my first *g-o-o-d* run. I wasn't making enough money to save a lot, but I lived for quite a while on it.

Where did you see The Thing *for the first time?*

I saw it in Pasadena, with Hawks' family—his mother and father were very old and they lived in Pasadena. I sat in the balcony with a couple of friends of mine, and I almost fell *out* of the balcony at the scene where the airmen open the door and the Thing is right there on the other side of it. I'd forgotten all about it, and the scene scared *me!*

Talk about John Carpenter's newer version of The Thing*.*

I saw it. I didn't care much for it. To me it was kind of *phallic*—all those tentacles or arms or whatever you want to call 'em. And I never could recognize any actors at all; except for Kurt Russell, I can't tell you who was in it.

What made Hawks such a great director?

He *listened.* And he had impeccable taste, and a wonderful sense of humor. He got sick fairly closely after that, and he didn't make all that many more pictures. I was supposed to be cast in *The Big Sky* [1952], which was a pioneer-type picture with Kirk Douglas that Hawks did next. I don't know what happened, but *some*thing happened and Dewey Martin played the part I was supposed to play in that. Hawks and Howard Hughes had multiple ownership of my stupid contract, but I never made a picture for Howard Hawks again.

But you were *in a few other RKO movies for Howard Hughes.*

Bill Self and director Christian Nyby give Tobey a hand at the 1982 reunion of key personnel from *The Thing from Another World.* **(Photo courtesy Ed Mangus.)**

And at about four times the money I made in *The Thing.* One was directed by Otto Preminger [*Angel Face,* 1952] and I got that part with no trouble at all, he just said, "Fine!" But during the picture he was kind of a stinker, in a way. I did something in one scene that made him laugh, and he spoiled the take. The next time I did the scene, Robert Mitchum did something funny, and *I* laughed. Mitchum was singing under his breath, *"Don't kick the actors in the balls, Mr. Preminger, don't kick the actors in the balls..."* [*Laughs.*] Well, I bust out laughing. And Preminger said, "What are you trying to do, ruin my picture?" I was never sure if he was serious or not, but he did have kind of a short fuse.

Christian Nyby still gives interviews where he takes credit for directing The Thing.

Chris has to sell himself, too. I've told the truth in about fifteen newspapers, magazines, etc., and on the air, so I don't mind telling you what I told them: Howard Hawks directed it, all except one scene. Chris Nyby directed us coming through a door, and it's the worst scene in the picture. I've worked with Chris on television and he was very nice to me. (And *I* was very nice to *him.*) He was an editor prior to *The Thing,* and he was learning how to direct from Hawks. But Hawks didn't let him learn by *doing [laughs]*! [Nyby died in 1993.]

Do you ever watch The Thing *any more these days? Or any of your science fiction films?*

Yeah, I watched *The Thing* recently in color—I didn't even know it *had* been colorized. I don't think it harmed it that much, *although* the black-and-white photography was really more conducive to the mood. (Whoever colorized it couldn't decide whether I had red hair or black hair, so they made it kind of reddish-black *[laughs]*!) I love to collect my movies [on video] because I let my folks see 'em, and show 'em to kids on Saturday afternoons. I don't have that many.

Why did you get out of your contract with Howard Hawks and Howard Hughes?

'Cause I wasn't being used. It may not have been a smart thing to do—I got a little hungry after that!—but career-wise I don't think it made a damn bit of difference. And I don't know if they'd have renewed me or not anyway.

What can you recall about The Beast from 20,000 Fathoms?

It was produced by a fellow that was originally a Dead End Kid, Hal E. Chester—nice guy—and they had a short schedule. I got along fine with everybody *except* a second assistant director who accused me of drinking, which I hadn't been doing. (I never drink while I'm working, I have my drinks *after* work *[laughs]*)! He spread the rumor that I was a drinker, and that kind of thing is anathema to your career. But I got along fine with everybody else: Paul Christian was the star and the girl was Paula Raymond, who became a friend of mine later. She was in a horrible automobile accident after the picture, but she was able to get back into pictures and she's still around.

That was Eugene Lourie's first film as director. Did he do much directing of the actors?

Well, he put us in position and then kind of let *us* work it out. He was a designer of special effects and art direction and things like that, an extremely talented man. He was another wonderful guy. I also met Ray Harryhausen on *Beast from 20,000 Fathoms,* and I'm very, very proud of that moment. He was extremely witty and very well trained in his profession. I enjoyed that whole picture very much.

You were in the next Harryhausen picture as well, It Came from Beneath the Sea, *for producer Sam Katzman.*

[Laughs.] Sam Katzman was a character, oh, my God. *It Came from Beneath the Sea* was a six- or seven-day picture: We had five days up in San Francisco and two days down here at the Columbia Ranch. Katzman comes over during the last day of shooting and says to the director, "How much more do you have to do?" The director, whose name was Robert Gordon, says, "We

only have three pages here"—it was my whole love scene with Faith Domergue. Katzman says, "Show me what you have to shoot," and Gordon
shows him the script and says, "Just these three pages here." Katzman tears
out the three pages and says, "*Now* how much do you have to shoot?" Gordon
says, "Now we don't have *any*thing left." And Katzman says, "*G-o-o-d*...!"
There went my whole love scene *[laughs]*!

Faith Domergue was another Howard Hughes "discovery." What was she like?
       She was a very nice lady. I didn't get to know her too well: I was married
to a gal that was very jealous, so I didn't get to know *any* of my leading ladies
too well. But we got along very nicely and she was a splendid girl. I remember
we had a scene on a beach which we shot on a stage on the Columbia back
lot; they had a truckload of sand brought in. And I weighing more than Faith,
I kept sinking through the sand, down to the stage floor, and then I'd be looking *up* at her! I kept scraping the sand together at the beginning of the scene,
packing it as hard as I could, and I'd start out looking over her head. But, by
God, I'd sink down through that sand *during* the scene, and she looked like
she was two feet taller than I was! I couldn't lick it, I just had to swallow my
pride and look short.

*What were you actually looking at when you were supposedly looking at the
monsters in* Beast *and* Beneath the Sea?
       The assistant director would walk around with something at the end of
a stick, and you would follow *that* with your eyes. I tried to visualize what the
monster might look like; we'd never even seen the giant octopus up till then.

The submarine scenes were shot on a real sub, correct?
       Absolutely. In fact, the fellow that played my executive officer *was* the
commander of the sub. (I thought *his* acting was better than *mine*!) We went
down under the ocean, so forth and so on, and it's pretty remarkable—the
quality of the picture—considering it was done in seven days, and going on
location to San Francisco!

Some scenes were photographed while the sub was actually submerged?
       Oh, yeah. They're lacking in room, submarines, so there were handheld
cameras, [shortcuts] like that.

*Did you stay with your folks while making that picture up in your old stamp-
ing grounds?*
       No, I stayed in the hotel—the St. Francis, a great old hotel.

*You were on Broadway in the nineteen forties, working with people like Ingrid
Bergman—do you ever wish that people would ask you about things like that*

Donald Curtis, Faith Domergue and Tobey, ready(?) for action in Sam Katzman's *It Came from Beneath the Sea*.

once in a while, and not just about The Thing *and the giant octopus and all this other nonsense?*

I hadn't thought of it. I did twenty-nine Broadway shows—don't ask me to name 'em *[laughs]*!—and a lot of people *do* remember me from Broadway. It's just nice that people remember you at *all*, it doesn't matter from *what*!

When you were on Broadway, were you earning a living by acting only?

When I was working, I never worked on the outside. Between jobs, I had several different jobs temporarily—I worked as a bartender, for instance, at the Commodore Hotel. There'd be periods of two or three months between jobs; if you didn't get something in the fall, you had to wait for summer theater.

You also went back to Broadway in nineteen sixty-four, for Golden Boy.

Oh, sure, with Sammy Davis. I was coming out of a jazz spot called Shelly's Manne-Hole in L.A. one night as Sammy was just going in, with his business manager, I think. The guy said, "There's your Tom Moody," and Sammy liked me ever since he saw *The Thing*. So they auditioned me—I had to sing a song, and I didn't do too well *[laughs]*. Then they had me come to

New York and audition again, and then they had me work with [conductor] Elliott Lawrence for an afternoon on one of the songs I had to sing in the show. I got the job.

You were also in one of the first reincarnation films of the nineteen fifties, The Search for Bridey Murphy.

I enjoyed it very much. I worked with Teresa Wright and Louis Hayward—I *loved* Louis Hayward, I worked with him several times in little tiny small-budget TV things at Ziv. I worked with a lot of wonderful people there at Ziv, people on their way down—like *I* am now *[laughs]*!

Reincarnation was a fad of sorts in the mid-nineteen fifties. Was the picture taken seriously by the people involved?

We *tried* to take it seriously. I went to one of the technical guys on it, a guy who knew all about hypnotism and stuff like that, and had him try to hypnotize me. Which he couldn't. I *pretended* he did—I didn't want to disappoint him too much. He said, "You're now starting to drool," so I pushed a bunch of spit out the side of my mouth to make it look right *[laughs]*! We had a real nice, big party at the director's house afterwards.

Any recollections of The Vampire *with John Beal?*

Yes, I enjoyed it very much. That was another six-day wonder, and we were at locations all over Hollywood. Most of the outdoor stuff was shot at an undeveloped lot, and all I remember is *running*. I'd run out one end of the lot, then we'd have to go back and set up at the *other* end of the lot, and shoot me running out the other end! What I also remember is John Beal, who is a very, very nice man; we've been friends ever since, although we don't see each other too much since he moved to New York. Coleen Gray was nice, too; she tried to get me into selling skin products and things like that door to door. I told her, "I may be unemployed, but I'm not *unintelligent!*" *[Laughs.]*

Was there any difference between working in these low-budget movies and working in TV?

W-e-l-l, not really. But I really did enjoy having my own series, *The Whirlybirds,* that was fun. In doing that series, I learned to fly, became a commercial pilot—I should say, I got a commercial *license.* All I needed was to take one flight test and I could have been a commercial helicopter pilot. But I didn't pursue it because it was so expensive; I hit a low spot about then and really couldn't afford to go that route.

Around the time of Psycho *you were the hero in a cheap thriller that tried to pass itself off as* Psycho-*ish,* Stark Fear.

Is that what it's called? I never knew the name of it! On that one, the director pooped out — the director was a drama teacher at the University of Oklahoma. He was inexperienced, he couldn't hold it, couldn't keep it together. The kid who was playing the villain, Skip Homeier, took over the direction. Oh, that was a miserable thing! They housed us in the hotel in Oklahoma City and we shot the film in Norman, Oklahoma, where the university is. We shot in sorority houses *[laughs]* — I don't know why, but we did. They built little sets or used the rooms that they had and so forth. And several times driving back from there, back to the hotel, I had to drive through thunderstorms. And, let me tell you, they were *wicked*! Tornadoes and stuff like that! I'd see cars *all over* — in the ditches beside the highway, *on* the highway — oh, it was awful. I got scared several times.

That's one film I'd like to see again, and show to people — show 'em I did some *bad* things, too *[laughs]*. Which I *did* — I've done some *awful* performances in this business. But in fifty years, you're allowed to have a few, you know.

In the nineteen seventies you had small parts in the Willard *sequel* Ben *and in a thriller called* Homebodies.

Oh, Jesus, *Ben*! I played a city engineer in that in a scene with Joe Campanella, and we shot that on one of the streets at Paramount at night, *all* night. And I want to tell you, it was the *coldest* night that Hollywood had ever seen — it set a record, it was below zero. Cold, wind — *awful*! I *hated* it. *Homebodies* was about a bunch of old people who don't want to be evicted from the tenement where they're living, so they start killing everyone who's trying to get 'em out. One of the old ladies was a gal named Paula Trueman; strangely enough, I went overseas with her doing a play with Moss Hart during the War, nineteen forty-four or forty-five, and *Homebodies* was the first time I'd seen her since. It was fun — she's a bird-like little thing, a little bit "tetched" here and there! I played a construction boss, and we shot that on a construction site in downtown L.A. And I hated that location, because the air was always full of cement dust.

You've played a number of sci-fi roles in the nineteen eighties, like Strange Invaders *and several Joe Dante pictures.*

I went to Toronto, Canada, for *Strange Invaders* and I enjoyed that very much. I don't think I was very *good* in it, but the director seemed to like it; I played the head cricket, and I was working as a little hotel keeper. I had a big part in that, I was on that for about five weeks.

And working with Joe Dante?

I enjoy Joe very much, but I really don't "work" with him, actually. He assigns me a part and he says, "Write a five-minute scene" when I show up — and writing's something I'm not too good at *[laughs]*! So I'm not sure I've ever really gotten to do my best, working for him. But I certainly don't mean that critically; he's one of my favorite directors, and very loyal to old actors. He hires the same ones all the time.

You worked with him for the first time on The Howling.

I played a policeman in that, a very, very tiny part. We were in the police car and they were taking shots of us traveling up and down the street. Three or four "custodians" of that street (if I can call 'em that) stopped us — prostitutes and bag ladies, drunks, all sorts of people. I almost ran over 'em — you can't see very well at night down Western Avenue. They came out into the street and flagged us down — either they needed help, or somebody was gonna shoot them, or some terrifying story, and they wanted our help! I was nonplussed — I didn't like to let 'em down, but I told 'em, "Well, we can't help you now, we're on a call!" *[Laughs.]*

I was also on Joe's *Innerspace,* which was a very funny movie — I had a famous scene in that. And it was only one tiny scene, just one line. Marty Short and I were in a men's room in a railway station; he's takin' a leak in a urinal and I'm coming out from takin' a crap. I'm putting on my coat and washing my hands, and it looks like he's talking to his dong 'cause he's looking right down there. He's had miniaturized people injected into his bloodstream and he's talking to them, but *I* don't know that. I say to him, "It's all right to play with it, but don't *talk* to it!" That got the biggest laugh in the show.

Any closing comment? Has it been a good career? Has it been everything you might have wanted or hoped for?

Yes, yes, no, no *[laughs].* I've loved being an actor — that's what I do, that's what I enjoy doing. It's hard work — most people think it's a cushy job, but it's really not. I've been in it for fifty-three years or something close to that, and I've enjoyed . . . most of it. The long waits *between* jobs sometimes are not much fun, and the long waits on the set waiting for a scene to come up are not enjoyable, either. But I've become accustomed to the way it works and I feel I've had a career. Maybe not a *great* career, but what the hell. I won't retire, I'll just be found one morning, dead, with one shoe on and one shoe off. And with a script clutched in my hand!

KENNETH TOBEY FILMOGRAPHY

The Man on the Ferry (Soundies Short, 1943)
Dangerous Venture (United Artists, 1947)
This Time for Keeps (MGM, 1947)
Beyond Glory (Paramount, 1948)
He Walked by Night (Eagle-Lion, 1948)
I Was a Male War Bride (20th Century–Fox, 1949)

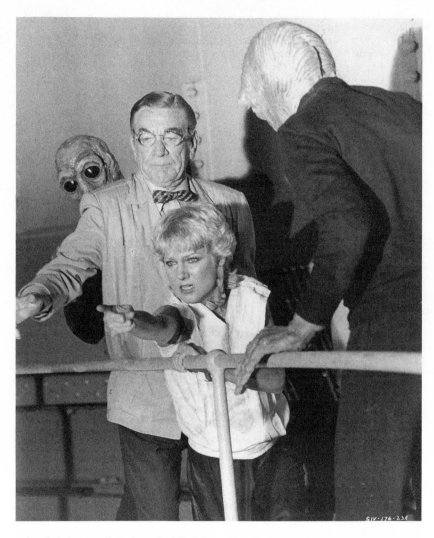

After fighting an alien threat in *The Thing,* Tobey was the humanoid leader of bug-like *Strange Invaders,* here contending with Diana Scarwid.

Task Force (Warners, 1949)
The File on Thelma Jordon (Thelma Jordon) (Paramount, 1949)
Free for All (Universal, 1949)
The Stratton Story (MGM, 1949)
Twelve O'Clock High (20th Century–Fox, 1949)
The Doctor and the Girl (MGM, 1949)
The Great Sinner (MGM, 1949)
Illegal Entry (Universal, 1949)
Love That Brute (20th Century–Fox, 1950)

Three Secrets (Warners, 1950)
When Willie Comes Marching Home (20th Century–Fox, 1950)
The Gunfighter (20th Century–Fox, 1950)
My Friend Irma Goes West (Paramount, 1950)
Kiss Tomorrow Goodbye (Warners, 1950)
Right Cross (MGM, 1950)
The Flying Missile (Columbia, 1950)
Up Front (Universal, 1951)
The Company She Keeps (The Wall Outside) (RKO, 1951)
The Thing from Another World (The Thing) (RKO, 1951)
Rawhide (Desperate Siege) (20th Century–Fox, 1951)
Angel Face (RKO, 1952)
The Beast from 20,000 Fathoms (Warners, 1953)
Fighter Attack (Allied Artists, 1953)
The Bigamist (Filmmakers, 1953)
Ring of Fear (Warners, 1954)
Down Three Dark Streets (United Artists, 1954)
The Steel Cage (United Artists, 1954)
Rage at Dawn (RKO, 1955)
Davy Crockett, King of the Wild Frontier (Buena Vista, 1955)
It Came from Beneath the Sea (Columbia, 1955)
The Steel Jungle (Warners, 1956)
The Man in the Gray Flannel Suit (20th Century–Fox, 1956)
The Great Locomotive Chase (Andrews' Raiders) (Buena Vista, 1956)
Davy Crockett and the River Pirates (Buena Vista, 1956)
The Search for Bridey Murphy (Paramount, 1956)
Jet Pilot (Universal, 1957)
Gunfight at the O.K. Corral (Paramount, 1957)
The Vampire (Mark of the Vampire) (United Artists, 1957)
The Wings of Eagles (MGM, 1957)
Cry Terror! (MGM, 1958)
Seven Ways from Sundown (Universal, 1960)
X-15 (United Artists, 1961)
Stark Fear (Ellis, 1962)
A Man Called Adam (Embassy, 1966)
40 Guns to Apache Pass (Columbia, 1967)
A Time for Killing (The Long Ride Home) (Columbia, 1967)
Marlowe (MGM, 1969)
Billy Jack (Warners, 1971)
The Candidate (Warners, 1972)
Ben (CRC, 1972)
Rage (Warners, 1972)
Walking Tall (CRC, 1973)
Dirty Mary, Crazy Larry (20th Century–Fox, 1974)
Homebodies (Avco Embassy, 1974)
Baby Blue Marine (Columbia, 1976)
W.C. Fields and Me (Universal, 1976)
MacArthur (Universal, 1977)
Goodbye Franklin High (Cal-Am, 1978)
Hero at Large (MGM, 1980)
Airplane! (Paramount, 1980)

The Howling (Avco Embassy, 1981)
The Creature Wasn't Nice (Creatures Features, 1981)
Strange Invaders (Orion, 1983)
Gremlins (Warners, 1984)
The Lost Empire (JGM Enterprises, 1985)
Innerspace (Warners, 1987)
Big Top Pee-wee (Paramount, 1988)
Freeway (New World, 1988)
Gremlins 2 The New Batch (Warners, 1990)
Honey, I Blew Up the Kid (Disney/Buena Vista, 1992)
Single White Female (Columbia, 1992)
Desire and Hell at Sunset Motel (Two Moon Releasing, 1992)

Halloween (Compass International, 1978) features clips with Tobey from *The Thing*.
Mr. Mom (1983) features clips with Tobey from *I Was a Male War Bride*.

I *didn't think that I was
sexy [in* Dracula], *but my youngest
grandson, when he finally saw the film,
said, "Grandma, I know now why Grandpa
married you!"*

Lupita Tovar

THE YEAR 1992 MAY GO DOWN IN THE Big Book of Horror History as the Year of the Vampire, and not just by virtue of the many new vampire films which invaded theaters that year. As fans of modern horror geared up for the unveiling of Francis Ford Coppola's eagerly awaited (and ultimately lousy) *Bram Stoker's Dracula,* followers of the classic chillers found cause to celebrate early: MCA Universal Home Video released the ultra-rare Spanish-language version of the 1931 horror milestone *Dracula.* Made in the days before the dubbing of Hollywood movies into foreign languages became commonplace, the Spanish *Dracula* was shot at Universal at night, on the same sets and locations where director Tod Browning put Bela Lugosi and the rest of his English-speaking cast through their paces during the day. Sparsely released (in the States) and seldom revived during the years since its original run, the film is being acknowledged by some fans as a more creative and cinematic rendition of Stoker's classic tale than Browning's stuffy museum piece; and one of the movie's only survivors, co-star Lupita Tovar, is still around to share 60-year-old memories of 1992's most notable horror release.

Born in Oaxaca, Mexico, Tovar appeared first in silent Fox films before making the move to Universal and co-starring in the Spanish-language version of 1930's *The Cat Creeps (La Voluntad del Muerto).* For the same producer, Czech-born Paul Kohner, she also appeared as Eva (the Spanish-language counterpart of Helen Chandler's Mina) in the Spanish *Dracula*; in 1932 she married Kohner, who later became one of the top agents in Hollywood. (Their daughter Susan Kohner was Oscar-nominated for her performance in Universal's 1959 *Imitation of Life.*) Widowed since 1988, still sharp-witted, always friendly, Lupita Tovar Kohner remembers vividly falling under the spell of Dracula (Carlos Villarias), the undead *conde* who never drank . . . *vino.*

Were the people involved on the Spanish Dracula *looking to "outdo" the Tod Browning* Dracula *that was shooting during the day?*

Yes, we were, and many of the critics say that we did. We were using the exact same sets, and we even had the same "marks" as the English cast, so that we would stand in the same spots.

Do you remember whether you ever bumped into Bela Lugosi or Tod Browning?

Oh, yes, Lugosi, he was terribly nice. I used to see him, usually on weekends. All the Europeans used to get together for a koffeeklatsch — they'd have coffee and pastries, and talk. And then sometimes they'd get together at small dinner parties, like at [actor] Victor Varconi's house — his wife was a wonderful cook. All the Hungarians would get together at places like that, and I was always invited because at that time Paul Kohner was sort of courting me; he was part of that group, and so whenever he was invited, he would bring me along. Even though they spoke German, and I hardly spoke English [*laughs*]!

Previous page: **Mexican actress Lupita Tovar brought a surprising level of sexy appeal to the Spanish-language version of Universal's** *Dracula.*

Paul Kohner was very romantic. Always there were flowers in my dressing room, and Sunday there were flowers at my house and boxes of candy. I started putting on weight, which I was not supposed to do *[laughs]*!

The cast of Dracula *knew that he had his eye on you?*

He was very, very careful, but of course everybody knew it. Everybody except me—I didn't realize it for a while because I was so worried about being good in the picture. When he came by, he said hello to everybody and he had dinner with us and sat next to me, but it was all business-like. I lived with my grandmother, so on Sundays he would take me out for coffee at Ernst Lubitsch's house or Mike Curtiz's—all of these Europeans. But he always came and asked my grandmother's permission, and he brought my *grandmother* flowers. You'd think he was courting my grandmother *[laughs]*! He had a very wonderful manner and he was quite a gentleman.

And Tod Browning?

No, I don't remember much about him. Naturally I met him afterwards, when we did publicity and all that. But not during work.

How about Carlos Villarias, "your" Dracula?

Villarias was a *wonderful* person. He was trying very hard to be as good as Lugosi. When you see the two versions, I think there's very, very little difference. They were both good actors—Villarias was really a good actor. The difference between the two was how they worked with their hands. Lugosi's fingers were very long, and Carlos Villarias had short fingers.

Did you have any inkling how Helen Chandler was playing her role in the English-language Dracula?

No, none of us had any opportunity to see the performances of the English actors. There *were* some movies I did where they'd have a moviola on the set and run the English-language versions, and we'd see what we were supposed to do. But on *Dracula,* we just didn't do that—it was a completely different interpretation. We didn't even see our own *Spanish* rushes, we never saw *any*thing.

Did Villarias stay "in character" between takes, the way Lugosi supposedly did?

He *was* concentrated on his performance and he kept to himself. He was determined not to get out of character. He was very serious. The only one that was always joking was young Barry Norton, who played my fiancé [Juan Harker]—he was always kidding and telling stories. Well, he was very young, and full of beans *[laughs]*! And Pablo Alvarez Rubio [Renfield] was wonderful. He was always very, very lively—and he had a *tough* role, very strenuous,

Cast photo from the Spanish *Dracula* with (left-right) Soriano Viosca, Carlos Villarias (Dracula), Carmen Guerrero, Tovar, Senorita Peza, Enrique Avalos, Barry Norton, Eduardo Arozamena (Van Helsing) and Pablo Alvarez Rubio (Renfield).

very demanding. I have wonderful memories of the making of this film. In between scenes, when there was a change of camera settings, all of these people used to tell stories about the theater and the plays they did, mostly in Spain. It was *fascinating*. They told different stories about actors and actresses and things that happened in the theater. I remember thinking that I had to "come up" to the other actors in the film, it was important to me that I didn't let them all down.

Looking back, do you think it was a good idea not *to show you Helen Chandler's performance?*

I think so, because I would have been very worried about copying her. I probably would have tried to imitate her performance, and we were two entirely different personalities. The way we did it, I was myself. I tried to understand George Melford, who was a wonderful director. We used to call him "Uncle George." Even though he did not speak Spanish, he somehow communicated with us what he wanted. There *was* an interpreter, but I tried to follow Melford, tried to understand what he wanted.

You see, I had no dramatic training. I came here to Hollywood from school; [director] Robert Flaherty came to Mexico City looking for talent, he went to my school and saw me doing gymnastics. Apparently he thought I had possibilities, because he had me make a test; Mr. Flaherty directed the test, *with* an interpreter. And a few weeks later, [Fox Films] came to me with a contract—which my father very quickly refused. He just would have no part of it. So they sent a second contract, and he still refused. No way could I go to Hollywood alone. So what happened was that I came to Hollywood with my grandmother, and I had a [Fox] contract which was supposed to be for seven years, with six-month options.

And so I had no [acting] training. At Fox, I did a couple of silent films where I didn't have to worry about dialogue or anything. But then when the "talkies" came along, everything changed. There was complete chaos at all the studios. They decided to bring in actors from New York, from the stage. And many of the big silent stars lost their careers because of the talkies. That was when I went to Universal, where I did first the Spanish version of *The Cat Creeps* [1930] and then *Dracula*. So there I was in *Dracula*, acting with wonderful actors, some of them stage actors very well known in their own countries for their theater work. I was still just a young girl, still very green, I still knew nothing. So I had to try very hard.

Helen Chandler is very prim in her Dracula, *and you're very sexy in yours.*
   [Laughs.] I didn't even realize that! As we were doing it, I had no idea! For one thing, we had different wardrobes, Helen Chandler and I. Entirely different wardrobes—mine *was* very sexy. *I* didn't think that I was sexy or anything like that, but my youngest grandson, when he finally saw the film, said, "Grandma, I know now why Grandpa married you!" *[Laughs.]*

Was Kohner on the set of Spanish Dracula *most of the time?*
   He was quite a bit. We were shooting at night, and naturally he worked there at Universal in the daytime, too. He used to come in as we got started, and then he'd go back to his office, I suppose to take a nap or something. We got a break about midnight for supper, and he used to come before that to see that everything was all right. Then about five o'clock in the morning he'd come around again and see how everything was going. He said he had a couch or something to nap on in between. So, yes, he came by every few hours. But, really, there was no need for him to come by because everything was going smoothly. We worked steadily until about seven-thirty in the morning, and then the English cast came in at eight.

So he was there at Universal twenty-four hours a day?
   He was a very ambitious young man, very conscientious.

Did the people who made the Spanish Dracula *earn as much as the English* Dracula *people?*
   No, no—we got a small salary. But that was the whole idea. The idea was to make the Spanish version for as little money as possible. So they used the

same sets and everything. And these [Spanish-speaking actors] were not demanding big salaries. We didn't know any better, and everybody was very happy to get a job. Most of them had been having little parts in silent films, and many of them had even played extras, even though they had a name in Spain and in Mexico. When Universal said, "The role pays so-much," you didn't argue, you said, "Fine!"

Also, I was always there almost an hour early, so that I would feel "at home" in the set, so that I would feel that I was secure. Many times I went in and the crew hadn't arrived yet, so I would sit there in the dark until they came and started lighting the place up. And it was very scary, the whole feeling of being in there alone! If someone had come up behind me, I would have let out a scream [laughs]!

Was there ever any concern about all the different accents in Spanish Dracula?

No. For their Spanish films, the Fox studio employed only people from Spain, because [Fox] thought they were the only ones that spoke proper Spanish. Universal didn't care. If we fit the role, it didn't matter where we were from — Mexico, Spain, Argentina — nobody worried. It was the same way at Columbia. I made a picture at Columbia with one Spaniard, one Cuban and myself, a Mexican. And it was a beautiful film.

What do you remember about the public appearances you made in connection with Dracula?

I made some appearances here in California when the picture opened, and then I went to Mexico to different states with the film. It was a terrific success and it made a lot of money.

Do you remember where you saw it for the first time?

I saw it at the studio. There was a screening for the whole cast — none of us had seen anything. So they had the special screening, and afterwards a little party at the commissary. We got a lot of compliments, and we were very excited about seeing the film.

When did you see the Lugosi Dracula?

I didn't see it right after the Spanish; I was busy and doing publicity things for the film, and I was concentrated in my job. But years later I saw it, and then I saw it again on television not long ago. I think the Spanish is better! The other one is a little *dull,* it's too passive. And the Spanish keeps you interested in it, it has a little more excitement in it.

If you could have picked your own roles in those days, what would you have played?

Oh, I liked very dramatic roles. I made the first talking pictures in Mexico.

Tovar and actor Barry Norton (playing "Juan Harker") between takes on *Dracula*.

I did a picture called *Santa*—it means "The Saint"—and that's still playing on television in Mexico. It's the story of a young, innocent girl that is seduced by an officer, and then becomes the most famous prostitute in town. (That was *my* role!) It's been remade twice, but the version that I made is the one that is still going on. Last November [1991] was the sixtieth anniversary and I was invited down there. I went to Mexico City, right to the spot where our first scene was shot. They had actors coming in on horses and a girl dressed like I was dressed in the film—they had the whole thing reenacted. It was very moving. And I received a gold medal for it. There were only two other survivors: One was the sound engineer and the other one was an extra in the film, they brought him in a wheelchair. There again, I thought to myself, "My

God—sixty years!" An awful lot went through my mind, my whole *life,* I think. I mean, I'm no spring chicken, I'm an old lady, with grown-up grandchildren. And all of these fantastic things keep happening.

Did you enjoy your acting days?

Oh, I loved to work. I did many Westerns, and for things like that I had to get up very early, like three in the morning. In those days, you had calls at four for makeup, and then you'd go on location. Paul [Kohner] used to drive me there, and then they'd bring me back to the studio and he'd pick me up in the afternoon. But his career was important, and we had to entertain. Many a time I'd come home and quickly take off my makeup, dead tired—and then be a hostess! Finally he said, "Look, this just won't work. I want a wife. You don't have to work." I said, "If that's what you want, fine." So I just completely ignored my career. I was interested always in what was going on when he stopped producing and became an agent; he was always with people who were in the business, so I didn't feel "out of it." Then I had my children, and that's a career in itself, to be a mother and raise two children and be a wife. I wanted my family to be happy, that was the most important thing to me. Once I gave up acting, I just lived for my husband, and I never thought about acting anymore.

Lately you've done some public appearances in connection with the Spanish Dracula.

I was asked to go to Dallas about a year ago, to go to the nineteen ninety-one USA Film Festival—Mr. [David] Skal's book *Hollywood Gothic* had come out, and the festival organizer Richard Peterson wanted to show the Spanish *Dracula.* They invited me, so I went with my son Pancho and two of my grandchildren. And I felt very peculiar, I can tell you, especially when I arrived at the [Lakewood Theater] and got out of the car, and people came toward me—people wanting autographs. Then we went in and it was a wonderful theater, a theater that was built in the thirties. They showed the movie—no subtitles, and with one reel missing. And you could hear a pin drop. Nobody walked out. I was a little nervous—in fact, let me tell you, I was very, *very* nervous. Then when it was over, they asked me to come up on the stage and my knees were shaking! I sat there thinking, "Oh, dear, what am I doing here?", you know? But after a little while I was able to control myself and answer questions, and it was all very, very exciting. It was like a *dream.* You don't expect that something you did sixty years before could ever catch up with you!

You did a special introduction for MCA's home video release of Spanish Dracula.

I hope that came out all right. I don't have any idea how I'll look on TV. You know, vanity. No matter how old you are, you still like to look good *[laughs].*

And you are enjoying the attention the film is now getting?

Oh, my goodness, *yes!* The University of Madrid invited me to go for a seminar; when they called, I thought somebody was fooling me! I thought somebody was pulling my leg, making fun of me! So I was very, very cagey; I told them that, yes, I would be interested, but would you be so kind as to talk to my son? I told them to arrange it with him. Then I called *him* and told him I thought somebody was playing a joke on me. Well, after about a half an hour he called me back and said, "Mama, it's no joke!" They wanted me to come and talk about my movies from twenty-seven to thirty-five, to make a speech, to talk to the students. I thought, "My Lord, I'm not sure I can do this, but—why *not?*" And so I did it, last July [1992]. To do things like this is a *challenge.* And instead of becoming a vegetable *[laughs],* I can do *some*thing!

LUPITA TOVAR FILMOGRAPHY

The Veiled Woman (Fox, 1929)
La Voluntad del Muerto (Spanish-language version of *The Cat Creeps*) (Universal, 1930)
King of Jazz (Spanish-language version) (Universal, 1930)
Serenata de Hollywood (Hollywood Serenade) (Universal, 1930)
Dracula (Spanish-language version) (Universal, 1931)
Un Sueño Fue Tu Amor (Just a Dream; Only a Dream) (Universal, 1931)
El Tenorio del Harem (Universal, 1931)
Carne de Cabaret (Spanish-language version of *Ten Cents a Dance*) (Columbia, 1931)
Border Law (Columbia, 1931)
East of Borneo (Universal, 1931)
Yankee Don (Daredevil Dick) (Capitol/Mercury, 1931)
Santa (Compania Nacional Productora de Peliculas/Rafael Calderon [Mexican], 1932)
Alas Sobre el Chaco (Spanish-language version of *Storm Over the Andes*) (Universal, 1935)
Vidas Rotas (Broken Lives) (Inca, 1935)
El Capitán Tormenta (Spanish-language version of *Captain Calamity*) (Regal/Grand
    National, 1936)
An Old Spanish Custom (The Invader) (J.H. Hoffberg, 1936)
Blockade (United Artists, 1938)
El Traidor (The Traitor) (Duquesa Olga release, 1938)
The Fighting Gringo (RKO, 1939)
Maria (PISA, 1939)
South of the Border (Republic, 1939)
Tropic Fury (Universal, 1939)
Green Hell (Universal, 1940)
The Westerner (United Artists, 1940)
Two Gun Sheriff (Republic, 1941)
Gun to Gun (Warners short, 1944)
The Crime Doctor's Courage (Columbia, 1945)

Tovar's 1931 credit *El Tenorio del Harem* was edited together from the unreleased shorts *Caballeros Árabes* (Arabian Knights) and *Let's Play.*

Index

Numbers in **boldface** refer to pages with photographs.

A

Abbott, Bud 40, 52
Abe Lincoln in Illinois (1940) 310
Abe Lincoln in Illinois (stage) 310
The Abominable Dr. Phibes (1971) 280
The Abominable Snowman see *The Abominable Snowman of the Himalayas*
The Abominable Snowman of the Himalayas (1957) 100, 102, 111–13, **111**
Ackerman, Bettye 215
Ackerman, Forrest J **304**, 305
Adams, Julie 37, **38**, 39, **40**
Adler, Buddy 214
Adventures of Superman (TV) vii
Agar, John 13, 197, 198
Aladdin and the Giant (unmade movie) 69
Alfred Hitchcock Presents (TV) 29, 134, 270–71
Alland, William 33, 41
Allen, Irwin 18, 21–22, 26, 27, 30, 221
Allen, Woody 121
The Alligator People (1959) **321**
Allison, Jean **244**
Alperson, Edward L. 256
Alton, Robert 33
"Amazing Stories" 197, 320
An American in Paris (1951) 292
Anchors Aweigh (1945) 196
Anders, Merry 1–16, **1**, **4**, **8**, **10**
Anderson, James 252, 254
Anderson, John 245
Anderson, Judith 310
Andress, Ursula 97, **97**

Andrews, Dana 24, 25
Angel Face (1952) 346
Angel Street (stage) 271
Ankers, Evelyn 39
Ankrum, Morris **211**
Antosiewicz, John xi
The Apartment (1960) 259
Arden, Eve 310
Arkoff, Samuel Z. 53, 58, 61, 64, 68, 74–75, 138, 140, 142, 143, 237
Arnaz, Desi 49
Arness, James 183, 342
Arness, Virginia 183
Arnold, Jack 33, 34, 35, 36, 39
Arnold, Wilfred 70
Arozamena, Eduardo **360**
Art Linkletter's House Party (radio) 251
Asher, Jane 106
Asher, William 134
Ashley, John 53–54
"Astounding Science Fiction" 197
Atlantis, the Lost Continent (1961) 7
Attack of the Crab Monsters (1957) 230, 233–34, **233**
Attack of the 50 Foot Woman (1958) 196, 198, 201–5, **202**, **204**, 207, 208
Attack of the Giant Leeches (1959) 239
Attenborough, Richard 114
Atwill, Lionel 270
Autopsia de un Fantasma (1967) 218, 219
Avalon, Frankie 136, **138**
Avalos, Enrique **360**
The Avengers (TV) 97, 98

B

Bacall, Lauren 171
Back from the Dead (1957) 326
Badiyi, Reza 148, 150, 152, 154
Bainbridge, William 32
Balcon, Michael 19, 114, 120
Ball, Lucille 49
Ball, Suzan 255
Bancroft, Anne 223, **224**
Band, Albert 214
Bandit xi
Bankhead, Tallulah 260
Barker, Lex 50
Barrett, Majel 177
Barrows, George **224**
Barry, Gene **289**, 292, 293, 294, 297, 298, 306
Barrymore, John 162
Bartok, Eva 216
The Basketball Fix (1951) 50
Batman (TV) 14, 76, 282
Battle of Blood Island (1960) 205
Battles of Chief Pontiac (1952) 48, 50, 58
Bava, Mario 140, 211, 215–16, 217
Baxter, Jane 20
The Beachcomber (TV) 219
Beal, John 350
Beall, Betty 329
Bean, Robert 189
Beast from Haunted Cave (1959) 189
The Beast from 20,000 Fathoms (1953) 347, 348
Beaudine, William 49
Beauty and the Beast (1963) 2, 6–7
Beckwith, Reginald 114
Bedroom Farce (stage) 66
Bela Lugosi Meets a Brooklyn Gorilla (1952) 49–50, 52
Ben (1972) 351
Benjamin, Richard 223, 264
Bennett, Charles 17–30, **17**, 137
Benny, Jack 56
Berger, Sidney 146
Bergerac, Jacques 5
Bergerac, Michel 5
Bergman, Ingmar 215
Bergman, Ingrid 168, 348
Bermudez, Irma 2–3
Bernds, Edward v, xi, 324, 326, 327

Bernstein, Elmer 57
Berserk (1967) 77–80, **78**, 82
The Beverly Hillbillies (TV) 134
The Big Sky (1952) 345
Birch, Paul 259
Bird of Paradise (1951) 33
Bissell, Whit 37, 39, 56, 60
Black Midnight (1949) 290
The Black Sleep (1956) **309**, 310–12, **311**, 313–16, **314**
Black Sunday (1961) 216
Black Zoo (1963) 72–74, **74**, 76
Blackmail (1929) 18, 30
Blackmail (stage) 18
Blake, Patricia **309**, **311**, 315
Bloch, Robert 333
Blood and Black Lace (1965) 211, 215–16
Blood Is My Heritage see *Blood of Dracula*
Blood Legacy see *Legacy of Blood*
Blood Link (1982) 223
Blood of Dracula (1957) 58, 59, 60–62, 61
Blood of the Demon see *Blood of Dracula*
The Blood Suckers see *Island of the Doomed*
Bloody Mama (1970) 136
Blumofe, Robert 52
Bobbikins (1960) 92
Bogarde, Dirk 114
Bogart, Humphrey 169, 171, 193, 279
Bonanza (TV) 53, 54
The Boneyard (1991) 246
Boni, John 264
Borglum, Gutzon 152
Born Free (1966) 75
Borzage, Frank 170–71
The Boss (1956) 259
Bowie, Les 106, 120
Boyce, William 132
Boyer, Charles 271
The Boys from Brooklyn see *Bela Lugosi Meets a Brooklyn Gorilla*
Bradbury, Ray 212
Brady, Scott 220
The Brain Eaters (1958) 230, 238–40, **239**
The Brain from Planet Arous (1957) 196, 197–98, 201, 203, 208

Bram Stoker's Dracula (1992) 358
Brando, Marlon 226
The Brass Legend (1956) 52
Break in the Circle (1957) 112
Brenda Starr (1992) 246
Bride of the Gorilla (1951) 46, 48–49, 52
The Brighton Strangler (1945) 169
Bristow, Billy 18
Britt, May 220
Broccoli, Albert R. 121, 123
Broder, Jack 46, 47, 48, 49, 50, 51, 52, 53, 57
Broidy, Steve 51
Bronson, Charles 270
Brooks, Mel 223
Brown, Georgia 76
Brown, Vanessa 50
Browne, Coral 262, **263**
Browning, Ricou 32, 34, 37, 41
Browning, Tod 329, 358, 359
Bruce, Nigel 26
Brunas, Ruth xi
Bryan, Peter 80
Buchwald, Art 200
A Bucket of Blood (1959) 205, 230
Buffum, Ray 197, 199
Buono, Victor **207**, 208
Burnt Offerings (1976) 208
Burr, Raymond 48, 52
Burson, Polly 37
Burton, Richard 153
Burton, Tim 268
The Bushwhackers (1952) 48, 50
Byrnes, Edd 63

C

The Cabinet of Caligari (1962) 332–33
The Cabinet of Dr. Caligari (1919) 333
Cabot, Susan **181**, 182, 237
La Cage aux Folles (stage) 295, 306
Cagney, James 262
Cahn, Edward L. 7
Caine, Michael 116
The Caine Mutiny Court-Martial (stage) 261
Cain's Hundred (TV) 129
Cairns, Jessica **87**

Calvert, Steve 52
Campanella, Joseph 351
Campbell, John W., Jr. 345
Can-Can (1960) 213
Carbone, Tony 185, **185**, 186, 188, **191**
Carey, Philip 9, 10, 11
Carlson, Richard 34, 39
Carnival of Souls (1962) 146–52, 154–56, **155**
Carnival Rock (1957) 235
Carousel (1956) 212–14, **213**
Carpenter, John 345
Carradine, John 13, 14, 94, 218, 219, 314
Carreras, James 60, 62, 101, 110, 122, 142, 143, 322
Carreras, Michael 102, 110
Carroll, Victoria 220
Carson, Johnny 73
The Case of Patty Smith (1962) 9
Casimir, Golda **78**
Casino Royale (1967) 100, 120–21
"Casino Royale" 120–21
Cason, Barbara 12
Castillo, Gloria 200
"Casting the Runes" 18, 23–24
Castle, William 79, 278
The Cat Creeps (1930) 358, 361
The Cat Creeps (1946) 171
Cat Women of the Moon (1953) 250, 256–59, **257**, 265
Cataclysm (1980) 222
Champagne for Caesar (1950) 273
Chandler, Helen 358, 359, 360, 361
Chaney, Lon, Jr. 14–15, 42, 48–49, 50, 193, 314, **314**, **327**
Chaney, Lon, Sr. 15, 42
Chapman, Ben 31–43, **31**, **35**, **38**, **40**
Chapman, Marguerite 211
Charlie's Angels (TV) 262
Chatelain, Didier 46, 67, 84
Chatto, Ros 108
Chatto, Tom 108, **109**
Chaves, Richard 290, 305
Chekhov, Anton 252
The Cherry Orchard (stage) 252
Chester, Hal E. 24, 347
Christian, Paul 347
Christiansen, Arthur 116
Cinderella (1950) 250, 251
Circus of Horrors (1960) 69, 77

The City Under the Sea see *War-Gods of the Deep*
The Clairvoyant (1935) 19–20
Clarke, Gary 63, **63**
Clarke, Robert 305
Clavell, James 323, 324
Claydon, George **78**
Cleopatra (1963) 214
Clift, Montgomery 226
Coates, Phyllis vii
Cocchi, John xi
Cohen, Herman 45–84, **45**, **63**, **70**, **74**, **78**, **81**, **83**
Cohen, Nat 50, 60, 64, 65–66, 69
Cohn, Harry 21, 56
Cohn, Robert 56
The Colgate Comedy Hour (TV) 40–41
Collyer, June 4
Colman, Ronald 22, 164
Coming to America (1988) 200
Conan Doyle, Adrian 75
Conan Doyle, Arthur 26, 75, 76
Conflict (1945) 169
Connors, Mike 231
Connors, Touch *see* Connors, Mike
Conqueror Worm (1968) 283
"The Conqueror Worm" (poem) 283–84
Conried, Hans 255
The Constant Husband (1955) 92
Conway, Gary 59, 63, **63**
Cooper, Alice 280–81
Cooper, Gary 153, 260
Copeland, Jodie 326
Coppola, Francis Ford 358
Corbett, Harry H. 80
Corey, Wendell 13
Corman, Gene 191, 242–43
Corman, Roger 52, 64, 75, 84, 176, 178–79, 180, 181, 182, 183–84, 185, 186, 187, 188, 189, 190, 191, 192–93, 205, 230, 231, 232, 234, 235, 236, 237, 238, 239, 240, 242, 243, 246, 268, 275, 276, **276**, 279
Cornelius, Joe **81**
Cornthwaite, Robert 341, 344
Corri, Adrienne 76
Corridors of Blood (1963) 86, 87, **91**, 92
Costello, Lou 40, 52
Costner, Kevin 49
Cote, Valerie 255

Cotten, Joseph 231
The Court Jester (1956) 313
Cowan, Will 33
Crabtree, Arthur 67
Craig, Harry 75
Crain, Jeanne 279
Crane, Les 153
Crane, Richard **244**, 301
Crane, Stephen 214
Crawford, Broderick 58
Crawford, Christina 79
Crawford, Christopher 79
Crawford, Joan 66, 77–80, **78**, 81, 82
Craze (1973) 82–84, **83**
Creature from the Black Lagoon (1954) **31**, 32, 33–40, **38**, **40**, 41, 42–43
Creature from the Haunted Sea (1961) **175**, 176, 178, 189–92, **191**, 206
The Creature Walks Among Us (1956) 42
The Creeping Unknown (1956) 100–3, 104–7, **105**, 110, 113, 322, 334
Crime of Passion (1957) 52, 53, 56, 57
Crimes in the Wax Museum see *Nightmare in Wax*
Crocodile (1979) 84
Crooks and Coronets (1969) 80
Crosby, Floyd 275
Cross, Henry *see* Spalding, Harry
Crossfire (1947) 250, 253
Crowley, Kathleen 3, 51, 52
Crowther, Bosley 93
Croydon, John 86, 88–89, 90
The Cry Baby Killer (1958) 237–38
"Cult Movies and Video" vii
Cummings, Irving 21
Curse of the Demon (1958) 18, 23–25, **23**
Curse of the Fly (1965) 320, 329, 335–36, **335**
The Curse of the Living Corpse (1964) 146, **151**, 152–54
Curtis, Dan 208
Curtis, Donald **349**
Curtis, Howard 244
Curtis, Tony 40
Curtiz, Michael 359
Cushing, Peter 97, 112, 113, 282

D

Daddy's Dyin'...Who's Got the Will?
(stage) 258
"The Daily Express" 115
Dalton, Abby 179, 181
Damato, Glenn xi
Damon, Mark 7
Dance with Me, Henry (1956) 52, 56
Dances with Wolves (1990) 49
Danforth, Jim 122
Daniel, Dennis xi
Daniels, Bebe 68
Dano, Royal 215
Dante, Joe xi, 268, 351–52
Davalos, Richard 13
Davis, Bette 79, 280, **337**
Davis, Bill C. 225
Davis, Sammy, Jr. 349
Day, Robert 85–98, **85**
The Day Mars Invaded Earth
(1962) 320, 328–29
The Day the Earth Caught Fire (1962)
100, 106, 113–20, **117**, **118**, 122
The Day the Earth Caught Fire (pro-
posed remake) 123–25
Days of Our Lives (TV) 305
"Deadly City" 50
Dean, Margia 101, 322
Death of a Salesman (stage) 210,
225–26
Death Takes a Holiday (1934) 169
Death Takes a Holiday (stage) 159,
168–69
de Havilland, Olivia 221
deKova, Frank 235–36
Del Vecchio, Carl xi
Del Vecchio, Debbie xi
Demara, Fred 6, **6**
DeMille, Cecil B. 20, 280, 294
The Demon (1981) 222
The Demon Planet see *Planet of the
Vampires*
Demons of the Swamp see *The Giant
Leeches*
De Niro, Robert 136
Denning, Richard 34, 39, 51, 52
Derek, John 52, 180
Desire and Hell at Sunset Motel
(1992) 340
de Toth, Andre 270

Devil and the Deep (1932) 260
Devil's Partner (1961) 230, 243–44, **244**
Devon, Richard 181, 182, 190, 230
Dexter, Maury 7, 327–28, 329, 331
Diary of a High School Bride (1959)
205
Dickerson, "Beach" 188
Dickinson, Desmond 67
Didio, Tony 221
Diffring, Anton 69
Diller, Phyllis 246
Dirty Mary, Crazy Larry (1974) 143,
144
Disney, Walt 251, 336
Dr. Cadman's Secret see *The Black
Sleep*
The Doctor from Seven Dials see *Cor-
ridors of Blood*
Dr. Goldfoot and the Bikini Machine
(1965) 128, 137–39, **138**, **139**, 140
Dr. Goldfoot and the Girl Bombs
(1966) 137
Dr. Jekyll and Mr. Hyde (1920) 162
Dr. Jekyll and Mr. Hyde
(1931) 161–65, **163**, **164**, 168
Dr. Jekyll and Mr. Hyde (1941) 168
Dr. Kildare (TV) 132
Dr. Phibes Rises Again (1972) 280
Domergue, Faith 13, 14, 348, **349**
Don Juan in Hell (stage) 261
Donlan, Yolande 100, 114, 116
Donlevy, Brian 110, 322, 329, 335–36
The Donna Reed Show (TV) 255
Dorian, Angela see Vetri, Victoria
Dors, Diana 82
Double Indemnity (1944) 52
Douglas, Kirk 345
Douglas, Susan 252, 254
Dracula (1931) 42, 43, 358, 359, 360,
361, 362
Dracula (Spanish-language version;
1931) **357**, 358–60, **360**, 361–62,
363, **364**
Dracula (1958) see *Horror of Dracula*
Dragonwyck (1946) 276–77, **277**, 278,
283
"Drop Dead" (album) 253
Duel in Durango see *Gun Duel in
Durango*
Duke, Maurice 49
Dukesbery, Jack xi

Duncan, Pamela 233–34
Dune (1984) 250
Dunlap, Paul 57

E

"Earth Abides" 333
The Earth Dies Screaming (1964) 320,
334, **334**
East of Borneo (1931) 160, 161
Easy Rider (1969) 223
Ebert, Roger 154
The Eddy Duchin Story (1956) 178
Edgar, Marriott 104
Edward Scissorhands (1990) 268
Edwards, Bill **90**
Edwards, Vince 292
Ege, Julie 83
Eisley, Anthony 47
Elam, Jack 256
Eldridge, Florence 162
Eleanor and Franklin (TV movie) 262
Elizabeth II 119
Elizabeth the Queen see *The Private
Lives of Elizabeth and Essex*
Elvey, Maurice 19, 20
Ely, Ron 96
Emery, Katherine 170
Enemy from Space (1957) 100, 107–8,
109, 110
Entertainment Tonight (TV) 154–55
Epstein, Julius 312
Epstein, Philip 312–13
Erdman, Richard 215
Erwin, Stu 4
Evans, Dame Edith 80, 82
Evans, Maurice 310
An Evening with Edgar Allan Poe
(TV) 276
Everitt, Dave vii
The Evil Mind see *The Clairvoyant*
Exner, Judith 259
Expresso Bongo (1960) 114

F

Face of Fire (1959) 214–15, **214**
Fairbanks, Douglas, Jr. 273
Families Are Like That (stage) 250

Family Planning (stage) 225
"Fangoria" vii, xi
Farrell, Charles 159–60, 170
The Fast and the Furious (1954) 52
Faulkner, William 341
Feldman, Charles K. 120, 121
Fenneman, George 344
Ferdin, Pamelyn 221
Ferrer, Jorje 218
Field, Virginia **334**
Fields, Verna 56
Fiend Without a Face (1958) 67
"films and filming" 120
Finlay, Frank 77
Finney, Albert 153
First Man into Space (1959) 86,
89–90, **90**, 92, 93
First of April (unmade movie) 3
The First Texan (1956) 259
Fisher, Terence 334
Five (1951) **249**, 250, 252–55, 256,
259, 265
Five Gates to Hell (1959) 323
Five Weeks in a Balloon (1962) 30
Flaherty, Robert 360–61
The Flash (TV) viii
Flight of the Lost Balloon (1961) 206–7
Flight to Mars (1951) 210–12, **211**
The Fly (1958) 282, 322–23, 324,
326–27
The Fly (1986) 282
"The Fly" 322
Flynn, Errol 280
Foch, Nina 146
Fontaine, Joan 22, 27, 28, **28**, 291
Fontanne, Lynn 210, 226
For Those Who Think Young (1964) 134
Ford, Derek 75
Ford, Donald 75
Ford, John 216
Foreman, Carl 75
Foster, John xi
Foster, Preston 9, 10, **10**
Foster, Ronald **8**
Fowler, Gene, Jr. 54, 55–56
Fowler, Marjorie 55, 56
Fowley, Douglas 256
Francis, Freddie 81, **81**, 83, 84
Frankenstein (1931) 42, 43, 166
Frankenstein Island (1982) 210, 223
Frankham, David **274**

Franklin, Hugh 153
Frankovich, Mike 76, 134
Franz, Arthur 211
Fraser, Ian 132, 133
Freaks (1932) 329
Freed, Herb 220
Freeman, Y. Frank 294
Freeman, Y. Frank, Jr. 294, 298
Frees, Paul 344
Frenchie (1950) 290
From a Whisper to a Scream see *The Offspring*
Frye, William 245
Fuest, Robert 280
Fuller, Robert 197
Fuller, Sam 57
Funnicello, Annette 136
Fury (TV) 296
Fury at Showdown (1957) 52

G

Gabby Hayes (TV) 176
Gable, Clark 32, 212
Gahagan, Helen 96
Gaines, Richard **211**
Galileo (stage) 251
Gangbusters (TV) 260
Gardner, Ava 218
Garland, Beverly 230, 231, 243, 246
Garland, Judy 213
Gaslight (1944) 271
Gassman, Vittorio 296
Gaye, Lisa 33
Gaynor, Janet 21, 160
Gemora, Charles 298
Genghis Khan (unmade movie) 140
Getty, Estelle 258
The Ghost in the Invisible Bikini (1966) 128, 140–41, 142, **142**
Ghost Ship (1953) 50
Ghost Story (TV) 97
Giancana, Sam 258
The Giant Leeches see *Attack of the Giant Leeches*
Gibbons, Ayllene 9
Gilda (1946) 272
Gilliat, Sidney 86, 92, 93, 104
Gilligan's Island (TV) 304
Gilling, John 80

Gilmore, John 7, 8
The Gin Game (stage) 230
The Glass Wall (1953) 290, 296
Glasser, Bernard xi, 326
Gleason, Jackie 244
Glenn, John 12
A Global Affair (1964) 134
Glory (1989) 81
Goddard, Paulette 20
Godsell, Vanda **334**
Goff, Ivan 262, 263
"The Gold-Bug" 276
Goldblum, Jeff 282
Golden Boy (stage) 349–50
Goldstein, Bob 52
Goldstein, Leonard 52
Gomez, Thomas 226
Gordon, Alex xi
Gordon, Bert I. 70
Gordon, Richard xi, 86
Gordon, Robert 347–48
Gordon il Pirata Nero see *Rage of the Buccaneers*
Gorilla at Large (1954) 223, **224**
Gorshin, Frank 237
Gough, Michael 60, 65, 66, 70, 73
Gozier, Bernie 37–38, **38**
Grant, Arthur 112
Grant, Cary 341
Graves, Peter 296
Gray, Carole 335, **335**
Gray, Coleen 350
The Great Gilbert and Sullivan (1953) 92
The Great McGinty (1940) 336
Green Hell (1940) 273
The Green Man (1957) 86, 93
Greene, Clarence 186
Greenstreet, Sydney 169, 170, 226
Greenway, Dan 342
Greenway, Lee 342
Greenwood, Jack 65, 71
Gregory, James 270
Gregory, Paul 260
Grey, Virginia 51, 52
Griffith, Charles B. 189, 234
Griffith, Hugh 82
The Grip of the Strangler see *Haunted Strangler*
Grubb, Davis 260
Guedel, John 255

Guerrero, Carmen **360**
Guest, Val 99–125, **99**, **124**
Gun Brothers (1956) 290
Gun Duel in Durango (1957) 290
Gunsmoke (TV) 342
Gwynne, Anne 200

H

Haggard, H. Rider 30, 96
Hall, James Norman 32
Hall, Jon 32
Haller, Dan 136, 137, 275
Hamilton, Kipp 179
Hand of Death (1961) 332
Handel, Leo 9, 12
Hanna, Mark 201
Hansen, Donald 129
Hardwicke, Sir Cedric 30
Harris, Denny 222
Harris, Lorraine **35**
Harris, Robert H. 63–64, **63**
Harris, Stacy 232
Harrison, Joan 29
Harrison, Rex 92
Harrison, Sandra **61**, 62
Harryhausen, Ray 347
Hart, Moss 351
Hart, Susan 127–44, **127**, **131**, **138**,
    139, **142**
Hartman, Margot 152
Harvey, Herk 146, 147, 148, 149, 150,
    152, 154, 155
Haskin, Byron 259, 292, 294, 295
Haunted Planet see *Planet of the
    Vampires*
The Haunted Strangler (1958) 86–89,
    87, **88**, 92, 98
Haunts (1977) 220
Havoc, June 290
Hawaii Five-O (TV) 262
Hawaiian Nights (1954 short) 33
Hawdon, Robin 122
Hawks, Howard 103, 341, 342, 344,
    345, 346, 347
Hayden, Sterling 52
Hayes, Allison 5, 201, 202, **202**, 203,
    204
Hayes, Helen 272
Hayward, Louis 350

Hayward, Susan 292
Haze, Jonathan **183**, 230, 236, **274**
Head, Edith 77
The Headless Ghost (1959) 68
Hearst, William Randolph 330
Heartbreak House (stage) 271
Hecht, Ben 121
Heinlein, Robert A. 240
The Helen Morgan Story (1957) 196
Helfer, Ralph 72, 73
Helm, Anne 220
Helmick, Paul 197
Henderson, Marcia 5
Hennesy, Tom 41
Henning, Paul 134
Henry, Buzz 264
Henry, Mike 95, 96
Hepburn, Audrey 153
Hepburn, Katharine 168–69
Herman, Norman 143, 144
Herron, Bob **131**
Hesse, Hermann 215
Heston, Charlton 280
Hewitt, David L. 11
Heydt, Donna 56
Heydt, Louis Jean 56
Heyward, Louis M. 137
Hicks, Seymour 19
The High Chaparral (TV) 210, 215
Highway Patrol (TV) 58
Highway to Heaven (TV) 7, 58
Hill, James 75–76
Hilligoss, Candace 145–55, **145**, **151**,
    155
Hilton, Arthur 257
Hinds, Anthony 100, 102, 103, 104,
    105–6, 107
His Kind of Woman (1951) 273
Hitchcock, Alfred 18, 21, 28, 29, 103,
    104, 270–71
Hively, Jack 256
Hobart, Rose 157–74, **157**, **163**, **164**,
    166, **173**
Hobbes, Halliwell 164, **164**, 165
Holden, William 292
"The Hollywood Reporter" 100, 197
The Hollywood Squares (TV) 280–81
Holm, Celeste 226
Holt, Patrick 122
Homebodies (1974) 351
Homeier, Skip 351

Honey, I Blew Up the Kid (1992) 340
Hope, Bob 56, 134
Hopkins, Miriam 162, 168
Horror of Dracula (1958) 65
The Horror of Party Beach (1964) 152, 153
Horrors of the Black Museum (1959) 46, 54, 64–68, **65**, 69
Horrors of the Black Zoo see *Black Zoo*
Hough, John 337
House of the Damned (1963) 7–9, **8**, 329–31, **330**
The House of the Seven Gables (1940) 273
House of Wax (1953) 50, **267**, 269–70
House on Haunted Hill (1958) viii, 278
Houseman, John 251
Houston, Donald 76
How to Make a Monster (1958) 46, 53, 54, 61, 62–64, **63**
Howard, Leslie 164
Howard, Trevor 82
Howdy Doody (TV) 176
The Howling (1981) 352
Hoyt, John 9
Hudson, Rock 37, 40
Hudson, William 203
Hudson's Bay (1940) 278
Hughes, Howard 21, 273, 342–43, 344, 345, 347, 348
The Hunchback of Notre Dame (1923) 42, 43
Hunter, Jeffrey 63, 196
Hunter, Tab 63, 135
The Hurricane (1937) 32
"The Hurricane" 32
Huston, John 121
Huston, Virginia **211**
Hutton, Robert 129–30, 132
The Hypnotic Eye (1960) 2, 4–6, **6**, 11

I

"I Am Legend" 110, 333
I Am Legend (unmade Hammer movie) 110
I Love Lucy (TV) 49
I, Mobster (1958) 235
I Was a Male War Bride (1949) 341

I Was a Teenage Frankenstein (1957) 46, 56, 58–60, 62, 64
I Was a Teenage Werewolf (1957) **45**, 53–58, **55**, 62
Idiot's Delight (stage) 146
Imitation of Life (1959) 358
Indusi, Jeff xi
Indusi, Joe xi
The Infernal Idol see *Craze*
Innerspace (1987) 352
The Invaders (TV) 97, 98
Invaders from Mars (1953) 250, 256
Invasion of the Body Snatchers (1956) 150
Invasion of the Hell Creatures see *Invasion of the Saucer Men*
Invasion of the Saucer Men (1957) 237
The Invisible Man (1933) 272
The Invisible Man Returns (1940) 272
The Invisible Mouse (1947 cartoon) 272
Ireland, John 50, 53
Island of Death see *Island of the Doomed*
Island of the Doomed (1967) **217**, 218
Isle of the Dead (1945) 170
It Came from Beneath the Sea (1955) 347–49, **349**
It Came from Outer Space (1953) 39
Ito, Robert 13
Ivy (1947) 27

J

JFK (1991) 116
Jacks, Robert L. 52
Jackson, Brad **181**
Jackson, Michael 36, 281
Jaffe, Leo 77
Jaffe, Sam 215
James, Montague 18, 23, 24
James, Sid 106
Jessel, George 3
Joan of Arkansas (unmade movie) 140
The Joey Bishop Show (TV) 129
Johnson, Russell 234
Johnson, Tom xi
Jones, Shirley 213
Jones-Moreland, Betsy 175–94, **175**, **181**, **183**, **185**, **191**
Jory, Victor 256, 257, 258

Journey to the Center of the Earth
   (1959) 25
Judd, Edward 116–7, **117**, 119
Juran, Nathan 198, 202–3, 206–7

K

Das Kabinett des Dr. Caligari see *The*
   Cabinet of Dr. Caligari
Kael, Pauline 93
Kahn, Ivan 2
Kandel, Aben 53, 56, 58, 62, 64, 68,
   69, 72, 80
Kane, Joe xi
Karloff, Boris 28, 41, 42, 86–88, **87**,
   92, 97, 141, **142**, 165–66, **166**, 167,
   170, 193, 245, 279
Katzman, Sam 347–48
Kazan, Elia 103, 186, 210, 215, 225, 226
Keaton, Buster 141
Kelly, Gene 292
Kendall, Suzy 83
Kennedy, John F. 10–11, 116, 258
Kenney, June 182
Kevan, Jack 34
Kid Galahad (1962) 333
Kiel, Richard 9, 256, 331
Killer Force (1975) 113
King, Henry 3
King Kong (1933) 20, 69, 71
King Rat (1965) 323
"King Rat" 323
King Solomon's Mines (1937) 30
"King Solomon's Mines" 29
Kings Row (TV) 296
Kirk, Phyllis 50
Kirk, Tommy 139
Kirshner, Don 123
Klinger, Michael 75
Klugman, Jack 13
Kneale, Nigel 100, 102, 106, 111
Knives of the Avenger (1967) 216
Knox, Harold **325**
Koch, Howard W. 310, 311, 312
Koehler, David 52
Kohner, Pancho 364, 365
Kohner, Paul 358–59, 361, 364
Kohner, Susan 358
Konga (1961) 69–72, **70**, 73, 74
Korda, Zoltan 92

Kowalski, Bernard L. 242
Kroeger, Berry 220
Kronos (1957) 326
Kruschen, Jack 259

L

L. A. Law (TV) 340
The Lady Vanishes (1938) 103, 104
Laemmle, Carl, Jr. 160–61
Laemmle, Carl, Sr. 161
Lamb, John 41
Lamour, Dorothy 32
Lanchester, Elsa 166–67, 258
Land of the Giants (TV) 18, 28
Landau, Richard 101–2, 322
Landi, Marla 89
Landon, Michael 7, **45**, 53, 54, **55**,
   58, 63, 328
Laramie (TV) 13, 129
Larsen, Keith 13
The Last Man on Earth (1964) 280,
   333–34
Last Woman on Earth (1960) 176,
   183–89, **185**, 190, 192, 205
Laughton, Charles 251, 252, 254, 260,
   261, 262
Launder, Frank 86, 92, 104
Laura (1944) 277, 278
LaVigne, Emile 5
Law, John Phillip 225
Lawman (TV) 13
Lawrence, Elliott 350
Lawrence, Marc 222
Leave Her to Heaven (1945) 278
LeBorg, Reginald 310, 311, 312, 315–16
Lee, Anna 30
Lee, Christopher 97, **97**, 282
Lee, Joanna **239**
Lee, Pinky 33
Leewood, Jack 326
Legacy of Blood (1973) 2, 13–14
Le Gallienne, Eva 158, 159, 310
The Legend of Hell House (1973) 143
Leifert, Don xi
LeRoy, Rita 2
Lester, Henry 75
Levy, Stuart 60, 64, 69
Lewis, Jerry 49–50
Lewis, Louise 62

Lewis, Milt 291
Lewton, Val 170, 331
"Life" 56
Lights Out (radio) 253
Liliom (1930) 158, 159–60, 170–71
Liliom (stage) 158, 159, 212
Linkletter, Art 251
Lippert, Robert L. 7, 101, 320–26, **325**, 327, 329, 331, 332, 333, 335–36
Litel, John 50, 211–12, **211**
Little House on the Prairie (TV) 7
The Little Shop of Horrors (1960) 192
The Littlest Hobo (1958) 243
Living Swamp (1955 short) 196
Loder, John 169
"Look" 56
Lorre, Peter 22, 27, 29, 170, 193, 273, 279
Lost Continent (1951) 322
The Lost Continent (1968) 143
Lost in Space (TV) 28–29
"The Lost World" 26
The Lost World (1925) 26, 320
The Lost World (1960) 18, 25–26, **27**
Lothar, Ernest 20
Lourie, Eugene 347
Love in the Afternoon (1957) 153
Lubitsch, Ernest 359
Lucas, George 67
Luce, Clare Boothe 214
Luce, Greg xi
Lugones, Alex xi
Lugosi, Bela 42, 49, 245, 312, 358, 359, 362
Lugosi, Bela, Jr. 49
Lugosi, Lillian 49
Lullaby (stage) 159
Lune, Ted **78**
Lunt, Alfred 210, 226
Lynch, David 250
Lyon, Ben 68
Lyon, Richard 68
Lytess, Natasha 3

M

Macbeth (stage) 310
McCarey, Leo 291
McCarthy, Joseph 41
McCarthy, Kevin 150

McCartney, Paul 106
McCrea, Ann 255
McDonnell, Dave vii, xi
McDowall, Roddy 290
MacGinnis, Niall 25
McKern, Leo 106
MacLaine, Shirley 212
MacMurray, Fred 221
McQueen, Steve 244
MacRae, Gordon 213, 214
Macready, George 167, 168, 272
Magginetti, Bill 326
Magnificent Roughnecks (1956) 52, 55
Maharis, George 193
Mahoney, Jock 95
Maibaum, Richard 121
Majors, Lee 42
Malone, Dorothy 5, 50, 53
Maltin, Leonard 155
Mamoulian, Rouben 161–62
Man on a Tightrope (1953) 226
The Man Who Knew Too Much (1934) 18, 29
Maneater of Hydra see *Island of the Doomed*
Mank, Greg xi
Mankiewicz, Joseph L. 277
Mankowitz, Wolf 114
Mannix (TV) 262
Manson, Mary **335**
The Many Loves of Dobie Gillis (TV) 134
March, Fredric 162, **163**, **164**, 165, 169
Marguetti, Victor 69
Mark of the Vampire see *The Vampire*
The Mark of Zorro (1940) 218
Marlowe, Scott 53
Marquette, Jacques 184, 191–92, 195–208, **195**
Marrazzo, Kevin xi
Marsh, Tani 33
Martin, Dean 49–50
Martin, Dewey 345
Martin, Quinn 96, 98
Martucci, Mark xi
Marvin, Lee 295
Marx, Groucho 23
La Maschera de Demonio see *Black Sunday*
The Masque of the Red Death (1964) 275

Master of the World (1961) **269**, 270
Matheson, Richard 333–34
May, Joe 272
Maynor, Asa 63
Medlinsky, Harvey 79
Meisner, Sanford 147
Melchior, Cleo 12
Melchior, Ib 9, 12
Melford, George 360
Menzies, William Cameron 256
Merivale, Philip 159
Meteor Monster see *Teenage Monster*
Mighty Joe Young (1949) 69
The Mike Douglas Show (TV) 295
Milland, Ray 275
Millay, Edna St. Vincent 158
Miller, Arthur 225, 226
Miller, Dick 230, 235, 236
Miller, Gilbert 272
Miller, Ron 336–37
Milli, Robert 153
Milner, Martin 291
Mirisch, Harold 51
Mirisch, Walter 211
Mitchell, Cameron 209–28, **209**, **211**, **213**, **214**, **217**, **219**, **224**
Mitchell, Duke 50
Mitchum, Robert 21, 260, 261, 346
Molnár, Ferenc 212
Mommie Dearest (1981) 77
"Mommie Dearest" 77, 79
Monkey on My Back (1957) 215
Monroe, Marilyn 3
"The Monster" 214
The Monster Meets the Gorilla see *Bela Lugosi Meets a Brooklyn Gorilla*
Montalban, Ricardo 279
Montbatten, Louis 108
Monte Cristo (TV) 24
Montez, Maria 32
Moreno, Rita 33
Moriarty, Michael 223
Moritz, Milt 58
Morley, Robert 76
Morning Star (TV) 192
Morris, Wayne 50
Morrow, Jeff 13
Morrow, Susan **257**, 259
Morse, Hollingsworth 301–2
Morton, Judee 132, 133

The Mothers-in-Law (TV) 310
The Mummy (1932) 43
Munro, Janet 117, 119
Murder by Decree (1979) 77
Mutiny on the Bounty (1935) 32
"Mutiny on the Bounty" 32
My Favorite Year (1982) 223
My Son John (1952) 291
Mystery! (TV) 282
Mystery of the Wax Museum (1933) 270

N

N.O.P.D. (TV) 232
Naked Paradise (1957) 189
Narizzano, Dino **151**, 153
Nash, Noreen 128
Neal, Tom 48
Nefertite, Regina del Nilo see *Queen of the Nile*
Nelson, Ed 229–47, **229**, **239**, **243**, **244**
Nelson, Gene 332
Neumann, Kurt 322, 323
Neville, John 76
New Orleans Uncensored (1955) 231
"The New Yorker" 173
Newhart, Bob 345
Newman, Alfred 213
Newton-John, Olivia 123
Niagara (1953) 196
Nichols, Kelly 221
Nicholson, Jack 136, 192, 222–23, 237, 238
Nicholson, James H. 51, 52, 53, 54, 57, 58, 59, 61, 64, 67, 68, 128, 132, 133, 134, 135, 136, 140, 141, 142, 143, 144, 237
Nicholson, Sylvia 142
Night of the Blood Beast (1958) 230, 242, **242**, **243**
Night of the Demon see *Curse of the Demon*
The Night of the Hunter (1955) 260–62
"The Night of the Hunter" 260, 261
Nightmare in Wax (1969) 219–20, **219**
Nimoy, Leonard 238, 255
"1984" 212
No Down Payment (1957) 222

Nordhoff, Charles 32
Norton, Barry 359, **360**, **363**
Nosseck, Max 169
Nyby, Christian 346, **346**

O

Oates, Warren 80
Oboler, Arch 250, 252, 253, 254,
  255, 260, 324
O'Brian, Hugh 52, 255
O'Brien, Willis H. 26
O'Connolly, Jim 71
O'Donnell, Bob 58
The Offspring (1987) 223–24
Oklahoma! (1955) 213
On the Beach (1959) 253
On the Waterfront (1954) 226
One Million Years B.C. (1966) 101
O'Neal, Ryan 245
Orbito, Alex 212
Orwell, George 212
"The Other One" 326
The Other Side of the Wind (1976)
  215–16
O'Toole, Peter 223
Out of the Darkness see *Teenage
  Caveman*
The Outer Limits (TV) 193, 245
Outlaw Planet see *Planet of the
  Vampires*

P

Pacific Destiny (1956) 93
Pagan Love Song (1950) 32
Paget, Debra **274**
Paiva, Nestor 39
Pajama Party (1964) 128, 135
Pal, George 7, 259, 290, 292, 293–94,
  295, 298, 304–5, **304**
Pal, Zsoka 293, **304**
Palance, Jack 82–84, **83**
Pallos, Steven 120
Panic in the Streets (1950) 103
Parfrey, Woodrow 262, **263**
Parla, Donna xi
Parla, Paul xi
Parsons, Jack 331

Parsons, Louella 68
Pate, Michael 7
Patrick, Dennis 9, 12
Paxton, John 253
Payton, Barbara 48
Peck, Gregory 312, 313, 340
Penn, Leo 252
Penn, Sean 252
Penny Princess (1951) 114
Perkins, Gil 199
Perkins, Millie 222
Peter and Paul (1981 mini-series) 98
Peterson, Richard 364
Petrillo, Sammy 49–50
Peyton Place (TV) 158, 168, 230, 245
The Phantom of the Opera (1925) 42,
  43
Phipps, William 249–66, **249**, **257**,
  263, **264**
Pidgeon, Walter 27, **28**
Pit and the Pendulum (1961) 275–76
A Place in the Sun (1951) 291
Planet of Terror see *Planet of the
  Vampires*
Planet of the Vampires (1965) 140
"Playboy" 129, 322
Playhouse 90 (TV) 280
Poe, Edgar Allan 25, 137, 275, 276,
  283–84
Poet's Corner (stage) 271–72
Police Woman (TV) 305
Pologe, Ruth 66, 139
The Poseidon Adventure (1972) 21
Powell, Dick 24
Power, Tyrone 218
Powers, Mala 206
Prather, Maurice 148
Preminger, Otto 162, 171, 277, 346
Presley, Elvis 6, 13, 333
Preston, Robert 292
Price, Vincent viii, 22, 50, 65,
  135–36, 137, 138, 165, 243, 262,
  263, **263**, 267–87, **267**, **269**, **274**,
  276, **277**, **281**, **285**, 327, 334
*The Private Lives of Elizabeth and
  Essex* (1939) 280
Provine, Dorothy 86, 96, 98
Psycho (1960) 29
"Psycho" 333
Psychomania (1964) 146, 152
"Psychotronic" vii

Pushnick, Freda 7, 8
Putnam, Jock 130

Q

Quark (TV) 264
The Quatermass Experiment see *The Creeping Unknown*
The Quatermass Experiment (TV) 100, 322
Quatermass II see *Enemy from Space*
Quatermass II (TV) 108
Quayle, Anthony 76, 77
Queen of the Nile (1964) 279
Quincy, M.E. (TV) 13

R

Rabin, Jack 257
Rage of the Buccaneers (1963) 279–80
Rains, Claude 20, 21, 26, 27, 272, 329, 335
Randall, Tony 340
Rathbone, Basil 26, **166**, 167, 218, 279, **311**, 312, 313
Rathbone, Ouida 167
Raw Force (1982) 222
Ray, Fred Olen 223
Raymond, Paula 347
Raynor, Bill 51
Reagan, Ronald 171
"The Red Badge of Courage" 214
Reed, Carol 92
Reed, Oliver 208
Reed, Roland 301
Rees, Yvette **332**
Reeves, Michael 283
Reeves, Richard 52
Reid, Milton **78**
Return of the Fly (1959) **321**, 326–27
Revenge of the Creature (1955) 41, 42
Revenge of the Vampire see *Black Sunday*
Reynolds, James **263**
Rhapsody in Blue (1945) 312
Richards, Dawn 54
Ride in the Whirlwind (1965) 222–23
Ride the Wild Surf (1964) 134, 135
Rigg, Diana 282

River Beat (1954) 50, 64
Robards, Jason, Jr. 192
The Robe (1953) 210
Roberts, Ben 262, 263
Robinson, Ann 289–307, **289**, **297**, **300**, **303**, **304**, **306**
Robinson, Bernard 108, 112
Rock All Night (1957) 234
Rocket to the Moon see *Cat Women of the Moon*
Rocketship X-M (1950) 322
Rocky Jones, Space Ranger (TV) 300, 301–2
Rodriquez, Ismael 218
Roeg, Nicolas 275
Rogers, Lorraine 146
Rombouts, Ben 14
Romero, Cesar 80
Rondeau, Charles 243
Rose, Kathleen 52, 55, 56
Rose, Sherman 51, 54–55, 56
Rosenberg, Max J. 81
Rosner, Milton 19
Ross, Barney 215
Ross, Mike 202
Rouse, Russell 186
Route 66 (TV) 193
Rubio, Pablo Alvarez 359–60, **360**
Rudley, Herbert 309–17, **309**, **311**, **314**
Ruick, Barbara **213**
Runser, Mary xi
Rush, Barbara 292
Russell, John 13, 14
Russell, Kurt 345

S

The Saga of the Viking Women and Their Voyage to the Waters of the Great Sea Serpent (1957) 176, 178–83, **181**, **183**, 190
The St. Valentine's Day Massacre (1967) 192
Saltzman, Harry 121, 123
Sanders, George 273–74
Santa (1932) 363–64
Savalas, Telly 80
Sayer, Diane 208
Sayer, Jay 180
"Scarlet Street" vii

Scarwid, Diana **353**
Scheer, Philip 54, 59, 63
Scheider, Roy **151**, 153
Scheuer, Steven 332–33
Schildkraut, Joseph 159
Schneider, Stanley 76
Schwalb, Ben 6
Scorsese, Martin 67, 68
Scott, Gordon 94
Scott, Peter Graham 68
Scrivani, Rich xi
Search for Bridey Murphy (1956) 350
The Secret of the Loch (1934) 18–19
Selander, Lesley 211–12
Self, William **346**
Sellers, Peter 96, 121
Selznick, David O. 20, 21
Sesame Street (TV) 264
77 Sunset Strip (TV) 129
Sharp, Don 331, 335
Shaw, George Bernard 261, 271
Shaw, Irwin 312
Shayne, Robert vii–viii
She (1899) 96
She (1935) 96
She (1965) 96–97, **97**
She Devil (1957) 326
She Gods of Shark Reef (1958) 234
Sheen, Martin 245
Shepard, Alan 12
Sheridan, Ann 296, 341
Sheridan, Margaret 341, **343**, 345
Sherman, Harry 51
Sherman, William Tecumseh 223, 224
Shields, Brooke 246
The Shoemaker's Holiday (stage) 271
Shogun Island see *Raw Force*
Shores, Del 258
Short, Martin 352
Shubert, Jacob J. 159
Shurlock, Geoffrey 59, 60
"Siddhartha" 215
"Sight and Sound" 331
The Silent Scream (1980) 222
Silver, Monty 146, 150
Simon, Robert F. 215
Simon, Sylvan S. 171
Sinatra, Frank 212–13
Sinclair, Ronald 141
Single White Female (1992) 340

Siodmak, Curt 28, 49
Siodmak, Robert 49
Siskel, Gene 154
The Six Million Dollar Man (TV) 42
The Sixth Sense (TV) 97
60 Minutes (TV) 172
The $64,000 Question (TV) 278
Skal, David J. 364
Skouras, Spyros 320–21, 327
The Slime People (1963) 128, 129–33, **131**
Small, Edward 7, 24, 296
Smith, John 13
The Snow Creature (1954) 250, 256, 260
Soldier in the Rain (1963) 244–45
The Solid Gold Cadillac (stage) 177
Sons and Soldiers (stage) 312
Sothern, Terry 121
The Soul of a Monster (1944) 167–68
Space Force (TV) 264
Space Master X-7 (1958) 326
Space Patrol (TV) 305
Spaceflight IC-1 (1965) 332
Spalding, Harry 319–38, **319**, **325**
Spalding, Jean 336, 337
Spencer, Douglas 341–42
Spenser, David **334**
"The Sphinx" 276
Spielberg, Steven 67, 156
Stabler, Robert 326, 333
Stalag 17 (1953) 235
Stanwyck, Barbara 52
Star Trek (TV) 2
Star Wars (1977) 144
Stark Fear (1962) 350–51
"Starlog" vii, xi
The Steel Trap (1952) 231
Steele, Barbara 216
Steele, Tom 345
Stevens, Dorinda **65**
Stevens, George 291
Stevens, Warren 3
Stevenson, Robert 21
Stewart, David J. 235
Stewart, George 333
Stiles, Norman 264
Stone, Andrew 231, 232
Stone, Oliver 116
Stone, Virginia 231
Storm Over the Nile (1956) 92

The Story of Gilbert and Sullivan see *The Great Gilbert and Sullivan*
The Story of Mankind (1957) 18, 22–23
The Story of Molly X (1949) 290–91
Strange, Glenn 40–41
Strange Invaders (1983) 351, **353**
Strangis, Greg 305
Strangis, Sam 305
The Strangler (1964) 207–8, **207**
Strasberg, Lee 147
Strauss, Robert 235
A Streetcar Named Desire (stage) 183
Strock, Herbert L. 58, 62
Strode, Woody 95
Strudwick, Peter 12
Struss, Karl 165
A Study in Terror (1966) 67, 75–77, 80
Stulberg, Gordon 114
Sturges, Preston 259
Sturges, Terry 259
Subotsky, Milton 81
Sullivan, Barry 140
Sullivan, Francis L. 25
Sunset Boulevard (1950) 220
Superman (1978) 221
Supersonic Man (1979) 221
Svehla, Gary J. xi
Swamp Diamonds see *Swamp Women*
Swamp Women (1956) 230, 231, 232
The Swarm (1978) 221
Swerdloff, Arthur L. 253

T

Tabu (1931) 32
Tales of Terror (1962) 273, **274**
The Taming of the Shrew (stage) 210, 226
Tamiroff, Akim 312
Target Earth (1954) 50–52, 55, 57
Tarzan (TV) 96
Tarzan and the Great River (1967) 96
Tarzan and the Valley of Gold (1966) 95
Tarzan the Magnificent (1960) 86, 93–95
Tarzan's Three Challenges (1963) 95
Tate, Dale 198
Taurog, Norman 137–38
Taylor, Elizabeth 153, 291

Taylor, Joyce 7
Taylor, Kent 329
Taylor, Robert 24
Teenage Caveman (1958) 235–37
Teenage Doll (1957) 235
Teenage Frankenstein see *I Was a Teenage Frankenstein*
Teenage Monster (1957) 196, 198–201, **199**
Teenage Thunder (1957) 197, 201
The Ten Commandments (1956) 280
Tenney, Del 146, **151**, 152, 153
Tenser, Tony 75
Theater of Blood (1973) 282
They Dare Not Love (1941) 21
The Thing (1982) 345
The Thing from Another World (1951) **339**, 340–45, **343**, 349
The 39 Steps (1935) 18
Thompson, Marshall 50, 67, 89, **90**, 206
Thriller (album) 281
Thriller (TV) 245
Thunder Over Hawaii see *Naked Paradise*
Tickle Me (1965) 2, 6, 13
Tierney, Gene 277, 278
"Time" 56
Time Express (TV) 262–63, **263**
The Time Travelers (1964) 2, 9–13, **10**
The Time Tunnel (TV) 29
Timpone, Tony vii, xi
The Tingler (1959) viii, 278
To Dorothy, A Son (stage) 114
Tobey, Kenneth 339–55, **339**, **343**, **346**, **349**, **353**
The Tomb (1985) 223
The Tomb of Ligeia (1964) 275, 276
Tomlinson, David 135
Tone, Franchot 32, 48
The Toolbox Murders (1978) 210, 221
Toomorrow (1970) 100, 123
Topper, Burt 207, 208
Tors, Ivan 291
Tourneur, Jacques 25, 136
Tovar, Lupita 357–65, **357**, **360**, **363**
Tower of London (1939) **166**, 167, 268, 279, **281**
Towne, Robert **185**, 185, 186, 187, 188
Townsend, Bud 219, 220

Tremayne, Les 12, 132, 295–96, **304**, 305

Trog (1970) 66, 77, 80–82, **81**
Trouble with Father (TV) 4
Trueman, Paula 351
Tucker, Forrest 112–13
Tufts, Sonny 256, 258–59
Turner, Lana 168
Turney, Catherine 326
The Twilight Zone (TV) 245
Two Dollar Bettor (1951) 50
Two Way Stretch (1960) 96, 98
The Twonky (1953) 250, 253, 255–56

U

Unconquered (1947) 20
Undercover Agent (1953) 50
The Unknown Terror (1957) 326

V

Valley, Richard xi
Valley of the Redwoods (1960) 240
The Vampire (1957) 350
Van Doren, Mamie 33
Van Dyke, Dick 232
Varconi, Victor 358
"Variety" 197
Varnel, Marcel 100
Vaughn, Robert 236
The Veil see *Haunts*
VeSota, Bruno 238, 239, 240–42
Vetri, Victoria 122
Vetter, Charles 86, 89
Victoria Regina (stage) 271, 272
Vidor, Charles 21
Villarias, Carlos 358, 359, **360**
Vincent (short) 268
Viosca, Soriano **360**
Vivian, Percival 158
La Voluntad del Muerto (1930) 358, 361
Vorkapich, Slavko 253
Voyage to the Bottom of the Sea (1961) 18, 22, 26–28, **28**, 29
Voyage to the Bottom of the Sea (TV) 18, 22, 29
Voyage to Venus (unmade movie) 212

W

Wagner, Robert 63
Wait Till the Sun Shines, Nellie (1952) 3
Walker, Robert 291
Wallace, Bryan Edgar 20
Wallace, Edgar 20
Wallach, Eli 340
Wallis, Hal B. 50, 154
War-Gods of the Deep (1965) 18, 25, 135–37
The War of the Worlds (1953) 250, 256, 259–60, 265, **289**, 290, 292–301, **297**, 304–6
The War of the Worlds (TV) 290, 305
"The War of the Worlds" 295
Warner, Jack 104
Warner, Jack L. 22, 23
Warren, Charles Marquis 326, 333
The Watcher in the Woods (1980) 336–37, **337**
"The Watcher in the Woods" 336, 337
Weaver, Jon xi
Webb, Jack 232
Weigel, Helene 251
Weill, Kurt 225
Weintraub, Sy 93, 95, 96
Weis, Don 135
Weissmuller, Johnny 94–95
Welcome to My Nightmare (album) 280–81
Welles, Mel 234
Welles, Orson 65, 103, 121, 139, 215, 271
Wells, H. G. 295
We're No Angels (stage) 270
Westcott, Helen 50
Westmore, Bud 34
Whale, James 21, 273
What Ever Happened to Baby Jane? (1962) 79
When Dinosaurs Ruled the Earth (1970) 100, 101, 121–23
When Worlds Collide (1951) 294, 304–5
Where Danger Lives (1950) 21
The Whirlybirds (TV) 340, 350
White, Robb viii
White Heat (1949) 262

White Shadows in the South Seas
(1928) 32
Whitmore, James 214, **214**, 215
"Who Goes There?" 345
Whorf, Richard 210, 226
The Wild One (1954) 253
The Wild Weird World of Dr.
Goldfoot (TV special) 139
Wilder, W. Lee 260
Willard, Fred 264
Willard (1971) 351
Williams, Wade 305
Willoughby, George 136, 137
The Wind Without Rain (stage) 291
Windsor, Marie 50, 256, 257–58
Winters, Shelley 261, 290
Wintle, Julian 69
Witchcraft (1964) 327, 331–32, **332**, 336
Witchfinder General see *Conqueror*
Worm
"Witchfinder General" 283
Without Warning (1980) 222
Women of the Prehistoric Planet
(1966) 2, 13
Wood, Natalie 4, 63
Wood, Sam 27
Woodbury, Joan **10**
Woodruff, Morris 96
Woodward, Joanne **213**

Woolner, Bernard 201, 206
Wordsworth, Richard **105**, 106
The World, the Flesh, and the Devil
(1959) 333
Wray, Fay 20
Wright, Frank Lloyd 252, 278
Wright, Teresa 231, 350
Wyatt, Al 37

Y

Yesterday's Enemy (1959) 108
Yordan, Philip 222
You Bet Your Life (TV) 255
Young, Aida 122
Young, Roland 164
Young Fury (1965) 15
The Young in Heart (1938) 21
The Young Rebels see *Teenage Doll*
Youngstein, Max 52

Z

Zabel, Edwin **213**
Zanuck, Darryl F. 3, 52, 214, 226
Zide, Mickey 143
Zucco, George 272

Keep going—you're only halfway

They Fought in the Creature Features

Interviews with 23 Classic Horror, Science Fiction and Serial Stars

by
Tom Weaver

McFarland Classics

McFarland & Company, Inc., Publishers
Jefferson, North Carolina, and London

Original Library of Congress Cataloguing-in-Publication Data (Book 2)

They fought in the creature features : interviews with 23 classic
  horror, science fiction and serial stars / by Tom Weaver
    p.   cm.
  Includes filmographies and index.

  [With Book 1:] ISBN 0-7864-1366-2 (softcover : 50# alkaline paper)

    1. Horror films—History and criticism.   2. Science fiction films—
History and criticism.   3. Motion picture serials—History and criticism.
4. Motion picture actors and actresses—United States—Interviews.
I. Weaver, Tom, 1958–
PN1995.9.H6T47   1995   791.43'616—dc20   94-48609

British Library cataloguing data are available

Manufactured in the United States of America

McFarland & Company, Inc., Publishers
  Box 611, Jefferson, North Carolina 28640
   www.mcfarlandpub.com

Amidst the many real-life people thanked
in the *Preface* on page ix, there are 13 "fictional"
names—characters in some of the SF and horror titles mentioned
in this book. If you're one of those remarkable people who can
pick out these 13 names, *and* provide the titles of the
flicks in which they appear, then this book
is very appreciatively dedicated to *you*.

Table of Contents

Acknowledgments   viii
Preface   ix

Julie Adams   1
John Agar   13
Richard Anderson   25
John Archer   37
Jeanne Bates   51
Billy Benedict   61
Turhan Bey   73
Lloyd Bridges   85
Ricou Browning   97
Robert Cornthwaite   111
Louise Currie   131
Richard Denning   145
Anne Francis   161
Mark Goddard   173
June Lockhart   187
Eugene Lourie   201
Jeff Morrow   211
Lori Nelson   221
Rex Reason   233
William Schallert   245
Don Taylor   263
George Wallace   277
Jane Wyatt   289

Index   303

Acknowledgments

Abridged versions of the interviews in this book were originally published in the following magazines:

Julie Adams: "Creature Love," *Starlog* #167, June, 1991

John Agar: "Creature Crusher," *Starlog* #164, March, 1991

Richard Anderson: "Tales of the Forbidden Planet," *Starlog* #156, July, 1990

John Archer: "Lunar Destiny," *Starlog* #202, May, 1994

Jeanne Bates: "The Phantom's Lady," *Comics Scene* #44, July, 1994

Billy Benedict: "Captain Marvel's Pal," *Starlog* #199, February, 1994

Turhan Bey: "Stardom at Bey," *Fangoria* #105, August, 1991

Lloyd Bridges: "Man of the Seas," *Starlog* #182, September, 1992

Ricou Browning: "Creature Man," *Starlog* #167, June, 1991

Robert Cornthwaite: "Friend of the Thing," *Starlog* #178, May, 1992

Louise Currie: "Cliffhanger Queen," *Comics Scene* #21, October, 1991

Richard Denning: "Creature Hunter," *Starlog* #164, March, 1991

Anne Francis: "Woman of the Forbidden Planet," *Starlog* #186, January, 1993

Mark Goddard: "Space Duty," *Starlog* #190, May, 1993

June Lockhart: "Outrageous Original," *Starlog* #198, January, 1994

Eugene Lourie: "Director of Dinosaurs," *Starlog* #193, August, 1993

Jeff Morrow: "Jeff Morrow—The Man from Metaluna," *Starlog* #118, May, 1987

Lori Nelson: "Creature Lady," *Starlog* #167, June, 1991

Rex Reason: "Memories of Metaluna," *Starlog* #140, March, 1989

William Schallert: "Character Star," *Starlog* #184, November, 1992

Don Taylor: "Director of Men-Apes," *Starlog* #165, April, 1991

George Wallace: "Call Him Commando Cody," *Comics Scene* #20, August, 1991

Jane Wyatt: "Mother Knows Best," *Starlog* #161, December, 1990

Preface

This companion volume to my earlier *Interviews with Science Fiction and Horror Movie Makers* (1988), *Science Fiction Stars and Horror Heroes* (1991) and *Attack of the Monster Movie Makers* (1994) could not have been written without the generous assistance of many of the same people who have helped me in the past. Sincere thanks go to Mark Martucci, Greg Luce, Tom Johnson, Kyra Zelas, Buddy Barnett, Ron Borst, Paul and Donna Parla, Louise Carey, David Skal, Will Murray, Captain Jim Maddison, Frank Coghlan, Jr., Eric Jacobs, Alex Gordon, Don Leifert, Isabel Lewis, Dan Scapperotti, the nice folks at Photofest, Fred Olen Ray, David Schow, *Fangoria*'s Tony Timpone and Mike Gingold, *Starlog*'s Dave McDonnell, Mitch MacAfee, John Foster, Quintillus Aurelius, Joe and Jeff Indusi, Carl Maia, Alex Lugones, Captain George LeMay, Dennis Daniel, Carl and Debbie Del Vecchio, Miklos Sangre, Glenn Damato, John Antosiewicz, Greg Mank, Tal Chotali, Gary and Sue Svehla (and the rest of the FANEX gang), Cal Meacham, Ruth Brunas, Rich Scrivani, Phyllis Allenby, Joe Dante, Jon and Julie Weaver, Erin Ray Fresco, Bandit and Tigger, Joe Kane and all the friendly people at Manhattan's Lincoln Center.

Research associates Mike and John Brunas did their usual, terrific job helping me whip this into shape, and John Cocchi and Jack Dukesbery furnished their always-invaluable assistance with the many filmographies. Thanks, too, to all of my new interviewees; and *special* thanks to the additional interviewees who were promised slots in this book, but (because of lack of space) had to be bumped. Needless to say, they'll all be on proud display in (gulp!) my fifth interviews book with McFarland.

Tom Weaver
North Tarrytown, New York

*The Creature scared people, but there was also a sort of
sweetness about it. In the real classics, there always is
that feeling of compassion for the monster. I think maybe
it touches something in ourselves, maybe the darker parts
of ourselves, that long to be loved and think they really
can't ever be loved. It strikes a chord within us.*

Julie Adams

IT'S BEEN ALMOST 40 years since Julie Adams was caught in the web-fingered clutches of the Gill Man, and she has not quite managed to wriggle free yet. It is the type of highly visible role that dogs an actress, even a talented one who has proven her dramatic worth in dozens of movies and enough television to fill that back lot Black Lagoon where the Creature, gulping like a lovesick schoolboy, suffered its initial attack of love-at-first-sight.

"Once I was working in Chicago in a play, *Father's Day* by Oliver Hailey, and I was peeved when I got this review that said, 'Julie Adams shows more depth than one would have suspected from the star of *Creature from the Black Lagoon*.' No matter what you do, you can act your heart out, but people will always say, 'Oh, Julie Adams — *Creature from the Black Lagoon*.'" Adams laughs, long and loud, but you have to wonder whether it isn't one of those crying-on-the-inside situations. She insists, convincingly, that it's not. "Oh, no, no, no. One must take all these things with humor. After all, it's amazing that the film connected with that many people. To be so closely connected with it is fine, just fine."

But like Lori Nelson, leading lady of *Revenge of the Creature,* Adams did squirm just a mite when she was first assigned to *Creature from the Black Lagoon.* "But then my attitude was, oh, all right. I was a contract player at Universal: Sometimes I did *this,* sometimes *that,* sometimes the other. I was working in four or five movies a year at that time, so it didn't seem like any big deal. I just went right along with it. I never really fought the studio much about things. And then I wound up having *such* a good time on the picture that there's no *way* I can say now that I was unhappy about it."

Still active and glamorous today, Julie Adams is probably Waterloo, Iowa's, greatest gift to the motion picture industry. Although born in the Hawkeye State, Betty May Adams grew up in Arkansas and made her acting debut in a third grade play. "I was in *Hansel and Gretel* and some milk spilled, and I ad-libbed and saved the day. This gave me a flush of power — in the third grade — and I think that's where it all began *[laughs]*! Then I was taking things like expression lessons when I lived in a town called Blytheville, Arkansas — a town of about 10,000 people — because I somehow knew that I wanted to be an actress. I went a couple of years to junior college, to please everybody, and then I came to California to try to be an actress. Nobody found me *[laughs]*, I had to go and find *them*!"

Working three days a week as a secretary to support herself, Adams concentrated the remainder of her time on taking speech lessons (to lose her Midwestern accent) and making the rounds at the various studios' casting departments. Her first movie role was playing a starlet, appropriately enough,

Previous page: Beauty (Julie Adams) consorts with the Beast ("Creature" Ben Chapman) in a between-takes pose. (Photofest)

Adams realizes that the Creature (Ben Chapman) just "longed to be loved," but doesn't seem too keen on the idea in publicity shots.

in a Paramount film called *Red, Hot and Blue* (1949), followed by a leading role in a 58-minute Lippert Western, *The Dalton Gang* (1949) with Don "Red" Barry. Over a period of five weeks, she appeared in six more quickie Lippert Westerns, co-starring with memorable(?) Western favorites(??) Jimmy "Shamrock" Ellison, Russell "Lucky" Hayden and Fuzzy Knight. "It was crazy! There were two leading men, Jimmy Ellison and Russell Hayden, and also a large cast of character actors, and we were all in all of the films. I was The Girl in all of them, so I had three outfits. I had a riding outfit, a stagecoach 'dress-up' outfit and a 'farm girl' outfit. We'd shoot all the farmhouse scenes for all six movies at once, then all the stagecoach scenes. I had a hard time remembering who I was. 'Am I the farm girl this time, or the cow girl?' It was very funny!"

Adams' first big show business break was at Universal, when she appeared in a screen test opposite All American footballer Leon Hart, a Detroit Lions end. It was Hart who was being considered by the studio, but the gridiron star flopped while Universal executives flipped over Adams. The studio changed her first name, possibly to cover up her prior history of low-caliber Westerns, and put her to work on the Universal lot. She co-starred in 21 Universal films over the next several years, including *Bright Victory* (1951) and *Bend of the River* (1952) — as well as the usual mixed bag of lesser-known, less respectable titles like the awful *Finders Keepers* (1951) and desultory Technicolor Westerns like *The Man from the Alamo* and *The Stand at Apache River* (both 1953).

She also had to put up with the harmless but tacky publicity ploys of the day, including having her legs, "the most perfectly symmetrical in the world," win an award, with the result that Universal insured them for $125,000. Of course, they were nowhere to be seen in the period dramas in which Universal kept placing her, so the studio obligingly gave her a bathing suit lead in *Creature from the Black Lagoon*. Richard Carlson was the nominal hero, but the *real* stars of *Creature* were Adams (in a white one-piece swimsuit that fit her far better than the title of "marine researcher") and a scaly foam rubber costume fabricated in the Universal makeup department.

"Bud Westmore and Jack Kevan made the Gill Man outfit in the lab. Bud particularly was a great friend of mine, I was extremely fond of Bud, and I liked Jack as well. Whenever I would go by, I would see them making their magic — pouring the foam rubber, working with molds, painting and fixing the costume and so on. They were quite marvelous, and in a way it was sort of an unrecognized art when you think of these things [like the Creature] that have become part of our culture. And it really *has* become part of everybody's psyche — people recognize it immediately.

"The first Creature suit was made in a certain way that was all wrong. Most of us knew it was wrong, but it was designed more to the taste of one of the executives at the studio, who wanted the Creature to look like the Oscar statuette. It was almost like a body suit; it just didn't have any menace or any kind of excitement about it. And when it was tested on film, it became clear that that was *not* going to be it! The day they tested it in the tank at Universal, I tried out the Aqualung — I swam around in the tank for about twenty-five minutes, and it was so wonderful. So the picture was closed down while Bud Westmore and Jack Kevan and whoever else made the monster suit that they'd had in mind in the first place. And because we had nothing to do until the new monster suit was made and approved, 'Scotty' Welbourne, who did the underwater photography, and Ricou Browning the man who played the Creature, and I, we lugged tanks from the studio and we went to Catalina and went diving. I had a wonderful time learning how to use what was then relatively new equipment."

Adams enjoyed working with Carlson as well as the other male leads, Richard Denning and Antonio Moreno. "It was a very, very pleasant movie, and we all laughed a lot. You *had* to! We were down on the beach on the edge of the water one day, doing the scene where the Creature has killed one of the natives. We were looking down at the body and there was this moment where we were all very still. Richard Carlson was in his bathing trunks and he had his face mask on his forehead, and in just the way people take off their hats for the dead, he reached up and took off his face mask. He doffed it so seriously that we all started to laugh, and it took us a long time to come back together again. It was just too absurd *[laughs]*! And then we had this wonderful guy who did the clapboard for the different shots, an old vaudevillian. The day that Whit Bissell's face was all bloodied up by the Creature, this fellow clapped the board and then he said to Whit *[out of the corner of her mouth]*, 'How ya fixed for blades?' *[laughs]*."

Director Jack Arnold, Adams reminisces, "I liked a lot. He's an extremely nice man and very easy to work with. In those days, we just sort of made movies—do you know what I mean *[laughs]*? We just got on with it, we just went forward. But Jack was extremely efficient. Pictures survive when they have an emotional impact, and I think that so often that is due to the director. That's really his job, because when a picture is finished shooting, basically it's just all this exposed film. The director had to have a picture of it in his mind, to know what's telling and what isn't. Jack really put together a film that touched people."

And William Alland, the too-often unsung producer of so many seminal fifties SF films, "was relatively quiet, soft-spoken, but seemed very efficient and very pleasant always. Now that I have two sons in production (one's in post-production and the other is a first assistant director), I've suddenly discovered that there really is an awful lot that actors don't know about. A producer works with the real nuts and bolts of the production and the actors know only what concerns them. I have to assume that William Alland was a good producer because *Creature from the Black Lagoon* came out looking so well, which is quite remarkable considering the fact that we didn't go on location. People are always quite astonished that we made it on the back lot."

While Jack Arnold put his cast and Creature (Ben Chapman) through their paces at Universal, director James C. Havens headed up the Florida-based second unit photographing underwater scenes at Wakulla Springs. "They ran some rushes of the Florida second unit stuff for us while we were doing *Creature*, and they were so wonderful. Especially the dive that Ricou Browning made, kidnapping the girl [Ginger Stanley] who was doubling me. A fifty foot

Beauty meets the Beast: Julie Adams and the *Creature from the Black Lagoon.*

dive! And after a fifty foot dive, you can't just come back up, you have to get air. So hidden behind some of the rocks at the bottom were breathing hoses, and they could breathe off of those — it forces the air through the side of your mouth. It was very exciting."

Less exciting was the morning when Adams found herself in a studio tank that no one had remembered to heat beforehand. "The day we shot on the stage where they had the Creature's underwater grotto, we were in this huge tank of water. They had forgotten to heat the tank, and the water was . . . *so*

... *cold. S-s-s-so c-c-c-cold!* It was sort of a disastrous morning all in all. It was freezing cold, and I was trying not to shiver as I was lying limp in this poor guy's [the Creature's] arms. And he could barely see, so as he carried me, he scraped my head on a plaster rock and skinned my head *[laughs]*! It was not the best morning of the picture!"

Even though she insists that she enjoyed working in *Creature,* Adams also admits that, "I didn't really want to be in the sequels, to tell you the truth. So I was happy that they didn't come to me anyway." Is *Creature from the Black Lagoon* a film that gets much play in her home video recorder? "No, never. But that's not saying anything against *Creature,* it's just that I'm really not one for watching my old movies. I never really like my work very much, I think about how I'd like to do it over—I'm very critical. I like to see something until I learn what I *can* learn from it, and then I put it away. I just don't believe in looking back."

Like both of the Creature's later female leads, Lori Nelson and Leigh Snowden, Adams also marked time as leading lady to another one of Universal's more unlikely leading men, Francis the Talking Mule. The gimmick that initially sparked the series had worn fairly thin by the time of *Francis Joins the WACs* (1954)—not that Adams missed much by failing to appear in the series during its dubious "prime." "*Francis Joins the WACs?* Well *[laughs],* what can we say? I enjoyed working with [series star] Donald O'Connor more than Francis! They had a little tiny wire under the lip of the mule, and from the side they would pull on the wire, move it around, to make him 'talk.'" Better roles lay ahead in pictures like the 1955 soaper *One Desire* (as the wicked wife of Rock Hudson, dying in flames at picture's end), the war actioner *Away All Boats* (1956) and the rackets exposé *Slaughter on Tenth Avenue* (1957). An added dividend of appearing in *The Looters* (1955) was meeting leading man Ray Danton, who "punched" her in the film and married her in real life in February 1955.

In 1958 she left Universal ("My contract was up and I was married and I had a baby, and I was just not as interested in working for a while"). But she soon made a comeback, appearing in movies and also on television, where her first regular role was opposite Jock Mahoney on CBS's short-lived *Yancy Derringer.* In 1962 she took the science fiction plunge again, playing a scientist in Columbia's *The Underwater City,* a soggy title-tells-all science-fact drama. Adams admits frankly that she has forgotten everything that happened to her on that forgettable picture, and from what she remembers of the one time she saw the film, "I'm very glad it hasn't been run on TV a lot." Columbia, who distributed the color film in black and white, apparently shared her misgivings.

The Allied Artists haunted house comedy *Tickle Me* (1965) was not much better, but what Elvis Presley leading lady could forget *that* experience? "He was such a gentleman, and surprisingly shy. There was a scene in the picture

where I pursued him around a desk and kissed him. All his friends from Memphis were standing around—all 'the guys'—and I suddenly felt like I was at a party where we were playing post office, and the boy was very bashful! But I was quite in awe of him because he would do a musical number in one take, and that was wonderful. And the most fun he had in the picture was when he and all his friends from Memphis staged a fight scene and tore up a barroom! They had great fun doing that!"

In the late sixties, she was a regular on the afternoon soap *General Hospital* and in 1971 she landed her best-remembered television role, as spouse to the star of *The Jimmy Stewart Show*. Curiously, one of the people she beat out in winning the role was Stewart's real-life wife, Gloria. "How did *I* get the role instead of her? That I don't really know *[laughs]*! I think Gloria is the most charming and delightful woman that I know, but that doesn't mean that you're necessarily an actress! But she is such a wonderful person and she has a real glamour about her that I've always loved—a really Class-A person."

Psychic Killer (1975) was a gruesome shocker bogged down by some cluckish moments of unwanted comedy relief. An obvious melding of *Psycho* and *The Exorcist*, it starred Jim Hutton as a one-time mental patient who uses newly acquired mystical powers to take "out-of-body" revenge on those he feels have wronged him. Horror film fans were delighted to find how chic Adams still looked, and probably a bit surprised by the mild bedroom scene she shared with co-star Paul Burke. "I enjoyed working on *Psychic Killer*. Ray Danton, who was by then my ex-husband, directed it; he was a wonderful director. I had some fun scenes to play, and I found it *not un*interesting to work on." The film was shot on actual locations (including a vacant house in Glendale and an unused jail), and Adams gave the best performance in it, prompting *Variety* to comment, "Adams does fine things with her part, making it one of the rare honorable outings for an actress in films this year."

One of her last pictures to date, *Black Roses* (1988), was also genre-related, with Adams as a small town resident opposed to the arrival of a visiting rock group. "We're of the opinion that their music is demonic. When the group finally does come to town, they seem very tame and we're all reassured. Then, of course, it turns out that they really *are* demonic! They turn into all kinds of nasty things."

Even today, Julie Adams laughs, she's "pressing on, pressing on," working on the stage and, more noticeably, in a semi-recurring role on the hit television series *Murder, She Wrote,* which she describes as "lots of fun." Now and forever, though, she will be mainly remembered by fans of *Creature from the Black Lagoon* as the girl in the brief shorts who almost became half of filmland's

Opposite: Adams remembers just enough about *The Underwater City* to be grateful that the film does not crop up on television much. Helping her out of a tight spot is William Lundigan.

most outlandish mixed marriage. So what is it about the Creature that accounts for its ongoing popularity? Julie Adams, the love of its million-year life, thinks she knows.

"The Creature scared people, but there was also a sort of sweetness about it. In the real classics, there always is that feeling of compassion for the monster. I think maybe it touches something in ourselves, maybe the darker parts of ourselves, that long to be loved and think they really *can't* ever be loved. It strikes a chord within us. That's what *Creature from the Black Lagoon* did."

JULIE ADAMS FILMOGRAPHY

As Betty Adams:

Red, Hot and Blue (Paramount, 1949)
The Dalton Gang (The Outlaw Gang) (Lippert, 1949)
Crooked River (Blazing Guns) (Lippert, 1950)
Hostile Country (Outlaw Fury) (Lippert, 1950)
West of the Brazos (Rangeland Empire) (Lippert, 1950)
Colorado Ranger (Guns of Justice) (Lippert, 1950)
Fast on the Draw (Sudden Death) (Lippert, 1950)
Marshal of Heldorado (The Last Bullet) (Lippert, 1950)

As Julia Adams:

Hollywood Story (Universal, 1951)
Bright Victory (Universal, 1951)
Finders Keepers (Universal, 1951)
Bend of the River (Universal, 1952)
Horizons West (Universal, 1952)
The Treasure of Lost Canyon (Universal, 1952)
The Lawless Breed (The Texas Man) (Universal, 1952)
The Mississippi Gambler (Universal, 1953)
The Man from the Alamo (Universal, 1953)
The Stand at Apache River (Universal, 1953)
The World's Most Beautiful Girls (Universal short, 1953)

Wings of the Hawk (Universal, 1953)
Creature from the Black Lagoon (Universal, 1954)
Francis Joins the WACs (Universal, 1954)

As Julie Adams:

The Looters (Universal, 1955)
One Desire (Universal, 1955)
The Private War of Major Benson (Universal, 1955)
Six Bridges to Cross (Universal, 1955)
Four Girls in Town (Universal, 1956)
Away All Boats (Universal, 1956)
Slim Carter (Universal, 1957)
Slaughter on Tenth Avenue (Universal, 1957)
Tarawa Beachhead (Columbia, 1958)
The Gunfight at Dodge City (United Artists, 1959)
Raymie (Allied Artists, 1960)
The Underwater City (Columbia, 1962)
Tickle Me (Allied Artists, 1965)
Valley of Mystery (Universal, 1967)
The Last Movie (Universal, 1971)
McQ (Warner Bros., 1974)
Psychic Killer (The Kirlian Force) (Avco Embassy, 1975)
The McCullochs (The Wild McCullochs) (AIP, 1975)
The Killer Inside Me (Warner Bros., 1976)
Goodbye Franklin High (Cal-Am, 1978)
The Fifth Floor (Film Ventures International, 1980)
Champions (Embassy, 1984)

Adams' scene was deleted from the final cut of *For Heaven's Sake* (20th Century–Fox, 1950). Her framed photograph hangs on the wall of Richard Denning's office in *The Glass Web* (Universal, 1953). She is seen in filmclips from *Creature from the Black Lagoon* in *Fade to Black* (American Cinema, 1980) and *It Came from Hollywood* (Paramount, 1982). *Black Roses* (1988) and *Backtrack* (1989) went directly to videocassette.

*Acting is something that I love to do, but it's a part of me
that's often dormant. So when I get an opportunity to go
on a set, it's like somebody pushing a button that's been idle
for a long time. And right away, I'm ready to get going at it.*

John Agar

IF ONE INDIVIDUAL were to be chosen as a human emblem for the science fiction movie boom of the 1950s and 1960s, that person would be John Agar. Typecast in the genre at the height of its popularity, he has appeared in more of that era's science fiction productions than any other actor, from favorites like *Revenge of the Creature* and *Tarantula* to notorious worst-film contenders like *The Brain from Planet Arous*, *Attack of the Puppet People* and *Curse of the Swamp Creature*.

Agar fought against this typecasting in the fifties, even walking away from a contract with a major studio (Universal-International) who saw him as their resident science fiction star. But Hollywood being what it is, he found himself back in the genre, time and again. If there was ever any bitterness on his part, it has apparently disappeared; he trades on the reputation now when he can, turning up with some regularity in newer science fiction films and thrillers and even appearing at science fiction conventions like Gary and Sue Svehla's Baltimore-based FANEX con. "If people want to see me, if they're interested in me, I'm more than happy to cooperate and get involved in things like that. Because the way I look at it, in essence the fan is really your boss, and they're the ones paying your salary *[laughs]*. But it does amaze me that there are people who like those sci-fi things we did thirty years ago and longer. *Tarantula*—the doggone thing is running on pay TV!"

Tall, lanky and always affable, Agar (now sporting a short white beard) is more than happy to swing down memory lane, pleased that the river of time has yet to sweep him downstream; the one question he is unable to answer, though, is just why people are still interested in John Agar. "For the life of me, I don't know! Last August [1989], I received a call from North Carolina, from a movie producer down there, Rick Brophy. A young man by the name of James Cummins wrote a script called *Winstrom*—it's a fantasy, a big-budget film, and they want me to play the third lead in it. That's why I've got the beard. Originally they had Dennis Quaid and Meg Ryan playing the two leads, and I think they were going to do it through Fox. But then Fox wanted to take control and these people down in North Carolina didn't want 'em to, so I guess Fox is out. I don't know what the particulars are now, but they insist that *I* am to be in the movie.

"Today, unless you're box office and your name is current, if you go in for a part, you read for the producer or the director. What amazed me was, these people in North Carolina wanted me to read the script and let them know if *I* wanted to do it *[laughs]!* That's something I just don't see that often anymore!"

Although *Winstrom* was never made, a steady string of recent movies have featured Agar in juicy supporting parts. The best known of this new bunch, *Miracle Mile*, did not set the 1989 box office on fire but got good word of

Previous page: **John Agar, science fiction's favorite leading man.**

mouth and enjoyed a second lease on life via pay television and videocassette. A sleeper about a group of Los Angeles nocturnal denizens reacting to news of an imminent nuclear strike, it featured Agar as Ivan Peters, grandfather of a coffee shop waitress (Mare Winningham) whose boyfriend (Anthony Edwards) inadvertently gets wind of the impending Armageddon. While Winningham and Edwards race to work out an escape plan, Agar and his wife, reconciling after years of separation, serenely drive to a restaurant for one last pleasant evening before The End comes. "*Miracle Mile,* I thought, was very well done. The writer/director Steve DeJarnatt—a very talented man—it took him *ten years* to get that picture into production, from the time when he first wrote the script. It was almost two years from the time they started to shoot before it was released. And then when they did release it, they released it at exactly the same time as *Batman, Ghostbusters II, Road House*—and it got lost."

Agar worked two weeks on the picture. "The two kids in it, Anthony Edwards and Mare Winningham, did a marvelous job. And then there was a gal from Texas, name of Lou Hancock, who played my wife, and I thought she also was wonderful in what she did. But, as I said, it got lost when it came out—partly, I think, because the subject matter of the film turned a lot of people off. But it's an exciting picture."

After years of battling monsters—the Creature from the Black Lagoon, the Mole People and Zontar, the Thing from Venus, to name a select few—Agar played a hermit who wanted to *become* a monster in director Clive Barker's *Nightbreed,* a 1990 release. "That was a strange situation. They had shot most of *Nightbreed* in England, and then they got to looking at the picture and in some ways it didn't make sense. The Nightbreed—some could be killed with gunfire, but some you could shoot and it wouldn't affect 'em at all. Some were affected by fire, and then with others, fire wouldn't affect them *[laughs].* There was no explanation about any of this. So I think what happened was, somebody said, 'We better explain this thing,' so I came in and I did a scene with David Cronenberg, the Canadian director—this was his first big role in a movie. They had me tied in a chair with Christmas tree wires and bulbs while he tortures me. I was tied up for an hour and a half to two hours, sitting in that chair with that stuff wrapped around me—and then it took 'em 15 or 20 minutes to get it all off of me, they had it so tangled up *[laughs]!*"

An icon of sorts to fans of the older science fiction films, Agar liked working with modern genre giants Clive Barker and David Cronenberg, although he admits that he just barely got to know them in the one day it took to shoot his scenes. "Barker seemed to be a very nice man, and Cronenberg, too. Cronenberg chose to underplay his part; that was his choice, and Barker went with him. I think he underplayed it too much—too much for *my* taste, anyway. But that's a matter of opinion." Speaking of opinions, what did Agar think of the finished film? Not surprisingly, he reached the same conclusion as did the ticket-buying public, which stayed away in droves.

"Back when we made it, the only thing I saw were the scenes that I was in — I didn't read the script or anything. So I wanted to see what it was like. So I saw it — watched the whole thing. *[Shakes his head.]* Uhn-uh. I pass. Didn't like the movie. They didn't go enough for story — it was just shock value.

"In all movies, I think the audience has the right to use their imagination. Today's pictures are just too graphic — they don't allow you to do that. Me, I won't go — rarely do I see a movie. I have cable, but I don't have any of the movie channels. There's a time and place for everything — we all go to the bathroom, but we don't need to photograph it."

A veteran of 50 films, Agar has been in the business since the late forties, when he signed a contract with Hollywood legend David O. Selznick. He never made a film for Selznick, but was lent to other producers and appeared in three of the decade's great action films — *Fort Apache, She Wore a Yellow Ribbon* and *Sands of Iwo Jima* — all opposite John Wayne. As a youth, however, acting — and career goals in general — were the farthest thing from John Agar's mind. "What would I have done if I hadn't gone into acting? To tell the truth, when I was growing up, I really, really hadn't any idea *[laughs]!* I used to play golf pretty well, and I might have gone in that direction — although I probably would have starved to death, the way Ben Hogan and guys like him played in those days."

The oldest of four children of a Chicago meat packer, Agar grew up during the Depression, although by dint of hard work his family remained upper-middle class. "My dad used to go down to that stockyard and try to keep his meat packing company going. He had angina, and all this pressure put on him caused his early demise — he died before he reached his 41st birthday, and he left my mom loaded with four kids at the age of 38. I was 14 — this was 1935." After the death of his father, the Agars relocated to California, where in 1945 John found himself in the headlines when he became engaged to "America's Sweetheart," former child star Shirley Temple. Temple, who divorced Agar in 1949, wrote about the marriage in her 1988 book *Child Star: An Autobiography,* but Agar insists he has not read it.

"Another book, *Shirley Temple: America's Princess,* was written by a lady in Massachusetts; she had asked some questions of me about our marriage, and I told her flat out, 'What is personal in Shirley's life and personal in my life is nobody's business. And I'm not going to tell you anything.' When we were separated, we made an agreement, Shirley and I, that we would not say anything against each other. I kept that promise. I will continue to keep it. I'm never gonna say anything detrimental — that's the way it is." Has Shirley Temple held to that promise? "She broke the agreement as soon as we went into court," Agar deadpans. "But that's *her* problem, not mine."

While they were still husband and wife, the Agars appeared in two films together, the first of which, *Fort Apache* (1948), was Agar's debut as well as

Pressbook ad for *Revenge of the Creature*

the first film in director John Ford's famous Cavalry Trilogy. "To me, John Ford was the epitome of screen directors. The first time I met Ford, he was on the same lot as David Selznick, who was my boss at the time—this was at RKO-Pathé over in Culver City. I went in his office and he had me standing at attention and turning right face, left face, about face. He said, 'Were you in the service?' and I said, 'Yes, sir. The Army Air Corps, sir.' 'Oh,' he said. 'You mean, off we go into the wild blue yonder—crash!' I said, 'Yes, sir. Were you in the service, Mr. Ford?' He said, 'Yep. The Navy.' I said, 'Oh, you mean, anchors aweigh—sink, huh?'

"So every time he would do something, I always considered he was kidding—and I'd kid him back! Duke, Hank Fonda, Ward Bond, Victor McLaglen, George O'Brien [the Ford regulars]—all these guys would say, 'We've known him for twenty-five, thirty years and we *never* know when he's kidding and when he's not.' But I always considered that he was kidding, and there's only one time I can remember that he really got mad at me *[laughs]*! He appeared tough, but I think Ford was a pussycat." Did Agar have first-picture nerves working with this giant of motion picture directors? "Listen, I was scared for the first twenty years," he laughs.

"You'd rehearse the scene before you'd shoot it, and John Ford wouldn't say a word to you. If you did the scene the way he thought it should be done, he still wouldn't say anything. And if you didn't do what he wanted, he would suggest *[softly]*, 'Why don't you do *this*?' 'Why don't you do *that*?' Allan Dwan *[Sands of Iwo Jima]* was the same way. So was Jack Arnold *[Revenge of the Creature, Tarantula]*. Those were people who knew what they wanted. In fact, John Ford never went to rushes, and he never allowed actors to go. If everything was technically okay, Ford knew exactly what was on film. He would go to the rough cut—that'd be the first time he'd see it. The only people who went to his rushes were the craft people. And the editor had only one way to cut that film—Ford's way—because that's all the film he had."

After a strong start, Agar's film career lost its momentum in the early fifties; in December 1950, he made his fantasy film debut playing the Scarlet Falcon in Columbia's *The Magic Carpet,* a Supercinecolor Arabian Nights programmer produced by low-budget legend Sam Katzman. "The Queen of Comedy, Lucille Ball, had a three-picture contract with Harry Cohn, who was the head of Columbia Pictures. She had made two pictures already [for $85,000 per film], and Cohn was trying to get out of having to make the third one. So he thought to himself, 'Well, I'll give her to Sam Katzman. He's making this movie called *The Magic Carpet*. She'll turn it down and I'll be out from under.' And Lucille Ball said, 'I'd *love* to do *The Magic Carpet*!' That movie took eighteen, maybe twenty days to shoot, and I don't think she worked over six—we were sitting there figuring out how much she was getting paid an hour! She was terrific, a lovely, wonderful lady."

Agar swashed and buckled his way through the film, dallied with harem

Gill Man (Tom Hennesy) towers, humans (Agar and Lori Nelson) cower. Publicity photo from *Revenge of the Creature*.

beauties and even rode on the titular conveyance. "They had it on a platform, and then they had wires to make it take off. We were on a stage, and I was thirty feet in the air on this thing! Because of my body weight, I had to lean forward to keep it moving — otherwise it would jerk along, and they wanted a smooth ride. So we tried it and it jerked, and they said, 'You've got to lean forward *further*.' I did, and the thing tipped — you should have seen me hanging onto those wires, looking thirty feet down! *That* got my attention!"

Agar freelanced for a few years, showing up in the science fiction comedy *The Rocket Man* (scripted by Lenny Bruce) as well as in the Caribbean-made voodoo adventure *The Golden Mistress*. In 1954 Agar signed with Universal-International, who were impressed with his work in *The Golden Mistress*. "I went under contract, and that was when I started into science fiction. I started out with *Revenge of the Creature*, the second Creature movie. We went to Florida, to Marineland, to shoot certain scenes, and that was lots of fun. There's one scene in there where Lori Nelson and I are swimming in a river, and that was done at Universal Studios in California. But besides that, all the underwater stuff was done in Florida. When the Creature grabbed Lori and carried her out of the Lobster House and I dove off the pier after them, that was in Florida, too. I remember there was a strong current in that river—when I dove in, it swept me quite a ways."

Swimming in the Marineland tank alongside its resident sharks did not faze Agar, Nelson or third lead John Bromfield. "In addition to Lori, John and myself, there was also Ricou Browning [the Creature], of course, and an underwater photographer. There might have been other people in there, too; in fact, I think some of the people who worked at Marineland were in the water with us, to keep creatures from getting into shots where they weren't wanted. We weren't really concerned about the sharks; Ricou was more concerned about the turtles. He had no peripheral vision at all while in that costume, and those dog-gone little suckers would come along and nip at him.

"Another thing that we were worried about were the moray eels—they hide in rock crevices and then jump out at you. That's the way they catch their dinner, by grabbing a fish or whatever comes by. They really weren't trouble, because we weren't about to go near the rocks where we knew they were hiding, but you could see their heads jumping out whenever a fish would go past." Plans to shoot scenes in the tank at night were discussed but quickly scuttled. "The people who were in charge said it wouldn't be a good idea. Those sharks were so well fed that you didn't have to be concerned about 'em during the daytime, but they didn't know what would happen at night."

When *Revenge of the Creature* made a splash at the box office, Universal was quick to place Agar in two other science fiction adventures, *Tarantula* and *The Mole People*. "The only picture that I made there that was not science fiction was *Star in the Dust* [1956], a Western. Then I got talking with them over there. I said, 'Gee, every time a science fiction picture comes along, you come after me.' They were building Rock Hudson and Tony Curtis at the time, and I wanted some of those kind of roles. But science fiction and the like was what they wanted me to do. So I said, 'Thanks a lot, but I'll go out on my own.'"

He made more money as a freelancer, but the reputation as a science fiction hero stuck as Agar waged war against the *Daughter of Dr. Jekyll*, *The Brain from Planet Arous* and the *Invisible Invaders*—as well as becoming a monster himself in *Hand of Death*. He hit rock bottom in the mid-sixties when he signed up to star in American International television movie remakes of the earlier AIPs *It Conquered the World*, *Voodoo Woman* and *Suicide Battalion*. "The director of those pictures, Larry Buchanan, was a man that was very infatuated with filmmaking, and in some manner or means he had become involved with Sam Arkoff—AIP. They worked a deal where he could take some of the films that AIP had done previously, change 'em around and do 'em again for however much money. (I don't know what the price was, but believe me, it wasn't very much!) As far as I was concerned, that was just a way for me to make a little extra money—that's why I did 'em. He'd fly me down to Texas, first-class accommodations, he met my salary—I had no kicks coming. Larry really was not a film director per se. He was learning his craft as we went along. I take my hat off to the guy, though—he tried. And from what I hear *[laughs]*, he's *still* trying."

By the mid-sixties, the fifties-style science fiction films were out of vogue, and Agar busied himself in the supporting casts of various Westerns: *Stage to Thunder Rock*, *Law of the Lawless*, *Waco*, the John Wayne vehicles *Chisum*, *Big Jake* and *The Undefeated* (from which Agar's footage was ultimately cut) and more. Film work was scarce in the seventies, with the notable exception of a cameo as the mayor of New York in Dino de Laurentiis's megabuck remake of *King Kong*.

"After I'd read for the role in *King Kong* and been accepted by [director] John Guillermin, I was told to go out to Metro at ten o'clock in the morning, to meet with Dino de Laurentiis. I get there quarter to ten, something like that, I'm sitting waiting, and all of a sudden Joyce Selznick, who is a casting lady and a niece of David's, says, 'Mr. de Laurentiis is not going to be able to keep the appointment.' I'd driven all the way from Burbank. She says, 'I'll call you later today, and we'll see if we can make it tomorrow.' So I go home, she calls me and says, 'All right, he can see you at ten o'clock tomorrow.'

"So I get out there again, about quarter to ten again, and about ten-fifteen he's ready to see me. Joyce takes me over to his office, we open the door, and I'll guarantee you, from the door to where his desk was, was a good forty feet—that's how deep it was. He's sitting there, and right next to him is a young man. Joyce introduces me to him, and then she introduces me to this young man, his son. That was *it*. He never said another thing. And I turned around and walked out. 'Hello, how are you?' 'Fine. How are you, sir?' And then I was ushered out. I went out there *twice* for that *[laughs]!*"

After some slow years, the offers are coming in again, and Agar is sifting through them, accepting the ones that "stick to my standards. I don't use four-letter words on the screen—no way." The thriller *Fear* with Ally Sheedy and *Perfect Bride* with Kelly Preston apparently met his criteria. "*Fear* is the story of a young lady [Sheedy] who is psychic. I play a psychopath. I've got a young girl tied up in the back of a car, and Sheedy's trying to convey to the police

Despite his popularity as Universal's resident monster fighter, Agar pined for "straight" roles. He and Richard Boone starred in the studio's *Star in the Dust* (1956).

where we are. Eventually she does—I've taken this young lady to a barn, I've got her tied on the floor and I've got a pair of shears, rubbing 'em against her face. Four cops break in, but instead of giving up, I go over to the workbench and get a gun, and they shoot me."

That's when the fun started. "The special effects people had squibs on me, and when the first one went off, I was going to hit the workbench with the lower part of my buttocks and throw myself up in the air. Then when the second squib went off, I was going to put my elbow on the workbench, roll off and fall to the ground. Well, I went up and my elbow missed, I hit hard — and I cracked my ribs. I wouldn't tell 'em — I wouldn't say a word. I was too embarrassed *[laughs]!* But I suffered for about three weeks after that."

Fear, directed by Rockne O'Bannon, premiered on cable television's Showtime rather than in theaters, but this bothers the self-effacing Agar about as much as the small size of his part. "To me, the idea of just working is what's fun. I don't give a doggone what kind of parts [I get]. Walter Huston said it years ago: 'I don't care about billing. If the show is good and I'm good in it, people are going to say, "Who *was* that?" And if it's *not,* I don't want 'em to know I was in it!'" *[Laughs.]*

And *Perfect Bride?* "That stars a gal by the name of Sammi Davis — an English actress — and Kelly Preston, who was in *Twins* [1988]. I play a ninety-year-old grandpa in this one; a friend of mine, an actor by the name of John Larch, said, 'Don't worry, Agar. They got makeup, they can tone ya down.' *[Laughs.]* Sammi plays a nurse, and in her childhood, her mother was mistreated by her father. It did something to her way of thinking, and now anytime she comes in contact with anybody (especially a man) that she thinks is doing her wrong, she takes a syringe and sticks it in their neck, and they appear to die of a heart attack. Now, she is engaged to my grandson. Kelly Preston is my granddaughter, and she becomes suspicious of Sammi. Everything was done on location, we shot over in West L.A., just off of Washington Boulevard. I had a good time doing it." (*Perfect Bride* also went directly to TV and videocassette.)

The careers of B movie stars do not often have happy endings, but John Agar is delighted to find that he has become an exception to that rule. "Acting is something that I love to do, but it's a part of me that's often dormant. So when I get an opportunity to go on a set, it's like somebody's pushing a button that's been idle for a long time. And right away, I'm ready to get going at it. It's fun for me to be able to get back into it, because it's a part of my life that I've really enjoyed."

JOHN AGAR FILMOGRAPHY

Fort Apache (RKO, 1948)
Adventure in Baltimore (RKO, 1949)
She Wore a Yellow Ribbon (RKO, 1949)
Sands of Iwo Jima (Republic, 1949)
I Married a Communist (The Woman on Pier 13) (RKO, 1949)
Breakthrough (Warner Bros., 1950)
Along the Great Divide (Warner Bros., 1951)

The Magic Carpet (Columbia, 1951)
Woman of the North Country (Republic, 1952)
Man of Conflict (Atlas, 1953)
The Rocket Man (20th Century–Fox, 1954)
The Golden Mistress (United Artists, 1954)
Shield for Murder (United Artists, 1954)
Bait (Columbia, 1954)

Revenge of the Creature (Universal, 1955)

The Lonesome Trail (Lippert, 1955)

Hold Back Tomorrow (Universal, 1955)

Tarantula (Universal, 1955)

Flesh and the Spur (AIP, 1956)

Star in the Dust (Universal, 1956)

The Mole People (Universal, 1956)

Joe Butterfly (Universal, 1957)

Daughter of Dr. Jekyll (Allied Artists, 1957)

Ride a Violent Mile (20th Century–Fox, 1957)

The Brain from Planet Arous (Howco, 1958)

Jet Attack (AIP, 1958)

Frontier Gun (20th Century–Fox, 1958)

Attack of the Puppet People (AIP, 1958)

Invisible Invaders (United Artists, 1959)

Raymie (Allied Artists, 1960)

Journey to the Seventh Planet (AIP, 1961)

Lisette (Fall Girl) (Medallion, 1961)

Hand of Death (20th Century–Fox, 1961)

Of Love and Desire (20th Century–Fox, 1963)

Cavalry Command (Parade, 1963)

The Young and the Brave (MGM, 1963)

Law of the Lawless (Paramount, 1964)

Stage to Thunder Rock (Paramount, 1964)

Young Fury (Paramount, 1965)

Women of the Prehistoric Planet (Realart, 1965)

Johnny Reno (Paramount, 1966)

Waco (Paramount, 1966)

The St. Valentine's Day Massacre (20th Century–Fox, 1967)

Chisum (Warner Bros., 1970)

Big Jake (National General, 1971)

How's Your Love Life? (Cal-Tex, 1971)

The Amazing Mr. No Legs (Cinema Artists, c. 1975)

King Kong (Paramount, 1976)

Miracle Mile (Hemdale, 1989)

Nightbreed (20th Century–Fox, 1990)

Agar's scenes were cut from *The Undefeated* (20th Century–Fox, 1969). Scenes of Agar in *The Brain from Planet Arous* and *Attack of the Puppet People* are seen in the compilation *It Came from Hollywood* (Paramount, 1982).

When I was four, I saw my first picture in New York City. . . .
Movies were my dream, and I always figured that was
the world that could be, not the world I was in.

Richard Anderson

RICHARD ANDERSON has been an actor for a long time, and like most actors, his career has gone through phases. In the 1950s he was one of the busier young supporting actors toiling at MGM, turning up in over two dozen movies and working alongside "more stars than there are in Heaven" (to quote the studio's most famous publicity line). In the 1960s, he turned to television with a workaholic's zeal, guest starring on every series imaginable. But it was in the 1970s that Anderson landed the role for which he is best known today, that of Oscar Goldman on television's *The Six Million Dollar Man*.

During his stint at Metro, Anderson was one of several up-and-coming young actors with a berth aboard the United Planets cruiser *C-57-D* in MGM's space adventure *Forbidden Planet*. Anderson was sixth-billed as Olonzo Quinn, chief engineer, klystron modulator repairman and Id-monster casualty, in the 1956 science fiction landmark.

Anderson has the sort of easygoing demeanor that immediately sets an interviewer at ease, and the way he does the softshoe around an occasional question tips you off that he is a believer in the old if-you-can't-say-something-nice credo. But, as they say in the Ozarks, he shucks right down to the cob when asked about *Forbidden Planet*.

"That was a B movie, made under the B unit. Nicholas Nayfack was the producer and Fred Wilcox the director, and a program picture was all it was," Anderson reminisces, sitting near the pool of his Beverly Hills home, one good scream away from the infamous Charles Manson murder house. "Everything was categorized — MGM even signed their actors that way. An actor had to have specific qualifications: He had to *look* a certain way, *be* a certain age, have a certain demeanor, or they wouldn't be interested. They'd say, 'This is not a Metro actor.' The same with their pictures. They rarely made Westerns; most of their films were what Western actors called 'carpet movies,' where you get to act in living rooms. So they made mostly mysteries and intriguing international movies and particularly movies with great emotional depth. Those were all formulas — everything was formula, and that included *Forbidden Planet*. They had A movies and B movies — this was a B movie. However, the thing that was interesting about Metro was, they made the B movie just as well as they made the A movie technically. That's what made *Forbidden Planet* exceptional."

It's been almost 40 years since Anderson roamed the deck of the *C-57-D* or trod the surface of Altair-4, but certain recollections of *Forbidden Planet* remain vivid in his mind ("We shot those scenes on Stage 30 at MGM," he says with a twinkle, showing off an excellent memory, of which he is rightly proud). In fact, one of the actor's pastimes during his Metro years was to hang around the studio's special effects and miniatures departments. "Oh, I used to go down

Previous page: **Richard Anderson in a recent shot.**

there a lot. They had a miniatures department you wouldn't believe — they had it down to a science. Metro was funding those people even when they weren't working [on a movie]; if you worked in special effects there and there was nothing to do, you would stay there and tinker around and experiment with new things. It was an extraordinary operation."

Memories of his fellow space pioneers are equally respectful, particularly those of talented veteran Walter Pidgeon. "My God, that guy was a splendid actor, I thought one of the best of them all. Anne Francis, Leslie Nielsen — there were some very good actors in that picture." Told that some of the actors in *Forbidden Planet* have shown a tendency to put the picture down any time it was mentioned, Anderson is taken slightly aback; he laughs out loud when he finds out that Earl Holliman says it was his worst movie. "Earl said that? Well, I'd better leave *that* alone!" he smiles, ducking the issue neatly. But for many actors, then and now, science fiction does tend to be viewed as a bottom-of-the-barrel genre.

"Control of the picture business was in the hands of five men, and what they decided to make was what the audiences saw," the actor explains. "They saw pictures in very simple terms: love stories, high adventures, 'scary' pictures, thrillers (like Hitchcock) and so on. And if anybody could come up with something new and it worked, they'd jump on it and make ten of 'em. But there were no new plots; everything was the same. The men became old and bored . . . and rich. Louis Mayer summed it up the best; at one point an interviewer asked him, 'Mr. Mayer, don't you want to try to make your pictures better? They're all formula.' And Mayer said, 'Let me tell you something. We make 52 pictures a year, and *none* of them has to be any good.' Think about it. That's how the business was run. They tried to make 'em better and they *wanted* to make 'em better and they competed against each other, but none of 'em had to be any good because the studios had a lock on the theaters. So with *Forbidden Planet* — they made it, but it didn't set the world on fire.

"When live TV came along, new ideas came along. Writers in New York had control of ideas, and they came out with a whole array of themes. All this rich, 'different,' literate stuff that the movies wouldn't dare do because it wouldn't 'sell' — the moviemakers thought the average mind was twelve years old. Television was the breeding ground for new ideas, and out of this 'golden age,' this literate time, came new experiments in how to make pictures. Science fiction was one of them. Science fiction was never 'big' before the fifties. I grew up on science fiction, but when I was a kid, you know what it was? The serials. When I was ten years old, I used to go to every Saturday matinee for ten cents, and we saw *Dick Tracy, Flash Gordon,* all of them." Anderson does not need to be reminded that the reverberations of these old chapterplays continue to be felt today. "Spielberg and Lucas sat on a beach in Hawaii and said, 'Let's get a bunch of those old serials and see what they were made of.' And they were right, because those serials were as good as the movies — and they were

MGM's ability to make classy-looking B movies was what made *Forbidden Planet* "exceptional," according to Anderson. *Left-to-right:* Jack Kelly, Warren Stevens, Morgan Jones (background), Leslie Nielsen, Anderson.

fifteen minutes. In *Indiana Jones and the Last Crusade* [1989], there's a scene where speedboats are racing between two ocean liners which are drifting together—that was a *Dick Tracy* cliffhanger. That kind of action and excitement, that's what movies are, and I happen to personally love those best: high adventure."

Returning to the subject of *Forbidden Planet,* Anderson adds that while the movie was in production, no one seemed to realize that its screenplay was a science fiction retelling of Shakespeare's immortal *The Tempest.* "The only one who could tell you if that was intentional would be the guy that wrote the screenplay. Everybody puts a lot of interpretations into these older films; maybe the guy was reading Shakespeare and figured he could reshape it into science fiction material. And when it got into Metro, obviously they decided to make it because it was an interesting idea. What they probably liked best about it was the robot.

"We shot all the scenes of the planet surface on a soundstage—nobody went anywhere. Audiences didn't know any better back then; you can't do that sort of thing anymore," Anderson continues. "I also remember that I liked the director, Fred Wilcox. He was a gifted man. He did the Lassie movies and had a great deal of talent—sensitive and a very, very fine director."

Overall, Anderson seems pleased with *Forbidden Planet* and with the fact that it is one of the movies for which he is best known, even though Chief Quinn was the lead-off victim for an Altair-4 monster that allowed the character only a handful of short scenes before tearing him limb from off-camera limb. "*Forbidden Planet* was very well made technically, and it had a very good idea. It dealt with the id and the superego and the ego, and the story was kind of interesting. But it was basically a science fiction film, although very, very well done in terms of the miniatures department, special effects and so on."

Anderson made his film debut in 1949, but the desire to become a movie actor had already been with him for nearly his entire life. "When I was four, I saw my first picture in New York City, where I lived with my parents, and it had a tremendous effect upon me. I didn't like New York City as far as I can remember — it's not a place for bringing up kids who like the outdoors, as I do. Movies were the escape — I was allowed to go to matinees with my brother. Movies were my dream, and I always figured that was the world that could be, not the world I was in. Of course, that can run into trouble later on in life *[laughs]*, but at the time that's what I was interested in. And I never lost that ambition to be in the movies, for I felt there was where my life was going to change for the better. Of course, it turned out that it wasn't all sunglasses and autographs, but at that time I decided I wanted to be a movie actor."

Anderson appeared in high school plays, served a hitch in the army and, upon his discharge, began doing summer stock, radio work, a movie bit part (as a wounded soldier in *Twelve O'Clock High* [1949]) and the other minor jobs required of your basic struggling thespian. "Then came live television," Anderson continues, recalling his Big Break. "There was a show called *Lights, Camera, Action,* which was an hour show on NBC in the winter of 1949. What it was, was a screen test — instead of making a movie screen test, you did it on live TV. This TV screen test was seen by everybody in town, because television was very new and interesting, and everybody watched it. I was doing comedy scenes, which I haven't done since *[laughs]*. I was on *Lights, Camera, Action* three times, and judged by many, many very well known celebrities in the business, particularly directors — one of which was Preston Sturges. I was seen by the Metro people, I was seen by Billy Wilder at Paramount — I got offers from a lot of people. And I finally went to the Metro studios — I made a screen test, a scene from *The Cowboy and the Lady* opposite Sally Forrest, and I signed a seven-year contract. It was kind of a dream come true; I had been a messenger boy with the publicity department there for a time, after I had gotten out of the army. So coming back to Metro was a kind of double victory."

Anderson looked forward to playing leading roles at MGM, but the studio saw him as a good, dependable supporting player. "The pressures of staying in the business demanded that you work, that you stay on the screen. So I chose to stay on the screen. I've seen a lot of them come and go because many of 'em just want to do a certain thing. But when that fades out or when you've had your chance at it, that's it — it's over. The average life expectancy of an actor was at that time seven years, and I don't think it's too different now. So my strategy was to *work*."

And work he did, in 25 Metro movies over a six-year period, although his roles did not improve much as the years went by. "What happened was unfortunate, and it had nothing to do with me or with them. The studio system broke down, and consequently it was no longer as good a business as it had once been. That was the end of their whole system of developing actors—putting them in supporting parts with leading people, then second parts, and then giving them a shot at something. In all the time I was there, they didn't groom any actors for stardom in that fashion, with the exception maybe of Debbie Reynolds, who was in their musicals. I decided that the best thing to do was to gain experience, so I played *everything*—if they assigned me to a part, I'd just go play it. Consequently, I became an actor that they knew they could use, and they kept picking up my option for that reason. They realized I was good business, that I could always do a reliable job. That's how I learned the business. And it came in handy later on, when I got into television, where you *had* to work fast. Most of the people who worked in those films don't work TV because it's a different technique. When they got into television, where you shoot fast, many of the Metro people weren't accustomed to that kind of shooting."

Dore Schary was in charge at MGM throughout most of the years that Anderson was under contract, but early on he had an opportunity to meet Louis B. Mayer, onetime junk dealer, cofounder of MGM and executive ruffian extraordinaire. "Ruffian? That kind of takes it out of context. There's a new book out on Sam Goldwyn where I think you'll find the same type of stories that you hear about Mayer, Harry Cohn and so on. These were men who simply got hold of an industry that was no industry at the time, just a fledgling toy. They took it and made it into something when no one else touched it. I would say that these men were a combination of a lot of things. First of all, they loved more than anything else being American, and they wanted everybody to know that they were respectable and successful Americans. Secondly, they saw a great opportunity to make money. It was a new business and therefore there were no rules; as George Washington said when he became the first president, 'I trod on ground that has never been walked on before.' They set the rules, they determined how the business was going to be operated, and they hired people that were talented. And the third thing was, they simply loved the idea of making good pictures. They were rough, but look at their backgrounds, and remember that it was a rough business in those days because everybody was after it. They were instinctive players. I met Mayer, and he was quite a man. He was an idea man—no, *more* than that, he was a *talent* man. He had an instinct for talent, and an instinct for doing it big and doing it right."

Anderson (and most of those other heavenly stars) left MGM in the mid-fifties, when the studio system broke down entirely, and Anderson began to freelance. With a juicy role in Stanley Kubrick's 1957 film *Paths of Glory* (Anderson was the first person cast, and served as dialogue coach), he was off to a strong start. "When the picture was agreed upon, United Artists did not like the idea of the men being executed at the end; they stipulated that the three soldiers must not die—they should be saved. But Kubrick was absolutely adamant: to make the picture work, those men had to be killed. Kubrick sent UA a copy of the final script, and in this script the men did die. *Nobody read it at UA.* So Kubrick went ahead and shot it his way. Of course, when UA saw the finished picture, they saw that the men did die, but all Kubrick had to do was to say, 'Look here, it's in the final script which was approved.' But nobody even asked after they saw it, because they realized how powerful it was."

Among the several movies Anderson made during the late fifties were *The Search for Bridey Murphy* and *Curse of the Faceless Man*, two minor pictures of the sort that he now refers to as "things I did on my way to something else." *Search*, based on the then-current reincarnation fad, had an interesting low-key approach but it was a wholly uncinematic subject. "I remember *Search* because I looked forward to working with Louis Hayward—I remembered him from when I was a boy and I saw him in *The Man in the Iron Mask* [1939]," says Anderson. He also recalls meeting Morey Bernstein, the real-life amateur hypnotist who regressed housewife Virginia Tighe and sparked the entire fad. "It's interesting when the actors meet the real people; I don't know why, but it's usually quiet, and no one has much to say. You shape parts to your personality—or at least most actors do—and then to meet the actual person...! For instance, on *The Six Million Dollar Man*, we met the man who was the real-life Six Million Dollar Man. We all greeted him and put our arms around him; Lee Majors and I have pictures of ourselves with him; suddenly he's gone and you never see him again *[laughs]!*" By the time *Search* came out, professional debunkers had done a number on the Bridey Murphy story, and the Paramount picture died a lingering death at the box office.

Anderson's much-vaunted memory (conveniently?) lets him down when the subject turns to *Curse of the Faceless Man*, the only one of his fifty feature films in which he is top-billed. The story of an Etruscan slave turned into living stone during the eruption of Vesuvius and reanimated in our modern world, it was strictly drive-in fodder, with Anderson ill at ease as the stereotypic hero/scientist. "That was another one I was doing just on my way to somewhere else; that trained me for television. Seven days shooting," he deadpans. "The director, Edward L. Cahn, was at Metro, in the shorts department, along with Fred Zinnemann, and I think he won an Academy Award for ... something."

It was at this same time that Anderson dove headfirst into television work, doing guest spots in every series under the sun (as well as working as a regular in such sixties shows as *Bus Stop, The Lieutenant* and *Perry Mason*. He was no stranger to horror and science fiction shows, either: *Thriller, The Alfred Hitchcock Hour, The Man from U.N.C.L.E., The Invaders, The Wild Wild West*,

Curse of the Faceless Man has slipped from Anderson's memory despite being his one-and-only starring film. *Left-to-right:* Elaine Edwards, Anderson, Jan Arvan, Gar Moore.

Land of the Giants and more. In the classic final episodes of *The Fugitive,* Anderson played brother-in-law to peripatetic escapee David Janssen, and when the moving finger of suspicion began to point to Anderson as the killer of Janssen's wife (rather than the One-Armed Man), Las Vegas oddsmakers started taking bets on his guilt or innocence.

Anderson was also a regular during the last season of *Perry Mason,* and in the last episode the actor (playing Police Lieutenant Drum) interrogates witnesses to a murder in a television studio—said witnesses being played by the *Perry Mason* crew. "The last day of that last episode, we had a courtroom scene. Every week they needed a different judge, and they brought in some day player. The fellow playing the judge this last week approaches me and says, 'Mr. Anderson, I've enjoyed watching you play this role the last year.' I didn't know who this guy was, but I could feel that he was something beyond just a day player—I knew I was into something, I knew something was coming. I said, 'Well, thank you very much.' We talked back and forth a little, he started to walk away and then he said, 'Oh, by the way, my name is Erle Stanley Gardner.' They had put him on the last day as the judge."

The number of movie roles dwindled when Anderson plunged into television, but he still managed to pop up in two of John Frankenheimer's most celebrated films, *Seven Days in May* and *Seconds*. "John is an exciting, eclectic kind of man. He has tremendous enthusiasm and he has an excitement about himself and his work — you can see it in his movies like *The Manchurian Candidate*. He exudes a great deal of energy. I think John mainly enjoys taking a piece of material that is in its simple stage and making something out of it — taking a simple plot and embellishing it.

"Motion pictures for the most part come from books — find a best-seller and make it. Both of those Frankenheimer films I was in were based on books. *Seven Days in May* was an intriguing political story. *Seven Days, The Best Man* [1964] — all those pictures are kind of limited in the sense that they're, well, not talking heads, but not what you'd call high adventure." *Seven Days*, scripted by Rod Serling, was a speculative suspenser about a covert military plot to overthrow the U.S. government. "An interesting idea. . . . It's happening this morning, right now, you know," Anderson remarks while, half a world away, all hell is breaking loose on the first day of riots in Tiananmen Square.

Asked about reported friction between stars Burt Lancaster and Kirk Douglas on the film's set, Anderson waxes philosophic. "Well, on the set, people are always trying to do their best. I'm not trying to sound like the ambassador for American films, but when people are trying to do their best, tempers run high, emotions go up, and also people are nervous. And in many cases *scared* — the best of 'em get scared. That's understandable. You have a concept, somebody else has a concept, that's what the director is there for. It's a highly volatile game, and when you get two visceral guys like that together, sure, there could be fireworks. I think Burt had just come off *The Leopard* [1963] for Visconti, probably was a bit frayed from the experience over there, and maybe he came in tired. But they have since worked on the stage together, they did *Tough Guys* [1986], so I don't think there was anything serious there. But they're guys that say what they think, that open their mouths and talk."

Anderson's other film for Frankenheimer was the offbeat *Seconds*, the story of a secret organization which (for a fee) will physically rejuvenate any individual and present him or her with a new identity. Anderson, playing the surgeon who transforms middle-aged businessman John Randolph into virile Rock Hudson, shared the world's opinion. "*Seconds* was intriguing but weird . . . *strange*. It became a cult movie. It didn't go over too well at the box office, but it wasn't a high budget movie. People say that was Rock Hudson's best performance. Well, at least it was different *[laughs]*."

One of the most famous scenes in *Seconds* featured Anderson wielding a scalpel in the surgical operation on John Randolph, with close-ups showing the blade slicing through the skin. "We used a double for John Randolph for the actual close-up stuff, and a doctor stood in for me and made the incisions," says Anderson. "The double had makeup skin above his own skin. The doctor made the incision, and the double didn't move. When it was over, I remember Frankenheimer saying to the double, 'You okay, Bill?' They took the makeup off, and the doctor had let him have it—he went a bit too deep. It was not the surgeon's fault, but he had never done that before and he didn't know how far down to go. The double was all right, but the interesting part was, the surgeon felt absolutely, terribly embarrassed!"

Anderson's claim to fame in the early seventies was playing Burt Reynolds' boss in the successful television police drama *Dan August,* but genre fans probably remember him better as Dr. Malcolm Richards, superpowered, ageless, vampiric foe of Darren McGavin's Carl Kolchak in the 1972 television movie *The Night Strangler.* "Richard Matheson saw the Underground City in Seattle and got the idea for the story: a doctor living beneath the city since 1868 who has to come up every twenty-one years to get some blood," explains Anderson. For his scenes in this top-rated television movie, Anderson worked at the Bradbury Building in Los Angeles and at a huge old mansion on the Pacific Coast. Stuntman Dick Ziker played the title role in action scenes where the fiend's face was unseen, but Anderson took over in a finale set in the Underground City. Makeup ace William Tuttle transformed him into a hideous hundred-year-old man for the film's climax.

Running in slow motion became the newest self-defeating pastime for America's youth as soon as Lee Majors's *Six Million Dollar Man* began inching his way across picture tubes tuned to ABC in 1973. A series sparked by the success of three 90-minute *SMDM* television movies was soon a hit, and Anderson settled into a comfortable niche as Oscar Goldman, bionic Steve Austin's (Majors) government boss. Anderson is casual in discussing his relationship with Majors and the depth of his emotional involvement with the show: "When Lee's lips stopped moving, I'd talk, and when *my* lips stopped, *he'd* talk. That was how it worked. We never discussed it, never talked about our characters, never discussed the show. Mostly we talked about football and someplace to go for a beer."

A spinoff series, *The Bionic Woman,* premiered in 1976, with Lindsay Wagner as a distaff bionic hero, and Anderson suddenly found himself a regular on *two* series simultaneously. Again Anderson is self-effacing concerning his minor distinction in television history: "A fast driver and a good memory is what's needed," he grins. On a single day, between pickup shots and other miscellaneous business, he worked on seven different episodes of the two series ("*That* I'll never forget!").

After a few years of double-barreled bionic action, however, both series began running out of gas. A bionic boy (played by Vincent Van Patten) debuted on *SMDM,* but according to Anderson, "That idea didn't work

Championing the cause of justice on 1970s television: Boss man Oscar Goldman (Anderson) and bionic Steve Austin (Lee Majors) in ABC's *Six Million Dollar Man*.

because kids started jumping off of roofs and fences." Bionic dog Maximilian (max.: one million—get it?) became a regular on *Bionic Woman* but failed to bolster faltering ratings. Both shows petered out in 1978. But bionic fever spread once again in the late eighties when NBC aired two movie follow-ups: *The Return of the Six Million Dollar Man and the Bionic Woman* (1987) and *Bionic Showdown: The Six Million Dollar Man and the Bionic Woman* (1989).

Anderson returned as boss Goldman and wore a second hat as well, that of producer. "And I learned more than I learned about anything in the film business before," he confides. "It's a very exciting side of the business." (A third made-for-television feature, *Bionic Ever After?*, co-starring and produced by Anderson, aired in 1994.)

You would think that maybe Anderson might be entertaining a notion to start kicking back and smelling the roses; after 45 years in the business, he must be lighting his cigars with residual checks. Tanned and easygoing and still handsome in his mid-sixties, Anderson fakes a look of confusion. "Retirement? What does that word *mean?* It doesn't seem to make any sense!"

RICHARD ANDERSON FILMOGRAPHY

Twelve O'Clock High (20th Century–Fox, 1949)
The Vanishing Westerner (Republic, 1950)
The Magnificent Yankee (MGM, 1950)
Grounds for Marriage (MGM, 1950)
A Life of Her Own (MGM, 1950)
The Unknown Man (MGM, 1951)
Go for Broke! (MGM, 1951)
Payment on Demand (RKO, 1951)
Cause for Alarm (MGM, 1951)
Rich, Young and Pretty (MGM, 1951)
No Questions Asked (MGM, 1951)
The People Against O'Hara (MGM, 1951)
Across the Wide Missouri (MGM, 1951)
Just This Once (MGM, 1952)
Scaramouche (MGM, 1952)
Holiday for Sinners (MGM, 1952)
Fearless Fagan (MGM, 1952)
The Story of Three Loves (MGM, 1953)
I Love Melvin (MGM, 1953)
Dream Wife (MGM, 1953)
Escape from Fort Bravo (MGM, 1953)
Give a Girl a Break (MGM, 1953)
Betrayed (MGM, 1954)
The Student Prince (MGM, 1954)
Hit the Deck (MGM, 1955)
It's a Dog's Life (MGM, 1955)
Forbidden Planet (MGM, 1956)
A Cry in the Night (Warner Bros., 1956)

The Search for Bridey Murphy (Paramount, 1956)
Three Brave Men (20th Century–Fox, 1957)
The Buster Keaton Story (Paramount, 1957)
Paths of Glory (United Artists, 1957)
The Long, Hot Summer (20th Century–Fox, 1958)
Curse of the Faceless Man (United Artists, 1958)
Compulsion (20th Century–Fox, 1959)
The Gunfight at Dodge City (United Artists, 1959)
The Wackiest Ship in the Army (Columbia, 1960)
A Gathering of Eagles (Universal, 1963)
Johnny Cool (United Artists, 1963)
Seven Days in May (Paramount, 1964)
Kitten with a Whip (Universal, 1964)
Seconds (Paramount, 1966)
Ride to Hangman's Tree (Universal, 1967)
Macho Callahan (Embassy, 1970)
Tora! Tora! Tora! (20th Century–Fox, 1970)
Doctors' Wives (Columbia, 1971)
The Honkers (United Artists, 1972)
Play It as It Lays (Universal, 1972)
Black Eye (Warner Bros., 1974)
The Glass Shield (Miramax, 1995)

Anderson is also seen in *The Metro-Goldwyn-Mayer Story* (1951), a 56-minute compilation of clips from then-current MGM movies.

I didn't give the business up,
it *gave* me *up.*

John Archer

WITH NEARLY 60 SCREEN ROLES to his credit, in addition to a long list of television parts, John Archer has played an assortment of characters in a wide range of genres. In horror and science fiction, however, the curly-haired six-footer generally played the good-natured but no-nonsense leading man who goes toe-to-toe with the forces of the unknown, whether it be zombies and Bela Lugosi on Poverty Row or the mysteries of the universe in George Pal's movie milestone *Destination Moon* (1950). As radio's Lamont Cranston (aka *The Shadow*), he knew *precisely* what evil lurked in the hearts of men.

The actor was born Ralph Bowman in Osceola, Nebraska (a suburb of Lincoln), on May 8, 1915. His family moved to California when he was five, and Bowman went to school at Hollywood High and the University of Southern California. He first set his sights on a job *behind* the cameras, taking a cinematography course at USC, but quickly learned just how tough it was to crack open those imposing studio gates, even in a low-paying entry-level position. "Times were tough then and I couldn't get a job for fifteen bucks a week in *any* area down there," Archer reminisces. "In fact, I had to leave USC in my junior year—I ran out of loot. So I finally went to work for an aerial photographer in Los Angeles for sixty bucks a month—I worked in an office, seeing clients and so forth. He went to New York and from there he sent me a wire, saying that some relatives of his from Texas were going to be in town; would I show them around and so forth? I *did* show them around Beverly Hills, and we stopped for lunch at a place at Wilshire and Fairfax. While we were dining, the hostess came over and said that there was a director in the room that wanted to ask me a few questions. His name was Ben Bard and he owned this little legitimate theater next door. He was having lunch with an actor, Jack Carson, and an agent, Frank Stemple. I made an appointment to see Bard the next day.

"Bard said, 'You've got all the qualities, all the attributes to do some acting. Have you ever thought of it?' I told him, 'No, I'm too self-conscious. I couldn't stand up next to my desk in school and read out of a book!' He said, 'Well, why don't you give it a shot?' and I said okay, and I did. In three months, I got my first job at Universal, and in six months, I started making a living at it!" Still using his real name, Bowman made his screen debut in *Flaming Frontiers* (1938), a Universal serial with cowboy star Johnny Mack Brown; "We shot an episode a day, practically." Other movie roles followed (including the serial *Dick Tracy Returns*), as well as parts in stage productions at the Ben Bard Playhouse, where Bowman worked alongside fellow newcomers Jack Carson, Alan Ladd, Turhan Bey and Byron Barr (aka Gig Young).

Another turning point for the young actor was competing in the unique talent quest program *Jesse Lasky's Gateway to Hollywood*, a CBS radio show

Previous page: While the science fiction fans of 1950 climbed the walls in anticipation of *Destination Moon*, star John Archer did, too—on the movie's "weightless" sets. (Photofest)

whose contestants vied to win a *nom de screen* coupled with a contract with a movie studio. "John Archer" was the name for which Bowman and other aspirants from all over the United States (including Hugh Beaumont) competed for 13 weeks, with Bowman eventually winning the screen moniker as well as a contract with RKO. ("I went from being a Bowman to an Archer!") His first film with the new name was RKO's *Career* (1939), a low-budget small-town drama starring Anne Shirley, Archer and "Alice Eden" (formerly Rowena Cook), another *Gateway to Hollywood* winner. *Variety's* Barn wrote of the contest winners: "In Archer, the *Gateway to Hollywood* has uncovered a lad with possibilities for development. He's a smooth looker, of clean-cut face and build, and with a bit of grooming has a chance to be heard from. With Miss Eden, it's another thing."

Archer's "grooming" continued, not only at RKO but at Republic, Monogram and other small companies as well. With horror films back in vogue after a late-thirties hiatus, Monogram producers Lindsley Parsons and Sam Katzman concocted cut-rate thrillers to capitalize on the new demand; Archer worked opposite black funnyman Mantan Moreland in Parsons's *King of the Zombies* (1941) and with horror king Bela Lugosi in Katzman's *Bowery at Midnight* (1942). "I enjoyed Monogram," admits Archer. "They were fast B pictures, but the people were all good. Working at Monogram, the techniques were all the same [as at larger studios], except that they would just shoot a *lot* faster. They didn't rehearse as much, and they'd shoot the whole picture in a week. In a larger studio, it would take three or four weeks to do a B picture. For instance, if you were in a B picture, actors didn't say 'God damn it!' or whatever if they flubbed a line. They just kept going, and created their own scene *[laughs]*, and the director would let 'em go as long as they wanted. Actually, that was good experience for *us*, too."

King of the Zombies, a horror comedy, was a mixed-up 67 minutes of low-cost fun, with heroes Archer and Dick Purcell encountering voodoo master Henry Victor on a mysterious jungle island near Cuba. Purcell is "zombified" early on, fifth-billed Archer handles most of the exposition, and comic Mantan Moreland, playing Archer's valet, shares his funniest scenes with Victor's band of zombies (typical dialogue: "If it was in me, I sure would be pale now!"). Besides doing his shtick in the movie, Moreland carried on and kidded between takes as well, and found a willing audience in Archer. "I liked having Mantan Moreland to work with—he was a funny little guy who just cracked me up. In fact, I thought he'd be a wonderful guy for Jack Carson to have as a sidekick on his radio show, like [Jack] Benny had Rochester. We kicked that around for a while, Jack Carson and [agent] Frank Stemple and I, but it didn't work out. They looked into it, and they realized the guy had tremendous talent and would have been very funny on the radio. But maybe it was the fact that they didn't want to get into something that would mimic Benny and Rochester."

Other *King of the Zombies* memories are less vivid, although Archer remembers Jean Yarbrough as "a good director — as a matter of fact, years later he directed a test I made for *The Egg and I* [1947] for Universal. (Fred MacMurray became available, so that stopped all conversation on the subject of me being in it!) I'm sure I saw *King of the Zombies,* and I probably enjoyed the film, but you must realize that they were still B pictures, and you could tell the difference."

While Archer's recollection of *Bowery at Midnight* is dim, the name Sam Katzman is one that the actor has not forgotten. "I worked with Sam several times after that; I think the last time was at Columbia, when he was producing a picture with Randolph Scott called *Decision at Sundown* [1957]. I'd worked for him in the interim, in a couple other pictures, too. He was a sweetheart, really, but he was a rebel. He was kind of a 'different' type of guy — a cigar-chompin' type of producer. Inwardly, he was a real nice man, but he didn't show it too often. I liked him." Bela Lugosi, the star of *Bowery at Midnight,* played a university professor who "moonlights" as a master criminal. Archer, playing one of Lugosi's students, is having trouble researching a term paper on the thoughts that cross a man's mind just before he dies; when Archer inadvertently learns about Bela's secret life of crime, the evil Lugosi gladly provides Archer with the opportunity to research the subject firsthand. Like other actors who worked opposite Lugosi, Archer concurs that "he wasn't around to have fun or to converse with, or even to rehearse with too much, until you got on the set. Then he would rehearse, and you'd do the scene. Maybe he was a shy man, I don't know — I have nothing derogatory to say about the guy, except that he was a loner."

Between *Zombies* and *Bowery,* Archer married actress Marjorie Lord, his costar in a stage production of *The Male Animal* (their daughter, born in 1947, is actress Anne Archer). Archer and Lord appeared together in *Sherlock Holmes in Washington* (1943), third entrant in Universal's series of Holmes adventures. Most audiences loved the Basil Rathbone–Nigel Bruce B series, but some critics (and finicky fans of the original Arthur Conan Doyle stories) decried the studio's decision to update the characters to the World War II era. "Those Sherlock Holmes fans — by God, they are rabid. They want everything to be just the way it was," says Archer. "But Universal was producing pictures to make money, and this was a question of making a buck. I'm sure that was their feeling — 'Let's update it or change it in some way, and see if we can make a little bit more money.' *That's* when all of the diehards got on them.

"I enjoyed that movie, even though the part was minimal," Archer continues. "Basil Rathbone and Nigel Bruce were both consummate pros, and a pleasure and a delight to work with. They were wonderful people to be around, and very helpful. They each had a subtle sense of humor, which was always kind of fun. Marjorie and I had a scene together where I said good-bye to her, and I did the usual thing, I patted her on the butt, 'See ya later' — you know

College student Archer gets some sage advice from Professor Bela Lugosi—an actor Archer remembers as a loner—in Poverty Row's *Bowery at Midnight*.

what I mean. And the director [Roy William Neill] said, 'Cut, cut! Oh, come on, John, what are you *doing?*' You can do those kinds of things in the movies today, but not *then [laughs].*"

Archer acted in a better grade of picture when he went under contract to 20th Century–Fox, but even there, he admits, "I realized that all the young actors out of New York were getting the good parts and more money. That's when I elected to go to New York, because New York in those days was the front door to Hollywood. *Hollywood* was the back door!" In New York he looked for stage and radio roles, and briefly considered jettisoning the name John Archer. "When I went to New York, I thought to myself, 'Well, I'll give up this John Archer thing,' because I thought it might have an onus, being a contest winner. I thought, well, shucks, if *that's* the case, let's dump Archer and go back to Ralph Bowman. That's when the radio people said, 'No, no— the John Archer name still means something. It still has a little marquee value because it's had so much exploitation. We *like* that.' So I said, 'I don't care what you call me, as long as you call me!'" he laughs.

And call they did: Archer quickly became one of the airwaves' foremost voices. "I was doing a *lot* of radio, going from studio to studio—soap operas in the morning, regular radio shows at night. There was a call for an interview for *The Shadow,* which I accepted just as I accepted any other interview. It didn't mean that much to me—I didn't know anything about *The Shadow,* really, except the name. I went in on my lunch hour and the director Bob Steel was just leaving for *his* lunch. I explained to him that I'd rushed over to have a quick interview with him (I was working), and he said, 'Well, come on in, John, we'll give you a shot.' He did, and he liked the way I read, he liked the laugh and whatever else was necessary. He said, 'Looks pretty good, John. We'll get in touch.' And they did, and I was the Shadow in 1944 and '45."

Archer took over in the role of the veteran sleuth at the beginning of the Mutual series' 14th year, following in the phonic footsteps of former Shadows Bill Johnstone, Bret Morrison and Orson Welles. His first installment, "The Ebony Goddess," was heard on September 24, 1944; his 30th and last, "The River of Eternal Woe," on April 15, 1945. (He also made guest appearances as the Shadow on a quiz program titled *Quick as a Flash.*) Archer's "Margo Lane" was actress Judith Allen. "She was married to Gus Sonnenberg, a wrestler," he adds. "She had a slight movie career before she came to New York and they cast her in that role.

"Myself, I did not have a specific approach for that [Shadow] role. I just treated it as any other job in radio, and that's what it was. I just wanted to go in and do a good job—and get my check *[laughs]!* I guess I did all right, but I'm not the judge of that." A number of the Archer *Shadow*s were scripted by Alfred Bester, but Archer never crossed paths with the noted science fiction author ("That's not unusual, though—you didn't see writers very often back then"). In addition to the radio roles, Archer also found work on the Great White Way; his Broadway bow was in *The Odds on Mrs. Oakley* (1944). He eventually left *The Shadow*—and New York—"to go to Ellitch's Gardens in Denver to be their leading man down there for the summer. Ellitch's Gardens was one of the best-known summer theaters in the country—I think it still *is.* We did ten plays, one every week for ten weeks. Then I came back *loaded* with scripts (I got over a dozen scripts for new Broadway plays while I was down there), and I selected a musical called *The Day Before Spring,* by Fritz Loewe and Alan Lerner. It was a semisuccess. It wasn't *too* great—Bill Johnson, Irene Manning and I were the leads. But it was a departure. I'm sorry I took it, really, because I had to turn down *Dream Girl* and a couple of other beautiful shows that turned out to be big hits. But it was an experience, and it didn't hurt me in the long run."

Archer's New York gambit paid off—in a way. "I was brought back to Hollywood at a good salary, at a good studio [Universal-International]—but I sat around for six months while they didn't cast me in *any*thing! They just loaned me out for one picture of Walter Wanger's, a picture with Bob Cummings and Susan Hayward called *The Lost Moment* [1947]." His other late-forties roles were in a pair of Warner Bros. features for director Raoul Walsh:

Colorado Territory (a Western remake of Walsh's earlier *High Sierra*) and the James Cagney classic *White Heat*.

Archer got star billing for the first time in the first of the fifties science fiction classics, producer George Pal's landmark *Destination Moon*. Based on a screenplay by science fiction novelist Robert Heinlein and screenwriter Rip Van Ronkel, the Technicolor space adventure was the first-ever Hollywood film to treat the subject seriously, with Archer starring as an aircraft industrialist "sold" on the idea of space travel by former army general Tom Powers and research scientist Warner Anderson (the nation that militarily controls the Moon controls the Earth as well). With additional financing furnished by other industrialists, an atomic rocket is constructed in the Mojave Desert, but insidious foreign-inspired propaganda turns the tide of public (and government) opinion against the project. Caution is tossed to the winds as Archer, Powers and Anderson—joined by electronics technician Dick Wesson—decide to make a hasty predawn liftoff in the untested spaceship *Luna* before the enemies of the project can use the law to bar the launching.

"I guess my agent got me an interview with George Pal, and I was signed," Archer surmises about the beginnings of his involvement. "I knew going into it who he was (everybody had tried to fill me in); he was one of the *best* in the [puppet animation] field originally. George Pal was a marvelous man, very thoughtful, very inventive. He wasn't on the set a *lot,* but he *was* there from time to time; he wanted to come down (I don't blame him!), and we were always happy to see him because he was such a pleasant man. He surrounded himself with such great talent; the writer, Robert Heinlein, was there a lot, and so was the man who designed the moonscapes, [space painter] Chesley Bonestell. They did some beautiful work. I thought they were highly intellectual and intelligent and interesting men. It was a pleasure to be with them, just to listen to them *talk.* Even though a lot of it was quite technical, it was understandable, and that's when you began to *believe* that these things were in the works, that they were going to happen. I really enjoyed those men very much, and I thought their talents were exceptional. And Lionel Lindon, the cameraman—*he* was exceptionally good. We were all kind of good friends, and we enjoyed working the movie."

The Irving Pichel–directed feature went into production November 14, 1949, at General Service Studio, where spaceship sets were ingeniously (and economically) constructed. "The spaceship set was a brilliant mechanism," Archer says. "They had this set that would turn over [like a rolling drum]. It was a fascinating set to be in. If you were required to walk on the wall, the set would be turning so that the wall was under your feet. We were just doing what we had to do, and the *set* was rotating. And we reacted as we went along. I thought that was very interesting. For scenes where we were floating around weightless in the cabin, they had tracks up in the ceiling area, and motors would just move us out to wherever it was we were supposed to be."

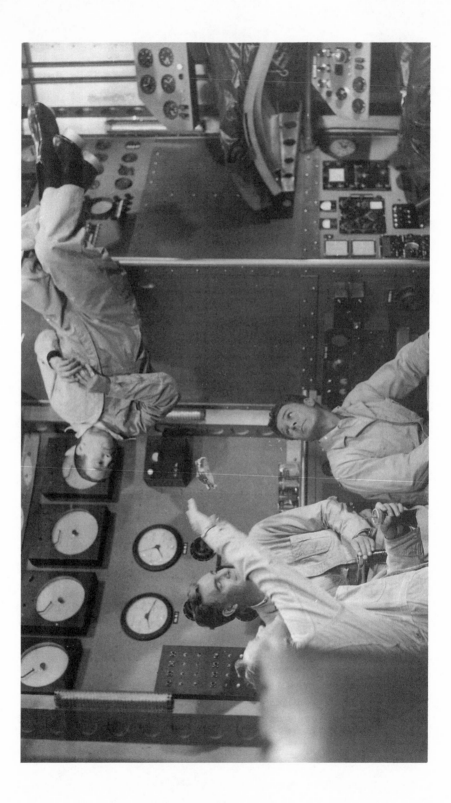

In the film's famous takeoff scene, the pressure of G forces distorts the faces of the pioneer astronauts—a special effect Archer remembers well. "That, I thought, was very interesting. Before shooting that scene, they put a wire and a piece of tape on each cheek and then they covered it with makeup. As the intensity increased, someone would be underneath us, out of camera range, pulling on these patches with the wire, which would force our faces back into that position. And, naturally, we cooperated as much as possible.

"In another scene, when we went outside the ship into space, Warner Anderson's character lost contact with the ship and floated off into space. I had to take a tank of oxygen and propel myself *to* him, and bring him back to the ship. Again, all that was done on a stage, with wires, and it was very exciting. That scene had a great, gorgeous background of brilliant stars—that was a backdrop that Bonestell had done. It was just breathtaking, the sight of it."

As for the moonscape set (representing the crater Harpalus), Archer recalls: "That was just a big, cracked-up thing, *unlike* what was actually found when they landed on the Moon. But this was their idea of it, big craggy areas and little valleys and hills. It was *very* effective. The problem with all those cracks was that they made our footing insecure and we had to look *down* too much, 'cause otherwise we'd have fallen on our faces! Remember, we were inside space suits, and our vision was hampered—we could only see so far with the helmets on. By the way, in those space suits, and under those lights, the actors got about as hot as you can get. Oh, it was insufferable *[laughs]!* But, oh, who cared? You did the work, it was no big deal."

Director Pichel (who directed Archer again a year later, in the Technicolor Western *Santa Fe*) is described by Archer as "a very easygoing, swell guy. He had an actor's approach because he *was* an actor—in fact, he appeared in *Santa Fe*. Very protective of his actors, very understanding—and very *good*. He could give you a lot. From being an actor, he knew the kind of stuff that we wanted *from* him, and we appreciated that." Pichel's set was constantly being invaded by press, scientists and other curious kibitzers, but according to Archer, the barrage of visitors did not seem to hinder production. "We knew these people were there—all the top guys from the top schools and laboratories were coming on, but we didn't know who they were and we didn't pay that much attention. They didn't seem to be interfering with anything, and you wouldn't even know they were there until you were told later." An occasional visitor would take a look around and comment that Pal was producing a *fantasy* film—an observation that would annoy the producer, who took great pains with what he called his "documentary of the future." "I can sympathize with

Opposite: "Weightless" Dick Wesson is about to catch a light snack on *Destination Moon*'s "rolling drum" spaceship set. Left–right: Tom Powers, Warner Anderson, Wesson, Archer.

George," Archer adds. "I'd have gotten pissed off and kicked 'em off the set *[laughs]!*"

To insure that the average Joe could relate to the futuristic goings-on in *Destination Moon,* a Woody Woodpecker cartoon simplistically described the principles of space travel, and actor Dick Wesson accompanied the space party as the low-comic Brooklynite radar-radio operator ("Go ahead, Oith!"). "I thought it distracted a *little* bit, but that's the way it was written, that's the way they wanted it and that's the way it was directed, so I guess that was supposed to have some kind of comic relief," Archer comments. "But, you're right, I don't know if it came off that well. By the way, Dick Wesson and I were good friends—the Wesson Brothers, Dick and his brother Gene, did a lot of vaudeville work around the country. Dick and his wife and my then-wife Marjorie and I used to do a lot of socializing."

More disastrous than Wesson's unfunny interludes was independent producer Robert Lippert's decision to cash in on the avalanche of publicity surrounding *Destination Moon*: Lippert knocked off a half-alike space travel movie and rushed it into release ahead of Pal's feature. Archer remembers the race for (theater) space well: "The Lippert picture with Lloyd Bridges, *Rocketship X-M*—they did that one in a hurry, because we were taking our time on *Destination Moon.* Ours was in color and it was just going to be great (and it *was*), so Lippert jumped the gun with that other movie and got it out a couple of weeks ahead of ours—and it *did* kind of steal our thunder a little bit. *Destination Moon* was getting a lot of attention [from newspapers, magazines, etc.] during production, and by coming out first, they stole a little of that for themselves. But there was nothing we could do about it."

One thing they *could* have done was rush through the balance of *Moon* when they saw Lippert's picture preparing for liftoff, but according to Archer, the pace of production did not change even when the imitation loomed. "No, that was never manifested at *all* during the shooting. We were on a schedule and Irving Pichel was doing a fine job *keeping* on schedule. We were never pressed at any time. If an audience saw our picture, and then walked next door to another theater and saw this *other* one, they'd say, 'Oh, my God— somebody's goofy *some*where.' What *[Rocketship X-M]* did was cut corners. We tried *not* to cut corners."

Almost a half century later, Archer is still able to look back on *Destination Moon* with pride: "I loved the movie and I *knew* that it was possible to someday get to the Moon. And later on, during the making of subsequent pictures, America *was* in space, making these wonderful orbits around the world in their spacecraft. And we on the set would always have a radio tuned in somewhere and we'd listen to this stuff, because a lot of us were interested in it. And then [in 1969], when a man finally *did* walk on the moon, I was amazed and awestruck at how little [the landing procedure in] *Destination Moon* differed from the actual landing." The $586,000 feature grossed $5.5 million

Archer dated Mari Blanchard in real life, and married and shot her in *reel* life—in the low-budget *She Devil*.

for distributor Eagle-Lion and won the 1950 Academy Award for special effects.

Archer worked throughout the fifties, on television and in movies big and small; his only other science fiction credit, *She Devil* (1957), has slipped from his memory other than the fact that it was made around the time that the divorced actor was dating the film's star, gorgeous Mari Blanchard. Television jobs included two stints on Ivan Tors' *Science Fiction Theatre* ("The episodes

I didn't think so much of—I don't think *Tors* did, either—but what the heck, we were all making a living") and Rod Serling's *The Twilight Zone* (in the classic episode "Will the Real Martian Please Stand Up"). "Rod Serling was on the set a few times, and he was a very interesting, fast-witted guy. Well, he had to be, because he wrote all those things overnight, practically. He was a nice man." Movie work ran the gamut from *The Big Trees* with Kirk Douglas to *Rock Around the Clock* with Bill Haley and His Comets and *Blue Hawaii* with Elvis Presley ("a great guy and a wonderful gentleman").

Another sixties movie role was as the father of teenager Sara Lane in William Castle's 1965 suspenser *I Saw What You Did,* starring Joan Crawford. "Joan did all of her stuff in a hurry and got out, and everybody else came to work then," Archer laughs. "I only saw her at the wrap party! I don't remember much else about that one, except that I've never known a picture to get so much exposure. I still get residuals from that, and I wonder where it in the heck it is they're still showing this thing *[laughs].*"

Archer's final feature to date was the Don Knotts comedy *How to Frame a Figg* (1971) and his last television role was in the "wonderful" *Rich Man, Poor Man.* "I didn't give the business up, *it* gave *me* up. I had a nice career and I felt that I should move along, so I went into something else which I enjoyed very much; in the sixties, I went into the trucking business with my brother, and we built that sucker up to quite an important arena in Los Angeles. I'd always go back and do a TV show if anybody hollered, but then I lost my agent and I just became disenchanted."

But John Archer isn't crabbing. Remarried (since 1956), he has four children (two by Marjorie Lord, two by second wife Ann), a new grandchild to visit and "some wonderful memories" of a long career in all media. If anybody wants to holler for him to do a television show *now,* their lungs had better be in shape: for the past four years, he's been living in the state of Washington, where one of his sons works for an engineering firm. "I'm also involved with the Radio Enthusiasts of Puget Sound. We had our first convention last June and it's a nice group, people who are just *nuts* about old-time radio, and naturally I'm part of it."

Obviously, fans of radio have not forgotten John Archer, the redoubtable Shadow—but will Universal, which is presently planning a big-screen version of the mysterious sleuth's exploits? Perhaps more pertinently, would Archer be tempted at this point by an offer of work? "You know, I've thought about that. For two or three years they've been talking about the movie, and I thought it was probably shelved. But *if* they do it, I *might* qualify as the Inspector—I'm the right age now. (They might want someone younger.) But, yeah, I'd like to be in it, and it couldn't *hurt* in a little exploitation way to say, 'Archer was the original Shadow.' Well, *one* of them!"

JOHN ARCHER FILMOGRAPHY

As Ralph Bowman:

Flaming Frontiers (Universal serial, 1938)
Letter of Introduction (Universal, 1938)
Overland Stage Raiders (Republic, 1938)
Dick Tracy Returns (Republic serial, 1938)
Spring Madness (MGM, 1938)
Barnyard Follies (Republic, 1940)
Cheers for Miss Bishop (United Artists, 1941)

As John Archer:

Career (RKO, 1939)
Curtain Call (RKO, 1940)
City of Missing Girls (Select, 1941)
Mountain Moonlight (Republic, 1941)
The People vs. Dr. Kildare (MGM, 1941)
King of the Zombies (Monogram, 1941)
Scattergood Baines (RKO, 1941)
Paper Bullets (Gangs Incorporated) (PRC, 1941)
Highway West (Warner Bros., 1941)
Sucker List (MGM short, 1941)
Hi, Neighbor (Republic, 1942)
Bowery at Midnight (Monogram, 1942)
Mrs. Wiggs of the Cabbage Patch (Paramount, 1942)
Scattergood Survives a Murder (RKO, 1942)
Police Bullets (Monogram, 1942)
Shantytown (Republic, 1943)
The Purple V (Republic, 1943)
Crash Dive (20th Century–Fox, 1943)
Guadalcanal Diary (20th Century–Fox, 1943)
Hello Frisco, Hello (20th Century–Fox, 1943)
Sherlock Holmes in Washington (Universal, 1943)
The Eve of St. Mark (20th Century–Fox, 1944)

Roger Touhy, Gangster (20th Century–Fox, 1944)
No Exceptions (20th Century–Fox / Office of War Information short, 1944)
I'll Remember April (Universal, 1945)
The Lost Moment (Universal, 1947)
Colorado Territory (Warner Bros., 1949)
White Heat (Warner Bros., 1949)
Destination Moon (Eagle-Lion, 1950)
The Great Jewel Robber (Warner Bros., 1950)
High Lonesome (Eagle-Lion, 1950)
My Favorite Spy (Paramount, 1951)
Best of the Badmen (RKO, 1951)
Santa Fe (Columbia, 1951)
Rodeo (Monogram, 1951)
The Big Trees (Warner Bros., 1952)
Sea Tiger (Monogram, 1952)
A Yank in Indo-China (Columbia, 1952)
Sound Off (Columbia, 1952)
The Stars Are Singing (Paramount, 1953)
Dragon's Gold (United Artists, 1954)
No Man's Woman (Republic, 1955)
Emergency Hospital (United Artists, 1956)
Rock Around the Clock (Columbia, 1956)
Three Brave Men (20th Century–Fox, 1957)
Affair in Reno (Republic, 1957)
She Devil (20th Century–Fox, 1957)
Decision at Sundown (Columbia, 1957)
Ten Thousand Bedrooms (MGM, 1957)
City of Fear (Columbia, 1959)
Blue Hawaii (Paramount, 1961)
Apache Rifles (20th Century–Fox, 1964)
I Saw What You Did (Universal, 1965)
How to Frame a Figg (Universal, 1971)

A painter can go and paint,
and a musician can practice by himself,
but an actor has to have an audience.

Jeanne Bates

HER ACTING CAREER BEGAN not with a bang but with a scream — something she has been doing regularly since. That's not all Jeanne Bates is known for: In addition to her radio and screen shrieks, in movies ranging from Bela Lugosi's *The Return of the Vampire* to the recent cannibal horror/comedy *Mom,* she has performed in dramas, Westerns and comedies, sung onstage, and played a regular role on television's *Ben Casey.* Serial and comic strip fans may first recognize her name from the credits of Columbia's jungle adventure *The Phantom* (1943).

Born in Berkeley, California, Bates began her acting career while a student at San Mateo Junior College, appearing on radio soap operas in San Francisco. She played the lead in an airwave mystery series, Lew X. Lansworth's *Whodunit* (Bates's scream was the show's signature), which became so successful that it (and Bates) moved to Hollywood in 1941. Bates and Lansworth married in 1943.

By the time the two were married, Bates was already under contract to Columbia Pictures, although she had no delusions that the studio intended to build her into one of their big stars. "I was just one more Columbia starlet," says Bates, now in her sixth decade of movies. "Max Arnow was the head casting man, and he took me in to meet Mr. [Harry] Cohn, the head of Columbia. Mr. Cohn looked up at me for a couple seconds, and then went *right back* to what he was doing *[laughs].* But even though I knew they had no 'big plans' for me, I did do about twenty-two films in the short time I was there. There was a very nice man in charge of Columbia's B unit and he liked me a lot, and he put me into some films."

Bates's debut was in a Boston Blackie mystery with Chester Morris, followed by a Charles Starrett Western on which she learned one of her earliest moviemaking lessons. "I love horses, but I never could afford to take riding lessons or anything. So the day I had to ride the horse, I practiced and practiced. But after practicing with the horse all morning long, when they said 'action,' the horse went one way when we were supposed to go the *other* way! I had no control over the horse whatsoever. So early on I learned not to say that I could do things I couldn't, because it's too dangerous." Other early roles included a precredits bit as a woman stalked by a vampire (Bela Lugosi's stand-in) in 1943 in *The Return of the Vampire* (screaming that scream again), comedy two-reelers, an Office of War Information short (*It's Murder*) and other bottom-of-the-bill features.

One of her first costarring roles was in Columbia's *The Phantom* (1943), based on the King Features syndicated comic strip. It took four writers to adapt Lee Falk's popular strip into the 15-episode adventure, which featured cowboy actor Tom Tyler as Godfrey Prescott and his masked alter ego, the Phantom. If the premise sounded glamorously exotic, the production, needless to say, was

Previous page: **Jeanne Bates (seen here in a Columbia glamour pose) never kidded herself that the studio had star-making roles in store for her.**

anything but. "We shot that at a studio called Darmour on Santa Monica [Boulevard], a really old, *old* studio. It must have been there in silent times. I think they had only *one* stage and the dressing rooms and it was all kind of out in the open—if it rained, forget it, folks—you'd be drowned between leaving the dressing room and getting to the soundstage *[laughs]*." Exteriors were shot "across from the Valley, in the hills up there, where Charles Manson killed all those people. Then there was another scene we shot at Malibu Lake, where all the natives climbed into the canoe—and the canoe sank! They had all these extras getting into this canoe and I thought to myself, 'They're not all gonna get in there, it's gonna sink.' And sure enough, it went down with all these guys trying to get into it. And, of course, the camera kept rolling as the boat and all these guys went down. It was *very* funny."

In the serial, directed by veteran soundstage speedster B. Reeves Eason, Professor Davidson (Frank Shannon) and his daughter Diana (Bates) arrive in Africa searching for the Lost City of Zoloz and its hidden treasures. Other self-interested parties with designs on the city and its riches include a local crook (Joe Devlin) as well as an international baddie (Kenneth MacDonald) who intends to build a secret air base there. Bates's fiancé (Tom Tyler) takes on his second identity (the Phantom) and, together with his dog Devil (played by Ace, the Wonder Dog), battles the villains throughout 15 "pulse-pounding" chapters before restoring peace to the jungles.

"Tom Tyler was very nice," Bates says of the *Phantom* himself. "Later on in life, he got some disease—elephantiasis or some other terrible thing! He was a nice man, very quiet and he did his job. And I was very impressed with the man who played my father [Frank Shannon, *Flash Gordon*'s Dr. Zarkov]. There was one scene where they were opening a treasure chest, and his hand got caught on a hinge and it cut the [webbing] of his hand, between the thumb and the forefinger. And he didn't stop. I would have screamed and yelled and hollered and so forth, but this actor, bleeding to death, went through this scene without a murmur. Only *after* the shot was completed did he say, 'Well, I've been cut.' And I thought that was wonderful, because he *was* an older man. I was very impressed with that.

"There was another incident where the heavies grabbed us and they were taking us up a ladder. Supposedly the Phantom was down below, being eaten by a gorilla—or whatever! The heavies went up this ladder, and it was nailed into the wall of this mountain. When I started going up—I remember that my boots were too big and my pants were too tight [for climbing]—the ladder started coming away from the wall. One of the actors at the top saw it happening and he grabbed it, so I finally got up. (They don't stop, you know—they keep shooting.) Then we were supposed to go over to the edge and look down to see the Phantom being eaten by the monster. Well, at the end of the shot, I couldn't *move*. I was frozen. My husband had been a reporter when the Bay Bridge was being built and he said that people would freeze—that's how they'd fall off the bridge and drown. Well, from that day on, I can't get up on a height without freezing, and I think it was all from that—it was kind of a traumatic experience."

Bates recalls working "three or four weeks" on the 15-chapter (30-reel) *Phantom,* including a period of a couple of days "when production was closed down because somebody caught cold or whatever, because it was freezing. It was *very* cold—they were shooting this in the winter, and we were in pith helmets and short sleeves. And every time we spoke, you could see our breath. On one of the first days of shooting, we were way up in the mountains, and they went downtown to Los Angeles to get 'natives'—extras. They bus-loaded these guys up there . . . and then they stripped 'em. And as I said, it was freezing cold. They were stripping 'em down to loincloths and painting their bodies brown to look like natives, and these guys were shivering to death. There was an Indian man who was in the picture, and he said that how you keep from catching cold is to keep standing, do not sit down. So I've always remembered that—I don't know whether it works or not, but it seemed to work then!"

B. Reeves Eason, who was better at directing action than actors (his second-unit credits include the chariot race in the silent *Ben-Hur,* the burning of Atlanta in *Gone with the Wind* and the charge in Errol Flynn's *The Charge of the Light Brigade*), "was an old-time director, from way back. He had a nickname, 'Breezy.' I don't remember him too well, but he was one of those rugged guys, I guess like John Ford, that kind of guy. He *never* stopped the camera." Bates, who never read the *Phantom* strip, also did not see her serial when it was originally released "because they showed at Saturday matinees, for the little kids. But I now have *The Phantom* on tape, all fifteen episodes, given to me on two tapes by a man out in Burbank. I've seen one tape, and *[laughs]* I haven't gone on to the other one yet!"

Elevated to B stardom, Bates played one of the leads in Columbia's 1944 horror movie *The Soul of a Monster,* about a dying surgeon (George Macready) whose foolhardy wife (Bates) prays that the Devil will save his life. A satanic emissary (Rose Hobart) appears and saves Macready, who is now a different man, cruel and mysterious. Bates has fond memories of her *Soul* costars, particularly "Rose Hobart—the poor thing. There was a scene where I was supposed to slap her. Well, I would grit my teeth and try and try and try. I'd get up to that point in the scene and I just couldn't do it. Instead of a slap, it would just be a pat—and a pat—and a *pat,* no good for the scene. And I guess the *pats* were just driving her up the wall, because finally she said, 'Will you please—will you p-l-e-a-s-e—just slap me!' And to tell the truth, I don't remember now if I was ever able to really hit her or not, but I know she pleaded with me to do it, just to get it over with!"

It was after her stint at Columbia that Bates had one of her best forties film roles, as the long-suffering wife of mad illusionist Erich von Stroheim in PRC's horror melodrama *The Mask of Diijon* (1946), directed by Lew Landers.

Serial star Bates stands ready for action with Tom Tyler and Wonder Dog Ace in Columbia's *The Phantom*.

"He was wonderful, von Stroheim," says Bates. "My husband had told me about him—I was fairly young at the time and I didn't know too much about von Stroheim. I guess von Stroheim did the picture just because he wanted the bucks. And he got his girlfriend [Denise Vernac] in the picture, too, so *she* got paid! I don't know how much he got paid, but I guess it was a goodly sum. This was shot just after the war [in November 1945] and he was on his way

Sinking canoes, rickety ladders and freezing location work were just a few of the *Phantom* pitfalls braved by Bates.

back to France, to Paris, and he had trunkloads of makeup and wigs and all kinds of things for the actors who had been deprived of all that stuff during the war. What impressed me was the fact that he would listen to what I had to say [in the scenes]. Most actors would ask you a question and you'd be answering them, and their eyes would drift off to see who was coming in or who was going out. I was very impressed with the fact that he would listen to anything I had to say *[laughs]*. I liked him very much, he was a very nice man."

Although *Diijon* is directed with more style than the average Lew Landers movie, Bates doesn't recall master director von Stroheim ever whispering in Landers' ear. "No, as far as I know, von Stroheim just was an actor. I think it was the cameraman, Jack Greenhalgh, who created the mood in *Mask of Diijon,* more (probably) than Lew, and it was absolutely wonderful. It was his lighting. In the close-ups, there was such a mood, and I think that was Jack, who I remember very well. At Columbia I didn't photograph that well, and here I thought I did—*very* well. (My husband once told me, 'It's too bad you don't photograph better,' which was a great help, I must tell you *[laughs]!*) At Columbia they just threw a bunch of light on you and that was that. Greenhalgh created a mood, and he probably was responsible for a lot of the [artistic] touches. With von Stroheim, I just remember one scene he wanted to take over—it was a scene where he was perspiring and he was crying, so there was a lot of water coming down. When I saw it in the rushes, it was very funny, and *he* laughed, too."

In the fifties she worked on television as well as in features, including a role that has completely faded from memory, as Peter Coe's wife in the jungle adventure *Sabaka* (1953) with Boris Karloff. She also worked regularly as a nurse—in the movies, that is—first in the supernatural *Back from the Dead* (1957), as midwife to ghost-possessed mom-to-be Peggie Castle, and again in *The Strangler* (1964), where mad mama's boy Victor Buono murders Bates for saving his ailing mother's (Ellen Corby) life. ("It was kind of spooky lying on that gurney, being hauled out like I was dead. I remember thinking, 'My God, how horrible that this could happen to a person!'") She wore white on television as well, playing the compassionate Miss Wills on the hospital drama *Ben Casey* (1961–66).

Other television roles included Rod Serling's *Twilight Zone* (in the classic "It's a Good Life" episode) and two visits to *One Step Beyond,* hosted by John Newland. "I knew Newland from radio," says Bates, who appeared twice on *Beyond,* the first time as Mrs. Abraham Lincoln in "The Day the World Wept." "I thought that was quite good—I liked doing that one. I remember that the makeup on the actor who played Lincoln, Barry Atwater, took *hours.* I did some research, of course, on Mary Todd Lincoln, but they wanted her to come across as a kind of dreary lady so I got that black wig—and, come on, folks, that ain't gonna make you look glamorous." In the sixties she also went back to her first love, stage work, appearing in "legitimate" productions (including several musicals) in the Los Angeles area as well as on the road.

Film work in the seventies included the satirical *Suppose They Gave a War and Nobody Came?* (1970) and one of her most unusual feature credits, David Lynch's experimental *Eraserhead* (1978). "That was quite an experience. One of the ladies in it, Judith Anna Roberts, who plays the girl in the room across the hall [from star John Nance] — she belonged to Theater West, which was a theater group that I belonged to, and she recommended me for *Eraserhead*. I then went on an interview for David, who was an art student, and he said, no, I was much too pretty. And I said, 'No, no, you don't understand. I can be pretty and I can be awful.' So I sold myself on how awful I could look *[laughs]*. And it worked! Also, the man that played my husband, Allen Joseph, was from Theater West, so Judith got us a *couple* of jobs.

"We worked at the Doheny mansion that the AFI [American Film Institute] used to rent for a dollar a year. David didn't shoot in the mansion itself, we shot in the stables — upstairs in the stables, they had living quarters for the grooms and so forth. It was great working for David. I think I only worked a week or so, and he insisted on paying us. Then I saw him a couple of years later, in the bank, and I asked him how it was going, and he hadn't finished it yet because he ran out of money. Finally he got somebody to finance it and he finished it."

The nightmare-like student film (Lynch's feature debut) reportedly took a year to shoot and another year to edit; Bates and her husband had the opportunity to catch an early cut of the cult-movie-to-be. "My husband, Lew, who was a writer, and I went to see it, the first showing, and Lew said to David, 'Don't you think it's a little long?' And it was like stabbing David in the heart. Since then, they've cut it — that first [cut] was forever, it went on and on and on. But *Eraserhead* was what got him his start — it's still showing today, and, needless to say, *Eraserhead* got him *The Elephant Man* [1980]."

Eraserhead also led to more film work for Bates, including the title role in the cannibal horror film *Mom* (1991). In the direct-to-home-video feature, Bates is the unsuspecting landlady of an unearthly flesh eater (Brion James) who bites her, turning her into a fellow carnivore (with fangs and yellow contact lenses). "Both the casting director of *Mom* and Pat Rand, who directed it, were ardently in love with *Eraserhead,* so that was part of the reason I got it. And also because I could scream good *[laughs]*!"

Primarily shot in a rented house in downtown Los Angeles, *Mom* was Bates' first brush with modern monster makeup. "They had to make a plastic mask of my face, and not knowing what that was like, I said, 'Sure, go ahead.' Well, I'm kind of claustrophobic, and when you're under that thing for forty-five minutes, you can get a little antsy. *That* wasn't too pleasant! I wore rubber appliances that were supposed to swell up, and I had hoses on my back that they pumped air through, to make the appliances inflate. (I didn't think they

Bates is still active in movies, on television and on the stage.

swelled up that much—I didn't think it looked *that* disastrous!) To put the makeup on, it took about two hours. So we started putting the makeup on at around five o'clock, and I didn't work until twelve-thirty the next morning. And carrying this stuff around with you, this whole appliance, it was excruciating."

"Mom's" victims included prostitute Stella Stevens as well as a homeless man from L.A.'s mean streets. "I believe they got an actual street person—his name was Bates, too, I remember. They hired a whole bunch of street people because they wanted to have people lying on the street for their shots. They fed them 'lunch' at 11 P.M. and after that, these street people decided they'd been there long enough and they all left! So all the ADs had to lie on the street with newspapers over 'em, because all the street people they'd hired got tired and left."

Despite the discomfort of the makeup, Bates enjoyed the experience of making *Mom* ("It was one of the first really good parts I'd had in a long, long time, and I liked doing it very much"), not to mention the fact that it led to another horror role, as the senior sorceress of a coven of modern-day witches in director Brian Yuzna's *Initiation: Silent Night, Deadly Night 4* (1990). "Oh, *that* disaster!" the actress scoffs. "I felt so sorry for that young actress [Neith Hunter] with all of those bugs crawling all over her—ai yi yi! That was a cheapie, shot at night. I got that from *Mom*, because I showed the tape of *Mom* to Brian Yuzna and he loved it. And Brian's little boy was in it, too—he was the little boy that we were going to kill."

Other roles in newer movies have included director Lawrence Kasdan's *Grand Canyon* (1991) as well as *Die Hard 2* (1990), as Bonnie Bedelia's sassy fellow plane passenger. Bates also still works on television (*The Commish*), in commercials and onstage (most recently in Jean Giradoux's *Ondine* in Los Angeles), so apparently retirement is not on the horizon. "But, you know, you're *semi*retired whether you want to be or not, when you get to be a mature lady!"

According to Bates (widowed since 1981), the important thing is simply to keep working, which is why, after a half-century in the business, she still belongs to acting workshops and does the occasional freebie play on the side. "I'm not ready to die yet!"

JEANNE BATES FILMOGRAPHY

The Return of the Vampire (Columbia, 1943)

The Chance of a Lifetime (Columbia, 1943)

The Phantom (Columbia serial, 1943)

The Black Parachute (Columbia, 1944)

Shadows in the Night (Columbia, 1944)

She's a Soldier, Too (Columbia, 1944)

Sundown Valley (Columbia, 1944)

The Racket Man (Columbia, 1944)

The Soul of a Monster (Columbia, 1944)

Tonight and Every Night (Columbia, 1945)

Sergeant Mike (Columbia, 1945)

The Mask of Diijon (PRC, 1946)

Death of a Salesman (Columbia, 1951)

Trouble In-Laws (Columbia short, 1951)

Paula (The Silent Voice) (Columbia, 1952)

The Hindu (Sabaka) (United Artists, 1953)

Marty (United Artists, 1955)

Trooper Hook (United Artists, 1957)

Back from the Dead (20th Century–Fox, 1957)

Blood Arrow (20th Century–Fox, 1958)

Vice Raid (United Artists, 1959)

The Strangler (Allied Artists, 1964)

Suppose They Gave a War and Nobody Came? (Cinerama, 1970)

Eraserhead (AFI/Libra, 1978)

Die Hard 2 (20th Century–Fox, 1990)

Grand Canyon (20th Century–Fox, 1991)

Wild Orchid 2: Two Shades of Blue (Triumph, 1992)

Dream Lover (Gramercy Pictures, 1994)

Jitters, the monkey, I'll never forget. One day he jumped out of a tree and landed on the top of my head . . . turned his tail around . . . and you know what happened next. All over me!

Billy Benedict

BILLY BENEDICT HAS A MODEST ATTITUDE about his acting career. He considers each of his 200 or so movie roles "just work" and the fabled stars he worked alongside only "coworkers"; the casual way he puts each role in its proper place, as a very small part of a very big picture, it is tough to disagree with him. But when he talks too modestly about his career as a whole, he is in for a fight. During Hollywood's Golden Age, and for decades afterward, he managed to keep his face in front of cameras, either in features or on television, and make it one of the most recognizable ones in the business; that is no small achievement. Fans probably remember him best as one of the East Side Kids (or the Little Tough Guys, or the Bowery Boys; he was part of all three "splinter groups"), but serial and science fiction aficionados know him, too, primarily for his costarring role in Republic's 12-chapter *Adventures of Captain Marvel* (1941).

"There wasn't much difference between working at one of the big studios and working at places like Republic and Monogram," Benedict, now 76, recalls in his Hollywood home, "not as far as the work itself was concerned, anyway. At Republic, you moved a little faster *[laughs],* and got a lot more done in a shorter length of time, but, really, it was all work any way that you look at it. Some of the schedules were short and others were longer, even at Republic and Monogram. Working fast or working slow, *I* had no preference — or, I should say, it didn't make any difference. It was work. In those years, we were young and it was a buck, and that was the important thing. I think *Adventures of Captain Marvel* was twenty-eight days, but that was early in the morning till late at night."

Like Red Ryder, Brenda Starr and other comic strip luminaries Benedict worked opposite, Captain Marvel too leapt from the printed page onto the silver screen, but the comic book Marvel was not one Benedict had kept up with. "No, I didn't read *Captain Marvel,* but *Brenda Starr* I looked at occasionally and *Red Ryder,* also. And *Tim Tyler's Luck* I'd read as a comic strip when I was younger; it was an exciting thing for me to read. But making *[Adventures of Captain Marvel]* was an enjoyable experience. Tom Tyler, who played Captain Marvel, was an exceptionally nice man and a very good actor, but he was very quiet on the set. He knew what he was doing and he always knew his dialogue very well — not that he had much of it in *that* thing *[laughs].*"

Curiously, Benedict himself did not have a word of dialogue in *Captain Marvel's* first chapter *(Curse of the Scorpion),* despite lots of screen time, but he found his voice again in subsequent episodes. His character, Whitey, was the sidekick to Billy Batson (Frank Coghlan, Jr.), a boyish newscaster who accompanies the Malcolm Archaeological Expedition on a trek into the barren wilderness of Siam. There the scientists discover the Golden Scorpion, an atom-smashing apparatus devised by the ancients, which has the power to turn

Previous page: **Benedict (on the right) warily watches for the monkey's next move.** (From *Perils of Nyoka*)

Benedict (holding hat) sizes up the bevy of suspects (George Pembroke, Robert Strange, John Davidson, Harry Worth) in *Adventures of Captain Marvel.*

base metals into gold. Motivated by greed and the lust for power, one of the scientists takes on the new identity of the masked Scorpion, an archvillain whose master plan includes laying evil hands on the Golden Scorpion and using it to rule the world. Batson, Whitey and Betty (Louise Currie), a secretary, are the youthful trio who battle the masked evildoer, with considerable help from Batson's alter ego, the superpowered, high-flying Captain Marvel (Tyler).

"Louise Currie was a lovely gal and it was nice working with her," Benedict continues. "I had met Frank Coghlan before we did *Captain Marvel* together, but we didn't become well acquainted until we did it; we've been friends ever since. [Stuntman] Dave Sharpe, who doubled for Frank and for Tom Tyler, was an exceptional man with tremendous talent, and as far as I'm concerned, he was one of the best stuntmen the business ever had. Dave's career went way, way back, almost as many years as Frank's; he did some comedies for Hal Roach and then he did some Westerns. Dave, unfortunately, had a voice that had rather a high pitch to it, and it was not really compatible as far as motion pictures were concerned. He was one hell of a guy, that's for sure.

"It was amazing what Dave did as Captain Marvel. For his takeoffs, he worked off a trampoline a lot of times, and the way it's cut together, it's pretty difficult to tell who was who. Dave had certain idiosyncracies [of movement] that if you *knew* him, it was easy to tell whether or not it's him doing a stunt in a picture or not. If I'm not mistaken, he even doubled for *me* once, in [the 1942 serial] *Perils of Nyoka*." Asked if he could have played Billy Batson as well as Coghlan did, Benedict scoffs. "No, I don't think so. For one thing, *physically* I was not right for it, I wasn't what the comic strip ordered."

As for directors John English *(Adventures of Captain Marvel)* and William Witney *(Marvel, Perils of Nyoka),* "I liked them very much; in fact, I saw Bill Witney up in Lone Pine [California] last year, at a convention, and I'll probably see him again this year. And Jack English [who died in 1969] was a delightful man, too—just the opposite of Bill Witney in dress and speech and everything. But they were very compatible, and it was a pleasure to work with them."

Benedict has lost count of how many movies he has been in; with the aw-shucks attitude he brought to many of his screen characters, he responds to the question with an embarrassed "Oh, gosh, no, I really couldn't tell you." He *does* know that he was born in Haskell, Oklahoma, on April 16, 1917. ("There are a lot of books that list me as being born in 1906; I'm aware of 'em, but there's not much you can do about 'em!") Asked what led him to a career in the picture business, the best the Panhandle State native can muster is a matter-of-fact "it just *happened.* One reason was the economic situation. I came out here to Hollywood during the Depression when jobs were hard to come by, and I figured that if I could do something in movies, I might make a couple of bucks. I graduated from high school in Tulsa—I had been active in the drama department there, and I also had been studying dancing. My older sister and I just decided that we would come to California—get out of the Dust Bowl—and we did, in 1934."

Benedict's sister did not go into showbiz, but Benedict did—and right away. "I had originally been a dancer [on the stage in Oklahoma], dancing at different spots—it was a rough go. I decided I'd attempt to do the same thing here in Hollywood, but I very quickly found out that dancers were a dime a dozen. So then I figured to try it as an actor. I went to the old Fox studio on Western Avenue to see a man by the name of Jim Ryan—he was the casting director. There was a lady there who was his secretary, Mary Yost, and she happened to be the aunt of a fellow from Tulsa whom I knew *[laughs]*. So we got in a conversation, and she said, 'Well, if anything comes up, I'll kind of jack up Mr. Ryan, and see if we can do anything.' About two weeks later I got a call from her, to come down and see Ryan. I went down and there was an interview. I went in, met Mr. Ryan and a director, George Marshall, and a producer (whose name I've forgotten). We talked for a while, and as a result of that, I got a part in *$10 Raise* [1935] with Edward Everett Horton. That was the first picture that I did."

Benedict went onto the Fox payroll as a "featured player," playing roles there at the studio (soon redubbed 20th Century–Fox) as well as at other lots;

his thirties credits include the classics *After the Thin Man, Bringing Up Baby,* and Universal's *The Road Back,* directed by James Whale. His first serial experience came at the same studio, when he costarred in their 12-chapter *Tim Tyler's Luck* (1937). "Frank Thomas was the star, and I liked working with him very much. Both his mother and father were in show business; in fact, his father and I became very well acquainted when we were both under contract at RKO." Benedict also would go to see his own pictures, as well as the serials in which he had acted, in the theaters. "I enjoyed going to the movies — I always have — and it was a big thrill for me to see myself on the screen. I even went to some of the kiddie matinees when I wanted to see a chapter of one of the serials I'd done. I'd sit with the kids — and I even got recognized occasionally!"

Characteristically, he never considered the possibility of stardom ("I really wasn't thinking about it"), for characteristic reasons ("Just to keep working, that was the important thing"). He insists that he did not have an in at the various casting offices, although he never seemed to lack for work; counting serials and shorts as well as features, he was in an amazing total of 80 titles between 1940 and 1944 alone. Many of them might have been one-day gigs, but others, like some of the serials and the East Side Kids pictures, had him in costarring roles. "How did I keep so busy? Again, I don't know — my ability, my talent (if I had any!), or whatever. Evidently they liked what I did, so they put me to work. It happened and I enjoyed it."

Benedict worked in serials not only at Republic but also at Universal and Columbia, and he shares the widely held belief that Republic's were by far the best of the bunch. "Oh, yes, they were, very much so. Republic had the ability to get a crew together that knew what the hell was going on. They made the moves — they could almost second-guess what the director would want. They went very smoothly, and they were a great, great crew to work with — fantastic."

Perils of Nyoka gave him another sidekick role, this time to two-fisted Clayton Moore and Kay Aldridge (Nyoka), in a tale no less exotic than *Captain Marvel's.* This scientific expedition takes our heroes to the deserts of northern Africa, where they search for the Lost Tablets of Hippocrates but find instead a villainous high priestess (Lorna Gray), her trained killer ape and hordes of angry tribesmen. "We shot that at Iverson's Ranch — the same place we went for Westerns and everything else Republic wanted to do," chuckles Benedict. "Clayton Moore and Kay Aldridge were both a lot of fun, and Jitters, the monkey, I'll never forget. One day he jumped out of a tree and landed on the top of my head . . . turned his tail around . . . and you know what happened next. All over me!" As for a favorite serial, Benedict cannot choose between *Marvel* and *Nyoka.* "I like both of 'em very much, and I enjoyed working in them. I've collected some of my serials on videocassette and I do dig 'em out occasionally and look at them. They're still pretty good.

Perils of Nyoka protagonists Benedict, Forbes Murray, Kay Aldridge, George Pembroke, Clayton Moore and Robert Strange await their next skirmish.

"I did a lot of my own stunts on *Perils of Nyoka*. But on some of the stuff I did down at Monogram, there were a couple of times where, after I had done my stunt, I wished that they had gotten a stuntman. I'm talking about the pictures with the Bowery Boys now. And there were also a couple of stunts they wanted me to do, which I did kiss off."

The early East Side Kids flicks were produced by Sam Katzman, the Hollywood moviemaker with the well-earned reputation of never meeting a corner he couldn't cut or a penny he couldn't pinch. "He also produced one of the serials I was in, *Brenda Starr, Reporter* [1945]," Benedict recalls of "Jungle Sam." "The Republic serials were by far much better directed, much better written, and the overall picture was much better [than *Brenda Starr*]. With Sam Katzman, they were on a strict budget, and they got by just as cheap as they could, and didn't worry too much about a lot of things that they *should* have. But Joan Woodbury, who played Brenda Starr, was a lovely gal and it was a lot of fun."

Returning to the subject of the East Side Kids, Benedict remembers, "Sam Katzman had latched onto all the Dead End Kids and signed 'em up. I had worked for Sam when he was an independent producer, years before, and he kind of liked me. He asked me to come down and go to work in one of these pictures. I said, 'Sam, you can't pay my salary.' And he said, 'Well, just try me.' So he got on the phone and called my agent, and I got the money I wanted.

"Katzman would hang around with his cane and beat the floor when things weren't going well. (Maybe some times he'd even try to beat you *[laughs]*.) I got along very well with Sam, and made a lot of movies with him." In the mid-forties the popular low-budget series got a much-needed facelift; budgets and shooting schedules were upped and the band of slaphappy hooligans was redubbed the Bowery Boys. "Sam Katzman and [series lead] Leo Gorcey couldn't get along, so Leo and his agent, Jan Grippo, made a deal together and started producing the pictures themselves. Now we were the Bowery Boys," says Benedict.

Not surprisingly, Benedict adds, Leo Gorcey and his "boys" were in real life nothing like the roughnecks they played—publicity to the contrary. "When they were away from the set, they were altogether different than when they were on. But they had to keep up appearances for publicity's sake. I got along with all of 'em very well." Various adventures found the slum kids pitted against horror-type actors in haunted houses and similar settings, giving Benedict an opportunity to see stars of this genre at work. "Glenn Strange [*Master Minds*, 1949] was a good actor and a nice guy. Bela Lugosi [*Ghosts on the Loose,* 1943] was in those, too, of course, and there again, he was a very pleasant individual. Before we did [*Spook Busters,* 1946], I had worked with Charlie Middleton at Republic—he was the villain in *Nyoka*—and he was a hell of an actor, that's for sure. So was Lionel Atwill [*Junior "G" Men of the Air,* 1942]. Both of those gentlemen were exceptionally good professional people."

"When I first started doing the East Side Kids pictures, we did 'em in three days and three nights. Later they got up to about four days, and then when the Bowery Boys came along, they went all the way up to five or six days. Toward the end, they were taking ten days, which no one had intended to happen, but it did." On his departure from the series (his last was *Crazy Over Horses,* 1951), he hesitantly admits, "I had just had enough. I suddenly decided I'd had enough of 'em, and it was getting a little rough doing 'em— emotionally—so I kissed 'em goodbye, and that was it. It got to be too much of a hassle. There was a lot of infighting going on with everybody concerned and I said, to hell with it, I don't need this."

By the early fifties, of course, Benedict was already acting on television in addition to tackling minor movie roles; one of his small-screen roles was as a baddie in the poorly produced (and short-lived) *Dick Tracy* with Ralph Byrd ("nice man"). *The Magnetic Monster,* a 1953 science fiction entry, had Benedict in the small part of a hardware store employee whose entire inventory has inexplicably become magnetized—the result of the presence of a deadly radioactive element hidden in an apartment above. "That was for [writer/director] Curt Siodmak, and it was made as an independent by Ivan Tors, before he moved on to his TV series. I found Siodmak very easy to work with; he might have

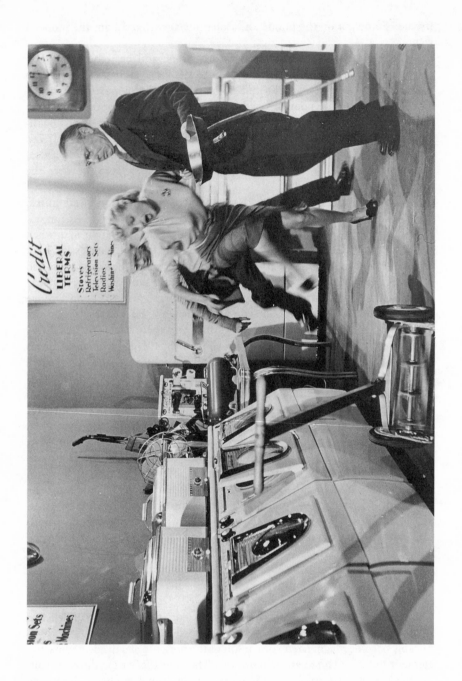

been a little hard to understand, but he was very pleasant with me. He was the man who had written *Donovan's Brain,* and he was a delightful man as far as I was concerned. That job went about three days, I think." On the opposite pole from *Magnetic Monster* (quality wise) was the Ed Wood concoction *Bride of the Monster* (1956), which Benedict recalls with a laugh and a "God Almighty! People get a laugh out of Wood's movies nowadays, they poke fun at 'em—and they *should.* He was a real hustler and a promoter. I don't know how many pictures he did, or attempted to do: I met him somewhere, don't ask me where, and he took a shine to me and wanted me to work in the picture. We started to work, and then the Guild shut it down because there was no money up front for the actors! (We finally *did* get paid.)"

Other television work has included *I Dream of Jeannie, Mission: Impossible, The Twilight Zone, Land of the Giants* and *The Incredible Hulk;* one of his last features (to date) is *Homebodies* (1974), which has a cast of veterans (Ian Wolfe, Ruth McDevitt, Peter Brocco, Douglas Fowley, more) and a horror/comic plot about oldsters resorting to murder to protect their condemned building. "*Homebodies* was directed by a man by the name of Larry Yust, with whom I'd worked before. That was one of the few commercial films that he made—the others that he had made were educational films. He was a good director—in fact, a very good director—and a nice man. I saw the movie, and it shakes you up a little bit, that's for sure!"

Billy Benedict, the man of many movies (and, generally, few words) describes himself today as "sort of kind of retired. I occasionally do a commercial. If something comes along, fine; if not, I go about my own business—I go fishin' *[laughs]!* And this is about as active as I want to be." Looking back over an almost-60-year career, he remarks, "All I can say is that it's been a lot of fun. If I had it to do all over again, I suppose I would do it the same way." Regrets? He's had a few; but then again, too few to mention. One of his only good *dramatic* parts was in William Wellman's *The Ox-Bow Incident* (1943); he would have liked to have played more roles like that. Other than that, he's been in plenty of other types of roles, in practically every sort of movie. In fact, there might be only one thing that Billy Benedict, the hoofer from Oklahoma who came to Hollywood with his eye on a dancing career, might have enjoyed doing in a movie, but never had the chance:

"Strange as it seems, I've never once danced in a picture!"

Opposite: Years before *The Lawnmower Man,* Benedict, Elizabeth Root and Byron Foulger were attacked in *The Magnetic Monster.*

BILLY BENEDICT FILMOGRAPHY

$10 Raise (Fox, 1935)
The Farmer Takes a Wife (Fox, 1935)
Steamboat 'Round the Bend (Fox, 1935)
Doubting Thomas (Fox, 1935)
Ladies Love Danger (Fox, 1935)
College Scandal (Paramount, 1935)
Silk Hat Kid (Fox, 1935)
Way Down East (Fox, 1935)
Your Uncle Dudley (Fox, 1935)
Show Them No Mercy (Fox, 1935)
Three Kids and a Queen (Universal, 1935)
Welcome Home (20th Century–Fox, 1935)
Can This Be Dixie? (Fox, 1936)
Meet Nero Wolfe (Columbia, 1936)
The Country Doctor (20th Century–Fox, 1936)
Theodora Goes Wild (Columbia, 1936)
Adventure in Manhattan (Columbia, 1936)
Crack-Up (20th Century–Fox, 1936)
After the Thin Man (MGM, 1936)
Ramona (20th Century–Fox, 1936)
M'Liss (RKO, 1936)
The Witness Chair (RKO, 1936)
Libeled Lady (MGM, 1936)
Captain January (20th Century–Fox, 1936)
A Son Comes Home (Paramount, 1936)
They Wanted to Marry (RKO, 1937)
The Last Gangster (MGM, 1937)
Jim Hanvey—Detective (Republic, 1937)
Rhythm in the Clouds (Republic, 1937)
That I May Live (20th Century–Fox, 1937)
Love in a Bungalow (Universal, 1937)
Tim Tyler's Luck (Universal serial, 1937)
Laughing at Trouble (20th Century–Fox, 1937)
A Dangerous Adventure (Columbia, 1937)
The Road Back (Universal, 1937)
Tramp Trouble (RKO short, 1937)
Flying Fists (Victory, 1937)

There's Always a Woman (Columbia, 1938)
Hold That Co-ed (20th Century–Fox, 1938)
Bringing Up Baby (RKO, 1938)
Say It in French (Paramount, 1938)
Walking Down Broadway (20th Century–Fox, 1938)
Young Fugitives (Universal, 1938)
King of the Newsboys (Republic, 1938)
Hold That Kiss (MGM, 1938)
No Time to Marry (Columbia, 1938)
Little Tough Guys in Society (Universal, 1938)
I Met My Love Again (United Artists, 1938)
Pack Up Your Troubles (20th Century–Fox, 1939)
Newsboys' Home (Universal, 1939)
Timber Stampede (RKO, 1939)
Code of the Streets (Universal, 1939)
Call a Messenger (Universal, 1939)
Man of Conquest (Republic, 1939)
Hollywood Hobbies (MGM short, 1939)
The Bowery Boy (Republic, 1940)
Legion of the Lawless (RKO, 1940)
My Little Chickadee (Universal, 1940)
Adventures of Red Ryder (Republic serial, 1940)
Lucky Partners (RKO, 1940)
Rhythm on the River (Paramount, 1940)
Grand Ole Opry (Republic, 1940)
Second Chorus (Paramount, 1940)
Prairie Law (RKO, 1940)
Stage to Chino (RKO, 1940)
The Great McGinty (Paramount, 1940)
Young People (20th Century–Fox, 1940)
Melody Ranch (Republic, 1940)
Give Us Wings (Universal, 1940)
Chicken Feed (RKO short, 1940)
And One Was Beautiful (MGM, 1940)
Citadel of Crime (Republic, 1941)
In Old Cheyenne (Republic, 1941)
The Richest Man in Town (Columbia, 1941)
Jesse James at Bay (Republic, 1941)
She Knew All the Answers (Columbia, 1941)

Unholy Partners (MGM, 1941)

The Man Who Lost Himself (Universal, 1941)

Variety Reels (*Meet the Stars* series) (Republic short, 1941)

Mr. District Attorney (Republic, 1941)

Bad Man of Deadwood (Republic, 1941)

Great Guns (20th Century–Fox, 1941)

Adventures of Captain Marvel (Return of Captain Marvel) (Republic serial, 1941)

The Great Mr. Nobody (Warner Bros., 1941)

The Mad Doctor (A Date with Destiny) (Paramount, 1941)

Tuxedo Junction (Republic, 1941)

Time Out for Rhythm (Columbia, 1941)

Confessions of Boston Blackie (Columbia, 1941)

Dressed to Kill (20th Century–Fox, 1941)

Home in Wyomin' (Republic, 1942)

Talk of the Town (Columbia, 1942)

A Night to Remember (Columbia, 1942)

Valley of Hunted Men (Republic, 1942)

Right to the Heart (20th Century–Fox, 1942)

A Tragedy at Midnight (Republic, 1942)

On the Sunny Side (20th Century–Fox, 1942)

Junior "G" Men of the Air (Universal serial, 1942)

Get Hep to Love (Universal, 1942)

Perils of Nyoka (Nyoka and the Tigermen) (Republic serial, 1942)

Rings on Her Fingers (20th Century–Fox, 1942)

Lady in a Jam (Universal, 1942)

The Glass Key (Paramount, 1942)

Wildcat (Paramount, 1942)

Two Yanks in Trinidad (Columbia, 1942)

Mrs. Wiggs of the Cabbage Patch (Paramount, 1942)

Almost Married (Universal, 1942)

Heart of the Golden West (Republic, 1942)

Affairs of Jimmy Valentine (Unforgotten Crime) (Republic, 1942)

Thank Your Lucky Stars (Warner Bros., 1943)

Clancy Street Boys (Monogram, 1943)

Aerial Gunner (Paramount, 1943)

Hangmen Also Die! (United Artists, 1943)

Mr. Muggs Steps Out (Monogram, 1943)

Whispering Footsteps (Republic, 1943)

Adventures of the Flying Cadets (Universal serial, 1943)

Ghosts on the Loose (Monogram, 1943)

The Ox-Bow Incident (Strange Incident) (20th Century–Fox, 1943)

Moonlight in Vermont (Universal, 1943)

Nobody's Darling (Republic, 1943)

All by Myself (Universal, 1943)

Million Dollar Kid (Monogram, 1944)

The Lady and the Monster (Republic, 1944)

Janie (Warner Bros., 1944)

The Whistler (Columbia, 1944)

My Gal Loves Music (Universal, 1944)

Follow the Leader (Monogram, 1944)

Goodnight Sweetheart (Republic, 1944)

The Merry Monahans (Universal, 1944)

Block Busters (Monogram, 1944)

That's My Baby (Republic, 1944)

They Live in Fear (Columbia, 1944)

Cover Girl (Columbia, 1944)

Follow the Boys (Universal, 1944)

Bowery Champs (Monogram, 1944)

Night Club Girl (Universal, 1944)

Brenda Starr, Reporter (Columbia serial, 1945)

The Story of G.I. Joe (G.I. Joe) (United Artists, 1945)

Docks of New York (Monogram, 1945)

Mr. Muggs Rides Again (Monogram, 1945)

Patrick the Great (Universal, 1945)

Come Out Fighting (Monogram, 1945)

Road to Utopia (Paramount, 1945)

Hollywood and Vine (PRC, 1945)

A Boy, a Girl and a Dog (Film Classics, 1946)

The Gentleman Misbehaves (Columbia, 1946)

No Leave, No Love (MGM, 1946)
One More Tomorrow (Warner Bros., 1946)
Live Wires (Monogram, 1946)
In Fast Company (Monogram, 1946)
Without Reservations (RKO, 1946)
Bowery Bombshell (Monogram, 1946)
Spook Busters (Monogram, 1946)
Mr. Hex (Monogram, 1946)
Gay Blades (Tournament Tempo) (Republic, 1946)
Do You Love Me? (20th Century–Fox, 1946)
Never Say Goodbye (Warner Bros., 1946)
The Kid from Brooklyn (RKO, 1946)
Hard Boiled Mahoney (Monogram, 1947)
The Hucksters (MGM, 1947)
Fun on a Weekend (United Artists, 1947)
Bowery Buckaroos (Monogram, 1947)
The Pilgrim Lady (Republic, 1947)
News Hounds (Monogram, 1947)
Merton of the Movies (MGM, 1947)
Jinx Money (Monogram, 1948)
Smugglers' Cove (Monogram, 1948)
Angels' Alley (Monogram, 1948)
Trouble Makers (Monogram, 1948)
Secret Service Investigator (Republic, 1948)
Night Wind (20th Century–Fox, 1948)
Fighting Fools (Monogram, 1949)
Hold That Baby! (Monogram, 1949)
Master Minds (Monogram, 1949)
Riders of the Pony Express (Kayson/ Screencraft, 1949)
Angels in Disguise (Monogram, 1949)

Blonde Dynamite (Monogram, 1950)
Lucky Losers (Monogram, 1950)
Triple Trouble (Monogram, 1950)
Blues Busters (Monogram, 1950)
Bowery Battalion (Monogram, 1951)
Ghost Chasers (Monogram, 1951)
Let's Go Navy! (Monogram, 1951)
Crazy Over Horses (Monogram, 1951)
The Magnetic Monster (United Artists, 1953)
Bride of the Monster (Banner, 1956)
The Killing (United Artists, 1956)
Rally 'Round the Flag, Boys! (20th Century–Fox, 1958)
Last Train from Gun Hill (Paramount, 1959)
Lover Come Back (Universal, 1961)
Dear Heart (Warner Bros., 1964)
Harlow (Paramount, 1965)
Zebra in the Kitchen (MGM, 1965)
The Hallelujah Trail (United Artists, 1965)
Frankie and Johnny (United Artists, 1966)
What Am I Bid? (Emerson, 1967)
Funny Girl (Columbia, 1968)
Big Daddy (Paradise Road) (Syzygy/ United, 1969)
Hello, Dolly (20th Century–Fox, 1969)
The Dirt Gang (AIP, 1972)
The Sting (Universal, 1973)
Homebodies (Avco Embassy, 1974)
Farewell, My Lovely (Avco Embassy, 1975)
Won Ton Ton, the Dog Who Saved Hollywood (Paramount, 1976)
Born Again (Avco Embassy, 1978)

Benedict's footage was deleted from *Metropolitan* (20th Century–Fox, 1935). He also acted in the unreleased *Rogue's Gallery* (Paramount, 1968).

Oh, horror films are wonderful.

Turhan Bey

TALL, DARK AND EXOTICALLY HANDSOME, Turhan Bey was emblematic of the breed of foreign-born leading men that flourished briefly in Hollywood during the World War II years. But Bey's home studio was Universal, the company whose most famous players had names like Dracula, Frankenstein and Kharis; unlike other Hollywood players who had lovely leading ladies in picture after picture, Bey occasionally found himself opposite such unglamorous costars as the Mummy, the Mad Ghoul and Boris Karloff. Surely the suave star of forties classics like *Ali Baba and the Forty Thieves* and Katharine Hepburn's *Dragon Seed* saw these B horror films as a decided comedown.

"No, I liked the horror films. I wish I could have kept it up," Turhan Bey declares emphatically. "I *always* liked horror films and I always liked playing heavies, when they were interesting. There are some heavies that are just mean, but I was lucky, I always played heavies that had some kind of a hidden cause to be mean. But dislike horror films? Oh, no, no! I *loved* them! I loved to see them and I loved to play in them."

It has been years since Turhan Bey has acted; even his "newest" film, a 1953 Sam Katzman quickie called *Prisoners of the Casbah,* is long gone into the limbo of forgotten celluloid. But Bey's memories of his movie days are still vivid. On an extended visit to Hollywood from his native Austria, seated poolside at his Beverly Hills hotel, he is only too happy to reminisce candidly about the highs (and lows) of his unique acting career.

Turhan Selahettin Schultavey (the "Bey" is actually a title) was born in Vienna, son of a Turkish father and a Czech mother. After his mother sold her lucrative glass manufacturing business in Czechoslovakia, the family moved to Paris, where they met a friendly American lawyer who recommended they visit California and gave Bey a letter of introduction to film director Arthur Lubin. The Beys left Paris because "my mother had the feeling there was going to be a war—and nobody else shared that opinion. But she had a wonderful sixth sense for those things, and she made us come to America."

Migrating to America in the late thirties, Bey spent his first several months in the States in Littleton, New Hampshire, where he lived with his mother and grandmother and studied English. The three later traveled west to California and presented the letter of introduction to Arthur Lubin, who proceeded to show them Hollywood. After that, Bey's decision to become an actor was not long in coming. "The fact that I had to perfect my English made me go to [acting teacher] Ben Bard's dramatic school. After a while, Ben Bard needed for one of his plays an actor to play a character that would fit me very well. And when the play was seen by two Warner Brothers talent scouts, I had my first role at Warner Brothers."

Bey earned $500 a week for his film debut, a supporting role in Warners' comedy-mystery *Footsteps in the Dark* (1941) with Errol Flynn. After making

Previous page: **Turhan Bey in a characteristic forties pose.**

a second Warners film, *Shadows on the Stairs* (1941), "I made a film at Universal and they liked what I did. At that time, they had a great many roles for people of my looks, which were Oriental ... could-be-Chinese, could-be-Japanese, all of which I played. And Universal signed me up." At first, the roles were not great, and neither were the movies: Bey had character names like Luchau, Muto, Chundra and Juma, and the pictures had titles like *Drums of the Congo* and *Raiders of the Desert*. (In the screen credits of *Raiders*, a typo makes him Tur*b*an Bey.) Excelling in minor villainous characters, he was the perfect choice to play the baddie in Universal's *The Mummy's Tomb*.

Second in Universal's series of Kharis films, *Tomb* moved the action from Egypt to America, as the Mummy (Lon Chaney) stalks and kills members of the expedition that desecrated his final resting place in the previous movie *(The Mummy's Hand)*. Chaperoning Kharis on his first trip abroad, Turhan's Mehemet Bey gave the Mummy his nightly wake-up call and brewed those eye-opening cups of tana fluid before sending him out on his murderous missions. "I felt terribly sorry for this excellent actor Lon Chaney, who had to wrap himself up every day, even in the greatest heat, in that fabulous costume of his. Except to speak with his body, he couldn't do anything. The costume was held together with a zipper in the back, so it wasn't all too difficult to get in and out of it—they didn't have to wrap all those bandages around him. Only one eye was showing through the mask, and there was a small slit for him to breathe through his nose and through his mouth. But that was all."

The Mummy was Chaney's least favorite monster role, and on the set of a later Kharis film, *The Mummy's Ghost,* the actor told a United Press visitor that people were crazy to spend their money to see Mummy films. On the set of *Mummy's Tomb*, however, Bey says that Chaney kept his dissatisfaction strictly to himself. "He was a real professional. He would never show anybody that. He may have felt that he couldn't do any acting [as the Mummy], but when you watch the way he moved, the rhythm of his various movements, he *did* do some acting with his body, as his father did."

Engagingly disingenuous, Bey insists—as he has in the past—that *The Mummy's Tomb* is perhaps his favorite among his own films. "I guess it's my favorite because it was a part closest to my own nationality—it was a young Egyptian who believed in something which we could not comprehend with our five senses. As I said before, I do like people who are in contradiction with all laws of human decency because of some reason, some inexplicable belief that they have. I don't mean that I would like to have people like that around me in life *[laughs]*, but I like to portray them. If I could have picked my own roles, I would have played these kinds of heavies, people who have a mental quirk or who, for some reason or another, are acting against the positive side of the plot of the picture. I like heavies with a cause, so I think *The Mummy's Tomb* was one of my favorite roles—really. But, to be perfectly honest with you, I

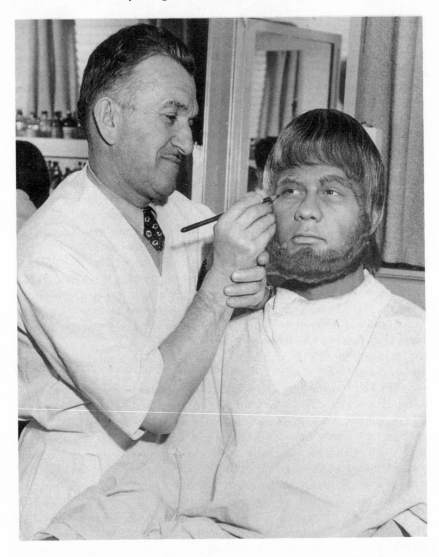

Jack P. Pierce makes up Turhan Bey for his role as the ape-like Aesop in Universal's *Night in Paradise*.

never saw the movie. For many of my films, I saw the rushes but never saw them finished. In fact, I never even kept a still picture of myself."

The films for which Turhan Bey remains best known are the Arabian Nights costumers Universal churned out in the early forties. Often paired with fellow camel jockeys Jon Hall, Sabu and, of course, Universal's Queen of Technicolor, Maria Montez, Bey costarred in the garish escapist romps *Arabian*

Nights, *White Savage*, *Ali Baba and the Forty Thieves* and *Sudan*. Today the movies themselves are regarded as kitsch, and Maria Montez has become the darling of the high camp set. Bey insists, however, that the people involved in the making of these films did not have their tongues in their cheeks.

"I didn't have that attitude, nor did the people I worked with. I took them very seriously; I think that's the only way to do anything, except when you play in a comedy. If you don't take these costume pictures seriously, they become a comedy, too." Bey—who, until this question, never heard of the word *camp*—is mildly distressed that the films have this sort of reputation today. "It would be terrible if you were to do something and to think that, in ten years, it would be ridiculous. You can't do that, you have to take it seriously. By the way, I saw *Ali Baba and the Forty Thieves* in Austria—nobody laughed at it; they enjoyed it. We wouldn't have made them if we thought they were 'camp.'" And as for the notorious Maria Montez, Bey is taken aback to hear that she's gone down in the Hollywood history books as a highly difficult and temperamental actress. "I enjoyed working with her very much. We were very dear friends. She wasn't always on time, but the difficulty with Maria was that she was brought up in a very Catholic and a very strict family surrounding, and some of the studio language isn't always the best *[laughs]*. So when somebody talked like that in front of her, she was shocked, and told him what she thought of him!"

By this time, of course, the six-foot-one Bey was known as one of Tinseltown's most eligible bachelors, frequently photographed arm in arm with Hollywood lovelies and endlessly profiled in movie magazines that dubbed him "Mystery Man," "Ladies' Knight" and, inevitably, "The Terrific Turk." Returning to horror, Bey furnished the closing narration for Universal's *Captive Wild Woman* before finally getting an opportunity to play hero, protecting Evelyn Ankers from the clammy clutches of *The Mad Ghoul*. Bey remembers remarkably little about the film, except that he enjoyed working with costars Ankers and veteran movie baddie George Zucco. "Zucco was one of the finest gentlemen I have ever worked with, and the last person in the world I would suspect to play horror parts. Except for his fantastic, menacing eyes and his voice, which he could manage so well, there was nothing horrible about him at all." And Ankers, reigning screen queen of the Universal lot, was "a very pleasant, wonderful girl with whom I had lunch once. We were talking about romance and things like that, and she said to me, 'Turhan, you're the kind of a man I'd like to have an affair with, but I'd hate to be married to.' *[Laughs]* That was her definition of Turhan Bey!"

The Ghoul himself, boyish leading man David Bruce, was "the sort of pleasant young man that was under contract to Universal at the time, a fellow who tried to make life as agreeable as possible for everybody. I think that at Universal, that was the tendency. We all got along fine and I don't remember ever having a serious clash with anybody. Not even an *un*serious clash." Bey's upbeat memories also extend to the people behind the camera at Universal, like prolific B producer Ben Pivar and *Mad Ghoul* director James Hogan. "Hogan was very matter-of-fact, but an excellent craftsman. And a craftsman was what you had to be when you directed B pictures. You could be an artist at the same time, but mainly you had to be a craftsman, because you had *X* number of scenes to shoot every day and you had to keep on schedule. And Ben Pivar was a wonderful man. The great thing about Universal at that time was that most of the producers were musicians—they loved music or wrote music or conducted it. And musicians are wonderful people."

On loan from Universal, Bey made his best-known film, MGM's *Dragon Seed* (1944) with Katharine Hepburn, a massive (145 minutes) production quite different from the ten-day B's that the Universal factory pumped out like automobiles from a Detroit plant. "*Dragon Seed* was different in the respect that it was very exciting to me. MGM was the studio of really big stars, so just to walk in there and to see Gable, Stewart, Spencer Tracy, Katharine Hepburn—! Maybe it was only the fact that it was different from Universal, but it excited me very much and I was very happy to be there. But as far as the work was concerned, I must admit that I almost preferred the way Universal worked, because it was faster and less time-consuming. *Dragon Seed* was very time-consuming. But maybe if it had been another MGM picture, I would have enjoyed it just as much."

Unlike the programmer-style *Mummy's Tomb* and *Mad Ghoul,* Bey's next Universal film, *The Climax,* was a comparatively major horror production. Prompted by the success of the studio's 1943 hit *Phantom of the Opera,* producer/director George Waggner dressed up this new opera-house horror film in Technicolor and lavish sets, filled it with songs and production values—and then forgot to put in the horror. "George Waggner was a wonderful, sensitive man, one of the most enthusiastic people I'd ever known," Bey reminisces. "I think you could have given him a Mickey Mouse picture to do—no offense to Mickey Mouse *[laughs]*—and he would have put just as much of his efforts and excitement and enthusiasm into that. I had one big row with him, and it was my own fault. There was a scene where he needed the camera to stay very long on me, for a dissolve, and I had to hold still. Then suddenly I said, 'This is too long for me. I just can't stand it anymore.' Poor George, he had to do something much different from what he had planned. That was our only row and it was my own doing."

Starring in *The Climax,* Boris Karloff was the sinister Dr. Hohner, full-time physician and part-time nut job, fiercely determined to thwart the Royal Theatre's plans to revive an opera that originally starred his sweetheart—whom he himself has since murdered. Susanna Foster, who played the female lead in both *Phantom of the Opera* and *The Climax,* scarcely enjoyed the experience of acting opposite Karloff ("Working with Karloff was like working with a slab of ice," Foster insists), but Bey begs to differ.

"He was an Englishman, and Englishmen are not as outgoing as Americans are on the set—he retired to his dressing room when he wasn't needed on the set. But, my God, he was a very pleasant, wonderful partner whom you could rely on to give you every cue—so disciplined! I didn't know Susie felt that way about him. I know I sound like Pollyanna in Hollywood, as if I loved everybody, but it's true, I've never encountered anybody whom I disliked. Boris I liked particularly, but he was a very shy man who I don't think associated really in what I would call a palsy-walsy form with anybody on the set." As for his own romantic role in the film (as Foster's chivalrous fiancé), "I enjoyed that part very much. It wasn't a very large role, but it was very interesting and quite different from what I had done before. I don't know how it went over with the public, but to me it was a great pleasure playing it." Critics lambasted *The Climax*; Arthur Lubin tells people that the film's failure hurt George Waggner's Universal career. "Certainly not that I noticed," Bey shrugs. "The only picture that ever hurt *me* was a picture that Arthur Lubin directed *[laughs]*."

The picture in question, *Night in Paradise,* was a gaudy fantasy placing the fabled storyteller Aesop (Bey) in the royal court of King Croesus (Thomas Gomez), circa 560 B.C. After appearing sleek and unruffled opposite such heavily greasepainted ghastlies as the Mummy and the Mad Ghoul, it was now Bey's turn to climb into Jack P. Pierce's makeup chair to be transformed into the apelike Aesop. "It was at least an hour that Jack Pierce spent on me. It wasn't as difficult as it might look; the wig was easy, but the beard had to be done very carefully, each hair on its own, not just a beard pasted on. I really am proud to say that I got along very well with Jack Pierce, because Jack was not a man who took a liking to everybody. Oh, no, not at all! He never was temperamental or anything, but to get him to laugh, you had to be very close. This I had the pleasure of being with him. He was definitely the specialist in horror makeups. He was never rude, but I never saw him really warm up to anybody, and some people were a little scared of him. And nobody ever dared to come late to Jack Pierce—even the big stars. When Jack said, 'Be here at five-thirty,' you had to *be* there *[laughs]!*"

Bey's romantic vis-à-vis in *Night in Paradise* was leading lady Merle Oberon; with his usual disarming candor, Bey admits, "I enjoyed working with her very much, but I doubt that she enjoyed working with me! This was at a time, unfortunately, when I was often very late on the set. Thomas Gomez, whom I loved, gave me hell every time I came late—he was very, very strict with me *[laughs]!* But I appreciated that; he was right, and he openly told me his mind. Merle Oberon behaved wonderfully, never said anything, but I know she was an absolute professional and she was always on time. There were several times when I was about an hour late. That's unforgivable, and I regret it tremendously now."

Night in Paradise was a tepid, almost vulgar fantasy, destined to die a slow

Bey (seated) cooked up a spiritualistic scam in the suspense film *The Amazing Mr. X.* Bey is flanked by Cathy O'Donnell and Lynn Bari; the ectoplasmic intruder is Donald Curtis.

death at the box office. "After the second week I knew it going to be a terrific flop, and I think everybody else knew it, too," Bey says. "So you can imagine that *that* was a little depressing. I think the thing that made me a little dubious about what [director] Arthur Lubin was doing was that he treated us more or less like robots. When we came to the set, everything was already there; our movements were already laid out for us. Nobody could say, 'Look, couldn't I do it *this* way?' or 'I would feel much better doing it a different way.' To make a change was impossible, because everything was already set up. I had never encountered this before; in all the B pictures that I worked on, nobody ever did this."

The postwar years were a time of decline for Turhan Bey; a hitch in the army interrupted his career momentum, and many long-established leading men, missing from the Hollywood scene in the early forties, were now back from the fighting and competing for the worthwhile roles. "When I came back from the army, Universal had been sold to an entirely new group of people. The first part they offered was impossible for me. I said to the producer, 'Look, couldn't we rewrite this a little bit?' and he said *[flatly],* 'Out of the question!' So I went on suspension, and they said, 'Not only do you go on suspension, but we also will sell your contract.' I said, 'All the better!' So after that, I had

two or three very happy years with Eagle-Lion, the studio they sold me to."
Asked for concluding comments on Universal, Bey offers, "Very pleasant; very
constructive; the end, unfortunately, a big flop, but c'est la vie." Special
memories? "Yes, of all my friends there. It was a studio of cooperation, where
the biggest producer never was too tired to talk to you or to listen to your problems." And regrets? "Well, yes. I should have been a little more serious about
my work, but I was very young and maybe I can be forgiven for that. I don't
think I did *bad* work; I could have done better, I think."

Just like those at Universal, the films in which the Eagle-Lion studios
placed Bey were often fluff and nonsense, but there was at least one diamond
in the rough, the moody suspense film *The Amazing Mr. X,* with Bey as a
phony spiritualist cooking up a plan to murder widow Lynn Bari for her
money. "The memory that I have of this film is that it was a fantastic role with
wonderful people to work with, and a lovely death scene which I completely
loused up. Absolutely. It was one of those days where I just didn't know
what acting was, and it was one of the best scenes that any actor could
wish for. When I saw it, I said to myself, 'Turhan, you've got to start all
over again.' But any actor will tell you that there are days when you just are
not fit to work. I just wish all of my roles would have been as interesting as
that one. *Amazing Mr. X* was a picture I wish we had had a little more time
to do."

By the late forties, with the war over, Bey was called upon to return to
Europe to handle business and property matters. "I told my agent I was going
to Europe and I'd be back in three months, because in three months I had a
picture lined up. Well, I stayed three *years.* Then, once I came back, I waited
for (I think) six months before I got a picture at Columbia, a Sam Katzman
picture with Cesar Romero called *Prisoners of the Casbah.*" It was not long
afterward, of course, that Turhan Bey threw in the towel acting-wise, returning
home to Austria and later turning his attention to fashion (and nude)
photography. "I've always been a photographer, even before I became an actor.
And now that's all I'm doing, so I'm extremely happy. That doesn't mean that
I wouldn't *like* to act again, but only the things I like to do."

Is Turhan Bey happy with the course his Hollywood career took? "No, I'm
not happy about it. It was a very short career, and because of my own doing,
it never got me to where every actor would like to be, which means being
recognized as an actor. Of course, the kinds of films I made were not
[*laughs*]—*not* the films that are nominated for Oscars or other kinds of awards,
but you can't think about things like that. Like everything else, it could have
been better."

And any closing comment for the contingent of horror film fans that have
always looked upon Turhan Bey as one of their favorites?

"Yes, that I'm honored if they regard me as a favorite. I've done very few
horror films, but I would like to have done many more. Of course, in all genres,

"I should have been a little more serious about my work [in films], but I was very young and maybe I can be forgiven for that." Turhan Bey in 1991.

there are good and bad. But basically, from *The Exorcist* down to *The Mummy's Tomb,* I enjoy seeing them, and I certainly would enjoy doing them again. Oh, horror films are *wonderful!*"

TURHAN BEY FILMOGRAPHY

Footsteps in the Dark (Warner Bros., 1941)
Shadows on the Stairs (Warner Bros., 1941)
The Gay Falcon (RKO, 1941)
Raiders of the Desert (Universal, 1941)

Burma Convoy (Universal, 1941)
A Yank on the Burma Road (MGM, 1942)
The Falcon Takes Over (RKO, 1942)
Bombay Clipper (Universal, 1942)
Destination Unknown (Universal, 1942)

Danger in the Pacific (Universal, 1942)

Arabian Nights (Universal, 1942)

Unseen Enemy (Universal, 1942)

Junior "G" Men of the Air (Universal serial, 1942)

The Mummy's Tomb (Universal, 1942)

Drums of the Congo (Universal, 1942)

The Adventures of Smilin' Jack (Universal serial, 1943)

Captive Wild Woman (voice only; Universal, 1943)

The Mad Ghoul (Universal, 1943)

White Savage (Universal, 1943)

Background to Danger (Warner Bros., 1943)

Ali Baba and the Forty Thieves (Universal, 1944)

Follow the Boys (Universal, 1944)

Dragon Seed (MGM, 1944)

Bowery to Broadway (Universal, 1944)

The Climax (Universal, 1944)

Sudan (Universal, 1945)

Frisco Sal (Universal, 1945)

Night in Paradise (Universal, 1946)

Out of the Blue (Eagle-Lion, 1947)

Adventures of Casanova (Eagle-Lion, 1948)

The Amazing Mr. X (The Spiritualist) (Eagle-Lion, 1948)

Parole, Inc. (Eagle-Lion, 1949)

Song of India (Columbia, 1949)

Prisoners of the Casbah (Columbia, 1953)

Stolen Identity (producer, Helen Ainsworth Corp., 1953)

Postscript: Bey has recently returned to acting after a 40 year hiatus, appearing on TV's *seaQuest* and *Babylon 5* and in direct-to-video *Possessed by the Night* (1994) and *The Skateboard Kid 2* (1995).

I don't remember that Rocketship X-M *did my career much good.*
It was considered a B picture, and you never make much
of an impression on the industry if you're in a B picture.

Lloyd Bridges

LLOYD BRIDGES—YOU CAN SAY *that* again. He bridges nearly all the media, having established himself time and again, and he spans the generation gap as well. He started out on stage in the 1930s, playing classical roles in college, in summer theaters and even on Broadway. In the forties he concentrated on his screen career, playing first in minor roles and later in solid supporting parts in some top Hollywood features. Baby boomers remember that in the fifties he became a household name thanks to *Sea Hunt*, then the most-watched syndicated television show in the United States. More recently, a whole new generation has come to know him for his befuddled roles in the zany spoofs *Airplane!*, *Hot Shots!* and now *Honey, I Blew Up the Kid*.

"They don't *really* blow the baby to pieces," Bridges is quick to correct. "What happens is, the baby gets ahold of something that increases his size, something that blows him up all out of proportion. He leaves the house, and is on his way to Las Vegas. And now it's a mad chase to get to him before he gets to Las Vegas, where the neon lights are going to make him God-knows-how-much taller than he is already."

As Disney's sequel to the hugely successful *Honey, I Shrunk the Kids* gears up for release, Bridges takes a break from the activity in his bustling Los Angeles home and talks about the real star of his upcoming feature: "The star of the whole thing is the wonderful special effects; it's just amazing what these effects men can come up with today," he affirms. "We worked some pretty late hours on the picture, but the cast was all very nice and it was a pleasure working with them. It was pleasant working with [star] Rick Moranis, who is a very nice man as well as a talented man. And I could say the same thing about the director, Randal Kleiser. He's someone who really knows his business. He's done quite a few of this kind of picture before, so it wasn't anything new for him."

Science fiction is also nothing new to Bridges, who has worked more than just occasionally in the genre. The star of many land, underwater and outer space adventures was born Lloyd Vernet Bridges, Jr., in San Leandro, California, and grew up in various Northern California towns. His father, who was in the hotel business in California, wanted him to become a lawyer, but young Lloyd's interests turned to acting while at the University of California at Los Angeles. (Dorothy Simpson, Bridges' wife of more than 50 years, was one of his UCLA classmates, and appeared opposite him in a romantic play called *March Hares*.)

"Working on the stage was my main ambition when I left college," he reminisces. "I did a lot of Shakespeare and Greek drama—as a matter of fact, I played the lead in *Oedipus* at UCLA, and played Hamlet and Romeo and all those things. That's what I was interested in when I went to New York to seek my fortune, but all I got was an extra part in [the 1937 Broadway produc-

Previous page: **Bridges over troubled waters: a posed shot for television's syndicated hit** *Sea Hunt.*

tion of] *Othello* with Walter Huston and Brian Aherne. But later on I did an adaptation of *Othello* and played Iago and directed it.

"A bunch of us New York actors couldn't get a job, and we started what *I* think was one of the first off-Broadway theaters. We found this old iron foundry and made it into a theater and put on about five plays. We were pretty well received—the big-time critics came down and reviewed us, and were very kind to us. It was there that the owners of a place called Green Mansions saw us and hired us. And so I was acting and directing and producing and *everything* there at Green Mansions, which was up in the Catskills. Sidney Buchman, who was the right-hand man to Harry Cohn at Columbia at the time, saw me in quite a few different things, and he felt that I had talent. He arranged for a screen test with Columbia, and my wife helped me—she played the gal in the test that I made. As a result of the test, I got started in pictures."

Although Bridges grew to miss stage work during the long motion picture and television career that ensued, he is quick to admit that "I did get kind of disenchanted with the stage because, on a couple of the plays that I was in, the atmosphere wasn't as good as I'd have liked it to be. And if a play 'runs,' if it's a success, you [the cast] are on top of one another for a year or two. There's a lot of backbiting that sometimes goes on. But it all depends on what kind of company you're in. Some of 'em were just wonderful, a lot of fun." Of course, once Bridges became established in pictures, there was a second consideration as well. "The other gamble that you have to think about is whether you want to take several months out of your life to do a play—and give up the possibility of doing a picture that might come up and mean a lot more money *[laughs]*. But the stage is still exciting, and certainly a great way to get started. When you've got a base like the theater, it always puts you in good stead working in pictures."

His stage background notwithstanding, Bridges's screen career got off to a fairly slow start at Columbia. Although the studio had him working constantly (almost 50 films in just four years, beginning in 1941 with *The Lone Wolf Takes a Chance*), they cast him in mainly minor roles in small, now-forgotten pictures: *I Was a Prisoner on Devil's Island, The Medico of Painted Springs, Two Latins from Manhattan, Sing for Your Supper,* even a two-reeler with the Three Stooges. ("Columbia got their money's worth out of me, you can believe that!") He played his first "fantastic" film role in the company's supernatural comedy *Here Comes Mr. Jordan* (1941), as the pilot of a Heaven-bound airplane, and made his horror film debut in Universal's *Strange Confession* (1945), an entry in the studio's heavy-handed Inner Sanctum series. Of the film's star Lon Chaney, Jr., Bridges recalls, "I enjoyed working with him very much. Of course, I'd been a great admirer of his father's. [Chaney, Jr.] was very sweet, very nice. The picture might not have been too much to brag about, but he was a very pleasant man to work with."

By this mid-forties period, Bridges was gone from Columbia and freelancing, landing two of this best early roles in *A Walk in the Sun* (1945), a thoughtful character study of men in war, and *Home of the Brave* (1949), with Bridges as the longtime chum of a black soldier (James Edwards) coping with racism during World War II. Then it was on to science fiction, as Bridges starred in the first postwar outer space adventure, *Rocketship X-M*.

Years before the expression "race to space" denoted the competition between the United States and the Soviet Union, two Hollywood moviemakers were locked in a competition of their own. Producer George Pal was taking pains with his production of *Destination Moon*: spending well over a half-million dollars on the film, working with scientists and space travel experts, creating an avalanche of advance publicity. B movie maven Robert L. Lippert decided that his company could quickly knock out a half-alike film, beat Pal to the finish line and take advantage of his rival's initiative and costly promotion. Lippert's film was *Rocketship X-M*.

"I don't know how much artistic value Lippert gave to a piece," Bridges recalls, "but he was crazy about motion pictures, and had seen just about every one that was ever made. Most of the things he did were the so-called B pictures of the day, but he made his impression on the business, I think. With *Rocketship X-M,* we *did* beat our competitor, *Destination Moon*. And they paid a *lot* more for their production. We kind of took advantage of the publicity that they were putting out—people weren't quite sure whether they were seeing *that* picture or *our* picture."

Lifting off from the Government Proving Grounds in White Sands, New Mexico, the multistage *RXM (Rocketship Expedition Moon)* was the first manned rocket into space, with a lunar landing and exploration planned. But a storm of meteors sends the rocket off in a new direction at incredible velocity, toward Mars. Taking advantage of the opportunity, the crew of five—pilot Bridges, designer John Emery, chemist Osa Massen, navigator Hugh O'Brian and engineer Noah Beery, Jr.—land and (in red-tinted scenes) scout the planet's barren surface, finding evidence of a long-ago civilization destroyed by atomic war. Savage Martian cave dwellers attack, killing Emery and Beery and wounding O'Brian. The survivors escape aboard the *RXM,* but a fuel shortage spells disaster. After shortwaving a full report to base, Bridges and Massen declare their newfound love for one another as the rocket plunges to a devastating crash landing on Earth.

"I begged the director not to shoot that love scene, when we're plummeting to the Earth and we pour out our hearts to one another," Bridges asserts. "I told him, 'You know, at a time like that, it just doesn't make sense.' It seemed so wrong to me to destroy the illusion; I was sure people would laugh at it. But he insisted, and who knows whether he was right or not."

The director, Kurt Neumann, is best recalled today for his science fiction films such as *Rocketship X-M*, *Kronos* and *The Fly*, but Bridges mostly remembers him as "a man who believed we had to do it fast *[laughs]*. We had

Lloyd Bridges got a taste of approaching "star"dom playing the top role in 1950's science fiction classic *Rocketship X-M*.

a very short schedule, I think maybe ten days or something like that. When we went out on location to film the scenes of Mars, we went out to Death Valley, and we had to put on our wardrobe and makeup en route, in the *plane,* so that as soon as the plane landed, we were ready to go to work right away.

   "Everything went smoothly and fast [in the Death Valley scenes]. It *had* to—or else they'd just skip the scene. I always felt that we should never have

Bridges' various story and directorial suggestions regarding *Rocketship X-M* were all treated with equal respect: Every last one was ignored! (Hugh O'Brian, Osa Massen and Bridges pictured.)

seen any of the Martians, they should have been just shadows. Imagination is stronger than actually seeing. (Not many of my suggestions were taken, as you may have noticed!) But I did think that the red tinting of the Martian scenes was a good idea, and Death Valley turned out to be a good location for us. It looked a bit like what we later found out that the Moon was like."

The *Rocketship X-M* spaceship interiors, Bridges continues, were shot "in the studio. I don't know how much of that [aeronautical equipment] was real; it was before its time, so I guess they figured they could be pretty freethinking about it. They were a bit crude, all of the *Rocketship X-M* effects, when you look at 'em today."

Bridges also remembers the cast of *Rocketship X-M* as a "very congenial" group of actors. "Osa Massen we don't see much of lately, but for quite a while we kept in touch. She was a very sweet person; she had been an editor for some time before she became an actress. She had a fascinating kind of personality, I thought, and she was a beautiful girl. In fact, Hugh O'Brian was very much in love with her—I guess we *all* were *[laughs]!* John Emery was quite the Shakespearean actor, always spouting Shakespeare, and as a matter of fact, a lot of people felt he was very much like John Barrymore. I remember that he kind of patterned himself after Barrymore to a certain extent; he always had some sort of Barrymore-like comment to make about everything. I think he was trying to figure out how he found himself in the desert, among the rocks, making *Rocketship X-M*, when he should have been in the theater doing Shakespeare!"

While many actors squawk about latter-day tampering with vintage films, Bridges has a casual reaction to news that new special effects scenes for *Rocketship X-M* were shot in the seventies. "Well, if it improved the film, I guess it doesn't matter," he says with a shrug. "It's the same kind of thing people are saying about colorization. With some of the classics, I think colorization would be a mistake. But for something like *Sea Hunt*, I think colorization would be an improvement. The first two *Sea Hunt* pilots that we did were in color, but because of the fact that they were going to cost a few thousand bucks more [per episode] to make 'em in color, the producers decided they didn't want to take the gamble."

Bridges adds quickly that the people behind *Rocketship X-M* had no idea that it would become any sort of classic. "I'm not sure that it has—*has* it? Well, because it was one of the first films of its sort, I guess it might have. I don't remember that it did my career much good. It was considered a B picture, and you never make much of an impression on the industry if you're in a B picture. Not even if you're in a good one." Does he consider *Rocketship X-M* "a good one"? "I like it, except that last love scene continues to bother me. I just can't imagine that any two people would be that calm about it all."

Another strong role came via producer Stanley Kramer's *High Noon* (1952), with Bridges as a conniving deputy who threatens not to back up town marshal Gary Cooper when outlaws invade their quiet Western town. But after *High Noon* came allegations that Bridges had been at one time involved with the Communist Party. After an FBI clearance, he resumed work, but once again he was in the clutches of the B moviemakers. Robert Lippert, producer of *Rocketship X-M*, was one who kept Bridges gainfully employed.

"Lippert was a lot of fun, a real promoter, a jolly, rotund kind of guy. I did several pictures for him; I especially remember one called *The Tall Texan* [1953] with Marie Windsor, Lee J. Cobb and Luther Adler. We were often rewriting that script the night before we were going to shoot, and Lee Cobb and Luther Adler, I guess because of their background in the Group Theater, were pretty adept at coming up with lines. So they were writing themselves into a lot more scenes *[laughs]*. We told 'em that was great, that we appreciated being able to take advantage of the tremendous talent they both had, but that we had better change the title to *The Short Texans [laughs]*."

Other producers who hired Bridges included England's Hammer Films and low-budget Hollywood maverick Roger Corman. Hammer's made-in-Spain *Deadly Game* (1954), according to Bridges, "was a lot of fun because it was a pleasure working with the English actors—they're always so good." And Corman, who directed Bridges in AIP's *Apache Woman,* "didn't know too much about directing at the time, and *[laughs]* I sort of pulled him through the whole thing. And I felt that I never got any thanks from him at all. He was one of the few guys I've worked with that I felt was very selfish—someone who wanted good results but didn't care how he got 'em."

Bridges's most enduring claim to fame remains *Sea Hunt* (1958–61), the Ivan Tors teleseries that grew in popularity until it became the country's most successful syndicated show. The series' one regular was Bridges as Mike Nelson, a one-time navy frogman who specialized in freelance underwater investigation. "When I first met Ivan Tors, I found out that he had seen a film of mine called *16 Fathoms Deep* [1948], where I played a sponge diver—'hardhat' diving gear. The whole interview, he didn't even ask me if I knew how to swim *[laughs]*. But he was a wonderful man. He was very smitten with all the latest things that science had to offer, and he incorporated most of that stuff in our shows.

"We started out filming the underwater stuff for *Sea Hunt* in the tank at Marineland out here. (They've torn it all down since.) Then we shot the topside scenes all up and down the coast nearby—Santa Monica piers, Malibu piers and so on. The underwater stuff for the first six episodes or so was done at the Marineland tank, but it got so that we recognized the same fish going by all the time *[laughs]*—we had to change the topography underwater. So we went to Nassau and shot underwater at a place called Lyford Cay. Lyford Cay turned out to be a beautiful place to do underwater photography. We'd do about eight [episodes' worth of topside scenes] and then go to Nassau and do underwater stuff for the eight."

Teaching Bridges the ins and outs of diving was done quickly, and not exactly by the book. "I had swum quite a bit in the ocean, 'cause we always had a place on the beach, but I didn't know anything about diving. So Courtney Brown [Bridges' underwater double] checked me out in a pool for one day, and the next day they threw me in the ocean *[laughs]!* That was all new and very exciting to me—it was a whole new world, as it was to everyone who saw the show." Another side benefit to having his own television series was being able to provide occasional employment to his acting sons, Beau and Jeff. "Yeah, they both got their feet wet in the business on *Sea Hunt,* and so did my daughter Lucinda."

Sea Hunt and other television tours of duty kept Bridges off the big screen throughout the late fifties and early sixties, and when he returned, it was in another subaqueous Ivan Tors adventure, *Around the World Under the Sea.* Introduced with a foreword by astronaut M. Scott Carpenter ("The sea is a tough adversary—much more hostile an environment than space"), the MGM production centered around the crew of the nuclear-powered submarine *Hydronaut* and their efforts to anchor earthquake sensors in strategic pressure points on the ocean floor. The premise may have been earthquakes but the film itself was less than earthshaking. "We did that in Miami, at Ivan Tors' studio there. David McCallum was in it, [Keenan] Wynn, the pretty English girl from *Goldfinger* [Shirley Eaton], Gary Merrill—they had a good cast for that one.

"The director was Andrew Marton, who did some of the *Sea Hunt*s, and who also directed my son Beau in (practically) his first movie, a Jon Hall thing called *Zamba* [aka *Zamba the Gorilla,* 1949]. The acting bug had bitten Beau, even that young. I remember on *Zamba* they gave us the script and I told him the story. And when Andrew Marton interviewed Beau, he asked, 'Are there any questions about the script? Is there anything that bothers you at all? Being with the gorillas and all that—does that worry you?' Beau said, 'No, but the thing that *does* bother me is when I have to parachute out of the burning plane.' He thought he'd have to do it himself—but he was ready regardless *[laughs]*!"

Another Bridges teleseries, *The Loner,* premiered on CBS in September 1965 and disappeared from the airwaves the following April. Bridges has fond memories of the short-lived program, and of writer Rod Serling. "I loved that man. It was a shame that he didn't last longer. He was a beautiful human being as well as a very talented writer—one of the most talented writers that we had in TV. I thought *The Loner* was a good show, and that it had an interesting format. It was just after the Civil War and I was an ex–Union officer trying to 'find myself'—I was very disappointed about the way the world was shaping up. I was restless, kept moving all the time, just me and my horse (a beautiful black stallion, a five-gaited American saddle bred). We had some very good scripts because Rod Serling was on top of it all."

Other Bridges series include *The Lloyd Bridges Show, San Francisco International Airport* and *Joe Forrester,* not to mention a host of television movies. Bridges, who explored Mars in *Rocketship X-M,* was cast as an extraterrestrial himself in ABC's movie *The Love War* (1970) with Angie Dickinson. "In that one, the idea was that, to save a lot of lives, there was going to be a war between my planet and the Earth, and it was settled with just about three of us. Angie Dickinson played a character with whom I fell in love. But she played a dirty

A series of outrageous movie comedies (such as *Hot Shots!* pictured 'ear) have made Bridges recognizable to a whole new generation of fans.

trick on me — she led me to believe that she was just a regular, normal gal, but instead she was an alien. And in the end, she shot me and I wound up in a puddle *[laughs]!*"

Above all, Lloyd Bridges just keeps on working, in movies, on television, and in seemingly every miniseries (*Roots*, *Movieola*, *East of Eden*, *The Blue and the Gray*, *George Washington* and *North and South, Book II*, just to name some). And the end, apparently, is nowhere in sight, with Bridges just recently winning yet more new fans with his portrayal of the addled Admiral Benson in *Hot Shots!* and *Hot Shots! Part Deux*, the smash-hit send-ups from the codirectors of *Airplane!* "*Hot Shots!* was a spoof on the Air Force, completely mad, a wonderful comedy, I thought. And as a matter of fact, deck scenes for the aircraft carrier in *Hot Shots!* were shot on the very spot where Marineland used to stand — where we used to film the underwater scenes for *Sea Hunt*. For *Hot Shots!* the ocean was in the distance, and so it saved a lot of expense and a lot of time; we'd have had to go back and forth on a boat to do it on a real carrier. And the navy wasn't too anxious to cooperate with us on that one, anyway—the film didn't paint a very flattering picture of the navy!"

LLOYD BRIDGES FILMOGRAPHY

Dancing Feet (Republic, 1936)
Freshman Love (Warner Bros., 1936)
The Lone Wolf Takes a Chance (Columbia, 1941)
The Royal Mounted Patrol (Columbia, 1941)
I Was a Prisoner on Devil's Island (Columbia, 1941)
Our Wife (Columbia, 1941)
Three Girls about Town (Columbia, 1941)
Sing for Your Supper (Columbia, 1941)
You Belong to Me (Columbia, 1941)
They Dare Not Love (Columbia, 1941)
The Son of Davy Crockett (Columbia, 1941)
Here Comes Mr. Jordan (Columbia, 1941)
The Medico of Painted Springs (Columbia, 1941)
Two Latins from Manhattan (Columbia, 1941)
Honolulu Lu (Columbia, 1941)
Harmon of Michigan (Columbia, 1941)
Canal Zone (Columbia, 1942)
Harvard Here I Come (Columbia, 1942)
Tramp Tramp Tramp (Columbia, 1942)
Counter Espionage (Columbia, 1942)
Cadets on Parade (Columbia, 1942)
Pardon My Gun (Columbia, 1942)
Riding through Nevada (Columbia, 1942)
Sweetheart of the Fleet (Columbia, 1942)
Alias Boston Blackie (Columbia, 1942)
A Man's World (Columbia, 1942)
Stand By All Networks (Columbia, 1942)
The Great Glover (Columbia short, 1942)
Blondie Goes to College (Columbia, 1942)

Shut My Big Mouth (Columbia, 1942)
Flight Lieutenant (He's My Old Man) (Columbia, 1942)
Atlantic Convoy (Columbia, 1942)
Talk of the Town (Columbia, 1942)
Riders of the Northland (Columbia, 1942)
Underground Agent (Columbia, 1942)
West of Tombstone (Columbia, 1942)
The Wife Takes a Flyer (A Yank in Dutch) (Columbia, 1942)
North of the Rockies (Columbia, 1942)
The Spirit of Stanford (Columbia, 1942)
The Daring Young Man (Columbia, 1942)
Commandos Strike at Dawn (Columbia, 1942)
They Stooge to Conga (Columbia short, 1943)
Sahara (Columbia, 1943)
His Wedding Scare (Columbia short, 1943)
The Heat's On (Columbia, 1943)
Passport to Suez (Columbia, 1943)
Hail to the Rangers (Illegal Rights) (Columbia, 1943)
Destroyer (Columbia, 1943)
A Rookie's Cookie (Columbia short, 1943)
Crime Doctor's Strangest Case (Columbia, 1943)
Once Upon a Time (Columbia, 1944)
Riding West (Columbia, 1944)
She's a Soldier, Too (Columbia, 1944)
Louisiana Hayride (Columbia, 1944)
The Master Race (RKO, 1944)
Saddle Leather Law (Columbia, 1944)
Mr. Whitney Had a Notion (MGM short, 1944)
A Walk in the Sun (20th Century–Fox, 1945)
Secret Agent X-9 (Universal serial, 1945)

Thunderbolt (narrator; Army Air Force/Monogram documentary, 1945)

Miss Susie Slagle's (Paramount, 1945)

Strange Confession (The Missing Head) (Universal, 1945)

Abilene Town (United Artists, 1946)

Canyon Passage (Universal, 1946)

Ramrod (United Artists, 1947)

The Trouble with Women (Paramount, 1947)

Unconquered (Paramount, 1947)

Secret Service Investigator (Republic, 1948)

16 Fathoms Deep (Monogram, 1948)

Moonrise (Republic, 1948)

Red Canyon (Universal, 1949)

Hideout (Republic, 1949)

Home of the Brave (United Artists, 1949)

Calamity Jane and Sam Bass (Universal, 1949)

Trapped (Eagle-Lion, 1949)

Colt .45 (Thundercloud) (Warner Bros., 1950)

Rocketship X-M (Lippert, 1950)

The White Tower (RKO, 1950)

The Sound of Fury (Try and Get Me) (United Artists, 1950)

Little Big Horn (Lippert, 1951)

Three Steps North (United Artists, 1951)

The Whistle at Eaton Falls (Columbia, 1951)

High Noon (United Artists, 1952)

Plymouth Adventure (MGM, 1952)

Last of the Comanches (Columbia, 1952)

The Tall Texan (Lippert, 1953)

City of Bad Men (20th Century–Fox, 1953)

The Kid from Left Field (20th Century–Fox, 1953)

The Limping Man (Lippert, 1953)

Deadly Game (Third Party Risk) (Lippert, 1954)

Pride of the Blue Grass (Allied Artists, 1954)

Wichita (Allied Artists, 1955)

Apache Woman (American Releasing [AIP], 1955)

Wetbacks (Bob Banner Associates/Realart/Gibraltar, 1956)

The Rainmaker (Paramount, 1956)

Ride Out for Revenge (United Artists, 1957)

The Goddess (Columbia, 1958)

Around the World Under the Sea (MGM, 1966)

Attack on the Iron Coast (United Artists, 1968)

Daring Game (Paramount, 1968)

The Happy Ending (United Artists, 1969)

To Find a Man (Sex and the Teenager; The Boy Next Door) (Columbia, 1972)

Running Wild (Deliver Us from Evil) (Golden Circle, 1973)

Scuba (narrator; Caribbean Films, 1973)

Behind the Iron Mask (The Fifth Musketeer) (Columbia, 1977)

Mission Galactica: The Cylon Attack (Universal, 1979)

Bear Island (Columbia, 1980)

Airplane! (Paramount, 1980)

Airplane II: The Sequel (Paramount, 1982)

Weekend Warriors (Hollywood Air Force) (The Movie Store, 1986)

The Wild Pair (Trans World Entertainment, 1987)

Tucker: The Man and His Dream (Paramount, 1988)

Cousins (Paramount, 1989)

Winter People (Columbia, 1989)

Joe versus the Volcano (Warner Bros., 1990)

Hot Shots! (20th Century–Fox, 1991)

Honey, I Blew Up the Kid (Buena Vista, 1992)

Hot Shots! Part Deux (20th Century–Fox, 1993)

Blown Away (MGM, 1994)

In as far as I see it, Creature from the Black Lagoon *was just another movie, just another job. I've done many things since then that I am much more proud of. But I've gotten more reaction out of the Creature thing than anything else. I guess that's life!*

Ricou Browning

IN THE MINDS OF SCIENCE FICTION film fans, there are not many actors who are tied as closely to a single role as Ricou Browning, the extraordinary swimmer who donned the scaly foam rubber suit of the *Creature from the Black Lagoon*. Browning played the role three times, in *Creature* and its two sequels, before going on to become one of the industry's most capable underwater stunt coordinators and directors of underwater sequences (as well as doing plenty of other film work topside), but the tight link between himself and the Gill Man role exists to this day. Not exactly proud but certainly not unhappy with his major claim to fame, Ricou Browning relives his Creature past (and other subaqueous adventures).

Born in Fort Pierce, Florida, in 1930, Ricou (pronounced Rico) grew up in nearby Jansen Beach and got a career start high diving and springboard diving in local water shows. By his early twenties, he was producing underwater shows at Weeki Wachee Springs and topside water shows at Rainbow Springs and other locations. A call from a coworker first alerted Browning to the fact that Universal Pictures was planning to photograph portions of their newest science fiction thriller (initially titled *Black Lagoon*) in the area.

"I was in college when that happened. A friend of mine who I used to work *with* and *for* phoned me and said that he had received a call about showing some Hollywood people a place called Wakulla Springs, which is south of Tallahassee. He couldn't make it, so he asked me if I wouldn't mind showing it to them. I said fine. So these people called me and told me when they were coming into town, and I met 'em at the airport in Tallahassee. It was Jack Arnold and the cameraman, 'Scotty' Welbourne, and a couple other people, I just don't remember who they were. Anyway, I took them to Wakulla Springs and showed 'em the area, and they loved it. 'Scotty' had his underwater camera and he asked me if I would get in the water with him and swim in front of the camera so they could get some perspective as to sizes of things with the background. I said sure, so I did. We had dinner that night, talked a little bit about the Springs, and they left.

"Later I received a call from Jack Arnold, and he said, 'We've tested a lot of people for this part, but I'd like to have you play the Creature—I like your swimming. Do you want to do it?' I said sure. So that was it."

The next stop, of course, was a trip to Universal Studios in California and the usual messy assortment of body molds, costume tests and time-consuming trial and error, with designers Jack Kevan and Tom Case doing most of the work. "It was a matter of making molds—body, face and so forth. Then, after molding the pieces, they made a latex suit, like a leotard, and they glued the pieces onto the latex. It was like a football uniform in the sense that they had thigh areas that they'd glue on, then the fin in the back, on and on—they piecemealed it together. They did it with the latex suit on *me* to begin with,

Previous page: The Man in the Foam Rubber Suit, Ricou Browning, doffs his Gill Man mask for a photo-op. (Notice the snaps along the costume's "collarbone.")

Browning tests out the Gill Man suit in the studio tank.

but then the glue started burning me badly; it went through the leotard and onto my body, and as it started setting up, it got very hot. So they made another mold of my body and then molded it onto that. The suit was foam rubber with a latex skin."

A first Creature suit, which Browning describes as "looking like a sausage," was quickly rejected. "It was kind of shaped like a man (of course) and it was just more streamlined: less scales, less fins, and the head was more like you were wearing a tight stocking over your face. A little bit more human in appearance."

Underwater test footage was shot of Browning in Universal's back lot tank, not only for showing to studio execs but also to allow Browning to gain experience swimming in the cumbersome outfit. "After the suit was finished, we would go in the water and I'd swim around. Then I would tell 'em what I needed for my purposes, and they would revamp the suit a little. Once we got it where we wanted it, we photographed it in the tank and then showed it to the studio heads, Jim Pratt and Ed Muhl, as well as the producer, William Alland."

Although the Creature's "look" had been agreed upon, numerous problems still had to be overcome, like how to get Browning to stay underwater in his buoyant foam rubber suit. "To get negatively buoyant, I had 'em make me a thing that was kind of like an armor vest. It was lead and it form fitted my upper body, from just below my neck down to just about the navel. I also had some lead plates that I wore in the Creature feet, and then I had little pockets on the back right side and left side, where I could insert a few weights, depending on whether I was in salt water or fresh water, because the buoyancy in fresh water and salt water varies. It was kind of like swimming in your overcoat.

"The most difficult part of the entire process was vision. I tried to wear little goggles, like pearl divers wear, but once you got water in the goggles, there was no way to get it out. That just didn't work. And then we tried a face mask, but that made the face of the Creature protrude too far. So we went without anything, and I just saw with my naked eyes. The eyes of the Creature mask were a couple of inches beyond my eyes, so it was kind of like looking through a keyhole. And looking through an underwater keyhole without a mask on, your vision is blurred—*very* blurred. It was very awkward seeing, and a lot of it was kind of hit and miss."

Yet another minor dilemma presented itself when Universal decided that at six feet, Browning was not tall enough to play a sufficiently menacing Gill Man in the underwater encounters with the movie's heroes and heroine. "We decided that when we did the underwater scenes, that we would scale the doubles for the 'human' actors down in size. In other words, if the stars were six feet tall, the doubles would have to be five-something. That way, I would appear much larger."

James C. Havens flew to Florida in the second week of October 1953 to direct the underwater second unit scenes with Browning and a trio of doubles. The underwater doubles for leading players Richard Carlson and Richard Denning were college students from Florida State University, and the double for Julie Adams was Ginger Stanley, a "mermaid" at Weeki Wachee. Jack Arnold—on whom praise for the direction of the underwater scenes has been heaped by science fiction film reviewers—was thousands of miles away, directing his portions of *Creature* at Universal, while Havens put Browning and the doubles through their underwater paces in Wakulla Springs.

An incredible swimmer, Browning still required underwater safety men, air hoses and a "distress signal" to ensure a speedy (and safe) production. "In order to breathe, I did what we call hose breathing. You have an oxygen tank or, coming from the surface, just an air hose. I'd stick the air hose in my mouth and breathe from it, like you would drink water from a hose in your backyard. There's kind of a little knack to it, but I learned it when I was very young, at Wakulla Springs, before they ever invented Aqualungs; we used it in the water shows at Weeki Wachee Springs. That's how the mermaids there would get air. Anyway, it was something I did very naturally, and so it came easy for me. I could insert the hose in the mouth of the Creature, then I'd have to go a couple of inches further, to get to my own mouth and then breathe.

"Let's say we were ready to do a scene: I would have a safety man with me and I'd be breathing, and when I was ready to go, I'd give the cameraman the okay sign — hand signals — and I'd keep breathing. When he would give me the signal he was rolling the camera, I would release the air hose, giving it back to the safety man, and then (if it was just a swim-through) I would swim by camera. On the other side, there'd be another safety man who'd give me a different air hose. So I had safety men in various places in order to get air."

If Browning got into trouble, a very basic signal was used to alert his coworkers. "If I got to where I was really desperate for air, I would just stop everything and go limp, and the safety man would swim in to me and give me an air hose. Or if I was in a fight scene, I would just stop fighting and not do anything, and then they would come in and give me an air hose. I had people that I had worked with underwater for years prior to this, so I had a lot of confidence in them. They were very good and it worked fairly well.

"We were shooting out in the middle of the Spring, and I had to go to the bathroom. They were going to take me ashore in a boat, but I said, no, I was gonna swim over. I swam underwater — sometimes it was easier to swim underwater in that suit than it was to swim on the surface. I swam to the ladder that was on the dock next to shore. I came up the ladder, and there was a lady and a little girl standing there. I came out, and this little girl started screaming. She started screaming and running and the mother went after her, and I went after *both* of 'em, trying to say, 'Hey, hey, it's okay, it's okay!' But me saying, 'It's okay!' didn't do a thing *[laughs]*. They took off, and that's the last I saw of 'em! But I never went out of my way to try and scare anybody, no; from then on, I made sure I kept the head off whenever I came ashore."

While the Gill Man suit is viewed by Creature fans as a marvel of design and execution, Browning is dismissive of the costume in comparing it to today's monster outfits. "Compared to what they do today as far as makeup and monsters' faces and so forth, the Creature would be considered the Model T. For instance, I had a little squeeze bulb that I held in my hand, and the tube from it ran up my arm. I could squeeze that and make the gills fluctuate in and out. I could move the lips a little by moving my chin, but the eyes I had no control over whatsoever. It was very crude compared to what they do today."

Universal apparently had great faith in *Creature from the Black Lagoon,* launching plans for a sequel even before the original's release. Lensed under the title *Return of the Creature,* the follow-up film *Revenge of the Creature* was made in midsummer 1954 — a welcome turn of events for Browning, who shot the first film during a Florida cold spell. "For my part, shooting *Revenge of the Creature* in the summer made it easier. It can get quite cold in Florida, and that suit's wet continuously. So, when it's wet and cold, *you're* wet and cold. On [the original] *Creature,* everybody was trying to be nice and they kept

giving me shots of brandy. And soon, they had a drunk Creature on their hands, so I had to cut *that* out! *Revenge* was easier. In the summer, you got hot, but you could pour water down the suit, or stay in the water."

Most of Browning's scenes in *Revenge of the Creature* were shot in a tank at the Marineland Studios, on the ocean south of St. Augustine. "On *Revenge,* we'd drive every morning from St. Augustine to Marineland, and on the way, there was a public beach. Charlie McNabb, one of the safety guys, had a bright idea: 'Why don't we take the suit back with us this weekend, and we'll take you out in the ocean? You jump in and swim to shore and come up, and we'll see what happens!' I said, 'Well, that'll be fine, but some idiot will think they can shoot me, and do it!' So, no, we didn't go through with that *[laughs]!*"

Headquarters for the troupe was a Marineland motel where, Browning concedes with *Revenge* stars John Agar and Lori Nelson, cast and crew whooped it up in grand style. "We used to have water fights and God knows what at the motel, big luaus on the beach—we had a great time. The cast and the crew just got along great, and it was a fun show."

Not even the fact that Browning, Agar and Nelson had to share the Marineland tank with sharks and other potentially dangerous deep-sea critters put a damper on things. "I really didn't have time to worry about 'em, I was too busy getting the air and taking of myself. I did have one thing happen: I had gone in the water and I was sitting down on a big anchor. They had the chain around my ankle in that scene, but I could get out of it anytime I wanted. Anyway, I was sitting there and I felt something tug on my foot. I looked down and, glory, it was a big turtle—he had taken a big hunk out of the heel of the Creature's foot and he was swimming off with it. Luckily, he didn't get *me*—he got the foam rubber, and he was trying to eat it. I realized that this was my last pair of flippers—I wore the other ones out, 'cause the way you swim and hit things, you tear 'em up pretty much. This was the last pair, so I got out of the chain, swam up fast as I could and I was yelling to Jack Kevan, but he couldn't understand me. So I finally swam over there and he finally understood me: 'The turtle's got the heel of the foot!' So everybody dove in the water and they went after the turtle *[laughs]!* They did get the piece back, and then I had to come out and they had to rinse it in fresh water and glue it back on."

As far as the land scenes shot at Marineland are concerned, Browning dismisses the recent rumor that Clint Eastwood—a budding bit player at the time, seen as a lab assistant in *Revenge*—squeezed into the scaly suit for some of the landlocked action. "The [land Gill Man] was a guy by the name of Tom Hennesy (nice guy). Hennesy was in the scene in the Lobster House in Jacksonville, and the reason I remember is because he had an alligator in the bathtub *[laughs].* We were rooming together, I walked in and found that he had

Opposite: The underwater camera crew catches Browning solo.

bought an alligator and stuck it in the tub. A cayman, actually — a South American alligator — 'cause you can't buy alligators."

The Lobster House scene, where the Gill Man (Hennesy) disrupts a jam session by crashing the party, was shot in Jacksonville, on the St. Johns River — but not without incident. "They used people from the insurance building next door as extras, and these people all came with their husbands, wives, girlfriends, whatever, all dressed in formal wear. They were shooting inside for about an hour and a half. I was sitting on top of the roof when suddenly I heard all this commotion. What had happened was, they had moved the arc lights up into the ceilings, and set off the sprinkler system. The entire bunch of people were just full of water and rust — the sprinkler system probably was never used, and was full of rusty water. So they had to wrap for the night."

Despite all the work Browning put in on the *Creature* movies, he was credited neither on-screen nor in publicity. "Universal's idea was, they didn't want people to think the Creature was human. When the second film came around, they called me again and I started to do the picture, and I said, 'Hey, I want to get credit for this, because it helps me to get other work.' We bickered and bickered — I think William Alland was involved, and Jim Pratt, and whoever else. They still didn't want to give credit, but they promised me that they'd get me publicity. So they started getting me interviews with people. And, sure enough, they really did — I must have been interviewed twenty times, by syndicated columnists, magazine writers, et cetera, et cetera. There were pictures and stories and a lot of publicity — they kept their word. But they still didn't give me credit *[laughs]*!"

While *Revenge of the Creature* was a slick-looking sequel overall, some of the underwater Gill Man scenes were slightly spoiled by the sight of a stream of bubbles floating up out of the top of the monster's head. "Well, that was unfortunate," admits Browning. "The Creature head fits over your head, and when you exhale as you're breathing inside, air goes up by your face and then goes up into the top of the head. Then it slowly goes up through that foam rubber — air is buoyant. Usually, I'd take a breath, give the air hose to the safety man, and then the safety man would grab the top of my head and squeeze it, and *I* would squeeze as much as *I* could (with those Creature hands, I couldn't do much). We were trying to squeeze all the air out of the top of the head, so that when I would go into the scene, no bubbles would be coming out. But sometimes we just didn't get 'em all out, and they'd come up out of the top during the scene."

Box office receipts for *Revenge of the Creature* called for a third Gill Man go-round, and *The Creature Walks Among Us* went into production in August 1955. By this point, however, Universal was beginning to economize in the

Opposite: **The Creature (Browning) and the Teamster from the Black Lagoon prepare for a scene.**

production of its science fiction films and the Gill Man was scaled down—quite literally—in this perfunctory sequel, in which its gills are accidentally destroyed by fire. Surgically converted into a land creature by screwy sawbones Jeff Morrow, the Gill Man was played on land by character actor Don Megowan, and Browning's underwater footage was minimal.

Returning to work at various Florida water shows, Browning got back into the swim of production a few years later as a result of an encounter with film and television producer Ivan Tors. "I worked for Ivan for about 15 years, and I wound up being president of his studios down here in Florida. He was a pretty great guy. The thing about him, more than anything else, is that once he got confidence in you as an employee of his, no matter who you were or what position you were in, he just let you go. He didn't stay on your back or anything. He and I got along famously. First I did three years of [Tors's television series] *Sea Hunt,* starting out as a stuntman. Courtney Brown doubled Lloyd Bridges, and in every show, Lloyd ran up against a heavy. Courtney did all the underwater for Lloyd and I did the underwater for all the heavies. They even started casting people that looked a little bit like me—dark hair, about the same size—because it made everything easier. Then Ivan did a show called *The Aquanauts* [aka *Malibu Run*], where I was the double for [series star] Keith Larsen, and Courtney started doubling the bad guys—that reversed our situation to where I was winning the fights and he was losing 'em! Courtney and I spent our whole career fighting each other *[laughs]!*"

In the early 1960s, Browning made another splash in the television/movie history books when he created *Flipper,* dolphin hero of two MGM feature films and four years' worth of episodic television. "That all started when I got the idea, as a publicity stunt, to go to South America and capture freshwater dolphin—they'd never been captured before. We formed an expedition over a period of a year, went to the Amazon, captured freshwater dolphin, brought them back to Silver Spring [a water park] and put them in the water there. We had 'em for about a year or so. In the process, I used to swim with them. Then I started thinking, they did a film about Lassie and a boy; why not do one with a *dolphin* and a boy? (In Grecian legends and so forth, they swam with dolphins.)

"I got together with Jack Cowden, who was a radio announcer in Ocala at the time, and we spent a couple of evenings jotting down an idea for a story. Then we thought about making the story into a book: I had the idea that if we did it into a book first, that I would have more protection if we went into making it as a movie. I flew to New York and spent about two weeks trying to peddle it as a book, and I got three or four companies interested—but none of them were interested enough to say, 'We'll do it.' So having known Ivan Tors, I got the bright idea to call him, get him to say he was considering it for a movie, then call a book company and say, 'I have someone interested in making it into a movie' to encourage *them* to make it into a *book.* Anyway, I called

Ivan and told him all about it, and I asked him if he would say that he was interested in it as a film. He said, 'Yeah, I'll say I'm considering it. But also send me a copy of it.' So I mailed him a copy, and sat back and waited to see if I'd hear anything from New York. About two weeks later, I got a call from Ivan, and he said, 'Let's make a movie,' and I said, 'What are you talkin' about?' He said, 'Let's make *Flipper.*' We did *Flipper* [1963] and after that *Flipper's New Adventure* [1964], then four years of *Flipper* on television."

A search for the right dolphin to play Flipper turned up nothing but the fact that aquarium-trained dolphins were frightened when humans joined them in the water. Browning, however, was undeterred. "During our travels, we went through the Keys and we found a guy named Milton Santini and his wife; he caught dolphins for a living and sold them to aquariums. But they had kept one dolphin, Mitzi, as a pet. When the other dolphins would arrive, they would see Mitzi feeding and they would start eating in captivity quicker than they would otherwise. I got in the water, Mitzi swam up right next to me and I put my arms on her—and as soon as that happened, we said, "*This* is the animal." Then we spent maybe six weeks working with the animal, trying to get her to do the things that we were going to need for the film.

"We knew nothing about [dolphin training], really, but we learned by hit and miss. I trained Mitzi down in Grassy Key, at a little motel with a natural pool coming into the center of the motel area from the sea. I had my son Ricky with me, he was nine years old at the time, and I was trying to get the animal used to a boy. And I couldn't figure out how he could ride her. I tried and tried to get something to happen, and I couldn't. But I had gotten her to retrieve a ball—several balls, as a matter of fact—and towels and whatever. And so one afternoon I got a bright idea: If I threw Ricky in the water like you'd throw a ball in the water, and say, 'Fetch!' maybe Mitzi would bring him back. I threw him in the water and I told Mitzi to fetch, and she swam over there and she grabbed a loop in his cutoff jeans and tried to pull him back. But he wasn't streamlined—it was kind of awkward. His arm fell on her back and I said, 'Hold her fin!' He held her fin—and she pulled him right to me. And from that day on, we had a boy riding a dolphin. Anyway, that was the process in which we trained her.

"After *Flipper* [the first movie], we didn't use her anymore. We got five dolphins from the Miami Seaquarium. They were new dolphins, all female—the reason we got females was that we heard that females were easier to train. We started training 'em, and the first one I was able to train was Suzy, and we used Suzy all through the *Flipper* series. I then acquired a bunch of trainers and I made a boy named Ric O'Feldman head trainer, and he trained another one called Kathy; about halfway through the series, we quit using Suzy and used Kathy. So actually there were three animals involved in all of the filming. You could do a book on it—they've only scratched the surface as to what you can do with dolphins. They're wonderful, wonderful animals."

Taking advantage of Browning's unique experience, the makers of *The Day of the Dolphin* (1973) hired him as technical adviser, but the association was short-lived. "When they got ready to film, Mike Nichols and I couldn't quite agree on things, so I left the film."

Fans of science fiction / action films also remember Browning's name from the credits of the James Bond adventure *Thunderball* (1965) as well as its 1983 remake, *Never Say Never Again*. "I got involved in *Thunderball* through Kevin McClory, who was one of the writers on it. He knew me and Ivan, and he had [Bond producer] 'Cubby' Broccoli call me. Kevin and I went over to London and we had four or five meetings and discussed what we were going to do, and they said, 'You got the job.'"

Shooting the underwater sequences in the Bahamas took three months, culminating with the harrowing aquatic free-for-all which remains the film's highpoint. "There aren't really many anecdotes I can tell you about it because it was so serious, because we had so many chances of somebody getting hurt. And we did have a few people hurt—nothing deadly or that serious, but it was a very serious shoot. In one scene Bond scuba-dives down and swims into a bomber that had crashed and sunk into the sea. We had caught a lot of sharks for this and other scenes. I was on the deck of a ship over the submerged plane and I said to one of the guys I work with, 'Big John, When Bond swims into the bomb bay, I want a shark coming down. Get a shark up in the bomb bay.' He said, 'What shark?' and I said, 'Get the biggest one.' So I was standing around on deck and John came back up and he said, 'The shark won't fit in the bomb bay. He's too big.' I said, 'Well, stick his tail in the pilot's cabin.' And John said, 'Are you kidding me?' *[Laughs.]* Well, we did it, and it worked out fine."

And series star Sean Connery? "Oh, he was a super guy, a gentleman and very professional. He's an excellent diver and did a very good job—he did all of his own stuff in close-ups, and we had doubles for the scenes where he was involved with sharks and so forth. He would have done whatever we asked him to do, but we didn't want to ask him to do stuff that was hairy." Browning's direction of the undersea segments helped *Thunderball* win the Academy Award for Special Visual Effects.

Film work has not been sparse for Browning in more recent years, either: He has been a director (*Island of the Lost, Salty* and more), second unit director (*Nobody's Perfekt, Caddyshack, Raise the Titanic!* and others), stunt coordinator (*The Heavenly Kid, Opposing Force*), stuntman (*The Six Million Dollar Man, The Bionic Woman*), writer (with Jack Cowden) of the 1980 science fiction film *Island Claws* and much more. "And I'm *still* directing; just recently, I finished a couple of commercials in the Bahamas."

With these credentials behind him, it is not surprising that Ricou Browning does not enjoy being primarily remembered as the Man in the Green Rubber Suit, but he's not about to make waves over it. "When we did the Creature films, no one ever thought they would remain popular; we thought, it was a movie, it's over and that's it. But it's a thing that just kind of lingers, and *[laughs]* nobody seems to forget it! Years later, I directed a feature called *Salty* [1975], about a sea lion. I put a lot of heart and soul into this film, and it was a good, G-rated family film, and it turned out real well. We were publicizing it and traveling with a Winnebago that we made for the sea lion to live in, and going to TV stations and so forth. Well, the PR people sent my résumé ahead of me to these different places. We'd go into these TV studios and I wanted to talk about *Salty,* but from my résumé they saw I had played the Creature, and all *they* wanted to talk about was the Creature! So I finally had to get the PR people to scratch that off, so I could talk about the film we just made *[laughs]!*"

Ricou Browning sets the record straight: "So you can get some kind of reality out of this picture, in as far as I see it, *Creature from the Black Lagoon* was just another movie, just another job. I've done many things since then that I am much more proud of. But I've gotten more reaction out of the Creature thing than anything else. I guess that's life *[laughs]!*"

The secret behind The Thing's *staying power?*
Gosh, I don't know. I cannot read
the public; I only know my own reactions.
When I saw it, I thought, "Ah, it's a good movie.
Thank God *it's a good movie!" Because,*
I confess, I really didn't know what *to expect!*

Robert Cornthwaite

FEW SCIENCE FICTION FILMS of the 1950s can compare to *The Thing from Another World* in the near brilliance of its writing and execution or in the opportunities it provided for some of the people involved. Apart from helping to establish the science fiction film genre in the fifties, it gave Christian Nyby an imposing initial directorial credit; made a fan favorite of star Kenneth Tobey; added to the legendary canon of producer (and de facto director) Howard Hawks; and even gave some early notoriety to James Arness, who played the space invader that terrorizes an Arctic base. But for film newcomer Robert Cornthwaite, the movie was more of a premature career peak than a stepping stone; he has been working constantly ever since, on the large and small screens as well as on the stage, but he has had few movie roles as meaty or as memorable as that of Dr. Arthur Carrington, the obsessive scientist who places the intellectual "carrot" Arness above the welfare of his fellow humans.

Born in St. Helen's, Oregon, Cornthwaite insists his first acting jobs happened "by accident, as I think it does to most actors. I have an older brother, one year older than I am, and Bill was my mentor in grammar school. He said, 'Don't let 'em get you into one of these school plays.' He had hated it, absolutely. So I took his word as gospel, and I carefully avoided it. When the school would send notes home, I wouldn't deliver 'em — I told the teachers, 'My mother doesn't want me to do that.' I don't think they really believed me, but they didn't force me to do it until the eighth grade, when I was about to graduate into high school. The teacher said, 'You can't get out of school without being in *one* play.' So I was in the Thanksgiving play, and had the deathless line, 'Thank God the ship has come!' I had this new thirteen-year-old voice, cracking all over the place most of the time, but I found that it was fine when I was on the stage *[laughs]*. And that hooked me — that was it. From then on, I was in plays wherever I could manage to be. I did my first work with professionals when I was eighteen, in a production of *Twelfth Night* up in Portland, on the Reed College campus. That was in 1935. My family moved to California in '35; as a matter of fact, the morning after we closed in *Twelfth Night,* we were on the road. (They weren't exactly waiting for me, but it coincided.) I worked on radio down here in Southern California."

Paramount showed what Cornthwaite calls "lukewarm interest" in signing him to a term contract, "but when they found I was 1-A on the draft status, that cooled that fast," he remembers. "Then there was the hiatus of almost four years in the air force [during World War II], three of which I spent overseas, which was really a great boon. They gave me the grand tour, let me tell you: We sailed from New York, around South Africa, put in at Durban and wound up in Egypt. (Of course, we didn't know where we were going till we got there.) We were flying air cover for the British Eighth Army; I was in a B-25 outfit, a radio gunner. Then they got me confused with a guy named Cornwall — leave it to the military to get things screwed up — and I wound up, off and on, with

Previous page: **Robert Cornthwaite in 1992.**

the RAF for the next three years, on detached service. It was a great adventure: We were all over the Mediterranean, we followed the Eighth Army west across the Sahara to Tunis, and linked up with the American forces there. Back with the British to Malta; then for the invasion of Sicily, I went *again* with the British. The Sicilian campaign, and then the Italian. Then I got into public relations—somebody found out I had worked in radio before the war, and they were setting up a new outfit called the Mediterranean Allied Air Forces, so I was in the headquarters of that, in public relations, and flying all over the place. Corsica, Sardinia—I covered the invasion of Southern France and got the Bronze Star for it. It was the adventure of my life."

Returning to Hollywood after the war resulted in what Cornthwaite calls "a terrible anticlimax. I found out that the people I knew in Hollywood radio had all gone in the four years that I was away. So I went back to radio announcing, which I had done as the bread-and-butter job: newscasting, disk jockeying, everything that came on your shift as a staff announcer. I did that, but got steadily more disenchanted with it, because there were very few acting opportunities. I did sneak off to Hollywood and used about half-a-dozen different names as an actor on network shows there, but I decided I wanted to be an actor full-time. So I just quit radio, cold.

"The agent who had handled me before the war—I told you about the Paramount deal that never came off—managed to sell me as a character actor. I was losing my hair by that time, and had always been a character actor anyhow. Within six months of quitting radio, I was doing pictures. That first year [1950], I did six movies, five of them before *The Thing*. And of course *The Thing* was a good, long period of employment, nearly five months on that."

Cornthwaite's involvement with the milestone science fiction film began with an interview at RKO with Howard Hawks and Christian Nyby (Hawks' longtime film editor), who would receive the "official" credit for direction of *The Thing*. "Then I started a picture called *Mark of the Renegade* [1951] at Universal, playing a Mexican. While I was working on that, Hawks decided he wanted to shoot a screen test, and Universal let me off to go over and shoot the screen test. It was supposed to be just a photographic test: They would shoot some film to see if I would photograph old enough for the role. They were shooting a number of tests on actors for the same part [Dr. Carrington], one after another. (Another actor up for the part was Philip Bourneuf, whom I later directed in a production of *Richard II*.) After they got me into makeup, Mr. Hawks said to me, 'We'd like to do it in sound because I want Howard Hughes to hear your voice.' So we did a test in sound, in *one* take, and I raced back to Universal, back to work. And I didn't hear anything for a few days. Then my agent brought the *[Thing]* script one day to this ramshackle place where I was living; he threw it down and said, 'Well, you've got the part.'"

RKO was at the time owned by Howard Hughes, the wealthy recluse who (disastrously) ran the studio by remote control. Cornthwaite, who never met or even saw Hughes during his acting stints at RKO, adds, "I heard rumors that he never actually set foot on the lot. He kept offices elsewhere and he met people in automobiles and things like that. Very secretive! But it was kind of funny, my Hughes connection. At the time, my mother was still living, down in Long Beach, and she was completely dependent on me—I'd go down on weekends and do the chores for her. I went down after that screen test (I still hadn't heard the results of it), and she wanted to know what had been happening during the week. I said I finished a picture at Universal, and I had a test at RKO and it sort of depended on what Howard Hughes said about it. She said, 'Howard Hughes? Is he from Texas?' I said, 'Yes, I believe so.' She said, 'Beaumont?' 'I don't know anything about Beaumont, but I've heard Houston.'

"She said, 'Well, of *course* Houston, that's where I *knew* him. How old is he?' I said, 'I haven't met him, but I guess he's probably in his late forties or around fifty now.' She said, 'No, no, no—too young. The Howard Hughes I knew would be much older than that,' and we dropped it. A couple of hours later, I was in the backyard doing something or other, and she came to the back door and said, 'But he had a *boy* named Howard, too!'

"This is the way it turned out: My mother's father was a building contractor and he had built the Southern Pacific railway stations across the South, among other things in his career. And he had done work building oil rigs for Howard Hughes, Sr., at Beaumont. Hughes would bring his little boy, six or eight years old, and my mother would mind him and play with him while the two fathers were doing business! So *she* knew him—but I never did!"

Production of *The Thing* began at RKO on October 25, 1950. On November 27, with RKO soundstage filming at an end, the company moved to the California Consumers downtown icehouse in Los Angeles. "That was where they'd shoot scenes where they had to have the breath showing; *Lost Horizon* [1937] was perhaps the first film shot in there, and then many pictures after. It's long since been destroyed. Then we did go up, just before Christmas time as I recall [December 9, 1950], to Montana, where they had built the huge set for the flying saucer sequence, and also the whole compound where the Arctic party was supposed to be—all the exteriors where the planes landed and so on. The locals made a big hoopla over us. Ken [Tobey] and Dewey [Martin] and I were adopted into the Blackfoot Tribe in a big ceremony with the chiefs, including the old chief who had signed the last treaty of peace between the Sioux nation and the United States. I couldn't believe he was still alive in 1950, but he was, a very dignified old man.

"Anyhow, we sat around doing *nothing*. We got acquainted with some of the local people, and a lady asked me, 'When are you going to start shooting?' I said, 'As soon as there's enough snow on the ground. We need eight or ten inches of virgin snowfall for what we need to shoot.' She said [*in a concerned voice*], 'Don't they *know* that the snow doesn't *stay* on the ground here?' It was a high plateau up there at Cut Bank, Montana; that's why the U.S. built a landing strip there for the takeoff to Alaska, because the snow is blown off by the winds. I told [associate producer] Eddie Lasker, who was putting up the money for the picture, and *[laughs]* it *disturbed* him—he couldn't deal with it. He said *[sputtering]*, 'N-n-no, we, we, we've got photographs, the snow stays on the ground here, it stays on the ground here, it stays on the ground here'—sort of an *incantation,* hoping it would happen! It never did—we never got a shot with actors. They did get a few brief shots with doubles. And then they had to rebuild the set in (I think it was) Minot, North Dakota; and they were *thinking* about building a set up in the Yukon (I don't think they ever did). But they did shoot some stuff in North Dakota, apparently, which I was not involved with at all, it was all doubles. I had about six doubles in that picture before it was done."

The fruitless stay at Cut Bank lasted, according to Cornthwaite, "a week or ten days, something like that. The whole cast was up there—that is, everybody that was concerned with the flying saucer scene. We shot that eventually in Encino, California, at the RKO Ranch. That was the last thing we shot, that was in early March of 1951, and they had a date in April that they *had* to have the film ready by, for exhibition at Radio City Music Hall. Dimitri Tiomkin, who did the score, was composing the music as we went along, toward the end. I met him when we got together and rehearsed for him this flying saucer scene, so that he could compose the score for it. He had, of course, been watching the dailies and the rough cut, so that he could time his music by each frame of film. When we met and shook hands, Dimi said, in his very thick Russian accent, 'Jesus Christ, you're just a boy!' He'd been used to the old man on screen!"

For that classic scene (in which Tobey's crew, Cornthwaite and his colleagues discover the flying saucer frozen beneath the Arctic ice), "a big expanse on the Ranch in Encino was where they built a huge backdrop which blended with the sky—at least, when you had the proper lenses on, and soft focus in the background/sharp focus in the front. It was simply done with fake snow against this huge cyclorama backdrop. I got an injured eye from that: They blew a mixture of Styrofoam and shaved ice in front of the wind machines for the snow stuff, and a bit of the Styrofoam stuck in my right eyeball. We got the shot *[laughs],* but I couldn't see out of that eye for twenty minutes afterwards, it was watering so much. That sort of stuff can happen very easily, and it's very painful. As a matter of fact, it pierced the eyeball in my case and formed what they call a pseudo-pterygium: A little bit of the eyeball structure extrudes through. It's visible now; it photographs. They could perform an operation in which they would slit the eyeball and tuck it back in; I said, 'No, thanks.'"

Wearing coats, hats and other gear beneath the California sun resulted in the expected discomfort for Cornthwaite and his fellow actors. "Well, March is not too bad, but it was no fun, I can tell you. It was sunny weather and there was not too much smog in those days in the Valley, and it was hard trying to play cold. I remember [actor] Bob Nichols was particularly good at playing cold. I thought, 'Well, Dr. Carrington, he wouldn't *allow* himself to be cold!'"

In addition to his Arctic raiment, Cornthwaite was also encumbered by a phony beard and other makeup in order to play the middle-aged Carrington. "They bleached my hair so that it would photograph gray, and I used to have to get to the studio at a quarter to five on the days when they had to touch up the bleach job," the actor recalls. "I'd go into women's hairdressing, where they did the bleaching. Janet Leigh, Gloria DeHaven and Ann Miller were shooting *Two Tickets to Broadway* [1951] at the same time, and while they were getting their hair done, *my* hairdresser was doing the bleach job on me. Ann Miller always called me 'the Professor,' because she couldn't remember my name. By the way, in the sequence where we're out around the flying saucer, *that* is my own beard, and that's the only sequence in the picture where it is. I had let it grow, thinking, 'Well, I can always shave it off, and they can paste the other one back on again.' Makeup man Lee Greenway decided that I had enough beard to work. I had to bleach it, because my beard was sort of a bright red in those days, red and black."

The excellent script of *The Thing,* credited to Charles Lederer, may also feature contributions by William Faulkner, whom Ken Tobey briefly met prior to the start of shooting. "I heard that rumor, too, but I don't know whether it was true," Cornthwaite says. "Quite possibly it was, because he did a lot of things for Hawks. At that time, he was working for several months there on the script of *The Left Hand of God,* which Hawks never made—he sold it to 20th, and Henry Hathaway directed it with Humphrey Bogart [in 1955]. Faulkner fascinated me, because I had read a great deal of his stuff. Ken was lucky; I never met Faulkner. I thought I'd better *not* meet him! I'd see Faulkner every day in the commissary, and he looked so morose, so dour. He would sit at this little table, by himself, and no one ever came *near* him except the waitress, who'd come and replenish his coffee from time to time. He looked *so* sour; I thought, 'One of these days, I may go up and say, "Mr. Faulkner, I admire your work very much," and then run like hell!' Because I thought he'd throw the sugar container at me!"

Possibly because of the overlapping dialogue in *The Thing,* another rumor started that Orson Welles had a hand in it behind the scenes, but Cornthwaite discounts that story. "I never heard *that,*" he scoffs. "I never saw Welles. *I* think that *Welles* was influenced by *Hawks'* filmmaking. Hawks was, in my book, the greatest filmmaker that I ever worked with, and I've worked with some pretty good ones: George Stevens, Billy Wilder, people with reputations like that. But Hawks had such complete control over all aspects [of his films]; he was a great writer, for instance. He never, to my knowledge, had screen credit for writing, even though he rewrote the scripts constantly. But he hired, in the first place, the best writers, like Faulkner, like I.A.L. Diamond. Charlie Lederer got the credit on *The Thing,* but Ben Hecht I know worked on the screenplay. I never met Hecht, but I heard that, definitely, that he had done one treatment at least, or maybe a screenplay of it."

The question inevitably asked of every veteran of *The Thing*—"How much directing did Christian Nyby actually get to do?"—is one that Cornthwaite is well prepared for. "Here's the way I look at it: Howard Hawks was launching Chris, who had been his cutter on several pictures, as a director. But on a Hawks picture, there was only one boss; he was an absolute autocrat. There were a few—*very* few—occasions when Hawks was *not* on the set and Chris *was* the actual director. But Chris *always* deferred to Howard Hawks— and for damn good reasons. Here was a great filmmaker, and Chris was not really in the same league. But as far as I was concerned, if it was between them that Chris was the director, then Chris was the director.

"There were times when Hawks would take me aside and give me direction, *away* from the set—which I took as a great compliment. He asked me to write the last scene—*my* last scene, that monologue with the Thing at the end of the corridor, just before they electrocute him." Did he write it? "I did very little; I cut it a bit, I rearranged it a little, but I didn't write a new one. I thought, 'No, these are good writers'—I had nothing better to offer *[laughs]!* But, getting back to your question about Hawks and Nyby, whenever that comes up, I answer always that, yes, it was Howard Hawks' picture, but Chris Nyby *was* the official director, and that's how it stands as far as I'm concerned.

"At that time, I think the people that worked *behind* the camera were much more interesting to me than the people in *front*. Don Steward was the special effects man; he had worked with Hawks on other things and was one of Hawks' 'regulars.' Hawks had favorite cameramen—Russ Harlan was cameraman on *The Thing,* and he did a lot of Hawks pictures. He was an excellent cameraman with a slew of Academy Awards. And Russell had *his* own crew. It was my first time out with 'em, but here was a crew of veterans who had worked together many times, and it was a very smooth operation. It was a pleasure working with all those people. They were damn good, top of their profession."

Cornthwaite's primary concern with his playing of the costarring role was "with playing with enough age and maturity. There've been rumors that I was in my twenties at the time, but I was thirty-three, which is not a kid. But the man's supposed to be fifty-five or so. I knew that, with film, it's not like theater where you can do a bit of faking; there's got to be a kind of reality in eyes and in movement. My principal concern was with that. Also, there are a few references in there to the fact that Carrington's a Nobel Prize winner. Well, *that* kind of puts you on the spot! If I had any images in mind, I suppose they were maybe a little of [J. Robert] Oppenheimer, who was in the news at that time (not specifically any mannerisms of his); and also Enrico Fermi, the Italian who was in on the atomic bomb. Such people. That was the image in my mind: A man of some dignity, but not without a sense of humor." Dr. Carrington had a sense of humor? "I thought he was not without a sense of humor, but *[laughs]* with a pasted-on beard, it's hard to smile without cracking the foliage off your face!"

In some respects, Cornthwaite's Dr. Carrington is the heavy in *The Thing,* standing up for the alien and thereby endangering everybody else. The actor remarks, "I thought to myself, 'The man believes what he says, and therefore in his own mind, he's not the heavy at all, he's doing the right thing.' Carrington was trying to increase the world's store of knowledge, and if there are going to be other Things coming in, we damn well better be prepared to deal with 'em for what they are. I think, actually, he was *right,* but from the point of view of a kid's matinee on a Saturday, he's the heavy." If Robert Cornthwaite were trapped in that Arctic base, what would he have thought of Carrington then? "Hard to say. Because people think only in terms of their own preservation, not about any future encounters. It's tough to be objective."

In an early draft of the script, the Thing decapitates Dr. Carrington, but according to Cornthwaite, "Hawks changed that, among many things, as we went along. Here was Hawks' method: While the actors' stand-ins went in and the gaffers lighted them, the actors would retire to a table that Hawks always had on any set where he worked. We would sit around and Hawks would say something like, 'Well, now, forget what's in the script. When *this* happens (whatever the scene entailed), what would *your* reaction be?' And if you had anything to suggest, you'd throw it in. It might be accepted, it might be rejected, it might be accepted in part and modified. That is the way the scene was developed, and this is how the overlapping dialogue was set up. Then we would go onto the set, the stand-ins would step out, and we would shoot the master shot (and then of course the two-shots and the over-the-shoulders). Meanwhile, Lorrie Sherwood, the secretary, would madly type up the scene we had put together around the table so that we could match what we had done in the master when we got around to closer shots and reverses.

"In *The Thing,* Hawks had very few individual shots, and no close-ups whatsoever—that also contributed to the sense of reality, I believe. That's the way he worked. When I worked with him again on *Monkey Business* [1952], it was the same way.

"Remember my first scene in *The Thing,* the scene where George Fenneman shows Ken Tobey slides of the saucer in flight? A great chunk of that dialogue initially was in my part. Hawks took me aside—that was my first day on the picture—and he said, 'You know, when I make a picture with John Wayne or Gary Cooper, they go through the script and they say, "How about taking this line of mine, having someone *else* say it, and I just react?" That way, *they* [Wayne and Cooper] come out looking better; the other people have the dull things to say, and all Wayne and Cooper do is react to 'em. I tell you this because I don't want you to feel bad: I'm going to take this long speech

Eduard Franz, Cornthwaite, Norbert Schiller and (squatting) Paul Frees share a tense moment during the search for the missing *Thing*.

and give it to George Fenneman.' So that's what we did. But I had learned this speech — I memorized it the night before. George got it *cold [laughs],* there on the set, this great big chunk of technological dialogue. He was a very experienced radio announcer, but he was used to having a script in front of him. And he simply couldn't get the words out *[laughs]!* I don't know *how* many takes we took! And finally Chris, who was a very considerate man, said, 'All right, that's a wrap for today. We'll start with that in the morning.' Then, of course, in one take the next morning, George had it. But he took such a kidding throughout the picture because of this, and he was so good-natured about it."

Less harmonious was the relationship between actor Douglas Spencer, who played reporter Scotty, and director of photography Russell Harlan. "Somehow or another, I don't know how, Doug rubbed Russ Harlan the wrong way — and suddenly his key light started disappearing. There are some scenes where you can see all the actors, but there's another face there *in the dark,* and it's Doug. In some scripts — I think in the Ben Hecht script, probably — the Spencer role, Scotty, was the central role of the film, the point-of-view character. Because Hecht, of course, had been a newspaperman himself." Cornthwaite adds that none of the actors had much difficulty overlapping dialogue. "No, I think we all enjoyed doing it. Sometimes it involved a certain amount of ad-libbing beyond the line, in order for the overlap to work. You'll notice that, in spite of the overlaps, what is necessary for you to hear comes out *crystal clear.* This was part of Hawks' technique. And it's a *witty* picture, isn't it? I had no idea until we saw a rough cut of about twenty-five, thirty minutes that it *was* witty. I didn't know that; I thought we were playing kind of a straight sci-fi melodrama. The fact that it was witty was escaping me during the making of it."

The self-animated Thing hand on the lab table "was made of latex rubber, like a glove. There was a girl with very slim hands and wrists who was under the table; she put her hand up through a hole in the top of the table, into this latex rubber forearm, and she did the movements from there. There was more than one of those latex rubber things; a collector named Bob Burns, who has a museum in his home, has one of those, and another one was found by someone else, under the soundstage floor. We shot on Stage 10 at RKO (where they shot *Citizen Kane,* by the way), and someone later found it during a cleanup." Even though he was not in the scene, "I watched the entire filming of the fire scene, and it was fascinating and *scary* to be there on the set. They had two stuntmen playing the Thing, so that they could change off. They were equipped with about a minute's worth of oxygen, so once they were sealed in that suit, they had to shoot immediately. I remember one of the guys being lighted on fire, and then they didn't call *action.* He just started jumping up and down with impatience; even though there was only so much oxygen, it puts you on the qui vive. It was exciting, *very* exciting, to watch that. And the electrocution was interesting, too. The electricity shrunk the Thing, from Jim Arness to [stuntman] Teddy Mangean, who was the middle size; then little Billy Curtis, the dwarf, was the smallest Thing. Then they just had a little doll or something. Teddy Mangean was my photographic double, and he did the fall for me there at the end of the corridor. Teddy looked uncannily like me in the makeup. I was amazed when I saw him."

As for James Arness' makeup, Cornthwaite says, "They spent two months experimenting before we started production, using Jim himself. He worked for a couple of months before we started principal photography, doing the variations on makeup and wardrobe and so on—they went through all kinds of changes before they settled on the quite-human-looking monster. Jim had done a few pictures; I think John Wayne had already taken an interest in him. Jim was a big guy, six-five, and Wayne liked to work with big men. What I heard from Lee Greenway, with whom I became very friendly during the course of the picture, was that they went from pretty outlandish ideas for the Thing, making it more and more human. I think that Hawks' reasoning, or *feeling,* was that if the Thing was not recognizably *like us,* it was not apt to be taken as seriously. Or its *intelligence* would be underestimated. You know, we have a great idea, human beings do, of our own superiority; we assume that we are about the brightest things around. So therefore, anything that doesn't look human can't be bright!"

As for Arness' attitude throughout shooting (rumor has it that the future *Gunsmoke* star was thoroughly embarrassed by his role), "I think Jim has perhaps *always* been a little embarrassed about being an actor; I don't think he was ever what you would call a dedicated actor. He hates horses, for instance; he's uncomfortable on horseback, and he just hates 'em. And on that last *Gunsmoke* special, a lot of the footage of Marshal Dillon is of Jim's photographic double, because he was in pain, and because *[laughs]* it's not what he wants to be doing. He's made a wonderful career out of it, had a great success, and I'm sure he enjoys that, but I don't think he ever particularly enjoyed making movies." And maybe he enjoyed *The Thing* even less than the others? "Well, he's on-screen, what, two minutes or less out of the picture. It's kind of an embarrassment, to have the title role and not have a word to speak, and your on-screen time is minimal. Perhaps from that point of view, it was an embarrassment to him; I don't know, he never said so to me. I had very good relations with him. When we were doing that confrontation scene, in the tunnel, just before the Thing whomps Dr. Carrington, he said something complimentary about how I was doing, and he said, 'They'll have to come in for a big close-up of you here.' And I said, 'No, they won't.' He didn't understand Hawks' way of making a picture."

Arness' Thing makeup included "a foam rubber helmet covering his head; it was built up to make him look even taller, just as his boots were built up to make him taller. He was almost seven feet in height with all these additions. He wore a green [makeup] base, I think the same green or grayish-green greasepaint that was devised for *Blithe Spirit* on the stage."

Science fiction was a new genre at the time, but Cornthwaite does not recall giving any particular thoughts to its possibilities. "I was so new at the game—it was my first year in pictures—that I don't remember having *any* attitude about it. I was working every day *[laughs]*—that's all that *I* knew. *The Thing* had a good-sized budget, but they weren't spending money on actors—we were a cast of unknowns. I think I was getting the top money in the picture; I don't think Ken ever knew that, I *hope* he didn't. I think the budget was $1,300,000 and they spent $1,600,000, so it wasn't a cheapie; the average A-picture was still under a million in those days. But on the other hand, it had no stars, and frankly I wondered if anybody would come to see it." Having a cast of unknowns in *The Thing* "was, I think, deliberate on Hawks' part. I think he wanted unknown faces, to get a freshness, a reality that you don't get when it's an identifiable star. I think that's why he used all of us.

"I think I saw *The Thing* for the first time on my birthday, which is April the 28th. It opened a few days before here in Southern California, and somebody in my family formed a little family group and we all went to see it together. I remember hunkering down in the seat and thinking, 'I don't know what this is going to be like!' *[Laughs.]* But very encouraging was the fact that the audience just whooped it up and liked it enormously." Their reaction to Dr. Carrington? "The kids' reaction was to *boo! They* knew who the hero was!"

And Cornthwaite's reaction to director John Carpenter's 1982 remake: "I thought the special effects were terrific, and the fact that they went back to [John W.] Campbell's original short story was a good idea. (I remember reading the short story early on in the shooting of our *Thing* and thinking, 'Gosh, this is an awfully good idea. I wonder why they departed from it?') All the gruesome special effects in John Carpenter's film sort of became overwhelming to me. I was not interested in the people. And I thought it would have been a nice gesture on Carpenter's part to invite survivors in and say, 'Look, we're doing a completely different version, and wanted to get your good wishes,' or something of the sort. But there was never any overture to *any* of us, that I ever heard of, from Universal or from Carpenter.

"When Universal released the remake, the Fox Venice in Venice, California — a huge, old 1920s theater — showed Hawks' *The Thing* (taking advantage of the release of the new picture) and they asked several of us to attend. I was there; Ken Tobey (I hadn't seen him in years); George Fenneman, who drove me home (I just had had a fender bender in my car); Chris Nyby and his wife, who came in from Hawaii; and others. Margaret Sheridan had died a couple of months before (we were all saddened by that), and Dewey Martin didn't want to come (he's become kind of reclusive, I understand). And the fans were there in hordes."

How often does Robert Cornthwaite rewatch his "signature" film credit? "I've got a video of it that I wanted to show some of my grandnieces and grandnephews, but their parents are leery about it; they think it's too scary for them. So I haven't shown it to them. I looked at it when I got it, and I liked it again, but — *The Thing* was many years ago. I don't identify with it, in a sense. There's not anything I'm dying to see again. After a certain period of time, they belong somehow outside of me; they're not me anymore. And that's kind of a comfortable feeling, not a sense of loss at all. I've had the experience of seeing a film that I've just done, when it's fresh in my mind what I *wanted* to do, and there's an awful sense of inadequacy and of frustration. In the actor's mind, he sees the scene one way, and the camera sees something else. Inevitably this is true."

Despite the popularity of *The Thing,* it did Cornthwaite's career little or no good. "In fact, I didn't work for eleven months after that *[laughs]*! It was a box office success from the beginning, and my agent was trying to up my salary, more than double. And getting no takers. But it was just an unfortunate time: Television was coming up strong, the major studios were falling apart, they were canceling their stock companies, letting contracts run out. Actors were becoming all freelancers. It was the wrong time to be asking for more money. When *The War of the Worlds* came along, it was the first job that I had after *The Thing*. I got very good billing for a nothing part.

"It was a dull picture to make, too. We saw none of the special effects, we were simply *told* what we were looking at. There weren't even sketches, George Pal was very secretive about it. Pal was a funny man. I had the interview for *War of the Worlds,* then heard nothing—and forgot about it, as a matter of fact. One day, my agent's office called to say, 'Go to Paramount for a wardrobe fitting.' I went over, and it was for *War of the Worlds.* I had my fitting, then went down to the studio street and was still talking to a wardrobe man—there were two or three of us there in a clump. A little man was kind of circling around the group, and he kept tapping me on the shoulder, saying *[speaking with a heavy accent],* 'I must speak to you. I must talk to you.' I said *[casually],* 'Yes, yes, fine.' He said, 'I am in Writers Building,' and he gave me a room number. 'Yes,' I told him, 'when I am finished here, I will see you.' Fortunately, I remembered before I left the lot—and the room was George Pal's office. It was George Pal! I hadn't remembered him from the interview at all.

"He said, very concerned, with a troubled frown on his face, 'You are a *bl-lond!*' (After *The Thing,* my hair was back to its normal color, almost black; and I was clean shaven, of course, no beard.) I said, 'No, this is my natural color—' He said, 'You are a *bl-lond!* I haff a photograph, you are a *bl-lond!*' And he brought out of a drawer one of my RKO photos, which they had taken at the end of the shoot of *The Thing,* where my hair was still bleached, before they dyed it back. Well *[laughs],* he had cast me in *War of the Worlds* because this minor scientist that I was playing entered in the same sequence with Gene Barry, their leading man, and they wanted someone that didn't have the same coloring as Barry; a leading character has got to stand out from the surroundings. So it was into the House of Westmore for another bleach job, but this time they bleached it a kind of Technicolor pink. And that's what I wore in *War of the Worlds.*"

Cornthwaite-wise, *War of the Worlds* is a switch from *The Thing:* In *War,* he is one of the scientists who cannot wait to *blow up* the Martians. "Yes, that *is* funny. But I don't think that was any sort of in-joke on anyone's part. I liked [director] Byron Haskin, but Byron was in an impossible situation: He was having to direct actors in scenes in which what they're looking at, what they're reacting to, has not even been created yet. (That was all done in postproduction.) The group of scientists I belonged to also included an old silent film actor named Ivan Lebedeff. He told me a wonderful Garbo story, he worked with her on *Conquest* [1937]. We all got along like a house afire, it was fun from that point of view, but we all had so little to do; we just stood around, we were background. We had a wonderful time among ourselves, but the actual filming was deadly dull."

The movie itself? "I didn't like it, frankly. But who am I? It's become kind of a classic, too, I guess."

Another scientist role came via a very different sort of science fiction movie, Howard Hawks' rollicking *Monkey Business* (1952), about a research scientist (Cary Grant) concocting a youth potion. "I reported for work on *Monkey Business* after they had been shooting for a few days, and when I came onto the soundstage, Howard Hawks was standing talking to Cary Grant and to John Wayne, who was visiting the set. So I just went over and found a chair to sit down in—I wasn't about to break in on *that*. And Hawks—such a strange man, really—he left these two stars to come and sit with me. He said, 'Glad to have you on the picture.' He had *fought* for me, fought to get me on the picture, for this nothing part. He had told 20th, 'If Robert Cornthwaite is available, I want him,' and 20th did not want to pay my salary. The part wasn't worth it. It went to the legal department, and finally I was in the picture—just because he *insisted!*

"He asked, 'Have you read the script?' (I.A.L. Diamond wrote that script.) I said, 'Yes, I have.' He said, 'Well, you know, we're just using that as a kind of springboard. Cary has some ideas, some things he's going to do; Charlie Coburn is always so good. And Virginia [Ginger Rogers] is going to have her hair *up* in the beginning of the picture, and then she's going to let it *down*.' And I thought, 'Oh, my God, *that's* what he thinks of Ginger Rogers' contribution to the picture!'

"At this point, Marilyn Monroe walked across the stage, and every eye was on her—it was quite a sight *[laughs]*! And Hawks said, 'I think that the overdeveloped quality in the little blond girl is going to be kind of funny.' That was his estimation of Monroe *[laughs]*! She was a lot of trouble. She was *so* insecure. I remember she and I were standing, waiting for an entrance together; we were going to come into a scene between Cary Grant and Ginger Rogers, who was playing his wife. Marilyn had four words to say in the scene, and she kept saying them over and over to me. And her diaphragm was just *vibrating*, like someone in great fright or at the end of a long run. She was scared to death! But then also, very stubborn. Joe DiMaggio was courting her at the time, and he was on the set sometimes. And when he wasn't there, she would get on the phone. They'd be shooting a scene and the second assistant would say to her *[whispering frantically]*, 'Honey! Get off the phone. We're shooting!' She would look at him with those big eyes and go right on talking.

"She kept saying that she was having attacks of appendicitis because she was scared of working; she would be late, or phone in and say she couldn't work, or whatever. And Hawks just ruthlessly wrote her out of scenes, he used her photographic double in long shots, and finally he gave the studio orders: He said, 'If she has appendicitis, send her to the hospital, have her appendix out.' There was a sequence coming up that he *had* to have her in, a scene of her and Cary Grant cruising around in a little sports car. I don't know that this is *true*, but I heard that they sent her to the hospital and she had her appendix out. That was Hawks' attitude toward her.

"Jean Peters told me a story about Marilyn that was kind of revealing, too. They were both under contract there at that time, and what the studio would

Cornthwaite was on our side (for a change) when Martians invaded in George Pal's *The War of the Worlds*. *Left-right:* Cornthwaite, Gene Barry, Alex Frazer, Ann Robinson.

do to save money was get all the girls [who were] under contract together and have a photo session — stills for publicity and magazines and whatnot — with the girls wearing all the glamorous duds that they'd wear in pictures. The wardrobe women were in attendance, and while one actress was being photographed, another would be changing; the photographer shoots, shoots, shoots, one girl after another. Marilyn and Jean Peters were in the dressing room together, changing, and Marilyn had tears in her eyes. She said, 'You other girls get to wear all the nice things. They just put me in the *sexy* things.' Now, *she* knew what she was selling, but that's the way she felt about it."

In addition to *Thing* holdover Cornthwaite, the previous film's Douglas Spencer and Bob Nichols also appeared in *Monkey Business*. "Hawks was very loyal to actors," says Cornthwaite. "He asked for me again when he did *Man's Favorite Sport?* [1964], which was a remake of his *Bringing Up Baby* [1938], and I couldn't do it. That was a great disappointment to me, but I was busy with something else. So I only worked with him the two times. I had enormous respect for him." As for Hawks' relationship with screen great Cary Grant, "I could see that Hawks had a great respect for Grant and that they loved working together. Hawks considered Grant one of the great film comedians, with his own bag of tricks, like an actor from the commedia dell'arte, a clown in a sense. And this is the way Grant looked upon himself, too, I believe. They had a long-term project which was never done, although they talked about it from time to time: They were going to make *Cinderella.* Howard Hawks was going to direct it, and Cary Grant was going to play the Wicked Stepmother *[laughs]!* It's a shame that it never got made, isn't it?

"Ginger Rogers has a talent for caricature, and she drew caricatures of everybody, cast and crew. In one set, there was a blackboard, and while Hawks was outlining a scene, she stood at the blackboard and did a very clever caricature of him—the long horse face. He was walking back and forth in front of it, he *had* to see it, but he *never* alluded to it, never gave any indication that he had seen it. So, sort of shamefacedly, she wiped it out with her hand. They went then into shooting the scene, and it was between her and Grant. They were doing a take, and in the middle of the take, Hawks walked from behind the camera, in front of the camera, and said, 'No, no, *no,* Virginia. *No-o-o-o.*' And nothing else! She stood there at attention, eyes wide open— and he walked behind the camera and said, 'All right, let's take it again,' without *ever* telling her what the 'no, no, *no*' was for. It shattered her—she was just aghast—and I thought, 'He punished her for drawing a caricature of him.' I can't be sure, but that's the way I read it. It was funny, and kind of scary."

Two of Cornthwaite's other films of this era were borderline genre, and both were for Robert Aldrich: *Kiss Me Deadly* and *What Ever Happened to Baby Jane? "Kiss Me Deadly* was the first time I worked for Aldrich. He told me that we had worked together when he was an assistant director on something or other, and that he had sort of liked my work. (I didn't remember it, and still cannot.) So when he made that independent, *Kiss Me Deadly,* he asked for me and I did that small part of the FBI man. Then the next thing I did for him was a major role, really about the third role in the picture although it was cut to ribbons, in a picture we made in Berlin, *Ten Seconds to Hell* [1959]. Hammer Films produced it, and they were used to making horror films. Here they were trying for a bigger market, a more . . . honorable art form *[laughs],* with this picture! And it was a very long picture, slow-paced. After Aldrich had finished his cut, Hammer hired Virginia and Andrew Stone to cut the film. And they cut it—*drastically!* The female star was Martine Carol, a French star who was very big on the Continent, and in the film,

Martine's character has a baby, which is central to the plot. They cut the baby, completely. They still left some scenes where there's a baby's crib in view *[laughs]*, but it's unexplained. And that baby was a motivating factor for many scenes; many scenes were built around it.

"I remember the first day that Martine worked on the picture, we were shooting in the Tiergarten, a big park in the center of West Berlin. It was a very cold day, the water was freezing on the lake. It was a scene with that baby—they had twins playing it, of course. The shot opened with me getting the baby out of its crib there on the lawn beside the lake, and holding it until she came up, and then giving *her* the baby. The baby was fine with me, I would hand the baby to Martine, and as soon as she took it, it would begin to cry. And it was supposed to be *her* baby *[laughs]*. Well, this was wrong, and that upset Martine greatly; we changed babies, took the other twin, and the same thing happened. Finally we got into the dialogue of the scene, two or three pages of dialogue between her and me, and *[laughs]* I could not understand a word she said, she was so upset! Eventually they dubbed her throughout the picture. Martine's English was not bad, but being upset, and with all these conditions—freezing cold, a baby that was reacting against her, her first day on the picture—it was a terrible psychological spot for her. We had a hellish time."

And in *What Ever Happened to Baby Jane?*, "I played the doctor who never arrives, like the marines who never land. Somebody else had played it— they had shot this particular scene once before, I found out later—but Aldrich called me to redo it. It was the last day of the shoot, with Bette Davis and Joan Crawford shooting close-ups for the beach scene. They had already shot it in long shots, down at Zuma, I think; for the close-ups, they rigged up a little spot of sand on the soundstage. That was my only contact with them. The two of them were very professional, and *so* conscious of what they were doing, so sure of themselves. It was kind of wonderful to see two such pros. In spite of all the publicity about their feuding (and I understand that they *really* did not like each other), they were very politely arranging a joint press conference, deciding whose house they would have it at, making these arrangements between themselves quietly and rather quickly.

"They showed the thing *[Baby Jane]* at the Directors Guild before it was in release, and we were all invited. At the time, I was going with a young lady who was kind of Hollywood-smitten, and I took her with me to see it. And as the picture ran, I thought to myself that it was the most heavy-handed, *awful* thing—I sank lower and lower in the seat. I could not think of a single good thing to say about that movie. And yet, it made nothing but money."

Like most other actors of his kind, Cornthwaite was also constantly busy on television, including (of course) the classic horror, science fiction and fantasy series like *The Twilight Zone*, *Thriller*, *Voyage to the Bottom of the Sea* and *Batman*. "One *Twilight Zone* I remember because it was with Dana

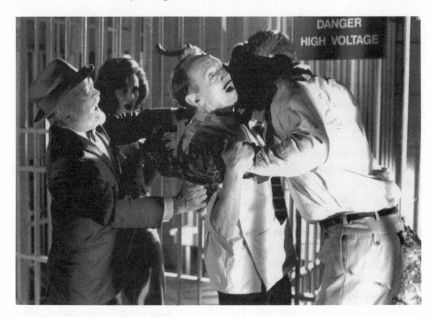

Cornthwaite and Cathy Moriarty watch as William Schallert falls prey to the ant-man in director Joe Dante's *Matinee*.

Andrews, with whom I had worked in 1936 at Pasadena Playhouse in a production of *Antony and Cleopatra*. I tried to use in that what I remembered of Wendell Wilkie's accent when he was running for president in 1940 against Roosevelt. *Thriller* I don't remember. *Voyage to the Bottom of the Sea*, that too is very vague. That kind of story is so remote from *human* values that I can't remember 'em; you do 'em, and that's it. But *Batman* had an awfully good script, and they thought this particular episode was going to be the best of them all. Art Carney was the villain [the Archer], but I really had a better role and I enjoyed doing it. But they turned it over to a director so stodgy, so unimaginative, that this good script came out as a flat piece of nothing."

He was also a regular—briefly—on the NBC spy spoof *Get Smart* with Don Adams. "I played Windish, the guy who invented all the gadgets that Agent 86, Maxwell Smart [Don Adams], used; Smart always screwed 'em up. We had shot a few of them, four or five, I guess, and Don Adams said to me, 'Do you think Windish gets angry with Agent 86 over his screwing up with the gadgets?' I said, 'Yeah, I think he gets angry, but he gets over the anger about this because he's always got *another* gadget he wants to promote.' And, after that conversation, I wasn't called for any more shows. Later I was working on something else on the Paramount lot, which is where we shot *Get Smart,* and Leonard Stern, one of the producers, came across the street toward me and said, 'Hey, Bob, I wanted to tell you that we were all very happy with what you were doing. But Don ... he's hard to please.' I don't know what Don's ideas were, but whatever I said wasn't the right thing."

The quintessential movie scientist, Cornthwaite added two more science fiction roles to his filmography in the 1970s, *Colossus — The Forbin Project* and *Futureworld*. "I thought *Colossus* was an awfully good script, but I had very little to do in it, and it was so isolated from the other people involved that I don't remember it with any particular feeling at all. I was on it for several weeks, but in a sense it was like *War of the Worlds*: The technology was so much a part of it — special effects — we were reacting to printouts. That's a pretty *sterile* kind of thing to do *[laughs]!* But I thought it was a very clever script, and I liked Eric Braeden; he had been Hans Gudegast up until that picture. Very nice guy." And as for *Futureworld*, AIP's sequel to MGM's *Westworld*, "I had a fair part in that, I worked several weeks on it. We shot at NASA for a week or two, in Houston. Angela Greene, who played my wife in it, called me after the preview and she said, 'Honey, we are *out!*' They had cut both our parts out. We're in background and that's about it. So it was take the money and run, as it turned out."

Nowadays, says Cornthwaite, "I do theater whenever I can, always have. I prefer theater; it is far more liberating for the actor than film. Writers, directors, editors and cameramen — those are the creative people in film. Actors are of necessity farther down on the totem pole, although they don't like to think so and a lot of them don't admit it. But they're relatively unimportant. They are things being manipulated by these other people. I like theater because *I've* got the reins in *my* hands, at least once the curtain goes up."

Forty-plus years after *The Thing*, it is still the one movie most fans instantly associate him with. Is that okay with Robert Cornthwaite? "Sure, I think it's a good picture, and I'm proud of it. The secret behind its staying power? Gosh, I don't know, I cannot read the public; I only know my own reactions. When I saw it, I thought, 'Ah, it's a good movie. Thank *God* it's a good movie.' Because, I confess, I really didn't know *what* to expect!"

ROBERT CORNTHWAITE FILMOGRAPHY

Union Station (Paramount, 1950)
Gambling House (RKO, 1950)
The Thing from Another World (RKO, 1951)
Mark of the Renegade (Universal, 1951)
His Kind of Woman (RKO, 1951)
Something to Live For (Paramount, 1952)
Monkey Business (20th Century–Fox, 1952)

The War of the Worlds (Paramount, 1953)
Day of Triumph (George J. Schaefer, 1954)
Stranger on Horseback (United Artists, 1955)
Kiss Me Deadly (United Artists, 1955)
The Purple Mask (Universal, 1955)
On the Threshold of Space (20th Century–Fox, 1956)

The Leather Saint (Paramount, 1956)
The Spirit of St. Louis (Warner Bros., 1957)
Hell on Devil's Island (20th Century–Fox, 1957)
Ten Seconds to Hell (United Artists, 1959)
Day of the Outlaw (United Artists, 1959)
All Hands on Deck (20th Century–Fox, 1961)
What Ever Happened to Baby Jane? (Warner Bros., 1962)
Reptilicus (voice only; AIP, 1962)
The Ghost and Mr. Chicken (Universal, 1966)
Ride to Hangman's Tree (Universal, 1967)

Waterhole #3 (Paramount, 1967)
The Legend of Lylah Clare (MGM, 1968)
Colossus — The Forbin Project (Universal, 1970)
The Peace Killers (Transvue, 1971)
Journey Through Rosebud (GSF-Cinerama, 1972)
Futureworld (AIP, 1976)
Deal of the Century (Warner Bros., 1983)
Dr. Detroit (Universal, 1983)
Disorderlies (Warner Bros., 1987)
Who's That Girl (Warner Bros., 1987)
Time Trackers (Concorde, 1989)
Matinee (Universal, 1993)

Halloween (Compass International, 1978) features clips from *The Thing from Another World;* Cornthwaite is heard but not seen.

*There has been, all through the years, a definite following
for many of the films that I was in, and they've never
given it up. And a lot of fans have kept up with me.
Believe me when I tell you that's one of the most
flattering things that can happen to an actress.*

Louise Currie

A GOLDEN ANNIVERSARY is a great excuse to celebrate. The year 1989 saw classic movies like *Gone with the Wind* and *The Wizard of Oz* hitting the half-century mark while the films themselves played to capacity crowds in revival houses; 1991 was the year of *Citizen Kane,* which also went the nostalgia route via new theatrical prints and much fan ado.

Actress Louise Currie did not have a substantial part in *Citizen Kane;* she was only one of a group of reporters seen in the film's closing scene, their faces obscured by shadows, puttering around amidst an ocean of crated objets d'art at Kane's palatial Xanadu estate. Closer to the hearts of science fiction and action fans than *Citizen Kane,* however, is another Louise Currie credit, one of the best and most famous serials of all time: *Adventures of Captain Marvel* (1941). Based on the popular Whiz Comics character and transposed from comic book page to silver screen by the action experts at Republic Pictures, the classic serial also recently turned 50, and Louise Currie helps to commemorate the occasion with reminiscences of this classic cliffhanger and of her brief but memorable career in serials and horror films.

"I can't believe it sometimes, but it seems as though *Captain Marvel* just isn't *ever* going to lose its appeal," the actress, fresh from a dip in her Beverly Hills pool, admits. "Recently a fan called me from the South; he was a school-teacher, taught third grade, and he said that he got amazing results with his class when he got the bright idea of running *Captain Marvel* the first thing every morning. When the children would come into the room, he'd turn on one chapter. Of course, they would be all settled down and he would have their rapt attention by the time the chapter would finish, and then he'd go into the lessons—'Okay, children, what's four and four?' and so on. They couldn't *wait* to get to his class every day, and he would get perfect attendance *[laughs].* He told me he had the best luck of his teaching career when he was using *Captain Marvel* to keep the children in line."

Of course, not all of us were fortunate enough to have *Captain Marvel* included as part of our grade school curriculum, and not every actress has been able to make the kind of crowd-pleasing movies that can win her a new generation of fans 50 years after the fact. Born in Oklahoma City, Louise Currie attended Sarah Lawrence College in Bronxville, New York, became interested in acting and then attended Max Reinhardt's drama school in Hollywood. ("At the time, I was not necessarily a movie fan, but once I came to California, of course, that's what California's all about, the movie industry," Currie remembers.) Talent scouts would spot the aspiring actress in the acting workshop's stage productions and press her to make the rounds of the Hollywood studios, but Currie remained adamant about staying out of the limelight, at least temporarily.

Previous page: **During her training at Max Reinhardt's Hollywood drama school, lovely Louise Currie could not have suspected that her eventual leading men would include superheroes, apes and voodoo men. (Photo from** *The Masked Marvel.***)**

"I said no because I felt I didn't know enough about it. I said, 'Well, if this is how it's done, I don't *want* to do it this way. If I'm going to be in pictures, I'd like to learn something *about* them first.' Several agents had asked me to sign with them, which I'd refused to do also — there again, I didn't want to start trying to get jobs if I didn't know my trade *[laughs]!* So I kept refusing until I graduated from Max Reinhardt's. At that point, I decided it was time to sign with an agent, and I went with Sue Carol. She was a very good agent and the wife of Alan Ladd, and she was developing Alan's career."

Currie's first movie (although not the first one to be released) was *The Pinto Kid* (1941), a Columbia B Western complete with post–Civil War cattle rustling, bank robberies, an attempted frame-up and wooden Western leading man Charles Starrett; *Variety* dubbed screen newcomer Currie "a neat looker." "At the end of that movie, the head of Columbia, Harry Cohn, offered me a contract. But my agent and I decided that, no, I wouldn't sign, it would maybe be more interesting to freelance. In those days, of course, the studios could build their people into stars; they had the wherewithal, the publicity and the money to do that. But we decided that I didn't want to be just a contract player at Columbia. So I went on to make about fifty movies, all freelance."

Another early role was a small but highly visible part as one of several debutantes in the song-filled mystery/comedy *You'll Find Out* (1940). Comic bandleader Kay Kyser and his motley College of Musical Knowledge were the stars of the film, and providing the menace were Hollywood's top three bogeymen, Boris Karloff, Bela Lugosi and Peter Lorre. "I appeared with Bela Lugosi three times; he was so different from the characters he played," says Currie. "He was quiet and unassuming off the screen, very studious and very sedate. Then the cameras would roll and he would be a *horrible* man *[laughs].* Boris Karloff I remember, too, but not as specifically as Lugosi, because I played with Lugosi so much more. Karloff I'm kind of vague about; I remember talking with him, and it seemed to me that he was also quite intelligent. He was actually a very nice-looking man, too, so to find him always in such weird parts was unusual. And Peter Lorre was very small and very . . . peculiar. Maybe his roles are more vivid in my mind than his actual personality, but my memory tells me he was a little weird in person."

While horror men Karloff, Lugosi and Lorre dished out their evil deeds on the set of *You'll Find Out,* a soundstage or two away, movie history was being made as 25-year-old Orson Welles gathered his Mercury Players together for their joint motion picture debut in the milestone production *Citizen Kane.* Currie and Alan Ladd were among the reporters discussing the life and times of the Hearst-like Kane (Welles) in the film's classic climax; Currie even gets to deliver the one line that perhaps best encapsulates the entire film ("If you could have found out what 'Rosebud' meant, I bet that would have explained everything").

"I remember being on that picture a long, long time, to do a sequence that seems so inconsequential," Currie says. "By the time they got through with it in the cutting room, there was not much left of the scene, but I think we were on that several months, which was amazing. It's quite a contrast to the work I *had* been doing, where I'd make a movie in ten days or something *[laughs]*. *Citizen Kane* went on and on and on and on, but it was a very educational, interesting experience. We watched Orson Welles work; his direction was remarkable, and quite unusual. He would get on the camera boom, way up, and decide how to angle his shots. He was a very demanding director; everything had to be done precisely his way. And he was not very patient unless you knew what you were doing *[laughs]*."

Of course, her minute role in *Citizen Kane* remains a footnote in Louise Currie's career; her enduring claim to fame remains *Adventures of Captain Marvel*, Republic Pictures' 12-chapter film version of the highly popular Fawcett Publications pulp hero and (according to many) the best serial ever made. "Serials were something that youngsters in those days would watch religiously, every Saturday; I remember my own son going every weekend to the movie theater in Westwood Village. That was something that all the neighborhood children did as a regular routine. When I was offered *Captain Marvel*, I thought it would be fun to try, just to see what it would be like. At that time, not being under contract, I just accepted whatever I felt might be interesting and worthwhile doing. And I ended up doing two serials, *Adventures of Captain Marvel* and *The Masked Marvel*."

The origins of Republic's Captain Marvel were markedly different from those of the comic book Marvel. In both, the caped superhero was the secret identity of Billy Batson, but in the comic book (*Whiz Comics* vol. 1, no. 2, February 1940), Batson was a newsboy who encountered the mystical wise man Shazam in a subway tunnel; invoking Shazam's name changed the wispy lad into the muscle-bound, bullet-proof Captain Marvel, champion of justice. A quintet of Republic screenwriters overhauled the comic book premise, depicting Batson (Frank Coghlan, Jr.) as a boyish radio newscaster accompanying the Malcolm Archaeological Expedition into a remote and volcanic section of Siam. There, the party discovers a secret underground tomb where Batson, exploring alone, encounters the wizened Shazam (Nigel de Brulier); the sage bestows upon Batson the ability to transform himself at will into the World's Mightiest Mortal (Tom Tyler).

Elsewhere, the remaining expedition members, accompanied by secretary Betty (Currie) and Batson's sidekick Whitey (Billy Benedict), have uncovered the tomb's greatest treasure, a large golden model of a scorpion holding in its claws five lenses. Directing sunlight through the lenses changes base metals into gold; realizing the incredible value of their find, the scientists divide the lenses and the scorpion model among themselves for safekeeping. But one of them takes on the second identity of the Scorpion, a hooded and robed super-criminal, and hatches a sinister plot to divest his former colleagues of their lenses. First in Siam, later in America, and finally once again in Siam, Batson/Captain Marvel battles the Scorpion and his henchmen, striving stoically to unmask the hooded fiend before the complete Golden Scorpion—and its destructive capabilities—are in his hands.

The plot of *Captain Marvel* was a perfect framework for action and suspense, and the Republic special effects and stunt teams operated at peak efficiency to cram the 12 episodes with unparalleled serial thrills. "The special effects men on *Captain Marvel* [Howard and Theodore Lydecker] were sensational; in fact, they were considered the best in the business at that time. They just did a fabulous job, especially with the flying dummy of Captain Marvel. I remember watching it in flight and being absolutely enthralled by the fact that they could do that. But the really interesting part was watching the stunt people work—they were brilliant. A stuntman named Dave Sharpe doubled for me—amazingly *[laughs]!* He was a smallish man but very, very versatile, and marvelous with his timing. Of course, I was there to watch them put on some of those big fight scenes we had in every chapter, but I didn't really like watching all that. I don't even like to watch fighting *today* on the screen. But they were remarkable, the way they could do it."

The hectic production pace of *Captain Marvel*—and of serials in general—presented no problem for Currie, who admits that she much preferred working that way. "Fortunately, I had enough training that I could do my scenes and not mess them up, not muff the lines. And I thought that was more stimulating and interesting than pictures like *Citizen Kane,* where you just sat on a set for endless hours, doing nothing—which to me was just a trial and a bore. So I sort of enjoyed the activity, and the fact that you could do something quickly and do it well, and have it finished—in fact, I rather liked that. (But I'm sure that most of the people that started with big A productions would never have understood that, or been able to cope with it!)

"*Captain Marvel* even had two directors [William Witney and John English], which was done, I'm sure, to save on time and budget," she continues. "The one who was not directing on a particular day could be studying what they were going to do next, or he could be off shooting on another location. I think that helped them to facilitate the thing and to make it all run faster. They were young and spirited and eager to do a good job. I believe I remember seeing the whole script at once at one point, but they were very innovative in those days and they would constantly change things *[laughs]*. You might *think* you were going to do one thing on a certain day, but they'd have you do sixteen others. So you had to be very fast and willing and ready just to go with whatever they happened to dream up."

At the conclusion of Chapter 1, the expedition members are fleeing in their cars from an angry horde of mounted natives, one of whom has mined a high chasm-spanning bridge with dynamite. The charge is detonated as the car containing Betty and Whitey is crossing the bridge, and the vehicle hurtles down into the river far below (an outstanding Lydecker miniature). Being expected to climb inside a submerged vehicle took Currie by complete, and not pleasant, surprise. "The station wagon was in the water, and I was supposed to get inside so that Captain Marvel could drag me out, rescue me. And I said to them, 'Uhn-uh. I'm not going down in that cold water, underneath a car, and wonder when I'm going to get out!' Well, that caused a little bit of discussion, but I stuck to my guns and refused to do it. It was beyond my capabilities—I studied acting, not stuntwork. So they acquiesced, and found some women's clothes for Dave Sharpe to get into. Dave ended up doing that stunt for me; once Captain Marvel carried Dave to shore, they went to a closeup of me reviving. So I was spared from doing that stunt by Dave Sharpe."

Currie's anecdote has an interesting and revealing postscript. "Years later, at a dinner party, I ran into one of the directors of *Captain Marvel*—I can't remember if it was Jack English or Bill Witney. I asked him, 'You can tell me now: How did you feel when I refused to do that stunt?' And he said, 'Well, we didn't like it, but you were absolutely in the right when you refused to do it.' *[Laughs.]* Everything was so fast and furious, you took enough chances doing a serial without doing things that were just plain dangerous like that. And the way I kept getting knocked out throughout [the serial], every time Billy Batson is about to say 'Shazam!' and change into Captain Marvel. I don't know how they thought of so many ways of destroying me. I was always getting knocked out, boards falling from the ceiling onto my head and everything—I look back at it and wonder how I did it. But at the time, you don't even realize it. That was the fun thing about doing those, the fast action—you never got bored."

Although generally regarded today as a Poverty Row studio, Republic, according to Currie, was a fun and exciting place to work. "Republic really had a lot going at that time. They were very active and had plenty of good people working there. They really were inventive, and kept doing different types of pictures: They would do extravaganzas with Vera Ralston, the ice skating star; the serials; lots of John Wayne Westerns—everything you could think of. They were always very busy and they did a good job at what they did."

Part of the fun was working alongside her youthful *Captain Marvel* costars, Frank Coghlan (Billy Batson) and Billy Benedict (Whitey). "They couldn't have been more pleasant," she states emphatically. "I still talk to them from time to time; in fact, Frank just sent me a tape of [American Movie Classics'] *The Republic Pictures Story* because I was out of town when it was shown and I couldn't record it. He really is a nice man. He and Billy were very, very cooperative and wonderful to work with. They both knew their trade and knew what they were doing, and it made working under those conditions a lot easier."

Tom Tyler, a cowboy star in a raft of B Westerns (and a supporting player in bigger productions like *Stagecoach* and *Gone with the Wind*) was ideally cast as Captain Marvel. The husky Tyler made for a unique superhero, one who combated criminals with a steely determination and showed no quarter to his defeated enemies; the serial's most notorious scene depicts Captain Marvel machine-gunning a pair of renegade natives in the back. Recalling the actor, Currie says, "Tom Tyler was very quiet and sort of reserved. Whereas Billy Benedict and Frank Coghlan were young and fun and full of enthusiasm, it seemed to me that Tom Tyler was very retiring. I don't remember talking or being with him that much, but working with him, he was very nice and very cooperative."

Currie wasn't able to see *Captain Marvel* when it was originally released for the simple reason that she was too regularly employed. "Funnily enough, I never saw any of my films; it just so happened that I worked rather constantly and rapidly. I think the one and only film that I spent any real amount of time on was *Citizen Kane* — where I had so little to do *[laughs]!* But the rest of 'em were just the opposite. So therefore, I was always working, and I really never saw them. But many years later, fans have found me and, little by little, they've sent me my films, and now I have a collection of about thirty — almost all of them I'm seeing for the first time because of all these nice fans! I would never have seen them if it weren't for all these young people."

Adventures of Captain Marvel is one that she's been able to see again in recent years, and "I really enjoy it. I think it really holds your attention, and that the cliffhanger endings are still exciting. Each chapter has a great deal of tension at the end, and I don't know how they were able to think up so many ways to be that suspenseful." Asked to rate her own performance in it, her enthusiasm wanes a bit. "Well, there was really very little performance — I was just there, being acted *upon!* There really was no acting on my part, and I don't feel that I was able to portray anything."

Her fans would, of course, disagree vehemently, and apparently so did her bosses: Two years later, she was once again selected to star in a Republic chapterplay starring a different Marvel — Tom Steele as *The Masked Marvel.* A big-city crimefighter who kept his identity a closely guarded secret, the Marvel squared off again Mura Sakima (Johnny Arthur), a Japanese spy/saboteur, in this wartime-era serial, which found Currie cast as Alice Hamilton, daughter of an insurance company executive murdered by Sakima's men. The role allowed Currie more screen time and a greater share of the action, a new arrangement she greatly preferred. "As far as my character was concerned, *Captain Marvel* was just running and screaming — or getting knocked out and being unconscious. I was more myself in *The Masked Marvel.* I had a part that was a little more normal."

Another unique serial, *The Masked Marvel* kept secret the true identity of its *hero* rather than that of its villain: Until the conclusion of Chapter 12, audiences did not know which of four young insurance investigators (Rod Bacon, Richard Clarke, David Bacon, Bill Healy) would turn out to be the

ADVENTURES OF CAPTAIN MARVEL

A REPUBLIC SERIAL

Chapter 7   HUMAN TARGETS

COPYRIGHT 1941
FAWCETT PUBLICATIONS, Inc.

Marvel (actually played throughout by stuntman Steele). The cast was equally in the dark. "Funnily enough, they kept the ending so secret that, while we were shooting it, none of us knew who was going to be the Masked Marvel. They wanted it to be such a secret, such a surprise—apparently even for us. The four investigators were played by a group of very interesting young men who were all starting their careers. All of them were very attractive and talented and nice. Johnny Arthur? Well *[laughs]*, he was very ominous, wasn't he? But I'm sure the Japanese probably wouldn't have thought too much of his portrayal! And Tom Steele, just like Dave Sharpe, was really very nice, very intelligent, very capable—I can't say enough good things about both of those fellows."

Talking about the directors of her B films and serials, Currie sounds almost like a spokeswoman for the low-budget film industry. "All those young directors were very good; just like the actors, they had to know what they were doing and do it quickly and not make mistakes and not hem and haw. I think some of the big A directors ended up being regarded as good because they took four thousand shots of everything; out of that number of shots, you'd have to find *some*thing that they could piece together to make it look good."

Well directed or not, most of Currie's other films of that period lack the staying power of *Captain Marvel* and *The Masked Marvel*; titles like *Billy the Kid's Gun Justice*, *The Bashful Bachelor* and *Stardust on the Sage* have long since dropped down the memory hole. Two exceptions to that rule are the pair of horror films in which she costarred with cult horror star Bela Lugosi, *The Ape Man* and *Voodoo Man*.

"Bela Lugosi seemed to enjoy doing that kind of work, or I don't know whether he'd have done it; I think he was a fine actor. But once you start playing those kinds of roles, I suppose you're kind of stuck with it. Also, he did definitely have a heavy accent, but the kinds of parts he played, he didn't need to speak perfect English. (Sometimes he didn't need to speak!) But he was an interesting man and certainly did a brilliant job on *The Ape Man*. He took it so seriously, he really wanted it to be believable, and I think it definitely was. His wife was around, too, and she was a very lovely, educated lady. It all seemed so strange, that they had such a wonderful marriage and nice home life, and here he was portraying mad scientists and voodoo men and apes!"

A real Golden Turkey contender, Monogram's *The Ape Man* starred Lugosi as Dr. James Brewster, a famous gland expert whose rash decision to inject himself with an ape's spinal fluid has devastating consequences: Brewster is covered with hair, walks like an ape, and occasionally has the beast's killer instincts. Devout Lugosi fans hold the film in contempt; for the more openminded, it is a camp classic of the highest order.

Opposite: **Doing what a superhero does best, Captain Marvel (Tom Tyler) rescues his swooning leading lady (Currie).**

One of the bad guys (George Suzanne) gets the drop on Currie (in black wig disguise) in the wartime serial *The Masked Marvel.*

Currie, who costars as a newspaper photographer caught up in the mystery, made an unfortunate decision in taking her young son to see the finished film. "After *The Ape Man* was finished, I did go to see a preview and I took my son with me — and he told me in later years that it scared him so much. He was six or seven when he saw *The Ape Man* and he had dreams for many years of the ape capturing his mother. Of course, I couldn't imagine that he'd have that kind of reaction — I was right there *with* him as he was watching it, so obviously the ape didn't 'get' me. But he vividly remembered the ape chasing his mother, and it left him with terrible dreams that had him waking up screaming for years."

Currie had a much smaller part in Lugosi's last Monogram film *Voodoo Man,* the story of a mad doctor (Lugosi) and his associates (John Carradine and George Zucco) resorting to black magic to restore life to Lugosi's dead wife. Currie, placed in a spell early on by the loony Lugosi, had little chance to contribute to the picture. "What I remember about *Voodoo Man* was walking around out in the woods with my eyes wide open, wandering around in a trance. And poor John Carradine — he played a halfwit in it. (And may I say he played it very *well* — playing a halfwit is not the easiest thing to do when you're a good actor.)"

Bela Lugosi stooped — literally *and* figuratively — to play the title role in Monogram's *The Ape Man,* with Louise Currie.

If Louise Currie had had the chance to pick her own roles, she admits horror films and cheap Westerns would not have been high on her personal list. "No *[laughs],* that wouldn't have been what I'd have had in mind at all! I did a film with Kent Taylor that was called *Second Chance* [1947], and I enjoyed that very much — I was a lady thief, and the picture had a to-catch-a-thief kind of theme. That I enjoyed tremendously, and that would be more or less the type of role that I would enjoy. Then I did one called *The Crimson Key* [1947] and another called *Backlash* [1947], and in those last two I played heavies. Instead of just the sweet young thing, I kind of liked playing more meaty parts, and all of those three pictures I just named I enjoyed very much — they were more my type."

Within a few more years, however, Louise Currie made the decision to leave the picture business once and for all. "I had married; my husband [John Good] had been on the stage and in some very good films at Metro and Fox. But when we decided to be married, we agreed it was not an easy industry to be in if you wanted to have a happy marriage and to raise children. So we decided we would start what we called our second career. I was a decorator (I had been doing it on the side, just for fun, for my friends), and my husband was an architectural designer. So we decided we would go into business at that — which we did — and we made a pact that we would not go back to films. And, funnily enough, of course the minute you decide something like that, then you get a fabulous offer *[laughs]!* Each of us got a *very* tempting offer, and we both turned it down. And from that day on, my husband remodeled houses and architecturally made changes, I decorated them, and we'd put them on the market and sell. We've had a long career of decorating and architecture. That's been our life since then."

She has been long retired from the picture industry, but Currie seldom goes for long without hearing from fans who have never forgotten her Westerns, her horror films, her serials — and the spunky, bright-eyed leading lady that graced them. Of course, it is almost always *Adventures of Captain Marvel* that heads her fans' lists of their favorite Louise Currie films. "Apparently, people have decided that *Captain Marvel* is one of the best serials that was ever made. I'm very, very surprised, and needless to say I'm delighted, that out of all the countless serials that were made, not one but *both* of mine have happened to come out on video. (That's also made it awfully easy for me to give gifts *[laughs]!*)

"I'm just so happy that people are still enthused, that they still like what they see; after all these many years, you would think that maybe they would have another trend, a desire to see something different. But there has been, all through the years, a definite following for many of the films that I was in, and they've never given it up. And a lot of fans have kept up with *me.* Believe me when I tell you that's one of the most flattering things that can happen to an actress."

LOUISE CURRIE FILMOGRAPHY

Billy the Kid Outlawed (PRC, 1940)
Billy the Kid's Gun Justice (PRC, 1940)
The Green Hornet Strikes Again (Universal serial, 1940)
You'll Find Out (RKO, 1940)
Citizen Kane (RKO, 1941)

Dude Cowboy (RKO, 1941)
Orchids to Charlie (Elizabeth Arden-Fine Arts Studios featurette, 1941)
The Pinto Kid (Columbia, 1941)
The Reluctant Dragon (RKO, 1941)
Look Who's Laughing (RKO, 1941)

Adventures of Captain Marvel (Return of Captain Marvel) (Republic serial, 1941)

Hello, Sucker (Universal, 1941)

Tillie the Toiler (Columbia, 1941)

Double Trouble (Monogram, 1941)

Bedtime Story (Columbia, 1941)

Call Out the Marines (RKO, 1942)

The Bashful Bachelor (RKO, 1942)

Stardust on the Sage (Republic, 1942)

Tireman, Spare My Tires (Columbia short, 1942)

Around the World (RKO, 1943)

The Masked Marvel (Republic serial, 1943)

A Blitz on the Fritz (Columbia short, 1943)

His Wedding Scare (Columbia short, 1943)

The Ape Man (Monogram, 1943)

Forty Thieves (United Artists, 1944)

Million Dollar Kid (Monogram, 1944)

Voodoo Man (Monogram, 1944)

Christmas Holiday (Universal, 1944)

Practically Yours (Paramount, 1944)

Sensations of 1945 (United Artists, 1944)

Love Letters (Paramount, 1945)

Wild West (Prairie Outlaws) (PRC, 1946)

Gun Town (Universal, 1946)

The Bachelor's Daughters (United Artists, 1946)

Three on a Ticket (PRC, 1947)

The Chinese Ring (Monogram, 1947)

Backlash (20th Century–Fox, 1947)

Second Chance (20th Century–Fox, 1947)

The Crimson Key (20th Century–Fox, 1947)

This Is Nylon (Nylon/Apex Film Corp., 1948)

And Baby Makes Three (Columbia, 1949)

Queen for a Day (United Artists, 1951)

When I was about to go into each of these science fiction
pictures, my reaction was, "Jeez, nobody's going to believe
this" — when I'd read the scripts, I had to shake my head.
But there is a certain type of fan that loves this stuff.
Including myself, in a way — I always enjoy watching them.
It's all imagination, and that's what's great about 'em.

Richard Denning

BOUNCE THE NAME RICHARD DENNING off the average movie fan and you'll get one of a half-dozen different reactions. Many will remember him best as the strapping, athletic lead in Technicolor fluff like *Beyond the Blue Horizon* (1942) with sarong queen Dorothy Lamour. Others will recall his B-grade detective or Western films, or maybe his early television series like *Mr. and Mrs. North* and *Michael Shayne;* baby boomers might think of him first as the governor throughout 12 seasons of *Hawaii Five-O.*

But science fiction fans have a different perspective, and to us Richard Denning was perhaps *the* most decorated soldier in the 1950s war against the armies of *Its* and *Thems* that rose from the depths of the oceans or the bowels of the Earth. Whether taking on the *Creature from the Black Lagoon* or the one *With the Atom Brain*, *The Black Scorpion*, robots who made their *Target Earth* or a three-eyed mutant on the *Day the World Ended*, Richard Denning fought the good fight, sometimes single-handedly, and has survived to bring back the inside story on a lifetime of movie heroics.

Born in Poughkeepsie, New York, in 1914, Louis Albert Denninger, Jr., was the son of a garment manufacturer who relocated and set up shop in Los Angeles when Louis was 18 months old. After finishing school, Denninger enrolled at Woodbury Business College and majored in foreign trade and accounting, graduating with a master's in business administration.

"Dad wanted me to take over the business, and I thought, 'Well, why not?'—I had nothing else. But I never liked accounting, never liked the confinement of being stuck at a desk. So I started joining high school / night school little theater groups, just as a hobby. At this point I was on the road as a salesman for my dad, driving around, calling on customers, but sometimes I'd go up into the Hollywood Hills and sit in the car and work on my script for the play that night. That was my avocation."

As a whim, Denninger decided to compete in a radio contest called *Do You Want to Be an Actor?*, sure that nothing would come of it. Auditioning along with "about four hundred other young people," he read a scene from the Paramount film *The Lives of a Bengal Lancer* (1935), playing the Franchot Tone part. "The contest ran for 13 weeks, and they had a different group of people each week. And I won my week. So the 13 of us won the prize, which was a screen test at Warner Brothers. This was in the spring of '36. I went to Warner Brothers—got there at nine in the morning, went through wardrobe fitting, makeup, shot the test, and I was through by noon. All 13 of us did it— the same morning, on the same set, with the same lighting, the same everything. And we each did a different scene—you figure *that* one out. I never saw the test—naturally—because I doubt if there was ever any film in the

Previous page: An unruffled Richard Denning, showing none of the scars of battles with *The Black Scorpion*, the *Creature from the Black Lagoon* or (pictured) the *Creature with the Atom Brain.*

camera *[laughs]!* I kept asking my agent, 'Why can't I see the test?' and he said, 'It's all confidential, it's top secret.' Well, finally I got a report from him, and he said, 'Warner Brothers said that you're too much like one of their new contract players, and there'd be a conflict.' I asked, 'Who?' and he said, 'They've got this kid Errol Flynn over there.' I didn't know who Errol Flynn was, but he was under contract to Warners and that took care of that."

By now, however, Denninger had what actors refer to as "the fever," not to mention an agent who began knocking on doors on his new client's behalf. "My agent had an interview for me to go to Hal Roach Studios, where they were going to do a picture with Carole Landis called *One Million B.C.* I was to costar in it with her. I had no experience, I had never even been in a picture except my quote-unquote screen test, and they offered to sign me and I was to go right into *One Million B.C.* And I was to get $75 a week for starring in this thing. I was elated. But my agent said, 'No, I don't want you to do it.' I said, *'What?!'* I was making $25 a week at the time, working for my dad in the garment business, as a salesman and what-have-you. But the agent said, 'You're not ready for this'—which was very true. Vic Mature finally did the picture, with Carole Landis, about four years later."

Thinking ahead, Denninger's agent convinced the fledgling actor that the best course of action would be to sign with a studio. "At that time, the studios had the talent pools—they'd sign all these young people and put them through training classes and coaching. So in 1936 I finally signed a contract with Paramount.

"When I first signed at Paramount my name was still Louis Albert Denninger, Jr., and Ted Lesser, who was the head of the talent department, said, 'The first thing you gotta do is change that name.' This was during the time when John Dillinger, the gangster/killer, was popular, and Ted thought Denninger was too close to Dillinger. So we started working with numerology and everything else, trying to come up with something. I asked all my friends, 'What do you think is a good name for me?' *[Laughs.]* It ended up where Ted said, 'Well, you're *definitely* a Richard. And since Denninger is too long, we'll drop the *er,* so you're Richard Denning.' So from that day I became Richard Denning."

Home to such screen greats as Gary Cooper, W.C. Fields, Mae West, John Barrymore and others, the imposing Paramount lot on Melrose Avenue in Los Angeles became a second home to Denning, who, over the course of the next five years, appeared in almost 50 pictures there—from bits to second leads, from fluff like *College Swing* and *Seventeen* to "prestige" pictures like DeMille's *Union Pacific* and *North West Mounted Police.* Half a century after the fact, Denning concedes, "I always had a little guilt complex because I never took on Dad's business. Dad lost interest in the business when there was no point in holding on to it. He finally sold out to one of his competitors and that was that."

Toiling on the Paramount soundstages, Denning helped to support his father as well as his younger brother throughout the early days of his acting career, even though he knew his seven-year Paramount contract was not necessarily worth the paper it was written on. "Yeah, it was a seven-year contract, but that's a laugh because it's only good if Paramount wants to *use* you for seven years. They had three-month options and six-month options, and they could drop you at any time. Every time an option would come up and you were supposed to get one of their fancy raises, they'd say, 'Well, we couldn't use you that much this past term and we've been talking about having to drop you. . . .' Of course, by this time you're panicky because you don't want to be out of a job. Then they'd say, 'Tell you what: If you're willing to work for the same money, then, okay, we'll give you another six months.' So you'd go on for maybe four years for the same money. Many of my peers thought they were going to get $800 a week or something like that, and they never got it. I remember one fellow who was signed about the same time I was — my gosh, he rented Lew Ayres' house up on the top of a hill, he threw big press parties and everything else *[laughs]*. I couldn't figure out how he could afford this, because he wasn't getting any more parts than I was. He told me *[belligerently]*, 'You gotta do this! You gotta spend it to make it!' Well, his option came up and they not only didn't take him at the same salary, they dropped him completely, and he was out of a job and that was the end of his career right then.

"I learned from my business background that you gotta save it when you're making it, 'cause when you're not making it, hopefully you'll have enough to carry you over until the next time. You don't spend it up to the hilt. I've been accused, every once in a while, like Jack Benny, of being a penny-pincher, but I'm able to have a home here [in California] and to live on Hawaii, and I don't have to work. The thrift and the saving paid off and, God willing, I know that I'll never be a burden on my family. I have always been independent enough that I don't want to have to be dependent on somebody else. And now *[pointing to his wife]* I've even married a wealthy woman *[laughs]!*"

Pat Denning laughs good-naturedly at this jibe, sitting in as Denning is interviewed for the first time since the days of television shows like *Michael Shayne*. Movie fans with their elephant memories know of course that Denning's first wife was Evelyn Ankers, queen of horror films during their 1940s heyday at Universal Studios. One of filmland's most enduring unions, Richard and Evelyn married in spite of initial disapproval on the part of Ankers' mother.

"Evie's mother never wanted Evie to get married, because Evie was her meal ticket. When I met Evie she was going with Glenn Ford, and supposedly engaged to him. (Incidentally, Glenn and I belonged to the Bachelors' Club, along with Bob Stack and everybody *else* that got married later!) Glenn was somewhere in Canada telling another girlfriend that the wedding was off and that he was going to marry Evie. In the meantime, Evie's mother figured, 'This is getting too serious with Glenn,' and she started building *me* up. She talked to Danny Linden, my press agent, and he said, 'I'll get 'em together.' So one night he brought Mrs. Ankers and Evie over to the Sunset Bowling Alley, where I was competing in a tournament. They're sitting up in the grandstands watching us bowl, and Danny came down and said, 'Dick, I've got Evelyn Ankers here and she's been dying to meet you for years.' I said, 'Great!' but I was more concerned about the tournament right then. And of course Danny had told Evie, 'This Richard Denning is anxious to meet *you!*' So Evie's sitting up there watching me, and I'm ignoring her completely because I'm bowling. *I'm* thinking, 'If she's that anxious to meet me, she'll keep.' And *she's* up there thinking, 'Who does he think he is?' But she did stay, after much persuasion from Danny.

"My best friend Bob Tappan, who was an agent, was there with me that night, and Bob and I had previously arranged to have a game after the tournament—like eleven o'clock or something—and now I *am* starting to get concerned about this dame that I still haven't met. Danny says, 'Why don't you at least go on up and apologize? Or ask her to bowl or something?' I go up there, and she's dressed for dinner—really gorgeous. I said, 'Gee, how 'bout bowling with Bob and me after the tournament is over?' She's got on this big picture hat and this tight black silk dress, high heel shoes—and she said, 'I'd love it!' So she stayed on, son of a gun, she kicked off her high heel shoes, picked up the ball—and ripped her dress, right up the side. And I thought, 'What a good sport!'

"Now, her mother is very conscious of trying to break Evie and Glenn up, so she says *[in a very British accent]*, 'Why don't you and Bob come up to the house, and we'll have a cup of tea?' They lived in a rented house in Beverly Hills. So we went up, and Evie and I clicked just like *that*. And about three o'clock in the morning Bob Tappan—who's been stuck with Evie's mother *[laughs]*—passes a note to me and it says, 'Get me the hell out of here, I've got to go to work!'"

Denning and Ankers began going out together, quickly became what the Hollywood columnists like to call "an item," and in September 1942, while Denning was in the midst of shooting *Quiet Please, Murder* at Fox, the pair tied the knot in an impromptu Las Vegas elopement. Part of what had attracted Denning to Ankers was the fact that she didn't like the picture business—"That was a *big* plus," Denning admits.

"Her mother pushed her into it as a girl. Evie never really liked it, but her mother was dependent on her. Her dad had left 'em when Evie was a little kid, so her mother had to raise her. Then when Evie started getting into the picture business, this was a good deal so Mama kept really promoting her heavy. But Evie couldn't stand the discipline of the picture business. She used to drive her agents right up the wall, because they'd set up an interview for her with some producer at ten o'clock, and about five minutes to ten she would say, 'Well, I guess I'd better get ready.' And she's supposed to be there in five minutes. So then it was a mad panic, and she'd dash out and get there late, and the agent and the producer would be fuming. She was a good actress, though, and if she'd liked the business, she could have gone a long way."

Sour on the Hollywood rat race in general, Ankers was even more turned off by the many horror films foisted upon her by the powers-that-be at her home studio, Universal. "Evie always wanted to do drama and, no, she *didn't* really like the horror films. But she did 'em. Evie, like all of us in the business, wanted to work, and even though you got the part that you didn't want, at least it's work." Occasionally a horror film like the Sherlock Holmes thriller *The Pearl of Death* would offer Ankers a good acting opportunity, but more often than not she found herself in minor items like *Captive Wild Woman*, *Jungle Woman* and *The Frozen Ghost*, occasionally in the company of one of her least favorite actors, Universal's "master character creator," Lon Chaney, Jr. He returned her sentiments.

"Evidently Universal gave Evie Chaney's old dressing room, and that got him shook up—he didn't like her, either. One day, writers from some of the major magazines were invited to a dinner party at Universal, where they would meet all the top Universal horror stars. Lon Chaney, who's all done up in this weird green makeup, ends up sitting next to me. I was in the service by then and I was in my uniform, my dress blues, and of course I'm kind of envious that they're all working in the picture business and I'm winning the war. And Chaney started making cracks. This was before I got into submarines, and he said, 'I see you're in uniform but you're stationed in downtown L.A.' So we started bickering back and forth.

"Now he starts pushing me. I say, 'Oh, you want to play!' I pick up my sundae and I say, 'Let's have some fun!' And I shove the sundae right in his face *[laughs]*. So Chaney reaches for his hot coffee and he shouts, 'Yeah, *let's!*' But before he can throw it, everybody's up there separating us. Afterwards I was supposed to go on the set of whatever picture it was they were making, and I didn't want to get into anything with Chaney because he was a big guy and he loved to find any excuse to get into a fight. So I just stayed on my side of the stage and he sat on the other side, and we got through the afternoon all right."

Returning to the picture business after four years in the service, Denning found it difficult to jump-start his career after the long absence. "Man, I couldn't get a job for eighteen months!" he exclaims. "By that time we'd used up all our savings, because the whole time I was in the navy I never made any money. We had to start all over again. We were in a house trailer at Paradise Cove—I have always loved the water and boats and everything else, so I set up a hundred lobster traps. I had this rowboat—I couldn't afford an outboard!— and I would row the traps out, set them in the evening and then go out and collect 'em at daybreak. We lived on lobster, and sold lobster, and were very happy. (Evie and I often would look back, years later, and realize that was the happiest time we had.) Finally, after eighteen months of unemployment, I was hired for a radio show, *My Favorite Husband,* with Lucille Ball. So I let somebody else take over the lobster business, and suddenly there were no more lobsters and the business just collapsed."

The radio situation comedy *My Favorite Husband* lasted three seasons before making the switch to television — and to a new title, *I Love Lucy.* Desi Arnaz, Lucy's real-life husband, stepped into the Denning role, but by then Denning was back on his feet career-wise, starring in B movies and also keeping busy in television.

As Denning's career picked up momentum once again, Evelyn Ankers dropped from the business — a career move partially prompted by an ugly confrontation with B movie mogul Sam Katzman, legendarily the cheapest man in Hollywood. "Oh, I tell you," Denning says, rolling his eyes, "he was Evie's demise in pictures. He produced *Last of the Redmen* [1947], which was one of Evie's last pictures, and they were on location on a hot, miserable, dusty day — they'd gotten up at four o'clock in the morning to drive up to the location. She's in a long dress, a long wig (it was a period picture), it was sweaty and miserable and everything was going wrong. And behind schedule. That would really get to Katzman — if you were five *minutes* behind schedule, you were in trouble. Everybody was tired and hungry, and of course all they had was little box lunches then. And Sam and his wife and his nephew Lennie, they're all sitting around having big ice cream sundaes. Just the Katzmans. And everybody else was watching 'em with their tongues hanging out!

"Well, they got through shooting that day, and Evie's hair was a mess. Katzman said, 'That's a wrap. Be here at daybreak in the morning.' Evie said, 'Well, what about my hair?' — she wanted to get it washed and cleaned up. Katzman said, 'Wash it!' Evie said, '*What?* You mean I gotta go home now and wash my hair and set it and everything?' And Katzman said, 'Well, you can't do it here!' And that's when Evie lost her temper — she really let him have it. She called him every name under the sun — 'You cheap, tight bastard! Sitting, eating ice cream in front of all of us, never thinking to bring us anything,' on and on. And I guess the word got around that Evie was difficult after that point...."

In 1948, Denning took the science fiction plunge, into the sky-blue waters that lapped at the beaches of Film Classics' *Unknown Island.* A dinosaur movie shot in garish Cinecolor, it starred Denning, Virginia Grey, Philip Reed and Barton MacLane as adventurers who discover a lost world–type land of prehistoric beasts on an uncharted Pacific atoll. "I admired Virginia Grey very much — she was a lovely girl. Barton MacLane, Philip Reed, we all had fun." Animation buffs have given *Unknown Island* a bum rap because the film employs men in dinosaur suits rather than costly stop motion, but Denning says that "the special effects on *Unknown Island* fascinated me—split screens and black screens and all. The scenes of the men in the dinosaur suits were shot by a second unit, before we started our shooting, and the first time I saw that footage was on the process screens, as Virginia Grey and I reacted to it all. I'd pick up some of these science fiction scripts and I'd think to myself, 'This could be good if the special effects are done right.' Boy, that is the key, to have good special effects like *Unknown Island* did, or *The Black Scorpion*. For those days, I felt that they had excellent effects, and I think the men who do that sort of thing are really marvelous. In my next life I'll probably come back as a special effects man."

It was in the mid-fifties that Denning cemented his science fiction reputation, costarring with Richard Carlson in Universal-International's *Creature from the Black Lagoon*. A modestly budgeted followup to the studio's earlier *It Came from Outer Space*, *Creature* was simply meant to capitalize on the then-hot 3-D and science fiction vogues, but the picture struck a chord with monster movie fans, and the Gill Man quickly took its place alongside Frankenstein's Monster, the Mummy and other bogeymen in the pantheon of classic Universal monsters. "I was impressed with that Creature suit, first while we were filming it, and then especially when I saw the picture. It was a great suit and the man inside was good—*really* good. *Creature from the Black Lagoon* was fun. I remember on the back lot at Universal, it was like October [1953] and it was freezing cold, and we were shooting at night on the Black Lagoon set. We were out in the water and we were tired and it was late, and the prop man kept bringing us brandy to keep us from freezing to death. It worked great, and we were going just fine. And then we finally wrap it up and we go to the dressing rooms—they're nice and warm. All of a sudden *[slurring his words]* that brandy just hit like a sledgehammer! But out in the cold and the wet and wind, it didn't bother us at all!"

Adding to Denning's enjoyment of the movie was the rare opportunity to play an unsympathetic role: the expedition leader who puts the capture of the Creature above the safety of his fellow adventurers. "It was good to get to change. My wife, Pat, when she sees me in something like that, says, 'Oh, *you're* not that way. I don't know why you played that.' But I enjoyed that role in *Creature*." Still happy with his performance and impressed with the film itself, Denning dismisses the 3-D process in which it was shot. "That was a fad, and I never thought it would last. But I still think probably someday it'll be natural—you'll be able to look at 3-D movies without the glasses. They'll get it, mark my words."

Constantly busy throughout the fifties, Denning's recollection of some of his lesser pictures is hazy; *Target Earth* and *Creature with the Atom Brain* are victims of the memory hole. Pressed about *Target Earth,* a Herman Cohen production about alien robots taking over an evacuated city, Denning offers, "To get the scenes of the empty streets, we had to get out there at four in the

Dick Wessel, Barton MacLane, Philip Reed, Virginia Grey and Denning watch with horror in Film Classics' Cinecolor *Unknown Island*.

morning—in those days, there wasn't that much traffic downtown. And we'd start shooting as soon as it got daylight, before the cars started coming through." And the robots (actually only *one* robot, and made to seem like more through the miracle of film editing): "I think for those days it was good. I remember I did marvel at it—it looked phony when you were right up close, but then when you'd see it on the screen, it looked pretty good."

Creature with the Atom Brain has disappeared from Denning's memory almost completely, except for the fact that he found the makeup unconvincing (the film's legion of zombies had sutured scalps) and that director Edward L. Cahn put speed above all other considerations. "On pictures like that you really didn't even *have* a director. Those directors are just there to see that the stuff gets done—a ringmaster. They kept things glued together, and [gave] very little direction." *Atom Brain* was written by Curt Siodmak, a name Denning remembers from the Universal forties fright films that starred (as often as not) Evelyn Ankers. "That sci-fi stuff was his knack, and he was good at that. I remember when I was about to go into each of these science fiction pictures, my reaction was, 'Jeez, nobody's going to believe this'—when I'd read the scripts, I had to shake my head. But there *is* a certain type of fan that loves this stuff. Including myself, in a way—I always enjoy watching them. It's all

Being treated for an on-set head injury during the filming of *Creature from the Black Lagoon,* Julie Adams gets moral support from director Jack Arnold, Gill Man Ben Chapman, Denning and Richard Carlson. (Photofest)

imagination, and that's what's great about 'em. It takes a great imagination to dream that stuff up."

Another director that Denning classifies alongside Edward Cahn was Roger Corman, who starred Denning in the end-of-the-world thriller *Day the World Ended.* "Oh, he'd tell you nothing except, 'Just *do* it,'" Denning scoffs. "All he was concerned about was, 'I've got *X* number of pages to do today.' That was it, boom. And no matter what happened in front of the camera, it was fine — '*Print! Print!*' But the picture itself was damn good, because it was way ahead of its time."

A man more to Denning's liking was the producer of *Day the World Ended,* veteran B moviemaker and film historian Alex Gordon. "I loved Alex Gordon. Alex was probably one of the sweetest, most congenial producers that I've ever worked for, and he certainly was the greatest fan anybody could want. He knew more than you could imagine, and I just marveled at his recall and his precision. Talking about older pictures, he knew who the assistant director was, who the cameraman was, this, that and the other thing. But always very sweet and pleasant, very quiet, friendly. He must have liked Evie and me because he's been a great and constant fan and friend. I also did a film in

England for his brother Richard—*Assignment Redhead* [1962]. He was very nice, too, but Alex—I think he's the tops." Denning also enjoyed working with Corman regular Mike Connors, the baddie in Denning's *Day the World Ended* and *The Oklahoma Woman* (1956). "Mike I loved, too, we were great friends. He's a very sweet guy, and I wish we could get together more often. We did quite a few things together; I remember coming home one night from *Oklahoma Woman* and I told Evie, 'This new kid Mike Connors—I think he's really gonna make it.' Then when he did [television's] *Tightrope!* and *Mannix,* I was so glad for him. He comes to Maui every once in a while, and we get together and commiserate *[laughs]!*"

Still at AIP, Denning also appeared in Alex Gordon's *Girls in Prison* (1956) and Corman's made-in-Hawaii *Naked Paradise* (1957)—an experience that helped Denning decide to make the move to Maui upon his retirement in the sixties. By the mid-fifties, of course, Denning was well used to lightning-fast production schedules, whether they be in television (*Mr. and Mrs. North,* *Michael Shayne, The Flying Doctor*), the Sam Katzman B unit or at AIP. "There again, my business education: I could look at it from the producer's point of view, and knew it was costing him money. After I finished *Mr. and Mrs. North*—three shows a week, two days a show—that's when I did *An Affair to Remember* [1957], with Cary Grant and Deborah Kerr. We'd sit on the set, Cary and everybody, sitting around, rehearsing. And Cary'd say *[Denning claps his hands together],* 'Well, I think that's enough for today,' and everybody would go home. My thought was, 'How can they *do* this? This is costing money!' In the time I spent on *An Affair to Remember*, I could have shot six feature films—and I'm only in the last half of the thing!"

Monster exterminating was a full-time job for movie heroes in the fifties, and Denning was pressed into service once again when *The Black Scorpion* menaced Mexico City in the 1957 Warner Bros. release. "Before I went down to Mexico for that picture, Evie and I had started building a new house in the Hollywood Hills. I could use the money they were going to pay me for *Black Scorpion* because I wanted to put it into the house. So I asked Evie, 'Can you handle things while I'm doing the picture?' and she said she could. (Evie could always do *any*thing.) So she took over the house, and I went down to Mexico."

In Mexico, however, taming the scorpion on film became less important than keeping leading lady Mara Corday at arm's length on the set. "Mara started to get very friendly. I'm down there over Thanksgiving—Christmas—New Year's—and she got more friendly all the time! And she was getting more and more *attractive* to me all the time!" Corday's boyfriend, actor Richard Long, was there in Mexico City as well, but not even his presence seemed to put a damper on things. "That didn't seem to bother Mara—and so I was getting less and less concerned about it *[laughs]!* Finally I got on the phone and I called Evie and told her, 'I think you better come down here.' 'Why?' she asked—she had the house project and her mom was sick and everything. I said, 'Well, there's a girl on the show and I'm afraid something's gonna happen—' 'I'll be right down!' she said.

"So she comes down, and after all these weeks away from her I'm *ready*—you know what I mean *[laughs]*? But first we go out to dinner. Evie loved oysters, and of course in Mexico they're cheap, so she had about a dozen and a half oysters, filet mignon, champagne, the whole bit. Now we're ready to go back to the hotel—the Hotel Bamer in Mexico City—and make up for lost time. I put my arms around her and all of a sudden *[Denning pretends to be on the verge of vomiting]*—she says, 'Excuse me!' and runs off. Well, she was sick in bed for four days!" *[Laughs.]*

Mara Corday eventually proved to be the least of Denning's problems in Mexico. "We shot out in villages, and I remember one day we had box lunches out in this village, outside of Mexico City. We broke for lunch and we're having sandwiches. I went to take a bite, and the flies were so thick on the sandwich I had to blow them away before I could take a bite, and *hope* I wasn't getting too many flies! We were in the town center, and it's the town rest room—there's no sanitation. You walk in there, and you just try to find a place to step so you're not stepping on a recent pile. And the flies are all over. So I wound up after that one with intestinal amoeba and dysentery and hepatitis. All from *The Black Scorpion*." Second lead Carlos Rivas was less than sympathetic. "I was so fed up with Carlos Rivas—he'd say, 'I don't understand why you get *seek. I* don't get *seek!*' I said, 'Well, your water—' and Rivas would say, 'I eat it all the time!' So about a year later he came up to Hollywood to do a picture, and I bumped into him. He said, 'Oh, I'm so *seek!* Your water!' I told him, 'I eat it all the time!'" *[Laughs.]*

A familiar face in science fiction films, Denning introduced himself to fans of horror movies in 1963 when he appeared in *Twice-Told Tales*, a stodgy Technicolor anthology horror film; Denning appeared in the third and final segment (*The House of the Seven Gables*) opposite the film's star, Vincent Price. "He was *[Denning hems and haws]* . . . kind of stuffy. But I never got to know him that well. I never really bothered people I worked with; if they didn't seem to be interested in getting any friendlier with me, well, then, so what? I could enjoy being a friend of the sound man or a cameraman just as much as the star—the name value never meant anything to me. That's why I wasn't that much of a fan of anybody, because I figured everybody was doing their job, just working. That was the only time I worked with Price. Beverly Garland was also in that—I still see her once in a while. A good, very efficient worker, and nice to be around."

After Denning's television series *Karen* expired in 1965, he made the decision to quit the business and move to Maui, Hawaii. "I told my agent, 'I can't believe this business anymore. I get scripts submitted to me, and I can't even figure out what they're about.' This was just when the change was starting, from the type of picture like *An Affair to Remember* to psychological things where the audience has to arrive at the conclusion of the story or something! Not long before that time, I had said to myself, 'What I need is a modern agent,' so I got one—porkpie hat, Sunset Boulevard, the whole bit. I went up to his office and he submitted his first script to me—'Oh, you're gonna love this!' he said. I read it . . . I gave it to Evie . . . and I said, 'What *is* it?' It was the weirdest thing. I was supposed to be a senator, and as the picture opens I'm plastering a wall, covering over something. Eventually you realize that I'm burying a woman, covering her bust with the plaster. Later I'm making violent love to a teenager on the beach—no reason, no explanation, nothing to it. I thought, 'Well, I guess the guy's a real weirdo.' Then the next scene I'm in the Senate, giving an oration, which has nothing to do with anything else. And then at the end, I'm plastering up another body in the wall! I couldn't even figure out how to play it—it was just a nut! The agent said, 'This is the new thing! This is the new era!' The business has changed so tremendously in fifty years that it's not the same in any sense of the word."

Denning was barely into his retirement when he was offered the semiregular part of Governor Philip Grey on television's *Hawaii Five-O*, starring Jack Lord. "*Five-O* was an added blessing and it worked out great. I had no idea it was gonna go twelve years, though!" Denning laughs. Evelyn Denning was offered the part of the governor's wife, but she "said no. She wanted no part of it! She had more fun when we'd go to Honolulu. I'd go there and be working on a *Five-O* and, of course, Evie would be in seventh heaven because now she was in Honolulu, which is the *big* city—she'd be in her car, shopping all over town for everything. That was much more fun for her than working *[laughs]!* She'd say, 'Somebody's gotta spend it if you're making it. I'm gonna spend it!' And she usually won, and spent more than I made! I have a knack for picking wives who like to shop!"

After the 12th season of *Hawaii Five-O,* the show's run finally came to an end and Denning remarked, "Evelyn and I are looking forward to the eighties as a new era—'retirement and pensions.' We hope it works out." But this new era was not to be: Evelyn developed cancer shortly afterward. "When Evie went through her two years with cancer, even with my Medicare and Screen Actors Guild Health Insurance, I'll bet there was still at least $75,000 left to be paid. Which, luckily, I had saved up, so it was all right." On August 28, 1985, Ankers succumbed at home.

"It was a great marriage—we were broke two or three times, but we'd always end up back on our feet again and we wound up very comfortably and raised our daughter. Evie was a wonderful wife, we had forty-three years together, and I think we got closer the last two years, when she had cancer, than we had ever been before. Our daughter Dee and Evie finally got to be close at the end as well. Evie and Dee never got along too well and they just didn't have a rapport that was what it should have been (Dee was antiestablishment).

Pat and Richard Denning in their California home, 1989.

Then when Evie got so sick, I think Dee suddenly realized, 'My gosh, I don't really know that much about Mom.' Dee finally had a reconciliation with Evie about two days before Evie died, so that was a miracle and a blessing. And she now wants to do a book on Evie and myself, and our life together."

Deeply religious, Denning thanks God for his many blessings. "I believe that with all my heart, and Pat believes it. And our relationship right now is a reward for a lot of things that we both went through. And no matter what happens, I don't feel alone because I know God is not only with me, He's with us, and God is our partner in our marriage."

Present connections with the industry: "None. I pick up *Variety* or *The Hollywood Reporter* and I might as well be reading the Chinese phone book—I hardly recognize a single name, unless it's in the obit column!"

Favorites among the movie people he's worked with: "I think Ingrid Bergman [*Adam Had Four Sons*, 1941] might be *the* favorite. She really was such an admirable person—nobody could swear in front of her. She was a lady and just a real charming person. I was also very fond of Deborah Kerr [*An Affair to Remember*], I thought she was great, and I loved Dorothy Lamour [*Beyond the Blue Horizon*]. We went through a lot together in the nine months it took to make that picture, I'll tell you."

On his days as a movie star: "I'm very greateful for a career that wasn't spectacular, but always made a living or filled in in between. I have wonderful memories of it, but I don't really miss it."

And the secret to a 45-year career in the movie business: "Get along with everybody. I never really had any trouble getting along with anybody I worked with, and I think that makes a difference. I enjoyed everything I've ever done, and when I look back I really have no regrets. It *was* a wonderful business."

RICHARD DENNING FILMOGRAPHY

On Such a Night (Paramount, 1937)
Hold 'Em Navy! (Paramount, 1937)
Daughter of Shanghai (Paramount, 1937)
Give Me a Sailor (Paramount, 1938)
The Big Broadcast of 1938 (Paramount, 1938)
The Buccaneer (Paramount, 1938)
Illegal Traffic (Paramount, 1938)
Her Jungle Love (Paramount, 1938)
Campus Confessions (Paramount, 1938)
College Swing (Paramount, 1938)
The Texans (Paramount, 1938)
King of Alcatraz (Paramount, 1938)
Say It in French (Paramount, 1938)
Touchdown Army (Paramount, 1938)
The Arkansas Traveler (Paramount, 1938)
Hotel Imperial (Paramount, 1939)
Undercover Doctor (Paramount, 1939)
King of Chinatown (Paramount, 1939)
Persons in Hiding (Paramount, 1939)
Zaza (Paramount, 1939)
Ambush (Paramount, 1939)
Union Pacific (Paramount, 1939)
Million Dollar Legs (Paramount, 1939)
The Night of Nights (Paramount, 1939)
I'm from Missouri (Paramount, 1939)
Some Like It Hot (Rhythm Romance) (Paramount, 1939)
Geronimo (Paramount, 1939)
Disputed Passage (Paramount, 1939)
Grand Jury Secrets (Paramount, 1939)
Sudden Money (Paramount, 1939)
The Gracie Allen Murder Case (Paramount, 1939)
The Star Maker (Paramount, 1939)
Our Neighbors—The Carters (Paramount, 1939)
Television Spy (Paramount, 1939)
Love Thy Neighbor (Paramount, 1940)

Emergency Squad (Paramount, 1940)
Queen of the Mob (Paramount, 1940)
The Farmer's Daughter (Paramount, 1940)
Golden Gloves (Paramount, 1940)
North West Mounted Police (Paramount, 1940)
Seventeen (Paramount, 1940)
Those Were the Days (Paramount, 1940)
Parole Fixer (Paramount, 1940)
Adam Had Four Sons (Columbia, 1941)
West Point Widow (Paramount, 1941)
Beyond the Blue Horizon (Paramount, 1942)
Ice-Capades Revue (Rhythm Hits the Ice) (Republic, 1942)
The Glass Key (Paramount, 1942)
Quiet Please, Murder (20th Century–Fox, 1942)
Black Beauty (20th Century–Fox, 1946)
The Fabulous Suzanne (Republic, 1946)
Seven Were Saved (Paramount, 1947)
Caged Fury (Paramount, 1948)
Lady at Midnight (Eagle-Lion, 1948)
Disaster (Paramount, 1948)
Unknown Island (Film Classics, 1948)
Harbor of Missing Men (Republic, 1950)
No Man of Her Own (Paramount, 1950)
Double Deal (RKO, 1950)
Flame of Stamboul (Columbia, 1951)
Secrets of Beauty (Hallmark Productions, 1951)
Insurance Investigator (Republic, 1951)
Week-End with Father (Universal, 1951)
Okinawa (Columbia, 1952)
Scarlet Angel (Universal, 1952)
Hangman's Knot (Columbia, 1952)

Target Hong Kong (Columbia, 1952)
The 49th Man (Columbia, 1953)
The Glass Web (Universal, 1953)
Jivaro (Paramount, 1954)
Creature from the Black Lagoon (Universal, 1954)
Battle of Rogue River (Columbia, 1954)
Target Earth (Allied Artists, 1954)
Air Strike (Lippert, 1955)
The Magnificent Matador (20th Century–Fox, 1955)
Creature with the Atom Brain (Columbia, 1955)
The Gun That Won the West (Columbia, 1955)
The Crooked Web (Columbia, 1955)
Day the World Ended (American Releasing [AIP], 1956)
The Oklahoma Woman (American Releasing [AIP], 1956)

Girls in Prison (AIP, 1956)
Naked Paradise (Thunder over Hawaii) (AIP, 1957)
The Buckskin Lady (United Artists, 1957)
An Affair to Remember (20th Century–Fox, 1957)
The Black Scorpion (Warner Bros., 1957)
The Lady Takes a Flyer (Universal, 1958)
Desert Hell (20th Century–Fox, 1958)
Million Dollar Manhunt (Assignment Redhead) (Tudor Pictures, 1962)
Twice-Told Tales (United Artists, 1963)
I Sailed to Tahiti with an All-Girl Crew (World Entertainment Corp., 1969)

A photograph of Denning is seen in *Night Club Scandal* (Paramount, 1937). Denning's footage was deleted from *You and Me* (Paramount, 1938). A clip of Denning and Deborah Kerr (from *An Affair to Remember*) is seen in *Sleepless in Seattle* (TriStar, 1993).

Robby the Robot got drunk one day at noon,
and his innards were promptly replaced! ...
Drunken robots are not to be countenanced!

Anne Francis

IT IS ONE OF THE INDELIBLE IMAGES of the 1950s: Against a backdrop of astral blackness and ringed planets, a fearsome-looking robot looms; lying unconscious in this metal monster's arms is a miniskirted girl with long ash-blond hair (and longer legs). Every science fiction fan worth his salt knows that this is the emblem for the film *Forbidden Planet*, MGM's one major contribution to the 1950s science fiction/monster movie boom, and that the fearsome mechanical man is actually the astounding Robby the Robot, poster boy for fifties science fiction. Does that make Anne Francis science fiction fans' favorite pinup girl?

"I got that part because I was under contract to MGM and I had good legs," the actress blurts out with no hesitation. "And still *do*, I might add!"

Over lunch at the Musso and Frank Grill, the popular and historic site of many a Hollywood meal and movie-related deal, Anne Francis looks back at the seminal outer space adventure with both fondness and fascinating insight. "I think that when I did the film, I *was* aware of its metaphysical implications. At that time, we did *not* have what is called today New Age thinking, which is very involved with metaphysical thinking. So for me, when I was doing *Forbidden Planet*, it seemed quite obvious that the Id was similar to what one in metaphysics would call the mass subconscious, and that what we put into this mass subconscious in our thinking comes back. Much as, in the Bible, it says, 'That which I have feared the most has come upon me.' So at that time it didn't seem dumb to me that the collective thinking could create a monster. It *still* doesn't seem dumb to me that our collective thinking is creating monsters — like nuclear bombs and everything else. The story made sense enough to me at the time."

Gulp. Lunch begins with bread, salads and that profound evaluation of *Forbidden Planet* — the sort of analysis that might sound odd coming from another fifties ingenue, but not from the cult actress whose list of credits includes *Forbidden Planet* as only *one* of many memorable titles. Born a stone's throw from Ossining, New York's, famous Sing Sing prison, Anne Francis' amazing career began when she was six months old and posing for calendar photos. Before she was five, she was a fashion model whose image appeared on the covers and pages of many national magazines; she made her television debut on an NBC Christmas show in *1939;* and she was on Broadway at age 11, playing Gertrude Lawrence as a child in the stage hit *Lady in the Dark.* Three thousand radio appearances during the 1940s earned the blue-eyed trooper the nickname the Little Queen of Soap Operas.

Eager to try acting in motion pictures, she made her first trek to Hollywood in 1946 and soon found herself under contract to MGM (where she also went to school with Elizabeth Taylor, Natalie Wood and Dean Stockwell, in the little schoolhouse on the Metro lot). "I was there under contract for one

Previous page: "Robby the Robot was the most expensive 'actor' in *[Forbidden Planet]*," says Anne Francis. "The *outer* robot, not the inner!"

year, and did two days' work in a picture called *Summer Holiday* [1948] with Walter Huston and Mickey Rooney. I went back to New York after that, into the Golden Era of Television—live TV back in New York, where they had really great writers."

She won movie roles in the East as well, appearing as a teenage prostitute in the female juvenile delinquency drama *So Young, So Bad* (1950); winning a small part in the documentary-flavored *The Whistle at Eaton Falls* (1951), made in Hanover, New Hampshire; and playing her first fantasy film role, a bit in director William Dieterle's classic *Portrait of Jennie* (1948). "I was still a kid when I did *Portrait of Jennie*, very obviously. It was just one quick scene, but I *am* glad that I shared the scene with Ethel Barrymore in a very minute way. She was very charming, very nice. And I remember William Dieterle wore white cotton editor's gloves—but I'm not certain why!"

Hollywood beckoned (and Francis reluctantly answered the call again) in the early fifties, this time landing a berth as a contract player at Darryl F. Zanuck's 20th Century-Fox. In December 1953, she played her first science fiction film lead in the Lenny Bruce–scripted science fiction comedy *The Rocket Man* (shooting title: *The Kid from Outer Space*), made at RKO by Panoramic Productions for Fox, but (like costars John Agar and Beverly Garland) she remembers little about the film. Far better and more memorable experiences awaited her once she changed studios and once again became part of the MGM "family"; for the Culver City studio, she appeared not only in *Forbidden Planet* but also in the 1955 classics *Blackboard Jungle* and *Bad Day at Black Rock*.

"*Bad Day at Black Rock* was hard," Francis recalls. "It was a very, *very* difficult show, because we were doing it in August in a place called Lone Pine, which is next to Death Valley, in the desert. The temperature was about a hundred degrees. And in those days, they used klieg lights to offset the sun. So, *with* those lights, we were working in 115, 120 degrees. We all lost a tremendous amount of weight; I mean, at the end of the day, who was hungry? You just dragged yourself back to the hotel. Spencer Tracy had a *very* hard time. They had to coax him more than once to please, *please* see it through, because it was terribly draining for him. For everyone! I mean, I was in my early twenties, so if it was hard for me, you can imagine how some of the others must have felt."

According to Francis, Tracy "would be very moody sometimes—the black Irish moods, you know. Then at other times, he'd be extremely accessible—he'd sit and work on a scene with you, and go over and over and *over* the lines. He was both an angel and—a stinker sometimes, depending what was going on in his own personal life with his physical problems and perhaps his personal emotional problems."

What might have been her least challenging MGM role has, of course, become her best known, as Francis played Altaira, the unworldly daughter of space pioneer Walter Pidgeon, in the studio's otherworldly *Forbidden Planet*. Preparing to play the naïve character with the scene-stealing legs required "no great preparation on my part; I wasn't that worldly-wise at that point myself. I remember that there were some costumes that they decided were too revealing. One was a silver lamé jumpsuit with silver boots—just absolutely gorgeous. It is rumored that [production head] Dore Schary's wife Miriam nixed it, saying that it was just too sexy, too extreme. It covered me from head to toe, along with the silver boots that matched this lamé suit. Kind of shows you how far we've come since then!"

Remembering her *Planet* costars, Francis smiles, "Walter Pidgeon loved to recite dirty limericks. He was a wonderful gentleman in every way, except for his proclivity for dirty limericks, which *were* really very, very funny—they were sort of 'the thing' back then, and none of the gentlemen on the show could match 'em. Walter and also George Sanders, who was on another film that I did [*The Scarlet Coat,* 1955], both loved dirty limericks. And Leslie Nielsen I was madly in love with. Les was a very gentle, kind, terrific guy, just as he is today. He had a great sense of humor; today it has become more extreme than it was when I worked with him in those days *[laughs]*! But Les, much like Burt Reynolds—they both have a wonderful basic outlook on life and they don't take themselves terribly seriously. Or, if they *do,* it's not noticeable on the outside."

And Robby the Robot? "Robby got drunk one day at noon, and his innards [actor Frankie Darro] were promptly replaced," she recalls, letting out another laugh. "He almost took a full nosedive, if three grips hadn't grabbed him in time. Robby was the most expensive 'actor' on the show—the outer Robby, not the inner! The facade was worth much more than any of the actors; the actors could have been replaced, but Robby would have been a terrible expense. Robby was really the star of the show, so the young man who was working him from the inside was replaced one afternoon after a five-martini lunch. Drunken robots are not to be countenanced!"

While Robby seems to be the threat to Francis on the film's poster, precautions were taken during production to protect the actress from a very different member of the cast. "They had the leopard behind glass, and made it look like I was touching the animal," she reveals. "They don't like to take chances; that's why they did it that way."

The hardest part of *Forbidden Planet,* Francis adds, was "reacting to things that weren't there. Disney's people did all of the special effects, the cartooning of the monster and all of that sort of thing. That was all postproduction. *We* were racing through the film, running away from things we had to imagine at all times. It was a matter of trying to grade our fear from one scene to another, from apprehension to *[laughs]*—to horrific extremes of facial expressions! I think that was the major challenge in the film, for all of us.

"[Producer] Nicholas Nayfack was a darling man. Fred Wilcox, the director, was fine, too, but his direction was, as I said earlier, 'Look scared. Look *more* scared.' It was not an in-depth study of character going on. I was the in-genue. It was pretty well defined, who each of us was. It was a science fiction fairy tale and I was the sleeping princess, no more, no less. I was awakened by the prince who landed in his flying saucer. I don't think anything more could be made of it; that's what the story was and there really wasn't much else to do. Yes, it's condescending, but that's what the story was. It's still going on today. Maybe women's roles have matured to a certain point, except that I think that a lot of the films are still playing the sex game. Instead of really hav-ing much growth with the women, I think their [idea of] 'feminine freedom' is that *now* one takes off more clothes. *That's* feminine freedom. I don't think there's that much more respect for women [in films] now than there was then. The attitude is that women don't have much to offer society. But that's gone on for centuries. There have been incredible women artists and composers, and folks are just becoming aware of them because more is being said about it, more is being brought forward. It's a big battle to get that information out."

Regarding *Forbidden Planet's* enduring appeal, Francis admits, "At the time, I don't think that any of us really were aware of the fact that it was going to turn into a longtime cult film, probably *much,* much stronger today than it was then." Costar Richard Anderson recalled that MGM thought of the film as a B movie, an opinion Francis doesn't dispute. "That's quite possible. But then I think at the time they also thought that *Bad Day at Black Rock* was a B movie. And *that's* become one of the big classics — which, again, I'm thrilled to have been in. So, even in those days, I think judgment was not always perfect as far as movies were concerned. *Forbidden Planet* just had a life of its own, something that none of us was aware was going to happen. I first saw the film in one of the screening rooms at the studio, and I think we were all im-pressed with what had been done by Disney; what they accomplished was quite phenomenal. Also, Joshua Meador's beautiful metal sculptings on the set were not nearly as appreciated as they should have been. He was a marvelous, marvelous artist who also had a lot to do with the sets and the backdrops."

Her favorite scene in the film? "Probably any scene where I kissed Les Nielsen, 'cause I had that terrible crush on him! And if Les does another *Naked Gun* movie, I think it would be wonderful fun for me to run through in the background with the lion — in the same outfit."

Looking back, Francis admits to having mixed emotions about her MGM years. "A lot of wonderful people, a lot of great crew people — but there was always the unfathomable hierarchy. I was never a very political individual; I was not able to play a lot of the games that were played in those days. I guess I was sort of a maverick in many ways. I had come out from New York, where the attitude was far more stress as far as being an actor, and looks were not really as important. Then I came out here where we were admonished to not be seen with curlers in our hair at the local market, to be made up at all times.

Jeans and tennis shoes and old shirts were not acceptable at the lot. So in many ways, it was kind of hard. Also, one would be taken to task for one's friends. I remember one day I was seen talking to a black actor at a restaurant quite close to the studio — it was a purely innocent meeting with other friends, but I was seen talking with him earnestly about a subject. And I was on the carpet the next day — I was not to be seen talking to any black actors, thank you very much. (Which I did not pay heed to.) So in many ways I didn't really fit what was expected, what the mold was supposed to be."

Freelancing after having left MGM by her own request, Francis turned up in the occasional movie but worked more steadily in television, where (among many other series) she acted on *Alfred Hitchcock Presents*, *The Alfred Hitchcock Hour*, *The Man from U.N.C.L.E.*, *The Invaders* and, perhaps most notably, *The Twilight Zone*. "Rod Serling was a wonderful man — a brilliant man, with a great sense of humor. That was back in the days when we rehearsed the show for a full week before we shot it, so we knew every shot that was going to be done. It was wonderful to be able to do that."

Her sixties film roles included the science fiction suspenser *The Satan Bug* and the melodramatic *Brainstorm* (both 1965). *The Satan Bug*, about a government search for a fanatic with a lethal supply of stolen lab-created virus, saw Francis replacing actress Joan Hackett as the female lead; just as in *Forbidden Planet* and *Bad Day at Black Rock*, she was the only woman in the cast. "I think there was some sort of altercation between Joan and the producers about how the character should be played, so I was called on a day's notice to go do it. I *liked* the script very, very much; it was an interesting script. John Sturges directed it; John had directed me in *Bad Day at Black Rock*. But John and [film editor] Ferris Webster were having meetings at lunch every day about another movie they were going to be doing, *The Hallelujah Trail* [1965]. Unfortunately, I think that *Satan Bug* kind of suffered a bit in the editing room because of this next project that they were into. I felt that *The Satan Bug* was not Ferris Webster's best job of editing: There are *long* drive-ins, *getting* out of the car, *walking* all the way up to the house, another person *opening* the door — they did not have cuts that would have kept that movie moving, and so the pace was dragged out tremendously. And it was the kind of a movie that *had* to have fast pacing. So I was very, very disappointed when I saw it. And the only thing I can consider is the fact that John and Ferris were pressed for time for this other biggie, *The Hallelujah Trail*, and that *Satan Bug* suffered. But, as I said, originally the script itself was terrific."

Brainstorm starred Jeff Hunter as a space scientist who hatches a bizarre scheme to feign insanity in order to get away with the murder of his lover's (Francis) sadistic husband (Dana Andrews). "That was directed by Bill Conrad, who is one of the brightest directors I've ever worked with in my life. He is absolutely incredible. Before a hysterical scene that I had in that film, Bill came up to me and he said, 'Now, when you get into the sobbing, I would like it

Francis (opposite George Maharis) thought *The Satan Bug*'s original script was "terrific," but that the movie suffered in editing.

to reach a peak' — and he gave me the *sound* of the highest pitch that he wanted in this sobbing scene. It was very exciting to work with somebody who had that much of an insight into the *sound* that he wanted. I had started in radio as a child, and *he* had been a radio actor for many years before he went into films and television, so he was very much involved with pitch. He also has a genius for making photographic decisions that were very unusual, on the spot. Brilliant, brilliant, brilliant director, and never really recognized as such."

In 1965 Francis also began her one-year run as a James Bond-ish private detective (complete with futuristic communicators and spy equipment) on television's *Honey West.* Based on the popular novels by Gloria Fickling and Forrest E. Fickling, the action-filled ABC half-hour series costarred John Ericson (as Honey's short-tempered partner Sam Bolt) and Irene Hervey (as her Aunt Meg). "*Honey West* was fun to do because we had such wonderful character actors on the show—I really enjoyed it for that reason. And also I loved the physical activity involved. I studied karate for the show and for about a month I worked out to get in shape for it. Actually, that came in handy many years later when I was doing a play at the Ahmanson Theater. I was going down the stairway into the bowels of the Ahmanson to get my auto—by that time, just about everyone else had cleared out—and I suddenly heard footsteps behind me. I went down one flight and I heard him; I went down a second flight and I heard him getting closer. I thought, 'Oh, baby, I'd better do something now.'

"About halfway down the next flight of stairs, as I heard the footsteps getting closer, I just whirled around and grabbed the bannister in one hand—and there was this guy. He stopped short, I looked at him and he looked at me—it felt like we were there for about a half hour, although it was probably only about three seconds. He said, 'Did I scare you?' and I said, '*No.*' And I was just waiting for him to make a move, because I knew from the karate training that, if he moved toward me, I might be hurt, but *he* would be hurt, too, because I would help him on down the stairs! So I just waited. Finally he turned around and went back up the stairs, and I went down and got in my car. *Then* I fell apart—just absolutely! But it *worked*, that instantaneous thing that just grips you, and you're prepared. I just knew instinctively that the best place for me to handle it was on the stairway with his being above me. On the flat, I would not have much of a chance."

Another part of the challenge of *Honey West* was keeping one move ahead of costar Bruce Biteabit, Honey's irascible 28-pound ocelot. "When cats get hot or tired, they start getting a little snarly. At times, it was like trying to hold a pair of cobras; each end of him was going one way or the other. From working with cats, I know that if one is happy, it bites and scratches, and if it's *un*happy, it bites and scratches. So it really doesn't make too much difference *[laughs]*! I learned pretty much to keep ahead of him when he was squirming, I do love animals, so we got along quite well. But a lot of character actors who came on the show were petrified of him." Francis was Emmynominated for her performance on the show ("I lost to a wonderful lady, Barbara Stanwyck—each one of us was rooting for the other"), and won a Golden Globe award. But, to everyone's surprise, the well-received and popular series was bumped by ABC at the end of its first year.

"Cancellation had nothing to do with the ratings—it was doing very well. But ABC was able to buy *The Avengers* for a lot less money than it cost to produce *Honey West*. Once they found that this genre would work, they dropped *Honey West* and brought over *The Avengers*—which did very well here. Its

Television's crime-busting *Honey West* could vamp information out of a suspect as easily as subdue him with a judo flip. Her enviable costar was Bruce Biteabit.

cancellation was a mixed blessing. I worked very hard on that show—day after day, seventeen or eighteen hours a day. I had a four-year-old daughter at the time, and I had very little opportunity to spend any 'quality time' at all with her. So in one way, the cancellation was a blessing in that I had that frustration behind me. And, for another thing, I think that if it had gone another season or two—who knows what direction anyone's life or career is going to take? I think that, when you have more than one interest in life, you can let certain areas lapse."

Another "notorious" credit for Francis was the 1968 *Funny Girl*, the Barbra Streisand–starring film bio of old-time stage comedian Fanny Brice. "The role that I was originally contracted to do was pretty much cut out of the movie, 'cut out' day by day, without shooting. So that was a very rough time for me. I don't think [director] William Wyler wanted that character in the movie to begin with, so the whole thing was unpleasant. People blamed it on Barbra; *I* did not blame it on Barbra. At that time, I had a public relations person who made a lot of statements about Barbra that were attributed to me. I *never* blamed Barbra, because I had absolutely no idea [why the cutting happened]; it may have been timing, the show may have been too long. But the role originally as written in the script was a wonderful, wonderful role—including a drunk scene which I *did* play, but they took it out of the film. It just turned into a whole mess."

In the seventies and eighties, her career took on yet more diversity, with Francis trying directing ("I didn't *try*—I *did* direct!") and turning her hand to writing. Her short film *Gemini Rising* (1970), about rodeo riders, has been seen on PBS, and her "spiritual exposé" *Voices from Home: An Inner Journey* was published in 1982. "Through my lifetime, I have had a lot of unusual experiences that would border on psychic and spiritual and such, and I have met many people along the way who were interested in such things. That's why I wrote the book, to share my experiences, so that other people who may have been going through similar things would not think they were *crazy*. (At least, I don't think *I* am!) Unfortunately, the publishers went bankrupt within a couple of months after it was published. The wild thing was, I had a ten-minute interview with Chris Wallace on *The Today Show*—and then there were no books in bookstores *[laughs]*!"

More recently, Francis has continued to act on stage and television, "and also to have fun with life as well." She much prefers looking ahead to looking back, and does not bother to collect her own movies or television appearances. "My movies are things that have been done; I'm through with them. I know what they are, and I move on to the next thing. Right now, I'm studying musical theater *singing*—and having a *lot* of fun with that. I'd love to do some musical work on the stage. I've sung in the past, but I've never *really* studied it for placement and endurance, which theater really takes. I've been working on it for a year now, and each lesson [my voice] gets stronger and stronger. And I love doing it, it's just great therapy."

She's heard the recent rumblings about a big-screen version of *Honey West*, but "nothing as far as *my* being involved with it! Actually, I really wouldn't have any idea where I would fit into something like that at this point. Yes, I'd be interested, but it would depend on what the role was. *Not* the Irene Hervey part, thank you very much!" She realizes that, for many people, she'll

According to Anne Francis, there *is* no down side to being a cult actress.

always be best remembered for her limited role in *Forbidden Planet*, but she takes the realistic stance that "I don't have much to say about that, really *[laughs]*! It's okay with me because I accept *life* as okay. To make it '*un*okay' would be spending time in a mood or an attitude that's not very beneficial."

According to Anne Francis, there *is* no down side to being a cult actress.

"I have fun; I sign posters and things that are sent to me; I answer letters from those who seem most sincere. Years ago I got a postcard which was just *crammed* with writing, how wonderful, how terrific, how great I was. 'Would it be possible, do you think, that I could ever meet you? I would love to marry you.' This was all squeezed onto the card, in tiny little letters. Then at the bottom, it said, 'P.S.: If you're not interested, would you send this to Debbie Reynolds?'"

ANNE FRANCIS FILMOGRAPHY

This Time for Keeps (MGM, 1947)
Summer Holiday (MGM, 1948)
Portrait of Jennie (Tidal Wave) (Selznick, 1948)
So Young, So Bad (United Artists, 1950)
The Whistle at Eaton Falls (Columbia, 1951)
Elopement (20th Century–Fox, 1951)
Lydia Bailey (20th Century–Fox, 1952)
Dreamboat (20th Century–Fox, 1952)
A Lion Is in the Streets (Warner Bros., 1953)
The Rocket Man (20th Century–Fox, 1954)
Susan Slept Here (RKO, 1954)
Rogue Cop (MGM, 1954)
Bad Day at Black Rock (MGM, 1955)
Battle Cry (Warner Bros., 1955)
Blackboard Jungle (MGM, 1955)
The Scarlet Coat (MGM, 1955)
Forbidden Planet (MGM, 1956)
The Rack (MGM, 1956)
The Great American Pastime (MGM, 1956)

The Hired Gun (MGM, 1957)
Don't Go Near the Water (MGM, 1957)
Girl of the Night (Warner Bros., 1960)
The Crowded Sky (Warner Bros., 1960)
The Satan Bug (United Artists, 1965)
Brainstorm (Warner Bros., 1965)
Funny Girl (Columbia, 1968)
Star! (Those Were the Happy Times) (20th Century–Fox, 1968)
Hook, Line and Sinker (Columbia, 1969)
More Dead than Alive (United Artists, 1969)
The Love God? (Universal, 1969)
Impasse (The Golden Bullet) (United Artists, 1970)
Pancho Villa (Challenge of Pancho Villa; El Desafío de Pancho Villa) (Bernard Gordon [Spanish/English], 1972)
Born Again (Avco Embassy, 1978)

My agent said, "Listen, you just do [the Lost in Space *pilot episode] and don't worry about it. Take the money. Because nobody's gonna see it and it'll never sell." I said okay.*

Mark Goddard

IT IS A COOL AUTUMN DAY on the boardwalk in Atlantic City, and inside one of the adjacent hotels, unnoticed by most of the slot-machine players, a small piece of television history is in the making. At the Taj Mahal, the entire surviving cast of *Lost in Space* is having one of their first full reunions in the quarter century since that CBS science fiction series disappeared from television airwaves in September of 1968, and followers from up and down the East Coast have congregated for the event. Most of these fans were still in school in the sixties, when the Space Family Robinson was at the height of their popularity. Now, in 1992, they are all grown up and surprised to find that costar Mark Goddard, Major Don West in the space series, has gone...

"Back to school!" He laughs, recognizing the irony in the situation himself. "Back when I was of school age, I went to Holy Cross College in Worcester, Massachusetts. I was in the dramatic society and I did some acting. I decided I wanted to try [to earn a living at it], so I left college in my junior year and I went to New York to study acting. Then I did stock in Florida and in New England, and I really enjoyed what I was doing, so I didn't go back and finish college. And that's something I always thought that I *should* do. I'm the youngest of five, my brother and my three sisters all graduated from college and I'm the only one who never did. I didn't feel too good about that, because we were all expected to go to college and finish. So, after I had my career as an actor, I began to think that I wanted to maybe get involved in education. I came back East and went to Bridgewater State College, and I've gotten a bachelor of arts in Communications and I graduated magna cum laude, which I'm proud of. Then I continued on and just last August ['92] got my master's degree in elementary school education. *Now* I'm going to school and starting my courses—it'll take me about a year and a half and I'll have my master's in special education.

"I'm committed to what I'm doing one hundred percent. It's a good life. I think that teaching is not only rewarding, but it takes a lot of time and effort, and it's very challenging. It's a growing process. I grew with the *Lost in Space* experience and I'm growing with the experience of teaching. I'm fifty-six years old and I'm still growing, and someday I'll decide what I want to do in life when I grow up!"

Obviously Mark Goddard has come a long way from the days of playing the two-dimensional Major West—piloting the *Jupiter 2*, dallying platonically with Marta Kristen's Judy Robinson and barking out the signature line, "Get back to work, Smith!" Born in Lowell, Massachusetts, July 24, 1936, the actor (real name: Charles Goddard) grew up in Scituate ("great little town") where his father owned a five-and-ten. He had been at Holy Cross three years when "Father Gallagher, who was my English professor and the head of the dramatic society, took notice of my acting and said, 'Hey, you've got something special.

Previous page: **During his three years *Lost in Space*, Mark Goddard wondered if he was not also Lost in Hollywood.**

It seems to come across the footlights.' Those were his exact words. And that was all the encouragement I needed—I was off to New York. That was 1958. James Dean died—when? '55?—and that was still a big influence. When I was doing dramatics in college, I felt like, 'Jeez, I'm gonna be the next Jimmy Dean.' And when I went to New York, there were about five hundred Jimmy Deans runnin' around *[laughs]*. We all had our red jackets and our little motorcycles. I lived at the Iroquois Hotel where Dean had lived, I got my hair cut by his barber, and it was like everybody was trying to be Jimmy Dean."

Goddard attended the American Academy of Dramatic Arts by day and worked at night as a floorwalker at a Woolworth's at 45th and Broadway. "I wasn't very successful at it," he recalls. "At Woolworth's I had to wear a suit—I had *one suit*, an old, funny-lookin' suit and tie. I remember taking my jacket off to help somebody move some cartons, and somebody stole my jacket. So I was the floorwalker and I didn't catch anyone stealing, but I lost my jacket *[laughs]*!"

Goddard soon moved from Woolworth's stock room to stock *companies*, where "basically what I was doing was running the lights or painting the scenery—I didn't get to do much acting. That was my apprenticeship. (I have a firm belief that you have to serve before you can *be* served, that you have to put that time in.) I got to Hollywood back in 1959. I was with the William Morris Agency, and the agency represented companies. They represented Dick Powell in Four Star Television, and while I was a client of theirs, they had *The Rifleman* with Chuck Connors. That was the first show I did—just a small part, I may have had one line. I was part of a posse and I got shot. I had to get on a horse for the first time and ride, and I didn't know how to do that, and the horse ran away with me. But, like I say, you learn as you go *[laughs]*. Acting or teaching or *any*thing is a process of learning as you're doing it."

The same agency also represented Aaron Spelling, who was at Four Star with Powell, and Goddard ended up with a costarring role in the first series Spelling produced, the CBS Western *Johnny Ringo*, in which Goddard appeared as lawman Ringo's (Don Durant) young deputy. "I did a pretty good job on that. It only lasted for one year, but in those days, we used to shoot 39 episodes a year. You'd be on the air for 39 weeks, and then in the summertime just 13 weeks of reruns. Nowadays, of course, they shoot 20 shows and then do 26 reruns—somehow *[laughs]*. In those days, we used to shoot more than we did reruns. I was on that show for a year, and when it went off the air, Dick Powell, who had become like a father figure to me, called me into his office at Four Star. He was a wonderful man and he had a generous heart, and his office door was always open. Actors, craft-service people, grips, *any*body that worked in his company could go into his office anytime they wanted and talk to him. He called me in and he said, 'Mark, *Johnny Ringo* is going off the air, but I have a new show coming on called *Michael Shayne* with Richard Denning, and there's also a part opening up on *The Detectives*,

Starring Robert Taylor.' (That show had already been on for a year.) 'Which one would you like to do?' I chose doing *The Detectives* because I really wanted to work with Robert Taylor, who I admired very much—I grew up watching movies like *Johnny Eager* and *Quo Vadis*, et cetera. I knew that he was the ultimate professional and that I would learn a lot from him. I was very happy and very fortunate to work with him for three years."

Joining the cast of the police drama in its second season, Goddard's sidekick character Chris Ballard was brought in to lure a younger audience to the ABC series (which until then was drawing mostly middle-aged viewers). "When I went into that show, it was like I was the star of the show and Robert Taylor was like the sidekick as far as the *publicity* was concerned. They threw a lot toward me during that first year. They wanted another 'Kookie' Byrnes; they wanted that 'look.' It wouldn't work today, but in those days it did." Of the experience of working opposite a major star like Taylor, Goddard recalls, "Let's say there was going to be a medium two-shot, Robert Taylor and myself. They'd spend about thirty-five, forty minutes lighting Robert Taylor *[laughs]*. I'd be just in back of him, my head over his shoulder. Then they'd say, 'Okay, let's go, let's shoot.' And they'd been lighting only Taylor all that time. I'd say to the cameraman Howard Schwartz, 'What about *me*? Do *I* get any light or what?' And Howard said, 'Mark, you just get all the leak light. All the light that's left over, that Robert Taylor doesn't use, *you* get!'"

After turning in his shield when the series wrapped up its caseload in 1962, Goddard continued to work in television, often in comedy: He guested on sitcoms like *Fair Exchange* and *The Beverly Hillbillies*, appeared in the unsold Desilu pilot *Maggie Brown* with Ethel Merman and was a regular on the short-lived *Many Happy Returns* (1964–65) with John McGiver. One of Goddard's infrequent film appearances was in Disney's *The Monkey's Uncle* (1965) with Tommy Kirk as the disaster-prone college whiz-kid Merlin Jones and Goddard in an unbilled supporting role as the head of a football-minded fraternity. "*The Monkey's Uncle* was fun because I was working at Disney—*everybody* wanted to work at Disney. It was just exciting to walk around the Disney lot because of its history."

Nowadays, of course, roles like these have become footnotes in Mark Goddard's career: In 1965 he was drawn (reluctantly!) into appearing in the pilot episode for a space-adventure series—a job the actor took only because he was assured that the show would never get off the ground. "I was with the General Artists Corporation agency and they represented Irwin Allen, who I didn't know at the time. My agent was named David Gerber, and David came to me one day and said, 'How would you like to do a pilot? A space pilot?' I said, 'I'm not really into space too much.' David said, 'Well, you've been everything else—you've been a detective, you've been a cowboy, you've done comedy. This is about a family going into space, and there's gonna be a lot of adventures, earthquakes—' I said, 'Gee, I don't know. I'm not sure, because of the subject matter.' And David said, 'Well, listen, you just do it and don't worry about it. Take the money. Because nobody's gonna see it and it'll never sell.' I said okay.

"It took about twenty-one days to shoot the pilot—that's a l-o-n-g time to shoot a pilot. It was a lot of earthquakes and water stuff, all physical—there wasn't really a lot of acting to do. I've always been athletic, so I enjoyed that part of it. *And they sold it.* So I went to find David Gerber, 'cause he'd said, 'I promise I can get you out of this if you don't like it.' But he wasn't around anymore. About six months had passed, and he had become a producer over at 20th Century–Fox, where Irwin was. So I just said to myself, 'Well, this is meant for me to do, so I'll just do it and I'll do the best job I can.'"

Goddard can joke about his early days on the show now, but he certainly was not laughing then. "The day that I went to wardrobe and they put the silver lamé space suit on me, I think I cried. I *cried*! My wife at the time put her hand on my shoulder and said, 'It's gonna be okay,' but I said, 'I don't know if I can do this.' She said, 'Yes you can, yes you can.' So I said to myself, 'Yes I can, yes I can!' I had realized that it was *not* going to be an acting challenge. It would be physical, and I wouldn't be getting the kind of direction that I wanted. I wouldn't be getting my teeth into material that had to do with [real] things, into the reality of emotional stuff. I just knew it had to do with outer space things and things that would be hard for me to relate to. I think I did okay, but—it's just different." (Coincidentally, one of Goddard's distant relatives is Robert Goddard, the professor and inventor known as "the father of modern rocketry.")

Unintentionally, Goddard almost *did* manage to avoid space duty aboard the *Jupiter 2*: a motorcycle accident nearly put the actor out of commission. "This was real early on in the show, maybe even just before the pilot. I used to drive motorcycles—Steve McQueen got me interested, 'cause he was also at Four Star. I was driving a bike back from the races and I hit an oil slick, and I went down on my left side. I skidded about forty feet. It took all the skin off the left side of my body ... took a piece of my thumb off ... cut a hole in my leg, stuff like that. (It also sheared practically all the metal off the left side of my bike—along with my skin!) There were four lanes of traffic and all these cars were just buzzin' by me. I was able to get up and cross the street and get to the side—and I went down there. The next thing I knew, I was in the ambulance.

"Later on, *months* later, I was at a party and an agent I knew said, 'I saw you that day you had your motorcycle accident.' I said, 'Oh?' He said, 'We were coming back from the races, too. God, you looked awful, you were all bloodied up there at the side of the road.' And then he said, 'We would have stopped to pick you up, but we didn't want to get any blood in the car.' How's that for a Hollywood story *[laughs]*?"

In costumes adjusted to allow for his bandages, Goddard began what would become a three-year stint on the 20th Century–Fox series, with every phase of the series (a popular part of CBS's Wednesday night lineup) supervised by veteran movie and television producer Irwin Allen (who also directed the pilot episode). "Irwin Allen was a good director when it came to 'vision,' and he knew what he wanted as an editor; he probably knew editing, he probably could envision things. But he wasn't a good director as far as actors were concerned, because he didn't *like* actors. And a director's *gotta* like actors, he's gotta *want* to work with them in some way.

"Doing a show like that is very difficult. I used to always put myself down, I'd say, 'Gee, I'm not very good. This is tough to do.' Then one day years later I was on the set of *The Towering Inferno* [1974] and I stood there and I watched Irwin directing Paul Newman and Steve McQueen in an office scene. Paul Newman is one of my favorite actors and one of the best actors who's ever been around, and one of the great things that you have to do as an actor is to be relaxed. That's very important. I was watching the scene being done, and I watched the tension in Paul Newman grow. I couldn't believe that *he* — even *he* — was having a hard time with this kind of dialogue, with this kind of directing, and what was happening. Of course, he was doing it because he was getting a million dollars or something. He did it for the money — he wasn't doin' it because he wanted to work with Irwin Allen *[laughs]*. But I saw that tension and I said, 'Boy, even with Paul Newman. Words that don't work are even hard for him. I guess I'm not doin' such a bad job after all!' That put things in perspective for me, in a way."

Goddard concurs instantly with the other *Lost in Space* veterans who have often described Allen as a man who considered his series regulars — and their performances — relatively low on his list of priorities. "With Irwin it was like, 'Get it all right technically, and if all the firecrackers go off, print it.' It didn't matter if I didn't get my line out right because a firecracker went off in the middle of it *[laughs]*, or if I just 'wasn't there with it' as an actor.

"I did a lot of series, and I found that the greatest support you get in a series usually is from the crew. When I did *Johnny Ringo* and *The Detectives*, I had great rapport with the cinematographer, the crew members, the writers and everyone that came down to the set, and everything was a pleasure. Everything fell in, everything was just nice, you know? We had our Friday afternoon parties, we all had a drink together and laughed about the week and had a good time, then went home to our families in a relaxed state. There was a whole family thing going on. With *Lost in Space*, there was tension all the time. There was tension with the cinematographer, there was tension with the writers coming down, there was always something going on. Tension with the actors, tension with the directors. *Always tension.* And, you know what they say, 'the fish stinks from the head'? This isn't fair to say because Irwin is dead and he can't defend himself, but I think that his kind of *perfection*, what he *wanted* and the *way* he wanted it, his very cold manner with everyone — this permeated right from him to the writers, to the directors, to the cast, to the crew. You could sense that.

"That was the three years on *Lost in Space* for me: 'Is the show good enough?' 'Is it getting the ratings?' And the cast was worried: 'Is this laughable?' (Especially after *Star Trek* came on—'Can we compete with this kind of a show?') Then we went up against *Batman* and *that* hit us—they got good ratings and we didn't, although we *did* come back later. '*Batman*'s a real camp show. *We're* not a camp show. Are we a real show? We're not a real show like *Star Trek*, and we're not a camp show like *Batman* ...' Tension! We didn't know where we fit, we hadn't found an identity. An identity came near the end, when finally it was Dr. Smith [Jonathan Harris] and the Robot doing silly things, and that's what the show became. But that's not what it set out to be. I always wanted to do a comedy, but I never knew [while I was on *Lost in Space*] that I *was* in a comedy *[laughs]*! One day I said, 'Hey, I've been doin' all this method stuff—I didn't know we were doin' a comedy here!'"

Another sore point for Goddard was the fact that, during the show's run, he never knew who its audience was. "The show *had* an audience, but I didn't know that. The audience was kids from (say) six to ten—and I didn't run around with those kids *[laughs]*! I wasn't out playin' golf with those kids, I wasn't playin' tennis with 'em, they weren't on motorcycles, I didn't see 'em at the racetrack, they weren't at the parties that I went to. The people that I *was* dealing with, it was almost like they looked down at [*Lost in Space*]. They didn't ever watch it, unless they had little kids (which they didn't). So I didn't know who I was reaching. It's not until recently that I realized [who the fans were]—they're now in their thirties and so forth. As kids, they loved it and got off on it and wanted to play *Lost in Space*. That is what I missed. If I knew that we were reaching an audience, and that they were really looking up to Don West and Judy and the Robot and Dr. Smith, and they were having fun with it, I'd have said, 'Gee, I'm doin' something worthwhile.' But I didn't know that, I didn't know *what* I was doing.

"We had a couple of directors I liked, like Sean Penn's father, Leo Penn; he directed a show and he was cool, he was a good director. I don't know why he did it—maybe his agent said, 'Hey, do it,' maybe he was in between jobs or something. Bob Butler was good, Harry Harris was good, so we had, sporadically, some good directors. But we also had directors who were just going by the numbers most of the time. You could say anything you wanted to some of these guys, and it was in one ear, out the other. One director, Sobey Martin, used to fall asleep on the set a lot, *while* he was directing! One day I woke him up and I said, 'Hey, Sobey, Sobey! Can I do this scene in the nude?' He said *[in a groggy voice]*, 'Oh, yeah, yeah, yeah, go ahead, whatever.' *[Laughs.]* It was like this: 'Say the lines, take the money and run. *That* was what we heard every day: 'Hey, don't question it. If you analyze these scripts, you'll go crazy.' But take the money and run is *not* why I became an actor. If

The stoic smiles of the *Lost in Space* stars were the false face of what Goddard recalls as an "angry show." (*Left–right:* Marta Kristen, Goddard, June Lockhart, Guy Williams.)

I wanted to take the money and run, I would have been a teacher, because I would have made more money as a teacher in those thirty years than I did as an actor. Even though I made good money some years, my *average* was half of what I would have made as a teacher. That sounds astounding, but it's true."

Goddard went from $1,150 to $1,350 to $1,750 a week during the three years (83 episodes) of *Lost in Space*. He was third-billed below Guy Williams and June Lockhart in the weekly saga of a "space family" (and their pilot,

**Giant footprints warn Guy Williams and Goddard that they are not alone on their new
planet in the *Lost in Space* pilot.**

Goddard) marooned on various planets in deep space. Williams was the osten-
sible star of the series, but when the decision was made to gear the series strictly
toward kids, "special guest star" Jonathan Harris (who played the "reluctant
stowaway" Dr. Smith) quickly moved to the fore. "It was a very difficult position for Guy," Goddard recalls of Williams' "demotion." "He was hired to be
the star of this show, the father of the family, then all of a sudden he *wasn't*

the star. Jonathan Harris was, Jonathan and the Robot. Hollywood has a way of 'getting' you: What they do is, they give you a lot of money, and *then* they say, 'Now that you've got all this money, now that you've got this lifestyle, *now* we're gonna tell you what you *can* do and what you *can't* do.' So Guy didn't have a lot of leverage, 'cause say he was making good money on this show; he had a family, he had a home—what was he gonna do? He needed to keep that money coming in, he had all that overhead. So when he wasn't the star of the show anymore, he'd get angry that Jonathan was getting most of the lines.

"And *one* time, Guy took some of *my* lines. I went in one morning to do a shot, and all of a sudden, when I was ready to do my lines, *Guy* had them all! So I got angry about that—of course. But Guy was havin' it pretty difficult. He'd come off *Zorro* [the 1957–59 Disney series] and that was a pretty big feather in his cap—he was a bigger star than *I* was, that's for sure, and probably the biggest star in the show, coming off of *Zorro*. And now he was being aced out by somebody nobody had ever heard of before, Jonathan Harris. (Maybe *some* people knew of Jonathan; I never had. But he wasn't like Guy.)

"So Guy was upset about that, and maybe some days he'd come in late, or maybe he'd walk off the set if something wasn't right. He was just angry about certain things and he threw his hands up in the air a few times. He never lost his temper about anything, at least not as far as I can remember; he was a gentleman. But he'd just *walk,* he'd just go. And so a couple of times, he and June were written out of shows, and I was written out of a show, for insubordination. It was like suspension time; it was like Irwin Allen was the headmaster of this co-ed school and we were getting our hands slapped if we didn't stay in line all the time."

Despite the discord brought on by the restructuring of the show, Goddard felt no rancor toward Harris other than *on*-screen, where pompous rascal Dr. Smith and hot-tempered Major West feuded incessantly. "Jonathan was the consummate professional. He did more than was ever asked of him, and you've gotta admire him. He developed that character, he worked on it, he came up with lines—he did *all* the kind of work that we as actors *want* to do, but we [other *Lost in Space* regulars] *didn't* do because we threw our hands up in the air. (At least *I* did.) If I had done the work that Jonathan did, maybe I would have come off better, but I really couldn't, my hands were tied. I'd get miffed at the Robot, because that was a piece of metal that was upstaging me *[laughs]*, but not at Jonathan; Jonathan deserved everything *he* got. He did the work and created a wonderful character."

Lost in Space was not a show that lent itself to big-name guest stars, but Goddard does remember a few favorites among the gallery of character actors who also did time on the Robinson family's galactic oasis. "Warren Oates and Albert Salmi were two of my favorites. Everybody has different favorites, but those were my two—those were *my* kind of actors, more than (say) a Michael Rennie or a Henry Jones. And I loved working with Kurt Russell. Kurt was

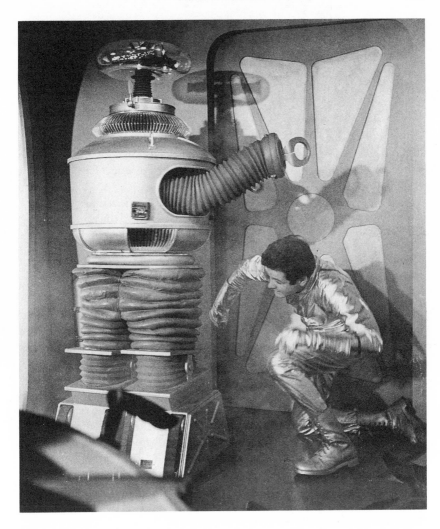

Goddard battles the out-of-control Robot (Bob May) in the initial *Lost in Space* episode, "The Reluctant Stowaway."

maybe 12 when he was on *Lost in Space*; his dad Bing I worked with a lot on *Johnny Ringo*. Kurt was a nice boy, a *great* kid, and a great *man* today — people say wonderful things about him. A lot of the *Lost in Space* guest stars I didn't get a chance to work with, because most of 'em worked with Jonathan.

"But, see, on *The Detectives*, I worked with Robert Taylor, with Edward G. Robinson — and I really *worked* with these people. On different shows, I *worked* with David Janssen, Chuck Connors, Myrna Loy, June Allyson, Tuesday Weld — a lot of people. So on *Lost in Space*, it wasn't like 'Oh, wow!' when they'd finally bring some guest star in." One unofficial *Lost in Space* semiregular was Dawson Palmer, who played many of the monsters during the series' three years, but "I don't remember him at all," admits Goddard. "See, by the time I'd get on the set, [the monster actors] were already in their outfits, and I wouldn't know Dawson Palmer if I *saw* him *[laughs]*. As a matter of fact, Michael Conrad was on *Lost in Space* once; in later years, he was the sergeant on *Hill Street Blues*. He played a monster in a show, made up like an ape kind of guy in a prison outfit. I had already worked with Michael at the Actors Studio, I *knew* Michael, but it wasn't until the last day that he finally told me it was him—I didn't know *[laughs]*. I *thought* the voice was familiar, but it was kind of muffled."

Remembering the *Jupiter 2* itself, Goddard reveals the actual layout of the (supposedly) two-level spaceship. "When we had scenes on the upper deck, we actually shot inside of the spaceship. Remember the big window that we looked out? The camera would just come up into there and shoot right in through the window at us, a big master shot. Then if they wanted to get close-ups, they could just set a camera up inside. They didn't cover close-ups too often, and if we were standing at the panels, they'd get our close-ups right there by shooting in through the view port. The elevator only went down about four feet, so to make it look like we were going down out of sight, we had to duck down and lie on the floor of the elevator. And if there were three or four of us going down, we'd be crammed down in there *[laughs]*. On another stage was the bottom floor, which we didn't shoot in as much."

After *Lost in Space* was canceled in 1968 at the end of its three-year run, Goddard found himelf driven into what has been called "a seven-year sabbatical from acting"—a description he balks at initially, then admits, "Well, maybe it's *not* all that far from the truth. When I finished *Lost in Space*, I wasn't happy with the prospect of what I was going to do next, because I knew that I would be typed as a 'space show' actor and I didn't know how I'd get out of it. And I figured the best way to get out of it was to go back into studying acting. So I wasn't on a sabbatical from acting, it was a sabbatical from trying to get *jobs*, a sabbatical from hopping around and getting a lot of rejection. That's when I did a lot of serious acting; that's when I started becoming an actor. I knew that if I was going to have a career in acting, I couldn't just do *Lost in Space* and then go out and bounce around from interview to interview; I had to step back, get ahold of myself, reestablish myself in the craft and gain my confidence back as an actor. I'd lost my confidence as an actor 'cause I wasn't doing any real acting. That's my own fault, not the fault of *Lost in Space. My fault.*"

Roles in the 1970s included a supporting part in the horror film *Blue Sunshine*, about people changing into bald-headed rampaging killers ten years after using an LSD-type drug in college. "I'm a straightlaced guy," Goddard explains, differentiating between himself and the drug peddler cum politician he played in the 1977 film. "I won't say I didn't inhale *[laughs]*, but I wasn't a smoker—you know what I mean?—and I wasn't into drugs and I've always been very straightlaced 'cause that's my generation. In *Blue Sunshine*, I played a character who had been involved in drugs and became a congressman. It was a good low-budget film, I thought. I liked the political part of it, because when I was young I thought that I would have liked to go into politics, and it gave me a chance to play a politician."

A far brighter high point in Goddard's career came a year later, when he costarred with Liza Minnelli on Broadway in *The Act*. "Doing that was the most exposure I ever had to stars," he recalls proudly. "Every night I knew that in the audience there'd be a star or a major person. It might be Jacqueline Kennedy, it might be Robert DeNiro, Sammy Davis, Henry Kissinger, Mia Farrow, Sinatra—'cause Liza was a draw, and anybody who was in New York was gonna see the show with Liza. So that was a wonderful year for me 'cause I thought, 'Wow, all these people I've been watchin' all these years, now they're gonna watch *me*.' Even if it's just for a few minutes, their eyes are going to be on *me* part of the time! I mean, they wouldn't remember watching me, they would watch Liza, but in *my* mind, they were watching me, too! That was a wonderful year." A *One Life to Live* casting director caught Goddard in *The Act* (so to speak) and lined up a role for him on the popular New York–based afternoon soap. "I enjoyed that year. I was working with a lot of good people and I did have the opportunity to get my teeth into something a little bit. My character was on for a year before he was killed—they wanted to keep me alive longer because I was really getting hot on that show. It was a good character and people loved it. But I had already made other plans to go back to California, so they killed me when they were supposed to. Then I went back to California and I did some writing—I wrote a couple of screenplays. I tested for a *General Hospital* part I *didn't* get, then I came back and tested again for a *different* part and I was signed to a two-year contract."

Between his two experiences in daytime drama, Goddard also added yet one more sci-fi credit to his filmography—albeit in a (very) supporting capacity. "I only did *Strange Invaders* [1983] because my daughter Melissa was an assistant on that movie. *Strange Invaders* was made by Orion, and Mike Medavoy, who was one of the owners of Orion, was my first wife's second husband. So my first wife was now married to him and my daughter was now his stepdaughter. (Are you following this?) She was up in Toronto, Canada, working as like an assistant director, just helping out, and I was in New York. I wanted to see her, so I flew up. And they had the part of a cop, and they asked me to do it, so I said yes. It was a one-day shoot. The same thing happened on *Play It Again, Sam* [1972] with Woody Allen. My second wife, Susan Anspach, was in that movie and I was there, and Woody asked me just to sit down in a scene. I sat down and said a line, and I've been getting residuals—every two years, I get a six-dollar check for *Play It Again, Sam [laughs]*!"

Throughout his acting career, in between jobs, Goddard worked with children, from Head Start programs in California to Sloan-Kettering Cancer Center in New York City; now, back in his home state of Massachusetts, he is turning his full attention to at-risk kids at the Longview Farm School. "These are kids who have come from broken homes, kids that don't *have* homes, kids who have been in foster homes, kids who have been abused in their infancy or in their early childhood, kids who have a learning disability but it's *really* based on economic factors or family problems, and they just haven't been able to get the learning that they should. These kids become the at-risk kids when they get into high school, kids who're going to drop out and kids that don't care about going to school and these kind of things. I love those kind of kids, I feel that they could be *me* except that I had a better break when I was a kid. I was able to go to high school and college because I had the family background. And because I *did* have a strong family background, I really have a lot of empathy and feeling for kids that didn't, and I feel I want to work with those kids. I think I'm pretty good with kids, so those are the kids that I want to work with in special education.

"At the Longview Farm School, I'm the behavioral specialist. 'My' kids come to me during the day when they can't make it in the classroom, and they pretty much spend the day with me. And it's probably the toughest job in education—*very* tiring. But I'm learning a lot, and I think I'm reaching some of them. They've certainly reached *me*. So it's challenging and it's wonderful, and I don't have a minute to think about, 'Why did I stop acting?'"

But it is not as though Mark Goddard has severed his showbiz ties: Daughter Melissa is now a producer (she produced *Poison Ivy* [1992] with Drew Barrymore as well as *Big Girls Don't Cry . . . They Get Even* [1992], a film about her father's work with his at-risk kids). Between his school duties and other responsibilities, he also finds time to do the occasional science fiction convention. "I never realized, never *dreamed* that I would be talking to fans at conventions about *Lost in Space* twenty-seven years later. I never dreamed that people would be interested still. So I'm grateful for that in a way, because it's nice to know that there are people who still want to read about me. I appreciate it in retrospect, everything that's happened, but at the time—*Lost in Space* was *not* the joy of my life."

MARK GODDARD FILMOGRAPHY

A Rage to Live (United Artists, 1965)
The Monkey's Uncle (Buena Vista, 1965)
The Love-Ins (Columbia, 1967)
Play It Again, Sam (Paramount, 1972)
Blue Sunshine (Cinema Shares, 1977)
Roller Boogie (United Artists, 1979)
Strange Invaders (Orion, 1983)

The agonies that some people go through, waiting for the phone to ring, wanting that great public success, has not been part of my makeup ... because of what I saw my parents do and what their concerns were with life as it should be lived.

June Lockhart

JUNE LOCKHART AND HER EXTENDED FAMILY are well on their way to setting some sort of record, if they have not done so already. "My daughter Annie is an actress, and it's quite possible that *her* two children will be the fifth generation [of Lockharts in the acting profession]," she recounts, filled with the sort of exuberance we all instinctively *knew* she had to have in real life. "Annie's two children are Carly, who's six, and a baby boy, Zane. Their father is Adam Taylor, who is an actor and a *very* good director—as a matter of fact, he's the first assistant on a movie that's being made in Tucson now called *Tombstone*, about the shootout at the O.K. Corral. *Adam*'s father is Buck Taylor, who was for 17 years on *Gunsmoke* and after that on *Dallas*, and *his* father is Dub Taylor. [Adam and Dub Taylor both died in 1994.] Annie added up all the years of the two families in show business and figured there's 287 years between us."

The voice—and the long, hearty laugh that punctuates the anecdote—is unmistakable, a voice that nearly all of us have grown up hearing. Those distinctive tones beseeched Lassie to find Timmy and sternly instructed Will and Penny to stay away from that mysterious cave. Movie fans know the voice from MGM classics of the 1940s, and folks who grew up during television's Golden Age have heard it on most of the top dramatic shows. Nowadays, of course, she is best remembered for the mothers (Ruth Martin and Maureen Robinson) she played on *Lassie* and *Lost in Space*, although it is a disservice that an actress who has essayed such a wide variety of roles should now be known mostly for that one facet of her work. "One of my favorites was an episode of *Gunsmoke* where I played an alcoholic nymphomaniac murderess with the mind of a twelve year old, and I 'offed' Wayne Morris," she enthuses, laughing that laugh again. "I wore a dress which was cut way low, with the boobs hanging out, and, oh, it was nifty—Crazy Beulah was the name of the character!

"I just take the roles as they come, and when you get a role in which you're able to do that sort of acting—and I *have* certainly done some of them—they're fun. But in the long run, because of what my image is, I think that playing the [maternal] roles has been far more remunerative for me. Dan Rather said, 'I can control my reputation, but not my image, because my image is how *you* perceive me.' And that's really true."

Maureen Robinson, *Lost in Space*'s understanding, brow-knitting mom, was one of those maternal (and "remunerative") acting stints, one in which Lockhart could show all the motherly concern she could muster—but none of the wifely affection. "Guy Williams [Professor John Robinson] and I *did* have scenes of intimacy in the beginning. Great affection was shown—hand-holding and kisses—in the pilot, it's all there. But the dictum came down from CBS that we were not to touch each other because, they said, it embarrassed

Previous page: "Born in a trunk," June Lockhart continued her family's acting tradition—often in "goody" roles that do not reflect her oft-outrageous personality.

children watching at home to see their parents kissing. Well, we could *not* believe it. We had a new network guy come on, and I said, 'Do you know what is going on here with these parts?' He thought it was preposterous when I told him about it—he said, 'My God, I can't believe it!' Guy and I had put in all these little things to try to give this family a *warmth* like that—being demonstrably affectionate was something I was raised with, as was Guy, being an Italian. In my family, I never saw my father *pass* my mother without touching her, patting her, hugging her."

The touchy-feely father she describes is, of course, Gene Lockhart (1891–1957), the veteran vaudeville and stage actor and writer, and her mom was actress Kathleen (1894–1978); the two were introduced by Thomas Edison. (It was Gene's father, John Coates Lockhart, a concert singer, who represented the first generation of the family in showbiz.) Born in New York City, only-child June made her professional debut at age eight in a Metropolitan Opera production of *Peter Ibbetson*, playing Mimsey in the dream sequence. In the mid-thirties, the Lockharts relocated to California, where father Gene enjoyed a long career as one of the screen's great character actors. Being the child of famous parents has frequently furnished Hollywood brats with an excuse for unproductive lifestyles, but June flourished rather than floundered in this unique environment.

"It was my parents, of course, because they were *in* but not *of* the business. It was how my father made his living—he was awfully good at it and he really loved it—but when he came home, he was concerned with his writing and his correspondence and what had happened in the house, and he was *always* outwardly motivated toward people and causes. And the people that they entertained at the house were journalists, physicians, publishers, singers, composers, columnists—they were there every Sunday, playing badminton *[laughs]*. Growing up in this sophisticated atmosphere was really an extraordinary thing to be able to do. And the *laughter* in the house, all the time, *such* laughter. My maternal grandparents lived with us, and a maiden aunt. We had just a neat time. So it was always kept in perspective, and I was *never* part of that Hollywood society that one read about in the movie magazines. It was quite well balanced, just a rich, wonderful education and family life."

She made her screen debut in MGM's 1938 version of Charles Dickens' timeless tale, *A Christmas Carol*, playing—appropriately enough—the daughter of stars Gene and Kathleen Lockhart. "It was lovely to be working with my mother and father, and it just seemed quite a natural thing to do because all my life we had always celebrated Christmas with a reading of *Christmas Carol*, done concert style. My father wrote a script and the dinner guests would take parts, and we would play it. I would play Tiny Tim until I got old enough to be one of the sisters, my mother and father were Mr. and Mrs. Cratchit, and Leo G. Carroll would play Scrooge, because he was *always* a dinner guest. So we had done this all my life and it was lovely, and then there we were doing it at MGM! And it certainly turned out to be a classic." The experience of setting foot in front of MGM's cameras was not at all daunting for the 13 year old "because I was with my parents. The thing I remember vividly is that, in my very first scene, we were all set and ready to go, the assistant said, 'Roll 'em' and I started to move — I was *that* eager. And the director, Ed Marin, said to me, 'No, June, you have to wait till *I* say *action.*' And *that* stayed with me a l-o-n-g time *[laughs]*!"

Two years later, while still in high school, June was offered a supporting role in Warners' *All This, and Heaven Too* (1940), a Bette Davis–Charles Boyer vehicle. "I was at Marlborough School, which was one of the two top schools at the time in Los Angeles. Daddy and I went to Miss Blake, the principal, and he said, 'June would like to do this part for the experience, regardless of whether she ever becomes an actress when she grows up. This is a really lovely opportunity for her, and a first-class production.' Miss Blake listened to all this. He went on, 'What I would like, please, is if you would arrange so that June can keep up with her class by doing the classwork *on* the set with the tutor.' At that point, Miss Blake said, 'Well, Mr. Lockhart, I personally would have no objection to June doing the film, but I *really* don't think the parents of the other girls would want *their* children going to school with anybody in the movies.' There was this *pause*, and then my father turned to me and said, 'June, go to your locker and get your books.' I went, and by the time I got back, I was no longer a Marlborough student.

"Daddy was an educated man — he was an author and a composer, and just the most marvelously gentle man. And the insult that she had slapped him with was really, really awful. As we drove home after that, he said, 'Well, Juney, today you had an experience of the disregard with which the acting profession is held in some circles.' Marlborough School was old Los Angeles money — which meant probably seventy years *[laughs]* — old *oil* money. So I went to an interim school, Immaculate Heart, which I'd been at before (and loathed), and then I went finally to Westlake, the *other* top school, which I adored, it was wonderful. Also there while I was were Shirley Temple and Elizabeth Montgomery." Around the time of June's eight-week acting stint in *All This, and Heaven Too*, Gene Lockhart authored the article "A Doting Father and His Talented Daughter." "He wrote in that that my acting training had consisted mostly of making signals to my mother behind the old man's back *[laughs]*!"

At no point during these formative years, June Lockhart insists, did she ever make a conscious decision to become an actress. "My opportunities came along so easily that there was never any sweating and striving and anxiety over it all. It was not until my first marriage [in 1951] that I really knew how much I enjoyed it, and that I really knew what I could accomplish with it." Other early forties movie roles that came her way included *Sergeant York* (as Gary Cooper's sister), *Miss Annie Rooney* with Shirley Temple, *Forever and a Day*, in a scene written by her father, and then in a succession of roles at MGM (among others, *Meet Me in St. Louis*, *The White Cliffs of Dover* and, portentously, *Son of Lassie*).

A different type of dog was at the center of the plot of her first costarring film. "Oh, *She-Wolf of London* was fun to do," Lockhart laughs about this mutt of a movie, found wagging at the tail end of Universal's monster cycle. "If I'm remembering right, I was just submitted for it by my agent. I did it, and—I was *not* very good in it. But the following year, I was *the* hot ingenue on Broadway in a wonderful comedy, so I guess what I needed [in *She-Wolf*] was good direction." Lockhart pauses, realizing she has just cast an aspersion, regroups and then adds, "Well, I guess the director of *She-Wolf* was a good one, but the film was of the genre that they did at Universal—I think it only took two weeks to shoot. That was so early in my experience, I was still learning the technique of film acting."

In the 1946 B movie, Lockhart is a woebegone English lass whose family, legend has it, was cursed by wolves; when vicious attacks occur in a nearby park, she convinces herself that she is the female lycanthrope responsible. "There were a lot of English people in it who were friends of my father's— people who would come around the house and play badminton *[laughs]*—so there again it was not strange or unusual or awkward. Don Porter was my leading man, and he was a dear." The shooting of some retakes necessitated that Lockhart, Porter, director Jean Yarbrough and a technical crew work on Christmas Eve (1945), with all concerned champing at the bit to get home to their families. "Don and I were in a horse and buggy, with rear-screen projection behind us. We finished the final take, and *before* Don could help me down out of the buggy, everybody was gone. Just *gone*! And we both laughed about it—there was no help with your costume or 'Merry Christmas' or anything. It was like an evacuation!" Other than this one incident, Lockhart insists, B studio Universal was as efficient and businesslike a workplace as "studio of the stars" MGM. "It was all the same—we broke for lunch and had toilets and dressing rooms *[laughs]*, and they treated you quite nicely. I was not aware of anything being less than most professional."

The following year, 1947, Lockhart made her Broadway bow, playing the ingenue in the comedy *For Love or Money* with John Loder. The play itself was mediocre by all accounts, but Lockhart got a standing ovation opening night and immediately became the toast of Broadway; one critic compared her debut to the first big hits of Helen Hayes and Margaret Sullavan. Soon played up in all advertisements as the main attraction of the production, she went on to win a Tony, the Donaldson Award, the Theatre World Award and the Associated Press citation for Woman of the Year for Drama.

When television's unblinking eye first opened on America, she was there, too, playing roles in many of the top dramatic programs (some of them live from New York). One was a 1951 *Robert Montgomery Presents* adaptation of

Lockhart admits to needing better direction on *She-Wolf of London*: "I was still learning the technique of film acting."

Nathaniel Hawthorne's *The House of the Seven Gables* — again opposite father Gene. "Daddy and I got the giggles in one scene — we always had trouble getting through it in rehearsal. The line that my father had to say to me was *so* convoluted that I remembered it forever: He was the villain and he was leaving the house, and the line was, 'Tell your cousin I will return betide, for the benefit of her and hers, to further discuss the matter of which we spoke.' He did it beautifully on the air, of course, but we knew that we had broken up and laughed hysterically all during rehearsal over it—and they never *changed* it. That's one thing wonderful about working with a relative—when you look deep into the eyes, you *know* there is all that subtext, and it's just Daddy there tryin' to get through a bad piece of dialogue *[laughs].*"

Lockhart worked steadily throughout the fifties, on television and the stage, and every now and then obeyed an impulse to branch out. She worked for a year or two on *Guideposts*, an interfaith religious magazine, in order to learn about the publishing business, and in the mid-fifties she was granted permission to travel with newspaper reporters covering the presidential candidates. Ever since then—except for a short break during the time that "people started shooting at our presidents"—she has attended Washington briefings every time an opportunity has presented itself. "Even today, whenever I'm in Washington, no matter *what* the administration or *who* the press secretary is, I call up and I'm invited to attend the briefing. April 1991 I was there and I was staying for over a week, so I got to a lot of briefings. This sort of filtered around town—nobody's ever made a fuss over this at all. The *Washington Post* wanted to run a little blurb about it, so they called different White House photographers to see if anybody had a picture of me in the briefing room. Finally one of the photographers said, 'A picture of *June*? Nobody takes a picture of June when she's here—she's just one of the guys!' And I thought that was the greatest compliment I'd ever had in my life—isn't that *terrific?*"

In sharp contrast to her busy, vivacious life was her role as the demure, gingham-clad, stay-at-home mom on television's *Lassie*, an acting stint that began in 1958. She remained with the show until 1964, but did guest shots on other series during those years, including the aforementioned *Gunsmoke* episode and a 1958 version of *Beauty and the Beast* on *Shirley Temple's Storybook.* "Oh, God, did we have a good time in that, with Chuck Heston as the Beast and Claire Bloom as Beauty. Barbara Baxley and I were the wicked and ugly sisters, and we had the most fun on that—it was neat."

It was a guest spot on ABC's *Voyage to the Bottom of the Sea* that led to Lockhart's *other* most-famous television role. Acting in the episode "The Ghost of Moby Dick," she met veteran producer Irwin Allen. "I had not met him before, to my knowledge. I was doing that *Voyage to the Bottom of the Sea* guest appearance in like maybe August or September [1964], and on the second day, Irwin saw the rushes of the first day. He came down and found me and he said, 'We're doing a series called *Space Family Robinson*. Would you like to do another series?' I said yes, and so he gave me the script and I called my agent and said, 'This looks interesting.' So we did it."

Rechristened *Lost in Space*, the original series pilot—at that time one of the most expensive in the history of television (over $600,000)—began shooting January 6, 1965, on the 20th Century–Fox Westwood lot. It starred Guy Williams as astrophysicist John Robinson and Lockhart as his biochemist wife, Maureen; accompanied by their children Judy (Marta Kristen), Penny (Angela Cartwright) and Will (Billy Mumy) and by Dr. Don West (Mark Goddard), the space pioneers set out aboard the *Gemini 12* to colonize the planet Alpha Centauri, only to be sidetracked by a meteor storm that sends them into the uncharted depths of outer space. Mark Goddard, who was not much interested in starring in a space show, has said that he accepted the role in the pilot when he was assured that the series would never sell, but Lockhart suffered under no such delusion. "Oh, I knew it would sell. Well, they already had an air date—this was set. CBS was part owner and I *knew* that it was going on the air for at least a year."

Before the series reached the airwaves, extensive changes were made, including the addition of Jonathan Harris as the saboteur caught aboard the spacecraft (renamed *Jupiter 2*) just before liftoff. Convoluted plots and intricate special effects caused delays, with the reported result that (for a time) the show was running only seven days ahead of air time. "Seven days ahead of air time in *Canada*," Lockhart corrects. "Sometimes we'd finish on Monday and it would be on the air in Canada the following Saturday night. And if the show wasn't ready, 20th Century–Fox or CBS would have been fined $50,000. But we made it every time, because Irwin kept everybody there working twenty-four hours a day, practically—the postproduction and everything."

Lockhart dismisses published accounts of a registered nurse visiting the set three days a week, and also denies another report that she took out a Lloyds of London policy against serious injury—but she admits that, early on, working on *Lost in Space was* a strenuous and often physical task. "The hours were very, very long. And there *was* a lot of physical stuff—there was less of that to do later in the run, because the story line changed, but, yes, the pilot was *very* physical, and all the flying on wires— *that* was an experience! And it was very hot, of course, in the silver lamé suits. However, we just accepted it all and did the job—you do your best to just keep yourself comfortable under those conditions. Bitching is not one of the things I do on a set, anyway, because *everybody's* doing the same thing. We had some very good directors on *Lost in Space* that first season, but they usually only did one or two shows, and then *probably* went to a halfway house *[laughs]*!"

The addition of Jonathan Harris to the cast would, of course, eventually take the series in a whole new direction; Lockhart is not certain whether the show would have been more successful had it stayed serious rather than going the "camp" route. "I don't know—it's hard to say what the length might have been. But *that* is what they chose to do with the show, to make it a comedy show about an old man [Harris] and a little boy [Mumy] in space. So there's still a lot of unmined area there, to have a *real* show about a family colonizing a new planet. That certainly would have been a different show! Would it have *run* as long—or longer—I don't know." Her role diminished in size the more the series concentrated on the misadventures of Harris and Mumy (and the

Robot, played by Bob May), but Lockhart does not admit to being disappointed by the change. "It took a while to realize that that was the direction they were going in. But I certainly would not agitate to leave the show. I believe in contracts, and certainly was happy to stay until the finish of it." Hers was also the only character who was never once the centerpiece of an episode. "Yes, I think that's right, and—you know—that *never* occurred to me before. That shows you about where my ego is, I guess!"

Other *Lost in Space* cast members have talked about the constant tension on the sets—caused, some say, by the influence of Irwin Allen—but according to Lockhart, "I wasn't aware of it. I went to work, I brought all the things I wanted to read, and I had a marvelous time with Guy. We used to play music in the dressing rooms, and people would come and join us and sit there and we'd listen to Tchaikovsky or Rachmaninoff or something. (Guy was a brilliant musicologist.) Then I'd go in and do my stuff, and come *back out* to my dressing room. So I wasn't aware of whatever was going on. I knew we were *always* under the gun, time-wise. (For example, if we were doing a scene with an explosion in it and you fluffed a line and the *explosion* was perfect and they had to do it over, you *really* felt bad *[laughs]*!) But about all that other stuff—I don't take that stuff on, because it can drive you nuts if you do."

Even if *Lost in Space* did represent long hours and an undemanding role, there were plenty of rewards, like the opportunity to bring her daughters Anne Kathleen (born 1953) and June Elizabeth (1955) to the set. "Oh, they loved coming to the set. But we *all* loved the set, it was just *amazing*—all that great silver hardware and lights blinking and things going up and down. It was really quite wonderful." The series was canceled at the end of its third season, but the "family" can still be found together at an occasional convention or—more regularly—gathered for lunch on the same Fox lot where they filmed their extraterrestrial adventures a quarter century ago. "We get together at least once every three or four months," Lockhart smiles. "In fact, we all had lunch together last week at Fox—Marta and Jonathan and Billy and myself, and even Bobby May was there for that one, the man in the robot suit. (Angela couldn't come this time, and of course Mark is back East.) But we're looking forward to us all being together again soon. We're all in touch all the time, we talk on the phone and we correspond and we've never ceased to be involved closely with each other."

The one absent "family" member is of course Guy Williams, who died in 1989, but Lockhart says that he's still "close to their hearts" as well. "This I think is quite unique in the business: I arranged a dinner with Jan Williams, Guy's widow, and her son and daughter and their mates and all of us [the remaining *Lost in Space* regulars], and Angela's husband and Marta's husband and Billy's wife. We all took them out to dinner, to a place in Santa Monica, and we all sat around and talked about Guy Williams. Talked about *Guido*, which is what we used to call him. It was the loveliest, sweetest, most senti-

The family created by the show (*Lost in Space*) is still one today, according to Lockhart.

mental evening—of course, we knew Guy's family through Guy while we were shooting. To be able to do this, to bring us all together like that, was really neat, and I *think* quite an original, unique idea. At no other time has a television family taken out the *real* family under those circumstances—for the sentimentality of it. It was a sweet evening."

As for the series itself, Lockhart has "a *few* of them on tape—I don't have them all—and I recently was given the original pilot, and that's grand to have.

I was given it by the Sci-Fi Channel prior to my hosting the premiere of it—it had never aired before. Hosting it and doing some interviews, that was great fun to do."

Retirement—or even just the thought of it—is apparently nowhere on the horizon for the actress, who says she cannot think of a single regret associated with her 50-odd-year career. "I never had a desire to be famous, I *never* had that driving force—gotta act! gotta get out there! It has just unfolded *so* naturally in my life. The agonies that some people go through, waiting for the phone to ring, wanting that great public success, has not been part of my makeup—again, because of what I saw my parents do, and what their concerns were with life as it should be lived." She has watched her own daughters grow, and now enjoys seeing acting daughter Anne's career develop. "She was Sheba in *Battlestar Galactica*. She's a very good actress, and has great potential still, I feel. She's awfully good on the stage—we did *Butterflies Are Free* and *Forty Carats* together. She's also a marvelous horseback rider—she appears at rodeos with her husband riding cutting horses, that's her particular favorite. She also is one of the busiest and most sought-after actresses for ADR work, which is postrecording of dialogue. You'd be very surprised at the number of films that you've seen in which you've heard Annie's voice on the sound track, often over-dubbing dialogue for famous actresses." Mother and daughter both appeared in 1986 in *Troll*, with Anne playing the younger version of her white-wigged mother. The *Gremlins*-like film did not get a great reception from fans, but Lockhart—who *swears* in the movie (gasp!)—also swears by the experience. "God, I had the best time! We shot it in Italy, and on days when we weren't working, they made all the arrangements for the most fabulous sightseeing—off to Rome, off to Florence, off to Venice. Lordy me, it was wonderful and I'd go again in a New York minute!"

Obviously, the *real* June Lockhart is a very different person from many of the poised, serene, housebound women she has played in her long career. She still stands by her long-ago quote, "I really have no understanding or patience for people who won't expose themselves to the innovative"—although, asked to name something *she* would never have tried, she is quick to specify bungee jumping. A *TV Guide* article once called her a "happy nut," a description that might ruffle a lot of actresses, but Lockhart just laughs it off. "Well, I don't know if *nut* is quite the word now, because *nut* may have a different connotation these days than it did years ago, when that was written. But I certainly am . . . *outrageous!* One of my greatest compliments in life was when Annie called me an eccentric, and I shouted, 'Hallelujah! I've been waiting for eccentric-hood all my life!' She didn't mean it as a compliment at all, but *by God* it was neat. Who wouldn't want to be an *original*?"

Lockhart has never had an acting lesson, nor the "gotta act! gotta get out there!" compulsion that drives many performers.

JUNE LOCKHART FILMOGRAPHY

A *Christmas Carol* (MGM, 1938)
All This, and Heaven Too (Warner Bros., 1940)
Adam Had Four Sons (Columbia, 1941)
Sergeant York (Warner Bros., 1941)

Miss Annie Rooney (United Artists, 1942)
Forever and a Day (RKO, 1943)
Meet Me in St. Louis (MGM, 1944)
The White Cliffs of Dover (MGM, 1944)

Keep Your Powder Dry (MGM, 1945)
Son of Lassie (MGM, 1945)
Easy to Wed (MGM, 1946)
The Yearling (MGM, 1946)
She-Wolf of London (The Curse of the Allenbys) (Universal, 1946)
It's a Joke, Son (Eagle-Lion, 1947)
Bury Me Dead (Eagle-Lion, 1947)
T-Men (Eagle-Lion, 1947)
Time Limit (United Artists, 1957)
Lassie's Great Adventure (20th Century–Fox, 1963)

Just Tell Me You Love Me (1979)
Butterfly (Analysis, 1982)
Strange Invaders (Orion, 1983)
Troll (Empire Pictures, 1986)
Rented Lips (Cineworld, 1988)
The Big Picture (Columbia, 1989)
Dead Women in Lingerie (AFI/USA, 1991)
Sleep with Me (MGM, 1993)

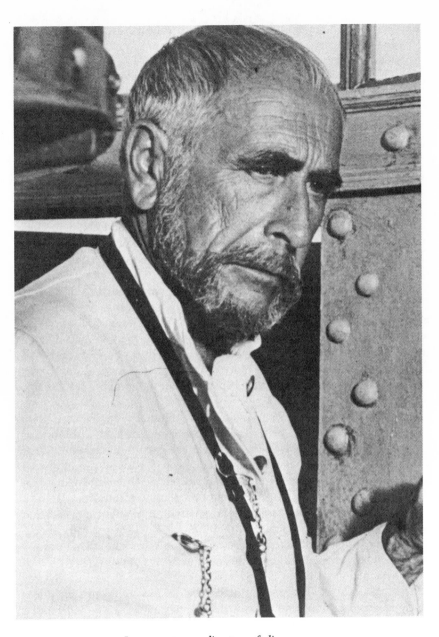

I was cast as a director of dinosaurs.
Like I was a lion tamer — but with dinosaurs!

Eugene Lourie

EUGENE LOURIE ENJOYED A FASCINATING and wide-ranging career in movies. In 1919 Yalta, while still a teenager, he worked as a bit player in an anticommunist movie called *Black Crows*; in 1930s France he was a renowned production designer collaborating with legendary screen directors Jean Renoir, René Clair and Max Ophuls. Arriving in Hollywood in the early forties, he resumed his career as art director (often working with fellow émigré Renoir); designed films as diverse as Chaplin's *Limelight* (1952) and Clint Eastwood's *Bronco Billy* (1980); even returned to acting with a bit in Richard Gere's *Breathless* (1983). "And yet," Lourie added, with a touch of regret, "*The Beast from 20,000 Fathoms* typecast me as a director of science fiction."

Lourie (who died on May 26, 1991) became involved with the classic 1953 dinosaur-on-the-loose thriller when a trio of low-budget producers approached him to handle the art direction on their upcoming slate of films. "They were called Mutual Films. They had three pictures to do — very cheap pictures — and they asked me if I would be interested in [art directing]. Jack Dietz, Hal Chester and Bernie Burton — they were the three that headed the company. That *was* the company *[laughs]*! They told me, 'We don't have any scripts, we have short outlines.' One outline was amusing to me; it was a subject that very seldom was done. It was the dinosaur coming out of the water. And I told them, 'I am interested in this picture. Who would direct it?' They said, 'We don't know. We don't have anybody to direct it yet.' I said, 'I doubt that anybody will know how to direct this picture. But if you like, I feel capable to do it, and I will do it.'

"They said okay, and that was all. Two weeks later, the call came from these same people: 'Gene, were you joking when you spoke of directing this film for us?' I said, 'No, I wasn't joking. I really can do it.' And they said, 'Well, then, it's your picture. Now find a writer to write the script.' I said okay. I found a friend who worked with me, and we wrote the screenplay in a very short time, one or two weeks. And then we made the picture."

The Beast from 20,000 Fathoms was the first of three dinosaur movies that Lourie would eventually direct, and the film that would stamp the eminent production designer as "a director of science fiction" — an association he found limiting in later years. Born in czarist Russia in 1905, Lourie's first brush with the movie medium came in 1911 when a cinema theater opened in Kharkov ("It was an unforgettable moment in my life"). Lourie remained an ardent young moviegoer throughout those turbulent years; escaping Russia, he found himself in Istanbul, where he drew and painted posters for a local movie theater to earn money for his fare to Paris and (to cut expenses) slept in the theater, atop its grand piano. "I had a kind of an adventurous youth because I was raised and I lived through the First World War and the Russian Revolution," Lourie recalled. "Like many young people of my generation, I wished

Previous page: **Director Eugene Lourie (seen here acting in *Krakatoa, East of Java*) grew to regret his reputation as a "dinosaur specialist."**

to leave Russia, to find my own life. I escaped through Turkey, from Crimea to Istanbul, and I lived in Istanbul one and a half years without money, trying to earn money. And then finally I went to Paris. My idea was to become a painter."

After working as a painter and a ballet set designer in France, Lourie turned to films and began a long association with famed French director Jean Renoir (*La Grande Illusion* [Grand Illusion], *La Bête Humaine* [The Human Beast], *La Règle du Jeu* [The Rules of the Game]). In 1941, during the Nazi occupation, French filmmakers (including Lourie, Renoir, Clair, Ophuls and others with whom Lourie had worked) fled for Hollywood. "I was a very known art director in France, and when a lot of people escaped from France, I decided to go where the films are made. Jean Renoir came here [to the United States], and I came here. Hollywood was like a giant magnet."

Lourie quickly found employment in Hollywood: he reteamed with Renoir on his stateside films, and also art directed such forties fare as *The House of Fear* (a Basil Rathbone/Sherlock Holmes mystery) and Abbott and Costello's *In Society*. (He even vaguely remembered working on an Invisible Man film, presumably *The Invisible Man's Revenge* [1944].) One difference between making films abroad and churning them out in Tinseltown, according to Lourie, was the fact that he "didn't like the dictatorial power of the production office. The studio dictated many things. I remember working at Warners and being told, 'Listen, this scene takes place in France. You go to the back lot and shoot it in our Paris street.' Their Paris street was made by a German art director, and it looked like a Bavarian village *[laughs]*. But you had to accept it. This was a little surprising."

It was in 1952 that Lourie was offered the director's chair on *The Beast from 20,000 Fathoms* (titled *The Monster from Beneath the Sea* during production). "Chester, Dietz and Burton were going to produce three films and release them through regional distributors," Lourie remembered. "They knew of my work for Renoir, and they knew also that I was designing cheap TV pictures at the Hal Roach studios. They were of no help to me [in directing the movie]. The one who was *pretending* to [be helpful] was Hal Chester; he provided the money, but he didn't try to influence me in any way. He was at one time one of the East Side Kids. I did have a *little* help from Bernie Burton because he was a very experienced filmmaker and a film editor. Otherwise, I was on my own. It was shot in a studio [the Motion Picture Center]. The Arctic scenes were shot on the stage. The amusement park was Long Beach. That picture was extraordinarily fast; I had a very quick cameraman named [Jack] Russell and I think we did it in twelve days. It cost about $200,000."

Lourie also helped to write the movie, although he did not take screen credit for his writing contribution (credit went to Lou Morheim and Fred Freiberger). "I was not full of vanity as I am now," Lourie joked. "[A writing credit] was not important to me. It was important at that point for me to make an interesting picture. A friend worked with me on the screenplay, and he also did not want his name on the film. I still remember his name, but as he didn't want credit then, I don't know if it would be discreet to name him." Asked about Ray Bradbury's contribution, Lourie recounted, "Bradbury got a story credit because, as we were working on the story, we came across a short story of his where a dinosaur answers the call of a lighthouse. I told my producers, and they decided the name of Bradbury would be good to add, and they bought his story. That's why his name is on the prints."

Beast, directed by Lourie and animated by Ray Harryhausen, opens in the Arctic with a nuclear blast freeing a prehistoric monster (a "rhedosaurus") after countless centuries suspended in ice. The creature promptly begins to wend its way south, from the snowy wastes at the top of the world toward New York City, its ancestral breeding ground. *Beast*'s large-scale crowd scenes (New Yorkers fleeing in panic from the rampaging creature) "were shot partly on location in New York City and partly on the back lot of Paramount Studios — Paramount had a big New York set. I went to New York with Bernie Burton [to shoot process plates and some of the mob scenes]. We shot on a weekend when there would be not much traffic. We had hired extras to play stevedores and dockworkers, and when we saw them we saw that they were puny men, they did not look like a stevedore should look. So we hired some real stevedores. When we were done, they asked for me to pose with them in a photo. They wished to show the photo to their wives; this would prove that they were working [in the film], not getting drunk in a bar *[laughs]*.

"The next day we shot on Wall Street with a crowd of twenty-five people. There were supposed to be many more, but the production manager said that it was a Sunday and extras would have to be paid double, so twenty-five was all we could afford. But I knew that we would be shooting [additional crowd scenes] at Paramount, so it was unimportant. The largest amount of extras I remember at Paramount was four hundred for one day. [Producer] Bernie Burton was the editor on it, and as he was cutting the film he said, 'Gene, you don't give me any prerogative. You shot the scenes [in such a way] that I can only put them together the way you shot them.' I said, 'That was the idea!'"

The official stars of *Beast* were Paul Christian and Paula Raymond, but the *real* star was the monster itself, brought to "life" by Harryhausen. "Hal Chester, one of the producers, told me that they had investigated all means of animating the beast and they had the name of a young animator who had worked already with Willis O'Brien, who made *King Kong*. Chester said, 'I think it would be useful for you to meet him and speak to him and decide if he will be part of our crew.' So I met Harryhausen; at that time he was animating fairy-tale [shorts] for children. We spoke and I liked him very much, and I saw the pictures he made and the animation was usually without jerks. So I said, 'Let's do the picture together.' I was amazed how long it took, the frame-by-frame animation. The time it took to shoot the picture was twelve days; to animate it, it took two or three months! But I enjoyed working with Harryhausen very much."

On the subject of his "official" stars, Lourie recalled, "Paul Christian is a German actor; his real name was Hubschmid, and he was very known in Switzerland. He was a very charming man. I remember I had a photograph of me with him; as he is very tall and I am quite short, the photograph was of me using a stepladder to speak to him [*laughs*]. Paula Raymond was a mediocre actress; she was very rigid. But Cecil Kellaway was very, very charming; he gave the picture a little humor and a nice kind of tone."

When the film was completed, producers Chester, Burton and Dietz were all pleased—and a bit surprised—that *Beast* had exceeded their expectations. "They were all *extremely* happy with the picture," said Lourie. "But when Dietz saw that it was better than they expected, he didn't want to release it through a small organization. He went to Jack Warner and offered *him* the picture. But Warner didn't want to release the picture; he wanted to buy it outright. And he *did* buy it outright, for $450,000, and Warners changed the title to *The Beast from 20,000 Fathoms*. Then, when the returns started coming in, Jack Dietz was very *unhappy* that he had lost the rights, because it was number one at the box office. Each time he read about it in *Variety*, he said, 'Oh, I am stupid!'"

Harryhausen's amazing effects also exceeded the expectations of everyone involved—invluding Lourie. "He invented some scenes that were very good. The scene of the Beast in the burning roller coaster was like a big opera act, like a tenor who dies in a very dramatic scene. That roller coaster was another miniature, like the Beast itself. It was eight feet high. We put rubber cement on the roller coaster so it would burn and we had pieces precut so that they would fly off in flames. Then Harryhausen added the Beast into the scene, attacking the roller coaster, and it all fit together. I saw the film at a matinee; Jean Renoir came with me. The ending of it affected my daughter. She was about six years old when I took her to see the picture. And coming home, she started to cry and said, 'You are bad, Daddy! You killed the big nice Beast!'"

The huge success of *Beast from 20,000 Fathoms* instantly typed Lourie as a science fiction specialist. "It was very strange. Many people came with projects for me to do, and they all wanted copies of *The Beast from 20,000 Fathoms*. Finally a producer named Dave Diamond came to me; he had seen *The Beast* and he had a film project where, instead of one villain-beast, it would be strange radiation coming from the river. I started to work with his writer on the story; it was going to be a coproduction between Allied Artists and an English company called Eros Films. But Eros Films insisted that I use the same type of beast and the same type of tricks as I did in *Beast from 20,000 Fathoms*—they wanted a physical monster. My friend Daniel Hyatt and I spent ten days [putting together] a rough draft that was a copy of *Beast*, and I told Dave Diamond that after the contracts with Eros Films were signed, the script would

Armed with a radiation field (and obvious mold seams), *The Giant Behemoth* **invades London.**

have to be redone. That did not happen, and so the film *[The Giant Behemoth]* was a copy of *The Beast from 20,000 Fathoms*. I *did* resent this—but not *too* much. Visually, it's much easier to see the villain-beast than to see radiation *[laughs]*."

Obviously, minus the involvement of stop-motion genius Ray Harryhausen, *Giant Behemoth's* prehistoric animal was strikingly inferior to the incomparable rhedosaurus seen in *Beast*; Lourie himself knew that *Behemoth's* special effects did not begin to compare with Harryhausen's. "I think the beast itself was not interesting in *The Giant Behemoth*. It's a visual thing, and very difficult to explain; you *feel* that [something] is wrong, but you don't know exactly what it is. It was bad animation and a bad animal—the model itself, I mean. Originally, I was to do [the effects] myself together with Harryhausen or with Willis O'Brien. O'Brien was still alive, and he worked together with Pete Peterson on animating. Dave Diamond decided to give [the effects work] to an outlet on a contract basis. So they listened to me when I spoke, but what they did, they did what they wanted. Essentially *The Beast* and *The Giant Behemoth* were *both* cheap pictures anyhow. The difference was, one was cheap in dollars and the other, cheap in English pounds *[laughs]*." (Was Willis O'Brien, "father" of *King Kong* and the dean of stop-motion animators, an interesting man to get to know? "No," Lourie responded flatly. "He was a one hundred percent technician.")

The Giant Behemoth (released as *Behemoth, the Sea Monster* in England, where it was made) was redundant both in title *and* story line, a carbon copy of *Beast*, with the dinosaur (here spawned by radiation) leaving a wake of destruction between Cornwall and London. Remembering the English crews he worked with on *Giant Behemoth* and (later) on *Gorgo*, Lourie offered, "Basically, they were no different from a Hollywood crew. Different in the kind of personal relations you had with them, maybe, but I liked them very much. They're a little slower, and a little more *stubborn* — especially the special effects men. The special effects men worked like a group of engineers: They all wore white smocks, and they all had very definite ideas about what could be done and what could not be done." Unlike *Beast*, which included a conventional boy-girl subplot, *The Giant Behemoth* (which starred Gene Evans and Andre Morell) avoided that well-traveled lane. "I didn't see what love relations between two humans had to do with a dinosaur."

The seeds of Lourie's third dinosaur film, *Gorgo*, were sown the day the director's daughter complained that her daddy had killed "the big nice Beast [from *20,000 Fathoms*]." "That is why, in *Gorgo*, I tried not to kill the beast," Lourie explained. "Gorgo escapes alive back to the sea. My daughter should have a writer's credit *[laughs]*."

In *Gorgo* (based on a story by Lourie and Daniel Hyatt), a volcanic eruption at the bottom of the Irish Sea rouses a giant beast, who wanders onto nearby Nara Island before being driven off by villagers. Salvage divers Bill Travers and William Sylvester capture the 65-foot beast and deliver it to London, where it is placed on display at an amusement park. But the beast proves to be just an infant — one with a very angry 250-foot mother in close pursuit. Explaining his involvement on the film, Lourie reminisced, "I was called to meet the King Brothers [the producers]. They were two nice chaps and they made my life quite easy with *Gorgo*. We met, and they had a writer in mind to write the story, but I didn't like his idea. I told them I would write it with my friend Hyatt. The King Brothers liked our story. They were very attached to their mother, and I do believe that the project appealed to them because the mother comes to save her baby.

"At first the King Brothers wanted to destroy a big town. They said, 'Let's go to Paris. Let's have the beast climbing the Eiffel Tower!' I worked with a sketch artist who made numerous sketches with the beast climbing the Eiffel Tower and destroying the Notre Dame of Paris. I said to Frank King, 'The problem is, we don't have a sea in Paris. The beast would have to walk knee-high in the Seine River!' *[Laughs.]* Now we went with the King Brothers to Germany, because they said they'd shoot the picture in Germany. We met a man over there who had a studio in Berlin, but his studio was too small. At this time, they had an offer from an English company to make *Gorgo* with them,

The man-in-a-monster-suit idea for *Gorgo* originated with Lourie, who believed it would give him much more control.

in their English studio. Part of it was shot in Ireland, too, in a port near Dublin. That is how it happened."

Unlike *Beast* and *Behemoth*, *Gorgo* fell back on the economical man-in-a-monster-suit technique rather than employing time-consuming (and costly) stop motion. "The man in the suit was my idea," Lourie added. "I thought—wrongly—that I would have more control, and it would be much faster anyhow. It would not necessitate the long delay of frame-by-frame animation. I wanted to have a lightweight suit for Gorgo, so that the man inside could use his physical strength to move the thing. I did not want to rely [on remote controls]. But the King Brothers employed [effects engineers] whose idea was hydraulic. The man who played the beast had to carry enormous weight on his back. I would have preferred the other idea."

Other people—namely, the King Brothers themselves—had had other, even *worse* ideas. "In spite of being ex-gangsters, they were very naïve in real life. Frank King often said, 'Gee, why don't we do a monster in rubber, like Macy's parade? We could carry it through the London streets, this big beast passing by.' He wanted to use *that* for the monster!

"We put the stunt man who played the monster on miniature sets to give

The Colossus of New York has the upper hand over creator Otto Kruger in Lourie's one nondinosaur directorial credit.

him the proportions," Lourie continued. "They cost a lot of money — and a lot of work! The biggest miniature set was the Thames River set, with the Bridge — it occupied MGM's biggest stage in London. The 'river' was not very deep, just knee-high water. It was a comical scene, because the stunt man who played the beast had trouble walking through the water with the big, clumsy dinosaur's feet. So we cut the costume, and from the knees down were human legs with tennis shoes. It was a very strange beast *[laughs]*!"

The filmmakers' ingenuity also came into play when it came time to shoot scenes of a flatbed truck carrying the supine Gorgo through London's bustling streets. "We had the problem of how to take through the streets of London a beast that we didn't have. We had only a [full-sized] head and the paws. King said, 'Let's put the beast under a tarpaulin on a truck. I will put a truck with an orchestra in front of it, and we will pass through Piccadilly and the streets will be full of people trying to see what it is.' We could get our shots of crowds that way and not have to employ extras for the scenes. On Sunday morning, we put the beast on a big platform truck—the head and the paws, and the rest was just tarpaulin. We hid the camera inside of the beast to shoot the reactions of people—and nobody came! This Sunday morning was very dismal—the scenes we got were of empty streets, and occasionally a few people *[Lourie made a scowling face]*, 'What the hell is *that?*'"

Lourie fondly remembered the stars (Travers and Sylvester), but held out reservations about Vincent Winter, who plays an Irish youngster throughout the film. "I was not very happy with the little boy. I had an idea to use another boy, but this boy Winter had a little bit of experience—and he was an old ham already *[laughs]*. I had a big pleasure to shoot the picture, especially making the crowd scenes in real streets, and then destroying the miniatures. But I was not so satisfied with Gorgo itself, because frame-by-frame animation makes the animal more alive than the stuntman in the rubber suit." Of his three dinosaur films, Lourie claimed that *The Beast from 20,000 Fathoms* remained his favorite.

Lourie remained active (as an art director again) throughout the 1960s and 1970s, working on a characteristically wide variety of projects, including director Sam Fuller's cultish *Shock Corridor* and *The Naked Kiss* ("Sam is a little crazy, but a very nice man"); he also worked as a miniatures and special effects unit director for such films as *Crack in the World*, *Battle of the Bulge* and *Krakatoa, East of Java*. His autobiography, *My Work in Films*, was published by Harcourt Brace Jovanovich in 1985, with full chapters devoted to the Renoir classics, *Limelight, Beast from 20,000 Fathoms* and many more. Toward the end of his life, largely incapacitated by strokes, he still kept busy, granting interviews and writing about his early life. "On my way from Russia to Paris, I had many experiences that would be good for interesting stories, and I am writing a series of short stories. I am contemplating sending them to New York. It will be great if they will accept them. If they do not accept them, I will be one more rejected writer."

With typical openness, he also admitted that—prior to *The Beast from 20,000 Fathoms*—he had no interest in science fiction films whatsoever, a fact which surely added to his discomfort with being typecast as a science fiction specialist. "I *was* very unhappy about that, because I was cast as a director of dinosaurs. Like I was a lion tamer—but with dinosaurs! All my life, *The Beast from 20,000 Fathoms* was hanging like an albatross around my neck."

There are two different audiences for science fiction pictures:
One is made up of the kids . . . and the other is made up
of older, intelligent, concerned people who are genuine
sci-fi fans. They're not what I call "the idiot Godzilla fan."

Jeff Morrow

IT IS A LONG WAY FROM BROADWAY to Hollywood to Metaluna, but during the 1950s monster boom, actor Jeff Morrow made the transition in easy strides. An accomplished stage actor, Morrow made an indelible mark on science fiction history via his portrayal of Exeter in Universal's *This Island Earth* (1955). Other genre credits include a strong performance as the paranoid protagonist in the same studio's *The Creature Walks Among Us* (1956), director Kurt Neumann's *Kronos* (1957) and the notorious science fiction cheapie *The Giant Claw* (1957).

The New York–born Morrow developed an interest in the theater as a result of his studies at art school. As Irving Morrow, he made his stage debut in the 1930 production of *Penal Law*, and later appeared in such plays as *Once in a Lifetime*, *A Midsummer Night's Dream*, *Twelfth Night*, *Romeo and Juliet* and *Macbeth*, treading the boards opposite stars like Katharine Cornell, Maurice Evans, Katharine Hepburn, Luise Rainer, Mae West and many others. He also racked up an imposing total of three thousand airwave performances, including two years as radio's redoubtable Dick Tracy.

Morrow made his film debut in 20th Century–Fox's Biblical epic *The Robe* (1953), with Richard Burton and Jean Simmons. His effective portrayal of the scowling, scarred centurion impressed both viewers and critics, and the fledgling screen actor followed up on this early credit with supporting roles in Paramount's 3-D *Flight to Tangier* (1953), a contrived foreign intrigue drama, and Universal's clichéd jungle adventure *Tanganyika* (1954). Struck with Morrow's screen possibilities, Universal approached the actor with a two-picture-a-year contract.

Over lunch at DuPar's in Encino, California, a lanky, bearded Jeff Morrow recalled the genesis of his first role as a Universal contract player. "My contract went into effect some time in February 1954, and just prior to that date Universal suddenly decided they wanted me to play the lead in a science fiction picture, *This Island Earth*. They sent me the script, I read it and went in to talk with the producer, Bill Alland, who is a very nice chap, quite able and talented, and the writer, Franklin Coen."

Morrow was intrigued by Coen's script but disappointed to find that his character, Exeter, an interplanetary emissary, had been written as a one-dimensional heavy. "You had no idea why Exeter was doing any of this stuff, except that he was an ornery character. I didn't have to do the picture because it was going to start ten days before my contract went into effect, so this was one of the few instances in all the times I've signed for pictures that I had a little bit to say about it! I told them, 'I'm interested in doing it, but he's such a heavy. Can't we do something about it—show that he is, let's say, the epitome of a true scientist, and really concerned about the effect of what he does upon the world?' So we talked for about an hour, and there was a sort of

Previous page: Jeff Morrow immediately saw all the possibilities inherent in the role of the noble Exeter in *This Island Earth*. (Photofest)

general agreement that it wasn't a bad idea. And when we walked down the street to the parking lot, Frank Coen said, 'I'm so glad you were there, because I've been trying to sell them on that concept for a month!'"

As a consequence, the rewritten screenplay, which Morrow received a week or ten days later, depicted the Exeter character in a more favorable light. The screenplay revisions, combined with Morrow's larger-than-life performance, resulted in one of the most memorable film characters of fifties science fiction.

Special makeup designed for Morrow necessitated his arrival at the studio a full two hours before cameras rolled. "They gave me a slightly enlarged forehead, which had to be put on very, very carefully, and then a white wig over that. It was the kind of look where, if you walked down the street, people wouldn't notice you, but then twenty feet later they would suddenly stop, turn around and say, 'He looked a little odd, didn't he?'" Later, unfortunately, the white wigs worn by Morrow and others in his cosmic coterie presented some unforeseen difficulties. "The wigs we wore were so white that we were all very worried, especially the woman hairdresser, about how they would wind up looking on film. I did a test, and that was printed and delivered on a Monday — the same Monday that we started shooting the picture. And, as we predicted, when we saw the dailies, we saw that my hair came out pure white — it looked like cotton candy. It was terrible! Well, after the producers and executives all went into a bit of shock, they decided, 'We'll just print the film darker, and the hair won't look so white.' So they printed it darker, but then my skin looked as though I had been out in the sun all my life! The consequence was that every day, little by little, the hairdresser would twist and comb so that there was a wave in the white hair — not for any cosmetic appearance, but simply so there'd be a little light and shade, and it wouldn't look this ghastly pure white. They also softened the lights on the hair, and after a short time I looked fairly human."

Dazzling special effects provided most of the highlights of *This Island Earth*; *New York Times* critic Howard H. Thompson perceived this when he closed his review by acknowledging technical artists Clifford Stine, William Fritzsche, Alexander Golitzen, Richard H. Riedel, David S. Horsley, Russell A. Gausman and Julia Heron as "the real stars" of the picture. The film's story, with its male-and-female Earthling protagonists, trips through space, enthroned space despot (Douglas Spencer) and gratuitous monster, is a bit closer to comic book pap like *Flash Gordon* than to any sort of "serious" science fiction. Morrow's Exeter is the film's one intriguing character, much of his appeal deriving from Morrow's sympathetic performance; the Franklin Coen–George Callaghan script is otherwise weak in characterization, and Newman fails to draw anything but wooden, wonderstruck performances from most of the rest of his cast. But whatever the film's minor failings, *This Island Earth* has stood the test of time and is today regarded as a milestone of the genre.

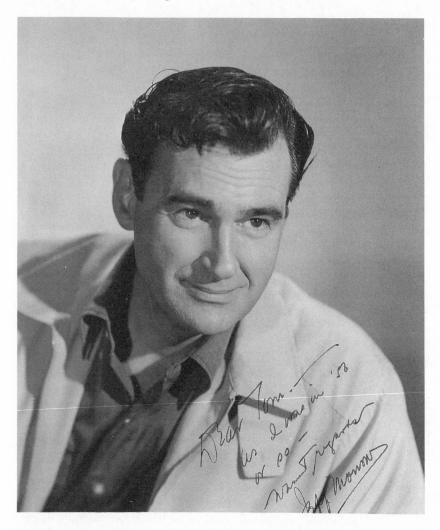

Broadway actor cum B movie star Jeff Morrow took on monsters from outer space in the fifties films *This Island Earth*, *Kronos* and *The Giant Claw* (pictured).

Morrow looked back on *This Island Earth* with affection. "By and large, the film was quite good; as a matter of fact, I think it was slightly underrated by some of the New York critics. To the best of my knowledge, it cost about $750,000, the shooting schedule was about six weeks, and it had extremely good special effects, much in advance of most of the science fiction pictures of that time. It certainly had a lot more to say than practically any of the science fiction pictures that I've seen recently — ones that cost $25–$30 million — which are not only not-positive but extremely negative in their point of view. And,

Morrow and Leigh Snowden react to off-camera commotion in a posed shot from Universal's *The Creature Walks Among Us*.

oddly enough, I know I did get more fan mail from that picture than any other I ever did." The one jarring note that Morrow detected was the last-reel appearance of the Metaluna Mutants. "[Universal] felt they had to have the insurance of audience reaction on the part of the kids, and they wrote in a monster. That really could've been cut out of the script, but we lived with it."

Morrow's next role for Universal was in the lively costume adventure *Captain Lightfoot* (1955), a Rock Hudson starrer made on location in Ireland. Morrow cut a dashing figure as the Irish rebel leader Captain Thunderbolt in this Douglas Sirk–directed swashbuckler, and *Captain Lightfoot* remained his favorite filmland experience. Returning to science fiction, he was reteamed with his *This Island Earth* costar Rex Reason for director John Sherwood's *The Creature Walks Among Us*, third and last film in Universal's Gill Man trilogy. Morrow starred as a famous surgeon who organizes an expedition to track down the notorious Creature from the Black Lagoon, presently residing somewhere in the Florida Everglades. A certifiable neurotic, Morrow's Dr. William Barton is full of nutty notions on subjects ranging from the evolutionary process to his buxom blond wife's (Leigh Snowden) fidelity, and he receives just desserts for his on-screen unpleasantness in the film's roof-raising finale. "I had done all my dialogue scenes, and on what I believe was the last day of shooting they gave me a script of 'new scenes' for the day. I was a little horrified, thinking that they'd thrown a lot of new dialogue at me, but I opened it and there was not a single line. It was a map of the house that we were in — the stairs, the gallery, the balconies, the rooms where I am chased by the Creature, finally caught and thrown off the balcony — which, needless to say, was the end of my character." Asked about the stunt, Morrow explained, "They had me on a wire that led up to a pulley on the ceiling. When Don Megowan — the Creature — reached down and grabbed me, they pulled me up with the wire as he lifted me. Needless to say, he did not throw me over; he raised me up to the ceiling and then they stopped — thank goodness! — and put a dummy up there in my place."

Due to his roles in *This Island Earth* and *Creature Walks*, Morrow's name was now apparently linked with science fiction in some producers' minds. For Robert Lippert's Regal Films, Morrow starred with Barbara Lawrence in *Kronos*, the story of a giant extraterrestrial robot absorbing energy and growing in size as it stalks up the West Coast from Mexico. An unenthusiastic critic for the *New York World Telegram* hit the nail exactly on the head when he griped that *Kronos* "presents an electronic monster too complicated to be very terrifying," but Morrow was fond of the finished film. "*Kronos* was a very good little low-budget picture. We made it in a couple weeks. The concept, I thought, was interesting, and it made good sense. I did a little fast research beforehand so that when I wrote down on the blackboard the figures of the alphas and the betas and the gammas, I think I knew what I was talking about and I think I *sounded* as if I knew. That was a very good, simple little picture."

Morrow's keenest memory of *Kronos* centered around the type of embarrassing situation actors are often unable to avoid. "Barbara Lawrence and I were shooting a scene on the beach, and I was supposed to run into the water. I stripped off my slacks and shirt and started to run, and then they yelled *cut* and in came a double, in bathing trunks, who was going to go into the water for me. But as I was walking off, heading for another section of the beach for

Morrow, his actress-wife Ann Karen and their daughter, Lisa, behind the scenes on Universal's final Gill Man stanza, *The Creature Walks Among Us.*

my next shot, I happened to look back and I saw that he was terribly bow-legged. And of course, seen from the back, everyone would assume that that was me!"

Morrow visibly cringed at the mere mention of his next film. "The less that's said about *The Giant Claw*, the better" *[laughs]*! Actually, we had a very good cast, and the basic concept of the story was also good. It was based upon a new development in science: the concept of the mirror image in outer space." The Samuel Newman–Paul Gangelin screenplay took the antimatter principle and applied it to the film's story of a colossal prehistoric bird emerging out of the depths of space to wreak havoc on a helpless modern world. "We poor, benighted actors had our own idea of what the giant bird would look like — our concept was that this was something that resembled a streamlined hawk, possibly a half a mile long, flying at such speeds that we could barely see it. That was the way *we* envisioned it. Well, the producer, Sam Katzman, decided for economy reasons not to spend the $10–$15,000 it would take to make a really good bird — he had it made in Mexico, probably for $19.28! I went to a sneak preview in Westwood Village, and when the monster appeared on the screen it was like a huge plucked turkey, flying with these incredible *squawks!* And the audience went into hysterics. I shrunk down in my seat, hoping that no one would realize that I was that man up there on the screen. My only consolation was that, when the picture was over and the lights finally came up, I heard somebody in front of me say, 'And it's such a shame, too, because he's such a very good actor.'" Morrow laughed, "After hearing that, I walked out feeling a little more hopeful."

While Morrow appeared to have a certain regard for science fiction films, the actor looked back on the fifties brand of science fiction with a harsh critical eye. "There are two different audiences for science fiction pictures: One is made up of the kids, many of whom are not the brightest in the world at that period in their lives, and the other is made up of older, intelligent, concerned people who are genuine sci-fi fans. They're not what I call 'the idiot Godzilla fan.' I think at that time [the fifties] there were about five or six science fiction pictures that had considerable merit — *The War of the Worlds*, *The Day the Earth Stood Still*, *Forbidden Planet* and perhaps a few others. But by and large the rest were pretty junky pictures."

Morrow's film and television appearances grew less frequent in recent years, but in the early seventies he marked time in two low-budget genre productions. Writer-director Harry Essex's *Octaman* was a shoddy semiremake of Essex's *Creature from the Black Lagoon*, with Kerwin Mathews and Pier Angeli battling a ludicrous octopus man in a primitive Latin American fishing community. Fortuitously removed from the film's main action, Morrow was confined to a single dialogue scene with Kerwin Mathews. "The producer, Mike Kraike, and the writer-director Harry Essex contacted me and said that one of their actors was sick and that they were in a jam, and would I do this small part as a special favor? So I did that one scene in a half a day, and it's one of the few pictures of mine that I've never seen."

His last fantasy film credit was director Carl Monson's *Legacy of Blood* (1973), a lurid murder-in-the-mansion melodrama filmed on location on an estate in Pasadena. Despite a strong cast (Jeff, John Carradine, Faith Domergue,

John Russell, Merry Anders, John Smith, Rodolfo Acosta), the results were disappointing. "That was a real horror picture—no great ethical value to it. I attended a screening of it, and the horror shots, which should have been just a few frames, just a fraction of a second, were instead lingered upon for perhaps a beat of three—which ruined the picture. It was just that the director and the cutter, everybody connected with it, were quite devoid of any kind of artistic taste."

Although largely absent from films and television in his later years, Jeff Morrow remained active by working as a commercial illustrator and taking the occasional acting assignment (most notably, a recent *Twilight Zone* episode that teamed him with fifties standbys John Agar, Kenneth Tobey and Warren Stevens). Morrow was open and enthusiastic about his long, wide-ranging career, and while he had no overwhelming affinity for science fiction subjects, he recognized and appreciated the fact that many of his biggest fans were from that contingent of film buffs. As for a favorite among his own science fiction credits, Morrow was emphatic in his obvious choice.

"*This Island Earth*, very definitely. The thing that I felt was important about *This Island Earth* was the fact that there was a sense of hope—that if we *do* ever come to meet people from another planet, in some way we'll be able to communicate on a human level of understanding. At least, let's hope to!"

JEFF MORROW FILMOGRAPHY

The Robe (20th Century–Fox, 1953)
Flight to Tangier (Paramount, 1953)
Siege at Red River (20th Century–Fox, 1954)
Sign of the Pagan (Universal, 1954)
Tanganyika (Universal, 1954)
Captain Lightfoot (Universal, 1955)
This Island Earth (Universal, 1955)
Hour of Decision (Astor, 1955)
The Creature Walks Among Us (Universal, 1956)
World in My Corner (Universal, 1956)
Pardners (Paramount, 1956)

The First Texan (Allied Artists, 1956)
Copper Sky (20th Century–Fox, 1957)
Kronos (20th Century–Fox, 1957)
The Giant Claw (Columbia, 1957)
Five Bold Women (Citation Films, 1960)
The Story of Ruth (20th Century–Fox, 1960)
Harbor Lights (20th Century–Fox, 1963)
Octaman (Filmers Guild, 1971)
Legacy of Blood (Blood Legacy) (Universal Entertainment, 1973)

Clips of Morrow in *This Island Earth* are seen in *The Incredible Shrinking Woman* (Universal, 1981).

Morrow, 86, died December 26, 1993, in a Canoga Park, California, nursing home after a long illness.

*To do science fiction in those days was like a step
down, career-wise. You generally started with something
like that — you didn't want to build up to it!*

Lori Nelson

A LARGE NUMBER OF STARRING FILM ROLES may make a talented actress popular, but it is no guarantee of lasting stardom. Universal's youngest contract player in the early 1950s, pretty Lori Nelson, displayed considerable charm and ability in many of the studio's bread-and-butter pictures: Ma and Pa Kettle movies, Audie Murphy Westerns, a Francis the Talking Mule epic and even the 3-D *Revenge of the Creature*. But shortsighted studio execs perceived Nelson as an actress suited only to these colorless ingenue roles, and she broke with Universal to find more diversified work as a freelancer.

These days she is looking to make a comeback: going on interviews, taking acting workshops and carrying the other behind-the-scenes baggage fans never consider when they think about a movie star's lifestyle. A good dramatic role is what she would like to land; although still radiant, she thrives on the character roles she plays in her workshop, like the unhappy widow in *The Trip to Bountiful* ("gray wig, an old sweater, the oxford shoes and all") and the frumpy mom in *'night, Mother*. "Those are the kinds of things that I'd dearly love to do. But I'm finding it very difficult to get back into the business again because it's very difficult for women my age—there aren't enough parts. For me it's almost like starting all over. Not because I don't have the experience; my major credits speak for themselves, and whenever I go on an interview, they do remember the stuff I was in. But there are so many women in my category and so few roles for women of any age, character or glamorous. Roles are few and far between, and there's a tremendous amount of competition. It's almost a crapshoot. What we have to do is just keep going out on the interviews until it's your turn—until the roulette wheel stops at you."

Born Dixie Kay Nelson in Santa Fe, New Mexico, she began her showbiz career at the tender age of two and a half, dancing in a hometown show. She was voted Santa Fe's most talented and beautiful child, and toured the state billed as "Santa Fe's Shirley Temple." At the age of four, Dixie moved to Hollywood with her mother and father and there was named Little Miss America. With the continuing help and encouragement of her mom, she worked as a fashion and photographer's model and in the early forties made her first bid for a movie career, testing (unsuccessfully) for a role in Warner Bros.' *Kings Row* (1941). A second false start came a few years later, when Dixie caught the fancy of Arthur Landau, a well-known Hollywood producer and self-proclaimed discoverer of thirties star Jean Harlow. Landau expressed interest in casting teenage Dixie as Harlow in a movie account of the platinum bombshell's life and times; but Dixie was too young and Landau unprepared to go into production, and the project never got off the ground.

Finally it was Hollywood agent Milo Frank who helped the aspiring actress get her foot inside a studio door. Frank wangled a Saturday appointment with

Previous page: **After years of regretting her starring stint in *Revenge of the Creature*, Lori Nelson has made peace with her one "cult" credit.**

one of the casting people at MGM, but when the day of the interview arrived, they learned that their Metro contact had been whisked away for an emergency appendectomy. Undeterred, Frank hurried Dixie over to Universal, where she and the agent met with front office and casting people. Dixie trained with studio dramatic coach Sophie Rosenstein over the next several weekends, enacted a scene for the front office and ultimately was offered a seven-year contract, which was approved in court on her 17th birthday.

"In those days, the most ideal, the most wonderful situation to be in was to be under contract," the actress (quickly redubbed Lori Nelson by Universal) stresses. "Actors today just don't know what they're missing. Because it was real training, it was like being at a university for actors. I was 16-going-on-17 when I was signed at Universal, and in fact I finished high school at Universal — I went each morning to the little schoolhouse that was right on the studio lot. I was the only student in school, and it was like having my own private tutor. I learned more in the short time that I was there finishing high school at Universal than in all the years previous to that, when I was in 'regular' school. I graduated second year college grades when I graduated from high school.

"I would go to the studio early in the morning and go to school three hours a day in the schoolhouse. Then I would go up to the dancing class with Hal Belfer — we'd learn routines. Next I would go to the gym and work out a while. On certain days we'd go out to the back lot, and the wranglers would teach us how to mount, dismount and ride horses. Then we had voice and diction and singing lessons. Then to Sophie Rosenstein's class, to work on scenes with other contract players. Put on little shows, little skits. Do scenes with other prospective actors that were being considered for possible contracts. We would also go to the screening rooms and critique old movie classics and acting techniques. It was like going from one class to another. And then in between we'd make a picture *[laughs]*! It was just the greatest training you could have ever imagined."

Enjoying what she still calls "the most fun in all the world," Nelson was not about to fret that most of her early pictures were silly confections like *Ma and Pa Kettle at the Fair* (her debut film, as the Kettles' oldest daughter Rosie, 1952), *Walking My Baby Back Home* (1953) and *Francis Goes to West Point* (with future television stars David Janssen and Leonard Nimoy in small parts, 1952). "When I first went to Universal, I had never done movies before, and it was all new and exciting to me. So starring in a movie with Donald O'Connor, or with Marjorie Main and Percy Kilbride [Ma and Pa Kettle] — or with Francis the Talking Mule *[laughs]*! — was very exciting, especially since I had never done featured roles. Right from the very beginning I was put in starring and costarring roles."

Better parts eventually ensued, like her role as the daughter of Barbara Stanwyck in the heart-tugging period piece *All I Desire* (1953) or her romantic lead in *All American* (also 1953) with the up-and-coming Tony Curtis. Their acting stables swelling with young talent, Universal saw fit to loan Nelson out to RKO for the deep-sea diving adventure *Underwater!* Typical of the wasteful extravagance for which that studio's Howard Hughes regime is remembered, RKO retained Lori's services for a full eight months but used her in only the one film. When Nelson returned to Universal in the latter part of 1954, she found herself a veritable stranger on the lot. "Milton Rackmil and Capital Records had bought Universal while I was doing *Underwater!* over at RKO. When I came back after those eight months, I knew practically no one and practically no one knew me."

Hoping for strong roles as a sort of welcome-back present, Nelson was placed in *Destry* (a remake of the 1939 *Destry Rides Again*, with Audie Murphy and Mari Blanchard in the James Stewart and Marlene Dietrich roles) before being taken aback when Universal lined up as her next leading man a scaly, dark-green prehistoric beast hailing from the jungles of South America. "In the beginning I didn't want to do *Revenge of the Creature* because I felt like it was almost a comedown for me. Most of the other movies that I did at Universal were a much better caliber than that. To do science fiction in those days was like a step down, career-wise. You generally started with something like that—you didn't want to build *up* to it *[laughs]*! But then I did find while I was making the movie that I really enjoyed the experience, and that it was above the average, a very high-caliber science fiction film."

Announced (under the title *Return of the Creature from the Black Lagoon*) by Universal even before *Creature from the Black Lagoon* was released, *Revenge* picks up the story where *Creature* left off, with adventurous John Bromfield scouring the Amazon for the Gill Man. Captured, the Creature is transported to Florida's Marineland, where scientists John Agar and Nelson poke and probe the Devonian relic, and later track the rampaging beast after its inevitable breakout. Much of *Revenge of the Creature* was shot in Florida at Marineland, where Agar, Nelson and Ricou Browning (the Gill Man) descended into tanks filled with denizens of the deep.

"I had learned how to use an Aqualung while I was making *Underwater!* I didn't have to do any scenes in *Underwater!* . . . underwater *[laughs]*, but because [stars] Richard Egan and Jane Russell were learning how to use the Aqualung, I got to learn how, also. I took all the lessons, never dreaming that it would come in handy when I did *Revenge of the Creature!* I did all my own diving in the Creature picture."

Being asked to swim amidst sharks would test any actress' mettle, but Nelson's hesitations were short-lived. "I had a little trepidation about it in the beginning. In the tank they had moray eels, stingrays, manta rays, bat stingrays, sharks—and of course all of the other various and sundry fish large and small. But the Marineland people told us that all those fish get fed every hour, and unless they're hungry, they're not going to bother you. And of course they made sure that they *were* fed just before any of us went in to do any underwater scenes. And therefore it was not dangerous, and it didn't bother me. It was a little scary the first time I went down, but after that I couldn't wait to get back in again. It was the most exciting thing in the world, to go down in those tanks with all those fish and see what was going on. As everyone else who has ever done it says, it's a fascinating world down there.

"Most of the time, the camera photographed us from an indoor viewing area that was below water level, through portholes that were designed for the tourists to see through. But there was also a professional diver with an underwater camera in the tank with us. He took close-up shots and so forth, and then also shots from the Creature's point of view, where he's looking out the windows at the people that are looking in at *him*. But most of the shots were shot from that viewing area outside. I remember that there were also a couple of professional underwater swimmers in the tank with us—off-camera, as protection, in case anything happened."

Nelson got wet not only in the tank scenes, but later in the picture as well, when the Creature abducts her from Jacksonville, Florida's, Lobster House and leaps with her in his arms into the St. Johns River. "There was a real strong current, and we had a hard time swimming back to the dock—a few times I didn't know whether I was gonna make it or not. Then we did another scene where John Agar and I dive off a boat and go for a swim, not knowing that the Creature has followed us. They had us swim way, way out, because they wanted us to be far away from the boat when the Creature came up underneath us—out so far that we couldn't conceivably be able to get back to the boat. That made it more suspenseful. John and I would swim way out and then cavort a while, and then we'd have to swim back, and a few times it got pretty hairy—I was awfully tired before I got back. I looked good in the water—I had good form—but I've never been a stamina swimmer *[laughs]*!"

Like John Agar, Nelson remembers the contribution of Creature portrayer Ricou Browning with awe. "He was a professional underwater swimmer, and he wore the suit and did all the underwater swimming. He was an incredible swimmer and a talented guy. He's the one that developed the Creature's way of swimming. There was an air tank off on the side—either another swimmer would be holding it or it would be stationed down there someplace. He would go off-camera and take a breath out of the tank using the mouthpiece, and then he would come back into the shot to do whatever business he had to do. Then back to the tank for another breath. They would just keep the camera rolling as he would swim off to take breaths, and then come back into the shot." Nelson recalls that the actor who played the Creature on land (Tom Hennesy) had a difficult time moving around in the heavy latex rubber suit, "so can you imagine swimming around in it underwater, like Ricou Browning did? And Ricou was not a big man. They had an actor who was very tall play the Creature on land."

Memories of her fellow cast members and of director Jack Arnold? "John

Location shooting at Florida's Marineland Studios gave Nelson and the rest of the *Revenge of the Creature* **contingent some unique R & R opportunities.**

Agar was probably one of the sweetest people I had ever met, a dear, dear man. His wife, Loretta, was on location in Florida with us; as a matter of fact, she had a bit part in the film. We had a lot of fun because I got along with both of them very well. And John Bromfield was a nice guy, too. I had a real crush on John Bromfield, but he was dating a dancer named Larri Thomas and they were quite close at the time. He was such a gentleman that nothing ever materialized between us; he was definitely true to Larri." And director Arnold "was another person I enjoyed working with, very much. Primarily because I thought he was quite a good director. I felt that he did very well with that film, with the shots and the angles, the suspense and the way he set everything up. And he was good with the actors, too."

Even though Nelson had fun making *Revenge of the Creature*, she remained slightly miffed at Universal for having assigned her to the type of role which she hoped she had outgrown. "I wanted to expand and move on and do bigger and better things. And I'd begun to figure that I probably wouldn't be able to do that at Universal, especially when I had done *Underwater!* and then I came back and they stuck me in *Revenge of the Creature*. So that was another reason why I decided that I wanted to leave Universal, and when my contract came up for renewal, I did. I'd been there for a number of years, and I wanted to move on. The movies that I did at Universal—they *were* good movies, but in those days they weren't top-notch, high-caliber motion pictures like some of the other studios were doing."

Revenge of the Creature is certainly no longer the sore spot it once might have been. "I'm much happier with it today than I was then," Nelson laughs. "In those days, I don't think I was terribly proud of the movie, but today I am. It really is one of the better science fiction movies."

Working as a freelancer kept Nelson bouncing from studio to studio: for Warners she costarred in a pair of remakes, *I Died a Thousand Times* (1955) with Jack Palance (a reworking of the Bogie classic *High Sierra*) and *Sincerely Yours* (also 1955) with Liberace (a second version of Warners' *The Man Who Played God*), and at Paramount she played Dean Martin's romantic interest in the next-to-last Martin and Lewis comedy, *Pardners* (1956). "After I left Universal, I had some good years when I did really good movies, and also some fantastic TV shows like *Climax!*, *Playhouse 90*, *G.E. Theater*, *20th Century-Fox Hour* and guest shots on lots of other shows. And then times began to get a little lean, for whatever reason, and I was not able to hold out for the plums. And so, as many actors do at some time in their careers *[laughs]*, they start doing what they consider schlock. And even though you're advised against it by whatever people are advising you, you wind up doing stuff that you wish you didn't have to do, in order to eat. And to keep your face in front of the public. Sometimes it's like that old adage, 'I don't care what you say about me, as long as you spell my name right.'"

Her name was spelled right in a variety of low-budget pictures, but Nelson remembers not all of them fondly. "*Untamed Youth* and *Outlaw's Son* [both 1957] I did for Howard Koch—Koch-Schenck Productions. *Outlaw's Son* was a pretty good movie, and I was not really unhappy with doing that; *Untamed Youth* I was kind of unhappy about. And *Hot Rod Girl* [1956] I was *very* unhappy about. And *Day the World Ended* was probably the thing that I was *least* happy about *[laughs]*!"

Day the World Ended is rich in B-movie significance: it was Roger Corman's first science fiction film as director as well as the picture that helped pull American International Pictures (then still calling itself American Releasing Corporation) back from the brink of collapse. Understandably, however, these historical niceties were lost on Lori Nelson at the time. "It was a very, very cheaply done, very low-budget movie. Roger Corman's movies in those days were not the caliber of the ones that followed—he later became quite the filmmaker. But in those days his pictures were not considered top-notch in any sense of the word.

"Roger and his brother Gene were two very, very nice guys; I can't remember now in what capacity Gene worked on *Day the World Ended*, but I met him at that time, too. Roger produced and directed that, and he was fun to work with. And working fast? Gosh, I think we did the whole picture in two weeks, maybe not even that long. It seemed like we had just barely started, and it was over *[laughs]*! And everything was so—*economical*! Even the monster costume that they used—the three-eyed mutant—was just not the caliber that the Black Lagoon Creature was. I'm sure I'm not offending Roger by saying that—surely that shouldn't be news to anyone *[laughs]*! He's a certain kind of filmmaker, and that is what he is famous for. He has a specialty, and nobody does it like he does."

In *Day the World Ended*, a ragtag assortment of survivors of an atomic war scurry to the comparative safety of a secluded valley shielded from the lingering radioactivity. Tensions flare among the survivors, and a three-eyed mutant spawned by the radiation (and played by AIP standby Paul Blaisdell) appears to menace the dwindling group.

"The actor inside the monster suit was very small, and not very strong. He was kind of wimpy-armed, not muscular at all, and not much taller than me. We were doing the scene by the lake, and he was carrying me down the bank. He was kind of staggering around—his knees were buckling. I think he stepped in a hole or tripped on a stick—he fell and I fell on top of him. I landed on his chest, and because the costume was made of rubber I started to bounce up and down. I started laughing, and I could hear the 'mutant' laughing, too—muffled—within the suit *[laughs]*! Luckily we fell down on the bank, right on the edge of the water; that was a good thing, because I don't know how well that monster suit would have stood up if it got wet. Also, he might have drowned, the suit was so heavy."

Stars Richard Denning and Touch (Mike) Connors were, again, "a couple of nice guys. It seems like I'm always saying that about these actors I've worked with, but they really were. I don't think there was anyone, in any of the films

Opposite: Nelson, who was unhappy with several of her mid-fifties roles, was *"least* happy about" the low-budget *Day the World Ended*. That is creature Paul Blaisdell on bended knee.

that I did, that was not a gentleman." Oh, come on—not even one? "I'm *serious*. Even Jack Palance [*I Died a Thousand Times*]—he had a terrible reputation for being kind of difficult to work with. Everybody worried how he'd get along with Shelley Winters, because they were both temperamental and that seemed like a lethal combination. But I never saw any of that in the scenes I did with Jack; he was always wonderful. I loved working with him, he's so good at what he does."

Television fans remember Lori Nelson best for her starring role in the syndicated series *How to Marry a Millionaire*. An extension of the 1953 20th Century–Fox movie, the 30-minute sitcom starred Nelson, Merry Anders and Barbara Eden as sexy New York bachelorettes waging a campaign to trap wealthy husbands. But Nelson quickly wearied of the day-to-day rut of a sitcom; her discontent mounted when her bosses insisted that the three actresses go without pay on their personal appearance tours. After 39 episodes, Nelson and the owners of the series, NTA, were not able to reconcile their differences, and Lori exited the show. Lisa Gaye replaced her, and the series expired after only 13 more episodes.

A guest shot on television's *Riverboat* led to romance and an engagement to series star Burt Reynolds, then at the beginning of his career. Six months after their breakup, Nelson married composer/conductor Johnny Mann in 1961 and gave birth to daughters Lori Susan (in 1962) and Jennifer Lee (in 1965). Picturemaking took a backseat to baby raising, although Nelson did little theater and a few workshops through the years to keep from losing her dramatic edge. After a series of separations and reconciliations, she and Johnny Mann divorced in 1971. Wanting to resume her career but realizing now more than ever how much her daughters needed her, she decided that show business would have to wait.

Encouraged by her new husband (since 1983) Joe Reiner, who is retired from the Los Angeles Police Department, Lori Nelson Reiner is determined to return to the acting fold, but roles for older women are depressingly scarce. "It is excruciatingly frustrating and anguish producing, because it's still predominantly a male-oriented business. There have been a few inroads, but just not enough and not fast enough. I feel that I am better than ever now, ten times the actress I was back then [in the fifties]. Through time and experience and through just living life, you get better at whatever you do. I think an actor or an actress very definitely gets better. So what a terrible time to find out that there are less roles for a woman, and that your hands are tied!

"I was starring in movies years before Barbara Eden ever came to Hollywood, and if I had hung in there like Barbara did, I would probably still be working today. But even *she* has to produce her own stuff now, to get any roles at all; Faye Dunaway, too. Meryl Streep talks about this every chance she gets. And it seems so unfair that this seems to be one of the only businesses in the world where you can have all the training and all the experience and all the

LORI NELSON

Looking to reenter the acting profession, Nelson is finding that the 1990s is "a terrible time to find out that there are less roles for a woman."

expertise, but if you stop working even for a while, they rarely make a place for you if you are a woman, especially an older woman. It's a hard pill to swallow."

Like it or not, for now, one of Lori Nelson's major claims to fame remains *Revenge of the Creature*—the one out of all her movies she was perhaps most reluctant to do. "I figured, okay, I might as well go ahead and do it, get it over with. There was no sense in fighting a studio like Universal because they had you under contract, and whatever film it was, they would have insisted that you do it. They never had to twist my arm very hard — I was pretty compliant in those days — but I'd have turned down *Revenge of the Creature* if I had been given a choice. Then time went on, of course, and I realized that it had become a cult film, and that it was considered by most science fiction people as quite an extraordinary and quite a good movie. *[Laughs.]* It just goes to show that actors don't always know what's good for 'em!"

LORI NELSON FILMOGRAPHY

Bend of the River (Universal, 1952)
Ma and Pa Kettle at the Fair (Universal, 1952)
Francis Goes to West Point (Universal, 1952)
All I Desire (Universal, 1953)
All American (Universal, 1953)
Walking My Baby Back Home (Universal, 1953)
Tumbleweed (Universal, 1953)
Destry (Universal, 1954)
Underwater! (RKO, 1955)
Ma and Pa Kettle at Waikiki (Universal, 1955)

Revenge of the Creature (Universal, 1955)
I Died a Thousand Times (Warner Bros., 1955)
Sincerely Yours (Warner Bros., 1955)
Day the World Ended (American Releasing [AIP], 1956)
Mohawk (20th Century–Fox, 1956)
Hot Rod Girl (AIP, 1956)
Pardners (Paramount, 1956)
Outlaw's Son (United Artists, 1957)
Untamed Youth (United Artists, 1957)

The Pied Piper of Hamelin (1957), a 90-minute television special starring Van Johnson, Claude Rains and Nelson, received limited theatrical release in 1961.

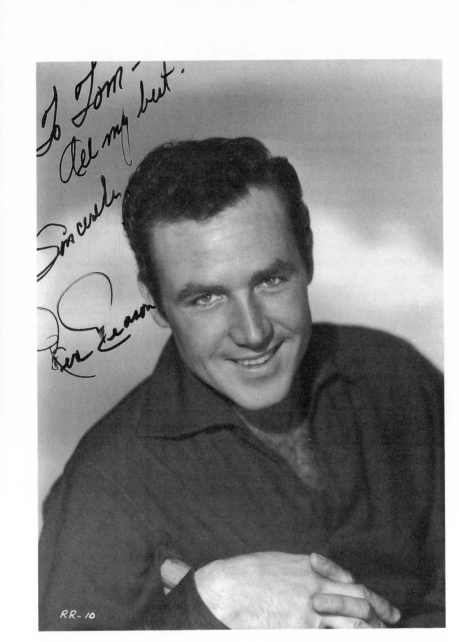

This Island Earth has done a lot for me as far as giving me
a little notoriety, keeping me alive in the minds of fans
and giving me a feeling that my work in films had a little worth.

Rex Reason

SOMETIMES AN ACTOR CAN TOIL in Hollywood for years without achieving recognition, and sometimes lasting fame can come from a single production. Rex Reason appeared in a score of fifties films, starred in two popular television series and guested in numerous television episodes, but film fans tend to remember him first and foremost as the staunch scientist-hero of 1955's *This Island Earth*. Reason does not resent the instant association, although he is quick to name other films and television appearances of which he is equally proud. The husky six-foot-four Reason now makes his living through real estate but is happy to reminisce about his stint as a Hollywood heavy/hero/he-man. Tanned, relaxed and affable, he settles into a favorite chair in the den/office of his Walnut, California, home and basks in science-fiction slanted memories of his film career.

Reason was born on November 30, 1928, in Berlin, Germany, while his family was in Europe on a business trip. He grew up in Los Angeles but, early on, his show business aspirations were nil. "I was never truly interested in the theater," the deep-voiced actor recalls. "It was my mother who had the interest and who was hoping that her two boys, my brother Rhodes and myself, would become interested." Maternal influences notwithstanding, Rex's acting career grew partly out of an inferiority complex that he developed during his high school years. A six-foot-three 15 year old with the voice of an adult, he frequently found himself the center of attention and became self-conscious as a result. His mother took him to a dramatic coach who, in working with Rex, recognized his stage and screen potential.

Apparently acting was in the cards for the teenage Reason: he transferred from Hollywood High to Glendale's Hoover High School, and on his first day in this new setting, the school dramatic coach spotted him in the hall and told him, "You are the one I want for the lead in my next play."

"The play happened to be *Seventh Heaven*, which my mother was in love with. She knew the role I was going to play, which was Chico — just the kind of romantic, dramatic part she was probably praying I'd get. She was very happy — tearfully happy — and she took ahold of me and said, 'Rex, you're going to *do* this play!' There were only two weeks to prepare, and she drummed those lines into my head, worked me until I was in bed, sick, and even *then* she kept at it!"

At 17, Reason enlisted in the army and used his time in uniform trying to figure out what he wanted to do with his life. His father's wish was that he become a civil engineer, while his mother kept after him to try for a career in acting. After his discharge, he opted for the latter, enrolling at the Pasadena Playhouse. Tiring of acting studies after a year and a half, he moved on and became involved in little theater. The big break came when an agent spotted him in a stage production of *Monserrat* and asked him whether he would like to try out for a picture.

Previous page: **Actor Rex Reason turned his back on his movie and television career when he decided that it was not giving him "a chance to grow up."**

Fantasy film fans remember Rex Reason exclusively for *This Island Earth* and *The Creature Walks Among Us*, tending to forget that his very first film, *Storm Over Tibet* (1952), also boasts mild supernatural overtones. Top-billed Reason played the role of an Air Transport Command pilot who, in preparing to be mustered out of the service and return home from the Himalayas, pilfers as a souvenir the skull mask of the Tibetan God of Death. When his copilot, Myron Healey, questions his right to steal the sacred symbol, the two tussle, Reason is slightly hurt, Healey takes over the flight and is killed in a crash. Reason becomes convinced that Healey suffered the fate the Death God had ordained for him. "From that point on, I did a search within my soul: I went back home, I saw Healey's wife [Diana Douglas], so on and so forth. In need of an answer, she and I took a trek back to the Himalayas, joined a UNESCO expedition and undertook the search. I climbed the mountains, got up to the top and challenged the Sinja god, and in the end I found my answer. That was the gist of it."

Directed by Andrew Marton, *Storm Over Tibet* was largely built around stock footage from a Himalaya-set feature that Marton had directed 20 years before (some of this stock had previously turned up in Columbia's *Lost Horizon*). Reason's mountain-climbing scenes were actually shot indoors, on a huge stage in a rented studio on Los Palmas in Los Angeles. "The snow in those scenes was corn flakes, painted. And I remember that when the wind machines started and those corn flakes were flying and we had to talk and react in the face of all of that, that these corn flakes got in our nostrils and got stuck *[laughs]*! So it was very difficult to cope with that." Reason also has fond memories of the film's producer, the late Ivan Tors. "Ivan, as I recall, was quite interested in animals at the time. In fact, he was studying a lot about porpoises, and as you know he later did a television series called *Flipper*. He and Laslo Benedek were the producers of *Storm Over Tibet*, and Marton was the director. They all were extremely interesting and helpful to me."

While at Columbia, Reason also played supporting roles in pictures such as *Salome* with Rita Hayworth, *Mission Over Korea* and *China Venture* (all 1953). Of his minor role in *Mission Over Korea*, the *New York Times* wrote, "In exactly two scenes, totaling approximately three minutes, a newcomer named Rex Reason wins top acting honors" over a cast that included veteran players John Hodiak, John Derek, Audrey Totter and Maureen O'Sullivan.

When Reason's tenure at Columbia reached its end, his agent talked him up at Universal. "Universal said they had a part which might get me a seven-year contract. It was the part of the Indian brother to Rock Hudson in *Taza, Son of Cochise* [1954]. They tested me, and they seemed to be very excited about the results. It was a rape scene with Barbara Rush—which, needless to say, was exciting to *me* [laughs]! And so, a few days later, they signed me to a seven-year contract and set up three pictures immediately for me to do; *Taza, Son of Cochise* and *Yankee Pasha* [1954] were the first two. And, although I didn't

The Flash Gordon and Dale Arden of the 1950s three-strip Technicolor era: Reason and Faith Domergue in *This Island Earth*. (Photofest)

know it at the time, for the third they had me penciled in as a possibility for *This Island Earth*."

In the latter half of the 1950s, Reason would become typecast as a movie and television hero, but early on, Universal heaped villainous roles on the stern, stentorian actor. In the 3-D *Taza, Son of Cochise*, he was Naiche, the hot-blooded Chiricahua savage who refuses to honor the peace his tribe has made with white men ("I want to live like an Apache warrior—by the lance, the arrow and the knife!"); and in the seriocomic costume adventure *Yankee*

Pasha, he was the bearded Islamic nobleman Omar Id-Din, who buys Rhonda Fleming for his harem and meets a gruesome impaling death that he had intended for hero Jeff Chandler.

Reason has fond memories of the early days when he dished out dastardly deeds as a Universal contractee. "It was wonderful there," he grins. "There were acting workshops where we would memorize a scene, do some improvisation; there was dancing; there was fencing—the whole grooming process. All the Miss Americas and Miss Universes would come out, and we would host all those lovely ladies, so on and so forth. I did love it because it kept us busy. Being a part of it and having roles in pictures and seeing your name up there on the screen is all very exciting, and I felt kind of blessed to be a part of that whole life." The one negative aspect of a contract player's life was that he was constantly subject to the whims of the front office. "Milburn Stone walked in on me one morning with a trade paper spread open in front of him, and he said, 'Hi, Bart.' I said, 'What do you mean?' and he read to me, '"Rex Reason's name now changed to Bart Roberts."' Well, that made me a little disturbed. So I went and talked to Ed Muhl, who was head of production at Universal, and I said, 'You know, if my name were Bart Roberts, I bet you'd change it to Rex Reason!' I told him Rex Reason was a good name and he didn't argue—he said, 'Fine, you can have it back.' However, as it ended up, those first two pictures [*Taza, Son of Cochise* and *Yankee Pasha*] went out with the Bart Roberts name on 'em."

It was by being in the right place at the right time that Reason won his best, and best-remembered, role as the hero of *This Island Earth*. Actress Piper Laurie was making a test for a Western picture and Reason was asked to play opposite her in a short scene set on a stagecoach. The scene belonged to the actress, Reason was relaxed and casual in his supporting part and today he cannot even recall what the picture was or if Piper Laurie got the part. "But Ed Muhl watched that scene and seemed to like it very much, and I think as a result of that he thought of me for the role of Meacham in *This Island Earth*. I read the script and I found it very interesting, I started testing and the rest you know."

Technicolor cameras rolled on Universal-International's most lavish science fiction production in January 1954. Reason and another screen newcomer, Jeff Morrow, starred respectively as hero and extraterrestrial tragic hero, sultry Howard Hughes discovery Faith Domergue assumed the female lead and supporting parts were filled by such fifties reliables as Russell Johnson, Lance Fuller and Robert Nichols. But it was the Universal special effects technicians who would emerge as the true stars of the film as *This Island Earth* began to grow in importance in the eyes of studio executives. "I know they put a lot of money into the special effects, and day after day the more it progressed toward getting ready for the screen, there was a lot more talk about it. It seemed to be a very important project at the time—important enough for them to put the money into it and make it as first-class as possible."

What Reason calls his "good vibes" over the picture and its possibilities were furthered bolstered as his relationships with cast and crew began to develop. "The producer, William Alland, had a lot of imagination. He was always fascinated with whatever it was he was doing, and he was always giving us his ideas regarding what we were going to do. He was quite an imaginative gentleman and always quite energetic. Joseph Newman I would call a comfortable director. A few of the directors I worked with did a lot of screaming and yelling, but Joe was very comfortable and easy to work with."

Regarding his costars, Reason is unstinting in his praise. "Jeff Morrow was, to me, *the* professional—he was very stimulating to watch and to work with. He was 'in' his part, and he had a lot of respect for his fellow actors. And as a result of this, I was better—he was 'high,' and this called forth every bit of my attention and involvement as an actor. His few remarks to me during the shooting of *This Island Earth* helped me. He said, 'You know, you have looks, Rex, but if you think that you do have looks, it's going to take away from your acting. You're the kind of person who's going to have to work a little harder.' I did the best work I knew how on *This Island Earth,* and I think I held up my end of the picture to his satisfaction. He is to be categorized as an 'actor's actor.'" And leading lady Faith Domergue "was quite a sport," Reason continues. "There was a scene where I had to dunk her down into some dirty water and a chase where I had to yank her along, and she didn't ever complain. She never once played the 'Hollywood Queen' with me—she did a good job, she was a lovely lady and she was real nice. I'm sorry I didn't get to know her better."

Production went smoothly over what Reason remembers as a six-week shooting schedule, with enthusiasm for the project continuing to grow and Reason enjoying the change of pace from his usual villainous roles. Questioned about reports that an uncredited Jack Arnold was partially responsible for the film's direction, Reason dismisses the rumor. "Jack Arnold was there, and he was very excited about being part of the picture," the actor allows, but to the best of his recollection, Arnold was in charge for only a few stray pickup or insert shots.

Reason continues to look back on *This Island Earth* with pride although he (like Jeff Morrow) regards Universal's decision to shoehorn monster scenes into the film's climax as an unhappy miscalculation. "I would say that those scenes definitely detracted from *This Island Earth*," he nods. "They didn't have the realism that the rest of the picture did—you could tell immediately that this was just a stuntman in a bug uniform, and that took away from the picture. If they had perhaps showed the monsters only in close-ups, if they had kept the camera up around their heads, it might have had more impact, but the long shots spoiled the moment. For the small kids it was all right, but *This Island Earth* was in some ways a rather thoughtful story, and I felt it was just too bad that they had to have those in there."

Metaluna mutants to the right of them, bogus backdrops to the left of them, Rex Reason, Faith Domergue and Jeff Morrow wish they were back on *This Island Earth*.

If Reason hoped that his heroic role in *This Island Earth* would change his screen image, Universal quickly dashed his hopes by returning him to deep-dyed villainy in pictures like *Kiss of Fire* (1955, as the ruthless governor of New Mexico) and the same year's *Smoke Signal* (as a conniving cavalry lieutenant). "But I enjoyed those villainous roles because I could lose myself. To my mind, I wasn't good looking enough to be a Rock Hudson or somebody like that, so I felt much more comfortable with some of those character roles. I knew how to act—I came off the stage, so to me acting was important. To know your job, do your job well. And I always did my job as well as I could. But I never really had any objective of getting to be a star or anything; I felt it was just part of the activity of growing up."

Asked what type of niche he had hoped to fill as a Hollywood actor, Reason pooh-poohs the question. When pressed as to what he would have considered an ideal role, he waxes metaphysical. "I've always had a philosophical attitude that I was hoping to find in a script: something that had a wonderful message, something that would fit my type and that I could carry. I like to say a few things about my relationship with Someone higher than I, Something divine. I don't want to use the word God because everybody uses it, misuses it and places it outside themselves where it shouldn't be. Once I really got into acting, I wanted to have that one certain role."

Neither Reason nor his Maker could have been overly pleased with the actor's next science fiction assignment, *The Creature Walks Among Us* (1956). Third installment in Universal's popular and profitable Gill Man trilogy, *Creature Walks* is notches below the earlier Creature films in quality, and to this day remains a slightly sore spot for its stalwart star. "If I had known that it would be shown on television and been around, I wouldn't have done it, to tell the truth. I did the film feeling it was just a job, but I really hadn't anticipated the possibility of it getting on television—there weren't too many movies of that type on television at the time, and I thought of it as a picture I'd be able to simply put behind me. I personally thought it was kind of corny."

Former assistant director John Sherwood assumed directorial duties on this final Creature outing while Reason was reunited with Jeff Morrow in the leading roles. A Gill Man–hunting expedition into the Florida Everglades is organized by Morrow, a slightly batty surgeon who spends most of his time bickering about evolution and casting fishy stares in the direction of his sorely tried bride, Leigh Snowden. Between verbal sparring matches, Morrow and fellow scientist Reason track down and capture the Gill Man, who is transformed by fire into an air-breathing, smooth-skinned Frankensteinian brute in a baggy sailcloth jumpsuit. Eventually the Creature rebels, kills Morrow and lumbers instinctively back to the sea and a presumed drowning death.

Like Jeff Morrow, Reason remembers precious little about his Creature encounter except that there were no opportunities for him in the picture and no challenges as an actor. "It was a comedown after *This Island Earth* and *Kiss of Fire*—a downer," he says, and once again wishes aloud that he had had the foresight to turn thumbs down on the assignment. Adding to his unhappiness is the fact that he still carries a scar from his Creature experience: "We had an accident while we were shooting the scene on the motorboat. There was a little lantern on board which fell over and started a fire. I jumped out, but there was a little piece of metal on the side of the boat that ripped open my left ankle."

Like John Agar, who quit Universal when he realized that science fiction roles were all the studio planned for him, Reason was becoming extremely wary of genre assignments. When Universal initially announced *The Deadly Mantis* in mid–1956, Reason and Mara Corday were slated for the leads and Rex finally put his foot down. "That was one picture when I finally spoke up and told them I didn't want to do it. To me it was very corny. I knew that the monster would be the star and I felt that I was worth a little more than just to support a praying mantis." As it turns out Reason need not have made a fuss over the proposed role: *The Deadly Mantis* was not shot until after the mid-fifties Universal shake-up in which most of the studio's contract players were dropped from the payroll. When the picture finally went into production in July 1956, Craig Stevens and William Hopper were sharing the top male slots opposite female lead Alix Talton.

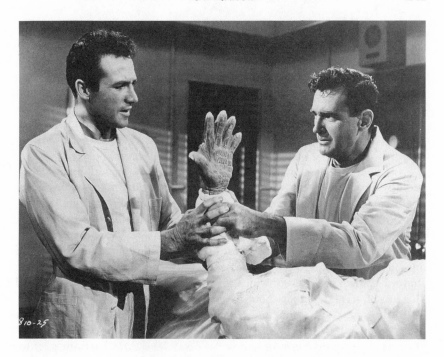

Scientists Reason and Jeff Morrow examine the injured Gill Man in the tawdry *The Creature Walks Among Us*, a film assignment Reason remembers as "a downer."

A freelancer after parting with Universal, Reason continued to work in pictures (mostly Westerns) and then in television. His first television series was the syndicated Western *Man Without a Gun*, which lasted 52 episodes, and his second, *The Roaring Twenties*, a Prohibition Era adventure series that ran on ABC-TV from 1960 to 1962. (He turned down the lead in television's *Maverick*, the show that established James Garner.)

After *The Roaring Twenties* wrapped up, Rex Reason, the man who once told an interviewer that "if I couldn't act, I wouldn't know what to do with my life," suddenly turned his back on acting. Reason explains his unexpected move: "At age twenty-two, I landed the lead in *Storm Over Tibet*, and I was considered a leading man in Hollywood all of a sudden, to some people a star. To me I was just a working actor, but the Hollywood life is very demanding and very magical. In those ten years I spent as an actor I didn't ever have a chance to grow up — to experience the normal processes of getting out, finding a job, working, dealing with people and so on. That was all sort of held in abeyance. If you're a leading man in Hollywood, that's all kept away from you: whether people like you or not, they *bow*. A few of my friends that I went to school with, who I would see from time to time during my acting career — I could see a growth, a *something* happening within them that was not happening within me. I didn't like not knowing or experiencing that growth. So that was part of the reason that I left and started really soul searching. It was very difficult to leave, and to try and find another profession. Three years it took me before I actually became receptive." His search for a new direction in life was complicated by the fact that many people still tended to look up to him as an actor and to associate him with the roles he had played in television. "At any time, if I ever got frustrated, I could have easily turned around and said, 'The heck with it' and moved back into acting. But I couldn't let myself do that."

Although his acting days are now permanently behind him, Reason recently has been talking to agents about the possibility of getting back into the business and doing some voice-over work. He made his last film in 1959, but occasionally he will pop up in a picture like *The Incredible Shrinking Woman* or *E.T. The Extra-Terrestrial*—in clips from *This Island Earth*. (Reason went to see *E.T.* because he had heard that he was in there somewhere, and missed the scene while buying popcorn.) Clearly *This Island Earth* has become and will remain the film for which the actor will always be best known, and Rex Reason has no qualms about the permanent link. "Well, you're here today!" he laughs. "I've done several interviews on the subject of *This Island Earth*, and I still get a lot of fan mail, believe it or not, from people who also mention *This Island Earth* constantly. So *This Island Earth* has done a lot for me as far as giving me a little notoriety, keeping me alive in the minds of fans and giving me a feeling that my work in films had a little worth. So, yes, I do have very fond memories and an appreciation of *This Island Earth* and what it's done for me."

REX REASON FILMOGRAPHY

As Bart Roberts:

Taza, Son of Cochise (Universal, 1954)
Yankee Pasha (Universal, 1954)

As Rex Reason:

Storm Over Tibet (Mask of the Himalayas) (Columbia, 1952)
Scaramouche (MGM, 1952)
China Venture (Columbia, 1953)
Salome (Columbia, 1953)
Mission Over Korea (Columbia, 1953)
Sign of the Pagan (voice only; Universal, 1954)
Smoke Signal (Universal, 1955)

Lady Godiva of Coventry (Universal, 1955)
Kiss of Fire (Universal, 1955)
This Island Earth (Universal, 1955)
Raw Edge (Universal, 1956)
The Creature Walks Among Us (Universal, 1956)
Badlands of Montana (20th Century–Fox, 1957)
Under Fire (20th Century–Fox, 1957)
Band of Angels (Warner Bros., 1957)
Thundering Jets (20th Century–Fox, 1958)
The Rawhide Trail (Allied Artists, 1958)

The Sad Horse (20th Century–Fox, 1959)

The Miracle of the Hills (20th Century–Fox, 1959)

This Island Earth clips featuring Reason are seen in *The Incredible Shrinking Woman* (Universal, 1981) and *E.T. The Extra-Terrestrial* (Universal, 1982).

*Actors really don't retire in the usual sense, because there's nothing
to prevent you from working until the day you die. If they need
an old person and you're old, maybe you'll get the part. And another
thing: At that point, your competition will soon begin to disappear!*

William Schallert

FOR THE PAST 35 YEARS, he has occupied a comfortable niche as one of television's most avuncular family men/father figures; those twinkling eyes can be seen in hundreds of sitcom episodes, that friendly voice (heard in countless commercials) enthusiastically invites us to try/taste/test drive every product under the sun. Is this all there is to actor William Schallert?

Hardly. The easygoing on-screen personality he has perfected might be a reflection of Schallert the man, but it does not do justice to Schallert the actor, who takes his craft *very* seriously. Years before his lucrative stints as Patty Duke's television father and *Get Smart*'s tottering Admiral Hargrade, he honed his talents on the stage, studied British repertory theater in England, even lectured at Oxford. And during the early days of his career, he also turned up regularly in science fiction — the film genre that, in fact, gave him his first big-screen break, when Schallert played one of the leads in the low-budget science fiction favorite *The Man from Planet X*.

"I've always felt very beholden to [producers] Aubrey Wisberg and Jack Pollexfen for recognizing that I was a usable actor and putting me into several of their pictures," Schallert recalls. "The first time they used me was in *The Man from Planet X*, which we made in 1950. At that point, I'd been working on the stage for four years, and I'd built a *kind* of a reputation in town. I was starting to climb the ladder: I wasn't famous or well known or anything, but as a beginning character actor, a few casting directors knew who I was. And that's all that matters. It's not who you know, it's who knows you. They begin to think of you more and more regularly, especially if you're reliable. So somebody probably suggested me to Wisberg and Pollexfen, or maybe they had seen me work. At the time, I also had a beard, and maybe that helped; the guy I played in *Man from Planet X* was the villain of the piece. I was called over to Hal Roach Studios, read for them and got the part."

The moody film, set amidst the rising mists of Scotland's moors, found Schallert fourth-billed as a scientist who is on hand when a small space vehicle — manned by a single, dwarf-sized occupant — sets down in the nearby wilderness. Fellow scientist Raymond Bond and reporter Robert Clarke attempt to communicate with the seemingly friendly alien, but Schallert, obsessed with learning its secrets, antagonizes and abuses X, which then turns against the humans. The film, a cult favorite today, was the first production for writers Wisberg and Pollexfen, who were on the Hal Roach lot sets constantly, supervising their maiden effort.

"They were an oddly matched couple of guys. Jack Pollexfen was a really strange looking guy; we used to kid and call *him* the Man from Planet X *[laughs]*. Jack was American and Aubrey was British, and they cowrote the thing. They were primarily writers, and they were trying to leverage themselves

Previous page: **From struggling bit player to television mainstay to Screen Actors Guild president: The William Schallert Story. (Photo from *Innerspace*.)**

A villainous role in *The Man from Planet X* (with Robert Clarke, left) represented a big career step forward for Schallert.

up into the producing end, which they did on this thing. And of course Edgar Ulmer, who directed it, has quite a good reputation among cineastes as the King of the B Pictures, for doing film noir low-budget movies. Edgar was . . . okay. I didn't think the picture was a particularly stylish film or anything like that, but I guess it accomplished what it needed to. We shot it in six days, all on a single soundstage at the old Hal Roach Studios, which are not there anymore."

Like many actors who have labored in this type of ultracheap cult picture, Schallert does not think as highly of it as its diehard fans do. "That's true. *The Man from Planet X* was exciting for me *at the time*, representing as it did a big step forward for me, but I didn't think it was a stunning picture or anything like that. Of its genre, it's probably okay. But I must say that Edgar Ulmer made the picture *look* quite interesting. I don't know how good he was with actors, to tell the truth; I think it was mostly that he was pretty good with the camera and with the lights, and could do things on the cheap." Schallert cannot clearly recall whether Ulmer ever attempted to guide his performance but "I'm sure he *must* have had ideas about what I should be doing and he probably communicated them to me. All directors, whether they're good with the actors or *not*, will let you know whether you're doing something that satisfies them or not. And if they can't tell you what to do, you just have to *invent* something else."

Third-billed, Schallert was acting in support of stars Robert Clarke and Margaret Field, who were paired in several B movies of that early-fifties era. "I knew Bob for a number of years after that; he later married one of the King Sisters," says Schallert. "Maggie I used to see once in a while; she later married Jock Mahoney, and of course she's Sally Field's mother. She was a *very* sweet person, I thought, and they were both nice to work with. I also remember working with Raymond Bond, who played the older professor. He and I once discussed how to make yourself cry, and he was describing what he did to do that."

The one burden shared by every one of *Planet X*'s leads was that of coping with their ornate, overwritten dialogue. "I'm afraid that's true, it *was* hard to make that dialogue your own, as we say in the acting profession. You always try to make whatever it is you have to say feel as though it's something that you are saying at the moment because you're responding to whatever the situation is. It's very difficult to make the kind of dialogue Wisberg and Pollexfen wrote 'your own.' Now, in a later picture of theirs [*Sword of Venus,* 1953], I played a drunken attorney in a jail cell. Somehow in *that* scene, the rather elaborately written, didactic, formal language was okay; it worked very well for that guy. But in some of the other pictures—oh, Jesus!"

"Cheap," according to Schallert, was the key word for *Planet X:* The $41,000 film was shot in less than a week, on reused sets from Ingrid Bergman's *Joan of Arc,* and with special effects which were primitive even by early 1950s standards. "When you shoot a whole feature film in six days, you don't have a lot of time to think about it. You just have to put in long days. And we were not paid handsomely, either. I think I got $225 for the week, and that was at a time when we had a six-day week. I also remember X himself. He [the actor] was a very small guy, kind of middle aged. He mostly just *looked* interesting; I don't know that he was much of an actor. In a way, you look back on pictures like *Man from Planet X* and you say, 'God, that whole thing was just a *joke,*' but it *has* lived on. It was made for less than $50,000 in six days, and Wisberg and Pollexfen sold it to Sherrill Corwin, who ran a chain of theaters. I guess Corwin got his money out of it okay; Wisberg and Pollexfen got enough money out of it to go on and make the next picture [*Captive Women*], with Albert Zugsmith."

Planet X capitalized on the big publicity push RKO was giving Howard Hawks' *The Thing from Another World,* insuring a warm box office reception. "*Planet X* didn't ride on the coattails of *The Thing*; it actually rode on the wave just ahead of it. *The Thing* had this enormous publicity campaign; it was the first really big, serious science fiction film in quite a while. (And a very stylish film, too, very well done.) *Planet X* took advantage of all *The Thing*'s publicity; we opened the week before *The Thing* did and gained a lot of benefit from all its publicity. *The Thing from Another World* and *The Man from Planet X*, they sounded vaguely alike to people, I guess. A friend of mine was in New York and he told me that there was a larger-than-life-sized head portrait of me in the lobby of one theater that was running *Man from Planet X*. 'There you were,' he said, 'a *star!*' *[Laughs.]* So, yeah, it *was* a big deal for me; I had good billing in the film and all the rest of that."

Encouraged by the success of *Planet X*, Wisberg and Pollexfen hustled to put a second science fiction film into production, reuniting Clarke, Field and Schallert in the postapocalyptic *Captive Women*. "That was originally called *3000 A.D.*," Schallert reminisces. "It was kind of a *dumb* film, but I thought that it had an interesting premise, the idea of people surviving after the Bomb and living in New York City subways. It was an unusual notion. The same plot was used later in one of the *Planet of the Apes* films [*Beneath the Planet of the Apes*]; *Captive Women* anticipated that. I don't know that Wisberg and Pollexfen ever had any *original* ideas, but they were very good at grabbing on to ideas that had some merit. I thought *Captive Women* had some possibilities. My wife [Leah — now Lia — Waggner] was also in that, incidentally, in a bit part. We played characters who were not called mu*tants* — we were called mu*tates*. I don't know whether that was just illiteracy or some perverse notion on the part of Wisberg or Pollexfen that that was a better word *[laughs]*."

In the film, the survivors of a devastating atomic war fight amongst themselves in and around the rubble of Manhattan. Schallert, a radiation-scarred member of the Mutate tribe, is banished after contesting Ron Randell's leadership and turns traitor, leading the warlike Up-river men against his own people. "The fellow who did the makeup was named Steve Clensos. He had invented a makeup remover which was called Clens *[laughs]*, so it was advantageous that his name was Clensos, I guess. Steve worked pretty quick: He would make up one side of my face with silver, to show the effects of radiation, and then he also added a scar to it. We probably shot that in ten days or two weeks, something like that." Production was hectic, with new scenes being written daily and an inexperienced director, Stuart Gilmore, having difficulty maintaining order. "Stuart had been an editor, and I don't know how much directing he'd done prior to this. *Captive Women*, I guess, was his break, but I *vaguely* remember Gilmore as being a man with not very much patience. He was under a lot of pressure. I don't have a lot of recollection of it, though, because we *all* had our problems with that picture. It was tough to make.

"Albert Zugsmith was one of the producers on that, along with Wisberg and Pollexfen. After I did *Captive Women* and a couple of other pictures for them, Zugsmith got the notion that I could do just about anything, and he became quite a champion of mine. He really did do his best to get me into everything he made, in one way or another. In fact, when he was at Universal, he tried to put me into his films, in parts that I was totally unsuited for. He tried to force me on Orson Welles in *Touch of Evil* [1958], to play the part that was played by Joseph Calleia, for God's sake *[laughs]*! Calleia was thirty years older than I, and he also was Mexican, which is what the character was *supposed* to be. It was just insane. Zugsmith used me in a thing called *The Girl in the Kremlin* [1957], and I played Joseph Stalin's brother. I remember trying to do this dumb Russian accent, and I must say that when I finally saw it, I thought to myself, 'Oh, God...!' (In it, I killed Stalin by driving off the road with him.) Well, all I can say is, a job is a job, and at a certain stage of your life, you just take what comes.

"You could almost say that Aubrey Wisberg and Jack Pollexfen were to blame for bringing Albert Zugsmith into the motion picture business—depending upon how you feel about Zugsmith's pictures. But he did make *Written on the Wind* [1956], which garnered Dorothy Malone an Oscar, and a couple of other things at Universal that might have been okay. In general, his pictures had a strong sense of schlock about 'em, but then *[laughs]*, Wisberg and Pollexfen were not exactly the top of the heap, either!"

One of Schallert's best-remembered small roles was his supporting part in Zugsmith's later *The Incredible Shrinking Man*. "*That* was a very good film, I thought. Jack Arnold directed that, and I thought Jack was a very stylish director. *The Incredible Shrinking Man* had an interesting story by Richard Matheson. *Shrinking Man* was a superior piece of writing; Matheson also did some very good writing for *Twilight Zone* and other shows. I played the doctor who diagnosed that Grant Williams was shrinking.

"It was nice that Albert Zugsmith used me so often, even though I used to end up playing roles that maybe I wasn't right for. But I was usually quite grateful, because I was trying to *survive* during that early- to mid-fifties period. The key thing about an actor who was in my position—the position I was in until I started to click in the late fifties in television—was staying alive without doing anything but acting. That's really tough to do, but I managed, partly because my wife was willing to tolerate it. But by 1954, we had three kids. You would step from one slowly sinking rock to another as you crossed the stream of life, and keep hoping for a new rock. It was always very dicey until about 1957, '58, when I began to work more, and especially in '59—that year I really worked a lot. From then on, I was okay."

Early on, before television typecast him as the affable sitcom dad, Schallert had a number of good heavy roles. Does he miss those opportunities? "I must say that I always found parts like that interesting. I continued to do that kind of thing in television a lot; I did a lot of interesting character work in TV even after *The Patty Duke Show*. But when it came to serious work, I was really typed for the warm, fatherly kind of guy. The 'heavier' parts do still come up from time to time: I've played a couple of sleazy lawyers recently on episodic television, so they haven't completely disappeared. So, yes, of course I've always enjoyed them; any actor does."

The son of Edwin Schallert, former drama editor of the *Los Angeles*

Times and the dean of West Coast critics, William became interested in an acting career while at UCLA in 1942. "I had been trying out various things while I was there—I worked on the newspaper, studied composing, did some singing, things like that. And I didn't feel that I was really very well suited to any of them. One night I was at a party, and there was an actress named Blossom Akst, whose father was Harry Akst, a well-known song lyric writer. She said, 'Listen, why don't you come down and audition for a part in a play I'm doing?' I had never thought about acting, but she kept at it: 'Sure, c'mon, you'd be very good for that.' (I used to kid around a lot, show off in various ways—typical actor's behavior.) So I went to the reading and tried out for the part; it was a play at UCLA, an adaptation of Ben Jonson's *Volpone*, and the role I was trying for was Corbaccio, an old miser and a lecher. A very interesting, fun character to do.

"I got it, and I guess I was reasonably good in it because they called me out to 20th Century–Fox about a week later. Ivan Kahn, who was the talent scout there, said it was a very interesting performance. He sent me into another room with a fellow who was their acting coach; I don't remember much about that except that we read together, and he kept saying to me, 'Don't move your hands so much!' *[Laughs.]* I guess I passed whatever minimal test they were laying on me, and Kahn said, 'So what's your status with the draft?' I said, 'Oh, I've probably got two or three months before the ROTC gets called up.' Kahn said, 'Well, be sure to look us up after the war.' I realized afterwards that they were lookin' for *any* warm male body in those days, with so many Hollywood actors off fighting the war! But, still, they *had* shown interest in me and I figured that was a good sign. So while I was in the service, I did start to plan on giving acting a shot.

"When I came back, I went back to UCLA to finish up, and I did two or three more plays there. I also got in a directing class—*why* I don't know; there was no acting class at the right time, I guess. Boris Sagal, who later became quite a well-known director before he was killed, was in the same class. And in the course of working in that class, I got cast in a lot of projects that other directors were doing. I would just play these little scenes, but in that one semester I did maybe ten or twelve scenes and I probably learned the fundamentals of how to act in doing that. Or, I should say, I found out what I could do. (You know, you really can't *learn* acting—you can either do it or you can't. You can get *better* at it, and training can certainly help, but you find out very quickly whether you can do it.) By the time that semester was over, I had a kind of a sense of myself, especially in comedy.

"Right after I got out of school, I got in with a group that had formed at UCLA, the Circle Theatre. I went down and read for them, and they took me on. I worked there for the next four years, and gradually became one of the owners of the place. By the time those four years were over, I had gotten into the Screen Actors Guild and AFTRA, and the year after we closed the

Being strangled by a robot is Schallert's main memory of playing a lab assistant in science fiction producer Ivan Tors' *Gog*.

theater, I joined Equity and did a lot of stage work. From then on, I was committed. By then I was married and had a child, so I had to work. I didn't have any choice *[laughs]*!"

The first of Schallert's approximately 80 movies was *The Foxes of Harrow* (1947), a period drama starring Rex Harrison. "William Bacher, the producer of *Foxes of Harrow*, and John Stahl, the director, each had one daughter who was part of our Circle Theatre; William Bacher's daughter talked to her father about the people at the Theatre. (We were doing *Ethan Frome* at the time, and people *were* rather impressed with the production.) Bacher and Stahl either came to see the play or they took their daughters at their word, because several of us were called out to Fox. I got a one-line bit, and *[laughs]* I still remember it: 'Gentlemen, gentlemen! The bank of the United States and Philadelphia has closed its doors.'"

During his early years, Schallert frequently played bit or supporting parts in science fiction and fantasy films, some of which he remembers (*Mighty Joe Young*, *Them!*, *Gog*), others of which he does not (*Port Sinister*, *Invasion USA*, *The Monolith Monsters*). Working in the genre suited him just fine, since "I was a big reader of *Astounding Science Fiction* from about the end of the war on up through the early fifties. I used to read it all the time; in fact, I remember when L. Ron Hubbard first appeared. The first advertisements for Dianetics appeared in *Astounding Science Fiction*, which really defined it for me pretty well *[laughs]*. I did read one of Hubbard's space operas, I think. I used to read *all* that stuff: I remember A.E. Van Vogt and Isaac Asimov, the *Foundations* stories in particular.

"I worked for [producer] Ivan Tors, who did a lot of that kind of thing; I did some stuff for him that was kind of junky, but it was good fun. *Gog* I remember, because I got strangled by a robot *[laughs]*. They had robot suits for that film, with people inside them. I don't remember the picture too well otherwise, except that I worked with a guy named John Wengraf, who was a very good Viennese actor; I'd already worked on the stage with him. I thought he was very stylish and had an interesting voice."

Schallert initially hooked up with Tors through the efforts of his then-agent Leon Lance — "who never really would sign me," he laughs. "I didn't ever have a signed contract with an agent until 1954, when I'd been in the business for seven years. That's not unusual for a character actor; it takes a long time to get off the ground. Leon was a very funny guy who had a rare way of speaking. He handled Jim Arness in (as Leon would say) *The Ting* and *Dem [The Thing* and *Them!]*; I once heard him say to an actress over the phone, 'Listen, you should do it, darlingk. It's a *fireproof* part!' ('Fireproof' being somewhere between surefire and foolproof, I suppose *[laughs]*!) Leon knew Ivan Tors — Tors was a European himself, so they kind of knew each other."

Working for Tors again, this time on television's *Science Fiction Theatre*, Schallert had his one chance to act opposite character star Edmund Gwenn. "We played Martians. He was a rather benign Martian and I was his assistant, trying to keep him under control and not let him do too much good. Edmund Gwenn was a really wonderful guy to work with. He'd already done all of his great movie stuff and had retired, but he had terrible arthritis in his knees from having played football when he was younger. He was a very distinguished actor — he'd been in the first productions of a couple of George Bernard Shaw's plays, besides winning the Academy Award for *Miracle on 34th Street*. And here he had to come out of retirement and work in this cheap *Science Fiction Theatre* thing because he needed the money—he needed arthritis treatment. It was really sad—his knees were killing him, he was having a really hard time. We [actors] didn't have a pension and health plan back then. Even in those days, if you got a really crippling disease, it could exhaust your funds."

A second robot movie, Republic's *Tobor the Great*, provided Schallert with a day's work at a very opportune time. "I was really having a tough time right about then. I'd been out of the country for a while—Lia and I had gone with two kids to England. I had a Fulbright Fellowship for a year, and I was studying British repertory theater. (*Why* I was doing that is beyond me; I was hoping I could work over there, I think.) Anyway, I'd come back and it was very slow. Leon Lance, my agent, called me one morning and said that a client of his named Charlie Wagenheim had gotten sick, and could I go to Republic to replace him? It was the part of a reporter, just a few lines or something like that, in *Tobor the Great*. It was probably a hundred, a hundred twenty-five dollars for the day, and I said, 'You *bet*, I'll be there!'—we could use that to pay the rent! Now, I've always suspected that maybe Charlie Wagenheim wasn't really sick, that Leon had simply said to him, 'Listen, I've got somebody who *desperately* needs the money. Would you mind?' and Charlie must have said okay. I've always had a feeling that it was just a good turn, but I've never known for sure and nobody would ever tell me. That's just a characteristic story of what it was like to be a struggling actor."

On television, Schallert was also briefly featured as a regular on the small-screen *Commando Cody*, playing sidekick to Judd Holdren, who wore Republic's familiar bullet-helmeted rocket suit. "I did a fair amount of work at Republic, which was a kind of a beginner's studio—they didn't have a lot of money. It was the bottom of the ladder, but they cranked out Westerns and serials. In 1952, they were still making serials, and they decided they would make a science fiction serial called *Commando Cody*. (Commander *Cory* was the star of a live television science fiction show called *Space Patrol*, and I used to play heavies on that on a regular basis—I must have worked for 'em a half a dozen times. Commander Cory was a well-known character, and I think Republic just ripped the name off for *Commando Cody*.) The fellow who played the lead in *Commando Cody*, Judd Holdren, had been a bookkeeper, and I bumped into him again years later when he was the bookkeeper at a commercial agency when I first began to do voice-over commercials. That was an interesting coincidence.

"*Commando Cody* was going to be done as a serial, in twelve episodes. But in the back of their minds, Republic also was thinking that they might release it as a television show. So it was kind of a hybrid, partially made as a theatrical serial and also partially made as a television series. It was kind of a Buck Rogers–type series about traveling in a spaceship. They had a big mock-up of a spaceship, split in half; we would climb up in there and do whatever we had to do. It was dumb writing. There was an actress named Aline Towne who was in it, too; she was actually quite a good actress, I thought. And Judd Holdren was okay; Judd was not a terrific actor, but he was a manly looking guy, the kind of guy you would cast in that. I played his sidekick/assistant; I did those types of 'other guy' roles at Republic, generally somebody with a sense of humor because I could do comedy pretty well."

Schallert appeared only in the first three segments of *Commando Cody* before he managed to pry himself out of the series. "I realized that, in order to continue to do it, I had to sign a term contract with Republic. Once I found out what they were going to pay me, and thought about it, I said to Leon Lance, 'We gotta get out of this.' I didn't think I could live on it—even though it was probably as much money as I was going to make that year anyway *[laughs]*. (Maybe it was just the fact that I didn't want to be trapped at Republic.) They were going to pay me $150 a week for 40 weeks, which was $6,000 for the whole year. I had one child and I knew what our rent was and all of that, and I didn't see how I was going to survive on that, especially since I couldn't do anything else. So I managed to get out of it—which was, in a way, insane. I don't know what I thought my prospects were that made me think I was going to make more money than that in the course of the year; in fact, I think I went to England later that year on the Fellowship. But it was one of those quickly sinking rocks that I managed to stand on for a short time. And after that, the casting director at Republic did not have a friendly feeling toward me for a while, because I had sort of reneged. I eventually went back to work for them."

Between jobs, Schallert often found time to take in some of his own movies; he attended the premiere of the John Wayne–starring *The High and the Mighty* [1954]. "I walked into the lobby of the Egyptian Theater in Hollywood, in a rented tux, with my wife. (We had driven up in our old Morris Minor that had a torn roof, and she had borrowed the formal dress she was wearing from a girl upstairs.) We came into the lobby, and there was a crowd of people there—premieres used to be that way. There was a rope holding the people back, and somebody cried out, 'There he is! There he is!' Some guy came under the rope and came *racing* toward me and held out something for me to sign, which I did. And as he was going back, the people who had been saying, 'There he is! There he is!' were now saying, 'Who *is* he? Who *is* he?' And the guy who got my autograph read it and groaned, 'Aw, it's *nobody!*' *[Laughs.]* I would say that that defines my situation in terms of the business, in terms of the general public, anyway, in those days, about as well as anything. I was really on the ragged edge, just eking out a living.

"One other thing about *The High and the Mighty*. I had one day's work on it, and again I was getting paid like maybe $150 for that one day. It was for William Wellman, a top-notch director, it was a very classy picture, and the scene was quite good—it was a brief scene, but I thought I'd done a good job in it. The same day that I worked on that, I had an offer to work at MGM for *two* days—in a nothing role, and not in a good picture, but it would have paid me $125 a day and I'd have made $250. And unfortunately (from *my* standpoint), I'd already committed to doing *The High and the Mighty*. I did not work for about two *months* on either side of it, and it was typical of the actor's struggle to survive that I would have a conflict on the same day I worked."

Other 1950s films roles included an early Roger Corman quickie (the switched-sex Western *Gunslinger*) and the notorious all-star Irwin Allen production *The Story of Mankind*. "In *Gunslinger*, I was the marshal, Beverly Garland was my wife, and once I got shot—in the first scene *[laughs]*—she became the marshal. That was the only time I ever worked for Corman, so I guess he was not impressed *[laughs]*. Beverly went on to do several things for him. She's a really good actress, and an intelligent person, too. And a good businesswoman—she's got a chain of hotels out here. I like Beverly a lot, she's a real down-to-earth person. And *The Story of Mankind*—God! I played the Dauphin in a scene with Hedy Lamarr, who was playing Joan of Arc. *[Laughs.]* I'm laughing, because Hedy Lamarr's reputation was as this sexpot, and here she was playing Joan of Arc. I made a lot of money on it, because I had to be in very early for makeup—I had a bald wig in that—and we did it all in one day. I worked until like eleven at night, *very* late; it was a long, long day and I got a lot of double time and overtime and all of that. So I was very happy with the film, simply because of the money I made on it."

While Schallert worked (somewhat) steadily in pictures throughout the fifties, he insists that he never sought any special niche in the movie business or tried to model himself after any other actor. "I don't think I ever approached the business that way. To tell the truth, I never thought about things like that, I was really very naïve when it came to thinking about myself in terms of a career. I felt like I could do almost anything that anybody asked me to do. That's *nonsense*, but that's what I thought. As to whether I ever tried to model myself after any other actor, *no*, although I have of course admired a great many actors for the kind of work they did. I guess if I saw *any*body who I thought it would be nice to be like, it would be Alec Guinness. When I was first starting, Guinness was also starting; I remember seeing *Kind Hearts and Coronets* [1949], in which he played eight roles, and thinking, 'Gosh, I would love to get a shot at something like that, because I think I could do it.' Actually, the thing that I had the most success with when I worked on the stage was comedy. There's a certain kind of comedy that I think I can do as well as anybody; if there was any way that I was ever going to be a star, it would have been from doing stuff like that."

From 1963 to 1966, Schallert played Martin Lane, the sorely tried but always patient father on television's *The Patty Duke Show*. The ABC half-hour sitcom remains, like it or not, Schallert's claim to fame, but action and science fiction fans probably prefer his shorter stints in other shows, *The Wild Wild West* and *Star Trek*, in particular. "I enjoyed working on *Wild Wild West*; there I got to play an assortment of different roles. When Ross Martin had a heart attack, he was out for about five episodes, and Charles Aidman and I replaced him serially. They offered that to me mainly because I had played such a variety of characters and they thought I could do almost anything; 'Okay, Schallert, we'll stick you in there and you can play all these wild characters the way that Ross did.'"

Asked about reported friction between stars Robert Conrad and Ross Martin, Schallert can offer little input. "There was never any evidence of that on the set; from what *I* saw, it seemed to me that they got along okay. Conrad's a kind of a prickly guy, and he would go through phases where he was doing what seemed to be rather foolish things, but actually he's a pretty good actor. People don't give him credit for very much, but I've seen him do some good things in movies of the week and that kind of stuff. He didn't have the technical resources of Martin, who was a very wide-ranging actor with a lot of facets to his personality and his skill, but Conrad does what he does very well. To tell you the truth, I always thought they got along pretty well, and seemed to have a lot of fun on the show. Maybe I missed some of the bad stuff."

Star Trek must be a subject about which Schallert is asked regularly, because he recalls the experience *and* the episode title without the slightest prompting. "'The Trouble with Tribbles'! I remember those little furry balls that they used for the Tribbles—they were all over the place—and you had to treat 'em as though they were alive in some way or another. Stanley Adams, who played the trader who sold them, was one of the funniest guys I'd ever met in my life. He was a comedy writer—I think he used to write for Red Skelton—and I enjoyed working with him always. He was a very funny guy on the set, and also a very good actor. And Charlie Brill, who's also a very funny fellow, played my lieutenant, who of course turned out to be the nasty guy who started all the trouble."

In the episode, a favorite among Trekkies, Schallert played Nilz Barris, official in charge of the delivery of a huge supply of grain to a distant planet. Some of the episode's humor derived from insults arrogantly tossed by Captain Kirk (William Shatner) at the uptight Barris; fans prefer to ignore the fact that Barris' misgivings about Kirk are well founded, since Kirk *does* in fact do a thorough job of bungling his important assignment.

Schallert recalls, "The character *I* played was characteristic of the way they sometimes cast me, which is as a stuffy sort of bureaucrat. Those are *not* rewarding roles, they're really not. It was okay, I played it, but it's not the kind of part I'd like to be remembered for, the rest of my life. (Unfortunately it *will* be, I guess *[laughs]*!) I probably saw an episode or two of *Star Trek* prior to working on there, but I was not a great devotee of science fiction shows; there are very few of 'em that I watch regularly. I was not a Trekkie. For whatever reason, that show never grabbed me."

Schallert even had his own shot at a starring role in a series in 1963, when Richard Donner directed him in the television pilot *Philbert*. "That was the first thing that Dave DePatie and Friz Freleng did together; they're the people who created the Pink Panther character. I played a cartoonist who drew a daily strip, and the character that I drew was Philbert — a little wiseass guy with a snap-brim hat and a perky attitude. He suddenly came to life and walked off the page, in the magical fashion of the sitcom, and entered my life. We had somewhat the same sort of relationship that Bill Bixby and Ray Walston did in *My Favorite Martian*: He would sort of mess up my life and then get me *out* of the mess. The problem with the show was that it cost about 50 percent more than anything else that was being done at the time, because of the animation. The average half-hour show in those days cost $50,000 an episode (roughly one-twelfth of what they cost today), and mine was going to be $75,000. Friz Freleng told me that that's what killed it; ABC just wasn't willing to spend that kind of money on it. I thought, when I saw it, that what I did was quite good, and if it had gone, who knows where it would have led."

The actor had the distinction of being assassinated with a hydrogen bomb in *Colossus — The Forbin Project*, 1970s entrant in the computers-take-over science fiction subgenre. "That was directed by a good friend of mine, Joe Sargent; I've worked for him a couple of times since. I thought Joe did a stylish job with that, and it was a very interesting idea, too. I don't think that picture made much money, which is too bad; it really deserved a better fate, because it was very well done. Speaking of that picture, I'm the only person I know of who was assassinated with an H-bomb — they usually don't go to that extent of overkill to get rid of one person *[laughs]*. Computers took over the world, and found out that I was the government official who was trying to defuse all the H-bombs that the computers were holding over us. I'm sitting there smoking a cigar when the computers unleash one of the bombs on us; the countdown starts and all the other people get up and start running away screaming, but I just sit there with a cigar in my mouth, knowing there's no point in running a few feet *[laughs]*. Then the flash comes. So there I was, assassinated by an H-bomb."

In a much lighter vein, Schallert played Professor Quigley in the Disney live-action comedy/fantasies *The Computer Wore Tennis Shoes* and *The Strongest Man in the World*. "Those were very satisfying. I thought, number one, that the films themselves were always very well done and a lot of fun to watch; you really could have a good time seeing them. Number two, the experience of working on 'em was very good. Disney was a pretty good quality lot to work on. It's a nice place, very democratically organized. I think because it was started as an animation studio, they didn't have much of a class system there. When they went to the commissary, there wasn't an executive dining room—Disney got in the line with everybody else, apparently. That tradition sort of carried over. It had a nice feeling, that lot. Also, I thought the writing on those shows was very good; in fact, I knew the writer, Joe McEveety, who went to school with my brothers. Joe had a bad heart; he was living on borrowed time when he was working at Disney, and he did die not long after that." Schallert adds that he definitely saw the "writing on the wall" for Disney's Kurt Russell, who starred in both movies (as well as in the Schallertless *Now You See Him, Now You Don't*) as the accident-prone college whiz Dexter Riley. "He was my idea of an extremely talented young actor. I thought, 'This guy really can act'—and, God knows, that's really been proven with time. For a long time I didn't think he got his due, but he is now."

From 1979 to 1981, Schallert was the president of the Screen Actors Guild, an organization with which he is still affiliated. In the 1980s, three of the five features in which he appeared were helmed by fantasy filmmaker Joe Dante. "I like Joe a lot. I think he's a very inventive and creative director. I didn't want to do *Twilight Zone—The Movie* when they first approached me because they were paying minimum. At that stage in my life, I said, 'I'm not going to work for minimum. It's ridiculous.' And 'Why is Spielberg so cheap?' is what I *really* wanted to know *[laughs]*. But that's the kind of a shop they were running, because they didn't know how this picture was going to turn out and everybody was working on the cheap. Everybody in the cast was getting the same thing— everybody, that is, except the individual star of each episode; they were getting more. But anyone who was playing a supporting role got minimum—that included people like Patricia Barry and Kevin McCarthy. There was also a girl in it named Nancy Cartwright, who is the voice of Bart Simpson now. *Twilight Zone* was one of the first things she did here in town; she played the girl who got her mouth sealed up.

"It was a kind of wild experience working on that thing because the sets were all done like cartoons. They used forced perspective, and nothing was real looking. For instance, when you went up the stairs, the steps kept getting smaller the higher you went. So it was very difficult to go up 'em. Those sets were really fascinating, because I'd never worked in that kind of an environment; it had a very cartoonlike *feeling* that Joe did deliberately—that's what he was after. He had a real definite sense of style for this thing. And he wanted me, and some of these other people, in it because he's a great devotee of old films, and especially of old science fiction films. He particularly wanted to have people in it who were in those films; I *have* done my share of 'em *[laughs]*. I found working with Joe on that to be quite a good experience."

Working for Dante again in *Gremlins* (1984) was "kind of accidental. I had asked Joe for a favor: I was helping a group of people raise some money for the deaf, and they thought that if we could have a premiere showing of *Twilight Zone* someplace, they could raise some money. Joe provided the film, and then he said, 'Okay, now you owe me one. I want you to be in *Gremlins*.'

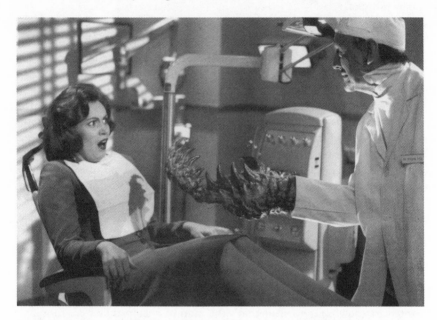

Schallert offers Cathy Moriarty a hand in the science fiction takeoff *Mant*, the movie-within-a-movie in director Joe Dante's *Matinee*.

It wasn't much of a part: He wanted me to play the kind of old guy I used to play on *Get Smart*. I played an old priest, spent most of a day doing a lot of stuff (some of it scripted, some of it invented right there). It was really funny stuff. All of it got cut, except for one event at a mailbox — that's all that's left of me in the picture. Joe told me that was all that was left, and he asked me if I wanted billing, and I said, 'Absolutely not!' *[Laughs.]* I'm just there for that one quick shot. I'm sorry that the other stuff didn't stay, but I understood why — it didn't advance the story. Obviously they knew what they were doing, because *Gremlins* did very, very well."

Schallert acted for Dante a third time in *Innerspace* (1987), in a scene reminiscent of his *Incredible Shrinking Man* doctor gig, examining hypochondriac patient Martin Short. "Working with Martin was terrific. He's such a funny guy and very inventive. And in addition, he's a very good actor; not just a funnyman, but also a very honest actor who's very much in touch with himself. Even though he does rather exaggerated things, I always *believe* him; he's got a good sense of *truth*, which some comics don't have."

Today, besides his work in front of the camera, Schallert keeps active with SAG-related projects: He's still the trustee of the Pension and Health Plan, and also one of the trustees of the Motion Picture and Television Fund. "Also, once a year for about six or eight weeks, I serve on the Allocations Committee of the Permanent Charities Committee, which is like the Hollywood version of the United Way. We in fact *give* money to the United Way, too, but we also fund a large number of projects of various kinds, mostly having to do with the health area. We've expanded now to deal with homelessness and in particular with AIDS."

William Schallert never gives retirement a thought. "Oh, no!" he scoffs, as if (at 69) he is surprised at the question. "I'm old enough to retire, but to tell the truth, I'm working so steadily that as long as people keep asking for me, I guess I'll keep working. Actors really don't retire in the usual sense, because there's nothing to *prevent* you from working until the day you die. If they need an old person and you're old, maybe you'll get the part. And another thing: At that point, your competition will soon begin to disappear *[laughs]*! Surviving is everything! And when you survive *long* enough, you do become a kind of an icon. I've been around long enough, and everything I've ever done in my life is being recycled on cable, particularly on Nick at Nite. Eventually, *all* of this stuff comes home to roost, and unless you were really ghastly, people are very fond of you for it. It's a nice feeling."

WILLIAM SCHALLERT FILMOGRAPHY

The Foxes of Harrow (20th Century–Fox, 1947)
Mighty Joe Young (RKO, 1949)
The Reckless Moment (Columbia, 1949)
Lonely Hearts Bandits (Republic, 1950)
The People Against O'Hara (MGM, 1951)
The Man from Planet X (United Artists, 1951)
Belle Le Grand (Republic, 1951)
Bannerline (MGM, 1951)
The Red Badge of Courage (MGM, 1951)
The Jazz Singer (Warner Bros., 1952)
Hoodlum Empire (Republic, 1952)
Paula (Columbia, 1952)
Storm Over Tibet (Mask of the Himalayas) (Columbia, 1952)
Captive Women (1000 Years from Now) (RKO, 1952)
Holiday for Sinners (MGM, 1952)
Rose of Cimarron (20th Century–Fox, 1952)
Just This Once (MGM, 1952)
Sally and Saint Anne (Universal, 1952)

Flat Top (Monogram, 1952)
Sword of Venus (RKO, 1953)
The Girls of Pleasure Island (Paramount, 1953)
Invasion USA (Columbia, 1953)
Torpedo Alley (Allied Artists, 1953)
Port Sinister (Beast of Paradise Isle) (RKO, 1953)
Down Three Dark Streets (United Artists, 1954)
Captain Kidd and the Slave Girl (United Artists, 1954)
The Raid (20th Century–Fox, 1954)
Them! (Warner Bros., 1954)
Riot in Cell Block 11 (Allied Artists, 1954)
The High and the Mighty (Warner Bros., 1954)
Gog (United Artists, 1954)
Tobor the Great (Republic, 1954)
Shield for Murder (United Artists, 1954)
Black Tuesday (United Artists, 1954)
Bobby Ware Is Missing (Allied Artists, 1955)
An Annapolis Story (The Blue and the Gold) (Allied Artists, 1955)

Smoke Signal (Universal, 1955)

Top of the World (United Artists, 1955)

Hell's Horizon (Columbia, 1955)

Glory (RKO, 1956)

Friendly Persuasion (Allied Artists, 1956)

Raw Edge (Universal, 1956)

Gunslinger (American Releasing [AIP], 1956)

Written on the Wind (Universal, 1956)

The Tattered Dress (Universal, 1957)

Band of Angels (Warner Bros., 1957)

The Story of Mankind (Warner Bros., 1957)

The Girl in the Kremlin (Universal, 1957)

The Incredible Shrinking Man (Universal, 1957)

The Tarnished Angels (Universal, 1957)

Man in the Shadow (Pay the Devil) (Universal, 1957)

The Monolith Monsters (Universal, 1957)

Man on Fire (MGM, 1957)

Torpedo Run (MGM, 1958)

Juvenile Jungle (Republic, 1958)

Cry Terror! (MGM, 1958)

Some Came Running (MGM, 1958)

The Beat Generation (This Rebel Age) (MGM, 1959)

Blue Denim (Blue Jeans) (20th Century-Fox, 1959)

Pillow Talk (Universal, 1959)

Day of the Outlaw (United Artists, 1959)

The Gallant Hours (United Artists, 1960)

Lonely Are the Brave (Universal, 1962)

Paradise Alley (Sutton, 1962)

Philbert (Warner Bros. featurette, 1963)

Shotgun Wedding (Pat Patterson Productions, 1963)

In the Heat of the Night (United Artists, 1967)

Hour of the Gun (United Artists, 1967)

Will Penny (Paramount, 1968)

Speedway (MGM, 1968)

Sam Whiskey (United Artists, 1969)

The Computer Wore Tennis Shoes (Buena Vista, 1970)

Colossus – The Forbin Project (Universal, 1970)

Tora! Tora! Tora! (20th Century-Fox, 1970)

The Trial of the Catonsville Nine (Cinema V, 1972)

Charley Varrick (Universal, 1973)

The Strongest Man in the World (Buena Vista, 1975)

Tunnelvision (World Wide Films, 1976)

The Jerk (Universal, 1979)

Hangar 18 (Sunn Classic, 1980)

Peege (USC/Phoenix Films short, 1982)

Twilight Zone – The Movie (Warner Bros., 1983)

Gremlins (Warner Bros., 1984)

Teachers (MGM/United Artists, 1984)

Innerspace (Warner Bros., 1987)

House Party 2 (New Line, 1991)

Matinee (Universal, 1993)

Schallert's scenes were cut from *Singin' in the Rain* (MGM, 1952) and *Bigger Than Life* (20th Century-Fox, 1956). *The Terminal Man* (Warner Bros., 1974) features the actor in a clip from *Them!* He narrated *Doomsday Chronicles* (1979).

*When I decided I wanted to direct, I couldn't even get
to first base; to get a half-hour show, I practically had
to kiss Dick Powell in the middle of Santa Monica Boulevard!*

Don Taylor

THEY ARE A DIME A DOZEN TODAY, but up until the 1950s, with the obvious exception of major names like Chaplin, Olivier and Welles, the actor-director was a genuine rarity in Hollywood. In the fifties, however, the floodgates opened, and in the forefront was a light leading man who remembers only too well the stumbling blocks that were once placed in the path of would-be directors.

"It took me quite a while, because in those days, nobody would let *any*body new direct," Don Taylor recalls. "Today, all you have to do is say, 'I wanna direct,' and the next thing you know, you got a movie. Back in the fifties, it was a hell of a lot tougher. Dick Powell, who was then one of the regulars on a television anthology series called *Four Star Playhouse*, gave me the chance to start directing.

"It started out slow, but I parlayed things. In other words, somebody would ask me to act in something, and I'd say, 'Sure, if you'll let me direct.' But after a while, that didn't work any longer because people weren't taking me seriously, and I had to really say, 'I'm a director.' I was a trailblazer. Paul Henreid, Ida Lupino, Dick Powell—we were the forerunners of actors becoming directors in that period. But it was very difficult—*very*. We really had to prove ourselves."

Of course, the days when Don Taylor had to prove himself as a director are long gone, with his list of features running to double digits and the roster of television directing jobs to the hundreds. Few directors that prolific have avoided dabbling in the science fiction and fantasy genres, and Taylor has done more than his full share in that field, helming such well-remembered science fiction titles as *Escape from the Planet of the Apes*, *The Island of Dr. Moreau* and *The Final Countdown*—not to mention the supernatural shocker *Damien—Omen II* and numerous episodes of television's *Alfred Hitchcock Presents*.

Born in Freeport, Pennsylvania, Don Taylor studied law, then speech and drama at Penn State University, where as a freshman he began taking part in college stage productions. ("There was never any question about it once I put my foot on a stage. I knew I was going to be an actor.") Hitchhiking to Hollywood in 1942, the youthful Taylor screen-tested at Warner Bros. but was rejected because of his draft status. MGM, not quite as fussy, signed him to a contract and immediately put him to work, assigning him the minuscule role of a soldier in director Clarence Brown's sentimental slice of Americana, *The Human Comedy* (1943). "They sent me downtown and put me on a train. I said, 'Where's my dialogue?' and they said, 'You don't have any dialogue. When the train stops in Pasadena, there'll be a family there. They'll shout, 'Don! Don!' and you'll greet them—you're coming home from the war.' So I got to Pasadena and got off and, boy, I kissed my 'family.' I had a merry old time! And then I suddenly heard Clarence Brown screaming: 'Get him out of

Previous page: Actor Don Taylor fought to turn director back in the days when it just was not done.

there! Get him the hell *out* of there!' The actor who they were really trying to photograph, John Craven, couldn't get off the train because I'd monopolized the whole area *[laughs]*!"

More minor roles followed before Taylor enlisted in the army, but even there he continued acting. Playwright/screenwriter Moss Hart chose him to play one of the leading roles in the Army–Air Force production of his play *Winged Victory*, which opened in November 1943. Amidst a bevy of rising stars (Lon McCallister, Jeanne Crain, Edmond O'Brien, Judy Holliday, Lee J. Cobb, Karl Malden, Gary Merrill, Martin Ritt), Corporal Don Taylor repeated his stage role in 20th Century–Fox's film version of the play, directed by George Cukor, in 1944.

Returning to civilian life, Taylor resumed his work in pictures with a top role in the trendsetting crime drama *The Naked City* (1948), which still stacks up as his favorite among his own films. "*Naked City* was a classic, one of the first of its kind. It was improvisational in many, many ways; now it's very ordinary to go and shoot anywhere, but *Naked City* we did long before anybody else." *The Naked City* was shot on actual locations throughout New York City with director Jules Dassin utilizing a hidden camera, although on at least one occasion all did not entirely go well. "I was walking down Fifth Avenue and keeping in view of the hidden camera—stepping around people, so forth and so on," Taylor recalls. "All of a sudden, a college fraternity brother of mine came along—'Hey, Don, how are you?' I said *[firmly]*, 'Get out of the way, I'm makin' a movie.' But he wouldn't leave me alone, and finally he even grabbed me!" The role for which he is best remembered remains the MGM comedy *Father of the Bride* (1950), as fiancé to Elizabeth Taylor ("That's still going strong—and so's Liz *[laughs]*!"). He reprised the character in 1951's *Father's Little Dividend* as well as playing other leading parts in fifties films at RKO (*Flying Leathernecks*, *The Blue Veil*), Fox (*Japanese War Bride*, *Destination Gobi*) and Paramount (*Stalag 17*, as the missing prisoner around whom the plot pivots).

Most actors have at least one skeleton in their closet of film credits, and Taylor has a dilly. "I was getting a divorce at the time, so I called my agent and I said, 'Listen, I've had it. I want to get out of the country. Do you have anything?' He said, 'Yeah, we've got a picture that's going in Brazil—' I said, 'That's for me.' Turned out to be a thing called *Women of Green Hell*. I didn't even read it; when I got to Brazil, they gave me the script. And when I read it *[laughs]*, I was ready to cut my throat!"

The notorious fantasy-adventure (written, produced and directed by Curt Siodmak) was shot under the title *Women of Green Hell* but released by Universal as *Love Slaves of the Amazons*. The top-billed Taylor was captured by a tribe of green-skinned warrior women in the unexplored jungles of South America. "Curt Siodmak—the brother of Robert Siodmak—had written a famous novel called *Donovan's Brain*, and he wrote a bunch of films. But this one—oh, God! *Terrible*! He was a good writer, but he didn't know how to direct. But there was a dear old actor down there, Eduardo Ciannelli, and he and I just had a great time together. We said, 'What the hell, let's do it.' We kidded each other and we got through it. I got along with Siodmak—almost—but Ciannelli was very rude to him—'Why don't you go back to school?' and comments like that *[laughs]*. And yet I was having a ball because I was 'out of commission'—really, that's all I was doing, hiding out."

He ended up hiding out a lot longer than he expected. "That damn movie never ended—shooting went on and on and on. For a cheap movie, it was amazing—I was down there in São Paulo for a long time. I swam in waters that I don't think I'd want to go in anymore; I remember a guy saying, 'Watch out for the piranhas' just as I was diving in *[laughs]*! Brazil uses the Portuguese language, and we had a crew from Argentina, which speaks Spanish. And the Brazilians didn't like the Argentineans anyway!"

In the film's one good scene, our heroes' boat, is boarded by a gang of cutthroats and a lively brawl ensues. "That scene, I think, was almost an ad-lib. We'd been out all day and we were coming home, and the unit manager (an American out of Universal, there to protect the money) said, 'Shoot something.' Siodmak said, 'What do I shoot?' and the unit manager said *[sharply]*, 'Put the camera there and turn it on!' Then he yelled at some guys, 'Hey, *you* guys start chasing *these* guys.' That's why that was probably the best scene: Siodmak didn't direct it!" Temple scenes for *Love Slaves* were shot in the Vera Cruz Studios in São Bernardo ("It didn't have any soundproofing, so when I came back here I think I had to loop most of the picture!").

"I believe Universal did *Love Slaves* because they had 'frozen funds' in Brazil, just sitting there, and so when somebody said, 'I can make a film in Brazil,' they said right away, 'Sure! Go ahead!' I told myself that nobody would ever see it—a movie like that would never make it. Then television bought it, and that son of a gun's on all the time! God, I have people call me at four or five o'clock in the morning, laughing so hard they can barely get the words out. They say, 'Guess what! *Love Slaves of the Amazons* is on!'" The *Love Slaves* experience had a happy ending when Taylor was asked by the Johnston Office to travel through South America on a goodwill tour upon completion of the picture. "I flew to almost every country, and there was a mob waiting for me every time. I really felt like I was back to being a star. It was fun, and I had a good time."

His acting career in a slump thanks to pictures like *Love Slaves* and Hammer's drecky *The Men of Sherwood Forest*, Taylor's desire to switch career gears and direct continued to grow. "I'd been in about two dozen films, and starred or costarred in most of 'em. But the creative forces that I was not feeling as an actor were all in the director's path. That's really why I did it. I had spent a lot of time watching directors, and I knew a lot more about directing than I thought I did." With Dick Powell's help, he made his directorial debut with an episode of *Four Star Playhouse* and soon branched off into other shows such as *Telephone Time* and *Alfred Hitchcock Presents*.

"I'd known Mr. Hitchcock because I had been up for a couple of his films. *Rope* [1948] was one of them; I had just finished *Naked City* and I went to see Hitchcock about *Rope*. We just talked — he had just seen *Naked City* and he wanted to know how they made this shot, that shot and the other shot. He marveled at the fact that we shot on Fifth Avenue.

"Anyway, I didn't get *Rope*, but I'd been interviewed by him. And once I got to do that first *Hitchcock* episode, then I used to sit and watch him direct — he was taking all the good scripts. My first year, he and Arthur Hiller and myself were among those directing. Arthur and I were way down at the bottom — if Hitch didn't want to do it or couldn't do it, then Robert Stevens got it, and if he'd already had one, then it came down to Arthur or me. Once in a while we'd get a good one; a lot of times we were struggling. But basically those were good scripts — when I think of the stuff that goes by me today, those were *excellent* scripts. The only thing that was wrong with them was what was wrong with most of the shows at that time — there was absolutely no production. They'd put up two walls and put a picture on the wall, a chair and a table and say, 'Shoot.' No books, no magazines, no papers, no frills. You couldn't get any production worth a damn."

The CBS show yielded another dividend for Taylor, one far more important than the directing jobs and the experience of working with Hitchcock: Directing the 1958 episode "The Crocodile Case" brought him in contact for the first time with red-haired actress Hazel Court, reigning scream queen of British horror films. Romance eventually blossomed; Taylor and Court tied the knot in 1964 and the happy marriage endures to this day.

After several years of directing in television, Taylor made his behind-the-scenes feature bow with the fantasy-comedy *Everything's Ducky* (1961), starring Mickey Rooney and Buddy Hackett as sailors who team up for a series of adventures with a talking duck. The film could hardly have been more minor, but Taylor was still happy to get the assignment. "It was a big step at that point. I was directing a TV series called *Hong Kong* with Rod Taylor when Mickey Rooney called me and said, 'Would you please direct this?' — I'd directed him four or five times in television at that point. I was hesitant, but Hazel said, 'Oh, go ahead and do it,' so I did. I got Arthur Hiller to direct the *Hong Kong*s so I could get released.

"*Everything's Ducky* was too tough — we had to do it in eleven days. Mickey and Buddy were good in it, but they were clowning and I had a terrible time — I couldn't stop 'em from clowning, and yet I didn't have the time for it. Mickey was the producer — it was his company making the film — so what could I do? And the duck didn't work — they finally tied his beak with a rubber band and made him eat cigarettes, that's the only way we could get him to open and close his mouth as though he was speaking. Talk about cruelty to animals *[laughs]*!"

Directing for television was not always a pleasure, either, especially when working with a series star who had definite ideas of his own. "That was always one of the difficulties of directing a series," Taylor grimaces. "Richard Boone had a TV series *Have Gun, Will Travel* that I had been asked to direct. At one point during an episode I said to him, 'Why don't we do such-and-such?' Boone said, 'Nope.' *[Pause.]* I said, 'Then, how 'bout so-and-so?' 'Nope.' About five 'nopes' later, I asked, 'Well, what do *you* want to do?' He said, 'I'll just walk over here and sit down.' And I said, 'Okay!' *[Laughs.]* He's directing—I'm only directing traffic, a stop-and-go director. There's no joy in that. I was supposed to do four *Have Gun, Will Travel*s, but I think I only did one—that was enough of that."

More to Taylor's liking were his two episodes of Rod Serling's *Night Gallery*, "They're Tearing Down Tim Riley's Bar" with William Windom (Taylor was Emmy-nominated for his direction) and "The Messiah of Mott Street" with screen great Edward G. Robinson. "'Messiah of Mott Street' was tough—I couldn't get Eddie Robinson to be Jewish. And he *was* Jewish! As a matter of fact, he was my technical adviser, because he was a Levitical student at one point—he helped me a tremendous amount. But he'd spent years being an Italian gangster, and now he wouldn't give me the Yiddish flavor. He was very sweet, but he wouldn't bend at all."

Taylor's other sixties films as director were *Ride the Wild Surf* (1964), a *Beach Party*-inspired surfing romp (Taylor replaced the original director Art Napoleon, who was injured in a fall) and the U.S./German *Jack of Diamonds* (1967) with George Hamilton. He directed one of his best and most popular films in 1971 when he signed on to handle the second sequel to Fox's profitable *Planet of the Apes*.

"*Escape from the Planet of the Apes* was just glass all the way, smooth as silk," Taylor reminisces. "Good script (no, a *beautiful* script), the actors were divine, everything went right. It was one of those instances where I just couldn't wait to get to the studio every day. There should be more pictures like that, but you don't get 'em anymore. In those days, all the people hadn't gotten in the act. Today, you do a picture like that and you have twenty people wanting to get their hands in, wanting to be creative, wanting to have a say. In the old days, it was easy—there'd be a producer and maybe one other person. You can handle two or three or four people, but you can't handle 15, 20."

Taylor had not seen either of the first two *Apes* films when he was approached to direct *Escape*. "When they suggested I do *Escape*, [producer] Arthur Jacobs, who I knew for years, said, 'Well, we can set it up for you to run at the studio, or you can come to my house tomorrow night for dinner and I'll run it for you.' So we ran *Planet of the Apes*, and I thought it was marvelous. Eventually I saw the second one, *Beneath the Planet of the Apes*; Ted Post directed that. It was a real bastardized version of the first one and it didn't really work, didn't have a story. But *Escape* was one of the best scripts—Paul Dehn was a good writer. I liked our script for *Escape* as much as I liked the first *Apes* script; in fact, ours was more humane."

Aside from the strong story, Taylor's job was facilitated by cooperative stars who knew their characters inside and out. "They were so pro, Kim Hunter and Roddy McDowall, and they knew their characters—I never *told* them what to do, I always *asked*. Sometimes Roddy'd say, 'No, I don't think our characters would do (whatever it was),' and how could I disagree? This was their second, third time out! Makeup-wise, though, Kim and Roddy had a terrible time— they had to get in about three o'clock in the morning for makeup, and then when they were done for the day it took an hour and a half to get it off. They'd be sitting there at night after they were finished, having the makeup taken off, and I'd go in and talk to them about the next day's work. With little drops of alcohol, the makeup men were able to dissolve the glue that held the makeup on and, inch by inch, they'd peel it off. It was painful."

Escape had its share of lighter moments—more so than any other film in the five-film series—but it also posed some interesting philosophical questions. "That's right, the profundity suddenly came through at one point. It was a plot where Somebody Had to Be Dumb, and in this case it was the human beings. In this film it worked. But that gets boring after a while; in almost every television show today, Somebody Has to Be Dumb—say something or do something that's so stupid, because that's the only way the show can develop or progress. It's true of a lot of movies, too."

Extensive makeup played an even larger role in Taylor's next science fiction film. "I had just done *The Great Scout and Cathouse Thursday* [1976] for American International, and they wanted me to do *The Island of Dr. Moreau* for them. But I inherited something that I couldn't do anything about, and that was the appliances that had been made—chin, nose and forehead for all these man-animals. The idea was that these animal men should have been grotesque—half-human and half-beast. But they weren't—they were all Disney. Cuddly. You wanted to kiss 'em *[laughs]*. I couldn't make any grotesquerie out of 'em at all! We had about eight makeup men, with John Chambers and Dan Striepeke in charge; they created all the stuff for the *Planet of the Apes* films. They made it in their cellars *[laughs]*—it was one of those things. And again, you couldn't reuse the appliances; by the time they came off, that was it, you just threw 'em away."

AIP's *Dr. Moreau* got an added box office boost from the casting of Burt Lancaster as the vivisectionist, even though Lancaster was far from the first choice for the role. "We were going for an English actor—the fact that it was based on an H.G. Wells story and all, we thought an Englishman should play the part. [Richard] Burton and [Peter] O'Toole and people like that were considered; we never got turndowns from any of them, they just weren't available.

Burt was available. Back in the days when I made *Naked City* and he made *The Killers* [1946] for Mark Hellinger, Burt and I were very close, but even so, when he was brought up in connection with *Dr. Moreau*, I said, 'Jeez, I don't think this is a part for Burt.' Somebody turned to me and said, 'You wanna make the picture?' and I said, 'Yeah.' He said, 'Well, don't turn down *every*body.'

"Right around that point, Burt showed up in Cannes, and he tore the place apart just walking down the street—the people went ape, because he's an old star, and I guess they don't get many old stars there anymore. That convinced us that we should use Burt. But even he had some hesitation, so I went and I talked to him. He said, 'You got a problem with the script.' I said, 'Yeah, but what picture have you done lately that didn't?' We did have a problem with the script, and we did a serious rewrite on it that . . . didn't work, unfortunately. But Burt was very good, because he was secure with me; I took care of him, watched him. That's my whole theory of directing; security. Give the actor security and, to a great degree, let him go. Sometimes you're able to do that completely, like I did with Burt, and sometimes you're not—that's when you get into trouble. Burt worked very hard, and we had a good relationship."

Hero Michael York, Taylor opines, also did a good job in the film, but "he was out there on a wing and a prayer. And when it came time for him to start wearing the [man-animal] makeup, was he scared! 'What are you doing to me? Christ, I'm a leading man! I don't wanna be a bear'—or whatever it was. We had to hold his hand!" And Barbara Carrera "was about fourteen feet off the ground in those days—she was swingin' somewhere that I wasn't *[laughs]*. But she's so gorgeous, she was perfect casting for it."

Shot in the Virgin Islands and costing far more than the average AIP exploitation item, *Island of Dr. Moreau* "was a big picture for Sam Arkoff, and it didn't do that well. Sam had a good little company, a family-oriented kind of company. I saw letters that went out to his distributors, and they were like, 'Hi, Joe. How's Mrs. Doakes this week? Hope she's feeling better.' It was like a high school newspaper *[laughs]*, but it was very sweet, the way that company worked. And they made money—a *lot* of money. On small investments—they didn't make big money, but for the investment, they made three hundred, four hundred percent. That's not bad. AIP movies generally ran in drive-in theaters, and I remember when the rushes on *Dr. Moreau* got to Sam, he started sending cables saying, 'More light! More light! It's too dark!' He was afraid they couldn't run in at the drive-ins."

Taylor is nothing if not consistent on the subject of *Dr. Moreau*: He doesn't think the Wells story was much good ("Wells wrote it, I think, on a weekend *[laughs]*"), nor was the 1932 Paramount version ("It's terrible! But critic after critic saw ours and said it wasn't as good"), nor his own AIP effort. "But I've seen it now a couple times on television, and it looks better now than

Taylor on location in the Virgin Islands for AIP's *The Island of Dr. Moreau*.

it did when I made it — I don't know how to explain *that* one, but it's true. For what it was, it worked. But there wasn't enough horror in it."

There was no shortage of horror in *Damien — Omen II*, 20th Century–Fox's sensationalistic follow-up to their 1976 box office winner *The Omen*. That li'l devil Damien (Jonathan Scott Taylor), no worse for wear after the bloodbath of *Omen*, was back, this time in the charge of William Holden and Lee Grant, and all Hell was breaking loose once again in a picture that seemed determined

to outgruesome its predecessor. "That's one thing that I think was wrong with the script, the idea that More Is Better. There was too much gore—every time you changed a reel, there was another character that you knew was gonna get it. I inherited all that—I would have eliminated at least two of those killings. All the stuff that I did (the kid being killed by the train, the doctor cut in half in the elevator, and so on) was good—I just thought it was too much. Then it got really gruesome at the end. Suddenly Bill is stabbed to death, and Lee Grant gets burned up—Jesus! More is *not* better."

Replacing British director Michael Hodges, who had worked on the film for about two weeks ("He and the producer just weren't seeing eye to eye as to what was being done, and he was fired"), Taylor shot the film in Chicago and on location in Wisconsin, with many interiors also shot on the Fox lot. "I had to redo quite a bit—I would say out of the two weeks work Michael Hodges did, I augmented or reshot about a week."

Star Holden had been offered the lead in the first *Omen*, but turned up his red nose at the idea of doing a horror film. This all changed, of course, two years and an offer of $750,000 later. "Getting Bill for *Omen II* was a plus value; we had made two movies together [as actors: *Submarine Command* (1951) and *Stalag 17* (1953)] and we were old friends. Bill and I used to drink like it was going out of style. *Everybody* used to drink in the business." All Holden did during *Omen II* was complain about it ("...sick-sick excesses ... unhealthy ambience..."), leaving Taylor a bit mystified. "He thought it was pretty good when we did it—I ran it for him about three times, so I don't know why he complained."

A *Twilight Zone*-ish type of science fiction story, Taylor's next, *The Final Countdown*, was set aboard the *U.S.S. Nimitz*, an ultramodern aircraft carrier that passes through a time warp and winds up in the Pacific on the eve of the December 7, 1941, Pearl Harbor attack. Should Captain Kirk Douglas and the men of the carrier prevent the Day of Infamy and change the entire future history of the world? "When my agent sent me the script and I read it, my first thought was that it was going to be difficult. And it *was* tough—it was a big picture. It was a good picture, except we had no ending—it just went nowhere, the air came out of the balloon. Everything was interesting getting *into* it; I thought it was just dreary getting *out* of it. About halfway through, you knew that Pearl Harbor was such a historical entity, that it had to happen." *Escape from the Planet of the Apes* had posed the same type of hypothetical science fiction question, but Taylor is quick to point out that "the thing about *Escape* is that both Roddy McDowall and Kim Hunter are killed—at least there's an ending. The ending in *Final Countdown* had nothing to do with the whole

Opposite: Taylor's complaint with *Damien—Omen II* is that "every time you changed a reel, there was another character that you knew was gonna get it." (Pictured: Lew Ayres.)

Don Taylor and Hazel Court Taylor today.

picture, of being in a time warp. Suddenly they're just back in their own time period, sailing blithely along!"

Shot aboard the *Nimitz*—a privilege the filmmakers paid a quarter million dollars for—*Final Countdown* bears a producer credit for Peter Vincent Douglas, "but it turned out to be Kirk. Kirk was great for about two-thirds of it, and then Peter was getting kind of in the way and in trouble, and so Kirk exercised his muscles. Of which he has quite a few. He made a lot of noises. Kirk was very difficult. As an actor, he's superb; as a producer, he's a pain in the ass. That's meant nicely *[laughs]*. He's a good actor, easy to direct, no problems."

In 1987 Taylor directed the made-in-Toronto television movie *Ghost of a Chance* with Redd Foxx and Dick Van Dyke, a *Here Comes Mr. Jordan*–type fantasy that was meant to spark a series. Taylor admits that it was a film that probably shouldn't even have been made, at least not under the circumstances. "We didn't have a [workable] script, and it was the start of a writers' strike. We should have never started. We were rewriting the whole time."

Taylor is not as busy with directing as he once was, often turning down television directing offers and devoting more and more time to writing; he and

Hazel Court Taylor also will not watch television or new movies the way they used to, subsisting instead on a video diet of PBS. "Outside of a movie here and there, most of the new stuff is just terrible," Taylor says. "There is a great need—a *cry* is the word for it—for something different, especially in TV. But when you go and give 'em something different, they say, 'Oh, no, we can't make this.'"

Right now his wish is to return to his first love, the stage. "I know I'll direct a couple more pictures—as a matter of fact, I'm contemplating doing one right now—but I feel like acting again and I'd like to do a play. But I haven't found a play that I particularly want to do." For a writer/director like Taylor, the solution is simple: "I think I'm gonna write myself a part!"

And he is equally happy with his acting and directing careers. "I love seeing some of those movies that I was in, but I would have died not directing. As I told you, I broke into it when it wasn't easy. It upsets me now that Kevin Costner, for God's sake, has gone and done a twenty-five million dollar picture *[Dances with Wolves]*—he's starring, he's producing, he's directing.... When I decided I wanted to direct, I couldn't even get to first base; to get a half-hour show, I practically had to kiss Dick Powell in the middle of Santa Monica Boulevard! But at least I helped to break that barrier down, in a way. It *is* a director's medium."

DON TAYLOR FILMOGRAPHY

The Human Comedy (MGM, 1943)
Girl Crazy (MGM, 1943)
Thousands Cheer (MGM, 1943)
Swing Shift Maisie (MGM, 1943)
Salute to the Marines (MGM, 1943)
Winged Victory (20th Century–Fox, 1944)
Song of the Thin Man (MGM, 1947)
For the Love of Mary (Universal, 1948)
The Naked City (Universal, 1948)
Battleground (MGM, 1949)
Ambush (MGM, 1949)
Father of the Bride (MGM, 1950)
The Blue Veil (RKO, 1951)
Father's Little Dividend (MGM, 1951)
Flying Leathernecks (RKO, 1951)
Submarine Command (Paramount, 1951)
Target Unknown (Universal, 1951)
Japanese War Bride (20th Century–Fox, 1952)
Destination Gobi (20th Century–Fox, 1953)

The Girls of Pleasure Island (Paramount, 1953)
Stalag 17 (Paramount, 1953)
Johnny Dark (Universal, 1954)
I'll Cry Tomorrow (MGM, 1955)
The Bold and the Brave (RKO, 1956)
Ride the High Iron (Columbia, 1956)
Love Slaves of the Amazons (Universal, 1957)
Men of Sherwood Forest (Astor Pictures, 1957)
Everything's Ducky (director, Columbia, 1961)
The Savage Guns (MGM, 1962)
Ride the Wild Surf (director, Columbia, 1964)
Jack of Diamonds (director, MGM, 1967)
The Five Man Army (director, MGM, 1970)
Escape from the Planet of the Apes (director, 20th Century–Fox, 1971)
Tom Sawyer (director, United Artists, 1973)

Echoes of a Summer (director, Cine
   Artists, 1976)
*The Great Scout and Cathouse Thurs-
   day* (director, AIP, 1976)
The Island of Dr. Moreau (director,
   AIP, 1977)

Damien — Omen II (director, 20th Cen-
   tury–Fox, 1978)
The Final Countdown (director, United
   Artists, 1980)

I think [Radar Men from the Moon] *is a gas. It's hard to relate it to the science fiction films of today — we didn't have the equipment, didn't have the knowledge of a lot of things. But I think that what we did, for that time, was good. The dialogue was hokey, but back then, it fit. And if people liked it, that was the important thing.*

George Wallace

HE IS ONE OF THOSE ACTORS who has seen both ends of the success ladder and all the rungs in between. At the age of 13, George Wallace was working in a West Virginia coal mine; years later, he was up for the New York Drama Critics Award for playing the male lead in Broadway's *New Girl in Town*. In between, in the guise of Commando Cody, he saved our Earth from devastating conquest and lunar invasion in the serial *Radar Men from the Moon*. A veteran of stage, television and almost 50 movies, Wallace is more than happy to look back on his days in the flying suit, his adventures on the Moon and on Altair-4, and the pitfalls of being an action hero in the days of Republic serials and Saturday matinees.

The New York City–born Wallace, who played the inventor of the flying suit (as well as an interplanetary spaceship) in *Radar Men from the Moon*, does not hesitate to talk about his upbringing during the Great Depression or the fact that as a kid he did not get the chance to go to high school. "I started to go to high school in Far Rockaway, Long Island, but that was right after the Depression, 1933 or '34. I just couldn't afford to finish going through school, because I had no dad — my dad left when I was six months old. I never saw my father — it was just my mother and me, so I had to go to work. I finished maybe three months of high school, and that was it. Then my mother remarried when I was thirteen, and the man she married was a coal miner from West Virginia. As soon as she married him, he packed us from Far Rockaway and we moved to outside of Wheeling, a place called McMechen, which is a sort of coal mining town. At thirteen, I started to work in the coal mines, and I've been workin' ever since."

Wallace joined the navy in 1936 and got out by 1940, although when World War II got underway he was right back in again. ("I was chief bosun's mate in the navy, which is like a master sergeant in the army. In the navy, they claim a bosun's mate is like a sea gull — all he does is eat, shit and squawk all day *[laughs]*!") Beaching himself in Los Angeles after a total of eight years in the service, Wallace supported himself with an array of odd jobs: working for a meat packer ("knockin' steers in the head"), as a lumberjack in the High Sierras, a truck driver, a bouncer, et cetera. "Finally I became a bartender here in Hollywood. In the navy, I always liked to sing, so when I would tend bar, I used to sing along with the jukebox. That was always good for a tip: Some guy would say, 'Hey, George, sing "Heartaches,"' he'd put down 15, 20 cents, and I'd sing 'Heartaches' with the jukebox. One day a guy came in and had a drink, and when he left, he gave me his card and said, 'Call me tomorrow.' I looked at the card the next day, and it was a man called Jimmie Fidler. Fidler was a famous Hollywood columnist, like the Walter Winchell of the West Coast. I

Previous page: Commando Cody (George Dewey Wallace) patrolled America's imperiled skies in Republic's *Radar Men from the Moon*. (The actor's great-grandfather/ namesake, George Dewey, was the U.S. naval commander whose victory over the Spanish fleet at the Battle of Manila Bay in 1898 led to the U.S. acquisition of the Philippines.)

went to see Fidler, and he said, 'How would you like to sing in a Jewish benefit?' I said, 'I'm not Jewish.' He said, 'Who cares?'" *[Laughs.]*

Fidler introduced Wallace to Mickey Katz (the father of Joel Grey), who played the clarinet. "I started with Mickey Katz, singing at Jewish benefits, but after a while somebody said, 'You better take lessons—you don't know how to sing.' So I started to study with an instructor, 'paying' her for my lessons by taking care of her yard and her house. Her husband was kind of sick, so I got two lessons a week by doing all that kind of stuff. Then after a while I went to dramatic school on my G.I. Bill of Rights, to help my singing, and that's how I got in the business."

Wallace enrolled in drama school while earning his living during the day tending the greens at MGM at the time of movies like *The Sea of Grass*, *Green Dolphin Street* (1947) and *The Kissing Bandit* (1948). His first television role was as an army sergeant in an episode of one of television's earliest filmed dramatic shows, *Fireside Theatre*—a performance that won him the Sylvania Television Award. Small parts in movies (*The Sun Sets at Dawn*, *Up Front*, *The Fat Man*) followed before Wallace landed what has come to be known (by science fiction fans, at any rate) as his "signature" role: the two-fisted super-scientist Commando Cody in the Republic serial *Radar Men from the Moon*.

"I was with a little English agent, and she sent me out to Republic for a role as a heavy in *Radar Men from the Moon*," the actor recalls. "I went out in the morning around ten o'clock and spoke to the producers, and they said, 'Do you have any film on yourself?' I said, 'Yes, a *Fireside Theatre*, which won me an award.' They said, 'We'd like to look at it. Just hang around.' So they sent for the film, and in the meantime, I was getting very upset, hanging around—they kept me there all afternoon, just to get a crummy part in *Radar Men* as a heavy. They called me in again about three o'clock and said, 'We saw the film. How would you like to be Commando Cody?'"

Seizing the starring role, Wallace and the rest of the *Radar Men* company began production on the 12-chapter serial October 17, 1951, with Wallace as Cody (no first name, not even among his on-screen friends), Aline Towne as loyal Girl Friday Joan Gilbert, and William Bakewell as lab assistant Ted Richards. Furnishing the film's requisite villainy, Roy Barcroft climbed back into his old Purple Monster tights as Retik, ruler of the Moon, bent on waging war with the Earth and beginning a mass migration of Moonmen from Luna's barren, sunlit(!) surface to our greener world. Clayton Moore took fifth billing as Graber, an earthling ex-convict in the employ of the Moonmen (the part for which Wallace was being considered before he landed the role of Cody).

"Aline Towne and Billy Bakewell were such nice people," Wallace remembers. "We did a lot of stuff that actors today just wouldn't *do*; in those days, you just *did* it, it was part of the job. (In the old days, if you went in for a Western, the director would say, 'Do you ride?' You'd say, 'Yeah.' 'Do you fight?' 'Yeah.' That was *it*!) So we became a unit, a group, and we got

Wallace doffs his helmet to take on Earthbound crooks in *Radar Men from the Moon*.

along just wonderfully. Roy Barcroft had been well known as a Western heavy for so many years, and he was a big, lovable bear, a sweetheart of a guy. And Clayton was just fine, except in one of the fight scenes, he broke my nose accidentally! It was a good group, we all had fun in those days."

Scenes of Cody and Ted (Wallace and Bakewell) fighting the Moonmen's agents in their own Earthly backyards were shot at or around the area of Republic Studios, but scenes set amidst the rocks and cliffs of the Moon surface were shot at Red Rock Canyon, a rugged area in the desert miles from Los Angeles. "Up in Red Rock Canyon, it was 112 degrees in the day, and running around in that hot weather with the heavy leather jacket and all this other stuff on, you sweated quite a bit. We had to stay out there all week to shoot. We'd start first thing in the morning, as soon as the sun came up, and work until the sun went down that night. Of course, I didn't know anything about the business then, because it was like the second thing I ever did. Up at Red Rock Canyon, we stayed in some little dinky motel right alongside of a freight yard. And every night we'd hear the boxcars being changed around for different destinations—clanging and banging all night long. We didn't get much sleep [*laughs*]!"

A highlight of *Radar Men from the Moon* is, of course, the flying scenes, most if not all of them culled from the earlier serial *King of the Rocket Men*. Some new close-up shots of Wallace's Commando Cody in airborne action, however, were filmed in front of a rear-projection screen. "For the scenes of Cody flying through the clouds, they sent a plane up and they took shots of clouds going by. Then they rear-projected this footage onto a screen, and I'd work in front of the screen. They built a platform just off-camera and they attached a two-by-four to it, extending it out into camera range maybe three feet. Very easily, I would crawl out onto this two-by-four, on my belly, and then they'd close my jacket around the two-by-four. And there I'd be, 'flying' in front of these clouds. But sometimes — quite a *few* times! — I'd lose my balance and I'd flip, and I'd be hanging upside-down by my jacket, off this two-by-four!" Wallace laughs.

"Then there were my takeoff scenes. They had a trampoline just in front of the camera, and I would jump and hit the trampoline and go sailing past the camera — and land in a big heap on a couple of mattresses. Then the director [Fred Brannon] said, 'George, you're not flying straight up, you're flying level. We want you to get more straight up.' So they put up a sort of high bar, like eight feet off the ground, and now I would be bouncing off the trampoline and jumping up past the camera for the high bar — which was a good shot. But being so hot and sweaty, I'd grab the high bar and my feet would swing free, 'cause I was clear of the ground, and every so often I'd lose my grip and fall from it [*claps hands together*] down onto my back!"

Radar Men's futuristic props, simplistic by 1990s high-tech standards but still effective, included Cody's bus-sized spaceship and a compact tank in which the evil Moonmen pursued Cody across the rocky lunarscape. "The first time you see the rocketship is in Chapter 1, where Aline, Billy and I drive up to it with a couple of cops who are seeing us off. The thing was probably twenty feet long and maybe eight feet high. It was just a front, a facade, not circular all around. Then they had a smaller rocketship, like maybe ten feet long, that they put on a wire which they had strung up between a couple of cliff rocks. They'd stick a sparkler in the rear end of it, give it a shove and down it would go. For the scenes on the Moon where Retik's henchmen were chasing after us in their tank, they took an old Chevy or something and built a plywood silhouette of a tank around it."

No Republic serial would be truly complete without a fistfight (or two) in every chapter, and in these once-a-reel brawls, Wallace was generally doubled by stunt ace Tom Steele while Dale Van Sickel replaced William Bakewell in the fisticuffs. "The thing that helped me was the fact that in the navy, before the war, I was a boxer — I fought light heavyweight in the Pacific Fleet, 1939–40. For the movies, I had to learn how not to hit somebody when I threw the punch, and also how to telegraph the punch. In a real fight, you throw the punch maybe six or eight inches, but in films or on television, you have to reach back and throw the punch, like maybe three *feet*, so it really shows."

Wallace (as Commando Cody, left) and William Bakewell, poised for action in *Radar Men from the Moon*.

Two of *Radar Men*'s fistic encounters were set in a restaurant, with Wallace and buddy Bakewell taking on baddie Clayton Moore and his criminal companion, Bob Stevenson. "Because it was one of the fights in the restaurant, I didn't have the Commando Cody flying helmet on. It was about five minutes to twelve as we were doing the fight scene, and all of a sudden *[Wallace punches palm of left hand]* Clayton Moore whacked me, and I heard a crack. We kept right on going, finished the scene. They called lunch, put me in a car and took me to St. Joseph's Hospital out in the Valley, where a doctor set my nose and gave me a shot so it wouldn't swell. Then we came back to the set, they had a coffee and a sandwich for me, and at five minutes to one, they said, 'Places!' I had a towel that I'd hold up to my nose, because it was dripping blood a little bit. They'd say, 'Action!' and I'd take the towel down and start the dialogue, until it started to bleed again. But, so that we wouldn't lose five minutes on the show, we kept right on going, me with a broken nose *[laughs]*!"

Less than four months after the filming of *Radar Men*, the character of

Cody was back in front of the cameras for the Republic television series *Commando Cody — Sky Marshal of the Universe* —with not Wallace but Judd Holdren, once serialdom's *Captain Video*, playing the role (Wallace was not offered the part).

Wallace does not try to put lesser screen credits behind him or to ignore the older films altogether. "I saw *Radar Men* again maybe a year ago—every so often, I have somebody over and they want to look at a chapter or two. I think it's a gas. It's hard to relate *Radar Men* to the science fiction films of today—we didn't have the equipment, didn't have the knowledge of a lot of things. But I think that what we did, for that time, was good. The dialogue was hokey, but back then, it fit. And if people liked it, that was the important thing."

Most of Wallace's other early fifties roles were in Westerns, with Wallace generally siding with the bad guys in such outdoor adventures as *Destry*, *Drums Across the River* and *The Lawless Breed* (in which Wallace's character, Bully Brady, climactically shoots star Rock Hudson in the back). Asked if he enjoyed playing these villainous roles, Wallace turns on his darkest look as he hisses a sinister *yes-s-s*. "When you're an actor, you're almost like a kid in a way. Like a little kid in the backyard in a cardboard box, and the mother says, 'Willie, come in the house,' and Willie says, 'I can't,' 'cause he's driving that cardboard box a hundred miles an hour and he can't go in right now! Being a heavy, you can bring to it a limp, an eyepatch; you can snarl, you can grow a beard; you can do all type of things that maybe you always wanted to do as a kid. It's almost sort of fun to hide behind the character, the makeup. I did a film called *Six Black Horses* [1962], with Audie Murphy and Dan Duryea, in which I played a *real* mean heavy. I was so mean, I scalped Indians, and I had Indian scalps hangin' from my belt! Heavies are fun to do."

What Wallace really wanted to do, however, was sing, an opportunity he had never had in films, so when Broadway beckoned, he was right there to answer the call. He debuted in Richard Rodgers' *Pipe Dream*, replaced John Raitt in *Pajama Game*, and was award-nominated for his leading role in *New Girl in Town*, a musical version of *Anna Christie* with Gwen Verdon (all in the fifties). Other stage roles have included *The Unsinkable Molly Brown* opposite Ginger Rogers in Dallas, *Jennie* with Mary Martin, *Most Happy Fella* (during production of which he met his present wife, Jane A. Johnston), *Camelot* (as King Arthur), *Man of La Mancha*, *Company* and more.

"Stage is wonderful because you get the audience reaction right as it's happening. Film or TV, all you get is *cut*, *print* and that's it, and you don't know what has happened. Then, too, you're torn because of money—after all, that's what we *all* work for. The theater, unfortunately, does not pay the type of money films and TV do. It does if you're a big name star—like when I did *Molly Brown* with Ginger Rogers. Ginger was getting I think $5,000 a week, plus a percentage, plus an apartment, plus an automobile, plus, plus, plus.

For playing Johnny Brown, which was the male lead opposite her, I was getting $1,250, paid for my own car, paid for my own apartment, paid for everything. So you're torn between making an existence and doing what you like to do. A lot of the stars today will go back and do off–Broadway stuff because they can afford it, and they *like* to do it. I've been offered many off–Broadway shows, but I can't afford it because I don't live in New York anymore. They only pay a couple of hundred dollars a week—I couldn't get a hotel *room* for that, let alone food and live there!"

Wallace never played Commando Cody a second time, but he did take a second trip into space in 1955 when he joined the crew of the United Planets Cruiser *C-57-D* on their trip to MGM's *Forbidden Planet*. "A man named Leonard Murphy was casting *Forbidden Planet*, and I went in for an interview. He said, 'George, when you were here several years ago [as a greensman], I heard that you were a bosun's mate in the navy.' I said, 'That's right. Why?' He said, 'Well, there's a bosun's mate in this rocketship. I thought of you, and that's why you're here.' That's how I got the part, because he remembered I was a bosun's mate and they needed a bosun's mate!" Wallace laughs.

"The spaceship and the planet surface were built on Stage 15, which was the largest stage at Metro. Way at the end of the stage, they had the backdrop, the skies in the distance. I was very aware of the bushes and things because years before that had been my job. Near the spaceship, the few little bushes they had were maybe two-and-a-half, three-feet high, and as you looked out in the 'distance,' across the stage, the bushes were smaller and smaller and smaller, to give the set more depth. And then they had a couple of midgets in space suits back there, too, to complete the illusion. You would swear that you were looking out for miles.

"Inside Robby the Robot, they had a guy who used to be a child actor, Frankie Darro. In the old pictures, he used to play jockeys, little tough guys, roles like that, but as years went on, he couldn't get a job and he ended up inside Robby the Robot. During lunch, I guess, Frankie would belt down a few, and after lunch, two, three o'clock in the afternoon, we'd go back to working. Robby would come walking into a scene and stop, then start to waver back and forth a little bit. And then all of a sudden, Robby would fall over backwards *[laughs]*, 'cause Frankie got a little drunk and he would fall over under the weight of the costume. So they fired him and they got somebody else and put him into the robot."

Wallace's opinion of science fiction in general is that "it's great, because all the stories have a futuristic theme to them. When I was a kid, we'd look at the comic books and they'd be full of rays and rockets and this and that, all beyond our scope at that time. Today, here they are: We *go* to the Moon, we *have* lasers, we *have* this and that. Look at the [Persian Gulf] war that just finished: a tank shooting another tank thirty miles away. So I think science fiction is great, very inventive, a terrific look ahead at things that could be in the future. I enjoy it."

Wallace's career was stalled in 1960 when the horse he was riding on television's *Swamp Fox* series reared and fell on him, breaking his back. After a painful seven-month recovery, film and television offers were slow to come in, Wallace now being considered a risk. He returned to the theater and to driving a cab in order to make ends meet while the incident passed from memory.

More recently, science fiction credits for Wallace have been scarce outside of television, where he has played a general in the 1973 television movie *The Six Million Dollar Man* and a captured human in the seventies teleseries *Planet of the Apes*. "The poor people playing the apes were constantly sweating because they were under all that makeup and wardrobe. Roddy McDowall had to stop shooting every day about 12:00 because he was allergic to the makeup and the spirit gum and all that stuff, and a heavy rash would break out if he played any longer than till about noon. That was interesting to do, though."

These days he calls himself George D. Wallace, to avoid confusion with the comic George Wallace (not to mention the ex-governor of Alabama). His eighties films have included *The Stuntman*, *Protocol*, *Just Between Friends*, *Punchline*, the fantasy-comedy *Defending Your Life* and the horror film *Prison*; on television he was most recently featured as a regular on *Sons and Daughters*. Less was seen of Wallace's character (Grandpa Hank) when the CBS series moved from an early evening, family oriented time slot to ten P.M., and adult themes ("all the young people in bed and having sex and this and that") began to prevail. Frequently preempted by Gulf War coverage and other special events, viewership dwindled and the show was axed.

Despite Wallace's work in the business for over 40 years and his rather impressive stage credits, die-hard science fiction fans continue to think of him, in knee-jerk style, as Commando Cody, protector of America's endangered skyways. Is our somewhat lowbrow orientation an annoyance to him? "No, I think it's just fantastic," Wallace grins. "A few years ago I went to Knoxville, Tennessee, for the annual Riders of the Silver Screen Western convention. It was amazing—they get this big convention hall and there must be two hundred, three hundred dealers selling memorabilia. So much from *Radar Men*, things that I never knew even existed. And the people are just as nice as can be.

"I was at an autograph table and I looked up and I saw two big guys in line, about six-three, big beards, dirty T-shirts, just staring at me. *Staring*. Gradually they came closer and closer in the line, looking like they're going to tear me in half. They finally got up to me and leaned forward onto the table, looked me in the face and one of 'em said, 'You've *always* been our hero.' I just wanted to kiss these guys, they were so sweet, I wanted to hug 'em! They told me that, as kids, they wanted to make Rocket Man helmets out of coat hangers and things like that! I'm awed and very pleased that after that long a time, people still remember, still care. I think that's just great."

George Wallace poses with a familiar photo.

GEORGE WALLACE FILMOGRAPHY

The Sun Sets at Dawn (Eagle-Lion, 1950)
Up Front (Universal, 1951)
Submarine Command (Paramount, 1951)
The Fat Man (Universal, 1951)
Man in the Saddle (Columbia, 1951)
We're Not Married (20th Century–Fox, 1952)
Sally and Saint Anne (Universal, 1952)
Million Dollar Mermaid (MGM, 1952)
Meet Danny Wilson (Universal, 1952)
Japanese War Bride (20th Century–Fox, 1952)

The Big Sky (RKO, 1952)
Kansas City Confidential (United Artists, 1952)
Radar Men from the Moon (Republic serial, 1952)
The Lawless Breed (Universal, 1952)
The Lusty Men (RKO, 1952)
Back at the Front (Willie and Joe Back at the Front) (Universal, 1952)
Arena (MGM, 1953)
Francis Covers the Big Town (Universal, 1953)
The Star of Texas (Allied Artists, 1953)

The Homesteaders (Allied Artists, 1953)

Vigilante Terror (Allied Artists, 1953)

The Great Adventures of Captain Kidd (Columbia serial, 1953)

Pardon My Wrench (RKO short, 1953)

The French Line (RKO, 1954)

The Human Jungle (Allied Artists, 1954)

Border River (Universal, 1954)

Drums Across the River (Universal, 1954)

Destry (Universal, 1954)

Rage at Dawn (RKO, 1955)

Soldier of Fortune (20th Century–Fox, 1955)

Man Without a Star (Universal, 1955)

Strange Lady in Town (Warner Bros., 1955)

The Second Greatest Sex (Universal, 1955)

Forbidden Planet (MGM, 1956)

Slightly Scarlet (RKO, 1956)

Six Black Horses (Universal, 1962)

Dead Heat on a Merry-Go-Round (Columbia, 1966)

Texas Across the River (Universal, 1966)

Caprice (20th Century–Fox, 1967)

Skin Game (Warner Bros., 1971)

Clay Pigeon (MGM, 1971)

The Swinging Cheerleaders (Centaur, 1974)

The Towering Inferno (20th Century–Fox/Warner Bros., 1974)

Lifeguard (Paramount, 1976)

The Private Files of J. Edgar Hoover (AIP, 1977)

The Stuntman (Melvin Simon Productions, 1980)

Protocol (Warner Bros., 1984)

Just Between Friends (Orion, 1986)

Prison (Empire, 1988)

Punchline (Columbia, 1988)

Defending Your Life (Geffen Film Co./Warner Bros., 1991)

Diggstown (MGM, 1992)

Fans were first introduced to Amanda during a "Journey to Babel."

My agent called up and said, "Do you want to be on Star Trek*?" and I said, "What* is *it?"*

Jane Wyatt

SHE IS BEST REMEMBERED TODAY as the mom on the long-running television sit-com *Father Knows Best*, but every movie buff worth his salt knows there is a lot more to her than the Emmy-winning role of Margaret Anderson: First came several seasons of Broadway and a contract with Universal Pictures, followed by years of freelancing in movies and television. So it is odd, and not entirely fair, that her second-best-known role should spring not from one of her many movies or celebrated stageplays, but from a single television episode that she herself has not seen since it was first broadcast. The show is *Star Trek*; the role, that of Sarek's earthling wife; and the actress, it goes without saying, is Jane Wyatt. The mother of Spock and Starman (and the First Lady of Shangri-La), Wyatt has enjoyed a career in fantasy and science fiction that has spanned a full half-century.

Born in Campgaw, New Jersey, Jane Waddington Wyatt came from a New York family of social distinction (her father was a Wall Street investment banker and her mother a drama critic). Jane was raised from the age of three months in New York City, attended the fashionable Chapin School and later Barnard College. After two years of college she left to join the apprentice school of the Berkshire Playhouse at Stockbridge, Massachusetts, where for six months she played a varied assortment of roles. One of her first jobs on Broadway was as understudy to Rose Hobart in a production of *Trade Winds*—a career move that cost her her slot on the New York Social Register. "It didn't bother me being dropped, but I hated being bracketed with whoever else was being dropped at the same time because of scandal or something," she laughs.

Making the transition from stage to screen was an easy step for a photogenic actress in the early thirties, but at first Wyatt resolutely resisted the move. "In those days, if you made any sort of little splash you were asked to go into the movies. And we'd all say, 'Oh, no, no, we couldn't stand it!' Leave the theater? We wouldn't *think* of it! I was kind of the little white hope of the ingenues in New York, and I was in demand for all these studios. But I stayed with the stage for quite a little while, and then one year I had kind of a bum year. This was the time of the Great Depression and it was a very bad year in New York, so I thought, 'Oh, well, I might as well try [Hollywood].'"

Wyatt landed a berth at Universal, but the circumstances of her deal at the studio were highly unconventional. "I made a stupid arrangement—at least, my agent did. I'd come out to Hollywood but only for the summer months; Universal would use me in the summer and then I'd go back to the Great White Way. And of course that was ridiculous; it was not realistic at all. Movie studios don't operate that way—they can't have a picture ready for a minor person. It's absurd!"

The arrangement would not work for long, but Wyatt did get some valuable filmland experience under her belt and began to learn some of the ways that working in films differed from working in the theater. "When you're

Previous page: Star Trek fans were introduced to Spock's (Leonard Nimoy) mother (Wyatt) in the episode "Journey to Babel."

in the theater you make yourself up, there's no makeup man or anybody. I came out to Hollywood and I went into makeup at Universal for the first time, and the makeup man was little Jack Pierce, who was quite celebrated (which I didn't know at the time). Ugly as sin, you know, and he had the worst breath — that's what I'll always remember about poor Jack Pierce *[laughs]*! And he started pulling out all my eyebrows! I cried out, 'Stop! Stop! I don't *want* you to pull out my eyebrows!' He said, 'Listen, little girl: I have made up the greatest. Don't you tell Jack Pierce what to do. Look!' And he waved his arm toward all the pictures he had up on the wall. Well, they were not glamour pictures, they were Boris Karloff and Bela Lugosi and I don't know who else *[laughs]*! He was a wonderful little guy and I got to be very, very fond of him."

Wyatt made her film debut in *One More River* (1934), a "veddy British" drawing-room drama directed by James Whale, Universal's prime purveyor of classic thirties horror. "Diana Wynyard and I played sisters, and in the picture Diana was divorcing her husband, Colin Clive. And in the courtroom scene, when she got up on the stand, they asked her why and she said *[in a stage whisper]*, 'Because he did . . . *unmentionable* things to me!' *[Laughs.]* I *still* remember that line! We had a marvelous cast. We had Mrs. Patrick Campbell as our aunt and Sir Aubrey Smith as our father, Colin Clive, Lionel Atwill, a whole lot of very good people."

Wyatt made a favorable impression with viewers and critics alike despite a mild case of first-picture jitters. "I did have the jitters, I'm sure, but everybody was very helpful. James Whale was the most charming man — he wasn't a warm man, he was kind of austere. But he was great with Mrs. Patrick Campbell, who *did* have the jitters — she *really* had the jitters! He was wonderful with her, and he did beautiful things with the picture — he was a real artist. The interiors of the houses were just beautiful because they spent hours lighting them and getting the flowers just right. I thought *One More River* was a very good picture, but they shouldn't have paired Frank Lawton and Diana Wynyard [for romantic scenes] because she looked like she could have been his mother. In fact, they had just finished *Cavalcade* [1933], where I think she *did* play his mother *[laughs]*! She was never an ingenue, she was always a tall, wonderful-looking woman. And Frankie was *tiny*! So there wasn't any romance, there wasn't any tension. Frankie Lawton could be very good, but in *One More River* he was so wimpy and Colin Clive was so much more attractive! He was strong and very masculine, a macho kind of guy."

Wyatt wrapped up her first two-picture summer with Universal's adaptation of the Dickens classic *Great Expectations*, starring (as Estella) with Henry Hull (Magwitch) and Phillips Holmes (Pip). "You know what's interesting about *Great Expectations*? There were two girls that tried out for the part of Estella — I was one, the other one was Valerie Hobson. And for whatever reason, I got the part — I think it was because Valerie was so imperious looking that she really wouldn't have been right for it. And then years later, in the great

Great Expectations, Valerie Hobson finally got the part. And Francis L. Sullivan was in *both* pictures, playing the lawyer." Of course the film that Wyatt calls the great *Great Expectations*, the classic David Lean version of 1946, has dwarfed Universal's rendition to the extent that many film fans are unaware that Wyatt's earlier version even exists. "But, you know, ours really isn't a bad picture, not bad at all. But that was the first time I ran into drugs — Phillips Holmes. He wasn't showing up and there were all sorts of whisperings about him going on, that the trouble was that he was on some kind of drugs. He was so attractive and so good looking."

Still an exile from the New York Social Register, Wyatt got another reminder of the social status of actresses during the making of *Great Expectations*. "The director was Stuart Walker. I met Walker's son and I went out with him. He asked me one weekend to go with him to the Bel-Air Bay Club — have lunch and go swimming and so forth. We got within about five miles of the place and all of a sudden he said, 'Oh, darn it!' I said, 'What's the matter?' and he said, 'I just remembered you can't take *actresses* to the Bel-Air Bay Club.'"

Back and forth between Universal and Broadway Wyatt hopped; one of the films Universal planned to place her in was *Dracula's Daughter* (1936), but delays and problems with the script caused a cast shake-up and Wyatt was dropped in favor of Marguerite Churchill, lent to the studio by Warner Bros. The Universal deal began to collapse entirely during the summer of 1936. "That particular summer they didn't have anything for me, absolutely nothing. On the advice of my agent I had a big brouhaha with Universal, because there was nothing for me in the future at Universal either. So they said, 'All right, you can make *one* outside picture. You just find the picture.' And I was lucky enough to get *Lost Horizon*. They were having auditions of some kind; and I-don't-know-how-many other people tested. There was an awfully nice Englishman who stood in for Ronald Colman and played these various scenes. And then I was chosen, I think because I was not well known at all and I was very young."

Was it the Frank Capra name that attracted her to *Lost Horizon*? "Oh, listen, I was attracted to anybody who would *hire* me, what are you *talking* about?"

Based on the 1934 novel by James Hilton, the Columbia production of *Lost Horizon* still remains a high-water mark in the careers of everyone involved, from director Capra, photographer Joseph Walker and maestro Dimitri Tiomkin to the superb cast, which included Ronald Colman, Wyatt, John Howard, Margo, Thomas Mitchell and Edward Everett Horton. Wyatt first read the Hilton book when it was recommended and sent to her by actor Walter Connolly, who tried out for the role of the High Lama in the picture. "It was really a charming book. Of course, my part wasn't in the book, and that's what made my part difficult to act. They just manufactured this character, and she really had no connection with anything. She was just someone for the star [Colman] to be able to talk to and have a romance with. I was used to playing parts in plays where I was part of the plot, and my role in *Lost Horizon* wasn't anything like that. I was just wandering through there. But I was thrilled to get the part, obviously."

Even after more than 50 years, Wyatt's memories of director Capra are warm and respectful. "Oh, Frank Capra was just a love. Isn't it remarkable to think that his mother never learned how to read, and *he* graduated from Cal Tech? Frank was lovely; he let you pretty much have your way; he's not a director like Elia Kazan, who has brilliant ideas and then says something to you that lights up the whole thing for you. Frank more or less let you do what you wanted and then told you what was wrong, or 'Why don't you do it *this* way?' Capra was very sweet; he wrote me a letter many years later, and in it he said, 'I just want to tell you I admired so much what you did in *Lost Horizon*.'"

An opulent production by any yardstick (and particularly by the tatty yardstick of Columbia, then Hollywood's least-prestigious major studio), *Lost Horizon* was shot on the Columbia ranch where an elaborate Tibetan lamasery was constructed for the film. "Those sets were quite stark, and there was a lot of criticism that they didn't look like a lamasery," Wyatt recalls. "But I've seen pictures in books, and they certainly *did* look like lamaseries — but the lamaseries were more dilapidated looking!"

One of the many famous scenes in *Lost Horizon* featured Wyatt's character taking a nude dip in a lake as Ronald Colman watches from a distance, a scene that you would think must have taken the actress aback when she first read the Robert Riskin script. "I just didn't think it was going to happen — but it *did*!" Wyatt laughs. A nude double was used in extreme long shots and Wyatt did her swimming in a strapless, flesh-colored suit. "They got a girl to do the dive, and she was really starkers standing up there. And she dove in, and it was flat. I was really quite a good swimmer and I always resented that *[laughs]*!"

While Wyatt did not do her own diving in *Lost Horizon*, she prides herself on having done her own horseback riding. "I may not have been much of an actress, but I was an awfully good horseback rider," she bubbles enthusiastically. "My sister saw the picture in New York at some sort of big opening. There were two men behind her and one of them said, 'Look at that girl! What a wonderful seat!' They meant my seat on the horse [manner of riding], but it doesn't sound very flattering *[laughs]*! But Ronnie Colman didn't like horses at all, he was terrified. He had a double who did most everything."

Working on *Lost Horizon* also brought Wyatt in contact with James Hilton himself, who hung around the sets as the film version of his best-selling novel was being produced. "He was around quite often. Little, thin guy, very nice. My husband [investment banker Edgar B. Ward] had broken his leg in Switzerland, very badly — it was a compound fracture with the bone sticking

"Ronnie was really a thoroughly charming man, very, very intelligent," Wyatt recalls of her *Lost Horizon* co-star Ronald Colman.

out. This was in the days before penicillin, before any kind of antibiotics. The doctors thought they'd have to cut off the leg — they didn't, but he was two months in that clinic. And when he read *Lost Horizon*, the descriptions were exactly the view he had from the clinic in Switzerland. So I asked Hilton, and he said yes, that was the very valley he described in writing about Shangri-La!"

Another visitor to the set of the film was Columbia chief Harry Cohn, legendary film mogul/tyrant and (according to Hedda Hopper) the man you had to stand in line to hate. "The way Frank handled him was, Harry Cohn would come on the set and Frank would say, 'Cut.' And we'd all gather and we'd all talk to Harry Cohn and just stand around. And Harry Cohn would get more and more nervous—it was costing him a thousand dollars every half a second—until he left the set. And then we'd begin again *[laughs]*."

Conversely, Wyatt (and Capra) had nothing but the highest regard for star Ronald Colman. "Ronnie was really a thoroughly charming man, very, very intelligent; he was well cast when he did *The Halls of Ivy*, his television series. I don't know whether he wrote poems but he *read* poems all the time (he would read aloud); he had a beautiful sense of humor. And it was always so entertaining when you think that he married Benita Hume later on, because she was really bouncy and open, she played in music halls and she was none of the things *he* was *[laughs]*. She was just wonderful, and they were such an entertaining couple."

According to Edward Bernds, who was sound man on *Lost Horizon* and other classic Capra films of the thirties, the director and Colman got along well, even though Capra regretted the fact that once Colman prepared for a scene, he was not open to last-minute suggestions or line changes and inflexibly stuck to the material he had memorized. "Colman also wasn't very happy in great, huge dramatic scenes," Wyatt adds. "When he had to make up his mind to leave Shangri-La, it was done in silence—no background music, nothing. He did the whole thing with his eyes, those wonderful, marvelous eyes. And I think Frank really admired that because it was an amazing scene. Of course, Ronald Colman had started his career in silents; in a way, that added a lot to some actors' stature, because they could do things that other actors couldn't.

"Tommy Mitchell and Eddie Everett Horton I liked very much, and they were good actors, but it seemed such routine casting to us then because they had both played those two parts over and over and over *again* in a million different things. But seeing the picture now, I like them, because Tommy was the quintessential businessman and Eddie was the quintessential ... whatever-he-was *[laughs]*, with the double takes and everything. They were wonderful."

While *Lost Horizon* put a new word (Shangri-La) into the English language, the film itself was treated with less than reverence during World War II, when it was reissued with many pacifist references excised. Other cuts were also made over the years until eventually the film was a shadow of its former 132-minute self. Much of the footage was (and still is) missing, but the American Film Institute and the UCLA Film Archives managed to piece *Lost Horizon* back together: finding scenes, locating the entire sound track and using stills to illustrate scenes where sound but no picture exists. In an odd postscript, the man who restored *Lost Horizon* then admitted that "some of the new footage just slows things down," and Wyatt agrees: "I think it *is* a little bit too long now, but I don't know where they should cut it. Not *my* scenes again, I hope *[laughs]*. But those are the ones they had cut, and quite rightly so. Those scenes weren't in the book; they were just jammed into the film. And it's not a very interesting character, really and truly."

One of the best-restored scenes depicts the first meeting of Colman and Wyatt in the Shangri-La apiary, where amidst the flutter of pigeons Wyatt tells Colman that it was her notion to shanghai him to the mountain retreat. "Ronnie had been to Bali, and he said that in Bali they had whistles tied onto the back legs of the pigeons, so that when they went up in the air and the wind came through, you'd hear this wonderful whistling sound. So that idea of his was incorporated into the film. Of course, Columbia nearly died after they brought the pigeons, because they never have been able to get *rid* of the pigeons out on that ranch *[laughs]*!"

After having frequently confessed that she is less than pleased with her performance in the film, Wyatt is finally beginning to mellow: "When I see it at the august age I am now, I see exactly why I was right and what was good about what I did. I just didn't feel when I saw it initially that I was any good." Her negative reaction to the remake, however, is unchanged. "Oh, I don't even *think* of that!" she scoffs, taken slightly aback. "I was working at Universal at the time when that was being made, and someone said to me, 'Wouldn't you like to go out and see the sets?' Now, I had nothing against them doing a musical remake, but I knew it wasn't going to be any good when I saw the sets. We had all real flowers in our *Lost Horizon*; they had fake flowers. And they had fuchsias and sweet peas blooming at the same time that they had all the autumn flowers like dahlias. I thought, 'This is just plain fake and it's gonna be awful.' I felt terribly sorry for Liv Ullmann—there was nothing for a great actress like her to dig her teeth into in any way, shape or manner. At least I had the horse—she didn't have *any*thing! And Peter Finch—a fine actor, but no good in that. He looked soft, and he couldn't possibly have fought his way back to Shangri-La like Ronnie Colman did. Ronnie was trim and taut, and you knew he could return. But poor Peter Finch, there was no way he was gonna march back! That was really a disaster."

The secret of *Lost Horizon*'s ongoing popularity? "Oh, I think it's the message, don't you?" Wyatt smiles. "Everybody's looking for Shangri-La."

Wyatt took a few years off from films after *Lost Horizon*, returning in 1940 to do a series of fluffy comedies and minor Westerns. Roles in major pictures like Clifford Odets' *None but the Lonely Heart* (1944) and Elia Kazan's *Boomerang!* and *Gentleman's Agreement* (1947) helped to raise her stock in Hollywood once again. For director Fritz Lang she appeared opposite Louis Hayward and Lee Bowman in Republic's *House by the River* (1950), an atmospheric and morbid suspense story. "Fritz Lang was a great director, no question about that, but *House by the River* wasn't one of his great pictures," Wyatt recalls. While Wyatt liked Lang and got along well with him, she saw

Wyatt in the 1950s.

firsthand his legendary bullying of actors, and got a taste of it herself. "When he started treating Lou badly, Lou would just go into a fit— he'd really begin to twitch. He was awfully nervous through that picture, but I think he would do this *[Wyatt shakes and twitches]* just to protect himself from Fritz Lang! Then Fritz started with Lee, and *[gritting her teeth]* Lee planted his two feet down and gave Fritz the gimlet look and wouldn't do a *thing* Fritz asked him to do. So Fritz had to give up on that. So then he started on *me*! One day I was in a rocking chair and I was rocking, and I was crocheting, and I was also doing something else. And he just kept after me and after me and *after* me. I had never in my life done this before, but in the middle of a take I got up and walked out of the shot."

From 1954 until 1960 Wyatt co-starred with Robert Young in *Father Knows Best*, the classic television sitcom chronicling the life and times of the Anderson family in the midwestern town of Springfield. After a slow start, *Father Knows Best* hooked viewers with its homey charm and remained a ratings champion throughout the fifties. A 1959 episode commissioned by the U.S. Treasury Department, *24 Hours in Tyrant Land*, showed how the Anderson children (Elinor Donahue, Billy Gray, Lauren Chapin) attempted to cope with a make-believe dictatorship. The episode was never aired but circulated to schools, churches and other organizations "to show the importance of maintaining a strong American democracy."

Today, squeaky-clean, idealized-family fifties sitcoms like *Father Knows Best* and *The Donna Reed Show* are being looked back upon by cynics more as camp than for their human or comic elements, but Wyatt (who won three successive Emmys for her *Father Knows Best* role) feels differently. "I travel around an awful lot for the March of Dimes, and I've been to every little place in the country. And right up to today people are looking at it and telling me, 'Gee, we want our children to look at it' or 'I just wish it was like that today.' No, I'm amazed at how solemnly they take it and, truly, I don't think that it's looked upon as camp. Of course, I don't like to be bracketed with *The Donna Reed Show*, because I don't think it compares *[laughs]*—but then I don't think *any* of the family shows compare to *Father Knows Best*."

Among the several television appearances Wyatt made during the sixties was a stint on *The Alfred Hitchcock Hour*, in the classic episode "The Monkey's Paw—A Retelling." An updated but otherwise faithful reprise of the well-known tale, it starred Wyatt and Leif Erickson as a married couple whose wish for wealth results in the insurance money they receive from the fiery death of their son in a race car accident. "Oh, I loved doing that, that was really fun. And my son in that was Lee Majors—he had never been before the camera at all, and was he nervous! He was always holding his little Bible *[laughs]*."

The television guest shot for which she is most frequently remembered is as Amanda, wife of Vulcan Sarek (Mark Lenard) and mother to Spock (Leonard Nimoy) in the *Star Trek* episode "Journey to Babel." "My agent called up and said, 'Do you want to be on *Star Trek*?' and I said, 'What *is* it?' I had a look and they sent a script and I thought it would be fun. I went there the first time thinking, 'Well, we'll all have a good laugh over this,' but not at all. Everybody in makeup, having their ears put on and everything else, was so serious. That's what made it so good, they were dead serious."

Although that serious attitude was maintained on the set, Wyatt says she enjoyed the *Star Trek* experience. "Oh, it was great fun. Mark Lenard [Sarek] was very good—I see he's going to be in the new TV series *[The Next Generation]*. He's going to be two hundred years old, but they've killed Amanda off—she was human. Mark is so good looking when he gets his *Star Trek* clothes on, and his ears are so good looking! And I think my 'son' [Leonard Nimoy] is better looking with his ears, too—I think all men ought to wear pointed ears; they're very becoming, aren't they?"

Wyatt is no Trekkie: She has not seen "Journey to Babel" since it was first aired, she could not tell you the first thing about the current state of Vulcan-Klingon race relations and she did not even know her name was Amanda in the show until fans started yelling it at her at a *Trek* convention. "No, I'm no Trekkie, but I have a grandson who is, so if I ever have any doubt about anything, I call him up and he tells me over the phone." She had little contact with series creator Gene Roddenberry, but shortly before his death attended a function where Roddenberry was honored as Humanitarian of the Year of the March of Dimes. "The party turned out very well, and Roddenberry was an awfully nice guy. He was so moved by this whole thing, he could hardly speak at the end. I was there and I introduced Ray Bradbury, the great science fiction writer. I had great fun with Ray—he was very entertaining and funny.

"I remember years ago going to UCLA to hear Ray Bradbury and Aldous

Huxley and somebody else talk—I guess it must have been about science fiction. I went to hear what Mr. Huxley was going to say, but the only thing I remember now is Ray Bradbury, because among the things he said was that the science fiction writers were writing about things to come—but it all comes true. And you see they *do*—the astronauts, when they walk on the Moon, look just the way the science fiction people said they would. And the Moon itself looks just the way it was described. And the rockets and all the other things that they dreamed up beforehand. Ray's feeling was that they had given the great scientists some good ideas to pursue *[laughs]*—which might be true! He's a very witty guy."

Wyatt also enjoyed working with series regulars Nimoy and William Shatner, either on the "Babel" episode or in the more recent *Star Trek IV: The Voyage Home.* "Shatner I'd seen in New York in several plays, and he was a very nice, light comedian, and very good. I don't know how good he is now in it, but he was a very good actor on the stage and he'd been trained in classic things. He did light comedy very well—it was the time of the drawing room comedy, and he was really entertaining. I had great fun with him on the set. My 'son'—he was more dour. I've gotten to know him since then and like him very much, but at that time he didn't really talk much. He was always busy on the telephone with a new deal or something or other *[laughs]*!"

Wyatt reprised the character of Amanda in *Star Trek IV*, 1986's popular installment in the continuing series of *Trek* films. "[Producer] Harve Bennett called me up to ask me to do *Star Trek IV*—they called it a cameo and I called it a bit, but never mind. I said, 'Oh, I'd love to.' But then it turned out they wanted me to do it at the time that I was going with my husband fishing at Christmas Island in the Pacific, and I said, 'I'm sorry, I couldn't.' Harve said, 'Oh, no, no, we can rearrange it'—which they did. And when I walked on the set after coming back from Christmas Island, Harve Bennett wasn't there but I had a telegram from him that said, WELCOME HOME, MOMMIE DEAREST!"

Wyatt's cameo/bit in *Star Trek IV* reunited her with Nimoy, who was directing the film as well as costarring. "I liked Leonard very much on that. He was an extremely good director and I thought the picture was good. But I don't really like acting with somebody who's also directing, because you're talking to them and in your close-up he's looking to make sure the lights are all right, et cetera, and he's not concentrated. When he did his close shots, he did it with so much more intensity; if I'd known he was going to do it like that, I would have done mine a little differently. But he was thinking about other things. I think that's always true if you're directing and acting in the darn thing, unless you have a stand-in that acts for you." Wyatt worked two days on *Star Trek IV*: the first day on the scene in which Amanda is reunited with Spock, and the second day on a silent shot of Amanda and Saavik (Robin Curtis) waving good-bye as the *Enterprise* crew heads back toward Earth.

More recently, Wyatt has attended a pair of *Star Trek* conventions; not being a Trekkie, did she really enjoy the offbeat experience? "Not very much." She smiles apologetically. "I did them because the young fellow who runs these things was so nice on the telephone. I've only been associated with *Star Trek* twice, and I honestly don't understand what's going on. Leonard was with me at one out here, and when we stood up together the place went wild, absolutely wild. He had a whole script—he reads his script and he reads his poems, and he has a whole routine that's been written for him to do. I just get out there and the fans ask these questions and so forth. The question they asked me in New York really threw me for a loop: 'What is it like making love to a Vulcan?' Oh, I just didn't know what I was going to say, and then all of a sudden I heard myself answering, 'Well, I'm not the kind of girl that kisses and tells!' They know everything, those people! In New York, there was a delegation from Paris that came, and they had the *Star Trek* clothes on! It was jam-packed, it was really extraordinary! But I doubt if I'd ever do another one."

One extraterrestrial son would be enough for most actresses, but Wyatt went beyond the call of duty playing Stella Forrester, mother to television's *Starman* (Robert Hays)—or, rather, mother to the human photographer whose identity Starman assumed. "I saw one or two episodes before I shot my *Starman*—when they asked me to do it, I made an effort to see the show and I saw an awfully good one. I thought Robert Hays was very good in it and I liked the series. We shot on location in Northern California, in an old mining town—it's a tourist place now, a very attractive town, and it was wonderful. We had a good time on that."

Jane Wyatt obviously is not one to dwell in the past; maintaining her beautiful gardens means more to her than cultivating a collection of videotapes of her own films, which in most cases she will not bring herself to watch. "I have more trouble looking at myself...!" she sighs with an emphatic shake of the head. "Like with *Father Knows Best*—I looked at each one as they came out, but the idea of sitting down and looking at them again *[laughs]*—well, the garden calls, or something else calls! I'm not terribly interested in seeing [my work] and I'm always disappointed in myself, so there you are." *Task Force* (1949) is still her favorite from among the 33 films in which she appeared ("We started in young and then grew old, and Gary Cooper was so marvelous").

She's still swamped with fan mail and autograph requests ("Hundreds of pictures from *Star Trek*!") and there's always work to be done in the garden (she rattles off the names of her exotic plants with a horticulturalist's zeal) and she just can never manage to remember her anniversary ("We've been married since 1935 and never once remembered—except our 50th!"); there just do not seem to be enough hours in Jane Wyatt's day. But this still-lively, still-lovely septuagenarian is not complaining.

John Howard and Jane Wyatt, the two surviving stars of *Lost Horizon*, reunited for the first time in 50 years at a 1986 Hollywood screening.

JANE WYATT FILMOGRAPHY

One More River (Universal, 1934)
Great Expectations (Universeal, 1934)
The Luckiest Girl in the World (Universal, 1936)
We're Only Human (RKO, 1936)
Lost Horizon (Columbia, 1937)
Girl from God's Country (Republic, 1940)

Kisses for Breakfast (Warner Bros., 1941)
Weekend for Three (RKO, 1941)
Hurricane Smith (Double Identity) (Republic 1941)
Army Surgeon (RKO, 1942)
The Navy Comes Through (RKO, 1942)

Buckskin Frontier (United Artists, 1943)

The Kansan (United Artists, 1943)

None but the Lonely Heart (RKO, 1944)

The Bachelor's Daughters (United Artists, 1946)

Strange Conquest (Universal, 1946)

Boomerang! (20th Century–Fox, 1947)

Gentleman's Agreement (20th Century–Fox, 1947)

No Minor Vices (MGM, 1948)

Pitfall (United Artists, 1948)

Bad Boy (The Story of Danny Lester) (Allied Artists, 1949)

Canadian Pacific (20th Century–Fox, 1949)

Task Force (Warner Bros., 1949)

House by the River (Republic, 1950)

My Blue Heaven (20th Century–Fox, 1950)

Our Very Own (RKO, 1950)

The Man Who Cheated Himself (20th Century–Fox, 1950)

Criminal Lawyer (Columbia, 1951)

Interlude (Universal, 1957)

The Two Little Bears (20th Century–Fox, 1961)

Never Too Late (Warner Bros., 1965)

Treasure of Matecumbe (Buena Vista, 1976)

Star Trek IV: The Voyage Home (Paramount, 1986)

Index

Page numbers in **boldface** indicate photographs.

Acosta, Rodolfo 219
The Act (stage) 185
Adam Had Four Sons (1941) 158
Adams, Don 128, 129
Adams, Julie ii, 1–11, **1**, **3**, **6**, **8**, 100, **154**
Adams, Stanley 257
Adler, Luther 92
Adventures of Captain Marvel (1941 serial) 62–64, **63**, 65, 132, 134–37, **138**, 139, 142
An Affair to Remember (1957) 155, 158
After the Thin Man (1936) 65
Agar, John 13–24, **13**, **19**, **22**, 103, 163, 224, 225–26, 219, 240
Agar, Loretta 226
Aherne, Brian 87
Aidman, Charles 257
Airplane! (1980) 86
Akst, Blossom 251
Akst, Harry 251
Aldrich, Robert 126, 127
Aldridge, Kay 65, **66**
The Alfred Hitchcock Hour (TV) 31, 166, 298
Alfred Hitchcock Presents (TV) 166, 264, 267
Ali Baba and the Forty Thieves (1944) 74, 77
All American (1953) 223
All I Desire (1953) 223
All This, and Heaven Too (1940) 190
Alland, William 5, 99, 105, 212, 238
Allen, Irwin 176, 177, 178–79, 182, 193, 195, 256

Allen, Judith 42
Allen, Woody 185
Allyson, June 183
The Amazing Mr. X (1948) **80**, 81
Anders, Merry 219, 230
Anderson, Eddie "Rochester" 39
Anderson, Richard 25–36, **25**, **28**, **32**, **35**, 165
Anderson, Warner 43, **44**, 45
Andrews, Dana 127–28, 166
Angeli, Pier 218
Ankers, Evelyn 77, 148, 149–50, 151, 153, 154, 155, 156, 157, 158
Anspach, Susan 185
Antosiewicz, John xi
Apache Woman (1955) 92
The Ape Man (1943) 139–40, **141**
The Aquanauts (TV) 106
Arabian Nights (1942) 75–6
Archer, Anne 40
Archer, John 37–49, **37**, **41**, **44**, **47**
Arkoff, Samuel Z. 21, 270
Arnaz, Desi 151
Arness, James 112, 120, 121, 253
Arnold, Jack 5, 18, 98, 100, **154**, 225, 227, 238, 250
Arnow, Max 52
Around the World Under the Sea (1966) 93
Arthur, Johnny 137, 139
Arvan, Jan **32**
Asimov, Isaac 253
Assignment Redhead (1962) 155
"Astounding Science Fiction" 253
Attack of the Puppet People (1958) 14
Atwater, Barry 57

Atwill, Lionel 67, 291
The Avengers (TV) 168
Away All Boats (1956) 7
Ayres, Lew 148, **272**

Bacher, William 252, 253
Back from the Dead (1957) 57
Backlash (1947) 141
Bacon, David 137
Bacon, Rod 137
Bad Day at Black Rock (1955) 163,
  165, 166
Bakewell, William 279, 280, 281, 282,
  282
Ball, Lucille 18, 151
Bandit xi
Barcroft, Roy 279, 280
Bard, Ben 38, 74
Bari, Lynn **80**, 81
Barker, Clive 15
Barnett, Buddy xi
Barry, Don "Red" 3
Barry, Gene 123, **125**
Barry, Patricia 259
Barrymore, Drew 186
Barrymore, Ethel 163
Bates, Jeanne 51–60, **51**, **55**, **56**, **59**
Batman (1989) 15
Batman (TV) 127, 128, 179
Battle of the Bulge (1965) 210
Battlestar Galactica (TV) 197
Baxley, Barbara 193
The Beast from 20,000 Fathoms (1953)
  202, 203–5, 206, 207, 208, 210
Beaumont, Hugh 39
Bedelia, Bonnie 60
Beery, Noah, Jr. 88
Behemoth, the Sea Monster see *The
  Giant Behemoth*
Belfer, Hal 223
Ben Casey (TV) 52, 57
Ben-Hur (1926) 54
Bend of the River (1952) 4
Beneath the Planet of the Apes
  (1970) 249, 268–69
Benedek, Laslo 235
Benedict, Billy 61–72, **61**, **63**, **66**, **68**,
  134, 136, 137
Bennett, Harve 299
Benny, Jack 39

Bergman, Ingrid 158, 248
Bernds, Edward 295
Bernstein, Morey 31
The Best Man (1964) 33.
Bester, Alfred 42
La Bête Humaine (1938) 203
The Beverly Hillbillies (TV) 176
Bey, Turhan 38, 73–83, **73**, **76**, **80**, **82**
Beyond the Blue Horizon (1942) 146,
  158
Big Girls Don't Cry . . . They Get Even
  (1992) 186
Big Jake (1971) 21
The Big Trees (1952) 48
Bill Haley and His Comets 48
Bionic Ever After? (1994 TV movie) 36
*Bionic Showdown: The Six Million
  Dollar Man and the Bionic Woman*
  (1989 TV movie) 35
The Bionic Woman (TV) 34, 35, 108
Bissell, Whit 5
Black Roses (1988) 9
The Black Scorpion (1957) 146, 152,
  155–56
Blackboard Jungle (1955) 163
Blaisdell, Paul **228**, 229
Blanchard, Mari 47, **47**, 224
Blithe Spirit (stage) 121
Bloom, Claire 193
Blue Hawaii (1961) 48
Blue Sunshine (1977) 184–85
The Blue Veil (1951) 265
Bogart, Humphrey 116, 227
Bond, Raymond 246, 248
Bond, Ward 18
Bonestell, Chesley 43, 45
Boomerang! (1947) 296
Boone, Richard **22**, 268
Booth, Adrian see Gray, Lorna
Borst, Ron xi
Bourneuf, Philip 113
Bowery at Midnight (1942) 39, 40, **41**
Bowman, Lee 296, 297
Bowman, Ralph see Archer, John
Boyer, Charles 190
Bradbury, Ray 204, 298, 299
Braeden, Eric 129
The Brain from Planet Arous
  (1958) 14, 20
Brainstorm (1965) 166–67
Brannon, Fred 281

Breathless (1983) 202
Brenda Starr, Reporter (1945 serial) 66
Brice, Fanny 170
Bride of the Atom see *Bride of the Monster*
Bride of the Monster (1956) 69
Bridges, Beau 93
Bridges, Dorothy 86
Bridges, Jeff 93
Bridges, Lloyd 46, 85–96, **85, 89, 90, 94**, 106
Bridges, Lucinda 93
Bright Victory (1951) 4
Brill, Charlie 257
Bringing Up Baby (1938) 65, 126
Brocco, Peter 69
Broccoli, Albert "Cubby" 108
Bromfield, John 20, 224, 226–27
Bronco Billy (1980) 202
Brophy, Rick 14
Brown, Clarence 264–65
Brown, Courtney 92, 106
Brown, Johnny Mack 38
Browning, Ricou ii, 5, 20, 97–109, **97, 99, 102, 104**, 224, 225
Bruce, David 77
Bruce, Lenny 20, 163
Bruce, Nigel 40
Brunas, John xi
Brunas, Mike xi
Brunas, Ruth xi
Buchanan, Larry 21
Buono, Victor 57
Burke, Paul 9
Burns, Bob 120
Burton, Bernard W. 202, 203, 204, 205
Burton, Richard 212, 269
Bus Stop (TV) 31
Butler, Bob 179
Butterflies Are Free (stage) 197
Byrd, Ralph 67
Byrnes, Edd 176

Caddyshack (1980) 108
Cagney, James 43
Cahn, Edward L. 31, 153, 154
Callaghan, George 213
Calleia, Joseph 250
Camelot (stage) 283

Campbell, John W. 122
Campbell, Mrs. Patrick 291
Capra, Frank 292, 293, 295
Captain Lightfoot (1955) 215–16
Captain Video (1951 serial) 283
Captive Wild Woman (1943) 77, 150
Captive Women (1952) 248, 249
Career (1939) 39
Carlson, Richard 4, 5, 100, 152, **154**
Carney, Art 128
Carol, Martine 126–27
Carol, Sue 133
Carpenter, John 122
Carpenter, M. Scott 93
Carradine, John 140, 218
Carrera, Barbara 270
Carroll, Leo G. 189
Carson, Jack 38, 39
Cartwright, Angela 194, 195, **196**
Cartwright, Nancy 259
Case, Tom 98
Castle, Peggie 57
Castle, William 48
Cavalcade (1933) 291
Chambers, John 269
Chandler, Jeff 237
Chaney, Lon, Jr. 75, 87, 150
Chaney, Lon, Sr. 87
Chapin, Lauren 297
Chaplin, Charles 202, 264
Chapman, Ben **1, 3, 5, 154**
The Charge of the Light Brigade (1936) 54
Chester, Hal E. 202, 203, 204, 205
"Child Star: An Autobiography" 16
China Venture (1953) 235
Chisum (1970) 21
Christian, Paul 204, 205
A Christmas Carol (1938) 189–90
Churchill, Marguerite 292
Ciannelli, Eduardo 266
Citizen Kane (1941) 120, 132, 133–34, 135, 137
Clair, René 202, 203
Clarke, Richard 137
Clarke, Robert 246, **247**, 248, 249
Clensos, Steven 249
The Climax (1944) 78–79
Clive, Colin 291
Cobb, Lee J. 92, 265
Coburn, Charles 124

Cocchi, John xi
Coe, Peter 57
Coen, Franklin 212, 213
Coghlan, Frank, Jr. xi, 62, 63, 64,
　134, 136, 137
Cohen, Herman 152
Cohn, Harry 18, 30, 52, 87, 133,
　294–95
Colman, Ronald 292, 293, **294**, 295,
　296
Colorado Territory (1949) 43
Colossus — The Forbin Project (1970)
　129, 258
The Colossus of New York (1958) **209**
*Commando Cody — Sky Marshal of the
　Universe* (TV) 254–55, 283
The Commish (TV) 60
Company (stage) 283
The Computer Wore Tennis Shoes
　(1970) 258, 259
Conan Doyle, Arthur 40
Connery, Sean 108
Connolly, Walter 292
Connors, Chuck 175, 183
Connors, Mike 155, 229
Conquest (1937) 123
Conrad, Michael 184
Conrad, Robert 257
Conrad, William 166–67
Cooper, Gary 91, 147, 190, 300
Corby, Ellen 57
Corday, Mara 155, 156, 240
Corman, Gene 229
Corman, Roger 92, 154, 155, 229,
　256
Cornell, Katharine 212
Cornthwaite, Robert 111–130, **111**, **119**,
　125, **128**
Corwin, Sherrill 248
Costner, Kevin 275
Court, Hazel 267, **274**, 275
Cowden, Jack 106, 108
Crack in the World (1965) 210
Crain, Jeanne 265
Craven, John 265
Crawford, Joan 48, 127
Crazy Over Horses (1951) 67
Creature from the Black Lagoon (1954)
　ii, 1, **1**, 2, **3**, 4–7, **6**, 9–10, **97**, 98–
　103, **99**, **102**, **104**, 108–109, 146, 152,
　154, 218, 224

The Creature Walks Among Us (1956)
　105–6, 212, **215**, 216, **217**, 235, 240,
　241
Creature with the Atom Brain (1955)
　145, 146, 152, 153
The Crimson Key (1947) 141
Cronenberg, David 15
Cukor, George 265
Cummings, Robert 42
Cummins, James 14
Currie, Louise 63, 131–143, **131**, **138**,
　140, **141**
Curse of the Faceless Man (1958) 31,
　32
Curse of the Swamp Creature (1966 TV
　movie) 14
Curtis, Billy 120
Curtis, Donald **80**
Curtis, Robin 299
Curtis, Tony 20, 223

Dallas (TV) 188
The Dalton Gang (1949) 3
Damato, Glenn xi
Damien — Omen II (1978) 264, 271–
　73, **272**
Dan August (TV) 34
Dances with Wolves (1990) 275
Daniel, Dennis xi
Dante, Joe xi, 259, 260
Danton, Ray 7, 9
Darro, Frankie 164, 284
Dassin, Jules 265
Daughter of Dr. Jekyll (1957) 20
Davidson, John **63**
Davis, Bette 127, 190
Davis, Sammi 23
The Day Before Spring (stage) 42
The Day of the Dolphin (1973) 108
The Day the Earth Stood Still (1951)
　218
Day the World Ended (1956) 146, 154,
　227–29, **228**
Deadly Game (1954) 92
The Deadley Mantis (1957) 240
Dean, James 175
de Brulier, Nigel 134
Decision at Sundown (1957) 40
Defending Your Life (1991) 285
DeHaven, Gloria 116

Dehn, Paul 269
DeJarnatt, Steve 15
de Laurentiis, Dino 21
DeMille, Cecil B. 147
Denning, Pat 148, 152, **158**
Denning, Richard 5, 100, 145–160, **144**, **153**, **154**, **158**, 175, 229
DePatie, David H. 258
Derek, John 235
Destination Gobi (1953) 265
Destination Moon (1950) **37**, 38, 43–47, **44**, 88
Destry (1954) 224, 283
Destry Rides Again (1939) 224
The Detectives, Starring Robert Taylor (TV) 175–76, 178, 183
Devlin, Joe 53
Dewey, George 278
Diamond, David 205, 206
Diamond, I. A. L. 117, 124
Dick Tracy (TV) 67
Dick Tracy Returns (1938 serial) 38
Dickens, Charles 189
Dickinson, Angie 93–94
Die Hard 2 (1990) 60
Dieterle, William 163
Dietrich, Marlene 224
Dietz, Jack 202, 203, 205
Dillinger, John 147
DiMaggio, Joe 124
Disney, Walt 259
Domergue, Faith 218–19, **236**, 237, 238, **239**
Donahue, Elinor 297
The Donna Reed Show (TV) 297, 298
Donner, Richard 258
"Donovan's Brain" 69, 266
Douglas, Diana 235
Douglas, Kirk 33, 48, 273, 274
Douglas, Peter Vincent 274
Dracula's Daughter (1936) 292
Dragon Seed (1944) 74, 78
Dream Girl (stage) 42
Drums Across the River (1954) 283
Drums of the Congo (1942) 75
Duke, Patty 246
Dukesbery, Jack xi
Dunaway, Faye 230
Dunne, Griffin 186
Durant, Don 175

Duryea, Dan 283
Dwan, Allan 18

E. T. The Extra-Terrestrial (1982) 242
Eason, B. Reeves 53, 54
Eastwood, Clint 103, 202
Eaton, Shirley 93
Eden, Alice 39
Eden, Barbara 230
Edison, Thomas 189
Edwards, Anthony 15
Edwards, Elaine **32**
Edwards, James 88
Egan, Richard 224
The Egg and I (1947) 40
The Elephant Man (1980) 58
Ellison, James 3
Emery, John 88, 91
English, John 88, 91
Eraserhead (1978) 58
Erickson, Leif 298
Ericson, John 168
Escape from the Planet of the Apes (1971) 264, 268–69, 273
Essex, Harry J. 218
Evans, Gene 207
Evans, Maurice 212
Everything's Ducky (1961) 267–68
The Exorcist (1973) 9

Fair Exchange (TV) 176
Falk, Lee 52
"Fangoria" xi
The Fat Man (1951) 279
Father Knows Best (TV) 290, 297–98, 300
Father of the Bride (1950) 265
Father's Day (stage) 2
Father's Little Dividend (1951) 265
Faulkner, William 116, 117
Fear (1990 TV movie) 21–22
Fenneman, George 118, 119, 122
Fermi, Enrico 117–18
Fickling, Forrest E. 168
Fickling, Gloria 168
Fidler, Jimmie 278–79
Field, Margaret 248, 249
Field, Sally 248

The Final Countdown (1980) 264, 273–74
Finch, Peter 296
Finders Keepers (1951) 4
Fireside Theatre (TV) 279
Flaming Frontiers (1938 serial) 38
Flash Gordon (1936 serial) 53
Fleming, Rhonda 237
Flight to Tangier (1953) 212
Flipper (1963) 106, 107
Flipper (TV) 106, 107, 235
Flipper's New Adventure (1964) 106, 107
The Fly (1958) 88
The Flying Doctor (TV) 155
Flying Leathernecks (1951) 265
Flynn, Errol 54, 74, 147
Fonda, Henry 18
Footsteps in the Dark (1941) 74
For Love or Money (stage) 191
Forbidden Planet (1956) 26–27, 28–29, **28**, **161**, 162, 163–65, 166, 171, 218, 284
The Forbin Project see *Colossus — The Forbin Project*
Ford, Glenn 148, 149
Ford, John 18
Forever and a Day (1943) 190–91
Forrest, Sally 29
Fort Apache (1948) 16–17
Forty Carats (stage) 197
Foster, John xi
Foster, Susanna 78, 79
Foulger, Byron **68**
Four Star Playhouse (TV) 264, 267
Fowley, Douglas 69
The Foxes of Harrow (1947) 252
Foxx, Redd 274
Francis, Anne 27, 161–72, **161**, **167**, **169**, **171**
Francis Goes to West Point (1952) 223
Francis Joins the Wacs (1954) 7
Frank, Milo 222–23
Frankenheimer, John 33, 34
Franz, Eduard **119**
Frazer, Alex **125**
Frees, Paul **119**
Freiberger, Fred 203
Freleng, Friz 258
Fresco, Erin Ray xi
The Frozen Ghost (1945) 150

The Fugitive (TV) 32
Fuller, Lance 237
Fuller, Sam 210
Funny Girl (1968) 170
Futureworld (1976) 129

Gangelin, Paul 218
Garbo, Greta 123
Gardner, Erle Stanley 33
Garland, Beverly 156, 163, 256
Garner, James 241
Gaye, Lisa 230
Gemini Rising (1970 short) 170
General Hospital (TV) 9, 185
Gentleman's Agreement (1947) 296
Gerber, David 176, 177
Gere, Richard 202
Get Smart (TV) 128–29, 246, 260
Ghost of a Chance (1987 TV movie) 274
Ghostbusters II (1989) 15
Ghosts on the Loose (1943) 67
The Giant Behemoth (1959) 205–7, **206**, 208
The Giant Claw (1957) 212, 214, 217–18
Gilmore, Stuart 249
Gingold, Mike xi
Giradoux, Jean 60
The Girl in the Kremlin (1957) 250
Girls in Prison (1956) 155
Goddard, Mark 173–86, **173**, **180**, **181**, **183**, 194, 195, **196**
Goddard, Melissa 185, 186
Goddard, Robert 177
Gog (1954) **252**, 253
The Golden Mistress (1954) 20
Goldfinger (1964) 93
Goldwyn, Samuel 30
Gomez, Thomas 79
Gone with the Wind (1939) 54, 136
Good, John 142
Gorcey, Leo 67
Gordon, Alex xi, 154, 155
Gordon, Richard 155
Gorgo (1961) 207–10, **208**
Grand Canyon (1991) 60
Grand Illusion see *La Grande Illusion*
La Grande Illusion (1937) 203
Grant, Cary 124, 126, 155

Grant, Lee 271, 273
Gray, Billy 297
Gray, Lorna 65
Great Expectations (1934) 291–92
Great Expectations (1946) 292
The Great Scout and Cathouse Thursday (1976) 269
Green Dolphin Street (1947) 279
Greene, Angela 129
Greenhalgh, Jack 57
Greenway, Lee 116, 120
Gremlins (1984) 259–60
Grey, Joel 279
Grey, Virginia 151, **153**
Grippo, Jan 67
Gudegast, Hans *see* Braeden, Eric
Guideposts 193
Guillermin, John 21
Guinness, Alec 256
Gunslinger (1956) 256
Gunsmoke (TV) 121, 188, 193
Gwenn, Edmund 253–54

Hackett, Buddy 267
Hackett, Joan 166
Hailey, Oliver 2
Hall, Jon 76, 93
The Hallelujah Trail (1965) 166
The Halls of Ivy (TV) 295
Hamilton, George 268
Hancock, Lou 15
Hand of Death (1961) 21
Harlan, Russell 117, 119
Harlow, Jean 222
Harris, Harry 179
Harris, Jonathan 179, 181, 182, 194, 195
Harrison, Rex 252
Harryhausen, Ray 204, 205, 206
Hart, Leon 4
Hart, Moss 265
Haskin, Byron 123
Hathaway, Henry 116
Have Gun, Will Travel (TV) 268
Havens, James C. 5, 100
Hawaii Five-O (TV) 146, 157
Hawks, Howard 112, 113, 116–17, 118–19, 120, 121, 123, 124, 125–26, 248
Hayden, Russell 3
Hays, Robert 300

Hayward, Louis 31, 296, 297
Hayward, Susan 42
Hayworth, Rita 235
Healey, Myron 235
Healy, Bill 137
The Heavenly Kid (1985) 108
Hecht, Ben 117, 119
Heinlein, Robert 43
Hellcamp see *Opposing Force*
Hellinger, Mark 269
Hennesy, Tom **19**, 103, 105, **221**, 225
Henreid, Paul 264
Hepburn, Katharine 74, 78, 212
Here Comes Mr. Jordan (1941) 87
Hervey, Irene 168, 170
Heston, Charlton 193
The High and the Mighty (1954) 255–56
High Noon (1952) 91
High Sierra (1941) 43, 227
Hill Street Blues (TV) 184
Hiller, Arthur 267
Hilton, James 292, 293, 294
The Hindu see *Sabaka*
Hitchcock, Alfred 267
Hobart, Rose 54, 290
Hobson, Valerie 291–92
Hodiak, John 235
Hogan, Ben 16
Hogan, James 78
Holden, William 271, 273
Holdren, Judd 254, 255, 283
Holliday, Judy 265
Holliman, Earl 27
Holmes, Phillips 291, 292
Home of the Brave (1949) 88
Homebodies (1974) 69
Honey, I Blew Up the Kid (1992) 86
Honey, I Shrunk the Kids (1989) 86
Honey West (TV) 167–70, **169**
Hong Kong (TV) 267
Hopper, Hedda 295
Hopper, William 240
Horton, Edward Everett 64, 292, 295
Hot Rod Girl (1956) 227
Hot Shots! (1991) **90**, 94–95
Hot Shots! Part Deux (1993) 94
House by the River (1950) 296–97
The House of Fear (1945) 203
How to Frame a Figg (1971) 48
How to Marry a Millionaire (1953) 230

How to Marry a Millionaire (TV) 230
Howard, John 292, **301**
Hubbard, L. Ron 253
Hubschmid, Paul Christian, Paul
Hudson, Rock 7, 20, 33, 215, 235, 283
Hughes, Howard 113–14, 224, 237
Hull, Henry 291
The Human Beast see *La Bête Humaine*
The Human Comedy (1943) 264–65
Hume, Benita 295
Hunter, Jeffrey 166
Hunter, Kim 269, 273
Hunter, Neith 60
Huston, Walter 23, 87, 163
Hutton, Jim 9
Huxley, Aldous 298–99
Hyatt, Daniel 205, 207

I Died a Thousand Times (1955) 227, 230
I Dream of Jeannie (TV) 69
I Love Lucy (TV) 151
I Saw What You Did (1965) 48
In Society (1944) 203
The Incredible Hulk (TV) 69
The Incredible Shrinking Man (1957) 250, 260
The Incredible Shrinking Woman (1981) 242
Indiana Jones and the Last Crusade (1989) 27–28
Indusi, Jeff xi
Indusi, Joe xi
Initiation: Silent Night, Deadly Night 4 (1990) 60
Innerspace (1987) **245**, 260
The Invaders (TV) 31, 166
Invasion USA (1953) 253
Invisible Invaders (1959) 20
The Invisible Man's Revenge (1944) 203
Island Claws (1980) 108
"The Island of Doctor Moreau" 269, 270
The Island of Dr. Moreau (1977) 264, 269–71, **271**
Island of Lost Souls (1933) 270
Island of the Lost (1967) 108

It Came from Outer Space (1953) 152
It Conquered the World (1956) 21

Jack of Diamonds (1967) 268
Jacobs, Arthur P. 268
James, Brion 58
Janssen, David 32, 183, 223
Japanese War Bride (1952) 265
Jennie (state) 283
Jesse Lasky's Gateway to Hollywood (radio) 38–39
The Jimmy Stewart Show (TV) 9
Joan of Arc (1948) 248
Joe Forrester (TV) 93
Johnny Ringo (TV) 175, 178, 183
Johnson, Bill 42
Johnson, Russell 237
Johnson, Tom xi
Johnston, Jane A. 283
Johnstone, Bill 42
Jones, Henry 182
Jones, Morgan **28**
Joseph, Allen 58
Judas Was a Woman see *La Bête Humaine*
Jungle Woman (1944) 150
Junior "G" Men of the Air (1942 serial) 67
Just Between Friends (1986) 285

Kahn, Ivan 251
Kane, Joe xi
Karen, Ann **217**
Karen (TV) 156
Karloff, Boris 57, 78–79, 133, 291
Kasdan, Lawrence 60
Katz, Mickey 279
Katzman, Leonard 151
Katzman, Sam 18, 39, 40, 66–67, 74, 81, 151, 155, 218
Kazan, Elia 293, 296
Kellaway, Cecil 205
Kelly, Jack **28**
Kerr, Deborah 155, 158
Kevan, Jack 4, 98, 103
Kilbride, Percy 223
The Killers (1946) 269
Kind Hearts and Coronets (1949) 256
King, Frank 207, 208

King, Maurice 207, 208
King Kong (1933) 204
King Kong (1976) 21
King of the Rocket Men (1949 serial) 281
King of the Zombies (1941) 39–40
Kings Row (1941) 222
Kirk, Tommy 176
The Kirlian Force see Psychic Killer
Kiss Me Deadly (1955) 126
Kiss of Fire (1955) 239, 240
The Kissing Bandit (1948) 279
Kleiser, Randal 86
Knight, Fuzzy 3
Knotts, Don 48
Koch, Howard W. 227
Kraike, Michael 218
Krakatoa, East of Java (1969) **201**, 210
Kramer, Stanley 91
Kristen, Marta 174, **180**, 194, 195, **196**
Kronos (1957) 88, 212, 216–17
Kruger, Otto **209**
Kubrick, Stanley 31
Kyser, Kay 133

Ladd, Alan 38, 133
Lady in the Dark (stage) 162
Lamarr, Hedy 256
Lamour, Dorothy 146, 158
Lancaster, Burt 33, 269, 270
Lance, Leon 253, 254
Land of the Giants (TV) 32, 69
Landau, Arthur 222
Landers, Lew 54, 57
Landis, Carole 147
Lane, Sara 48
Lang, Fritz 296–97
Lansworth, Lew X. 52, 53, 55, 57, 58
Larch, John 23
Larsen, Keith 106
Lasker, Edward 115
Lassie (TV) 188, 193
Last of the Redmen (1947) 151
Laurie, Piper 237
Law of the Lawless (1964) 21
The Lawless Breed (1952) 283
Lawrence, Barbara 216
Lawton, Frank 291
Lean, David 292
Lebedeff, Ivan 123

Lederer, Charles 116, 117
The Left Hand of God (1955) 116
Legacy of Blood (1973) 218–19
Leifert, Don xi
Leigh, Janet 116
Lenard, Mark 298
The Leopard (1963) 33
Lerner, Alan 42
Lewis, Jerry 227
Liberace 227
The Lieutenant (TV) 31
Lights, Camera, Action (TV) 29
Limelight (1952) 202, 210
Lindon, Lionel 43
Lippert, Robert L. 46, 88, 91–92, 216
The Lives of a Bengal Lancer (1935) 146
The Lloyd Bridges Show (TV) 93
Lockhart, Anne 188, 195, 197
Lockhart, Gene 189, 190, 191, 192–93, 197
Lockhart, John Coates 189
Lockhart, June 180, **180**, 182, 187–99, **187**, **192**, **196**, **198**
Lockhart, June Elizabeth 195
Lockhart, Kathleen 189, 190, 197
Loder, John 191
Loewe, Fritz 42
The Lone Wolf Takes a Chance (1941) 87
The Loner (TV) 93
Long, Richard 155
The Looters (1955) 7
Lord, Jack 157
Lord, Marjorie 40, 46, 48
Lorre, Peter 133
Lost Horizon (1937) 114, 235, 292–96, **294**
Lost Horizon (1973) 296
"Lost Horizon" 292, 293, 294
Lost in Space (TV) **173**, 174, 176–84, **180**, **181**, **183**, 186, 188–89, 193–97, **196**
The Lost Moment (1947) 42
Lourie, Eugene 201–10, **201**
Love Slaves of the Amazons (1957) 265–66
The Love War (1970 TV movie) 93–94
Loy, Myrna 183
Lubin, Arthur 74, 79, 80
Lucas, George 27

Luce, Greg xi
Lugones, Alex xi
Lugosi, Bela 38, 39, 40, **41**, 52,67, 133, 139, 140, **141**, 291
Lundigan, William **8**
Lupino, Ida 264
Lydecker, Howard 135, 136
Lydecker, Theodore 135, 136
Lynch, David 58

Ma and Pa Kettle at the Fair (1952) 223
McCallister, Lon 265
McCallum, David 93
McCarthy, Kevin 259
McClory, Kevin 108
McDevitt, Ruth 69
MacDonald, Kenneth 53
McDonnell, Dave xi
McDowall, Roddy 269, 273, 285
McEveety, Joseph 259
McGavin, Darren 34
McGiver, John 176
McLaglen, Victor 18
MacLane, Barton 151, **153**
MacMurray, Fred 40
McQueen, Steve 177, 178
Macready, George 54
The Mad Ghoul (1943) 77–78
Maggie Brown (unsold TV pilot) 176
The Magic Carpet (1951) 18–19
The Magnetic Monster (1953) 67–69, **68**
Maharis, George **169**
Mahoney, Jock 7, 248
Main, Marjorie 223
Majors, Lee 31–34, **35**, 298
Malden, Karl 265
The Male Animal (stage) 40
Malibu Run see *The Aquanauts*
Malone, Dorothy 250
The Man from Planet X (1951) 246–49, **247**
The Man from the Alamo (1953) 4
The Man from U.N.C.L.E. (TV) 31, 166
The Man in the Iron Mask (1939) 31
Man of La Mancha (stage) 283
The Man Who Played God (1932) 227
Man Without a Gun (TV) 241

The Manchurian Candidate (1962) 33
Mangean, Teddy 120
Mank, Greg xi
Mann, Johnny 230
Manning, Irene 42
Mannix (TV) 155
Man's Favorite Sport? (1964) 126
Manson, Charles 26, 53
Many Happy Returns (TV) 176
Margo 292
Marin, Edwin L. 190
Mark of the Renegade (1951) 113
Marshall, George 64
Martin, Dean 227
Martin, Dewey 114, 122
Martin, Mary 283
Martin, Ross 257
Martin, Sobey 179
Marton, Andrew 93, 235
Martucci, Mark xi
The Mask of Diijon (1946) 54–57
Mask of the Himalayas see *Storm over Tibet*
The Masked Marvel (1943 serial) **131**, 134, 137–39, **140**
Massen, Osa 88, **90**, 91
Master Minds (1949) 67
Matheson, Richard 34, 250
Mathews, Kerwin 218
Matinee (1993) **128**, **260**
Mature, Victor 147
Maverick (TV) 241
May, Bob **183**, 195
Mayer, Louis B. 27, 30
Meador, Joshua 165
Medavoy, Mike 185
Meet Me in St. Louis (1944) 191
Megowan, Don 106, 216
Merman, Ethel 176
Merrill, Gary 93, 265
Michael Shayne (TV) 146, 148, 155, 175
Middleton, Charles 67
Mighty Joe Young (1949) 253
Miller, Ann 116
Million Dollar Manhunt see *Assignment Redhead*
Minnelli, Liza 185
Miracle Mile (1989) 14–15
Miracle on 34th Street (1947) 253
Miss Annie Rooney (1942) 190

The Missing Head see *Strange Confession*
Mission: Impossible (TV) 69
Mission Over Korea (1953) 235
Mr. and Mrs. North (TV) 146, 155
Mitchell, Thomas 292, 295
The Mole People (1956) 20
Mom (1991) 52, 58–60
Monkey Business (1952) 118, 123–26
The Monkey's Uncle (1965) 176
The Monolith Monsters (1957) 253
Monroe, Marilyn 124–25
Monson, Carl 218
Montez, Maria 76, 77
Montgomery, Elizabeth 190
Moore, Clayton 65, **66**, 279, 280, 282
Moore, Gar **32**
Moranis, Rick 86
Moreland, Mantan 39
Morell, Andre 207
Moreno, Antonio 5
Morheim, Lou 203
Moriarty, Cathy **128**, **260**
Morris, Chester 52
Morris, Wayne 188
Morrison, Bret 42
Morrow, Jeff 106, 211–19, **211**, **214**, **215**, **217**, 237, 238, **239**, 240, **241**
Morrow, Lisa **217**
Most Happy Fella (stage) 283
Muhl, Edward 99, 237
The Mummy's Ghost (1944) 75
The Mummy's Hand (1940) 75
The Mummy's Tomb (1942) 75
Mumy, Billy 194, 195, **196**
Murder, She Wrote (TV) 9
Murphy, Audie 222, 224, 283
Murray, Forbes **66**
Murray, Will xi
My Favorite Husband (radio) 151
"My Work in Films" 210

The Naked City (1948) 265, 267, 270
The Naked Kiss (1964) 210
Naked Paradise (1957) 155
Nance, John 58
Napoleon, Art 268
Nayfack, Nicholas 26, 164
Neill, Roy William 41

Nelson, Lori 2, 7, **19**, 20, 103, 221–232, **221**, **226**, **228**, **231**
Neumann, Kurt 88, 212
Never Say Never Again (1983) 108
New Girl in Town (stage) 278, 283
Newland, John 57
Newman, Joseph 238
Newman, Paul 178
Newman, Samuel 218
Nichols, Mike 108
Nichols, Robert 116, 125, 237
Nielsen, Leslie 27, **28**, 164, 165
Night Gallery (TV) 268
Night in Paradise (1946) 76, 79–80
'night, Mother (stage) 222
The Night Strangler (1972 TV movie) 34
Nightbreed (1990) 15–16
Nimoy, Leonard 223, **289**, 298, 299
Nobody's Perfekt (1981) 108
None but the Lonely Heart (1944) 296
North West Mounted Police (1940) 147
Now You See Him, Now You Don't (1972) 259
Nyby, Christian 112, 113, 117, 119, 122
Nyoka and the Tigermen see *Perils of Nyoka*

Oates, Warren 182
O'Bannon, Rockne S. 23
Oberon, Merle 79
O'Brian, Hugh 88, **90**, 91
O'Brien, Edmond 265
O'Brien, George 18
O'Brien, Willis H. 204, 206–7
O'Connor, Donald 7, 223
Octaman (1971) 218
The Odds on Mrs. Oakley (stage) 42
Odets, Clifford 296
O'Donnell, Cathy **80**
O'Feldman, Ric 107
The Oklahoma Woman (1956) 155
Olivier, Laurence 264
The Omen (1976) 271, 273
Ondine (stage) 60
One Desire (1955) 7
One Life to Live (TV) 185
One Million B.C. (1940) 147
One More River (1934) 291
One Step Beyond (TV) 57

1000 Years from Now see *Captive Women*
Ophuls, Max 202, 203
Oppenheimer, J. Robert 117
Opposing Force (1986) 108
O'Sullivan, Maureen 235
Othello (stage) 87
O'Toole, Peter 269
The Outlaw Gang see *The Dalton Gang*
Outlaw's Son (1957) 227
The Ox-Bow Incident (1943) 69

Pajama Game (stage) 283
Pal, George 38, 43, 45–46, 88, 123
Palance, Jack 227, 230
Palmer, Dawson 184
Pardners (1956) 227
Parla, Donna xi
Parla, Paul xi
Parsons, Lindsley 39
Paths of Glory (1957) 31
The Patty Duke Show (TV) 250, 256
The Pearl of Death (1944) 150
Pembroke, George **63**, **66**
Penn, Leo 179
Penn, Sean 179
The Perfect Bride (1991 TV movie) 21, 23
Perils of Nyoka (1942 serial) **61**, 64, 65–66, **66**, 67
Perry Mason (TV) 31, 32–33
Peters, Jean 124, 125
Peterson, Pete 206
The Phantom (1943 serial) 52–54, **55**, **56**
Phantom of the Opera (1943) 78
Philbert (1963 TV pilot) 258
Pichel, Irving 43, 45, 46
Pidgeon, Walter 27, 164
Pierce, Jack P. 76, 79, 291
The Pinto Kid (1941) 133
Pipe Dream (stage) 283
Pivar, Ben 78
Planet of the Apes (1968) 268, 269
Planet of the Apes (TV) 285
Play It Again, Sam (1972) 185
Poison Ivy (1992) 186
Pollexfen, Jack 246–47, 248, 249, 250
Port Sinister (1953) 253

Porter, Don 191
Portrait of Jennie (1948) 163
Post, Ted 268–69
Powell, Dick 175, 264, 266, 275
Powers, Tom 43, **44**
Pratt, Jim 99, 105
Presley, Elvis 7, 9, 48
Preston, Kelly 21, 23
Price, Vincent 156
Prison (1988) 285
Prisoners of the Casbah (1953) 74, 81
Protocol (1984) 285
Psychic Killer (1975) 9
Psycho (1960) 9
Punchline (1988) 285
Purcell, Dick 39

Quaid, Dennis 14
Quick as a Flash (radio) 42
Quiet Please, Murder (1942) 149

Rackmil, Milton 224
Radar Men from the Moon (1952 serial) **277**, 278, 279–83, **280**, **282**, 285
Raiders of the Desert (1941) 75
Rainer, Luise 212
Raise the Titanic! (1980) 108
Raitt, John 283
Ralston, Vera 136
Rand, Patrick 58
Randell, Ron 249
Randolph, John 33, 34
Rathbone, Basil 40, 203
Ray, Fred Olen xi
Raymond, Paula 204, 205
Reason, Rex 216, 233–43, **233**, **235**, **239**, **241**
Red, Hot and Blue (1949) 3
Reed, Philip 151, **153**
La Règle Du Jeu (1939) 203
Rennie, Michael 182
Renoir, Jean 202, 203, 205, 210
Return of Captain Marvel see *Adventures of Captain Marvel*
The Return of the Six Million Dollar Man and the Bionic Woman (1987 TV movie) 35
The Return of the Vampire (1943) 52
Revenge of the Creature (1955) 2, 14,

17, 18, **19**, 20, 101–5, **221**, 222, 224–27, **226**, 231–32
Reynolds, Burt 34, 164, 230
Reynolds, Debbie 30, 172
Rich Man, Poor Man (TV) 48
Ride the Wild Surf (1964) 268
The Rifleman (TV) 175
Riskin, Robert 293
Ritt, Martin 265
Rivas, Carlos 156
The Road Back (1937) 65
Road House (1989) 15
The Roaring Twenties (TV) 241
The Robe (1953) 212
Robert Montgomery Presents (TV) 191–93
Roberts, Judith Anna 58
Robinson, Ann **125**
Robinson, Edward G. 183, 268
Rock Around the Clock (1956) 48
The Rocket Man (1954) 20, 163
Rocketship X-M (1950) 46, 88–91, **89, 90**, 93
Roddenberry, Gene 298, 299
Rodgers, Richard 283
Rogers, Ginger 124, 126, 283, 284
Romero, Cesar 81
Rooney, Mickey 163, 267
Root, Elizabeth **68**
Rope (1948) 267
Rosenstein, Sophie 223
The Rules of the Game see *La Règle Du Jeu*
Rush, Barbara 235
Russell, Bing 183
Russell, Jack 203
Russell, Jane 224
Russell, John 219
Russell, Kurt 182–83, 259
Ryan, Meg 14

Sabaka (1953) 57
Sagal, Boris 251
Salmi, Albert 182
Salome (1953) 235
Salty (1973) 108, 109
San Francisco International Airport (TV) 93
Sanders, George 164
Sands of Iwo Jima (1949) 16, 18

Santa Fe (1951) 45
Sargent, Joseph 258
The Satan Bug (1965) 166, **169**
Scapperotti, Dan xi
The Scarlet Coat (1955) 164
Schallert, Edwin 250–51
Schallert, William **128**, 245–62, **245, 246, 252, 260**
Schary, Dore 30, 164
Schiller, Norbert **119**
Schow, David xi
Schwartz, Howard 176
Science Fiction Theatre (TV) 47–48, 253–54
Scrivani, Rich xi
Sea Hunt (TV) **85**, 86, 91, 92–93, 94, 106
The Sea of 'Grass (1947) 279
The Search for Bridey Murphy (1956) 31
Second Chance (1947) 141
Seconds (1966) 33–34
Selznick, David O. 16, 18
Selznick, Joyce 21
Sergeant York (1941) 190
Serling, Rod 33, 48, 57, 93, 166, 268
Seven Days in May (1964) 33
The Shadow (1994) 48
The Shadow (radio) 38, 42, 48
Shadows on the Stairs (1941) 75
Shakespeare, William 28
Shannon, Frank 53
Sharpe, Dave 63–64, 135, 136, 139
Shatner, William 257, 299
Shaw, George Bernard 253
She Devil (1957) 47, **47**
She-Wolf of London (1946) 191, **192**
She Wore a Yellow Ribbon (1949) 16
Sheedy, Ally 21–22
Sheridan, Margaret 122
Sherlock Holmes in Washington (1943) 40–41
Sherwood, John 216, 240
Shirley, Anne 39
"Shirley Temple: America's Princess" 16
Shirley Temple's Storybook (TV) 193
Shock Corridor (1963) 210
Short, Martin 260
Simmons, Jean 212
Sincerely Yours (1955) 227

Siodmak, Curt 67–69, 153, 265, 266
Siodmak, Robert 265
Sirk, Douglas 216
Six Black Horses (1962) 283
The Six Million Dollar Man (1973 TV movie) 285
The Six Million Dollar Man (TV) 26, 31, 34–35, **35**, 108
16 Fathoms Deep (1948) 92
Skal, David xi
Skelton, Red 257
Slaughter on Tenth Avenue (1957) 7
Smith, C. Aubrey 291
Smith, John 219
Smoke Signal (1955) 239
Snowden, Leigh 7, **215**, 216, 240
So Young, So Bad (1950) 163
Son of Lassie (1945) 191
Sonnenberg, Gus 42
Sons and Daughters (TV) 285
The Soul of a Monster (1944) 54
Space Patrol (TV) 254
Spelling, Aaron 175
Spencer, Douglas 119, 125, 213
Spielberg, Steven 27, 259
The Spiritualist see *The Amazing Mr. X*
Spook Busters (1946) 67
Stack, Robert 148
Stage to Thunder Rock (1964) 21
Stagecoach (1939) 136
Stahl, John M. 252, 253
Stalag 17 (1953) 265, 273
The Stand at Apache River (1953) 4
Stanley, Ginger 5, 100
Stanwyck, Barbara 168, 223
Star in the Dust (1956) 20, **22**
Star Trek (TV) 179, 257–58, **289**, 290, 298, 299, 300
Star Trek: The Next Generation (TV) 298
Star Trek IV: The Voyage Home (1986) 299, 300
"Starlog" xi
Starman (TV) 300
Starrett, Charles 52, 133
Steel, Bob 42
Steele, Tom 137, 139, 281
Stemple, Frank 38, 39
Stepkids see *Big Girls Don't Cry . . . They Get Even*

Stern, Leonard 128–29
Stevens, Craig 240
Stevens, George 116
Stevens, Robert 267
Stevens, Stella 59
Stevens, Warren **28**, 219
Stevenson, Bob 282
Steward, Don 117
Stewart, Gloria 9
Stewart, James 9, 224
Stockwell, Dean 162
Stone, Andrew 126
Stone, Milburn 237
Stone, Virginia 126
Storm Over Tibet (1952) 235. 241
The Story of Mankind (1957) 256
Strange, Glenn 667
Strange, Robert **63**, **66**
Strange Confession (1945) 87
Strange Invaders (1983) 185
The Strangler (1964) 57
Streep, Meryl 230
Streisand, Barbra 170
Striepeke, Dan 269
The Strongest Man in the World (1975) 258, 259
The Stuntman (1980) 285
Sturges, John 166
Sturges, Preston 29
Submarine Command (1951) 273
Sudan (1945) 77
Suicide Battalion (1958) 21
Sullivan, Francis L. 292
Summer Holiday (1948) 163
The Sun Sets at Dawn (1950) 279
Suppose They Gave a War and Nobody Came? (1970) 58
Suzanne, George **140**
Svehla, Gary xi, 14
Svehla, Sue xi, 14
Swamp Fox (TV) 285
Sword of Venus (1953) 248
Sylvester, William 207, 210

The Tall Texan (1953) 92
Talton, Alix 240
Tanganyika (1954) 212
Tarantula (1955) 14, 18, 20
Target Earth (1954) 146, 152–53
Task Force (1949) 300

Taylor, Adam 188, 197
Taylor, Buck 188
Taylor, Don 263–76, **263**, **271**, 272, **274**
Taylor, Dub 188
Taylor, Elizabeth 162, 265
Taylor, Jonathan Scott 271
Taylor, Kent 141
Taylor, Robert 176
Taylor, Rod 267
Taza, Son of Cochise (1954) 235, 236, 237
The Tempest (stage) 28
Temple, Shirley 16, 190
$10 Raise (1935) 64
Ten Seconds to Hell (1959) 126–27
Them! (1954) 253
The Thing (1982) 122
The Thing from Another World (1951) 112, 113–22, **119**, 123, 125, 129, 248–49, 253
Third Party Risk see *Deadly Game*
This Island Earth (1955) **211**, 212–15, 216, 219, 234, 235, 236, **236**, 237–239, **239**, 240, 242
Thomas, Frank 65
Thomas, Frank, Jr. 65
Thomas, Larri 226, 227
Thriller (TV) 31, 127, 128
Thunder Over Hawaii see *Naked Paradise*
Thunderball (1965) 7–9
Tickle Me (1965) 7–9
Tidal Wave see *Portrait of Jennie*
Tigger xi
Tighe, Virginia 31
Tightrope! (TV) 155
Tim Tyler's Luck (1937 serial) 65
Timpone, Tony xi
Tiomkin, Dimitri 115, 292
Tobey, Kenneth 112, 114, 115, 116, 118, 121, 122, 219
Tobor the Great (1954) 254
The Today Show (TV) 170
Tombstone (1993) 188
Tone, Franchot 146
Tors, Ivan 47, 48, 67, 92, 93, 106, 107, 108, 235, 253
Totter, Audrey 235
Touch of Evil (1958) 249–50
Tough Guys (1986) 33

The Towering Inferno (1974) 178
Towne, Aline 255, 279, 281
Tracy, Spencer 163
Trade Winds (stage) 290
Travers, Bill 207, 210
The Trip to Bountiful (stage) 222
Troll (1986) 197
Tuttle, William 34
Twelve O'Clock High (1949) 29
Twice-Told Tales (1963) 156
The Twilight Zone (TV) 48, 57, 69, 127–28, 166, 250
Twilight Zone—The Movie (1983) 259
Twins (1988) 23
Two Tickets to Broadway (1951) 116
Tyler, Tom 52, 53, **55**, 62, 63, 134, 136–37, **138**

Ullmann, Liv 296
Ulmer, Edgar G. 247
The Undefeated (1969) 21
Underwater! (1955) 224, 227
The Underwater City (1962) 7, **8**
Union Pacific (1939) 147
Unknown Island (1948) 151–52, **153**
The Unsinkable Molly Brown (stage) 283, 284
Untamed Youth (1957) 227
Up Front (1951) 279

Van Dyke, Dick 274
Van Patten, Vincent 34
Van Ronkel, Rip 43
Van Sickel, Dale 281
Van Vogt, A. E. 253
Verdon, Gwen 283
Vernac, Denise 55
Victor, Henry 39
Visconti, Luchino 33
"Voices from Home: An Inner Journey" 170
von Stroheim, Erich 54, 55, 57
Voodoo Man (1944) 139, 140
Voodoo Woman (1957) 21
Voyage to the Bottom of the Sea (TV) 127, 128, 193

Waco (1966) 21
Wagenheim, Charles 254

Waggner, George 78, 79
Waggner, Lia 249, 254, 255
Wagner, Lindsay 34
A Walk in the Sun (1945) 88
Walker, Joseph 292
Walker, Stuart 292
Walking My Baby Back Home
　(1953) 223
Wallace, Chris 170
Wallace, George 277–87, **277**, **280**,
　282, **286**
Walsh, Raoul 42, 43
Wanger, Walter 42
The War of the Worlds (1953) 122–23,
　125, 129, 218
Warner, Jack L. 205
Wayne, John 16, 18, 21, 120, 124, 136,
　255
Weaver, Jon xi
Weaver, Julie xi
Webster, Ferris 166
Welbourne, Charles "Scotty" 4–5, 98
Weld, Tuesday 183
Welles, Orson 42, 116, 133, 134, 249,
　264
Wellman, William A. 69, 255
Wells, H. G. 269
Wengraf, John 253
Wessel, Dick **153**
Wesson, Dick 43, **44**, 46
Wesson, Gene 46
West, Mae 212
Westmore, Bud 4
Westworld (1973) 129
Whale, James 65, 291
What Ever Happened to Baby Jane?
　(1962) 126, 127
The Whistle at Eaton Falls (1951) 163
The White Cliffs of Dover (1945) 191
White Heat (1949) 43
White Savage (1943) 77
"Who Goes There?" 122
Whodunit? (radio) 52
Wilcox, Fred McLeod 26, 28, 164–65
The Wild Wild West (TV) 31, 257
Wilder, Billy 29, 116

Williams, Grant 250
Williams, Guy 180, **180**, 181–82, **181**,
　188, 189, 193, 195, 196, **196**
Windom, William 268
Windsor, Marie 92
Winged Victory (1944) 265
Winged Victory (stage) 265
Winningham, Mare 15
Winstrom (unmade movie) 14
Winter, Vincent 210
Winters, Shelley 230
Wisberg, Aubrey 246–47, 248, 249,
　250
Witney, William 64, 135, 136
Wolfe, Ian 69
Wolff, Ed **209**
Wood, Edward D., Jr. 69
Wood, Natalie 162
Woodbury, Joan 66
Worth, Harry **63**
Written on the Wind (1956) 250
Wyatt, Jane 289–302, **289**, **294**, **297**,
　301
Wyler, William 170
Wynn, Keenan 93
Wynyard, Diana 291

Yancy Derringer (TV) 7
Yankee Pasha (1954) 235, 236–37
Yarbrough, Jean 40, 191
York, Michael 270
You'll Find Out (1940) 133
Young, Gig 38
Yust, Larry 69
Yuzna, Brian 60

Zamba (1949) 93
Zamba the Gorilla see *Zamba*
Zanuck, Darryl F. 163
Ziker, Dick 34
Zinnemann, Fred 31
Zorro (TV) 182
Zucco, George 77, 140
Zugsmith, Albert 248, 249–50